Y0-DLI-581

# THE SABBATH SHIUR

*Rabbi Mordechai Miller*
GATESHEAD

# THE SABBATH SHIUR

SABBATH SHIURIM
volume 3

FELDHEIM PUBLISHERS
JERUSALEM NEW YORK

Quotations from Tanach are printed in boldface.

Compiled and prepared for publication by Avigail Sharer.

ISBN 1-58330-391-x



FELDHEIM PUBLISHERS
POB 43163
Jerusalem, Israel

208 Airport Executive Park
Nanuet, NY 10954

www.feldheim.com

*Printed in Israel*

**RABBI B. RAKOW**
RAV OF GATESHEAD
150 WHITEHALL ROAD,
GATESHEAD, Co. Durham
TEL. 73012

**בצלאל בהרה"ג ר' יום טוב ליפמאן ראקאוו**
אב"ד דגייטסהעד

ב"ה ..........................................

שמחתי בשומעי שיצא לאור חלק שני משיעורי שבת של ידי"נ הגה"צ מוה"ר מרדכי מילער זצ"ל
כבר נפוצו ספריו בכל העולם וכל דבריו בנויין על יסודי חז"ל ובראשם המהר"ל דרכו של מורו ורבו
מרן הגרא"א דסלר זצ"ל ובודאי כמעשהו בשני ספרים הקודמים גם ספרו השלישי כן
ושמעתי אשר חלק ממנו כבר הכין הוא עצמו בחייו. וצאצאיו עוסקים בזה הרבנים המופלגים שי'
להשלים הספר, ובודאי יהי' לתועלת גדולה לרבים בס"ד

והנה הרב מילער זצ"ל שבק חיים לכל חי והלא חז"ל אמרו גדולים צדיקים במיתתן יותר
מבחייהם
וכבר פירשו התוס' בחולין: דהרי בחייו של צדיק כמו אלישע הוי [illegible] יכולים להשיב [illegible]
לאלישע בו, ולאחר מיתתו רק [illegible] לעצם אלישע בו עד שהחיהו
[illegible] ענני חיים בעולם הגשמי והגופני ובזה מכוסה ממנו שיעור קומתו
האמיתית של צדיק ובעולם העליון [illegible] כמו חיים הלא לא הי' אפשר להכניס
[illegible] עם ההכבד חיים נצ"ל רק הכיסוי הגופני ועתיים נגלפנים לנו
עולם צדיקים שאחר מיתתן מעולם הגופני ענין כאן אלא שיעור קומתו הרוחני
הלא המו גדול מהנס שאין לנו שום דמיון והשגה
כן צדקיו ידידנו הגה"צ אינו בעולם הזה אפשר להכיר קצת את שיעור קומתו
של מרדכי טוב כמוהו
הי' אדם השלם בתכלית השלימות ת"ח מובהק ועל עניני גדול הלא כלאו להכניס לקום
תפו"ד של גבוה מדת כבושה שלו מדוקדק מאד ובין אדם לחבירו הנקיאות
והאכת פנים של שמחה לכל אחד ואחד, והוא הי' דוגמת הדמות של המשפחה שלם
בכל צורתו כתלמיד מובהק לרבו שהי' דבוק אליו בלב ונפש
וגם את מרן הגה"צ מבוזר נפתלי שקופ זצ"ל שהי' אב"ד דק"ק גייטסהעד הכיר כרבו מובהק
ואני ידעתי היטב הקשר העמוק את התלמיד. מרן זצ"ל הי' התלמיד של שני גדולי דורו הגה"צ
והפרנו מפלגנובקה, והי' מציגה עולו שני הדורים ובודאי גם התלמיד הזוכה קיבל
הרבה ממנו
ובזה הי' השפעתו לא רק בשיעורים הנפלאים שנתן לפני אלפי תלמידות וגם לבני תורה
של עירנו אלא הוא הרים את מצב ודרגתו הרוחנית של עירנו ואני בעצמי הייתי סומך
עליו לקבל ממנו עצה והדרכה לעת הצורך
ותנני בזה לאמץ ידיהם היקרים שיזכו לעלות על המוציאים ולהוציא לאור עולם
ספרו הנחמד של הגה"צ הנ"ל
ידידכם הק' בצלאל ראקאוו

איד הסגן [illegible]

RABBI B. RAKOW
RAV OF GATESHEAD
150 WHITEHALL ROAD,
GATESHEAD, Co. Durham
TEL. 73012

בצלאל בהרה"ג ר' יום טוב ליפמאן ראקאוו
אב"ד דגייטסהעד

ב"ה ..............................

שמחתי באומרים לי שיצא לאור חלק שלשי משיעור שבת של ידיד נפשי, הגאון הצדיק מהור"ר מרדכי מיללר זצ"ל. כבר נפוצו ספריו בכל העולם. וכל דבריו בנויין על אדני חז"ל וביאורם הם לפי דרכו של מורו ורבו מרן הגרא"א דסלר זצ"ל. ובודאי, כמעשהו השני ספרים הקודמים גם ספרו השלישי כן, ובפרט אשר חלק ממנו כבר הכין הוא עצמו בחייו. ועכשיו עוסקים בניו הרבנים המופלגים שי' להשלים הספר, ובודאי יהיה לתועלת גדול לרבים, בס"ד.

והנה הרב מיללר זצ"ל שבק חיים לכל חיי, והלא חז"ל אמרו גדולים צדיקים במיתתן יותר מבחייהם; וכבר פרשו התוס' חולין ז: דהרי בחייו של צדיק, כמו אלישע, היו רשעים יכולים לישב אצלו ולנגוע בו, ולאחר מיתתו לא ניתן רשות לרשע לנגוע בו עד שהחיהו. זאת אומרת, אנו חיים בעולם הגשמי והגופני, ובזה מכוסה ממנו שיעור קומתו האמיתית של צדיק. ואילו היו לנו עיניים רוחניים, הלא לא היה אפשר להכנס למחיצה של החפץ חיים זצ"ל, רק הכיסוי הגופני ועיניים גופניים לנו. אולם צדיקים לאחר מיתתן, שרושם הגופני אינו כאן אלא שיעור קומתו הרוחני, הלא כוחו גדול מאד, שאינו לנו שום דמיון ואחיזה. כן עכשיו שידידנו הגה"צ אינו בעולם הזה, אפשר להכיר קצת את שיעור קומתו של גברא רבא כמוהו.

היה אדם השלם בתכלית השלמות, ת"ח מובהק, אבל עניו גדול שלא רצה להכנס לשום תפקיד של כבוד. מדת האמת שלו היה מדוקדק מאד, ובין אדם לחבירו, הנעימות והארת פנים של שמחה לכל אחד ואחד. הוא היה באמת הדמות של המשכת קלם בכל זוהרו, כתלמיד מובהק לרבו שהיה דבוק אליו בלב ונפש.

וגם את מו"ח הגה"צ מהור"ר נפתלי שקוביצקי, שהיה אז אב"ד דק"ק גייטסהעד, הכיר כרבו מובהק. ואני ידעתי האיך העריך מו"ח את תלמידו. מו"ח ז"ל היה תלמידו של שני גדולי דורו, הח"ח זצ"ל והסבא מסלבודקה, והיה מזיגה אצלו שני הדרכים, ובודאי גם תלמידו האהוב קיבל הרבה ממנו.

ובזה היה השפעתו לא רק בשיעורים הנפלאים שנתן לפני אלפי תלמידות, וגם לבני תורה שם עינו, אלא הוא הרים את מצב ודרגא רוחנית של עירנו. ואני כשלעצמי הייתי סומך עליו לקבל ממנו עצה והדרכה לעת הצורך.

הנני בזה לאחל לבניו היקרים שיזכו לברך על המוגמר ולהוציא לאור עולם ספרו הבהיר של הגה"צ הנ"ל.

ידידכם הק' בצלאל ראקאוו
אייר תשס"ג לפ"ק

# A TRIBUTE

**by Rabbi Betzalel Rakow *zt"l***
**Former Rav of Gateshead, England**

I AM DELIGHTED TO hear that the third volume of the *Sabbath Shiurim* series by my close friend, the late *gaon* and *tzaddik* Rabbi Mordechai Miller *zt"l*, is soon to be published. His previous books, which have attracted a world-wide readership, are based on the teachings of *Chazal,* elucidated using the methodology of his great teacher, Rabbi E. E. Dessler *zt"l.* Undoubtedly, this is also true of the present volume — particularly as it was partly prepared by Rabbi Miller himself. Rabbi Miller's illustrious sons have now undertaken to complete this work, which will certainly be of great benefit to all.

Now that Rabbi Miller *zt"l* has departed from this world, we can apply the teaching of *Chazal,* "*Tzaddikim* are greater in death than in life."...Tosafos explain this concept to mean that our perception of a *tzaddik* in this material world is somewhat obscured by our focusing on his physical dimension, which conceals his true spiritual stature. After his death, however, nothing physical remains to conceal his awesome greatness. In this vein, it is only now, after Rabbi Miller's, passing, that we can truly begin to appreciate this giant of a man.

Although Rabbi Miller possessed a sterling character and excellence in Torah scholarship, due to his extreme humility he never sought positions of honour. He was scrupulously truthful and honest, and in dealing with people, his demeanour was always joyful and pleasant. He truly personified the "Kelm tradition" as a devoted desciple of his beloved rebbe, Rabbi Dessler *zt"l.*

Rabbi Miller also recognized my late father-in-law, Rabbi Naftali Shakovitzky, *zt"l,* the previous Gateshead Rav, as his rebbe, and I myself can testify to the high esteem in which Rabbi Miller was held and valued by him. My father-in-law was a *talmid* of two great leaders of his time, the

Chafetz Chaim and the Alter of Slabodka, and consequently himself was a composite of both approaches — approaches with which his cherished *talmid* in turn became imbued.

Besides Rabbi Miller's influence through his brilliant lectures delivered to thousands of seminary students as well as to countless *bnei Torah,* he also elevated the spiritual level of our town, and I myself would seek his sage advice and direction whenever necessary.

I wish his dear sons success in completing this project of publishing their saintly father's luminous work.

With friendship,
Betzalel Rakow
Iyar 5763

ע״ש ר׳ חיים מנחם להמן ע״ה
רח׳ הרב סורוצקין 39 ירושלים
מיסודו של תנועת שוחרי מוסר, ירושלים

Institute for Torah Ethics
IN MEMORY OF R'CHAIM MENACHEM LEHMANN
39 Harav Sorotzkin St., Jerusalem

בס״ד

כ׳ טבת תשמ"ח

הר"כ ידידי הדגול הרה"ג מוהר"מ מילר שליט"א
שלום וברכה מרובה !

שמעתי כי בקרוב יצא ספר כתר"ה "שעורי שבת" בלשון הקודש, ומאד שמחתי על בשורה טובה זו. שעורי כת"ר שכבר יצאו לבם מוניטין בעולם בהיותם מלאי חכמה ודעת, מוסר ויראת שמים – למה יגרע חלקם של דוברי עברית להתבסם מדברים יקרים אלה ! כת"ר, תלמידו המובהק של מרן הגרא"א דסלר זצללה"ה, מצא את הדרך לקרב דברים רמים ונשגבים ללב צעירים, וכעת בצאת ספרו בע"ה בקרוב בלה"ק הנני לברכו מקרב לב על זיכוי-רבים זה.

יהי רצון שכת"ר יזכה להמשיך בהפצת תורתו ביתר שאת וביתר עוז, להאיר לדורנו היתום ולהיות ממצדיקי הרבים ככוכבים לעולם ועד,

כעתירת ידידו מוקירו ומכבדו
כרום יקרת ערכו

הרב שלמה וולבה

*Haskamah from Rabbi Shlomo Wolbe for the previous Hebrew edition*

**ישיבת פוניבז'**
גבעת זכרון מאיר
ע"י קרית הישיבה
בני־ברק, ארץ־ישראל
ת. ד. 26

בנשיאות והנהלת:
הרב יוסף ש. כהנמן מפוניבז'

**PONEVEZ JESHIVA**
GIVAT ZIKHRON MEIR
NEAR KIRYAT HAYESHIVA
BENEI-BERAQ, PALESTINE
P. O. B. 26

DEAN:
RABBI J. KAHANEMAN OF PONEVEZ

בתשובה נא להזכיר:
No. ..... ת

ב"ה. יום ד' ר"ח מנ"א תש"ט.

ידידי ומכירי קא אמינא, זה תלמידי היקר הרה"ג המצוין מוה"ר מרדכי
מילר הי"ו. מעיד אני עליו כי הנהו א' מעולי התלמידים היותר גדולים, וגדל בתורה וגם
במדעים החיצוניות יתרה. מלבד בקיאות הי' טהרה, ומרבה עמלים לתורה והוראה. כעת
הוא מגיד שעור בקהלת בישיבת גייטסהעד (הגדולה שבישיבות אנגליא), וסגן המנהל בסמינר
למורות שם, זה הסמינר שהוא מפורסם באיכותו הרבה ברוח בהוראה ובמורות.
בהיות שזה כמה שנים התאוננתי הרבה בסמינר הזה מולא הוסבו לאוקס. שמח לבי אל
עבודת הרה"ג מילר הי"ו ונוכחתי לדעת כי מצליח הרבה בהשפעתו הגדולה הן באופן
ההוראה והן ביראת שמים. הוא מצוין ביותר בהוראת תנ"ך, השקפות והיסטוריא,
הכל עפ האמונה הטהורה ובאופן מסודר ומבוסס אשר יניח את הלבבות מסופקות
ומתוקנות. במדע, הנה גמר את חלק הלמודים באוניברסיטה דבלין (חלק המשפטים)
וזכה בשלשה דיפלומות L.L.B., B.A., וגם M.A. לא השתמש במדעיו אלה, כי חשקה נפשו
בחנוכה של תורה להפיץ בתורה ובאמונה כי זה עמו.

הכו"ח לכ' התורה ולומדי'

אליהו אליעזר דסלר
משגיח פוניבז
לשעבר מנהל כולל הרבנים דבריטניא

*A Letter of Recommendation by Rabbi E.E. Dessler, 1949*

**Rabbi N. SHAKOVITZKI,**

RAV OF GATESHEAD.

175, WHITEHALL ROAD,
GATESHEAD, Co. Durham,
(ENGLAND)

**נפתלי בהר"הג ר' לניטין הכהן שאקאוויצקי**

אב"ד דגייטסהעד.


ב"ה יום ו' [illegible] לחודש [illegible] שבט שנה הש"ז

הנני להעיד על הבחור המופלג ונעלה בכל מעלה מו"ה מרדכי מילער נ"י

תלמיד הישיבה הק' דפה גייטסהעד.

כי עסק בעת האחרונה בלמוד הענינים [illegible] בשקידה רבה ומצא [illegible] בדיעות והבנת האמונה
ובמשך הזמן שישב קבוע אצלי שמעתי [illegible] בעל פה כל החלק הראשון
משו"ע יו"ד מהחלק [illegible] כל דברי המחבר והרמ"א עם נושאי כליהם,
וגם לרבות כל הענינים המחודשים המובאים בס' פתחי תשובה.
ומובטחני כי כאשר ילך בעזה"י בדרכו זו לשקוד על התורה, יהי' לנחת גדול
כי [illegible] רבה [illegible] בכשרונותיו המצוינים ונעלה מדותיו יחד עם יראתו
הקודמת לחכמתו.

החותם בברכה נפתלי הכהן [illegible] שאקאוויצקי [illegible].

*An Appreciation of the Author by Rabbi Naftali Shakovitzki, 1947*

Rabbi S. J. RABINOW,
107, KYVERDALE ROAD,
STAMFORD HILL, N.16.
'PHONE: STAMFORD HILL 5861.

שמואל יוסף ראבינאוו
החופ"ק לונדון,
רב דביה"מ „גראוו ליין",
סטעמפארד הילל והגליל.

בעז״ה

הנה האמת והצדק ניתן לכתוב ולהעיד בשער בת רבים של ת״ח.
על האי בחור הצעיר באלפי ישראל ינוק וחכים בחכמת התורה והיראה
המוכתר בכתר שם טוב מרדכי [illegible] נ״י.
הנה בא לפני והראה לי מכתב תעודה מהרב הגאון הגדול [illegible]
שליט״א. [illegible] על כור המבחן על חלק [illegible] של יו״ד.
[illegible]
[illegible]
הק׳ שמואל יוסף ראבינאוו

Ktav Semichah from Rabbi Shmuel Yosef Rabinow to the Author, 1947

# Acknowledgments

THIS VOLUME IS THE completion of a project begun by Rabbi Miller *zt"l* himself, having selected these *shiurim* and entrusted them to Avigail Sharer, a loyal, faithful and dependable *talmidah*, to transcribe and prepare for publication. The family of the author extends their deep appreciation to Mrs. Sharer, for her masterful execution of a vastly difficult assignment.

Special thanks are due to:

Rabbi Akiva Tatz, for his time, effort and concern that this book should be nothing less than perfect;

Rabbi Yitzchak Miller, for his insightful comments and suggestions;

Sorele Beaton, for reviewing and correcting the manuscript.

Finally, the Miller family would like to express their gratitude to R' Yaakov Feldheim and the members of his staff, particularly Yocheved Lavon, Yossi Ben Shachar, Eden Chachamtzedek, Chana Devorah Sklar, Penina Langsam, Bracha Steinberg and Deena Nataf. Their outstanding professionalism, coupled with sensitivity and accessibility, made it a pleasure to work together.

ישלם ה' פעלם ותהי משכרתם שלמה מעם ה' אלקי ישראל

# CONTENTS

## *BEREISHITH*



## *SHEMOTH*



## *VAYIKRA*



## *BEMIDBAR*



## *DEVARIM*

# BEREISHITH

# BEREISHITH

IN OUR PARASHAH — the blueprint of world history — a basic flaw in human nature is depicted.

וַיְהִי מִקֵּץ יָמִים וַיָּבֵא קַיִן מִפְּרִי הָאֲדָמָה מִנְחָה לַה׳. וְהֶבֶל הֵבִיא גַם הוּא מִבְּכֹרוֹת צֹאנוֹ וּמֵחֶלְבֵהֶן וַיִּשַׁע ה׳ אֶל הֶבֶל וְאֶל מִנְחָתוֹ. וְאֶל קַיִן וְאֶל מִנְחָתוֹ לֹא שָׁעָה וַיִּחַר לְקַיִן מְאֹד וַיִּפְּלוּ פָּנָיו. וַיֹּאמֶר ה׳ אֶל קָיִן לָמָּה חָרָה לָךְ וְלָמָּה נָפְלוּ פָנֶיךָ. הֲלוֹא אִם תֵּיטִיב שְׂאֵת וְאִם לֹא תֵיטִיב לַפֶּתַח חַטָּאת רֹבֵץ וְאֵלֶיךָ תְּשׁוּקָתוֹ וְאַתָּה תִּמְשָׁל בּוֹ. וַיֹּאמֶר קַיִן אֶל הֶבֶל אָחִיו וַיְהִי בִּהְיוֹתָם בַּשָּׂדֶה וַיָּקָם קַיִן אֶל הֶבֶל אָחִיו וַיַּהַרְגֵהוּ.

*It was after [some] days that Kayin brought an offering to the Eternal from the produce of the ground. Hevel also brought [an offering], from the firstborn of his sheep and from the fattest ones, and the Eternal showed regard to Hevel and his offering. But to Kayin and his offering He showed no regard, and Kayin became very angry and downcast. The Eternal said to Kayin, "Why are you angry and downcast? If you improve [your deeds], [you] will be forgiven, but if you do not improve [your deeds], then [your] sin is crouching [in wait] at the entrance [of your grave]. Its longing is to [entice] you, but you can dominate it." Kayin then had words with Hevel, his brother, and it happened when they were [both] in the field, that Kayin rose up against Hevel, his brother, and killed him.*[1]

These verses dealing with the actions of Kayin and Hevel present several difficulties. The phrase וְהֶבֶל הֵבִיא גַם הוּא — "And Hevel brought, also he," seems rather circuitous, since the simpler form,

1. *Bereishith* 4:3–8.

וְגַם הֶבֶל הֵבִיא — "And Hevel also brought," would convey the same meaning. There must, therefore, be a reason for the seemingly redundant phrase גַם הוּא, and it is incumbent upon us to discover what the Torah seeks to stress through these words.

The meaning of the words, לַפֶּתַח חַטָּאת רֹבֵץ must also be elucidated, as well as their connection with our subject matter, the primordial feud between Kayin and Hevel.

In addition, we must consider the question posed by the Maharal. Citing the principle stated in *Koheleth*, שׁוֹמֵר מִצְוָה לֹא יֵדַע דָּבָר רָע — "No evil will befall one who is engaged in a mitzvah,"[2] he questions how Hevel could have been killed in the first place while involved in the mitzvah of bringing an offering to God.

The idea of לַפֶּתַח חַטָּאת רֹבֵץ — "Sin crouches at the entrance," is dealt with by the Vilna Gaon in *Adereth Eliyahu*:

> לְפֶתַח הַבַּיִת שָׁם רוֹבֵץ חַטָּאת כֵּיוָן שֶׁפָּתַחְתָּ הַדֶּלֶת אָז הַחַטָּאת רוֹבֵץ כְּאַרְיֵה מִי יְקִימֶנּוּ.
>
> *Sin crouches at the entrance of the house. As soon as the door is pushed ajar, sin enters like a lion.*[3]

The ethical instruction book *Madregoth HaAdam* elaborates on the Gaon's succinct statement. As the author explains, one of the main tactics employed by the evil inclination to seduce man is to set up for him a פֶּתַח כָּשֵׁר, a "kosher opening," that is, an apparently proper motivation to embark on a certain course of action. It disguises evil with a veil of righteousness, thus misleading a person. Once this happens, one is immediately perverted from virtue and quickly led astray, without realising he has done anything wrong. The initial sense of rectitude bolsters one's conviction that he has chosen the right way and blinds him from perceiving that he has in fact fallen prey to evil persuasions. (A חֵטְא is an inadvertent sin where one is insensible to the wrong.) Even spiritual giants are thus induced to sin.

---

2. *Koheleth* 8:5.
3. *Adereth Eliyahu* on *Bereishith* 4:7.

The vice that brought about the sad fates of both Kayin and Hevel was that of jealousy. Although jealousy is considered to be a most ruinous character trait, it can also take a form that our Sages actually praise: קִנְאַת סוֹפְרִים תַּרְבֶּה חָכְמָה — "The envy of Torah scholars increases wisdom."[4] How may we recognise this "good" kind of envy? The distinction between the negative and positive manifestations of envy lies in the root of the emotion. The feeling of jealousy might stem from our perception of a commendable quality in another person, and this jealously might goad us to strive to make this quality a part of our own character, as well.

Alternatively, we might be overcome by a bitter feeling that the very idea of another person being in any way greater than ourselves is intolerable.

The founder of the Mussar movement, Rabbi Yisrael Salanter, once pointed out a real-life illustration of the negative form of jealousy while walking with his students. They passed two little children earnestly debating as to which one was taller. One of the boys settled the argument by pushing the other into the gutter and then quickly measuring himself while he had the advantage of greater apparent height. As the child preened himself victoriously, R. Yisrael observed that this boy would develop into a warped personality. The students thought that their master was referring to the trait of dishonesty that the boy obviously possessed, as he had attempted to win the competition in a false and perverted manner. But R. Yisrael explained, "Dishonesty is a common weakness among children. However, this child's behaviour is particularly despicable. Instead of lowering the other child into the gutter, he could have elevated himself onto a nearby stone." The child did not desire the actual quality of height; he merely wanted to make sure that no one else enjoyed any attribute that would eclipse his own.

We have stated that both Kayin and Hevel suffered from jealousy. Let us now turn to the wisest of all men to help us discern the nature of Hevel's jealousy.

---

4. *Baba Bathra* 21a.

**וְרָאִיתִי אֲנִי אֶת כָּל עָמָל וְאֵת כָּל כִּשְׁרוֹן הַמַּעֲשֶׂה כִּי הִיא קִנְאַת אִישׁ מֵרֵעֵהוּ גַּם זֶה הֶבֶל וּרְעוּת רוּחַ.**

*And I have seen that all labour and skilful enterprise stem from man's rivalry with his neighbour. This too is futility and a vexation of the spirit.*[5]

The Maharal elaborates upon this verse in answering his question mentioned above, namely, how could the performance of a mitzvah lead to Hevel's death?

כִּי רָאִיתִי מַעֲשֵׂה הָאָדָם אֲשֶׁר הָאָדָם טוֹרֵחַ בָּהֶם וְאֶת כָּל כִּשְׁרוֹן הַמַּעֲשֶׂה כִּי הוּא קִנְאַת אִישׁ מֵרֵעֵהוּ וְעוֹשֶׂה גַּם כֵּן מַעֲשֶׂה טוֹב צַד הַקִּנְאָה לַעֲשׂוֹת כְּמוֹ שֶׁעָשָׂה הָאַחֵר, וְאֵין זֶה מִכֹּחַ הִתְעוֹרְרוּת מֵעַצְמוֹ וּלְכָךְ הוּא הֶבֶל – וְאֶפְשָׁר כִּי רֶמֶז כִּי גַּם זֶה הֶבֶל, שֶׁגַּם כָּךְ עָשָׂה הֶבֶל מִכֹּחַ הַקִּנְאָה.[6]

The Maharal explains that the expression גַּם הוּא — "he also," signifies that the offering brought by Hevel was stimulated by envy. He did not personally feel motivated to offer something to God. Rather, his actions stemmed from the desire to imitate Kayin and thus equate himself with his brother. An action is only classed as a genuine mitzvah if it is rooted in the depths of ones's heart. Anything less than total sincerity is mere imitation. Without a firm foundation, a deed will be dissipated by the wind, leaving void, emptiness, and vanity. Hevel's very name, denoting vanity or futility, hints at this inherent characteristic. In this instance, therefore, there was no true mitzvah performed. Hevel's deed did not constitute a truly spiritual and Godly act. Thus the question of how harm could befall Hevel while he was engaged in a mitzvah ceases to exist. Hevel was not performing a deed that emanated from the depths of his own soul; thus he did not enjoy the accompanying protection.

A further point to notice is that Hevel himself fully believed that he was indeed performing a mitzvah in its finest manner. For he had made all the necessary efforts involved in bringing an offering to

---

5. *Koheleth* 4:4.
6. *Derashah* for *Shabbath HaGadol.*

God. However, the principle of לַפֶּתַח חַטָּאת רֹבֵץ here recurs. Hevel was deceived by the "kosher opening," the meritorious appearance of the action, without taking heed of the element of jealousy that goaded him into the action in the first place. The apparent rectitude was only on the surface level. But a deed motivated by a bad character trait, hidden at the root level, sets off a course of evil consequences that escalate until a tragic ending — in this case fratricide — results.

Let us now analyse Kayin's jealousy. Hevel had imitated Kayin's action and his mimicry had been accepted by God, whereas Kayin, who had originated the whole idea of bringing offerings to God, had seen his own offering rejected. Kayin thus considered his anger to be fully justified. Yet with the words, לָמָּה חָרָה לָךְ וְלָמָּה נָפְלוּ פָנֶיךָ — "Why are you angry, and why has your countenance fallen?" God rebuked him for responding in this way. This is highlighted by the classic commentator, the Seforno:

> וְלָמָּה נָפְלוּ פָּנֶיךָ. כִּי כְּשֶׁיֵּשׁ לַקִּלְקוּל אֵיזוֹ תַּקָּנָה אֵין רָאוּי לְהִצְטַעֵר עַל מַה שֶּׁעָבַר אֲבָל רָאוּי לְהִשְׁתַּדֵּל לְהַשִּׂיג תִּקּוּן לֶעָתִיד.
>
> *When some type of failure has occurred, it is not fitting to bemoan the past, rather one should exert oneself to correct one's character for the future.*[7]

Instead of indulging in resentment and becoming morose, Kayin should have been anxious to discover what was lacking in his offering and sought a remedy for the deficiency. Had his envy taken the positive form of קִנְאַת סוֹפְרִים, he would have been glad that Hevel's offering had been accepted, because this afforded him an opportunity to learn how he might improve his own offering.

God says to Kayin, הֲלוֹא אִם תֵּיטִיב שְׂאֵת, if you find a method of rectification and subsequently improve, you will rise and elevate yourself. Kayin's error lay in viewing the matter from a false perspective: anger rather than self-correction.

---

7. Seforno on *Bereishith* 4:7.

Once the evil inclination succeeds in pushing a person through a "kosher opening," one can no longer elude its grasp. The eventual result of an initially small sin is inevitably a grave one. In our incident, Kayin's initial sin was a bitter envy which gradually magnified, culminating in murder.

In accordance with this principle, the Seforno says:

וְאִם לֹא תֵיטִיב — גַּם כֵּן הַחַטָּאת מוּכָן לְפָנֶיךָ כִּי תּוֹסִיף עַל חַטָּאתְךָ פֶּשַׁע שֶׁכָּךְ דַּרְכּוֹ שֶׁל יֵצֶר הָרַע.

*If one does not constantly strive to improve oneself, inadvertent sin leads to premeditated transgression, for this is the way of the evil inclination.*[8]

This fact can be inferred through a close analysis of the following:

**וַיֹּאמֶר קַיִן אֶל הֶבֶל אָחִיו וַיְהִי בִּהְיוֹתָם בַּשָּׂדֶה וַיָּקָם קַיִן אֶל הֶבֶל אָחִיו וַיַּהַרְגֵהוּ.**

*Kayin then had words with Hevel, his brother, and it happened when they were [both] in the field, that Kayin rose up against Hevel, his brother, and killed him.*[9]

Striking in this verse is the absence of information concerning Kayin's conversation with his brother. We are explicitly told that Kayin spoke to Hevel, yet we are left wondering as to the content of the conversation. The Vilna Gaon gives a novel interpretation of the verse, based upon the statement of the Sages that the verb אָמַר, used in the above verse, always indicates soft speech. This tells us that Kayin always spoke to Hevel in a loving manner, continually demonstrating the brotherly feeling that he genuinely felt towards him (as the verse indicates with the phrase הֶבֶל אָחִיו).

However, because a degree of jealousy had always been rooted deep within his heart, once he was alone in the field, without external inhibitors, his vice could break through to the surface with apparent

8. Seforno on *Bereishith* 4:7.

9. *Bereishith* 4:8.

suddenness, overcoming natural brotherly love. Human life was taken. Kayin killed his brother Hevel.

Rabbi Simcha Zissel Ziv, one of the great Mussar teachers of the twentieth century, once stated that at heart everyone is a murderer. This sounds shocking. Yet, although most of us would not set about physically murdering anyone, one often harbours thoughts of envy and hatred upon seeing another advance further than oneself. Resentment is magnified when another's progress appears to come at one's own expense. If not for our awareness of the grievous consequences of venting our anger or jealousy on another person, perhaps these secret emotions would be outwardly, physically expressed, resulting in the devastation of civilisation.

Therefore we must scrutinise our hearts honestly and unflinchingly, with a view to discovering what our behaviour might be should we ever find ourselves בַּשָּׂדֶה — "in the field," removed from the external factors that normally serve to restrain our hidden impulses. For when the evil inclination gains access to a bad trait hidden at the root and sets it into motion, there is no limit to the devastation that ensues. We are obligated, therefore, to uproot any vestige of blemish or weakness from our hearts, and thus cultivate the ground for sincere performance of genuine mitzvoth motivated at the root level, deeds that will elevate us and our lives to spirituality.

# NO'ACH

UPON NO'ACH AND his family's exit from the ark, we read:

וַיִּבֶן נֹחַ מִזְבֵּחַ לַה' וַיִּקַּח מִכֹּל הַבְּהֵמָה הַטְּהוֹרָה וּמִכֹּל הָעוֹף הַטָּהֹר וַיַּעַל עֹלֹת בַּמִּזְבֵּחַ. וַיָּרַח ה' אֶת רֵיחַ הַנִּיחֹחַ וַיֹּאמֶר ה' אֶל לִבּוֹ לֹא אֹסִף לְקַלֵּל עוֹד אֶת הָאֲדָמָה בַּעֲבוּר הָאָדָם כִּי יֵצֶר לֵב הָאָדָם רַע מִנְּעֻרָיו וְלֹא אֹסִף עוֹד לְהַכּוֹת אֶת כָּל חַי כַּאֲשֶׁר עָשִׂיתִי.

*No'ach built an altar to the Eternal, he took some of every [kind of] pure animal and of every [kind of] pure bird, and offered [them] up as burnt-offerings on the altar. The Eternal [willingly accepted his sacrifice], and the Eternal said to Himself, "I will never again curse the ground on account of man['s sins], for the imagination of man's heart is [towards] evil [even] from his [earliest] youth; nor, will I ever again smite all living creatures as I did."*[10]

Rashi explains the seemingly unnecessary repetition of the words וְלֹא אֹסִף:

כָּפַל הַדָּבָר לִשְׁבוּעָה הוּא שֶׁכָּתוּב אֲשֶׁר נִשְׁבַּעְתִּי מֵעֲבֹר מֵי נֹחַ וְלֹא מָצִינוּ בָּהּ שְׁבוּעָה אֶלָּא זוֹ שֶׁכָּפַל דְּבָרָיו וְהוּא שְׁבוּעָה.

*The use in the verse of a double expression indicates an oath undertaken by God, promising never again to bring destruction upon the world.*[11]

It was No'ach's act of bringing offerings that prompted God's vow that He would never again destroy the earth. What special quality lies in sacrifices that would bring about this oath?

---

10. *Bereishith* 8:20.
11. Rashi *ad loc.*

In connection with this incident, we find in the Talmud:

אָמַר רַבִּי חֲנִינָא כָּל הַמִּתְפַּתֶּה בְּיֵינוֹ יֵשׁ בּוֹ מִדַּעַת קוֹנוֹ שֶׁנֶּאֱמַר וַיָּרַח ה' אֶת רֵיחַ הַנִּיחֹחַ וגו'.

*Said R. Chanina, "One who is persuaded by his own wine possesses a characteristic similar to God. For the verse states that God smelt the sweet scent of the offerings (and made an oath)."*[12]

Let us uncover the meaning behind this enigmatic statement. No'ach was instructed concerning the building of the ark:

**עֲשֵׂה לְךָ תֵּבַת עֲצֵי גֹפֶר קִנִּים תַּעֲשֶׂה אֶת הַתֵּבָה וְכָפַרְתָּ אֹתָהּ מִבַּיִת וּמִחוּץ בַּכֹּפֶר.**

*Make for yourself an ark of gofer wood...*[13]

Rashi questions the reason for the ark's construction:

עֲשֵׂה לְךָ תֵּבַת — הַרְבֵּה רֶוַח וְהַצָּלָה לְפָנָיו וְלָמָּה הִטְרִיחוֹ בְּבִנְיָן זֶה, כְּדֵי שֶׁיִּרְאוּהוּ אַנְשֵׁי דוֹר הַמַּבּוּל עוֹסֵק בָּהּ ק"כ שָׁנָה וְשׁוֹאֲלִים אוֹתוֹ מַה זֹּאת לְךָ וְהוּא אוֹמֵר לָהֶם עָתִיד הקב"ה לְהָבִיא מַבּוּל לָעוֹלָם, אוּלַי יָשׁוּבוּ.[14]

The Almighty has any number of methods through which He could save man. Therefore, Rashi asks, why was the elaborate construction involved in building an ark necessary? He answers that underlying No'ach's tremendous exertion was the ideal of working for the public good. When the people of the generation saw him engaged in his project, they would inquire as to the ark's purpose. No'ach would respond that if they did not repent God would bring a deluge upon the world. His prolonged process of construction tangibly conveyed a warning to civilization.

The Midrash[15] documents the people's reaction:

---

12. *Eruvin* 65a.
13. *Bereishith* 6:14.
14. Rashi *ad loc.*
15. *Bereishith Rabbah* 30:16.

The entire 120 years, the people saw No'ach planting and felling trees.

The people: "Why are you doing this?"

No'ach's response: "The Master of the World commanded me to do so, for He will bring a flood upon the world."

The people: "If He brings a flood, it will be your family who will perish. We will remain unaffected."

Upon the death of Methushelach, No'ach's grandfather, the people pointed an accusing finger at No'ach, as their claim that No'ach's family would suffer seemed to have been substantiated.

No'ach's tireless efforts seemed futile, having no visible effect upon civilization. No'ach continued to build; the people continued to mock. Nevertheless, No'ach remained steadfast in his all-embracing devotion to God.

Our Sages bring a different perspective on No'ach's effort to inspire his generation to repentance.

> וְלָא בָּעִי רַחֲמֵי עַל עָלְמָא וּנְחִיתֵי מַיָּא אֲבוּדוּ בְּנֵי עָלְמָא, וּבְגִין כָּךְ "מֵי נֹחַ" כְּתִיב, דְּלָא בָּעִי רַחֲמֵי עַל עָלְמָא.
>
> *No'ach did not beseech God on behalf of mankind. The world was engulfed with water and civilization was extirpated. The flood was called after No'ach — "Waters of No'ach," attributed to him due to his failure to pray for the people.*[16]

No'ach devoted 120 years of his life providing a graphic stimulus to repentance. Why then do our Sages hold him culpable? And why indeed did he not beseech the Almighty for the people's sake?

A passage from the prophet Michah will help us reconcile these difficulties:

> **מִי אֵ-ל כָּמוֹךָ נֹשֵׂא עָוֹן וְעֹבֵר עַל פֶּשַׁע לִשְׁאֵרִית נַחֲלָתוֹ לֹא הֶחֱזִיק לָעַד אַפּוֹ כִּי חָפֵץ חֶסֶד הוּא. יָשׁוּב יְרַחֲמֵנוּ יִכְבֹּשׁ עֲוֹנֹתֵינוּ וְתַשְׁלִיךְ בִּמְצֻלוֹת יָם כָּל חַטֹּאותָם. תִּתֵּן אֱמֶת לְיַעֲקֹב חֶסֶד לְאַבְרָהָם אֲשֶׁר נִשְׁבַּעְתָּ לַאֲבֹתֵינוּ מִימֵי קֶדֶם.**

16. *Zohar, Bereishith* 67.

*Who is a God like You, Who forgives iniquity and passes over the transgression of the remnant of His heritage? He does not maintain His anger forever, for He desires loving kindness. He shall return and grant us compassion; He shall hide our iniquities, and You shall cast into the depths of the sea all their sins. You have given truth to Ya'akov, loving kindness to Avraham, which You swore to our forefathers from days of yore.*[17]

The profound ethical book *Tomer Devorah* explains that these three verses contain thirteen qualities. We will deal with the last one of these qualities, that of מִימֵי קֶדֶם.

הֲרֵי מִדָּה שֶׁיֵּשׁ להקב"ה עִם יִשְׂרָאֵל. כְּשֶׁתַּמָּה זְכוּת אָבוֹת וְכַיּוֹצֵא, מַה יַּעֲשֶׂה, וַהֲרֵי מִצַּד עַצְמָם אֵינָם הֲגוּנִים. כְּתִיב [ירמיהו ב':א'] "זָכַרְתִּי לָךְ חֶסֶד נְעוּרַיִךְ אַהֲבַת כְּלוּלֹתָיִךְ" מַמָּשׁ זוֹכֵר הקב"ה יְמֵי קַדְמוֹנִים אַהֲבָה שֶׁהָיָה מִקֶּדֶם, וּמְרַחֵם עַל יִשְׂרָאֵל וּבָזֶה יַזְכִּיר לָהֶם כָּל הַמִּצְוֹות שֶׁעָשׂוּ מִיּוֹם שֶׁנּוֹלְדוּ וְכָל מִדּוֹת טוֹבוֹת שהקב"ה מַנְהִיג בָּהֶם עוֹלָמוֹ, וּמִכֻּלָּם עוֹשֶׂה סְגֻלָּה לְרַחֵם בִּשְׁבִילָם.

כָּךְ הָאָדָם יְתַקֵּן הַנְהָגָתוֹ עִם בְּנֵי אָדָם, שֶׁאֲפִלּוּ לֹא יִמְצָא טַעֲנָה בָּאֵלּוּ הַנִּזְכָּרוֹת, יֹאמַר "כְּבָר הָיָה שָׁעָה קֹדֶם שֶׁלֹּא חָטְאוּ, וַהֲרֵי אוֹתָהּ שָׁעָה, אוֹ בְּיָמִים קַדְמוֹנִים, הָיוּ כְּשֵׁרִים". וְיִזְכֹּר לָהֶם הַטּוֹבָה שֶׁעָשׂוּ בְּקַטְנוּתָם, וְיִזְכֹּר לָהֶם אַהֲבַת גְּמוּלֵי מֵחָלָב עַתִּיקֵי מִשָּׁדַיִם וּבָזֶה לֹא יִמְצָא אָדָם שֶׁאֵינוֹ רָאוּי לְהֵטִיבוֹ וּלְהִתְפַּלֵּל עַל שְׁלוֹמוֹ וּלְרַחֵם עָלָיו.

*This is the attribute with which God conducts Himself towards the Jewish nation when their merit and all other mitigating factors fail, and they are unworthy. What course of action can the Almighty then take?*

*The verse states (Yirmiyah 2:1), "I recall My kindness towards you in your youth, the love for you on the day of your marriage...." God recalls the days of old and the love He once felt towards His people, and His compassion is aroused. He remembers all the commandments they have fulfilled from the beginning of their nationhood, and all the good qualities with which God conducts His world. From all these, God fashions a*

---

17. *Michah* 7:18–20.

> *special treasure with which to show them compassion.*
>
> *A person should strive to improve his conduct towards others. For even if he cannot find a logical reason for showing love and compassion to his fellow, he should say, "There was surely a time when they had not yet sinned, and in that time or in former days they were worthy." He should recall the love of "those just weaned." This way he will not find a single person unworthy of kindness, prayer, or compassion.*[18]

No'ach is described as an אִישׁ צַדִּיק תָּמִים, an upright and righteous individual. The word צַדִּיק implies acting strictly in accordance with the letter of the law. A person in this category will not feel compassion towards one who does not legitimately deserve it.

It was because of this characteristic that No'ach could not pray wholeheartedly for a civilization which he felt was undeserving. Hammer onto nail, with every bang No'ach would try to return the people to God. And, once they had elevated themselves sufficiently, No'ach would find them deserving of his prayers on their behalf. No'ach spent 120 years toiling to present a genuine prayer on behalf of the nation. Prayer is defined as "service of the heart," and requires heartfelt emotion to qualify as the optimum act of prayer. No'ach had to develop a real compassion, which emanated from the core of his being, to facilitate a true act of prayer on behalf of the corrupt and perverted society in which he lived.

In contrast to No'ach, Avraham was called an אִישׁ חֶסֶד. This term implies that he went beyond the strict dictates of the law. Indeed we find he implored God on behalf of Sedom, those people who were completely embroiled in evil. The necessary quality in this situation was that trait elucidated above by the *Tomer Devorah*, of מִימֵי קֶדֶם — "days of yore." He searched for purity deep within the people of Sedom, regardless of how far back he had to probe. For this very reason, Avraham was able to beseech God to have mercy upon them. He was able to recall the times when they possessed Godliness and through this recollection, have compassion and pray for them.

---

18. *Tomer Devorah,* Ch. 1.

Relating to this theme, the commentator *Ohr HaChaim* brings the following parable:

One Friday night, a wealthy man encountered a destitute wayfarer and invited him home for a meal. After a truly satisfying Sabbath meal, the host, seeing that the pauper had nowhere to go, further extended his hospitality.

As days turned into weeks, the pauper's discomfort in being a constant recipient of his host's kindness turned into shame. His feelings intensified until, sitting at a Sabbath meal, he could no longer contain himself. With a bottle of crimson wine in one hand, and a silver goblet in the other, the pauper began pouring. As the cup filled to the brim, with a shaking hand, the pauper handed the goblet to his host. He pleaded with his host to accept his own property as a gift. He had no possessions of his own to offer to his host; he could only hand him what was already his, and pray that his benefactor accept the sentiment with which it was accompanied.

His host was "persuaded with his own wine," accepting that which was rightfully his. He garbed himself with the characteristics of the Almighty.

This parable corresponds to the underlying idea of sacrifices, as explained by the *Akeidas Yitzchak*. Imagine a person trying to buy a present for a friend who has everything. He seeks advice from a third party, who informs him of an appropriate gift for this affluent man. The one who seeks to give will be delighted with the information, and will consider the disclosure an act of kindness.

Similarly, we have an overwhelming desire to "give" to the Almighty. However, what can a lowly mortal bestow upon omnipotent God? The Torah informs us that we can bring offerings, granting us the opportunity to "give" to our Creator in some way, causing a רֵיחַ נִיחֹחַ לַה'. Man's constant existence, second after second, minute after minute, is a direct result of God's benevolence. Through the act of bringing sacrifices, we are taking God's crimson wine and silver goblet, the gifts He gives us, and returning them to Him, with the hope that He will accept the sentiments behind it. We give back to Him of His own. Thus our Sages' words are understood: כָּל הַמִּתְפַּתֶּה

בְּיֵינוֹ יֵשׁ בּוֹ מִדַּעַת קוֹנוֹ — "One who is persuaded with his own wine possesses a similar characteristic to God."

No'ach's year-long sojourn in the ark served to rectify a slight deficiency of his in the area of unconditional kindness and giving. His test, to feed and care for a multitude of animals, was quite impossible. Apart from the duty of caring for his family members, he now had to meet the many different requirements of caring for these multifarious species. This was a year replete with arduous tasks, straining No'ach to the limit.

The result: God brought the job to its completion by bestowing Divine aid. After his unbelievable exertion in the ark, God gave No'ach the assistance to obtain levels which were previously out of his reach.

There is a principle of הַכֹּל לְפִי רֹב הַמַּעֲשֶׂה, the repetition of a physical action makes a profound impression on one's essence, changing the person. No'ach, during this year of constant giving, underwent a metamorphosis from an אִישׁ צַדִּיק, a man of justice and exactitude, to an אִישׁ חֶסֶד, a man of kindness.

It was in this mode of giving that No'ach proceeded to build a new world in a new form, reflected in the physical realm through the sacrifices that he offered. Mankind now carried the ability to give for its own sake, by considering the מִימֵי קֶדֶם — "days of yore" — of each individual. This was a result of No'ach's intense work in the ark.

As emphasized by the *Tomer Devorah*, it is this trait of מִימֵי קֶדֶם which is vital for us to exercise in our lives. We must look at the original purity of every Jew, the spark of Godliness that all possess. Through this trait we become likened to our Creator and as in all areas, when we work to acquire it, we will receive Divine aid to progress further. The ramifications of cultivating this characteristic not only affect a lone individual, but build the entire world. For it was through acquisition of the quality of מִימֵי קֶדֶם that No'ach, in the days of old, built the world anew.

With the bringing of sacrifices at the world's new inception, God promised never again to destroy the universe. For the cosmos would now endure and be sustained through unmitigated kindness, as symbolized by those offerings which prompted God's vow. In our own lives, may we merit to build the world through cultivating this trait of compassionate kindness within each of us, within each "miniature world."

# LECH LECHA

IN GREAT DETAIL, the *parashah* describes the war between the Five Kings and the Four Kings, in which Lot, Avraham's nephew, is taken captive. Avraham comes to Lot's rescue and defeats the Four Kings. Reading between the lines, one discovers that this war was not caused only by political motives, nor is it documented in the Torah simply as a piece of history. Rather, this war holds a powerful message for all.

In this episode, Nimrod, one of the Four Kings, is referred to as Amraphel. Rashi explains the significance of this name: שֶׁאָמַר לְאַבְרָם פֹּל לְתוֹךְ כִּבְשַׁן הָאֵשׁ... — "Who said to Avraham, fall into the fiery furnace."[19] Avraham rejected the prevalent beliefs of his time, and instead spread belief in Hashem throughout the world. This new conviction was a fatal blow to the beliefs and religion of the society at large and particularly to Nimrod, as the king. In his efforts to ensure the survival of his beliefs and to save his position as a god, Nimrod tried to thwart Avraham's growing support. To this end, he cast Avraham into a fiery furnace and thus acquired the name אַמְרָפֶל.

As the battle progresses we read:

**וַיָּשֻׁבוּ וַיָּבֹאוּ אֶל עֵין מִשְׁפָּט הִוא קָדֵשׁ.**

*They then turned back and came to Ein Mishpat — that is Kadesh.*[20]

The Midrash explains the symbolic connotation of the name *Ein Mishpat*: לֹא בָאוּ לְהִזְדַוֵּג אֶלָּא לְתוֹךְ גַּלְגַּל עֵינוֹ שֶׁל עוֹלָם — "They were

19. Rashi on *Bereishith* 14:2.
20. *Bereishith* 14:7.

fighting against the focal point of the world..."[21] The *Mattenas Kehunah* states that "the focal point of the world" refers to our Patriarch Avraham, who eased the world out of its previous state devoid of belief and meaning. The Midrash implies that the war was in fact a "religious war," directed solely at Avraham, whose revolutionary ideas endangered the dogma of the era. When the Four Kings captured Lot, Avraham's nephew, their sole intention was to rid the world of Avraham and extinguish the belief that he had kindled.

**אַחַר הַדְּבָרִים הָאֵלֶּה הָיָה דְבַר ה' אֶל אַבְרָם בַּמַּחֲזֶה לֵאמֹר אַל תִּירָא אַבְרָם אָנֹכִי מָגֵן לָךְ שְׂכָרְךָ הַרְבֵּה מְאֹד.**

*After these events, the word of the Eternal was [addressed] to Avram in a vision, saying, "Avram, do not be afraid! I will act as a protection for you, [and] your reward will be very great."*[22]

Rashi explains that after the war between Avraham and the Four Kings, the Almighty appeared to reassure him and guarantee his protection. Avraham feared that as a result of the miracles that had ensured his victory, perhaps he had forfeited his Eternal reward, having received it already in this world. God removed this worry:

**אַל תִּירָא** — Do not worry.

**אָנֹכִי מָגֵן לָךְ** — You will not be punished for killing all those that you killed.

**שְׂכָרְךָ הַרְבֵּה מְאֹד** — You have not lost your Eternal reward.

The Midrash[23] elaborates:

*Avraham was worried that perhaps there may have been a righteous individual among all the people he had killed in the war. To this God answered* **שְׂכָרְךָ הַרְבֵּה מְאֹד** *— "Your reward is great..." R. Levi brings a parable of one who removed weeds and thorns from the King's orchard. The King saw this and the man was worried that perhaps he would be punished for his*

---

21. *Bereishith Rabbah* 42:11.
22. *Bereishith* 15:1.
23. *Bereishith Rabbah* 44:5.

*deed. The King reassured him, saying that had he not removed the thorns, the King would have had to hire workers to remove them. The man thus deserved payment.*

*So God said to Avraham. The people that he had killed were thorns in the garden of God. Avraham removed them and should now receive reward. R. Levi continues, saying that Avraham was worried lest the kings whom he had fought would form a military alliance against him. God answered him,* אַל תִּירָא... אָנֹכִי מָגֵן לָךְ *— "I will protect you."* אָנֹכִי מָגֵן לָךְ *and* שְׂכָרְךָ הַרְבֵּה מְאֹד *were guarantees and reassurances to stave off Avraham's fears.*

The Maharal[24] sheds light on the words אָנֹכִי מָגֵן לָךְ — "I will shield you," enumerating the specific criteria required to merit this Divine protection. These criteria find greatest expression in Avraham about whom we say in our prayers, בָּרוּךְ אַתָּה ה' מָגֵן אַבְרָהָם — "Blessed are You, God, shield of Avraham." What are these qualities that make Avraham the one person who is referred to as "the one whom God shields?"

Avraham battled valiantly against the Four Kings. And it was his quality of internality that enabled him to merit the Divine protection of "אָנֹכִי מָגֵן לָךְ" and thus emerge victorious. The Four Kings, personifying the external, opposed Avraham, the centre, internal point of the world.

As elucidated by the Maharal, every number is invested with profound significance, symbolizing a certain spiritual concept. The number four is symbolic of externality, while the number one always represents the inner, hidden, spiritual core of an entity. This can be seen in the verse: ...וּפָרַצְתָּ יָמָּה וָקֵדְמָה וְצָפֹנָה וָנֶגְבָּה — "And you shall expand to the west, and to the east, and to the north, and to the south."[25] Expansion always manifests in four directions that emanate from one central point. One can balance a cube only by finding its centre of gravity. The equilibrium of the cube is dependent on the

24. *Gevuroth Hashem* Ch. 6.
25. *Bereishith* 28:14.

internal, central point. The cube will be unable to balance on any of its external sides.

The whole world rests on the shoulders of Avraham, who injected the world with belief in God. This can be clearly seen in the following verse:

**אֵלֶּה תוֹלְדוֹת הַשָּׁמַיִם וְהָאָרֶץ בְּהִבָּרְאָם.**

*These are the offspring of the heavens and the earth in their creation.*[26]

Rearranged, the Hebrew letters בְּהִבָּרְאָם spelling "in their creation," form אַבְרָהָם — "Avraham." The world was created for the belief and ideals that Avraham propagated. In contrast, the Four Kings observed the world's multiplicity and concluded that the forces of nature were independent powers. They refused to see the centre point of all directions, the One Force controlling all, recognising only the shell without the inner meaning.

Only by constant probing could their error have been dispelled. In the words of Yeshayah:

**שְׂאוּ מָרוֹם עֵינֵיכֶם וּרְאוּ מִי בָרָא אֵלֶּה...**

*Lift up your eyes and see Who created these.*[27]

It is notable that one of the Hebrew names we use for God, אֱלֹקִים, is composed of the same letters as the two words מִי אֵלֶּה — "Who are these?" Only by constantly asking מִי בָרָא אֵלֶּה — "Who created these?" can one pierce through the superficial diversity and discern the Creator and the Guide of the World. Avraham did just this. He discovered the One and Only God. He discovered the unity, the internal point, despite the external multiplicity.

Another illustration of this idea is found in an exchange between Yosef and his father Yisrael (Ya'akov) immediately prior to Yisrael's passing.

---

26. *Bereishith* 2:4.
27. *Yeshayah* 40:26.

**וַיַּרְא יִשְׂרָאֵל אֶת בְּנֵי יוֹסֵף וַיֹּאמֶר מִי אֵלֶּה. וַיֹּאמֶר יוֹסֵף אֶל אָבִיו בָּנַי הֵם אֲשֶׁר נָתַן לִי אֱלֹהִים בָּזֶה...**

*Yisrael then perceived Yosef's sons, and he asked, "Who are these?" Yosef answered his father, "They are my sons whom God has granted me by means of this (בָּזֶה)."*[28]

Ya'akov's question, מִי אֵלֶּה, alludes to the words, אֵלֶּה אֱלֹהֶיךָ יִשְׂרָאֵל — "These are your gods, Israel," which were said during the Children of Yisrael's paganistic service of the Golden Calf. It is the multiplicity in nature (אֵלֶּה — "These") that leads to the fatal error of idolatry. In essence Ya'akov was questioning his son's ability to see through the אֵלֶּה, the multiplicity, through continuous study of מִי בָרָא אֵלֶּה, the unifying Force behind this world of confusion. Yosef hastened to assure Ya'akov by using the word בָּזֶה — "with this." This word is in the singular form to imply that Yosef and his offspring indeed possess the ability to recognise the underlying unity in the creation, the Unifier of creation.

Let us turn our attention back to the war of the Four Kings against Avraham. This was no mere physical war; it was a battle of faith, of essence. It was a clash of externality versus internality, paganism and the belief in powers of nature versus conviction in God, the Unifying force of the world.

A second thought deduced by the Maharal from R. Levi's words on אָנֹכִי מָגֵן לָךְ is as follows:

Avraham is the יְסוֹד הָרִאשׁוֹן — "The first foundation" upon which the world is built. A יְסוֹד — "foundation," is extremely strong, and cannot be uprooted. Even the intense force of many nations united is rendered useless against Avraham, the cornerstone of the world.

A third idea expressed by the Maharal on אָנֹכִי מָגֵן לָךְ is that Avraham was the pioneer of belief in God in the world. The significance of this idea is that initiation is not dependent on the thoughts of others. Were Avraham to have been affected by the ideas of others, he would not have been "first," but rather a follower of others, i.e.,

28. *Bereishith* 48:8, 9.

secondary. The existence of the number two is dependent on the preceding number one. In contrast, the number one is independent. Avraham was the first, number one, herald of a new era in which faith in God would prevail. He could not possibly have been influenced by anyone, because this would be antithetical to the idea of initiation.

Granted that these three concepts, of initiation, foundation, and internality — הַתְחָלָה, יְסוֹד, פְּנִימִיּוּת — are all stated concerning אָנֹכִי מָגֵן לָךְ, it is certain that there can be only one underlying theme connecting them all.

We say in our Sabbath prayers: סוֹף מַעֲשֶׂה בְּמַחֲשָׁבָה תְּחִלָּה. The thrust of this statement is that the end result is a physical manifestation of an abstract initial thought. Thought is clearly related to internality, one's hidden inner life. It is only through the existence of this internality that ideas can eventually be manifest, and plans can materialise. For if there was no initial thought, or internal life, nothing would exist! פְּנִימִיּוּת — internality, thought, is therefore clearly linked to initiation — הַתְחָלָה. As stated: בְּמַחֲשָׁבָה תְּחִלָּה — "first in thought."

Avraham also possessed the quality of יְסוֹד, being the "foundation" of the world. As explained above, Avraham was the initiator of monotheism, and as such, was independent of any external influences. He was a foundation, a bastion of faith because of his internality, because of the philosophical conclusion that he reached of his own accord.

The *Mesillath Yesharim* brings the relationship among the three concepts into sharper focus:

> יְסוֹד הַחֲסִידוּת וְשֹׁרֶשׁ הָעֲבוֹדָה הַתְּמִימָה הוּא, שֶׁיִּתְבָּרֵר וְיִתְאַמֵּת אֵצֶל הָאָדָם מַה חוֹבָתוֹ בְּעוֹלָמוֹ.
>
> *This is the foundation of piety and the root of perfect service of God: it should be clear to a person, and verified, what his duty is in this world.*[29]

---

29. *Mesillath Yesharim,* Ch. 1.

One's Divine service is founded (יְסוֹד וְשֹׁרֶשׁ) on one's internal thought — פְּנִימִיּוּת (שֶׁיִּתְבָּרֵר וְיִתְאַמֵּת) in first (הַתְחָלָה) clarifying what are one's obligations in this world. Hence the three concepts — הַתְחָלָה, יְסוֹד, פְּנִימִיּוּת — are in actuality only dimensions of the same underlying idea, אָנֹכִי מָגֵן לָךְ.

Let us elaborate on this profound and illuminating principle.

**וַיְהִי בַּיָּמִים הָהֵם וַיִּגְדַּל מֹשֶׁה וַיֵּצֵא אֶל אֶחָיו וַיַּרְא בְּסִבְלֹתָם וַיַּרְא אִישׁ מִצְרִי מַכֶּה אִישׁ עִבְרִי מֵאֶחָיו. וַיִּפֶן כֹּה וָכֹה וַיַּרְא כִּי אֵין אִישׁ וַיַּךְ אֶת הַמִּצְרִי וַיִּטְמְנֵהוּ בַּחוֹל. וַיֵּצֵא בַּיּוֹם הַשֵּׁנִי וְהִנֵּה שְׁנֵי אֲנָשִׁים עִבְרִים נִצִּים וַיֹּאמֶר לָרָשָׁע לָמָּה תַכֶּה רֵעֶךָ. וַיֹּאמֶר מִי שָׂמְךָ לְאִישׁ שַׂר וְשֹׁפֵט עָלֵינוּ הַלְהָרְגֵנִי אַתָּה אֹמֵר כַּאֲשֶׁר הָרַגְתָּ אֶת הַמִּצְרִי וַיִּירָא מֹשֶׁה וַיֹּאמַר אָכֵן נוֹדַע הַדָּבָר.**

*During that time Moshe grew up, and he went out to his brethren and saw their suffering. And he saw a Mitzri man hitting an Ivri man, [one] of his brethren. He turned this way and that and saw there was no one, so he struck the Mitzri [dead] and hid him in the sand. He went out the next day and there were two Ivri men quarreling. He said to the wicked one, "Why do you [wish to] hit your companion?" He replied, "Who appointed you as an officer and judge over us? Do you plan to kill me as you killed the Mitzri?" Moshe was afraid, saying [to himself], "Indeed the matter is known!"*[30]

Rashi elaborates:

דָּאַג לוֹ עַל שֶׁרָאָה בְּיִשְׂרָאֵל רְשָׁעִים דֵּילָטוֹרִין. אָמַר מֵעַתָּה שֶׁמָּא אֵינָם רְאוּיִין לְהִגָּאֵל.

*It worried him to see wicked people among the Jews who spoke evil of one another. He said to himself, perhaps they are no longer worthy of being redeemed.*[31]

Moshe now realised why the Jews deserved to suffer so: they quarreled and bore tales about one another.

---

30. *Shemoth* 2:11–14.
31. Rashi *ad loc.*

The Maharal[32] elaborates: "Whoever has the trait of revealing the hidden is undeserving of redemption." Redemption is dependent on a person's internal quality. A person's spirit can never be subjected to the rule or command of an oppressor. It is only when one exposes one's internality, losing the spirit to the world of superficiality and externals, that oppressors can have complete dominion over body, mind, and soul.

It seems impossible to fathom the survival and tenacity of Jews under the extreme torture and suffering inflicted by the Nazis. However, applying the explanation of the Maharal stated above, one can attempt to comprehend. The Nazis may have hurt us bodily, diminished our physical numbers by six million, affected our actions. But no amount of affliction and torment could impinge upon our souls. Our spirit reigned supreme, remaining free despite the physical bondage.

This idea is beautifully expressed in the actual words of the verse: אָכֵן נוֹדַע הַדָּבָר— "Indeed the matter is known." In this word "אָכֵן" the letter א is not pronounced, it being a silent letter. A permutation of the letter *alef* when spelled out in full — אָלֶף — is the word פֶּלֶא, meaning "hidden," signifying פְּנִימִיּוּת, internality. It is when one reveals the hidden, externalizing the internal, that the פֶּלֶא, or אָלֶף, is transformed to "כֵּן — this is so!" The *alef* is brought into a world of כֵּן; a world of the tangible, of physical dimensions.

The letter *alef* always signifies one. The numerical value of the word "כֵּן" is 70. The Jewish People are one and independent as long as they remain faithful to their natural habitat: the world of internality and depth. As soon as the Jewish nation divorces itself from internality, entering the realm of the physical, it is immediately vulnerable to the reign of the 70 nations — "כֵּן".

This is what Moshe implied when he stated "אָכֵן נוֹדַע הַדָּבָר". He saw wicked people amongst the nation, those who reveal the hidden, and knew that they could not be redeemed. They must remain under the dominion of seventy, of proliferation and externality.

---

32. *Gur Aryeh ad loc.*

Thus we view with clarity the war between Avraham and the Four Kings. Avraham was internality personified. The Four Kings were the embodiment of external physicality. The Four Kings, the "כֵּן", could have no power whatsoever over Avraham, the "א".

One who identifies with the outer world and sees everything with the associated superficial perception, is unable to appreciate true depth or recognise, "מִי בָרָא אֵלֶּה". A demonstration of this is found in the following:

**וְעֵמֶק הַשִּׂדִּים בֶּאֱרֹת בֶּאֱרֹת חֵמָר וַיָּנֻסוּ מֶלֶךְ סְדֹם וַעֲמֹרָה וַיִּפְּלוּ שָׁמָּה וְהַנִּשְׁאָרִים הֶרָה נָּסוּ.**

*The Valley of Siddim was full of clay pits, and [when] the King of Sedom and [the king of] Amorah fled, they fell there...*[33]

Rashi says that the Kings of Sedom and Amorah fell into a quagmire, and a miracle happened to them and they escaped from the pit. This miracle transpired because there were many amongst the nations who did not believe that Avraham was miraculously saved from the fiery furnace of Nimrod. Now that the King of Sedom was miraculously extricated from the quagmire, they retrospectively believed in the miracle that had happened to Avraham.

The Ramban is perturbed by the words of Rashi:

הָאֻמּוֹת שֶׁלֹּא הָיוּ מַאֲמִינִים שֶׁעָשָׂה הקב"ה נֵס לְאַבְרָהָם, בִּרְאוֹתָם נִסּוֹ שֶׁל מֶלֶךְ סְדוֹם לֹא יוֹסִיפוּ אֱמוּנָה בהקב"ה.[34]

The Ramban asks why the nations would believe in the miracle that God performed for Avraham, through seeing the miracle that happened to the King of Sedom. The King of Sedom was an idolater. One would logically think that the miracle which he experienced should, rather than strengthening faith in monotheism, cast aspersions on the power of God and reinforce his and others' belief in paganism and the powers of "chance."

---

33. *Bereishith* 14:10.
34. Ramban *ad loc.*

The Ramban suggests an answer to this question. The miracle experienced by the King of Sedom did not occur until Avraham passed the pit. The miracle clearly happened in the merit of Avraham, who desired to save the kings and return their possessions. Seeing this, one would now believe in the miracle that saved Avraham from the fiery furnace, because it was only due to Avraham that the King of Sedom was miraculously saved!

The *Nachalath Eliezer* highlights a parallel between the words of the Ramban and the Midrash:

When the King of Sedom emerged from the pit, he arrogantly declared:

"מָה אַתָּה יָרַדְתָּ לְכִבְשַׁן הָאֵשׁ וְנִצַּלְתָּ, אַף אֲנִי יָרַדְתִּי לַחֵמָר וְנִצַּלְתִּי..."

*"Just as you were saved from the fiery furnace, so too was I saved from this quagmire..."*[35]

Instead of having gratitude to Avraham, in whose merit he was saved, the King of Sedom attributed the miracle to his own merit. This was the direct result of a superficial outlook. He lacked the trait of acknowledging the origin, the abstract Source of everything, and therefore he could be confronted with blatant truth, and yet ignore it.

One's life is dictated by the forces in which he places his trust. The fluctuating winds of political life and current world events bespeak just this. Factions and individuals within society place their trust in other mortals, often individuals of the most immoral and degenerate calibre. And what strength does a person gain through this belief in "forces" of the external? His conviction renders him helpless.

The Chafetz Chaim takes this a step further. In reality, externals and physicality have no power at all. Consequently, if one has no trust in God, one is trusting void, vanity — nothing.

If one first has the internal thought, the פְּנִימִיּוּת, based on knowledge of his purpose in this world, he becomes a יְסוֹד, a cornerstone

35. *Bereishith Rabbah* 43:6.

that cannot be moved. He is one, working towards the Ultimate One. And it is only then that a person is guaranteed complete protection from all external forces: אָנֹכִי מָגֵן לָךְ — "I will shield you."

יִשְׂרָאֵל בְּטַח בַּה' עֶזְרָם וּמָגִנָּם הוּא.

*Yisrael, trust in God; He is their help and shield.*[36]

36. *Tehillim* 115:9.

# VAYERA

WHEN ANGELS APPEARED to Avraham three days after his circumcision, he exerted himself in the mitzvah of welcoming visitors, and the verse states:

יֻקַּח נָא מְעַט מַיִם וְרַחֲצוּ רַגְלֵיכֶם וְהִשָּׁעֲנוּ תַּחַת הָעֵץ.

*Let a little bit of water be brought now, and wash your feet and rest yourselves under the tree.*[37]

The Gemara expounds:

תַּנָּא דְּבֵי רַבִּי יִשְׁמָעֵאל בִּשְׂכַר שְׁלֹשָׁה זָכוּ לִשְׁלֹשָׁה. בִּשְׂכַר "חֶמְאָה וְחָלָב" זָכוּ לַמָּן, בִּשְׂכַר "וְהוּא עוֹמֵד עֲלֵיהֶם" זָכוּ לְעַמּוּד הֶעָנָן, בִּשְׂכַר "יֻקַּח נָא מְעַט מַיִם" זָכוּ לִבְאֵרָהּ שֶׁל מִרְיָם.[38]

In the merit of Avraham's actions, his progeny benefited in a number of ways:

1. They received manna in the wilderness as a result of Avraham's having fed the angels.
2. The cloud that stood over the Jewish nation to direct them through the desert corresponded to Avraham's standing over the angels to serve them.
3. They enjoyed water from the Well of Miriam, corresponding to Avraham's instruction, "Let a little bit of water be brought now."

Our Sages,[39] however, state elsewhere that the well from which the Jewish People benefited in the desert was given to them in

37. *Bereishith* 18:4.
38. *Baba Metzia* 86b.
39. *Ta'anith* 9a.

Miriam's merit. The Maharsha[40] questions this seeming discrepancy. In whose merit was the well bestowed upon the people, Avraham's or Miriam's?

A similar question arises when examining the mitzvah of *tzitzith*. After No'ach finally left the ark, he planted a vineyard. He produced wine, and subsequently became inebriated. The verse then relates:

**וַיִּקַּח שֵׁם וָיֶפֶת אֶת הַשִּׂמְלָה וַיָּשִׂימוּ עַל שְׁכֶם שְׁנֵיהֶם וַיֵּלְכוּ אֲחֹרַנִּית וַיְכַסּוּ אֵת עֶרְוַת אֲבִיהֶם...**

*And he, Shem, with Yefeth, then took the garment and placed [it] on the shoulders of both of them. They walked backwards, and covered their father...*[41]

Rashi questions the use of the singular form to refer to both brothers:

לְשׁוֹן יָחִיד – אֵין כְּתִיב כָּאן וַיִּקְחוּ אֶלָּא וַיִּקַּח לִמֵּד עַל שֵׁם שֶׁנִּתְאַמֵּץ בְּמִצְוָה יוֹתֵר מִיֶּפֶת. לְכָךְ זָכוּ בָנָיו לְטַלִּית שֶׁל צִיצִית.

וַיִּקַּח — *"And he took" in the singular form is used, for Shem exerted himself in this mitzvah more than did Yefeth. (The whole deed is thus attributed to him.) It was due to this that his descendants merited the mitzvah of tzitzith.*[42]

In direct conflict with this information is our Sages' comment concerning Avraham's statement after his conquest of the Four Kings. Avraham disdained to take the spoils of battle, declaring:

**אִם מִחוּט וְעַד שְׂרוֹךְ נַעַל וְאִם אֶקַּח מִכָּל אֲשֶׁר לָךְ וְלֹא תֹאמַר אֲנִי הֶעֱשַׁרְתִּי אֶת אַבְרָם.**

*[I will not keep] even a thread or a shoelace, nor will I take anything of yours, [so that] you will not [be able to] say, "I made Avram rich."*[43]

---

40. Maharsha *ad loc.*
41. *Bereishith* 9:23.
42. Rashi *ad loc.*
43. *Bereishith* 14:23.

We are told of the consequences of Avraham's behaviour:

דָּרַשׁ רָבָא בִּשְׂכַר שֶׁאָמַר אַבְרָהָם אָבִינוּ אִם מִחוּט וְעַד שְׂרוֹךְ נַעַל זָכוּ בָּנָיו לב׳ מִצְווֹת, חוּט שֶׁל תְּכֵלֶת וּרְצוּעָה שֶׁל תְּפִלִּין.

*In the merit of Avraham's refusal to gain benefit from even a string or shoelace, his descendants merited the mitzvoth of tzitzith and tefillin.*[44]

Was the mitzvah of *tzitzith* bestowed upon the Jewish People in the merit of Shem or of Avraham? How can we reconcile this blatant contradiction?

A key to understanding the above difficulties is found in *Parashath Chukas*, where the Well of Miriam inspired the Children of Yisrael to burst out in song.

**אָז יָשִׁיר יִשְׂרָאֵל אֶת הַשִּׁירָה הַזֹּאת עֲלִי בְאֵר עֱנוּ לָהּ. בְּאֵר חֲפָרוּהָ שָׂרִים כָּרוּהָ נְדִיבֵי הָעָם...**

*Then Yisrael were moved to sing this song: "Arise, O well! [All] sing praise to it! The well that nobles dug..."*[45]

In the Aramaic translation of this verse, the identity of these nobles is specified:

בֵּירָא דְחָפְרוּ יָתָהּ אַבְהַת עָלְמָא אַבְרָהָם יִצְחָק וְיַעֲקֹב רַבְרְבַנַּיָּא דְמִלְקַדְמִין חָפְרוּ יָתָהּ רֵישֵׁי עַמָּא מֹשֶׁה וְאַהֲרֹן סַפְרֵיהוֹן דְיִשְׂרָאֵל.

*The well dug by the fathers of the world: Avraham, Yitzchak, and Ya'akov. Nobles of old dug it: these were the leaders of the people, Moshe and Aharon.*[46]

Rabbi Chaim Shmuelevitz explains the underlying concept behind attributing the well to several premier personalities. There are many vital components to a tree's development. The process requires not merely the seed, but healthy roots, fertile soil, sufficient water, and sunshine. If any one of the above is missing, the tree will

---

44. *Sotah* 17a.
45. *Bemidbar* 21:17, 18.
46. *Targum Yonathan* on *Bemidbar* 21:18.

not flourish. The Jewish People operate in the same manner. The merits of Avraham, Yitzchak, Ya'akov, Moshe, Aharon, and Miriam were all vital for the existence of the well. The contribution of each, commencing with Avraham, was manifest later, culminating in the Well of Miriam.

The mitzvah of *tzitzith* parallels this phenomenon. In *Parashath No'ach*, the mitzvah of *tzitzith* is attributed to Shem. In *Lech Lecha*, bestowal of the mitzvah is credited to Avraham's declaration of "אִם מִחוּט וְעַד שְׂרוֹךְ נַעַל". Both were needed, the combination of merits culminating in the bequeathal of this mitzvah to the Jewish People.

Parenthetically, our Sages explain the significance of a single thread in the *tzitzith* being dyed with *techeleth*, a distinct blue color. *Techeleth* is the same shade as the sea, which should bring to mind the blue heavens, in turn leading one to remember his Creator. However, this line of association will only be entertained if a person is anxious to attain closeness to the Almighty. A person will only listen intently for a knock on the door if he is eagerly awaiting a guest. Similarly, if a person yearns for closeness to God, he will develop the above association; the blue will act as an aid to his Divine service.

Avraham refused the riches offered to him by the King of Sedom. It was his rejection of materialism which facilitated a desire to become close to God. It was only because he rejected one that he could acquire the other. Our Sages write that when standing in prayer, one who desires intelligence should turn South. One who wants riches should turn North. It is notable that these directions are mutually exclusive. If one is turned northward, he is facing away from the South. If one is turned southward, he is facing the furthest point from North. Therefore it is necessary to determine one's priorities, for a person can only have one true desire. When Avraham said, אִם מִחוּט וְעַד שְׂרוֹךְ נַעַל, his renunciation of material goods demonstrated his yearning for exclusively spiritual riches. The declaration identified him as foremost a dedicated servant of the Almighty. Had he been involved in the physical world for its own sake, the *techeleth* would be futile, for the relevant associations would not be entertained; but having demonstrated the spiritual focus of his life, Avraham revealed himself as a fitting candidate to receive this mitzvah.

Returning to our original point, it is the combination of many merits that brings dividends. Now that we have examined this principle in a positive light, let us investigate its negative manifestation.

We find the classic example of this in Moshe's words to the Jewish People on the day of his death.

> **פֶּן יֵשׁ בָּכֶם אִישׁ אוֹ אִשָּׁה אוֹ מִשְׁפָּחָה אוֹ שֵׁבֶט אֲשֶׁר לְבָבוֹ פֹנֶה הַיּוֹם מֵעִם ה' אֱלֹקֵינוּ לָלֶכֶת לַעֲבֹד אֶת אֱלֹהֵי הַגּוֹיִם הָהֵם פֶּן יֵשׁ בָּכֶם שֹׁרֶשׁ פֹּרֶה רֹאשׁ וְלַעֲנָה.**
>
> *Perhaps there is among you a man or woman, or a family or tribe, whose heart turns away today from [following] the Eternal, our God, by going to serve the gods of these nations? Perhaps there is among you a root sprouting gall and wormwood?*[47]

The Ramban[48] expounds:

> *There might be a bad fruit amongst you that will grow up and in the future produce bad flowers and bitterness. This is why the covenant was sealed with both those present today and those absent. The "father" is the root and the "child" is the growth developing from the root. The significance of the root being mentioned is that the root is here at present and in the future will develop into something bad, bringing forth poison. This alludes to the fact that bitter fruit cannot be produced by a sweet root. If a person's heart is completely dedicated to God, without any negative, paganistic thoughts or inclinations, none of his descendants will turn to idolatry or heresy. Conversely, if one's heart does have negative inclinations, later descendants will be detrimentally affected.*

---

47. *Devarim* 29:17.
48. Ramban *ad loc.*

We find an illustration of this principle in Acher, a Torah scholar who eventually rejected Judaism:[49]

תָּנוּ רַבָּנָן מַעֲשֶׂה בְּאַחֵר שֶׁהָיָה רוֹכֵב עַל הַסּוּס בְּשַׁבָּת וְהָיָה רַבִּי מֵאִיר מְהַלֵּךְ אַחֲרָיו לִלְמֹד תּוֹרָה מִפִּיו. א"ל מֵאִיר חֲזוֹר לַאֲחוֹרֶיךָ שֶׁכְּבָר שִׁעַרְתִּי בְּעִקְבֵי סוּסִי עַד כָּאן תְּחוּם שַׁבָּת. א"ל אַף אַתָּה חֲזוֹר בְּךָ. א"ל וְלֹא כְּבָר אָמַרְתִּי לְךָ כְּבָר שָׁמַעְתִּי מֵאֲחוֹרֵי הַפַּרְגּוֹד שׁוּבוּ בָּנִים שׁוֹבָבִים חוּץ מֵאַחֵר.

*It once happened that Acher was riding on a horse on the Sabbath, and his prime student was walking after him to learn Torah. [Our Sages explain that Rabbi Meir, his student, had the unique ability to "extract the juice from pomegranates while leaving the pips." He could learn from Acher's wisdom and knowledge while discarding anything with any heretical slant therein. In this manner was he able to learn from Acher.] While traveling they reached the* תְּחוּם שַׁבָּת *— the boundary beyond which one may not walk on the Sabbath, at which point Acher informed his pupil that he should turn back. Rabbi Meir replied that Acher, too, should "return" [meaning repent]. Acher replied, "Haven't I already told you about the Heavenly voice I heard, saying, 'Return, erring children — except for Acher.'"*

Acher plummeted from the heights of Torah scholarship to a state of spiritual depravity. How did he come to this situation?

Rabbi Elisha ben Avuyah (Acher's name before his descent) and Rabbi Meir were involved in a dispute concerning the verse, "טוֹב אַחֲרִית דָּבָר מֵרֵאשִׁיתוֹ". Rabbi Meir understood it as meaning, "The end is better than the beginning." Acher argued in the name of Rabbi Akiva that the verse should be understood as "A good end results from a good beginning."

Acher cited himself as proof for this interpretation, relating the following:[50]

---

49. *Chaggigah* 15a.

50. Tosefoth *ad loc.*

Acher's father, Avuyah, was one of Jerusalem's most prominent men, and consequently, many of the greatest Sages were present at his son's circumcision. During the celebration, R. Eliezer and R. Yehoshua were in another room, so deeply immersed in Torah study that they were encircled by a Heavenly fire. Avuyah became agitated at the sight of the flames, fearing that his house would catch fire. The Rabbis explained that they had been rejoicing in their study as when Torah was given at Sinai, when fire was also present. Astounded by the power of Torah learning, Avuyah vowed to dedicate his son to this holy pursuit. His intentions, however, were not totally pure, being sullied with the desire for the glory accompanying Torah, rather than the Torah itself. Therefore his wishes were not fulfilled in his son, who eventually became Acher the heretic.

The deficiencies present in Avuyah's intention developed and became magnified in his son. Thus Acher brought himself as sad proof of his interpretation of "טוֹב אַחֲרִית דָּבָר מֵרֵאשִׁיתוֹ".

The Talmud[51] elaborates upon the life of Acher, stating that while he was learning he enjoyed singing Greek songs. Acher used his intellectual aptitude to learn about other cultures, and while in the midst of learning Torah in the study hall, he would also read heretical books of Greek philosophy. According importance to both, he eventually came to the state where he could declare that repentance was an impossibility.

In another significant incident, Acher observed someone performing the mitzvah of sending away a mother bird before taking its young, in reward for which the Torah promises longevity. Then Acher witnessed this man who, as he descended from the tree after fulfilling the Torah's dictates, plummeted to the ground and died. He used this incident as grounds to reject Judaism. In truth, the promise of longevity — לְמַעַן יַאֲרִיכוּן יָמֶיךָ, does not refer to this transient world, as explained by R. Ya'akov, but refers to the Eternal world, rendering Acher's argument baseless. Acher, however, already

51. *Chaggigah* 15b.

possessing the root of heresy within, interpreted every incident in consonance with this leaning. His interpretation resonated with his heretical outlook. He would never have entertained the interpretation of R. Ya'akov, for it did not accord with his preconceived ideas.

The extent of this principle is demonstrated through a subtlety within a verse recounting the genealogy of Korach:

**וַיִּקַּח קֹרַח בֶּן יִצְהָר בֶּן קְהָת בֶּן לֵוִי...**

*Korach, the son of Yitzhar, the son of Kehas, the son of Levi, took...*[52]

Rashi comments:

בֶּן יִצְהָר בֶּן קְהָת בֶּן לֵוִי וְלֹא הִזְכִּיר בֶּן יַעֲקֹב שֶׁבִּקֵּשׁ רַחֲמִים עַל עַצְמוֹ שֶׁלֹּא יִזָּכֵר שְׁמוֹ עַל מַחֲלָקְתָּם שֶׁנֶּאֱמַר בִּקְהָלָם אַל תֵּחַד כְּבוֹדִי, וְהֵיכָן נִזְכַּר שְׁמוֹ עַל קֹרַח בְּהִתְיַחֲסָם עַל הַדּוּכָן בְּדִבְרֵי הַיָּמִים שֶׁנֶּאֱמַר בֶּן אֶבְיָסָף בֶּן קֹרַח בֶּן יִצְהָר בֶּן קְהָת בֶּן לֵוִי בֶּן יִשְׂרָאֵל.[53]

Rashi highlights that four, not five generations of Korach's genealogy are reported in the Torah. Although Levi is recounted, his father, the Patriarch Ya'akov, is omitted in accordance with his plea that his name not be associated with the dispute of Korach and his congregation. He wanted to preempt claims that Korach's behaviour stemmed from a flaw in his own character. His fear teaches the magnitude of our theme. Our sublime Patriarch was aware that a subtle flaw in Korach's ancestry could have developed and magnified, leading to the catastrophic destruction of his descendant Korach.

Noting a physical application in our own lives, pregnant women are advised against ingesting various types of food and medication due to their possible detrimental effects upon the fetus. While the child might be affected, a grandchild or even a great-grandchild would remain unscathed. However, in spiritual matters, evil affects not merely the individual, but children, grandchildren, and future generations. The seed is sown and the evil will be reaped.

52. *Bemidbar* 16:1.
53. Rashi *ad loc.*

Considering the extent people concern themselves with the physical welfare of a child, at least as much, if not more concern should be demonstrated with regard to a child's spiritual welfare. No evil can emerge from a sweet root. This should provide additional impetus to character perfection and incentive to correct any character flaws latent within us, which would otherwise manifest in the future of our people.

# CHAYEI SARAH

IN THIS PARASHAH, Avraham dispatches his servant Eliezer to seek a wife for Yitzchak. As the verses state, Eliezer took many material goods with him.

**וַיִּקַּח הָעֶבֶד עֲשָׂרָה גְמַלִּים מִגְּמַלֵּי אֲדֹנָיו וַיֵּלֶךְ וְכָל טוּב אֲדֹנָיו בְּיָדוֹ וַיָּקָם וַיֵּלֶךְ אֶל אֲרַם נַהֲרַיִם אֶל עִיר נָחוֹר.**

*The servant took ten camels of his master's camels, and he departed with [the deeds of] all his master's wealth in his hand...*[54]

Rashi explains the emphasis in the verse on "his master's" ownership of the camels.

נִכָּרִין הָיוּ מִשְּׁאָר גְּמַלִּים שֶׁהָיוּ יוֹצְאִין זְמוּמִין מִפְּנֵי הַגָּזֵל שֶׁלֹּא יִרְעוּ בִּשְׂדוֹת זָרִים.

*The camels were distinguishable from others' camels for they went out muzzled. This was to prevent them from grazing in other people's fields, and thus stealing from other people's crops.*[55]

Avraham's care concerning his camels echoes a previous incident, where a feud between the shepherds of Avraham and Lot centred around this point.

**וַיְהִי רִיב בֵּין רֹעֵי מִקְנֵה אַבְרָם וּבֵין רֹעֵי מִקְנֵה לוֹט. רַבִּי בֶּרֶכְיָה בְּשֵׁם ר' יְהוּדָה בַּר סִמוֹן אָמַר בְּהֶמְתּוֹ שֶׁל אַבְרָהָם אָבִינוּ הָיְתָה יוֹצְאָה זְמוּמָה וּבְהֶמְתּוֹ שֶׁל לוֹט לֹא הָיְתָה יוֹצְאָה זְמוּמָה.**

---

54. *Bereishith* 24:10.

55. Rashi *ad loc.*

> *...Any animal of Avraham's would go out muzzled, while Lot's animals went without any muzzle.*[56]

When Lot's shepherds were berated by the shepherds of Avraham for allowing their animals to graze in other people's fields, they justified themselves by claiming that it was only a matter of time until Avraham would die, and since he was childless, they would then inherit the land. Thus, they claimed, their act was not one of theft. Since the native Canaanites still inhabited the land, however, and Avraham had not yet taken possession of it, their excuse was rejected.

Although we may be impressed by Avraham's pious action, when considering the following incident, various difficulties arise:

> אִיקְלַע לְהַהוּא אוּשְׁפִּיזָא רָמוּ לֵיהּ שְׂעָרֵי לְחַמְרֵיהּ לָא אָכַל. חֲבָטִינְהוּ לָא אָכַל, נַקְרִינְהוּ — לָא אָכַל. אָמַר לְהוּ דִּילְמָא לָא מְעַשְּׂרִין עַשְּׂרִינְהוּ וְאָכַל. אָמַר עֲנִיָּה זוֹ הוֹלֶכֶת לַעֲשׂוֹת רְצוֹן קוֹנָהּ וְאַתֶּם מַאֲכִילִים אוֹתָהּ טְבָלִים.
>
> *After a long journey, R. Pinchas ben Yair stayed at an inn. His donkey was provided with grain, yet it refused to eat its food. They sifted and ground the grain, but to no avail; the food remained untouched. R. Pinchas then inquired as to whether or not the required tithes had been separated from the grain. The innkeeper obligingly separated tithes whereupon the donkey partook of the proffered food.*[57]

It is with this incident in mind that the Ramban asks a famous question:

> אִי אֶפְשָׁר שֶׁיִּהְיֶה הַחֲסִידוּת בְּבֵיתוֹ שֶׁל ר' פִּינְחָס בֶּן יָאִיר גָּדוֹל יוֹתֵר מִבֵּיתוֹ שֶׁל אַבְרָהָם אָבִינוּ, וְכַאֲשֶׁר חֲמוֹרוֹ שֶׁל ר' פִּינְחָס בֶּן יָאִיר אֵינֶנּוּ צָרִיךְ לְהִשְׁתַּמֵּר מִפְּנֵי הַדְּבָרִים הָאֲסוּרִים לִבְעָלָיו לְהַאֲכִילוֹ, כָּל שֶׁכֵּן גְּמַלָּיו שֶׁל אַבְרָהָם אָבִינוּ וְאֵין לְזַמְּמָם כִּי לֹא יְאֻנֶּה לַצַּדִּיק כָּל אָוֶן.[58]

---

56. *Bereishith Rabbah* 41:5.
57. *Chullin* 7a.
58. Ramban on *Bereishith* 24:32.

The above incident demonstrates the incredible spiritual level of R. Pinchas ben Yair; even his donkey would not come close to performing a misdeed. (Even further, it is doubtful that such a prohibition would apply to animal food.)

Is it possible to suppose that Avraham was on a lower spiritual level than R. Pinchas ben Yair, in light of the fact that Avraham found it necessary to take precautions against his animals actively stealing from other people's fields? Would Avraham's animals not naturally restrain themselves, as did the donkey of R. Pinchas ben Yair? Why was Avraham so careful concerning the muzzling of his animals?

We find another example of Avraham's extreme caution in the passage which relates the appointment of Eliezer as a messenger to seek a wife for Yitzchak.

**וַיֹּאמֶר אַבְרָהָם אֶל עַבְדּוֹ זְקַן בֵּיתוֹ הַמֹּשֵׁל בְּכָל אֲשֶׁר לוֹ שִׂים נָא יָדְךָ תַּחַת יְרֵכִי. וְאַשְׁבִּיעֲךָ בַּה' אֱלֹקֵי הַשָּׁמַיִם וֵאלֹקֵי הָאָרֶץ אֲשֶׁר לֹא תִקַּח אִשָּׁה לִבְנִי מִבְּנוֹת הַכְּנַעֲנִי אֲשֶׁר אָנֹכִי יוֹשֵׁב בְּקִרְבּוֹ. כִּי אֶל אַרְצִי וְאֶל מוֹלַדְתִּי תֵּלֵךְ וְלָקַחְתָּ אִשָּׁה לִבְנִי לְיִצְחָק.**

*Avraham said to his servant, the elder of his household, who was in charge of everything he owned, "...Swear by [the Name of] the Eternal, the God of the heavens and the God of the earth, that you will not take a wife for my son from the daughters of the Canaanite amongst whom I am living. You shall go instead to my country and to my kindred, and take a wife [from there] for my son, for Yitzchak."*[59]

Rabbi Simcha Zissel Ziv questions the necessity of the oath undertaken by Eliezer. Eliezer had been dispatched as a messenger with a very specific set of instructions to which he was required to adhere. Were Eliezer to deviate from Avraham's requirements, his role as a messenger would be rendered null and void, and no marriage would take place. Why then did Avraham make Eliezer swear that he would follow his instructions in seeking a wife for Yitzchak?

---

59. *Bereishith* 24:2–4.

Rabbi Yerucham Levovitz asks a related question. Considering, as our Sages inform us, that Eliezer played a central role in disseminating Avraham's teachings to the masses, would it be possible to entertain the idea that Avraham did not have full confidence and trust in him, his chief disciple? Again, why was this oath necessary?

Both Rabbi Simcha Zissel and Rabbi Yerucham Levovitz give the same cryptic answer. They tell us that Avraham's act of ensuring an oath was taken is an indication of the superior spiritual level of our Patriarch, not the reverse as we might expect. Let us discover what lies in this answer.

Rabbi Yisrael Salanter points out the distinction between Avraham and Eliezer. Our Sages comment on the words, וה׳ בֵּרַךְ אֶת אַבְרָהָם בַּכֹּל — "And God blessed Avraham with everything,"[60] that Avraham had full control over his evil inclination — שֶׁהִשְׁלִיטוֹ בְּיִצְרוֹ.[61] This description would superficially seem to set Avraham on a par with his servant, who merits a similar description from our Sages: שֶׁהָיָה שַׁלִּיט בְּיִצְרוֹ כְּמוֹתוֹ.[62] Eliezer, too, had complete reign over every one of his actions. But the distinction between master and servant must lie beyond their external actions, instead touching the essence of the two personalities.

The *Mesillath Yesharim* expounds upon two distinct spiritual levels through which man must travel on his journey to spiritual perfection: זְהִירוּת וּנְקִיּוּת — caution and purity.

וְהִנְּךָ רוֹאֶה עַתָּה הַהֶפְרֵשׁ שֶׁבֵּין הַזָּהִיר וְהַנָּקִי אַף עַל פִּי שֶׁקְּרוֹבִים הֵם זֶה לָזֶה בְּעִנְיָנָם. הַזָּהִיר הוּא הַנִּזְהָר בְּמַעֲשָׂיו וְרוֹאֶה שֶׁלֹּא יֶחֱטָא בְּמַה שֶּׁכְּבָר נוֹדַע לוֹ וּמְפֻרְסָם אֵצֶל הַכֹּל הֱיוֹתוֹ חֵטְא. אָמְנָם עֲדַיִן אֵינוֹ אָדוֹן בְּעַצְמוֹ, שֶׁלֹּא יִמָּשֵׁךְ לִבּוֹ מִן הַתַּאֲוָה הַטִּבְעִית שֶׁלֹּא תַּטֵּהוּ לְהֵרָאוֹת לוֹ הֶתֵּרִים בְּאֵיזֶה דְּבָרִים שֶׁאֵין רָעָתָם מְפֻרְסֶמֶת. וְזֶה, כִּי אַף עַל פִּי שֶׁהוּא מִשְׁתַּדֵּל לִכְבֹּשׁ אֶת יִצְרוֹ וְלִכְפּוֹת אֶת תַּאֲווֹתָיו, לֹא מִפְּנֵי זֶה יְשַׁנֶּה אֶת טִבְעוֹ וְלֹא יוּכַל לְהָסִיר מִלִּבּוֹ הַתַּאֲוָה הַגּוּפָנִית, אֶלָּא שֶׁיִּכְבֹּשׁ אוֹתָהּ וְיֵלֵךְ אַחַר הַחָכְמָה וְלֹא אַחֲרֶיהָ. אַךְ עַל כָּל פָּנִים חֹשֶׁךְ הַחָמְרִיּוּת עוֹשֶׂה

60. *Bereishith* 24:2.
61. *Bereishith Rabbah* 59:7.
62. *Bereishith Rabbah* 59:8.

אֶת שֶׁלּוֹ לַהֲסִיתוֹ וּלְפַתּוֹתוֹ.[63]

To paraphrase the *Mesillath Yesharim*:

*The distinction between one who is careful in his actions and one who is clean of any impure taint is a subtle one. Although one who is cautious will not commit a sin, deep within him he still has the desire to do so. He overcomes any inclination to perpetrate a misdeed, yet because the will still exists at a root level, when doubt arises as to the correct course of action, and the situation could be viewed in a manner which will not obligate him at all, he will attempt to release himself from potential obligation and allow expression to his desires. This person has not yet conquered his lower self, for he must struggle with it; it is still a force to be reckoned with. The* זָהִיר *has not changed his nature; in cases when wrong is not readily apparent, or when an act seems optional, he will fall prey to his instincts and persuasive desires.*

In contrast, a person who has completely cleansed himself of base inclinations, a נָקִי, would never perform a questionable act, for the deed holds no attraction. Desire for anything but spirituality and goodness is simply not present; evil has lost its allure.

People in both of these categories perform the correct external deeds. A cautious person and a pure person both control their lower selves, yet a different fabric entirely constitutes their cores. And this difference is manifest in situations when the truth is obscured, when the horizons are hazy and grey. What then will be one's course of action?

This was the difference between Avraham and Eliezer. To categorize the two, Eliezer would be placed in the class of those who are cautious, or זָהִיר, in their actions. This placement is founded upon an analysis of the concerns Eliezer expressed to Avraham when given the mission of finding a wife for Yitzchak. The Midrash records Eliezer's secret calculations:

---

63. *Mesillath Yesharim,* Ch. 10.

וַיֹּאמֶר אֵלָיו הָעֶבֶד הֲדָא הוּא דִכְתִיב "כְּנַעַן בְּיָדוֹ מֹאזְנֵי מִרְמָה לַעֲשֹׁק אָהֵב", כְּנַעַן – זֶה אֱלִיעֶזֶר, בְּיָדוֹ מֹאזְנֵי מִרְמָה – שֶׁהָיָה יוֹשֵׁב וּמַשְׁקִיל אֶת בִּתּוֹ רְאוּיָה הִיא אוֹ אֵינָהּ רְאוּיָה. לַעֲשֹׁק אָהֵב – לַעֲשֹׁק אֲהוּבוֹ שֶׁל עוֹלָם זֶה יִצְחָק. אָמַר אוּלַי לֹא תֹאבֶה הַנַּעֲרָה וכו' וְאֶתֵּן לוֹ אֶת בִּתִּי וכו'.

*Concerning the fear Eliezer expressed over the possibility of the girl's unwillingness, our Sages apply the verse, "Canaan [referring to Eliezer] was in possession of false scales, wanting to grasp the beloved one [for his own family]." The "false scales" refer to Eliezer's inner conflict as to whether or not his own daughter was fit to marry Yitzchak. "The beloved one" refers to Yitzchak, the beloved one of the world. The conflict was manifest in the qualms Eliezer voiced to Avraham. If the girl Eliezer sought were to refuse to travel back and marry Yitzchak, Eliezer could then offer Avraham his own daughter as a suitable match for him. Avraham refused on the grounds that it was an inappropriate match, Avraham's family and Eliezer's family belonging to two completely separate leagues.*[64]

While on his mission, Eliezer was constantly considering his own suggestion. He fulfilled his task admirably, with zeal and sagacity — yet there was an inclination present within him which needed to be overcome. He was a זָהִיר, one who exercises the utmost caution in his actions, yet, not having changed his actual nature, still desires something other than what has been dictated.

Avraham surpassed this level, as demonstrated by his utmost vigilance against theft of any description. His care stands in stark contrast to Lot's shepherds, who employed the most circuitous reasoning and unlikely justification for some small material gain. They calculated that eventually Avraham would inherit the land and dispossess the Canaanite inhabitants. Avraham would then die, and leaving no heir, Lot would surely inherit Avraham's possessions. Thus it was obvious (to them) that Lot's cattle were permitted to

64. *Bereishith Rabbah* 59:9.

graze on land which not only did not belong to Avraham, but was even further from Lot! But with his unadulterated purity, Avraham did not seek any loopholes or leniencies. He fulfilled the word of God with wholesomeness. Avraham was a נָקִי, pure in every way.

The *Mesillath Yesharim*, elaborating on the saying of R. Pinchas ben Yair that Torah brings one to the level of זְהִירוּת, cites the Rabbinic maxim, לֹא עַם הָאָרֶץ חָסִיד.[65] A prerequisite for piety is Torah knowledge; thus, "An ignoramus cannot be pious." Rabbi Yechezkel Sarna questions the relevance of this statement in the context of a discussion of the level of זְהִירוּת, caution. The level of piety is one of an infinitely more lofty nature, and reference to piety at this stage seems an anomaly.

He questions further:

הֲלֹא הָיָה לַתַּנָּא לִשְׁנוֹת — וְלֹא עַם הָאָרֶץ זָהִיר. וְעַיֵּן פ׳ י״ב שֶׁהֵבִיא רַבֵּנוּ [הרמח״ל] מַאֲמָר זֶה [וְלֹא עַם הָאָרֶץ חָסִיד] בְּבֵאוּר מַפְסִידֵי מִדַּת הַנְּקִיּוּת, וּכְבָר הֵבִיאוֹ רַבֵּנוּ בפ׳ י״ח בְּבֵאוּר מִדַּת הַחֲסִידוּת. יֵשׁ לוֹמַר כִּי רַבֵּנוּ מְפָרֵשׁ "וְלֹא עַם הָאָרֶץ חָסִיד", כְּלוֹמַר שֶׁחָסֵר לוֹ הַזְּהִירוּת הַנְּחוּצָה לְמִידַּת הַחֲסִידוּת. כִּי אֵינוֹ דוֹמֶה זְהִירוּת הַזָּהִיר בִּלְבַד לַזְּהִירוּת הַנְּחוּצָה לֶחָסִיד. וְכֵן שֶׁחָסֵר לוֹ הַנְּקִיּוּת הַנְּחוּצָה לֶחָסִיד, כִּי גַּם כֵּן אֵינוֹ דוֹמֶה הַנְּקִיּוּת שֶׁל הַנָּקִי בִּלְבַד לִנְקִיּוּת הֶחָסִיד.[66]

The *Mesillath Yesharim* applies the above dictum, "An ignoramus cannot be pious," to the levels of caution, זְהִירוּת, then purity, נְקִיּוּת, and finally to the sublime level of piety, חֲסִידוּת. Rabbi Sarna reveals to us that every level requires a degree of watchfulness, yet this quality will differ fundamentally depending on which level one has reached. Whether on the level of זְהִירוּת or whether on the incomparably higher level of חֲסִידוּת, watchfulness and caution are required. A נָקִי, however, requires a greater degree of caution than a זָהִיר, and in turn a חָסִיד requires a greater vigilance than a נָקִי. The higher one climbs on the spiritual ladder, the more care and caution are required. The level of זְהִירוּת exercised on level one will be

65. *Pirkei Avoth* 2:5.
66. *Iyunim*.

totally insufficient having arrived in the world of level two.

With this principle we can comprehend how the watchfulness and caution required of Avraham was of a much more exacting and lofty standard than that demanded of R. Pinchas ben Yair. Avraham made Eliezer swear that he would remain faithful to his mission, despite the fact that any deviation would instantly invalidate Eliezer's quest and leave Avraham under no obligation to the potential match found for Yitzchak. However, Avraham exercised extra caution in order to prevent any negative consequences which could result from Eliezer's undertaking. Avraham wanted to totally remove himself from any suspicion that he was not scrupulous in upholding his promises and fulfilling his word.

Avraham did not impose an oath only on his servant, as seen after the battle between the Four and Five Kings. Victorious, Avraham spurned the spoils of battle, even taking a vow to this effect: "I raise up my hand [symbolic of an oath] that I will not take even a string or a shoelace from that which was captured in the battle." Not trusting even himself without the extra caution imposed by an oath, there was no reason for him to trust his servant. He possessed a superior level of זְהִירוּת, caution and watchfulness, which was commensurate with his sublime status.

This trait is seen also through Avraham's insistence that his cattle be muzzled to prevent theft. He did not trust himself, because of his elevated spiritual level of not only purity, but even piety, and his extreme care was a reflection of his elevation. The added caution docs not show that Avraham was on a lower spiritual level than R. Pinchas ben Yair, but rather indicates the more sublime nature of our Patriarch. The caution one exerts is proportional to one's spiritual level.

Avraham was on guard against anything which could have negative connotations or consequences, no matter how slight. This is a quality to be lauded; one should be ever vigilant against arousing the slightest suspicion towards oneself, or one's actions. A reflection of this concern lies in the law obligating each Jew to leave one corner of his field to the poor. The corner must visibly be left over — it would be forbidden to allow paupers to partake of their corner before one has harvested, for it would then appear as if the owner had been remiss in his obligation when he finally harvests the complete field. One must exercise caution not to do any actions which could cast even the slightest aspersions upon one's character or behaviour.

This was reflected on all levels in the Divine service of Avraham, and it is thus that we are commanded, וִהְיִיתֶם נְקִיִּים מֵה׳ וּמִיִּשְׂרָאֵל — "You shall be innocent in the eyes of God and man."[67] On whatever spiritual level we are presently situated, we must exercise caution, watchfulness and care. As we labour both in the area of service between man and God, and in serving God through our relationships with our fellow men, we must always bear in mind that this ingredient is a vital one for success.

---

67. *Bemidbar* 32:22.

# TOLDOTH

OUR PARASHAH CONTAINS the famous incident of the blessings bestowed upon Esav and Ya'akov.

> וַיְהִי כִּי זָקֵן יִצְחָק וַתִּכְהֶיןָ עֵינָיו מֵרְאֹת וַיִּקְרָא אֶת עֵשָׂו בְּנוֹ הַגָּדֹל וַיֹּאמֶר אֵלָיו בְּנִי וַיֹּאמֶר אֵלָיו הִנֵּנִי. וַיֹּאמֶר הִנֵּה נָא זָקַנְתִּי לֹא יָדַעְתִּי יוֹם מוֹתִי. וְעַתָּה שָׂא נָא כֵלֶיךָ תֶּלְיְךָ וְקַשְׁתֶּךָ וְצֵא הַשָּׂדֶה וְצוּדָה לִּי צָיִד. וַעֲשֵׂה לִי מַטְעַמִּים כַּאֲשֶׁר אָהַבְתִּי וְהָבִיאָה לִּי וְאֹכֵלָה בַּעֲבוּר תְּבָרֶכְךָ נַפְשִׁי בְּטֶרֶם אָמוּת.
>
> *When Yitzchak was old and his eyesight failing, he called Esav, his elder son, and said to him, "My son," and he answered him, "I am here!" [Yitzchak] said, "Look. I have now grown old [and] do not know the day of my death. So now, please sharpen your weapons — your sword and your bow — and go out to the field and hunt some game for me. Then prepare [it] for me [as] delicacies in a way that I love, and bring [them] to me [so that] I may eat, so that my soul may bless you before I die."*[68]

An examination of this episode raises a number of difficulties. Upon a superficial reading, our Patriarch Yitzchak would seem to be attaching great importance to the type of food that he commands Esav to prepare for him, specifying that Esav should hunt the venison he enjoys. It seems strange that our noble Patriarch Yitzchak would use the term אָהַבְתִּי — "love," in conjunction with meat.

Upon reflection, there are a number of considerations which serve to mystify us further:

This incident transpired when Yitzchak was old. When one is

68. *Bereishith* 27:1–4.

old, one's sense of taste is impaired, and delicate or subtle tastes are not appreciated. This is clearly demonstrated in the Scriptures.

**בֶּן שְׁמֹנִים שָׁנָה אָנֹכִי הַיּוֹם הַאֵדַע בֵּין טוֹב לְרָע אִם יִטְעַם עַבְדְּךָ אֶת אֲשֶׁר אֹכַל.**

*"I am eighty years old today. Can I taste that which I eat?"*[69]

We hear clearly the testimony of an old man who states that due to his age, the physical taste of food does not affect him. Why then, does Yitzchak attach such importance to the taste and type of meat prepared for him?

The commentators' observations seem to augment the difficulties:

**וַיֶּאֱהַב יִצְחָק אֶת עֵשָׂו כִּי צַיִד בְּפִיו...**

*Yitzchak loved Esav, for he would eat what [Esav] hunted...*[70]

The *Targum Onkelos*, an Aramaic translation of the text, elaborates:

וְרָחֵם יִצְחָק יַת עֵשָׂו אֲרֵי מִצֵּידֵהּ הֲוָה אָכִיל.[71]

Again, it was because of the meat Esav used to bring him that Yitzchak loved him.

In a similar vein, the Ramban states:

וְיִתָּכֵן לְפָרֵשׁ וַיֶּאֱהַב יִצְחָק אֶת עֵשָׂו בַּעֲבוּר כִּי בְּפִיו שֶׁל יִצְחָק צַיִד תָּמִיד, כָּל הַיּוֹם יִתְאַוֶּה לֶאֱכֹל אֶת הַצַּיִד, וְתָמִיד הוּא בְּפִיו, לֹא יֹאכַל דָּבָר אַחֵר וְהוּא הַמֵּבִיא לוֹ כַּאֲשֶׁר אָמַר אִישׁ יוֹדֵעַ צַיִד.

*...Yitzchak constantly desired to eat the meat, and it was always in his mouth. Yitzchak did not eat anything else, and it was Esav who fulfilled Yitzchak's craving. Therefore Esav is described as a hunter.*[72]

---

69. *II Shemuel* 19:33.
70. *Bereishith* 25:28.
71. *Targum Onkelos ad loc.*
72. Ramban *ad loc.*

It seems that Yitzchak constantly desired meat, and Esav fulfilled this craving. Was Yitzchak's love for his son based on the indulgence of his physical desires that Esav facilitated? To view the episode in this light would be to degrade our Patriarch Yitzchak to someone far less sublime than the reality. In fact, it would reduce Yitzchak, one completely separated from materialism, to someone dominated by earthly desires.

Let us further complicate the matter! Rivkah, hearing of the instructions which Yitzchak had given Esav, commanded Ya'akov as follows:

**לֶךְ נָא אֶל הַצֹּאן וְקַח לִי מִשָּׁם שְׁנֵי גְּדָיֵי עִזִּים טֹבִים, וְאֶעֱשֶׂה אֹתָם מַטְעַמִּים לְאָבִיךָ כַּאֲשֶׁר אָהֵב.**

*Go now to the sheep and take for me from there two good goats. I will then prepare tasty food for your father as he loves.*[73]

Rashi comments:

**כַּאֲשֶׁר אָהֵב — כִּי טַעַם הַגְּדִי כְּטַעַם הַצְּבִי.**

*As he loves — for the taste of goat meat is like the taste of venison.*[74]

R. Tzadok HaCohen questions: If the meat of domestic livestock tasted the same as deer, why did Esav exert so much effort in hunting venison? He could have easily prepared a domestic animal for Yitzchak, an act involving far less effort. As emphasized by Rashi, Yitzchak could not taste the difference in the meat.

The Shach questions the episode further, asking why the word "לִי", "for me," "to me," is repeated three times:

**וְצוּדָה לִי צָיִד. וַעֲשֵׂה לִי מַטְעַמִּים... וְהָבִיאָה לִי...**

*Hunt some game for me. Then prepare [it] for me [as] delicacies... and bring [them] to me...*

---

73. *Bereishith* 27:9.

74. Rashi *ad loc.*

The key to resolving all these difficulties lies in a Midrash concerning the holy Sabbath.

בֵּרְכוֹ בְּמַטְעַמִּים. רַבֵּנוּ עָשָׂה סְעוּדָה לְאַנְטוֹנִינוּס בְּשַׁבָּת. הֵבִיא לְפָנָיו תַּבְשִׁילִין שֶׁל צוֹנֵן אָכַל מֵהֶם וְעָרַב לוֹ. עָשָׂה לוֹ סְעוּדָה בַּחוֹל הֵבִיא לְפָנָיו תַּבְשִׁילִין רוֹתְחִין, א"ל אוֹתָן עָרְבוּ לִי יוֹתֵר מֵאֵילוּ. א"ל תַּבְלִין אֶחָד הֵן חֲסֵרִין, א"ל וְכִי יֵשׁ קלרין שֶׁל מֶלֶךְ חָסֵר כְּלוּם. א"ל שַׁבָּת הֵן חֲסֵרִין אִית לָךְ שַׁבָּת.

*God blessed the Sabbath with* מַטְעַמִּים*, delicacies. Rabbeinu HaKadosh [Rabbi Yehudah HaNasi] once prepared a cold meal for Antoninus on the Sabbath, and the emperor enjoyed it more than a hot meal that Rabbeinu HaKadosh had served him during the week. In response to Antoninus' inquiry, Rabbeinu HaKadosh explained that the food served during the week was missing one vital ingredient — the Sabbath.*[75]

It is the blessing of the Sabbath which imbues food with a special flavour.

This can be understood through the following story.

Two successful business partners play golf every Sunday to relieve themselves of the pressure of work. Enjoying the pastime immensely, they decide to appoint a manager over the business, leaving them free to lead a life of leisure, playing golf every day. On Sunday, as usual, they go to the golf course, eat lunch, continue playing, and return home. On Monday they go, eat lunch, continue playing, and return home. Tuesday is a replay of Sunday and Monday, and Wednesday is a repeat of Tuesday. Finally one of the partners broaches the topic with the other, explaining his feeling that they are becoming like animals. Animals come to the field in the morning, feed, and return home in the evening! Their lives were becoming bland and meaningless. Previously, the golf had a purpose: to provide a reprieve from the pressures of work. But once they had left work, the golf playing became meaningless. The two returned to their business!

---

75. *Bereishith Rabbah* 11:12.

The word טַעַם means both reason and taste, for when one's action is performed for a reason, with a specific intent and purpose, it is enjoyable and fulfilling. It has טַעַם.

There is a mitzvah attached to the pleasure of eating on the Sabbath. The eating is purposeful, it has a reason and it is this which gives taste to the food. It is therefore understandable that food eaten during the week does not taste the same as food eaten on the Sabbath. It was this lack of purpose, reason, and ultimately lack of taste, טַעַם, that Antoninus discerned in the food served to him by Rabbeinu HaKadosh during the week.

Returning to our episode, we can now begin to comprehend the unfolding events.

Esav had a specific set of clothes that he wore exclusively for serving his father. R. Shimon ben Gamliel praises this conduct.

> אָמַר ר' שִׁמְעוֹן בֶּן גַּמְלִיאֵל כָּל יָמַי הָיִיתִי מְשַׁמֵּשׁ אֶת אַבָּא וְלֹא שִׁמַּשְׁתִּי אוֹתוֹ אֶחָד מִמֵּאָה שֶׁשִּׁמֵּשׁ עֵשָׂו אֶת אָבִיו.
>
> *R. Shimon ben Gamliel compared his actions to Esav's behaviour, and exclaimed that he was unable to attain even one hundredth of the level of Esav's degree of* כִּבּוּד אָב, *honour of his father.*[76]

In reality, Esav did not serve his father in purity, having ulterior motives behind his actions. However, a deed performed even without the correct intentions breeds tremendous consequences. A demonstration of this is found in the book of *Melachim*, where we find forty-two renegades insulting the prophet Elisha. Elisha responded as follows:

> וַיִּפֶן אַחֲרָיו וַיִּרְאֵם וַיְקַלְלֵם בְּשֵׁם ה'.
>
> *He looked back and saw them, and cursed them in the name of God.*[77]

---

76. *Bereishith Rabbah* 65:12.
77. *II Melachim* 2:24.

The forty-two renegades subsequently all died. The *Yalkut Shimoni* expounds:

Balak, King of Mo'av, had brought a total of forty-two offerings when he attempted to curse the Jewish People. These offerings injected his curse with a potency which eventually resulted in the death of forty-two members of the Jewish People.

R. Yehudah provides an explanation of the above which is of profound significance. He states: A person should always engage in mitzvoth, even with incorrect motives (a principle we shall be returning to and elaborating upon). For although Balak's sacrifices were offered with the blackest and most evil of intentions, he nonetheless caused a tremendous light to shine in the world. As a consequence of Balak's action, he merited that Ruth — a woman of spiritual greatness — was one of his descendants. In turn, Ruth merited having among her descendants King Shlomo — who is described as a man who brought not forty-two, but one thousand offerings to the Lord. Both sweet and bitter fruit grew from the same tree, a tree planted by Balak.

Balak's deed was comprised of two parts: a praiseworthy action and a destructive intention. The positive action resulted in Ruth being brought into the world. The negative intention had literally fatal consequences for forty-two young men.

Esav performed the mitzvah of honouring his father, and although his motives were corrupt, the action itself was commendable. In fact, the great R. Shimon ben Gamliel could not match Esav's deed, which was of the highest calibre. It was Esav's action of honouring his father that imbued the food he prepared for his father with a special flavour. It was the taste of the mitzvah inherent in the food that Yitzchak loved.

With this understanding we can return to the episode of the מַטְעַמִּים and behold a depth and profundity in our forebears' actions.

**וְצוּדָה לִּי צָיִד. וַעֲשֵׂה לִי מַטְעַמִּים... וְהָבִיאָה לִּי...**

Yitzchak emphasizes that all of Esav's actions should be directed to his father. It was because the food was prepared for the mitzvah of honouring his father that it would contain the desired taste, the taste needed for Yitzchak to bless his son. The beloved צַיִד בְּפִיו was due to the meticulous and beautiful nature of the action, which was an expression of Esav's reverence for his father. However, the taste is conditional on the reason for exerting the necessary effort. Esav had to do it "לִי" — solely for the sake of this mitzvah. It was this which transformed the food from a piece of meat into the higher realm called מַטְעַמִּים, delicacies.

In this light, let us examine Rivkah's words.

**וְרִבְקָה אָמְרָה אֶל יַעֲקֹב בְּנָהּ לֵאמֹר הִנֵּה שָׁמַעְתִּי אֶת אָבִיךָ מְדַבֵּר אֶל עֵשָׂו אָחִיךָ לֵאמֹר. הָבִיאָה לִּי צַיִד וַעֲשֵׂה לִי מַטְעַמִּים וְאֹכֵלָה וַאֲבָרֶכְכָה לִפְנֵי ה׳ לִפְנֵי מוֹתִי. וְעַתָּה בְנִי שְׁמַע בְּקֹלִי לַאֲשֶׁר אֲנִי מְצַוָּה אֹתָךְ. לֶךְ נָא אֶל הַצֹּאן וְקַח לִי מִשָּׁם שְׁנֵי גְּדָיֵי עִזִּים טֹבִים וְאֶעֱשֶׂה אֹתָם מַטְעַמִּים לְאָבִיךָ כַּאֲשֶׁר אָהֵב.**

*Rivkah spoke to Ya'akov her son, saying: "Behold, I heard your father talking to Esav your brother telling him, 'Bring me the meat which you hunt and prepare it for me, and I will bless you.' Now my son, listen to my instructions which I will command you. Go now to the sheep and take for me from there two good goats for me, and I will then prepare tasty food for your father as he loves."*[78]

Ya'akov, in following his mother's instructions, would be performing the mitzvah of honouring his mother. It is this mitzvah which would inculcate the desired taste into the meat. The meat brought by Ya'akov would have that same taste of כִּבּוּד אָב וָאֵם as the meat brought by Esav. As stated by Rashi, the types of meat did not have a different taste. Yitzchak loved Esav's meat because of the כִּבּוּד אָב it involved. If meat was prepared by Ya'akov solely in response to Rivkah's command, the food would have the same flavour, and Yitzchak would love it.

King Shlomo states, בְּכָל דְּרָכֶיךָ דָעֵהוּ — "In all our actions we should know God."[79] Everyday life necessitates mundane actions:

---

78. *Bereishith* 27:6–9.
79. *Mishlei* 3:6.

eating, drinking, sleeping. However, from this episode we learn the secret of how to infuse holiness into every aspect of our lives. If we eat, drink and sleep only to enable us to serve God, each deed is elevated, for it has טַעַם, reason. טַעַם gives taste. Our lives will be filled with a taste that is lacking in the lives of people who do not live in this purposeful manner.

This principle is realised when we observe the Sabbath. The mention of the Sabbath conjures up images of a family enjoying a meal together on that day which is a culmination of the week. It is a day that is savoured. The gaping hole present in the lives of those who do not observe the Sabbath is unimaginable. Life holds a banal quality as each day passes like every other. Their existence lacks the sublime טַעַם, taste, which the Sabbath infuses into our lives.

However, the quality of the Sabbath must be carried into the week. If we do every action with a purpose, with the intention of serving God, we give a טַעַם, a taste to life unimaginable to one who does not live in this manner. It is meaning that makes life so beautiful.

Fulfilling the dictum of בְּכָל דְּרָכֶיךָ דָעֵהוּ, knowing Him in all our ways, makes us appreciate the beauty of our lives and thus brings love to every action. As a result, it brings us to love Him Who gives the commandments that fill our days. The formula to achieve the sublime level of אַהֲבַת ה' — "love of God," then, is to perform every action with intent. Life will then be blissful indeed!

**הַשָּׁמַיִם שָׁמַיִם לַה' וְהָאָרֶץ נָתַן לִבְנֵי אָדָם.**

*The heavens belong to God, but the earth is man's dominion.*[80]

The *Chiddushei HaRim* states that the earth was given over to mankind. We are given the earth to elevate it into שָׁמַיִם, to transform it into spirituality. It is through infusing our every action with holiness that life becomes no longer mundane, but rather takes on a beauty and excitement unfortunately unknown to many. With this appreciation we will attain a level of אַהֲבַת ה', loving Him Who gives us lives of beauty, lives of meaning.

---

80. *Tehillim* 116:16.

# VAYEITZEI

AFTER YA'AKOV HAS run away from Lavan at God's command, taking his family and his goods with him, Lavan pursues Ya'akov for seven days, eventually overtaking him on Mount Gil'ad.

> וַיָּבֹא אֱלֹקִים אֶל לָבָן הָאֲרַמִּי בַּחֲלֹם הַלָּיְלָה וַיֹּאמֶר לוֹ הִשָּׁמֶר לְךָ פֶּן תְּדַבֵּר עִם יַעֲקֹב מִטּוֹב עַד רָע. וַיַּשֵּׂג לָבָן אֶת יַעֲקֹב וְיַעֲקֹב תָּקַע אֶת אָהֳלוֹ בָּהָר וְלָבָן תָּקַע אֶת אֶחָיו בְּהַר הַגִּלְעָד. וַיֹּאמֶר לָבָן לְיַעֲקֹב מֶה עָשִׂיתָ וַתִּגְנֹב אֶת לְבָבִי וַתְּנַהֵג אֶת בְּנֹתַי כִּשְׁבֻיוֹת חָרֶב. לָמָּה נַחְבֵּאתָ לִבְרֹחַ וַתִּגְנֹב אֹתִי וְלֹא הִגַּדְתָּ לִּי וָאֲשַׁלֵּחֲךָ בְּשִׂמְחָה וּבְשִׁרִים בְּתֹף וּבְכִנּוֹר. וְלֹא נְטַשְׁתַּנִי לְנַשֵּׁק לְבָנַי וְלִבְנֹתָי עַתָּה הִסְכַּלְתָּ עֲשׂוֹ. יֶשׁ לְאֵל יָדִי לַעֲשׂוֹת עִמָּכֶם רָע וֵאלֹקֵי אֲבִיכֶם אֶמֶשׁ אָמַר אֵלַי לֵאמֹר הִשָּׁמֶר לְךָ מִדַּבֵּר עִם יַעֲקֹב מִטּוֹב עַד רָע.

> *God came to Lavan the Arami in a dream at night, and said to him, "Be careful not to speak with Ya'akov, neither good nor evil." Lavan caught up with Ya'akov; Ya'akov had set up his tent on the mountain, while Lavan encamped his kinsmen on [the same] Mount Gil'ad. Lavan then said to Ya'akov, "What have you done?! You deceived me and led away my daughters like prisoners of war. Why did you run away secretly and deceive me and not [even] tell me? I would have sent you away with rejoicing and songs, with drum and harp! You didn't [even] allow me to kiss my [grand]children and my daughters. You acted foolishly now by doing [this]. I have the power to do evil to you, and [just] last night, the God of your fathers spoke to me, saying, 'Be careful not to speak with Ya'akov, neither good nor evil.'"*[81]

Lavan, attempting to intimidate Ya'akov, told him that despite

81. *Bereishith* 31:24–29.

his burning desire to harm him, he would refrain from touching him, only because of God's restrictive order. This statement seems not only unnecessary, but also self-defeating. What was Lavan's purpose in conveying this information?

Furthermore, when reporting God's words, Lavan added the word לֵאמֹר, saying: אֶמֶשׁ אָמַר אֵלַי לֵאמֹר הִשָּׁמֶר לְךָ — "[God] spoke to me, saying, 'Be careful…'" The Ramban explains the implications of this word:

מִלַּת לֵאמֹר בְּכָל הַתּוֹרָה לֵאמֹר לְיִשְׂרָאֵל.

*Throughout the Torah, this word means to speak to Yisrael.*[82]

The word לֵאמֹר always refers to information to be reported to the Jewish People. The *Mechilta* brings further proof for this, explaining this word לֵאמֹר, "saying," as צֵא וֶאֱמֹר לָהֶם — "Go, and relay to them." In light of this, Lavan's use of the term לֵאמֹר is inappropriate, for he was not instructed to repeat the information to anyone. What, then, was the purpose of his insertion of this superfluous word?

Further in the episode, the verse states:

**וַיִּפְגַּע בַּמָּקוֹם וַיָּלֶן שָׁם כִּי בָא הַשֶּׁמֶשׁ...**

*He met the place and stayed there.*[83]

Rashi explains the word וַיִּפְגַּע, he met, as implying that Ya'akov prayed there. The unusual context of the word teaches us שֶׁקָּפְצָה לוֹ הָאָרֶץ — "The earth jumped towards him," that is, the spot towards which he was journeying came to meet him. Rashi's comment has profound significance when considering subsequent events.

After his monumental dream on Mount Moriah, Ya'akov declared, מַה נּוֹרָא הַמָּקוֹם הַזֶּה — "How awe-inspiring is this place!" The *Sefath Emeth* elaborates:

מַה נּוֹרָא הַמָּקוֹם הַזֶּה. תָּלָה אָבִינוּ יַעֲקֹב הִתְגַּלּוּת הַקְּדֻשָּׁה בַּעֲבוּר קְדֻשַּׁת הַמָּקוֹם. וּבֶאֱמֶת חֲכָמֵינוּ ז"ל הִגִּידוּ כִּי קָפַץ הַר הַמּוֹרִיָּה וּבָא

82. Ramban on *Shemoth* 6:10.

83. *Bereishith* 28:11.

> אֵלָיו. נִמְצָא הַכֹּל אֱמֶת שֶׁהִרְגִּישׁ שֶׁהַמָּקוֹם גּוֹרֵם וְאַף עַל פִּי כֵן הָיָה הַכֹּל בִּזְכוּתוֹ. וְהוּא מִפְּלְאוֹת הַבּוֹרֵא יתֹ' אֲשֶׁר הוּא שׁוֹמֵר אוֹהֲבָיו לְבִלְתִּי יָבוֹאוּ בְּמַעֲשֵׂיהֶם לִידֵי גַּבְהוּת. לָכֵן מְסַבֵּב סִבּוֹת שֶׁיִּנְהֲגוּ בָּהֶם הַתְּמִימֵי דֶּרֶךְ כנ"ל.[84]

To paraphrase the *Sefath Emeth*: On the one hand, Ya'akov bestowed honour on the place by attributing his dream to the inherent sanctity of the location. On the other hand, our Sages inform us on the word וַיִּפְגַּע, that the place moved towards Ya'akov, thus demonstrating its deference and subordination to him and giving him honour. This apparent contradiction as to who precisely paid homage to whom may be resolved as follows: we know that the Almighty guards His loved ones from falling into the trap of haughtiness. God therefore allowed Ya'akov to feel that his dream resulted from the sanctity of the place, so that he would not attribute it to his own spiritual stature and become proud. Thus, Ya'akov displayed the character trait of humility, being free of any pride, and God aided him in retaining this quality intact.

The examination of a second character trait will facilitate an explanation of the above. This is the character trait originating in Rachel and manifesting itself in her descendant Shaul, and once again, in a later generation, in her descendant Queen Esther. When Achashverosh urged Esther to disclose her origin, she was silent: אֵין אֶסְתֵּר מַגֶּדֶת מוֹלַדְתָּהּ וְאֶת עַמָּהּ — "Esther did not tell her birthplace or her people." The Midrash elaborates:

> אֵין אֶסְתֵּר מַגֶּדֶת. מְלַמֵּד שֶׁתָּפְשָׂה שְׁתִיקָה בְּעַצְמָהּ כְּרָחֵל זְקֶנְתָּהּ... וְעָמְדוּ כָּל גְּדוֹלֵי זַרְעָהּ בִּשְׁתִיקָה. רָחֵל... רָאֲתָה סִבְלוֹנוֹתֶיהָ בְּיַד אֲחוֹתָהּ וְשָׁתְקָה... וּבְשָׁאוּל בֶּן בְּנָהּ כְּתִיב (ש"א י',ט"ז) וְאֶת דְּבַר הַמְּלוּכָה לֹא הִגִּיד לוֹ.
>
> *Esther did not tell. This teaches us that she held herself in a grip of silence like Rachel, her ancestress...and all the great ones among [Rachel's] descendants stood up to the test of silence. Rachel... saw her gifts [which Ya'akov had sent her]*

84. *Sefath Emeth* on *Bereishith*, section 537.

*in the hands of her sister and was silent...and of Shaul, her descendant, it is written (I Shemuel 10:16), "He did not tell him about the matter of the kingship."*[85]

Esther, even when placed under intense pressure to speak, remained silent. She garbed herself with the same quality as her forbear Rachel, and did not reveal her royal origin. Rachel herself saw all the gifts being given to her sister at what was meant to be her own wedding. In an incredible act of self-control she suppressed her own desires, revised her dreams, and remained silent. Shaul, searching for lost donkeys, was privately anointed as king over the Jewish People. When he arrived at home, his family remained oblivious to this momentous event, for Shaul remained silent. The strength initiated by Rachel was actualised and manifested in her descendants Shaul and Esther.

Three areas of our conduct — thought, speech, and physical action — require the quality of modesty. Modesty in the area of speech involves restraint and consideration in that which one utters, a higher and more difficult level to attain than simply controlling external appearances. These prime personalities, Rachel, Shaul, and Esther, all possessed this quality of reticence, not speaking of their own greatness.

We have discussed two character traits: modesty as exemplified by Rachel, and humility as exemplified by Ya'akov. Both these qualities were absent in Lavan. His lack of humility is apparent in his response to being granted the privilege of having a prophetic dream. Although the dream was only in Ya'akov's merit and for Ya'akov's benefit, Lavan attributed the revelation to his own superior status. Additionally, Lavan could not contain his pride at this occurrence, eagerly informing Ya'akov of it at the first opportunity. Aware that relating this information could be perceived as a purposeless expression of pride, Lavan added the word לֵאמֹר, implying that God had instructed him to relate His revelation, and thus preempting any

85. *Esther Rabbah* 6:12.

accusations of pride. We see that modesty in speech and humility in thought are both found to be sorely lacking in Lavan.

A stark contrast is noticeable between the traits displayed by Lavan and those displayed by Ya'akov. A tangible demonstration of this lies in the placement of the future Temple on the same site as Ya'akov's dream. It was the declaration of מַה נּוֹרָא — "How awesome!" that distinguished the mountain as a fitting place for the *Beith HaMikdash.*

**כֹּה אָמַר ה' הַשָּׁמַיִם כִּסְאִי וְהָאָרֶץ הֲדֹם רַגְלָי אֵי זֶה בַיִת אֲשֶׁר תִּבְנוּ לִי וְאֵי זֶה מָקוֹם מְנוּחָתִי. וְאֶת כָּל אֵלֶּה יָדִי עָשָׂתָה וַיִּהְיוּ כָל אֵלֶּה נְאֻם ה' וְאֶל זֶה אַבִּיט אֶל עָנִי וּנְכֵה רוּחַ וְחָרֵד עַל דְּבָרִי.**

*The heavens are My throne, the earth My footstool. How can you build Me a house? Where can I rest?... With a poor person and one of lowly spirit...will I dwell.*[86]

Ya'akov's statement of מַה נּוֹרָא demonstrated his possession of the quality which enabled the holy Temple to be built in that place. Instead of taking credit for his awesome dream, he gave honour to the place, attributing his dream to its sanctity. Negation of self is a prerequisite for the very existence of the *Beith HaMikdash.* For it is only when we sacrifice our selfish desires and ego that we create a space which the Almighty can permeate. It is humility which allows God to dwell within us. God orchestrated the situation to give Ya'akov the opportunity to attribute spirituality to something outside himself, and it was this demonstration of his humility that established the place as a fitting site for the Temple.

The extreme damage caused by receiving even a small amount of honour is highlighted by Rabbi Dessler.[87] He cites the Vilna Gaon, who explains that honour is a spiritual pleasure, experienced by the soul, and thus it reduces one's Eternal reward much more than indulgence in physical pleasure, which by its very nature is limited. It is for this reason that glorifying oneself in the eyes of others has such

---

86. *Yeshayah* 66:1, 2.
87. *Inyanim*, no. 563.

ruinous consequences. Rabbi Dessler expands this idea in conjunction with the following events:

וַיַּרְא ה' כִּי שְׂנוּאָה לֵאָה וַיִּפְתַּח אֶת רַחְמָהּ וְרָחֵל עֲקָרָה.

*The Eternal saw that Le'ah was hated, so He opened her womb, while Rachel remained infertile.*[88]

Rabbi Dessler brings the verse, וַיֶּאֱהַב גַּם אֶת רָחֵל — "And [Ya'akov] *also* loved Rachel,"[89] as proof that Le'ah was indeed loved. The description of Le'ah as a hated wife means in essence that, although Ya'akov loved and honoured both Le'ah and Rachel, slightly more honour was bestowed upon Rachel than upon Le'ah. In fact this distinction was made with good judgment; Rachel was deserving of the honour given to her. A proof for this is found in the book of Ruth, where the descendants of Yehudah declared that Ruth should be כְּרָחֵל וּכְלֵאָה — "like Rachel and like Le'ah." Our Sages notice the order of the statement, Rachel being placed before Le'ah, in a seemingly inappropriate slight towards Ya'akov's first and in many ways most important wife. In their wisdom the Sages comment that Rachel is appropriately bestowed with more honour by being placed before Le'ah.

In fact Rachel did not seek or desire this honour. Before her marriage to Ya'akov she received signs through which Ya'akov could ensure he was marrying the right woman. Fearing Le'ah's humiliation if her true identity was exposed during the wedding, Rachel passed these signs on to her. Through this action, Rachel was not merely giving up her spouse, she was sacrificing her whole task in life and her essence as propagator of the Jewish nation. She rid herself of any last vestige of self, negating her loftiest aspirations for the sake of her sister's dignity. Her tremendous deed demonstrates that when honour was later given to her, it was of course without her seeking it. Furthermore, Rachel was a prophetess, a level requiring

88. *Bereishith* 29:31.
89. *Bereishith* 29:30.

complete perfection of all character traits. Seeking honour would disqualify a person from belonging to the lofty ranks of those who receive prophecy.

Rabbi Dessler explains Rachel's inability to have children as one of the terrible consequences of her having received additional honour. She thus lost the opportunity to bring into the world the tribe of Levites, which included the great leader Moshe and the priesthood, and the tribe of Yehudah as well, from which the royal dynasty sprouted, and from which the Mashiach will come. All these distinctions were transferred to Le'ah. If not for Le'ah's prayers that the last two tribes descend from Rachel, Rachel would have had fewer children than her handmaidens. All this resulted from the honour she received. An enormous moral lesson is evident, as we see the loss honour carries with it, and how much one should shun honour.

Fleeing from honour has been the hallmark of Torah giants throughout the ages. Paying close attention to the events of our Sages' lives, we can often discern tangible demonstrations of this principle. Time and time again we view remarkable events protecting these "beloved ones" from the spiritual destruction honour engenders. Eternal rewards are thus kept intact and preserved in their genuine glory.

May we merit being "loved ones" of the Almighty. May we, too, be prevented from receiving the fleeting honour which is so ruinous to our spirituality.

# VAYISHLACH

IN PREPARATION FOR the confrontation with his rival, Esav, Ya'akov exerted himself in three areas: by sending gifts to appease his brother, by praying, and by planning a military strategy. He subsequently experienced the primordial struggle with Esav's angel, as the verse recounts:

**וַיִּוָּתֵר יַעֲקֹב לְבַדּוֹ וַיֵּאָבֵק אִישׁ עִמּוֹ עַד עֲלוֹת הַשָּׁחַר... וַיֹּאמֶר שַׁלְּחֵנִי כִּי עָלָה הַשָּׁחַר וַיֹּאמֶר לֹא אֲשַׁלֵּחֲךָ כִּי אִם בֵּרַכְתָּנִי.**

*Ya'akov was left by himself, and a man wrestled with him until dawn... [The man] then said, "Let me go, for it is [already] dawn," but [Ya'akov] replied, "I will not let you go unless you bless me."*[90]

Rashi specifies that the blessings which Ya'akov desired were those same blessings he had originally taken from Esav. After the legitimacy of what Ya'akov did was disputed by his brother, who claimed that he had usurped the blessing from him unlawfully, Ya'akov sought confirmation of these blessings from the angel of Esav. In response to his request, the angel gives Ya'akov a new name.

**וַיֹּאמֶר לֹא יַעֲקֹב יֵאָמֵר עוֹד שִׁמְךָ כִּי אִם יִשְׂרָאֵל כִּי שָׂרִיתָ עִם אֱלֹקִים וְעִם אֲנָשִׁים וַתּוּכָל. וַיִּשְׁאַל יַעֲקֹב וַיֹּאמֶר הַגִּידָה נָּא שְׁמֶךָ וַיֹּאמֶר לָמָּה זֶּה תִּשְׁאַל לִשְׁמִי וַיְבָרֶךְ אֹתוֹ שָׁם.**

*[The man] then said, "It shall no longer be said that your name is Ya'akov, but rather Yisrael (great one of God), for you have become great before God and among men, and you*

90. *Bereishith* 32:25, 27.

*overcame [them]." Ya'akov questioned [the man] and said to him, "Tell [me] now your name." He replied, "Why do you ask me about my name?" He then blessed him there.*[91]

Rashi explains the connection between the change of name and the blessings:

לֹא יַעֲקֹב, לֹא יֵאָמֵר עוֹד שֶׁהַבְּרָכוֹת בָּאוּ לְךָ בְּעָקְבָה וּבְרְמִיָּה כִּי אִם בִּשְׂרָרָה וּבְגִלּוּי פָּנִים וְסוֹפְךָ שֶׁהקב"ה נִגְלָה אֵלֶיךָ בְּבֵית אֵל וּמַחֲלִיף אֶת שִׁמְךָ וְשָׁם הוּא מְבָרֶכְךָ, וַאֲנִי שָׁם אֶהֱיֶה וְאוֹדֶה לְךָ עֲלֵיהֶן וְזֶה שֶׁכָּתוּב "וַיָּשַׂר אֶל מַלְאָךְ וַיֻּכָל בָּכָה וַיִּתְחַנֶּן לוֹ." בָּכָה הַמַּלְאָךְ וַיִּתְחַנֵּן לוֹ. וּמַה נִּתְחַנֵּן לוֹ "בֵּית אֵל יִמְצָאֶנּוּ וְשָׁם יְדַבֵּר עִמָּנוּ" הַמְתֵּן לִי עַד שֶׁיְּדַבֵּר עִמָּנוּ שָׁם. וְלֹא רָצָה יַעֲקֹב וְעַל כָּרְחוֹ הוֹדָה לוֹ עֲלֵיהֶן. וְזֶהוּ וַיְבָרֶךְ אֹתוֹ שָׁם שֶׁהָיָה מִתְחַנֵּן לְהַמְתִּין לוֹ וְלֹא רָצָה.

*It shall no longer be said that the blessings were acquired with deceit or guile, but rather that they were openly and honestly attained. Ultimately, God will reveal Himself to you in Beth El and change your name, and bless you, and I will be there and I will acknowledge that the blessings do indeed belong to you. Thus it is written [in the book of Hoshea], "The angel cried and beseeched him." What does the beseeching refer to?" He beseeched him, saying, "We will soon be in Beth El, where God will speak with us; put off your demand on me until He speaks with us." But Ya'akov did not want to delay, and the angel was forced to give him the blessing on the spot. Therefore it says, "And he blessed him there," for he begged Ya'akov to delay, and Ya'akov was unwilling.*[92]

The question now begs to be asked, why was Ya'akov so insistent upon receiving confirmation from Esav's angel that the blessings were indeed rightfully his? Yitzchak had already confirmed the blessings he had unwittingly bestowed upon Ya'akov. What would be added by the admission of Esav's angel? Receiving the recommendation of a righteous individual would seem to render any

---

91. *Bereishith* 32:29, 30.
92. Rashi *ad loc.*

subsequent recommendation from someone of lesser calibre entirely superfluous and even detrimental. Why, then, was a recommendation from this representative of evil so avidly sought?

Ya'akov, as we have stated, made three preparations for the confrontation with Esav, the first of which was sending a large gift. The Midrash elaborates upon the idea behind this gift.

> וַיֹּאמֶר אִם יָבוֹא עֵשָׂו אֶל הַמַּחֲנֶה הָאַחַת וְהִכָּהוּ. בְּאוֹתָהּ שָׁעָה אָמַר יַעֲקֹב אָבִינוּ לִפְנֵי הקב"ה רבש"ע כָּתַבְתָּ בְּתוֹרָתְךָ "וְשׁוֹר אוֹ שֶׂה אוֹתוֹ וְאֶת בְּנוֹ לֹא תִשְׁחֲטוּ בְּיוֹם אֶחָד". אִם יָבוֹא רָשָׁע זֶה וִיאַבֵּד אֶת בָּנַי וְאֶת אִמָּם בְּאַחַת, סֵפֶר תּוֹרָה שֶׁאַתָּה עָתִיד לִתֵּן עַל הַר סִינַי מִי יִקְרָא בּוֹ. בְּבַקָּשָׁה מִמְּךָ הַצִּילֵנִי נָא מִיָּדוֹ שֶׁלֹּא יָבוֹא וְהִכַּנִי אֵם עַל בָּנִים, שֶׁנֶּאֱמַר "הַצִּילֵנִי נָא". מָה עָשָׂה עָמַד וְשָׁלַח לוֹ דּוֹרוֹן לְסַמּוֹת אֶת עֵינָיו שֶׁנֶּאֱמַר "כִּי הַשֹּׁחַד יְעַוֵּר עֵינֵי חֲכָמִים" וְאֵין חֲכָמִים אֶלָּא אֱדוֹמִיִּים שֶׁנֶּאֱמַר "וְהַאֲבַדְתִּי חֲכָמִים מֵאֱדוֹם וּתְבוּנָה מֵהַר עֵשָׂו".
>
> *[Ya'akov] said, "What if Esav comes and smites this whole camp?" He then said to God, "Master of the Universe, in Your Torah You wrote, '...Do not slaughter an animal and its offspring in one day'. If this wicked individual comes and puts my children and their mothers to death all at once, then who will learn and observe the Torah that You will give in the future on Mount Sinai? I beseech You, save me from his hand, let him not come and smite the mother with the children." What did [Ya'akov] then do? He sent Esav a lavish gift in order to blind his eyes, as it is written, "Bribery blinds the eyes of the wise." The "wise" people referred to here are the people of Edom [the progeny of Esav]. In conjunction with this it is written, "I will destroy the wisdom of Edom and the understanding of the mountain of Esav."*[93]

The encounter between Ya'akov and the angel of Esav was not a one-time historical event. Rather, it is the confrontation of each individual with his own evil inclination, the force at the root of his own personality that seeks to use the individual's potential for negativity.

---

93. *Bereishith Rabbah* 75:13.

The Satan's guise changes in every generation; the necessity of the wrestle, however, does not. Now, as then, preparing to confront the Esav within entails three things: a bribe, prayer, and readiness for war.

Let us focus on the first area of preparation, a gift or bribe. An analogy is given concerning the nature of this bribery. A fierce dog blocks the entrance to a house. Unable to bypass the terrifying creature, a visitor to the house throws some meat to the dog. While the dog is occupied with his treat, the visitor slips past him and enters the house. Similarly, our Sages inform us that a frontal attack is not necessarily the best strategy to employ against the evil inclination. Instead, one can slip past the Satan by offering it a bribe.

It is in connection with this idea that our Sages offer us their timeless advice:

> לְעוֹלָם יַעֲסֹק אָדָם בְּתוֹרָה וּבְמִצְווֹת אַף עַל פִּי שֶׁלֹּא לִשְׁמָהּ שֶׁמִּתּוֹךְ שֶׁלֹּא לִשְׁמָהּ בָּא לִשְׁמָהּ.
>
> *One should always occupy himself with Torah and mitzvoth, even if not for their own sake, for through this behaviour he will come to do these things for their own sake.*[94]

Even though one may have personal motives in doing mitzvoth, one should nevertheless begin by doing them on this level, because this will lead him in time to desire to do them for the correct purpose. A scenario is being presented to us here. A person does not truly want to perform a good deed. But a sweetener is added to the bitter medicine and the person then swallows it, eventually coming to recognise the value of the medicine. In this vein one can understand Rashi's comment[95] on the injunction to love God with all your heart, בְּכָל לְבָבְךָ. His elucidation: בִּשְׁנֵי יְצָרֶיךָ — "with both of man's inclinations," the evil and the good. Our obligation to serve the Almighty with all our faculties entails making use of our inclination towards negativity and physicality in our quest for goodness. Our sincere desire for a mitzvah may not be strong enough in itself to

---

94. *Pesachim* 50b.
95. Rashi on *Devarim* 6:5.

see us through the performance of the deed. But by including in our action some incentive for the evil inclination to perform the deed, an extra impetus is provided.

When scaling a mountain whose gradient appears impossibly steep, a stick can be used to help one climb higher. Pushing downwards with the stick is the most effective method to facilitate our ascent. Improper, "downward" motives can be utilised to push one ever onwards. However, this propelling action, the שֶׁלֹּא לִשְׁמָהּ, must be used for the purpose of reaching one's destination. In this case the שֶׁלֹּא לִשְׁמָהּ, the improper motivation, is the bribe we offer to the evil inclination, freeing us to perform the mitzvah unhampered.

While using these methods, the purpose and goal in their employment must always be clear: מִתּוֹךְ שֶׁלֹּא לִשְׁמָהּ — within the personal motivation must be a seed of the prototype deed, the desire to perform a mitzvah in purity and ardour. It is only when we have the goal in mind that we can use this method effectively to aid us on the way to our destination. To this end we beseech the Almighty, וְטַהֵר לִבֵּנוּ לְעָבְדְךָ בֶּאֱמֶת — "Purify our hearts to serve You in truth." Judicial use of war tactics and strategies is invaluable in our struggle to escape the clutches of the evil inclination, the angel of Esav.

Rabbi Yerucham Levovitz reveals to us an entirely new dimension in this idea of administering a bribe to the Satan. He explains that it is normal in the world for a father to take his son's part and support his actions. A father is blind to his beloved son's deficiencies. This observation is made by King Shlomo in the book of *Mishlei*: וְעַל כָּל פְּשָׁעִים תְּכַסֶּה אַהֲבָה — "Feelings of love obscure all wrongdoings."[96] Even in the blackest of deeds, a father will discern a glint of light, and some justification will be conceived. Conversely, a person's enemy will never place his stamp of approval on any action of his foe. Some deficiency will be detected even in the most altruistic and selfless of deeds.

A situation could arise, however, in which a person's deeds are of such sterling quality that an enemy's words would be discounted and

---

96. *Mishlei* 10:12.

rejected, branded as just that — the words of an enemy. Everyone would recognise that it is only the seed of hatred within the enemy that prompts him to speak in this manner.

Developing this theme, R. Yerucham discloses an awesome principle: "The Torah teaches us the quality required of our good deeds. Our actions must be of such calibre that even our most relentless enemy would be forced to give his stamp of approval and agreement upon them, acknowledging that they are good."[97]

For a positive action to be truly considered as such, our greatest enemy, the evil inclination — the Satan himself — must acknowledge the correctness of the deed. This is seen concerning Iyov. God praises His servant:

הֲשַׂמְתָּ לִבְּךָ עַל עַבְדִּי אִיּוֹב כִּי אֵין כָּמֹהוּ בָּאָרֶץ.

*Have you observed My servant, that there is none like him in the land?*[98]

Satan himself was then forced to declare, אֱמֶת הַדָּבָר — "Indeed the matter is true." Our greatest enemy must be forced to admit the greatness of the deed; if not, the action contains some flaw or deficiency which precludes its definition as a מַעֲשֶׂה טוֹב, truly a good deed in its optimum form.

Ya'akov asked the angel of Esav to acknowledge the correctness of his act of usurping the blessings intended for bestowal upon his twin. When his fiercest opponent was forced to admit the truth of his deed, he had a guarantee that the deed was, from all angles, one of shining light. The acquiescence and blessing of his father was insufficient for Ya'akov, who sought an admission that his deed was of the highest calibre, a true "good deed."

In connection with this idea, the Ramban explains one of the most mystifying of procedures, performed on the holiest of days in the time of the Temple. Two completely identical goats are selected. One goat is brought as an offering to God, while the other is cast off

97. *Da'ath Chochmah U'Mussar*, Vol. 2, p. 132.
98. *Iyov* 1:8.

a cliff, to an abyss called עֲזָאזֵל, Azazel.

**וְנָתַן אַהֲרֹן עַל שְׁנֵי הַשְּׂעִירִם גּוֹרָלוֹת גּוֹרָל אֶחָד לַה׳ וְגוֹרָל אֶחָד לַעֲזָאזֵל.**

*Aharon shall then put [two] lots on the two goats — one lot [marked] "for the Eternal" and the [other] lot [marked] "for Azazel."*[99]

רמב"ן – מְפֹרָשׁ מִזֶּה בְּפִרְקֵי דְּרַבִּי אֱלִיעֶזֶר הַגָּדוֹל לְפִיכָךְ הָיוּ נוֹתְנִין לוֹ לְסַמָּאֵל שֹׁחַד בְּיוֹם הַכִּפּוּרִים שֶׁלֹּא לְבַטֵּל אֶת קָרְבָּנָם שֶׁנֶּאֱמַר גּוֹרָל אֶחָד לה׳ וְגוֹרָל אֶחָד לַעֲזָאזֵל שְׂעִיר הַחַטָּאת... רָאָה סַמָּאֵל שֶׁלֹּא נִמְצָא בָּהֶם חֵטְא בְּיוֹם כִּפּוּר, אָמַר לִפְנֵי הקב"ה רִבּוֹן כָּל הָעוֹלָמִים, יֵשׁ לְךָ עַם אֶחָד בָּאָרֶץ כְּמַלְאֲכֵי הַשָּׁרֵת שֶׁבַּשָּׁמַיִם. מַה מַלְאֲכֵי הַשָּׁרֵת יְחֵפֵי רֶגֶל כָּךְ הֵן יִשְׂרָאֵל יְחֵפֵי רֶגֶל בְּיוֹם הַכִּפּוּרִים. מַה מַלְאֲכֵי הַשָּׁרֵת אֵין בָּהֶם אֲכִילָה וּשְׁתִיָּה כָּךְ יִשְׂרָאֵל אֵין בָּהֶם אֲכִילָה וּשְׁתִיָּה בְּיוֹם כִּפּוּר. מַה מַלְאֲכֵי הַשָּׁרֵת אֵין לָהֶם קְפִיצָה כָּךְ יִשְׂרָאֵל עוֹמְדִים עַל רַגְלֵיהֶם בְּיוֹם כִּפּוּר. מַה מַלְאֲכֵי הַשָּׁרֵת שָׁלוֹם מְתַוֵּךְ בֵּינֵיהֶם כָּךְ יִשְׂרָאֵל שָׁלוֹם מְתַוֵּךְ בֵּינֵיהֶם בְּיוֹם כִּפּוּר. מַה מַלְאֲכֵי הַשָּׁרֵת נְקִיִּים מִכָּל חֵטְא כָּךְ הֵן יִשְׂרָאֵל נְקִיִּים מִכָּל חֵטְא בְּיוֹם כִּפּוּר.

*Ramban – Pirkei D'Rabbi Eliezer explains on this verse that they would give Satan a bribe on Yom Kippur so that he should not cancel out the merit of their sacrifice, as it says, "One lot [marked] 'for the Eternal', and the [other] lot [marked] 'for Azazel', a goat for a sin offering." The Satan would see that no sin was found in them on Yom Kippur, and would say before the Holy One, blessed be He, "Master of All the Worlds, You have one people in the land like the ministering angels in Heaven. Just as the angels are barefoot, so Yisrael are barefoot on Yom Kippur. Just as there is no eating or drinking among the angels, there is no eating or drinking among Yisrael on Yom Kippur... Just as the angels are clean of all sin, so the nation of Yisrael is clean of all sin on Yom Kippur."*[100]

One's actions must withstand the fiercest and most critical scrutiny: that of one's worst enemy — the Satan, or one's own desire for

99. *Vayikra* 16:8.
100. Ramban *ad loc.*

negativity. Only then is the action truly a good one.

There are two distinct levels in bribing the Satan:

1. One uses the evil inclination as a tool to help one bring an action to its completion. One thus escapes the clutches of evil.
2. On a higher level, one does not merely slip past the dog that lies in wait, but uses it to announce one's arrival at the desired destination. One changes the accusatory claim of the Satan, transforming it from casting aspersions upon one's actions, to placing its stamp of approval upon the deeds performed, a stamp which is attained only through labour and complete honesty.

Ya'akov was not satisfied with attainment of the first level. His declaration of וְהָיָה ה' לִי לֵאלֹקִים — "The Eternal shall be a God to me," indicated his willingness to be judged by a measure of strict justice, unadulterated by any mercy or compassion. Ya'akov asked for the accusing Hand of אֱלֹקִים, invoking the Name of God which denotes His use of the strict judgment which scrutinises every action, holding it up to the glare of truth, a beacon which highlights any deficiencies or shortcomings only too clearly. Ya'akov asked for this, and he desired that in this light his deeds would still be determined to be of the highest quality.

Mankind as a whole cannot withstand the glare of this light. It was because of our human frailty and weakness that God, at the beginning of creation, fused this strict justice with mercy and compassion. It was thus that the world could endure. Ya'akov returned to the seminal moments of the world and was judged on the scale of exacting justice. וַיִּוָּתֵר יַעֲקֹב לְבַדּוֹ — Ya'akov was left alone, unaided. He served God through his own backbreaking toil. Through this labour he attained the level where the power of negativity incarnate was forced to admit the rectitude of his actions. "בָּרְכֵנִי," Ya'akov demanded. The angel then blessed Ya'akov, bestowing upon him the name יִשְׂרָאֵל, Yisrael. יִשְׂרָאֵל — the name containing the word יָשָׁר, meaning straight, upright. His actions were indeed wholesome and good.

On Yom Kippur, too, this is the process which unfolds. We attempt to transform the harsh accuser into the defendant. Our greatest enemy becomes our most potent ammunition. On this day even the prosecutor admits that the Jewish People are inherently righteous.

Our actions must be correct and flawless in the eyes of both God and man, בְּעֵינֵי אֱלֹקִים וְאָדָם. We might ask ourselves, which man is being referred to in this statement? Whose scale of rectitude need we adopt? R. Yerucham has provided the answer: in the eyes of all men and any man. Both those who love you and those who oppose you must acknowledge the correctness of your position. When our actions are of this calibre, we will be secure in the knowledge that they are deserving of being called truly good.

# VAYESHEV

AS OUR PARASHAH coincides with the festival of Chanukah, let us consider just some of the numerous themes of this holiday.

**וַיְהִי הַשֶּׁמֶשׁ לָבוֹא וְתַרְדֵּמָה נָפְלָה עַל אַבְרָם וְהִנֵּה אֵימָה חֲשֵׁכָה גְדֹלָה נֹפֶלֶת עָלָיו.**

*As the sun was setting, a deep sleep came over Avram, with the dread of a great darkness enveloping him.*[101]

רש"י — וְהִנֵּה אֵימָה וגו' — רֶמֶז לְצָרוֹת וְחֹשֶׁךְ שֶׁל גָּלֻוּיוֹת.

*This was a hint to the sufferings of the Jewish People and the darkness of our exile.*[102]

Our Sages elucidate this idea, detailing that אֵימָה refers to the Babylonian exile, חֲשֵׁכָה refers to the Median exile, and the adjective attached to the darkness, גְּדֹלָה, refers to the Greek oppression which the Jews endured at the time of the Chanukah story. Let us investigate what lies behind this חֲשֵׁכָה גְדֹלָה, the "great darkness" which so epitomizes the Greeks.

The Gemara discusses the nature of the elusive festival of Chanukah.

מַאי חֲנֻכָּה? דְּתָנוּ רַבָּנָן בכ"ה בְּכִסְלֵו יוֹמֵי דַחֲנֻכָּה תַּמְנַיָּא אִינוּן דְּלָא לְמִסְפַּד בְּהוֹן וּדְלָא לְהִתְעַנּוֹת בְּהוֹן שֶׁכְּשֶׁנִּכְנְסוּ יְוָנִים לַהֵיכָל טִמְּאוּ כָּל הַשְּׁמָנִים שֶׁבַּהֵיכָל וּכְשֶׁגָּבְרָה מַלְכוּת בֵּית חַשְׁמוֹנַאי וְנִצְּחוּם בָּדְקוּ וְלֹא מָצְאוּ אֶלָּא פַּךְ אֶחָד שֶׁל שֶׁמֶן שֶׁהָיָה מֻנָּח בְּחוֹתָמוֹ שֶׁל כֹּהֵן גָּדוֹל וְלֹא הָיָה בּוֹ אֶלָּא לְהַדְלִיק יוֹם אֶחָד נַעֲשָׂה בּוֹ נֵס וְהִדְלִיקוּ מִמֶּנּוּ שְׁמוֹנָה יָמִים. לְשָׁנָה אַחֶרֶת קְבָעוּם וַעֲשָׂאוּם יָמִים טוֹבִים בְּהַלֵּל וְהוֹדָאָה.

---

101. *Bereishith* 15:12.
102. Rashi *ad loc.*

*What is Chanukah? Our Sages state that from the 25th day of Kislev we celebrate eight joyous days. On these days we abstain from delivering eulogies and from fasting. This is because of what occurred after the Greeks entered the holy Temple and defiled all the pure oil therein (which was required for lighting the Menorah). After the Chashmonaim vanquished their enemies they searched the Sanctuary and they found only a single flask of oil which, with the seal of the High Priest intact upon it, was guaranteed to be pure. This single flask contained sufficient oil to burn only for one day. A miracle transpired and the oil in the Menorah burned for eight days. The following year these days were established as a festival of praise and thanksgiving.*[103]

Everything contained in Torah is not merely academic, but has significance for our own lives. How can we relate this miraculous event and the joyous days we celebrate to our contemporary lives in the society in which we live?

The above Gemara has a fascinating continuation:

תְּנַן הָתָם גֵּץ הַיּוֹצֵא מִתַּחַת הַפַּטִּישׁ וְיָצָא וְהִזִּיק חַיָּב גָּמָל שֶׁטָּעוּן פִּשְׁתָּן וְהוּא עוֹבֵר בִּרְשׁוּת הָרַבִּים וְנִכְנְסָה פִּשְׁתָּנוֹ לְתוֹךְ הַחֲנוּת וְדָלְקָה בְּנֵרוֹ שֶׁל חֶנְוָנִי וְהִדְלִיק אֶת הַבִּירָה, בַּעַל הַגָּמָל חַיָּב. הֵנִיחַ חֶנְוָנִי אֶת נֵרוֹ מִבַּחוּץ, חֶנְוָנִי חַיָּב. רַבִּי יְהוּדָה אוֹמֵר בְּנֵר חֲנֻכָּה פָּטוּר.

The following scenarios are presented:

If sparks from a blacksmith's smithy kindle another's flax, the blacksmith is liable to pay for damages.

A camel driver has overloaded his animal with flax, so that while traveling along a public thoroughfare the flax protrudes into a blacksmith's workshop. If a spark ignites the flax, causing the smithy to be burned down, the camel driver is responsible to pay for the damages to the shop.

If a shopkeeper placed a lamp outside his shop and it caused damage, the shopkeeper is liable to pay for damages. Rabbi Yehudah,

103. *Shabbath* 21b.

however, states that if this was done on Chanukah, he is not liable, and does not have to pay. For, on Chanukah, one has permission to station a lamp outside in public property.

What is the significance of this law?

Interestingly, a comment of Rashi in the beginning of our *parashah* echoes this excerpt:

הַפִּשְׁתָּנִי הַזֶּה נִכְנְסוּ גְּמַלָּיו טְעוּנִים פִּשְׁתָּן, הַפֶּחָמִי תָּמַהּ, אָנָה יִכָּנֵס כָּל הַפִּשְׁתָּן הַזֶּה, הָיָה פִּקֵּחַ אֶחָד מֵשִׁיב לוֹ, נִיצוֹץ אֶחָד יוֹצֵא מִמַּפּוּחַ שֶׁלְּךָ שֶׁשּׂוֹרֵף אֶת כֻּלּוֹ, כָּךְ, יַעֲקֹב רָאָה כָּל הָאַלּוּפִים הַכְּתוּבִים לְמַעְלָה, תָּמַהּ וְאָמַר, מִי יָכֹל לִכְבֹּשׁ אֶת כֻּלָּן, מַה כְּתִיב לְמַטָּה אֵלֶּה תֹּלְדוֹת יַעֲקֹב יוֹסֵף, וּכְתִיב וְהָיָה בֵית יַעֲקֹב אֵשׁ וּבֵית יוֹסֵף לֶהָבָה וּבֵית עֵשָׂו לְקַשׁ, נִיצוֹץ יוֹצֵא מִיּוֹסֵף שֶׁמְּכַלֶּה וְשׂוֹרֵף אֶת כֻּלָּם.

*A flax merchant was leading his camels which were heavily loaded with flax. The blacksmith wondered how the flax merchant would bring his bulky wares into any premises. A clever man commented that only one spark from the blacksmith's fire was needed to consume the entire load. Similarly, as enumerated in the Torah, the number of princes and captains stemming from Esav was enormous, and Ya'akov wondered how he could ever overcome them. The answer: "This is the progeny of Ya'akov: Yosef." Yosef, in contrast to Ya'akov who is compared to fire, is compared to a leaping flame. Merely one spark from Yosef is sufficient to consume Esav in its entirety.*[104]

This is seen more explicitly in *Parashath Vayeitzei*. There, Rashi comments:

מִשֶּׁנּוֹלַד שִׂטְנוֹ שֶׁל עֵשָׂו, שֶׁנֶּאֱמַר וְהָיָה בֵית יַעֲקֹב אֵשׁ וּבֵית יוֹסֵף לֶהָבָה וּבֵית עֵשָׂו לְקַשׁ. אֵשׁ בְּלֹא לֶהָבָה, אֵינוֹ שׁוֹלֵט לְמֵרָחוֹק, מִשֶּׁנּוֹלַד יוֹסֵף, בָּטַח יַעֲקֹב בְּהַקָּדוֹשׁ בָּרוּךְ הוּא וְרָצָה לָשׁוּב.

*It was when the leaping flame, Yosef, was born that Ya'akov felt sufficiently confident to leave the house of Lavan and confront Esav. For Yosef represented a leaping flame; an*

104. Rashi on *Bereishith* 37:1.

*entity which spans distances and makes an impact even from afar.*[105]

This then, is the distinction between Ya'akov and Yosef, between fire and flame. A fire burns in its place, the yellow flames consuming all that is present. In contrast, a leaping flame sends its sparks further afield, igniting even that which lies at a distance. We are informed that one spark of Yosef is sufficient to destroy all of the officers of Edom. What is the significance of this idea?

The key to the subjects raised above lies in a Gemara quoted and elucidated by the Maharal in his *Nethivoth Olam.*

*Rabbi Yehudah said: If one withholds knowledge from a thirsting student it is as if one has stolen from him, as it is written, "Torah was commanded to us by Moshe as an inheritance to the congregation of Ya'akov." It belongs to the entire people from the beginning of time, and thus is the rightful property of each member.*[106]

*If you do teach Torah, what reward is received? Said Rava in the name of R. Shesseth, "He receives the same blessing as that received by Yosef. As it says, 'Blessing is bestowed upon the one who sustains another.'" This verse refers to Yosef, who sustained others in Egypt, distributing to those in need during the years of famine in Egypt.*

The Maharal elaborates upon this, explaining the parallel between the blessings of Yosef and the blessings bestowed upon one who disseminates Torah. Yosef received his blessings because of his role as a distributor, a task undertaken not only in Egypt, but also amongst the Jewish People. This is demonstrated in the Aramaic translation of a verse which reads, "He sustained fathers and sons." The idea of radiating out and benefiting others with one's resources is such a lofty one that Yosef was blessed with the blessings of "Heaven and earth." This is all attributable to his expansive giving

105. Rashi on *Bereishith* 30:25.
106. *Sanhedrin* 91b.

to the entire nation. One who promulgates Torah and transcendent knowledge, affects the entire nation and is therefore likened to Yosef and is deserving of his blessings.

A related Gemara[107] states the following:

> *Said Reish Lakish, "One who teaches Torah to the son of one's friend is credited with making him. For the verse says (in reference to Avraham's spiritual work), 'And the souls which they made in Charan.' Through teaching people, Avraham actually made them."*
>
> *Rabbi Eliezer elaborated further, "One who teaches Torah adds an extra dimension to that which he has taught. For it states,[108] '...And you shall guard My covenant and make them* (וַעֲשִׂיתֶם אֹתָם)*.' This implies that one in some way actually makes the words of Torah."*

Rava said that when one disseminates Torah to others, וַעֲשִׂיתֶם אֹתָם — "And you shall make them," should be read as אִתָּם — "with them," implying that one develops and builds oneself through the sublime words which are shared with others. One who teaches others gains a degree of completion through this activity which would be otherwise unattainable. He brings Torah from potential into actuality. Prior to teaching others he had a potential within him which has now been brought to fruition, thus developing a part of himself which previously lay dormant. For the truth of Torah lies not in physicality, but in the domain of the intellect. Thus, one transforms oneself through giving in this manner to others. It is this actualization of one's potential, through relating Torah wisdom to others, which brings one ultimately to a state of perfection.

We can explain the words of the Maharal by contemplating the following. Any physical object is finite by its very nature, bound by space and time, and limited at any given moment to a particular location. An idea, however, is not a tangible entity, and we see that a

---

107. *Sanhedrin* 99b.
108. *Devarim* 29:8.

concept can be carried by one person, shared by two, or even spread around the entire world. The characteristic therefore of something that lies in the realm of the intellect is that unlike the physical world, it is not bound by any time or place. Torah, in the category of the intellect, also has these characteristics as its hallmark: it can be diffused and disseminated around the world and can sustain anyone, anywhere, in its unlimited fashion. To disseminate Torah is to bring one's own potential to fruition, and to refrain from giving in this way is to withhold from others that which rightfully belongs to them as members of the congregation of Ya'akov.

Rabbi Yitzchak Hutner used this principle to explain the statement of our Sages: "I have learned much from my teachers, a greater amount from my contemporaries, yet I have learned the most from my students."[109] Teaching and transmitting one's knowledge to others effects a vital change within a person, actualizing one's potential. This benefit is reaped only through nurturing and imparting knowledge to others, thus: "I have learned the most from my students." The act of giving changes the essence of the teacher.

The Greeks reached the pinnacle of intellectual achievement. The great Rambam himself lauds the faculty of logic possessed by Aristotle, one of the outstanding Greek philosophers. For many centuries, throughout the Western world, a thorough knowledge of the Greek classics was a prerequisite to entrance into the circles of high culture. Greek thought dominated not only fashionable society, but the entire civilised world. Intellect was their domain.

Yet, almost antithetically to this image of philosophical sophistication, the Greeks invented the Olympics, that tournament which served solely to glorify the achievements and allure of the body. High jump, long jump, sprinting — whose "machine" worked the most efficiently? That was the question posed by these games. With all their intellectual acumen, the Greeks nevertheless worshipped pure physicality, the opposite of the mind and the level of abstraction. They spurned the unlimited quality of the mind, replacing it

---

109. *Ta'anith* 7a.

with the finite nature of the body. They thus extinguished the light of the intellect.

Darkness is often defined as the absence of light. There is a different kind of darkness, however, an active night which pervades and penetrates into almost every corner. For this darkness is invited inside, welcomed, cultivated. Not only did the Greeks bring an absence of light into the world; they actively created darkness through snuffing out the light of the mind, the illumination of ideas and thought. They buried the abstract in the physicality in which they wallowed. A double darkness swept through the world, a חֲשֵׁכָה גְדֹלָה. This great darkness resulted from the Greeks' active transformation of light into darkness, day into night, mind into materialism. Their intellect was used for no higher purpose than glorification of the body.

At the beginning of the *parashah*, Rashi commented that merely one spark is needed to obliterate and consume an entire load of flax. Merely one small light will dispel much darkness. One spark of genuine light can disperse the multitude of Edom's armies. Yosef personified the idea of a distributor, spreading out resources and providing for others. One who benefits the world through disseminating Torah merits the same blessing as Yosef, that leaping flame with the capacity to spread and affect distant places from afar.

Moshe was instructed to gather seventy men who would constitute a *Sanhedrin*. Moshe's task was to pass on the resources and spiritual faculties that would enable this elite to fulfill their allotted duty. The Midrash informs us that:

> נִתְמַלְּאוּ רוּחַ הַקֹּדֶשׁ מֵרוּחוֹ שֶׁל מֹשֶׁה וּמֹשֶׁה לֹא חָסַר כְּלוּם, כְּאָדָם שֶׁמַּדְלִיק נֵר מִנֵּר.[110]

Each of the seventy men became filled with Divine inspiration which originated and stemmed from the Divine inspiration of Moshe. Despite having given of his own spiritual resources to these men, we are told that Moshe remained without deficit: "He lost nothing,

110. *Bemidbar Rabbah* 13:19.

like a candle that is used to kindle another." The original candle is unaffected despite spreading itself and affecting another independent entity, continuing to burn with the same vigour and strength. According to the above Gemara, not only does one not lose, but one positively benefits from spreading the light of Torah; the glow cast by the original candle is actually intensified.

At the time that the Chanukah story took place, the people "became lax in their Divine service."[111] They were complacent, and did not exert themselves to influence others. The following principle is learned from *Megillath Esther*: When a strength or trait exclusive to the Jewish nation is not utilised by them to the full, that advantage is transferred to the Gentiles, who use it against us. This is seen through the description of Achashverosh: כְּשֶׁבֶת אֲחַשְׁוֵרוֹשׁ..., literally meaning, "When Achashverosh sat." We are told by our Sages, that the word כְּשֶׁבֶת also alludes to the gift of the Sabbath which, profaned by part of the Jewish People, was transferred to the Gentiles, who are not party to this concept — וְלֹא נְתַתּוֹ לְגוֹיֵי הָאֲרָצוֹת. Neglected by the Jews, the power of the Sabbath was now seized by the Gentiles, who could wield it against us.

Torah is the collective possession of the entire Jewish nation. Each individual therefore has a duty to disseminate Torah to the people and influence others to follow the path of truth. In our prayers we request the ability, "to learn and to teach." In essence our request is to teach and spread the light of Torah, thus elevating the congregation of Ya'akov, and bringing out our own latent potential through the distribution of this priceless sustenance. The dissemination of Torah is intrinsic to the existence of our nation. However, when we become lax and neglectful of this characteristic, then it passes over to the Gentiles.

The Greeks refused to tolerate the inconspicuous, unobtrusive fire which was being stoked in the study hall. Illogically and irrationally, they acted as if the Torah learned and observed by the Jewish People would in some way harm them. Unprovoked, they sought

---

111. Bach on the Tur, *Orach Chaim* 670.

to snuff out the flames of truth and pulsating life; they sought to silence the sound of Torah which still rang clear. The Greeks wanted to replace ultimate wisdom with the logic and intellectuality of their philosophers; they wanted to replace Moshe and Aharon with Socrates and Plato. The Greeks were not content merely to overlook the Jews, for they felt an urgent need to influence, to disseminate, and to spread their wisdom throughout the land. The Jews were not using their gift. The Gentiles pounced upon it with a vengeance, and employed it against them — לְהַשְׁכִּיחָם תּוֹרָתֶךָ וּלְהַעֲבִירָם מֵחֻקֵּי רְצוֹנֶךָ.

Awareness of this unique characteristic, and utilisation of it, is particularly relevant in our present society. In his commentary on Torah, Rabbeinu Yonah explains that each of the Six Days of Creation is an antecedent of each millennium of the world's existence. Thus the era of the last thousand years, in which we presently find ourselves, corresponds to the sixth day of Creation. On this day was commanded, תּוֹצֵא הָאָרֶץ נֶפֶשׁ חַיָּה לְמִינָהּ — "Let the earth bring forth living beings."[112] Rabbeinu Yonah interprets this phrase figuratively, stating that in this era, earthly, materialistic people will develop into souls possessing the quality of true life. A metamorphosis will occur, as people who were entrenched in the muck and mire of this transient world will develop into groping, searching, growing beings, who will blossom and stretch out of the ubiquitous mud, reaching for the cultivated soil and the sunlight in which to bask.

Fifty years ago there existed merely one returnee to Judaism in England. Today, there are many hundreds, if not thousands, of returnees to Judaism, as all over the world the seeds burst forth from the earth. Our generation is a receptive one. They stand, waiting to hear. The challenge is now ours. Will we provide sufficient nourishment? Will we cultivate and encourage this new growth? Will we garb ourselves with the gift belonging to the Jewish People and act as disseminators of Torah? If we do not, we are perpetrating an act of robbery as we withhold that which is their due. A special challenge is presented to those endowed with the ability and opportunity to do

---

112. *Bereishith* 1:24.

so: to cast light where darkness reigned.

We kindle the Menorah outside the house. We light a flame which leaps upwards. It takes just a little light to dispel much darkness. Just one spark is sufficient to consume an entire load of flax. Through a spark, a genuine spark, a spark from the flame of truth, from the flame of Torah, we can kindle and illuminate the lives of those many people who still dwell in piteous darkness. When we disseminate those sparks, when we act as that vigourous leaping flame, we will influence and enlighten the world. We thus take the quality originally given to us as the Jewish nation and liberate it from the control of the Greeks, from the pervasive culture which they so determinedly attempted to spread. We kindle our lanterns, and in the face of great darkness we bear our torches. We anticipate the time when the nations will gather and express their yearning, נֵלְכָה בְּאוֹר ה׳ — "Let us go in the light of God."[113]

113. See *Yeshayah* 2:5.

# MIKEITZ

AT THE CONCLUSION of *Vayeshev*, we find an indication of the exactitude with which Yosef was judged. His appeal to the butler, זְכַרְתַּנִי... וְהִזְכַּרְתַּנִי — "If you remember me... mention me to Par'oh and effect my release from prison,"[114] is viewed as a deficiency, although the commentaries differ in pinpointing precisely what was the flaw in Yosef's request. All agree, however, that due to this subtle shortcoming Yosef was subject to two additional years in prison. This is highlighted by the Midrash:

> וַיְהִי מִקֵּץ שְׁנָתַיִם יָמִים — בְּכָל עֶצֶב יִהְיֶה מוֹתָר וּדְבַר שְׂפָתַיִם אַךְ לְמַחְסוֹר. עַל יְדֵי שֶׁאָמַר לְשַׂר הַמַּשְׁקִים זְכַרְתַּנִי וְהִזְכַּרְתַּנִי נִתּוֹסֵף לוֹ שְׁתֵּי שָׁנִים שֶׁנֶּאֱמַר וַיְהִי מִקֵּץ וגו'.
>
> *And it was at the end of two years.*
>
> *"In all reticence there will be gain, but talk of the lips incurs only loss."*
>
> *By virtue of his request to the butler to remember him, two further years of imprisonment were decreed upon him, as it is stated, "And it was at the end of two years..."*[115]

To elucidate the statement of King Shlomo quoted in the Midrash above:

"In all reticence there will be gain." All reticence results in tangible gain; however, "talk of the lips" brings no benefit in its wake and even leads to loss. Yosef learned this principle through personal experience: speaking the words זְכַרְתַּנִי וְהִזְכַּרְתַּנִי — "If you remember me, mention me," caused him to languish in jail for two extra years.

---

114. *Bereishith* 40:14.
115. *Bereishith Rabbah* 89:2.

Rabbi Leib Chasman compares the words of the Midrash to an incident recounted in the Talmud.[116]

*R. Pinchas ben Yair went to perform the mitzvah of releasing captives. He encountered the Ginai River. He said, "Split your waters that I may cross."*

*The river replied, "You are going to perform your Creator's will. I too am presently performing His will. The task you intend to accomplish may or may not come to fruition. My mission, however, is constantly fulfilled."*

*Said R. Pinchas ben Yair, "If you do not split your waters, I decree that no water continue to flow between your banks."*

*The waters parted.*

The above extract recounts a deep confrontation. The entirety of the physical world was created solely for the purpose of sanctifying the Almighty's Name. Indeed, all physicality aspires to realise this sublime goal. A river, water flowing downstream, fulfills a specific mission. Therefore the river did not "wish" to restrain itself, and resisted R. Pinchas' request. A clash here is taking place: two creatures want to serve the Almighty, yet their service conflicts.

The submission of the river demonstrates the particular importance attached to the mitzvah of redeeming captives. The Talmud continues, stating that the merit of R. Pinchas ben Yair in the performance of this mitzvah is comparable to the merit of Moshe Rabbeinu and the 600,000 members of the Jewish People for which the Red Sea split. It was in recognition of the magnitude of the deed that the river held its waters back from their natural path.

Let us examine a law concerning the redemption of captives in an attempt to elucidate this concept.

תָּנוּ רַבָּנָן הָיָה הוּא וְאָבִיו וְרַבּוֹ בַּשֶּׁבִי. הוּא קוֹדֵם לְרַבּוֹ, וְרַבּוֹ קוֹדֵם לְאָבִיו.

*A person is imprisoned with both his spiritual mentor and his father. He is presented with the opportunity to release just one*

116. *Chullin* 7a.

*of the three captives. The order of priority is himself, then his Rabbi, and then his father.*[117]

According to this law, were Yosef to have uttered two words — זְכַרְתַּנִי וְהִזְכַּרְתַּנִי — to save his father or Rabbi, he would not have been punished. If, according to the above, one's first priority is to save oneself, why, then, was Yosef criticised for asking the butler to remember him to Par'oh?

Further, the story related to us by the Talmud does not record the identity of the captive whom R. Pinchas was traveling to redeem. The absence of this information leads us to surmise that it was not a particularly venerated or prominent personality. Nevertheless, because of the value of this mitzvah, R. Pinchas merited an open miracle, as great as the splitting of the sea for the Jewish People upon their Exodus from Egypt.

As mentioned earlier, there is a difference of opinion among the various commentators as to Yosef's exact crime. Yosef is called צַדִּיק יְסוֹד עוֹלָם, a righteous individual upon whose merit the world endures. As is the general rule, the higher the stature of the man, the greater are God's expectations of him. A righteous individual is held culpable for a "hairbreadth's" aberration from the correct path. The subtlety of Yosef's error is emphasized by those commentators who claim that Yosef's sin lay in turning to a high-ranking officer. Upon this haughty butler's release from jail, he would immediately forget a lowly vagabond who had been his companion during a period he would rather consign to oblivion. It would be an abnormality, then, if such a proud officer were to remember Yosef. Thus, turning to the butler for assistance is deemed as seeking salvation by supernatural means, through a process which cannot be said to conform to the normal manner of events. When a person resorts to an inappropriate endeavour he puts himself in the situation of a drowning man who clutches at straws; his salvation is openly miraculous, for straws are futile to save one from the current. As the Chazon Ish explains, Yosef did not rely on the butler himself, but he chose a kind of effort

---

117. *Horayoth* 13a.

that would not hide the miracle of his redemption. Yosef is therefore faulted not for his lack of faith in the Almighty, but for choosing an inappropriate form of personal effort.

However, this explanation of Yosef's sin is surprising when we recall that R. Pinchas ben Yair also awaited a miracle to facilitate his fulfillment of the mitzvah of redeeming captives, a miracle comparable to the splitting of the Red Sea. Further, the text indicates that the captive concerned was not a character of note, yet these measures were still taken. Wherein lies the distinction between the two situations, the distinction between saving oneself and redeeming another? Why was Yosef punished and R. Pinchas rewarded?

Let us digress and examine the explanation of the Vilna Gaon upon a verse in *Yeshayah*:

אִמְרוּ צַדִּיק כִּי טוֹב כִּי פְרִי מַעַלְלֵיהֶם יֹאכֵלוּ.

*Say concerning a righteous person that he is good, for the fruit of their labour they shall eat.*[118]

The Vilna Gaon questions the grammatical discrepancy in the verse, which begins in the singular form, and concludes in the plural. He explains that although the reward for mitzvoth is principally reserved for the Eternal world, righteous individuals also reap dividends in this physical existence. The latter half of the verse, "The fruit of their labour they shall eat," refers specifically to this idea. This clause applies to a generation in which many righteous individuals live together. However, in a generation in which there is but one righteous individual, who alone fulfills his obligations with exactitude and devotion, although the entire world may be sustained in his merit, he himself will not benefit from his actions in this world.

While the grammatical difficulty has now been reconciled, we remain with a philosophical conundrum. According to our understanding, we would expect a lone individual, fighting valiantly against the prevailing wind of negativity, to receive additional reward for his

118. *Yeshayah* 3:10.

efforts, and benefit both in this world and the next. Why should the righteous man surrounded by people of purity and wholesomeness be rewarded more than his struggling counterpart, if in absolute terms they have both acquired the same spiritual level? For example, applying the Gaon's principle to the episode at hand, Yosef was a righteous individual upon whose shoulders the world rested. He had been placed in a degenerate society of crumbling values. He would thus fit into the category just described, of righteous individuals who find themselves alone in the world, and would be rewarded according to the principle stated above.

Analysis of the Talmudic character Nakdimon ben Gurion will shed light upon the issue at hand.[119]

> *It once happened that R. Yochanan ben Zakai was riding his donkey out of Jerusalem, followed by his disciples. He saw a maiden collecting barley amongst the droppings of Arab animals. Upon seeing him, the maiden, who was not dressed appropriately, wrapped her hair around herself and approached R. Yochanan. She implored him, "Rabbi, please provide me with a means of livelihood."*
>
> *"My daughter, from which family do you come?"*
>
> *"Nakdimon ben Gurion," she said, pronouncing the name of one of the wealthiest men of the time.*
>
> *R' Yochanan asked the girl, "What became of your father's riches?"*
>
> *"To preserve riches, one must give charity. My father was deficient in this area, and we are now suffering the loss." She further explained that other sources of financial aid had also been exhausted.*

Analysing this exchange, the Gemara asks a striking question:

"Can we believe this of Nakdimon ben Gurion? Concerning him it is recounted that he gave an abundance of charity, and made sure to give it in a way that would not embarrass his beneficiaries!"

---

119. *Kethuboth* 66b.

Although it seems that Nakdimon ben Gurion was extremely generous and considerate with his resources, the Gemara concludes that his deeds were for his own glory and honour.

Rabbi Chaim Shmuelevitz cites another incident in the Talmud which appears to contradict the above inference of our Sages.[120]

It once occurred that the Jewish People journeyed to Jerusalem on a pilgrimage to the Temple and had no water to drink. Nakdimon ben Gurion approached a wealthy squire. "Loan me twelve springs of water for the pilgrims, and I shall repay you with twelve wells of water. And if I fail to pay you back I will give you twelve units of silver." Nakdimon ben Gurion appointed a day by which the debt was to be repaid.

The deadline arrived and rain had not fallen. In the morning messengers were sent to Nakdimon with the following request, "Send me either the water or the money which you owe me." Nakdimon's reply: "The day is mine" (i.e. I still have today to repay you). In the afternoon, the emissaries returned with the same demand. Again Nakdimon replied, "There are yet a few hours." The squire mocked Nakdimon, "The entire year has been bereft of rain. Why should rain fall now?" As the squire entered the bathhouse in gleeful anticipation of twelve units of silver, Nakdimon ben Gurion entered the Temple with a heavy heart. He immersed himself in prayer, presenting the following plea. "Master of the Universe, it is revealed before You that it is not for my honour, nor for the glory of my father's house that I have done this. I acted for Your honour, that water should be available for the pilgrims."

Immediately, clouds covered the sky and rain fell until twelve wells of water were filled to overflowing.

How can we reconcile this story with the seemingly uncomplimentary appraisal of Nakdimon ben Gurion inferred from his daughter's words?

Rabbi Chaim Shmuelevitz suggests that although Nakdimon ben Gurion went to some lengths to hide his benevolence, and considered

---

120. *Ta'anith* 19b.

how to give indirectly to the paupers, he nevertheless did receive some honour for his actions. The glory bestowed upon him did, in some small way, detract from and infringe on the purity of his intentions. Let us elaborate further.

The Gemara states:

> א"ר יִרְמְיָה מִשּׁוּם ר' שִׁמְעוֹן בַּר יוֹחַאי. יָכֹל אֲנִי לִפְטֹר אֶת כָּל הָעוֹלָם כֻּלּוֹ מִן הַדִּין מִיּוֹם שֶׁנִּבְרֵאתִי עַד עַתָּה, וְאִלְמָלֵי אֶלְעָזָר בְּנִי עִמִּי מִיּוֹם שֶׁנִּבְרָא הָעוֹלָם וְעַד עַכְשָׁו. וְאִלְמָלֵי יוֹתָם בֶּן עֻזִּיָּהוּ עִמָּנוּ מִיּוֹם שֶׁנִּבְרָא הָעוֹלָם עַד סוֹפוֹ.
>
> *R. Yirmiyah states in the name of R. Shimon bar Yochai: "I can spare the world from the measure of strict justice from the day I was born until today. If my son El'azar is considered with me, we could shield the world from the inception of the universe until today. With Yothem ben Uziah with us, the world would be protected from the intensity of God's exacting justice from its beginning until the end."*[121]

Rashi elaborates upon the evidently great merit of Yothem.

Yothem ben Uziah was a more righteous and humble individual than any other king. It is concerning him that the verse states, "A son will honour his father," for he excelled in this mitzvah. Through the entire period in which his father was a leper, Yothem acted as the judicial authority in the land, as stated, "And Yothem the judge." Yothem would not accept the yoke of kingship during his father's lifetime, and when pronouncing any verdict, he would cite the law in his father's name.

The sage Rabbeinu Chananel writes that Yothem's exceptional merit was equivalent to that of R. Shimon bar Yochai and his son. These personalities are distinctive in that they received no dividends from their sublime actions while in this world. This feature is a prerequisite for fortifying the world, and it is this category of Divine service which can provide atonement for the entire world, releasing it from the gripping claws of strict justice. It is those individuals

---

121. *Sukkah* 45b.

who derive no pleasure and feel no personal benefit at all from the physical world, who are the pillars upon which the world continues to exist. This principle is clearly illustrated in the following statement of our Sages:

> בְּכָל יוֹם בַּת קוֹל יוֹצֵאת וְאוֹמֶרֶת כָּל הָעוֹלָם כֻּלּוֹ נִזּוֹן בִּשְׁבִיל חֲנִינָא בְּנִי, וַחֲנִינָא בְּנִי דַּיּוֹ בְּקַב חֲרוּבִים מֵעֶרֶב שַׁבָּת לְעֶרֶב שַׁבָּת.
>
> *Every day a Heavenly voice proclaims, "The entire world is sustained through My son Chanina. And Chanina is satisfied to subsist on a few carobs for the whole week."*[122]

It was R. Chanina's satisfaction with so little that caused the world to be sustained because of him — בִּשְׁבִילוֹ. The word שְׁבִיל literally translates as a pathway or a channel. R. Chanina provided a channel through which the world could be sustained. He was a conduit through which Heavenly blessings could be bestowed.

Any obstruction within a pipe automatically impedes the flow, and diminishes the quality or quantity of the outcome. Were R. Chanina to have received personal benefit from the world, the pipe would have been blocked to some extent, so that the world could not have been sustained through him, בִּשְׁבִילוֹ. The thicker the walls of a pipe, the less water is able to flow through the pipe at any one time, and the less will be received by those waiting to benefit from the flow.

With this principle in mind, let us return to the words of the Vilna Gaon. A single righteous person in a generation sustains the whole world, and it is for this very reason that he can enjoy no benefit in this world. His life is not his own, and he must rid himself of every last vestige of self, so that the channel of sustenance for the world remains unobstructed. One who is categorized as a יְסוֹד עוֹלָם has a pivotal role to play. Standing between Heaven and earth, he is a conduit for the flow of blessing. His sacred duty is to ensure that all his deeds are done purely for the sake of Heaven. Any personal gain would obstruct the flow.

In contrast, when many righteous people exist, each individual

---

122. *Ta'anith* 24b.

plays some role in drawing down holiness and blessing. For them to derive some benefit from the world would not inhibit the flow, as there are many pipelines through which God's bounty could stream. This was not the situation of R. Shimon bar Yochai and his son, who received nothing from this world. They disdained honour, resisted the allure of wealth, and spurned physical gratification. It was due to this that they had the capacity to shield the world from God's strict justice, and it was because of this that they could sustain, or rather act as the conduit through which the whole world was sustained.

Man can only transcend when he lifts himself above the swirling whirlwind of physical pleasures and worldly gratifications. He then achieves a level of complete self-abnegation before the Omnipotent One. Through his subordination he makes himself into an empty vessel, a tool in the hands of the Almighty. The Source of all blessing can then begin to pour, for a hollow receptacle is standing, waiting to receive and radiate forth, for the sake of His holy Name. The potential benefit bestowed upon the world in this manner is unlimited.

A corollary of this is the essential distinction between a mitzvah performed for the sake of others, and a deed which brings a personal benefit in its wake. Considering Yosef's situation from its halachic perspective, he cannot be faulted for his efforts to save himself from his horrible fate of captivity. However, Yosef, as we know, was in an entirely different league from the rest of humanity. He was in the class entitled צַדִּיק יְסוֹד עוֹלָם and as such, could reap no fruit from his actions while still in this transient world. He was the vital conduit for the world's blessing, and the pipeline had to remain unobstructed. He had to remove any trace of self to become a perfect channel for Divine goodness. Only by nullifying any personal interests could he continue in this capacity, and allow the flow to remain unimpeded.

Returning to Nakdimon ben Gurion, it is safe to state that this venerable individual gave charity neither for his own honour, nor for the glory of his household, a fact which God Himself showed. However, Nakdimon ben Gurion had not yet attained the stature of one through whom the world is sustained. The small amount of satisfaction and honour which he did enjoy impaired his ability to act as a conduit for the people during their time of need, when in the throes of famine.

This principle is awe-inspiring; one who awaits praise or honour for his actions impairs the intrinsic merit of the deed. The *Mesillath Yesharim* elaborates upon this:

> אָמְנָם מַה שֶׁצָּרִיךְ לָאָדָם יוֹתֵר עִיּוּן וּמְלָאכָה רַבָּה הוּא תַּעֲרֹבֶת הָאִסּוּר. דְּהַיְנוּ, שֶׁלִּפְעָמִים הָאָדָם הוֹלֵךְ וְעוֹשֶׂה מִצְוָה לִשְׁמָהּ מַמָּשׁ, שֶׁכָּךְ גָּזַר אָבִינוּ שֶׁבַּשָּׁמַיִם. אָמְנָם לֹא יֶחְדַּל מִלְּשַׁתֵּף עִמָּהּ אֵיזֶה פְּנִיָּה אַחֶרֶת אוֹ שֶׁיְּשַׁבְּחוּהוּ בְּנֵי הָאָדָם אוֹ שֶׁיְּקַבֵּל שָׂכָר בְּמַעֲשֵׂהוּ. וְלִפְעָמִים אֲפִלּוּ אִם לֹא יִהְיֶה מִתְכַּוֵּן מַמָּשׁ לְשֶׁיְּשַׁבְּחוּהוּ, בִּשְׂמֹחַ לִבּוֹ עַל הַשֶּׁבַח יַרְבֶּה לְדַקְדֵּק יוֹתֵר, כְּעֵין מַעֲשֶׂה שֶׁל בִּתּוֹ שֶׁל רַבִּי חֲנִינָא בֶּן תְּרַדְיוֹן שֶׁהָיְתָה פּוֹסַעַת פְּסִיעוֹת יָפוֹת, וְכֵיוָן שֶׁשָּׁמְעָה שֶׁאוֹמְרִים כַּמָּה נָאוֹת פְּסִיעוֹת שֶׁל רִיבָה זוֹ, מִיָּד דִּקְדְּקָה יוֹתֵר. הֲרֵי הַתּוֹסֶפֶת הַזֶּה נוֹלַד מִכֹּחַ הַשֶּׁבַח שֶׁשִּׁבְּחוּהָ, וְאָמְנָם אַף עַל פִּי שֶׁאִסּוּר כָּזֶה בָּטֵל בְּמִעוּטוֹ, עַל כָּל פָּנִים הַמַּעֲשֶׂה שֶׁתַּעֲרוֹבֶת כָּזֶה בְּתוֹכוֹ, טָהוֹר לְגַמְרֵי אֵינֶנּוּ.
>
> *Exclusion of any forbidden motive while performing good deeds requires great insight and effort. For sometimes one embarks upon a mitzvah truly for its own sake, because thus decreed our Father in Heaven, but does not prevent one from incorporating some additional motive, such a desire for praise or reward, into the deed. And sometimes, even if one is not seeking praise, nevertheless one's pleasure in the praise he has received leads him to take greater pains than before in performing the deed. Such was the case with the daughter of R. Chanina ben Teradyon. After overhearing praise concerning her graceful stride, she sought to display even more grace. Though an undesirable motive may be outweighed by the main intention behind a deed, the deed which contains such a motive is not completely pure.*[123]

Purification of one's motives is one of the most complex and demanding of man's obligations. Even an action performed sincerely

---

123. *Mesillath Yesharim*, Ch. 16.

for the sake of Heaven, injected with a genuine intent to fulfill God's will, can be detrimentally affected by secret hopes for praise or reward. These thoughts sully the purity of the action.

As is well known, the *Mesillath Yesharim* is structured upon a famous statement of R. Pinchas ben Yair:

> אָמַר ר' פִּינְחָס בֶּן יָאִיר: תּוֹרָה מְבִיאָה לִידֵי זְהִירוּת, זְהִירוּת מְבִיאָה לִידֵי זְרִיזוּת, זְרִיזוּת מְבִיאָה לִידֵי נְקִיּוּת, נְקִיּוּת מְבִיאָה לִידֵי פְּרִישׁוּת, פְּרִישׁוּת מְבִיאָה לִידֵי טָהֳרָה.

> *Said R. Pinchas ben Yair, "Torah brings one to the level of caution. Caution brings one to zeal. Zeal brings one to innocence. Innocence brings one to a negation of personal desires. This brings one to purity."*[124]

The rungs of the spiritual ladder continue, climbing to saintliness, humility, fear of sin, and holiness, culminating in the sublime level where one is worthy of receiving Divine inspiration. The level of purity which we have been investigating is the fifth rung on the spiritual ladder, yet it is, according to any standard, a lofty level indeed. Though our spiritual level may be impoverished in comparison, it is nevertheless incumbent upon us to exert ourselves in our efforts to eliminate thoughts of praise or transient gratification from our mind while performing good deeds. We must empty ourselves of ego, nullifying our base desires, effecting our own transformation into hollow receptacles before the Source of all blessing. A trait can be nurtured within us which will effect a metamorphosis. We can become hollow pipes and conduits for blessing, thus enabling the entire world to be sustained "בִּשְׁבִילֵנוּ" — because of us.

---

124. *Mesillath Yesharim*, Introduction.

# VAYIGASH

HEARING YEHUDAH'S PLEAS, and seeing his genuine concern for Ya'akov's wellbeing, Yosef could no longer contain himself.

> וְלֹא יָכֹל יוֹסֵף לְהִתְאַפֵּק לְכֹל הַנִּצָּבִים עָלָיו וַיִּקְרָא הוֹצִיאוּ כָל אִישׁ מֵעָלָי וְלֹא עָמַד אִישׁ אִתּוֹ בְּהִתְוַדַּע יוֹסֵף אֶל אֶחָיו.
>
> *Yosef could not abide [the presence of] all those standing around him, so he announced, "Remove every man from my presence!" Thus no man stood in Yosef's presence when he made himself known to his brothers.*[125]

Rashi[126] explains Yosef's motive for this command: "He could not bear that there should be Egyptians present to witness his brothers' mortification as he revealed himself to them."

Our Sages elaborate on the scene:

> אָמַר ר׳ שְׁמוּאֵל בַּר נַחְמָן לְסַכָּנָה גְדוֹלָה יָרַד יוֹסֵף, שֶׁאִם הֲרָגוּהוּ אֶחָיו, אֵין בְּרִיָּה בָּעוֹלָם מַכִּירוֹ. וְלָמָּה אָמַר הוֹצִיאוּ כָל אִישׁ מֵעָלָי. אֶלָּא כָּךְ אָמַר יוֹסֵף בְּלִבּוֹ מוּטָב שֶׁאֵהָרֵג וְלֹא אֲבַיֵּשׁ אֶת אַחַי בִּפְנֵי הַמִּצְרִיִּים.
>
> *Yosef placed himself in great danger, for if his brothers had killed him, no one in the world would have discovered his true identity. Why then did he issue the dangerous command, "Remove all men from the room"? He said in his heart, "Better to be killed than to shame my brothers in front of the Egyptians."*[127]

With incredible courage, Yosef risked his life rather than shame

---

125. *Bereishith* 45:1.
126. Rashi *ad loc.*
127. *Tanchuma*, *Vayigash* 5.

his brothers. Let us examine Yosef's considerations at the time of this challenge and thus have an insight into his awesome greatness. There is a further point to learn from this confrontation. The Torah reveals to us that the revelation of Yosef's identity stemmed from a surge of emotion which he was unable to contain. It appears from this that if Yosef had been able to suppress this tremendous yearning, he would have done so. But why would Yosef prefer to continue hiding behind the Egyptian mask that he had donned? Since his famous dreams had already been realised, had not the time arrived for a final reunion?

Yosef's position as leader of the land was the fulfillment of his teenage dream-vision.

**וְיוֹסֵף הוּא הַשַּׁלִּיט עַל הָאָרֶץ הוּא הַמַּשְׁבִּיר לְכָל עַם הָאָרֶץ, וַיָּבֹאוּ אֲחֵי יוֹסֵף וַיִּשְׁתַּחֲווּ לוֹ אַפַּיִם אָרְצָה.**

*Now, Yosef, who was the governor of the land, was the one who sold produce to all the people of the country, and Yosef's brothers came and prostrated themselves to him with [their] faces to the ground.*[128]

This transpired as he had seen in his dream. Nevertheless, Yosef did not yet wish to reveal his true identity. Had Yosef been able to restrain himself, the shape of history would have been dramatically altered.

The *Zohar* states that as a result of the sin of selling Yosef, exile and slavery were decreed on the twelve tribes. The period of slavery can be calculated to have been 210 years according to the following: Yosef was estranged from his family for 22 years. Correspondingly, each of the brothers incurred 22 years of exile. The sum of this would be 220 years. However, when the brothers died, ten years were deducted from the total, for since they were righteous individuals, their death atoned somewhat for their sin. The final result, therefore, is that the Jewish People deserved 210 years of exile.

Although here, the reason given for the Egyptian exile is the selling of Yosef, earlier in the Torah, a different explanation is supplied.

---

128. *Bereishith* 42:6.

Years before, long before the twelve tribes were born, Avraham received a promise from God. At the Covenant of the Parts, God decreed, "And they (the Egyptians) will enslave and torture them." In light of this, the question arises: What was the true reason for the Jewish People's terrible enslavement?

Contemplating the situation, it appears that even if Avraham had not received this promise, and even if the brothers had not sold Yosef, he would still have descended to Egypt. God had decreed that Yosef would rule, and that the brothers would bow to him. Does this not render both reasons irrelevant?

Our Sages[129] liken Yosef to a calf that is led wherever one wishes the mother to follow, to prompt the mother to follow a certain route. God "led" Yosef to Egypt so that Ya'akov would follow him. This would bring about fulfillment of the decree of exile foretold to Avraham. The affliction and suffering endured by the Jewish People were engineered by God, and revealed to the world hundreds of years previously, during the lifetime of Avraham. Considering this explanation, we can ask, why does the *Zohar* so closely relate the decree of exile to the sin of selling Yosef?

After considering these questions, we can conclude that there was indeed an original decree of exile. All was not black, however — a possibility still remained for the Jewish People to extricate themselves from this edict. The Children of Yisrael could have been saved from their fate. How could this have been achieved?

Let us digress and study the following Midrash.

קוֹל דּוֹדִי הִנֵּה זֶה בָּא. קוֹל דּוֹדִי זֶה מָשִׁיחַ. בְּשָׁעָה שֶׁהוּא בָּא וְאוֹמֵר לָהֶם לְיִשְׂרָאֵל בְּחֹדֶשׁ זֶה אַתֶּם נִגְאָלִים. אָמְרוּ לוֹ לֹא כָּךְ אָמַר הקב"ה לָנוּ שֶׁהוּא מְשַׁעְבְּדֵנוּ בְּשִׁבְעִים אֻמּוֹת. וְהוּא מְשִׁיבָן שְׁתֵּי תְּשׁוּבוֹת וְאוֹמֵר לָהֶם אֶחָד מִכֶּם גָּלָה לְבַרְבַּרְיָא וְאֶחָד לִבְרִיטַנְיָא, כְּאִלּוּ גְּלִיתֶם כֻּלְּכֶם. וְלֹא עוֹד, אֶלָּא שֶׁמַּלְכוּת הָרְבִיעִית מַכְתֶּבֶת טִירוֹנְיָא מִכָּל הָאֻמּוֹת. כּוּתִי אֶחָד בָּא וּמְשַׁעְבֵּד בְּאֶחָד, כְּאִלּוּ שִׁעְבְּדוּ כָּל אֻמָּתִי. וּבַחֹדֶשׁ הַזֶּה אַתֶּם נִגְאָלִים שֶׁנֶּאֱמַר הַחֹדֶשׁ הַזֶּה לָכֶם.

129. *Bereishith Rabbah* 86:2.

*"The voice of my beloved knocks, behold he has come." "The voice of my beloved" is that of the Mashiach, when he announces to Yisrael, "This month you shall be saved."*

*Yisrael reply, "What of the decree that we endure exile under seventy nations?"*

*The Mashiach provides two answers. "One of you was sent to exile to Barbary, and one to Britannia. It is considered as if all of you were there. Further, the fourth exile is considered the most grueling. One Kuthite shall come and enslave an individual, and it shall be considered as if he enslaved My entire nation. Thus in this month you shall be redeemed, as it states, "This month shall be to you."*[130]

From this Midrash we conclude that the decree of exile to which the descendants of Avraham were subjected could have been fulfilled through the oppression of one man alone. Thus, the suffering undergone by Yosef could have atoned for the entire Jewish nation. The nationwide calamities, the terrible tragedies that accompany exile, could have been prevented.

Yosef's sojourn in Egypt served a dual purpose. The primary purpose was to actualize the words of the covenant to Avraham,[131] "For your descendants will be strangers in a land which is not their own, and they (the Egyptians) shall enslave and torture them." There was a further reason, however. According to the *Zohar*, it was the brothers' sin that was the driving force behind the edict of exile. This sin awaited rectification and wholehearted repentance. For this reason, Yosef was dispatched to Egypt. Yosef's suffering, and his treatment of the brothers, would prompt a complete repentance from them. For every manner in which the brothers had mistreated Yosef, they were required to atone, and endure a similar suffering. The brothers despised Yosef for having spoken badly of them. They cast him into a pit and correspondingly, Yosef held them in prison for three days. The brothers then sold Yosef as a slave. This was atoned

130. *Yalkut Shimoni, Shir HaShirim* 986.

131. *Bereishith* 15:13.

for by their admission, "We are slaves to our master."

All that remained requiring atonement was the awesome anguish and indescribable pain that the incident caused Ya'akov. This was of such intensity that we are told that Ya'akov refused consolation. He could feel no comfort, and his pain was not numbed. What could possibly atone for this grievous misdemeanor?

The Rambam defines perfect repentance:

> אֵיזוֹ הִיא תְּשׁוּבָה גְּמוּרָה? זֶה שֶׁבָּא לְיָדוֹ דָּבָר שֶׁעָבַר בּוֹ וְאֶפְשָׁר בְּיָדוֹ לַעֲשׂוֹתוֹ, וּפֵרֵשׁ וְלֹא עָשָׂה מִפְּנֵי תְּשׁוּבָה.
>
> *What is complete repentance? When one encounters a situation in which he has the possibility of transgressing in the same area as previously, yet, due to his repentance, he overcomes his inclination to do so. This is a complete repentance.*[132]

Yosef places his brothers in a situation exactly mirroring a previous challenge, a test in which they had been unsuccessful. Binyamin, Rachel's younger son, is imprisoned in Yosef's hands. The burden now lies heavily on the brothers to bring back these tidings to their elderly father. Yehudah refuses to tolerate Binyamin's imprisonment. He heroically steps forward to beseech the Egyptian ruler. His words describe Ya'akov's intense love for his son Binyamin. Further, Yehudah offers his own freedom to Yosef in exchange for Binyamin's liberty. His words conclude with the following cry,[133] "For how shall I go up to my father if the lad is not with me? How can I witness the anguish my father will feel?"

Had Yosef restrained himself, and not revealed his identity to his brothers, but kept up his facade as a Gentile despot, his brothers would have withstood the trial. They demonstrated a preparedness to sacrifice their lives to prevent the anguish their father would feel if Binyamin were left in Egypt. Had Yosef continued to obscure his identity, the brothers would have triumphed in their challenge and achieved a complete repentance. Placed in the same situation as

---

132. *Hilchoth Teshuvah* 2:1.

133. *Bereishith* 44:34.

when they sold Yosef, where they displayed flagrant disregard of the anguish Ya'akov would feel, they were now ready to pass the test, as they sought to protect Ya'akov from potential sorrow. The necessity for continued exile in Egypt would have been removed, as a complete repentance would have been achieved.

However, וְלֹא יָכֹל יוֹסֵף לְהִתְאַפֵּק — "Yosef could no longer contain himself." Instead of continuing the facade and allowing his brothers the opportunity for complete repentance, he revealed his identity to them. Let us contemplate the outcome of Yosef's uncontainable emotion, and the longing for his father which overtook him at this point. His overflowing emotion precluded his brothers' attainment of a full atonement. It was only because of his revelation that the Egyptian exile continued.

**וַיַּעֲבִדוּ מִצְרַיִם אֶת בְּנֵי יִשְׂרָאֵל בְּפָרֶךְ. וַיְמָרְרוּ אֶת חַיֵּיהֶם בַּעֲבֹדָה קָשָׁה בְּחֹמֶר וּבִלְבֵנִים וּבְכָל עֲבֹדָה בַּשָּׂדֶה אֵת כָּל עֲבֹדָתָם אֲשֶׁר עָבְדוּ בָהֶם בְּפָרֶךְ.**

*The Mitzrim then subjected the Children of Yisrael to back-breaking labour. They embittered their lives with hard labour, with mortar and with bricks, and all kinds of agricultural work, [besides] all their [other] work, which [the Mitzrim] subjected them to do arduously.*[134]

The conditions of the slavery, and the affliction of the Jewish People were intolerable. Every male that was born was cast into the river Nile. Par'oh would slaughter Jewish babies and bathe in their blood. The harsh afflictions and bitter tribulations were borne by the Jewish People until their cries reached the Almighty. Yet the rectification for the sin of selling Yosef remained incomplete. Indeed, centuries later, the ripples emanating from the sin could still be felt. Ten spiritual giants were brutally killed by the Romans at the time of the destruction of the second Temple. This, too, was punishment for the selling of Yosef.

Our Sages inform us that every harsh decree placed upon the

---

134. *Shemoth* 1:13, 14.

Jewish People as a result of sins committed between man and his fellow atones in part for the primal sin of selling Yosef. In a similar vein, all punishment for sins performed between man and his Creator contains a degree of atonement for the sin of the Golden Calf. All that befalls us is because the sin of the brothers was not completely rectified. All that befalls us, resulting from sins from man to man, is because Yosef did not restrain himself.

These considerations were contemplated by Yosef, who knew all that would befall the Jewish People. In spite of this, he was unable to restrain himself, a restraint which would have facilitated his brother's complete repentance and removed the decree of exile from their descendants. He was unable to further bear the anguish he knew his father was suffering, still grieving his death. He yearned to inform his father of his existence; to reveal to him that he was still alive.

However, for one further moment Yosef was able to restrain himself. This was so that he could call out, "Remove every man from my presence." Rabbi Leib Chasman directs our attention to an awesome lesson.[135]

> *Although cognizant of the danger that the brothers might kill him, Yosef nevertheless assessed that it would be preferable to lose everything, even possibly cut short the wick of his life, to prevent any embarrassment to his brothers.*

The fear of shaming his brothers was a more profound emotion than even his yearning for his father. Yosef's swirling emotions and stormy sentiments expressed themselves in his cry, "I am Yosef. Is my father still alive?" Yet he held back this cry until he had ascertained that every single Egyptian had left the room. Restraining himself until a complete rectification had been effected, such that the Jewish nation would be spared all future torment and exile, was not a possibility. However, to prevent any embarrassment, to prevent his brothers undergoing any shame; for this Yosef could check his words and bridle his emotions.

---

135. *Ohr Yahel*, Part Three, p. 76.

In this vein, R. Chasman explains the statement of our Sages concerning the sin of shaming a fellow Jew.

נוֹחַ לוֹ לְאָדָם שֶׁיַּפִּילוּהוּ לְכִבְשַׁן הָאֵשׁ וְאַל יַלְבִּין פְּנֵי חֲבֵרוֹ בָּרַבִּים.

*It is better for a person to be thrown into a fiery furnace than to embarrass his fellow in public.*[136]

This dictum is not a halachic guideline; rather it indicates an attitude which must be cultivated in each and every one of us. The sentiment possessed by all should be that to shame one's fellow is a furnace of more intense heat than one in which physical fire roars. When the choice is presented to us, our inclination should be that it is the easier option to choose the physical fire, and thus avoid the licking flames inflicted upon another through shaming him. It is incumbent upon us to feel that shaming another person is worse than the heat of a furnace.

R. Chasman continues:

*It is thus that we see the lofty level and holiness of Yosef, it being easier for him to shatter all his hopes, and crush everything, rather than embarrass his brothers in front of the Egyptians. Yosef pursued this course of action to such an extent that he is faulted by our Sages for placing himself into mortal danger by removing any bodyguard or protection and exposing himself completely to his brothers' wrath. Yet this was something concerning which Yosef would not, and could not, compromise. For love overrides the logical course of action. Let a wise man hearken to this lesson, and draw the correct conclusions!*

---

136. *Sotah* 10b.

# VAYECHI

WITH THE PRESENT-DAY decline in moral values, parents all over the world wonder how to influence their children to choose moral, honest, and upright lifestyles. Countless child-rearing books have been authored; parenting classes abound. But our guide to life, the Torah, and our Sages who explain what is written therein, addressed these issues many hundreds of years ago. Let us look into their words about one fundamental principle, one that is so relevant to us today. To do this, let us turn to Ya'akov's words concerning the death of his wife. Ya'akov said:

**וַאֲנִי בְּבֹאִי מִפַּדָּן מֵתָה עָלַי רָחֵל בְּאֶרֶץ כְּנַעַן בַּדֶּרֶךְ בְּעוֹד כִּבְרַת אֶרֶץ לָבֹא אֶפְרָתָה וָאֶקְבְּרֶהָ שָּׁם בְּדֶרֶךְ אֶפְרָת הִוא בֵּית לָחֶם.**

*As for me, when I came from Padan, Rachel died on me in the land of Canaan, on the road, still a certain distance from reaching Ephrath, and I buried her there, on the Ephrath — that is Beith Lechem — Road.*[137]

The Talmud renders the word "עָלַי" as "in relation to me," and explains the significance of this translation:

תַּנְא, אֵין אִשָּׁה מֵתָה אֶלָּא לְבַעְלָהּ, שֶׁנֶּאֱמַר מֵתָה עָלַי רָחֵל.[138]

However, the word "עָלַי," as it is found in this context, is defined differently in the Midrash. There it is interpreted as meaning, "because of me." Through the Torah's use of this word, the Midrash discerns Ya'akov's startling feeling that he was in fact responsible for Rachel's death.

137. *Bereishith* 48:7.
138. *Sanhedrin* 22b.

אָמַר ר׳ שְׁמוּאֵל בַּר נַחְמָן, כָּל מִי שֶׁנּוֹדֵר וּמַשְׁהֶה אֶת נִדְרוֹ סוֹף שֶׁבָּא לִידֵי עֲבוֹדָה זָרָה וְגִלּוּי עֲרָיוֹת וּשְׁפִיכוּת דָּמִים וְלָשׁוֹן הָרַע. מִמִּי אַתָּה לָמֵד? כֻּלְּהוֹן מִיַּעֲקֹב, עַל יְדֵי שֶׁנָּדַר וְשִׁהָה אֶת נִדְרוֹ בָּא לִידֵי כֻּלָּן. עֲבוֹדָה זָרָה מִנַּיִן "וַיֹּאמֶר יַעֲקֹב אֶל בֵּיתוֹ הָסִירוּ אֶת אֱלֹהֵי הַנֵּכָר." גִּלּוּי עֲרָיוֹת מִנַּיִן, מִדִּינָה שֶׁנֶּאֱמַר "וַתֵּצֵא דִינָה." שְׁפִיכוּת דָּמִים מִנַּיִן, שֶׁנֶּאֱמַר "וַיְהִי בַיּוֹם הַשְּׁלִישִׁי בִּהְיוֹתָם כֹּאֲבִים וגו׳." לָשׁוֹן הָרַע מִנַּיִן שֶׁנֶּאֱמַר "וַיִּשְׁמַע אֶת דִּבְרֵי בְנֵי לָבָן." וְרַבָּנָן אָמְרֵי כָּל מִי שֶׁנּוֹדֵר וּמַשְׁהֶא נִדְרוֹ קוֹבֵר אֶת אִשְׁתּוֹ הֲדָא הוּא דִכְתִיב "וַאֲנִי בְּבֹאִי מִפַּדָּן מֵתָה עָלַי רָחֵל."

*R. Shemuel bar Nachman said, "Anyone who makes a vow, but tarries in carrying it out, will eventually come to be involved in the sins of idolatry, immorality, murder, and evil slander.*

*From whom can this be learned? These consequences are learned from Ya'akov. Due to tarrying over fulfilling his vow, Ya'akov eventually became involved in all of these sins.*

*From where do we learn idol worship? The verse states, "Ya'akov said to his household, 'Remove all the strange gods from your midst.'"*

*From where do we learn immorality? From the incident with Dinah (in which she was defiled by Shechem), as it states, "And Dinah went out."*

*From where do we learn bloodshed? It states, "On the third day (of circumcision), Shimon and Levi (killed all the people in Shechem)." ...*

*Our Sages state, "If a person vows, yet tarries in its fulfillment, he buries his wife, as it says, "And when I came from Padan, Rachel died because of me."*[139]

The vow concerning which Ya'akov is criticised was made in the *parashah* of *Vayeitzei*. After Ya'akov's famous dream, in which he saw angels ascending and descending a ladder that stretched from Heaven to earth, he made the following oath:

**וַיִּדַּר יַעֲקֹב נֶדֶר לֵאמֹר אִם יִהְיֶה אֱלֹקִים עִמָּדִי וּשְׁמָרַנִי בַּדֶּרֶךְ הַזֶּה אֲשֶׁר אָנֹכִי הוֹלֵךְ וְנָתַן לִי לֶחֶם לֶאֱכֹל וּבֶגֶד לִלְבֹּשׁ. וְשַׁבְתִּי בְשָׁלוֹם אֶל בֵּית**

---

139. *Vayikra Rabbah* 37:1.

**אָבִי וְהָיָה ה' לִי לֵאלֹקִים וְהָאֶבֶן הַזֹּאת אֲשֶׁר שַׂמְתִּי מַצֵּבָה יִהְיֶה בֵּית אֱלֹקִים...**

*Ya'akov made a vow, saying, "If God is with me, and protects me on the way I am going and gives me food to eat and clothes to wear, and I return in peace to my father's house and the Eternal acts for me as God, then this stone that I have placed as a monument shall be the House of God" [i.e. a place dedicated to bringing sacrifices].*[140]

This was the vow that led to such disastrous consequences. Ya'akov delayed offering the promised sacrifices, and thus incurred tragedy. Elaborating further on this theme, our Sages state that as a direct consequence of tarrying, בָּנִים מֵתִים כְּשֶׁהֵן קְטַנִּים — "Children will perish when they are young."[141] What do these words mean? How can we fathom why God would mete out such a severe punishment for a seemingly trivial oversight? In Ya'akov's case, how can we understand the justice of his suffering, in light of the fact that he did eventually fulfill his promise?

To shed some light on this difficulty, let us turn to the following statement of our Sages:

ר' שִׁמְעוֹן בֶּן אֶלְעָזָר אוֹמֵר יֵצֶר, תִּינוֹק וְאִשָּׁה, תְּהֵא שְׂמֹאל דּוֹחָה וְיָמִין מְקָרֶבֶת.

*R. Shimon ben El'azar says, "The evil inclination, a child, and a wife should be pushed away with the left hand and drawn near with the right."*[142]

Rabbi Dessler explains a concept, which we have previously encountered,[143] that can be employed to elucidate the above cryptic statement.

ע"כ בְּמִלְחֶמֶת הַיֵּצֶר צָרִיךְ לִלְחֹם בְּעָרְמָה רַבָּה, שֶׁלֹּא יָבוֹא עִם הַיֵּצֶר לְמִלְחֶמֶת פָּנִים בְּפָנִים. כִּי בְּמִלְחֶמֶת פָּנִים בְּפָנִים, הֲרֵי יִדְחֹק עַל גַּבֵּי

140. *Bereishith* 28:20–22.
141. *Shabbath* 32b.
142. *Sotah* 47a.
143. Essay on *Vayishlach*.

הַקְּפִיץ וְיָשׁוּב הַקְּפִיץ לִדְחֹק אוֹתוֹ כָּל עוֹד יוֹתֵר. וּמִן הָעֵצוֹת הַיּוֹתֵר מֻצְלָחוֹת בְּזֶה הוּא, לְהַשְׂבִּיעַ אֶת הָעַקְשָׁנוּת בְּאֵיזֶה דָּבָר קָטָן חִיצוֹנִי, שֶׁיִּהְיֶה נִרְאֶה כְּאִלּוּ ח"ו מָט צַדִּיק לִפְנֵי רָשָׁע, וְיַצְלִיחַ לְרַמּוֹת אֶת הַסִּטְרָא אַחְרָא וּלְחַסֵּל אֶת הָעַקְשָׁנוּת הַמַּחְרֶבֶת. וְזֶהוּ גֶּדֶר שֹׁחַד לַשָּׂטָן כְּשֶׁכַּוָּנָתוֹ לְשֵׁם שָׁמַיִם מַמָּשׁ.

*Guile and strategy are vital in combating one's evil inclination. One should never use a frontal attack in this war. To do so would be like depressing a spring that will rebound with greater force than the force with which it was originally depressed. Rather, one of the most effective strategies is to perform some minor external act to placate one's inclination. Thus it will appear that a righteous individual is beginning to falter in the face of evil. In this way a person can dupe his evil inclination, removing its obstinacy, reducing its potency. This is called "giving a bribe" to Satan to satisfy him, and thus ridding oneself of his dominion.*[144]

Rabbi Dessler is suggesting a practical technique for grappling with negative forces. When the evil inclination clamors for our attention, the correct approach is to procrastinate, appearing to consider the suggestion, rather than categorically refusing its blandishments. In this manner, one can ultimately triumph over the forces of evil.

On the other hand, the *Sefer HaChinuch* lays down an important rule in character development:

אַחֲרֵי הַפְּעֻלּוֹת נִמְשָׁכִים הַלְּבָבוֹת.

*One's heart is drawn after one's outer actions.*[145]

For example, to uproot miserliness from one's personality and replace it with generosity does not require hours of meditation on the negativity of stinginess and the positive aspects of giving (although this of course does help). Instead, we are advised to simply start giving. Consistent outer generosity will influence one's inner being, and although initially the giving may not stem from an inner desire to

---

144. *Michtav MeEliyahu*, Part One, p. 262.
145. *Sefer HaChinuch*, Mitzvah 16.

help another, this desire will develop. The outer action will stimulate inner change and growth.

However, this rule can also have a negative application. Returning to our subject, our Sages recommend procrastination, or some kind of outward acquiescence, when encountering Satan. But a certain danger is involved in this procedure. The external procrastination may affect one's internality, gradually bringing one to a state in which procrastination is part of one's character. That being the case, a person will procrastinate even when it is inappropriate to do so, as when faced with the opportunity to do a mitzvah or when confronted with his inclination towards good. A person may fall into the habit of delaying actions to such an extent that he will even vow to perform them at a later date. Rabbi Dessler's words on this topic continue:

> הַקֶּשֶׁר הַפְּנִימִי בֵּין חֵטְא זֶה לָעֹנֶשׁ הֶחָמוּר הוּא, כִּי הָרָגִיל לִנְדֹּר וְאֵינוֹ מְקַיֵּם, הֲרֵי זֶה לְאוֹת שֶׁנִּדְרוֹ אֵינוֹ בָּא אֶלָּא לִדְחוֹת הִתְעוֹרְרוּת פְּנִימִית עַל יְדֵי שֶׁמַּבְטִיחַ הַבְטָחוֹת שָׁוְא כְּדֵי לְהַשְׁקִיט אֶת הִתְעוֹרְרוּת מַצְפּוּנוֹ. נִמְצָא שֶׁעִקָּר נִדְרוֹ אֵינוֹ אֱמֶת, אֶלָּא אַדְּרַבָּא, בְּהַבְטָחַת שָׁוְא הוּא רוֹצֶה לְכַסּוֹת עַל הָאֱמֶת שֶׁהִכִּיר וְלִדְחוֹתוֹ.
>
> *The relationship between the sin of failing to implement a vow, and the resulting punishment, is as follows: One who persistently vows without fulfilling his words, silently testifies that his vow was only a means to dismiss his inspiration, a false promise to salve his conscience. It is evident that the foundation of his vow is not genuine; on the contrary, by using false promises he wants to hide from the truth that he recognises, and repel the obligations cast upon him.*[146]

In Heaven, this man is no longer trusted. He has demonstrated his unreliability, the betrayal of his own conscience. This being the case, he is unable to raise children to follow the truth and develop their service of the Almighty. As he cannot fulfill this mission, his family is taken from him. As R. Moshe Chaim Luzzatto explains:

---

146. *Sefer HaChinuch*, Part Three, p. 253.

כְּשֶׁאָדָם נוֹדֵר נֶדֶר טוֹב וְרָצוּי, הוּא מֵבִיא אֶת פְּנִימִיּוּתוֹ לִידֵי גִּלּוּי. וּכְשֶׁמְּאַחֵר לְשַׁלְּמוֹ הוּא חוֹזֵר וּמַעֲלִים הֶאָרָה זוֹ, כָּךְ שֶׁאֵינָהּ מְאִירָה עוֹד לְאֵלֶּה הַצְּרִיכִים לְקַבֵּל הַשְׁפָּעָתוֹ. דָּבָר זֶה מוֹנֵעַ הַחְדָּרַת הַפְּנִימִיּוּת אֶל אוֹתָם שֶׁהֵם כֵּלָיו לַעֲבוֹדַת ה׳, וּבָזֶה הוּא מְרוֹקְנָם מִתַּכְלִיתָם. וְעַל כֵּן גּוֹרֵם לְמִיתַת אִשְׁתּוֹ, שֶׁהִיא הָעֵזֶר כְּנֶגְדּוֹ בַּעֲבוֹדַת ה׳ שֶׁלּוֹ. כִּי אֵין הַמִּיתָה אֶלָּא הִסְתַּלְּקוּת הַנְּשָׁמָה מִן הַגּוּף, דְּהַיְנוּ הִסְתַּלְּקוּת הַפְּנִימִיּוּת מִן הַחִיצוֹנִיּוּת.

*When a man makes a vow for a virtuous purpose, he brings his good intention out from the realm of thought and internality into external speech. If he tarries in its execution, he has obscured the good intention that he had, and the internal root of goodness from which the promise originally emanated. He has betrayed his conscience, been disloyal to his inner being. Through the vow taken and left unfulfilled, he numbs his morality. He can no longer influence others.*[147]

The sin our Sages denounce so fiercely then, consists of two stages:

1. The vow itself; which involves delaying the physical expression of a good intention.
2. Once the vow has been made, one is castigated further if one tarries and thereby leaves the promise unfulfilled.

His internal world is irrevocably dulled; it has become hollow, and all his subsequent actions will be pitifully deficient. The person's nearest and dearest, who were originally present as tools for his spiritual mission of influencing and affecting others, those people who provided him with a spur for spiritual growth, have lost their function. Thus his wife, his helpmate in his life's mission, is taken away. His children, whom he should have guided along the path of growth, are buried.

Our Divine service must be an expression, an outer manifestation, of inner purity of heart. We must desire to perform the mitzvoth because we genuinely *know* them to be correct and good, not merely

---

147. *Megillath Sethorim, Vayechi.*

because it is the social norm, the accepted practice. It is through this sincere approach, stemming from our innermost being, that our children will be imbued with a feeling of the beauty and wealth of our lives. For others are affected and influenced by one's words only if they discern that they stem from real conviction. Possession of this conviction in turn enables our children to bequeath our heritage to a further generation, who will perform the mitzvoth from genuine desire.

Turning now to a Midrash in *Shemoth*, we are led to conclusions that, at first sight, seem incongruous with the words of R. Moshe Chaim Luzzatto: Having established that true purity of heart is a prerequisite for influencing others, let us now put this into even sharper focus.

מִי שֶׁקִּבֵּל עַל עַצְמוֹ לַעֲשׂוֹת מִצְוָה, אֵין אוֹתָהּ מִצְוָה פּוֹסֶקֶת מִבֵּיתוֹ. מִצְוָתוֹ שֶׁל יִתְרוֹ שֶׁקִּבֵּל בְּתוֹךְ בֵּיתוֹ גּוֹאֵל שֶׁבָּרַח מִפְּנֵי הַשּׂוֹנֵא. עָמַד מִבֵּיתוֹ שֶׁקִּבֵּל לַשּׂוֹנֵא שֶׁבָּרַח מִפְּנֵי הַגּוֹאֵל וַהֲרָגוֹ. אֵיזֶה זֶה, זֶה סִיסְרָא שֶׁנֶּאֱמַר וְסִיסְרָא נָס בְּרַגְלָיו אֶל אֹהֶל יָעֵל אֵשֶׁת חֶבֶר הַקֵּינִי וּכְתִיב וּבְנֵי קֵינִי חוֹתֵן מֹשֶׁה.

*When one accepts upon oneself to perform a good deed, that mitzvah will not depart from one's house. The good deed that Yithro performed was taking a redeemer (Moshe) into his house, on his flight from the enemy (Par'oh). There arose from his offspring one who took into her house an enemy who fled from a redeemer, and she slew him. Who is this? This is Sisera, as it says, "And Sisera escaped on foot to the tent of Yael, wife of Chaver the Kenite," and it is written [Shofetim 1:16], "And the sons of Keni, the father-in-law of Moshe."*[148]

The Midrash here parallels two separate incidents. The first: Yithro welcoming Moshe into his home, thus protecting him from danger. The second: Yael welcoming Sisera, the archenemy of the Jews, into her home, an act which gave her the opportunity to kill him and bring salvation to the Jews. The common factor of the two events, the mitzvah that is referred to, is that both Yithro and Yael

---

148. *Shemoth Rabbah* 4:2.

welcomed someone into their home. Further, the Midrash informs us that the seeds of Yael's action lie in that of Yithro: his performance of this mitzvah paved the way for Yael to later mirror his actions.

But this comparison seems illogical. Although both personalities performed the external act of bringing someone into their home, they did so for two divergent reasons. Yithro welcomed Moshe in an attempt to save him. Yael, on the other hand, was seeking to slay Sisera. Are these acts both valid instances of the mitzvah of welcoming a guest into one's home? Wherein lies the comparison? Furthermore, we have previously established the view of R. Moshe Chaim Luzzatto that children internalise the intention behind an action, rather than the superficial motions. How then can we say that Yithro transmitted this mitzvah to his descendants? Although Yael performed the same initial action, the thoughts behind her deed were the antithesis of Yithro's intention.

The solution to this anomaly becomes apparent by examining how the two concepts of כַּוָּנָה, intention, and פְּנִימִיּוּת, internality, complement each other. כַּוָּנָה can be defined as one's specific intention when performing the mitzvah. In contrast, פְּנִימִיּוּת implies the investment of one's inner self into the deed, and a wholehearted desire to follow God's will. Although Yithro's and Yael's actions differed in terms of כַּוָּנָה, intention, the two deeds were performed with a similar פְּנִימִיּוּת. Yithro's פְּנִימִיּוּת, his internal truth, ensured that Moshe was kept alive; his wholehearted desire was to save the Jewish People. Yael's פְּנִימִיּוּת is attested to by her willingness to endanger her own life for the sake of her people. She welcomed Sisera into her home, and then summoned up the courage to kill him, all to provide salvation to the Children of Yisrael. Although the intention, כַּוָּנָה, of Yithro and Yael were antithetical, the underlying desire behind both deeds, a vibrant פְּנִימִיּוּת, was the same in both cases.

פְּנִימִיּוּת, the internality of a person from which one's deeds stem, is intangible. It is nevertheless a prerequisite in order for the action to have any effect on others. To influence those around one, the essential ingredient is the genuine wholeheartedness of a pure soul. Yithro planted a seed; he performed a deed with sincerity.

This seed that was planted was passed through the generations and blossomed in Yael, who performed the same deed as her ancestor, albeit with different intentions. The פְּנִימִיּוּת, however, was present in both cases.

To return to our original topic: later in the *parashah* we find another consequence of Ya'akov's vow. After Ya'akov's demise, Yosef approached Par'oh with the following request:

**אָבִי הִשְׁבִּיעַנִי לֵאמֹר הִנֵּה אָנֹכִי מֵת בְּקִבְרִי אֲשֶׁר כָּרִיתִי לִי בְּאֶרֶץ כְּנַעַן שָׁמָּה תִּקְבְּרֵנִי וְעַתָּה אֶעֱלֶה נָּא וְאֶקְבְּרָה אֶת אָבִי וְאָשׁוּבָה. וַיֹּאמֶר פַּרְעֹה עֲלֵה וּקְבֹר אֶת אָבִיךָ כַּאֲשֶׁר הִשְׁבִּיעֶךָ.**

*"My father made me swear, saying, 'I am about to die. In my grave that I dug for myself in the land of Canaan, there shall you bury me.' So now, please let me go up [to Canaan], and let me bury my father and then return."*

*Par'oh replied, "Go up and bury your father, as he made you swear."*[149]

Our Sages make the following comment:

תַּנְיָא בְּשָׁעָה שֶׁאָמַר יוֹסֵף לְפַרְעֹה אָבִי הִשְׁבִּיעַנִי, אָמַר לֵיהּ אִתְשִׁיל אַשְׁבוּעֲתָךְ. אָמַר לֵיהּ וְאִתְשִׁיל נָמֵי אַדִּידָךְ דְּמִשְׁתַּבַּעְנָא לָךְ דְּלָא מְגַלֵּי דְּלָא שָׁמְעִית בִּלְשׁוֹן הַקֹּדֶשׁ. מִיָּד אָמַר לוֹ עֲלֵה וּקְבֹר אֶת אָבִיךָ כַּאֲשֶׁר הִשְׁבִּיעֶךָ.

*We learn that at the time that Yosef said to Par'oh, "My father made me swear," Par'oh countered, "Go and annul your vow." Yosef replied, "If I did so, I would have to reconsider another vow that I made. I promised not to reveal your ignorance of the Hebrew language." Immediately, Par'oh retracted, "Go up and bury your father, as he made you swear."*[150]

In this dialogue we hear the undertones of blackmail; it appears that Yosef manipulated Par'oh to obtain his own wishes. However, the Steipler Gaon זצ"ל, in his work *Birkas Peretz*, disagrees with

149. *Bereishith* 50:5, 6.
150. *Sotah* 36b.

this interpretation. He maintains that it is inadvisable to speak to any king, let alone a despot like Par'oh, in a threatening manner. He states that Yosef explained thus to Par'oh:[151]

> *If a person swears to perform a certain deed, he will be pricked by his conscience until he has carried out his word. A person would not betray his conscience and desecrate the purity of his heart by failing to discharge his obligation. However, this can only be guaranteed if a person is accustomed to fulfilling his promises. One who is lax in this area will have irrevocably numbed and desensitized his conscience. Consequently, all future promises will have lost a degree of potency and validity.*

With this understanding, it is clear that Yosef was not threatening Par'oh; nor was he subjecting him to blackmail. He was simply informing him of the inevitable consequence of breaking his oath. Yosef explained that if he obeyed Par'oh and dissolved the promise he had made to his father, the oath he had made to Par'oh would inevitably also be weakened. To annul a promise sullies the purity of one's internal realm, one's פְּנִימִיּוּת.

If we wish to influence our children, then, bequeathing our heritage throughout the generations, we must be genuine and sincere, or nothing will be transmitted. This sincerity must be constantly nurtured and cultivated, and thus false promises or delaying the fulfillment of an oath must be assiduously avoided. For this would diminish one's ability to influence, causing one's household to crumble away, fading into nothingness. In contrast, developing one's internality, remaining faithful to one's inner purity, enables one to steadily pass the glowing torch from one's own hand into the hands of one's children. It enables one to proudly watch as the torch is transmitted from children to grandchildren. It enables one to behold the glow, watching the torch of truth and purity burn brightly as it travels into the distance.

---

151. *Birkas Peretz*, *Vayechi*.

# SHEMOTH

# SHEMOTH

A MIRACLE! YELLOW flames licked the briars and yet the bush was not consumed. Upon witnessing this wondrous sight, Moshe drew near:

**וַיַּרְא ה' כִּי סָר לִרְאוֹת וַיִּקְרָא אֵלָיו אֱלֹקִים מִתּוֹךְ הַסְּנֶה וַיֹּאמֶר מֹשֶׁה מֹשֶׁה וַיֹּאמֶר הִנֵּנִי.**

*The Eternal observed that he had turned aside to look, so God called to him from within the bush and said, "Moshe! Moshe!" He answered, "Here I am."*[1]

The *Ba'alei Tosefoth* inform us that Moshe was criticised for his answer:

אָמַר יִתְבָּרַךְ אַתָּה עָנִיתָ הִנֵּנִי כְּמוֹ אַבְרָהָם זְקֵנְךָ וּכְתִיב בִּמְקוֹם גְּדוֹלִים אַל תַּעֲמֹד. אָמַר לוֹ יִתְבָּרַךְ אַל תִּקְרַב הֲלוֹם לֹא לִכְהֻנָּה דִּכְתִיב בָּהּ קָרַב אֶל הַמִּזְבֵּחַ וְלֹא לְמַלְכוּת דִּכְתִיב בֵּיהּ הֲלוֹם גַּבֵּי דָּוִד.

*God said, "You answered 'Here I am' as your ancestor Avraham did. Yet it is written, 'Do not stand in the place of those who are greater than you.' Therefore, you will not merit that which Avraham did, i.e. priesthood and royalty, as it says, 'Do not draw near.'" This expression is also found with reference to the priesthood of Aharon, as it says, "Do not draw near the altar," and with reference to the kingship of David.*[2]

Rabbi Zaitchek, in his work *Ohr Chadash*, poses a number of questions on the aforementioned comment of the *Ba'alei Tosefoth*. The first difficulty arises from a Midrash that states:

1. *Shemoth* 3:4.
2. *Ba'alei Tosefoth ad loc.*

זָכָה מֹשֶׁה לִשְׁתֵּיהֶן כְּהֻנָּה שֶׁשִּׁמֵּשׁ בְּז' יְמֵי הַמִּלּוּאִים, מַלְכוּת דִּכְתִיב וַיְהִי בִישֻׁרוּן מֶלֶךְ.

*Moshe merited both of these (priesthood and royalty). He merited priesthood when he served as High Priest during the seven days of the inauguration of the Sanctuary, and royalty as it is written concerning Moshe, "And it was when there was a king in Yeshurun."*[3]

These words seem to directly contradict the above statement of the *Ba'alei Tosefoth*, that Moshe was denied both of these privileges.

Secondly, Moshe was criticised for his imitation of Avraham's answer of הִנֵּנִי — "Here I am." However, when we examine the meaning that underlies this response, we are puzzled further as to Moshe's fault. Let us turn to this incident.

Rashi lauds this answer of Avraham as follows:

כָּךְ הִיא עֲנִיָּתָם שֶׁל חֲסִידִים לְשׁוֹן עֲנָוָה וּלְשׁוֹן זִמּוּן.

*Such is the answer of the pious. This is a humble expression and a demonstration of preparedness.*[4]

In a similar vein, Yosef answered הִנֵּנִי to his father's request that he travel to Shechem and inquire after his brothers' welfare, and he too is praised for his response. Rashi again highlights the traits of alacrity and modesty, which can be discerned from this expression.

לְשׁוֹן עֲנָוָה וּזְרִיזוּת. נִזְדָּרֵז לְמִצְוַת אָבִיו וְאַף עַל פִּי שֶׁהָיָה יוֹדֵעַ בְּאֶחָיו שֶׁשּׂוֹנְאִין אוֹתוֹ.

*An expression of humility and eagerness. He was quick to fulfill his father's command even though he knew that his brothers hated him.*[5]

It would appear from these two instances that הִנֵּנִי is in fact a correct and praiseworthy response. Moshe, though, is faulted for his use of this answer. Such criticism is puzzling.

---

3. *Shemoth Rabbah* 2:6.
4. Rashi on *Bereishith* 22:1.
5. Rashi on *Bereishith* 37:13.

Our Sages make the following famous statement, urging us to constantly set our sights on those who have attained more than we have.

חַיָּב אָדָם לוֹמַר מָתַי יַגִּיעוּ מַעֲשַׂי לְמַעֲשֵׂי אֲבוֹתַי אַבְרָהָם יִצְחָק וְיַעֲקֹב.

*One is obligated to say, "When will my deeds reach the level of my ancestors, Avraham, Yitzchak, and Ya'akov?"*[6]

One should always strive forward in an attempt to reach higher levels of spirituality. Our sights should be set upon the lofty stature of our Patriarchs as we gradually progress higher and deeper. Why then is Moshe faulted for his apparent emulation of Avraham?

Let us digress and examine a certain law, which will shed light upon the subject in question.

הָעוֹבֵר לִפְנֵי הַתֵּבָה צָרִיךְ לְסָרֵב וְאִם אֵינוֹ מְסָרֵב דּוֹמֶה לְתַבְשִׁיל שֶׁאֵין בּוֹ מֶלַח וְאִם מְסָרֵב יוֹתֵר מִדַּאי דּוֹמֶה לְתַבְשִׁיל שֶׁהִקְדִּיחַתּוּ מֶלַח. כֵּיצַד הוּא עוֹשֶׂה? פַּעַם רִאשׁוֹנָה יְסָרֵב שְׁנִיָּה מְהַבְהֵב שְׁלִישִׁית פּוֹשֵׁט אֶת רַגְלָיו וְיוֹרֵד.

*If one is asked to lead the community in prayer, he is required to refuse. If he does not do so, he is compared to a cooked dish that lacks salt. Yet, if he refuses too much he is compared to a cooked dish containing too much salt. How then is he expected to act? The first time he is asked he should refuse. At the second request, he should reluctantly begin to consider the offer. The third time he should accept immediately.*[7]

This law appears to oppose a recommendation of our Sages. We are told to perform mitzvoth at the first available opportunity, with alacrity and zeal. Yet, in this case, procrastination, and even trying to avoid the opportunity for a good deed, seem to be in place.

The apparent contradiction can be resolved through a famous story concerning Rabbi Yisrael Salanter, the founder of the Mussar movement. The world of Mussar is primarily a method of learning works pertaining to character development. At the time the movement

---

6. *Tanna D'vei Eliyahu Rabbah* 25.
7. *Berachoth* 34.

was introduced, much suspicion was cast on what was then viewed as a modern innovation, and the movement became the subject of much controversy. It once happened that R. Yisrael was scheduled to deliver a lecture in the main synagogue of a certain town, and in accordance with the protocol, he provided, in advance, a list of sources to which he would refer in the course of his delivery. Upon his arrival at the synagogue, R. Yisrael discovered that his opponents had tampered with the list of references, exchanging it for another list of unconnected and obscure sources. After examining the new list for a few minutes, R. Yisrael gave a brilliant and erudite lecture connecting all the new sources. He later informed his students that he had needed only the first moment to formulate the lecture. The rest of the time was spent overcoming any pride he may have felt as a result of his capabilities.

Certain mitzvoth may lead to pride. Amongst them are those that place one in a prestigious position such as that of a king, a High Priest, or one who leads the congregation in prayer. Since being offered such positions can lead one to feelings of pride, the recipient of these offers must first refuse, overcoming such negative feelings, and only then accept the position.

It was on that sublime day, Yom Kippur, that the High Priest could enter the innermost Sanctuary. Entrance was a privilege exclusive to him, and was permitted solely on this day. This knowledge could have engendered a feeling of pride; therefore, certain actions were prescribed as an antidote. The Torah tells us the course of behaviour commanded for Aharon in preparation for this unique event, and adds:

> **וְהָיְתָה זֹּאת לָכֶם לְחֻקַּת עוֹלָם לְכַפֵּר עַל בְּנֵי יִשְׂרָאֵל מִכָּל חַטֹּאתָם אַחַת בַּשָּׁנָה וַיַּעַשׂ כַּאֲשֶׁר צִוָּה ה' אֶת מֹשֶׁה.**
>
> *And this shall be for you as an eternal law to atone for all the sins of the Children of Yisrael, once a year. And he did all that God commanded Moshe.*[8]

---

8. *Vayikra* 16:34.

Rashi's comment on the last words of this verse is particularly revealing.

כְּשֶׁהִגִּיעַ יוֹם הַכִּפּוּרִים עָשָׂה כַּסֵּדֶר הַזֶּה וּלְהַגִּיד שִׁבְחוֹ שֶׁל אַהֲרֹן שֶׁלֹּא הָיָה לוֹבְשָׁן לְגַדְלוּתוֹ אֶלָּא כִּמְקַיֵּם גְּזֵרַת הַמֶּלֶךְ.

*When Yom Kippur arrived, Aharon performed the service in this order. This comes to praise Aharon, who donned the priestly vestments not for his own honour, but as one who fulfills the decree of the King.*

Aharon initially declined the position of High Priest, unable to accept it due to the humility he felt. It was only after being urged by Moshe that he agreed. His initial refusal demonstrates that his later acceptance of the role was indeed for the sake of Heaven. A pure acceptance is facilitated by an initial refusal.

The *Ohr Chadash* differentiates between the circumstances surrounding the reply of Moshe and that of Avraham. Moshe declared "הִנֵּנִי" to the attractive offer of priesthood and kingship. With the same word, Avraham was demonstrating his readiness to sacrifice his son for the sake of the Almighty.

Similarly, Yosef's "הִנֵּנִי" indicated his willingness to travel to his brothers who he knew hated him. In the latter two cases, the immediate acceptance of the task, the הִנֵּנִי, was praiseworthy, an indication of a willingness to serve God and follow His precepts in whatever form required, despite the difficulty involved. However, in the case of Moshe, the instruction was a mitzvah that could lead to pride. Moshe is thus censured for his initial acceptance, the correct course of action being to first refuse.

It is noteworthy that Moshe's next instructions were אַל תִּקְרַב הֲלֹם — "Do not draw near." Moshe obeyed this command, demonstrating his ability to abstain, and to restrain himself in a situation in which this was called for. It was only after this restraint that he was called near; a closeness which could be with motives of purity, only for the sake of Heaven. The "הִנֵּנִי" of Moshe caused a loss. After his subsequent restraint and refusal, Moshe could acquiesce to God's request with the correct intentions.

This explanation accords with the comment of our Sages upon the following verse:

**וַיַּסְתֵּר מֹשֶׁה פָּנָיו כִּי יָרֵא מֵהַבִּיט אֶל הָאֱלֹקִים.**

*Moshe hid his face, for he was afraid to look directly at God.*[9]

Our Sages state:

אָמַר ר' שְׁמוּאֵל בַּר נַחְמָנִי אָמַר רַבִּי יוֹחָנָן בִּשְׂכַר שָׁלֹשׁ זָכָה לְשָׁלֹשׁ. בִּשְׂכַר "וַיַּסְתֵּר מֹשֶׁה פָּנָיו", זָכָה לְקְלַסְתֵּר פָּנִים. בִּשְׂכַר "כִּי יָרֵא" זָכָה ל"וַיִּרְאוּ מִגֶּשֶׁת אֵלָיו". בִּשְׂכַר "מֵהַבִּיט" זוֹכֶה ל"תְמוּנַת ה' יַבִּיט".

*As reward for three, he merited three. As a reward for, "Moshe hid his face," Moshe merited a shining countenance. As a reward for, "For he was afraid," he merited "And they were afraid to draw near to him." As a reward for, "to look," he merited "And he looked upon the 'image' of God."*[10]

The greatest joy a prophet can have is to receive Divine revelation. Yet, Moshe was able to refuse even this pleasure, even this privilege. His initial refusal, however, was a prerequisite for his later acceptance, an acceptance in purity. Accepting immediately is an indication of being motivated by self-glorification. In this case, one ultimately loses.

**וַיִּקַּח מֹשֶׁה אֶת עַצְמוֹת יוֹסֵף עִמּוֹ כִּי הַשְׁבֵּעַ הִשְׁבִּיעַ אֶת בְּנֵי יִשְׂרָאֵל לֵאמֹר פָּקֹד יִפְקֹד אֱלֹקִים אֶתְכֶם וְהַעֲלִיתֶם אֶת עַצְמֹתַי מִזֶּה אִתְּכֶם.**

*Moshe took the bones of Yosef with him, as Yosef made the Children of Yisrael swear, saying, "God will surely remember you, and you shall bring up my bones from here with you."*[11]

The *Mechilta* states on this verse:

לְהוֹדִיעַ חָכְמָתוֹ וַחֲסִידוּתוֹ שֶׁל מֹשֶׁה שֶׁכָּל יִשְׂרָאֵל עוֹסְקִין בְּבִזָּה וּמֹשֶׁה עוֹסֵק בְּמִצְוַת עַצְמוֹת יוֹסֵף. עָלָיו הַכָּתוּב "חֲכַם לֵב יִקַּח מִצְוֹת".

---

9. *Shemoth* 3:6.
10. *Berachoth* 13:19.
11. *Shemoth* 13:19.

> *This informs you of the wisdom and piety of Moshe. While all Yisrael were busy taking the spoils, Moshe was occupied with the mitzvah of the bones of Yosef. Concerning him the Scriptures say, "A wise heart will take mitzvoth."*

Both collecting the spoils and recovery of the bones of Yosef were mitzvoth. However, wisdom is needed in deciding which mitzvah to fulfill. Despoiling Egypt could involve selfish motivations and personal benefit. Moshe demonstrated wisdom when he chose the mitzvah that did not promise personal benefit upon its performance.

One should look for the mitzvoth that do not involve self-glorification, and thus will not lead to pride. Concerning these deeds, one can immediately and enthusiastically declare "הִנֵּנִי", for there is no doubt that performance of these actions is solely for the sake of the Almighty; there is no possibility of earning stature in the eyes of onlookers. However, when mitzvoth involve acceptance of honour, glory, or positions of authority, one must not be too eager to accept. One's refusal however, must also not be too vigourous. After the initial abstention, one can and should acquiesce, and in doing so be secure in the knowledge that one's actions are not for one's own glory, but are undertaken only to enhance the honour and glory of the Almighty.

# VA'ERA

THE TEN PLAGUES that afflicted the Egyptian population were a response to Par'oh's defiant declaration of מִי ה' — "Who is God?" The plagues were grouped into three sets of three, with the final plague, the death of all firstborns, acting solely as a catalyst for the release of the Jewish People. The first two plagues of each set were preceded by a warning to allow Par'oh to repent and thus avert the predicted suffering. No notification was given for the third plague of each set; it served as a punishment for disregarding previous words of caution.

When focusing upon the second plague in each group, a difference in the third set can be noted. Concerning both the plague of frogs and that of pestilence, the warning opens with the words, וְאִם מָאֵן אַתָּה לְשַׁלֵּחַ — "If you refuse to release them."[12] However, with regard to the plague of hailstones, we find a change of expression: עַד מָתַי מֵאַנְתָּ לֵעָנֹת מִפָּנָי — "How long will you refuse to be humbled before Me?"[13] On the first occasion there was no mention of Par'oh humbling himself. What is the significance of this variation?

Concerning Par'oh, the Rambam makes a cryptic statement: פַּרְעֹה מֶלֶךְ מִצְרַיִם הוּא יצה"ר בֶּאֱמֶת — "Par'oh, king of Egypt, is the embodiment of the evil inclination."[14] Let us investigate why the Rambam defines Par'oh as the evil inclination incarnate.

In a passage laden with meaning, the Talmud discusses the question of when, in the development of an infant, the evil inclination becomes active.

12. *Shemoth* 7:27 and 9:2.
13. *Shemoth* 10:3.
14. *Iggereth HaMussar.*

וְאָמַר לֵיהּ אַנְטוֹנִינוּס לְרַבִּי מֵאֵימָתַי יצה"ר שׁוֹלֵט בָּאָדָם מִשְּׁעַת יְצִירָה אוֹ מִשְּׁעַת יְצִיאָה? אָמַר לוֹ מִשְּׁעַת יְצִירָה. אָמַר לוֹ אִם כֵּן בּוֹעֵט בִּמְעֵי אִמּוֹ וְיוֹצֵא אֶלָּא מִשְּׁעַת יְצִיאָה. אָמַר רַבִּי דָּבָר זֶה לִמְּדַנִי אַנְטוֹנִינוּס וּמִקְרָא מְסַיְּעוֹ שֶׁנֶּאֱמַר "לַפֶּתַח חַטָּאת רוֹבֵץ".

*Antoninus Pius (Emperor of Rome) asked R. Yehudah HaNasi, "At what stage does the evil inclination begin to dominate man? Is it from the moment the embryo is formed within its mother or at birth?" R. Yehudah HaNasi replied, "From the time the embryo is formed."*

*Antoninus objected, "If this were so, the fetus would kick against its mother and exit. Birth must herald the advent of the evil inclination's reign."*

*Rabbi acceded, "I learned this from Antoninus. Indeed his observation is supported by a verse: Sin crouches at the opening."*[15,16]

This conclusion is striking when considering the *gemara* in *Niddah* which reads as follows:

דָּרַשׁ רַבִּי שִׂמְלַאי לְמָה הַוָּלָד דּוֹמֶה בִּמְעֵי אִמּוֹ... וְנֵר דָּלוּק לוֹ עַל רֹאשׁוֹ וְצוֹפֶה וּמַבִּיט מִסּוֹף הָעוֹלָם וְעַד סוֹפוֹ... וְאֵין לְךָ יָמִים שֶׁאָדָם שָׁרוּי בְּטוֹבָה יוֹתֵר מֵאוֹתָן יָמִים.

*Rabbi Simlai describes the condition of an unborn child. There is a beacon above its head, with which it can perceive the world from one end to the other. No days in a person's existence are more blissful than those days.*[17]

We have previously established that if the evil inclination were present before birth, the child would struggle to be born. However, that would seem to contradict this *gemara*, which defines these days as ones unparalleled in their pleasure. For if these days offer the peak of pleasure, why would the evil inclination battle so fiercely to enter an inferior existence?

---

15. *Bereishith* 4:7.
16. *Sanhedrin* 96b.
17. *Niddah* 30b.

Considering the position of the child, we can discern one factor which impinges upon its otherwise blissful experience: the infant is confined. Particularly evident in today's society, restriction is universally resented, viewed as one of the worst evils. The desire for freedom in all areas is one of the most basic instincts possessed by man. As is reasoned by Antoninus in the above-cited *gemara*, this drive would take effect even in the most perfect of circumstances, when a child is ensconced within the mother.

Rabbi Dessler comments that this idea is contained within the name Par'oh itself. A hint to the meaning of the name "Par'oh" can be found in a phrase connected with the sin of the Golden Calf. (In fact there is an inherent connection between Par'oh and the Golden Calf, as is depicted by the verse in *Yirmiyah*: עֶגְלָה יְפֵה פִיָּה מִצְרָיִם — "A beautiful calf is Egypt.") After the sin of the Golden Calf was perpetrated, the verse states the following:

**וַיַּרְא מֹשֶׁה אֶת הָעָם כִּי פָרֻעַ הוּא כִּי פְרָעֹה אַהֲרֹן לְשִׁמְצָה בְּקָמֵיהֶם.**

*Moshe saw that the nation was exposed, for Aharon had uncovered them...*[18]

Rashi interprets:

פָּרֻעַ – מְגֻלֶּה, נִתְגַּלָּה שִׁמְצוֹ וּקְלוֹנוֹ.

פָּרֻעַ *[is to be interpreted as] "exposed." The nation's wickedness and shame were revealed.*

פָּרֻעַ denotes a breaching of the borders of the heart, a granting of free rein to the evil inclination. This is indeed an apt definition of Par'oh. It is to this evil inclination which the Rambam refers in his statement "פַּרְעֹה מֶלֶךְ מִצְרַיִם הוּא יצה"ר בֶּאֱמֶת". Man's resistance to confinement is a negative tendency which lies at the root of all sin. This idea is emphasized in the following famous Midrash:

ר' יוֹסֵי בַּר חֲלַפְתָּא פָּתַח (תְּהִלִּים ס"ח:ז) "אֱלֹקִים מוֹשִׁיב יְחִידִים בַּיְתָה". מַטְרוֹנָה שָׁאֲלָה אֶת רַבִּי יוֹסֵי בַּר חֲלַפְתָּא. אָמְרָה לוֹ לְכַמָּה

18. *Shemoth* 32:25.

יָמִים בָּרָא הקב"ה אֶת עוֹלָמוֹ? אָמַר לָהּ לוֹ' יָמִים כִּדְכְתִיב (שְׁמוֹת ל"א) "כִּי שֵׁשֶׁת יָמִים עָשָׂה ה' אֶת הַשָּׁמַיִם וְאֶת הָאָרֶץ." אָמְרָה לוֹ מַה הוּא עוֹשֶׂה מֵאוֹתָהּ שָׁעָה וְעַד עַכְשָׁו. אָמַר לָהּ הקב"ה יוֹשֵׁב וּמְזַוֵּג זִווּגִים. בִּתּוֹ שֶׁל פְּלוֹנִי לִפְלוֹנִי. אִשְׁתּוֹ שֶׁל פְּלוֹנִי לִפְלוֹנִי. מָמוֹנוֹ שֶׁל פְּלוֹנִי לִפְלוֹנִי. אָמְרָה לוֹ וְדָא הוּא אֻמְנוּתֵיהּ. אַף אֲנִי יְכוֹלָה לְזַוְּגָן. אָמַר לָהּ אִם קַלָּה הִיא בְּעֵינַיִךְ קָשָׁה הִיא לִפְנֵי הקב"ה כִּקְרִיעַת יַם סוּף.

הָלַךְ לוֹ ר' יוֹסֵי בַּר חֲלַפְתָּא מֶה עָשְׂתָה נָטְלָה אֶלֶף עֲבָדִים וְאֶלֶף שְׁפָחוֹת וְהֶעֱמִידָה אוֹתָן שׁוּרוֹת שׁוּרוֹת אָמְרָה פְּלוֹנִי יִסַּב לִפְלוֹנִית וּפְלוֹנִית תִּסַּב לִפְלוֹנִי. וְזִוְּגָה אוֹתָן בְּלַיְלָה אַחַת. לְמָחָר אָתוּן לְגַבָּהּ דֵּין מוֹחֵיהּ פְּצִיעָא. דֵּין עֵינוֹ שְׁמִיטָא. דֵּין רַגְלֵיהּ תְּבִירָא. אָמְרָה לְהוֹן מַה לְכוֹן. דָּא אָמְרָה לֵית אֲנָא בָּעֵי לְדֵין. וְדֵין אָמַר לֵית אֲנָא בָּעֵי לְדָא. מִיָּד שָׁלְחָה וְהֵבִיאָה אֶת ר' יוֹסֵי בַּר חֲלַפְתָּא אָמְרָה לוֹ לֵית אֱלָהּ כֵּאֱ-לָהֲכוֹן אֱמֶת הִיא תּוֹרַתְכוֹן נָאָה וּמְשֻׁבַּחַת יָפֶה אָמַרְתָּ אָמַר לֹא כָּךְ אָמַרְתִּי לָךְ, אִם קַלָּה הִיא בְּעֵינַיִךְ קָשָׁה הִיא לִפְנֵי הקב"ה כִּקְרִיעַת יַם סוּף.

*R. Yossi bar Chalafta opened with the words from Tehillim (68:7), "God settles individuals into a household."*

*A princess asked R. Yossi bar Chalafta, "How long did God take to create His world?"*

*He answered her, "Six days, as is stated (Shemoth 31:17): 'For in six days God made the heavens and the earth.'"*

*The princess returned to ask, "With what has He occupied Himself since then?"*

*R. Yossi replied, "God is arranging matches: this man's daughter for this person, that man's wife for another. This person's money for somebody else."*

*The princess exclaimed, "Is this indeed what He does? Even I could do so! I have many servants and maidservants whom I could pair up in but one hour."*

*R. Yossi countered, "You may imagine it to be an easy matter, but the Almighty finds it as difficult as splitting the Red Sea." R. Yossi bar Chalafta departed.*

*The woman took one thousand servants and maidservants, lined them up and paired off one with another in one night. The next morning they confronted her, one with his head bruised, another with his eye hanging out, a third with a broken leg. She exclaimed, "What has happened to you?" One complained, "I don't want this one." A second protested, "I don't want that one." She immediately sent for R. Yossi bar Chalafta and declared, "There is no God like yours. Your Torah is true, beautiful, and praiseworthy. You have spoken well."*

*He responded, "So I told you — it may be easy in your eyes but it is as difficult for God as splitting the Red Sea."*[19]

This princess had no difficulty accepting God as the Creator of the universe, as she certainly could not claim to have had any part in Creation. However, she was unwilling to recognise that it is the Almighty who arranges marriages; for this belief encroached on her own sphere of capabilities.

Man, by nature, resents any limitation of his own field of activity, and Par'oh, as the representation of the evil inclination, epitomizes this characteristic. Through the process of the plagues, in which the restriction of his own power became apparent, Par'oh was forced to confront this very limitation.

The Malbim highlights Par'oh's reaction to the tangible demonstration of God's omnipotence. As we find in his commentary, the purpose of the first three plagues was to demonstrate אֲנִי ה', the existence of Godly power. As is expressed in connection with the plague of blood:

**כֹּה אָמַר ה' בְּזֹאת תֵּדַע כִּי אֲנִי ה'...**

*So says the Lord of Hosts, "With this shall you know that I am the Lord."*[20]

The second set of three plagues was designed to demonstrate the concept of Divine Providence in this world. This is reflected in Moshe's words of warning to Par'oh prior to the plague of wild animals.

**לְמַעַן תֵּדַע כִּי אֲנִי ה' בְּקֶרֶב הָאָרֶץ.**

19. *Bereishith Rabbah* 68:4.

20. *Shemoth* 7:17.

*So that you shall know that I am God in the midst of the land.*[21]

This idea threatened Par'oh's identity as the undisputed controller of Egyptian life. It curtailed his self-invented power, restricted him in his capacity as the personification of unfettered freedom.

The last vestige of Par'oh's power crumbled with the advent of the third group of plagues, which testified beyond a doubt to the Almighty's absolute supremacy:

בַּעֲבוּר תֵּדַע כִּי אֵין כָּמֹנִי בְּכָל הָאָרֶץ.

*So that you shall know that there is none comparable to Me in all the land.*[22]

Thus, as the Malbim outlines the process, each stage in the plagues was a further demonstration to Par'oh, the quintessential opponent of personal limitation, of the limitations of his own power.

The *Chovoth HaLevavoth* enumerates a three-step process in a person's every deed. Firstly, an idea enters the mind. The mind then assimilates this idea and makes a conscious decision to act. Finally, the deed is performed; the intention is crystallised into action. The initial two stages are dependent upon the person himself. It is man who resolves to bring an idea into fruition. Its successful implementation, however, is beyond his control. God is the controller of circumstance, and it is only He Who can bring abstract intention into tangible fulfillment. Only the gift of free choice has been bestowed upon man; dominion over his own decisions. As the verse states: וּבָחַרְתָּ בַּחַיִּים — "And you shall choose life."

After the first five plagues, even this power of decision was withdrawn from Par'oh. As the verse states: וַיְחַזֵּק ה' אֶת לֵב פַּרְעֹה — "The Eternal strengthened Par'oh's resolve."[23] Par'oh was no longer master over his own heart. Yet Par'oh did not feel this loss. To recognise that this essential human power had been revoked would have meant admitting his ineffectualness, and Par'oh was loath to

21. *Shemoth* 8:18.
22. *Shemoth* 9:14.
23. *Shemoth* 9:12.

humble himself to this degree. Thus the verse:

**וַיִּשְׁלַח פַּרְעֹה וַיִּקְרָא לְמֹשֶׁה וּלְאַהֲרֹן וַיֹּאמֶר אֲלֵהֶם חָטָאתִי הַפָּעַם...**

*Par'oh sent for Moshe and Aharon and said to them, "This time I have sinned."*[24]

Par'oh still claimed dominion over his heart, as though it were his choice to sin. He refused to admit that the decision was out of his control. This explains the change of wording in the Almighty's warning after the second plague of each set. Originally, God cautioned: אִם מָאֵן אַתָּה לְשַׁלֵּחַ — "And if you refuse to release them..."[25] At this point, Par'oh was still capable of rendering his own decisions; his free choice remained unhampered. In the third set, however, this power is revoked. Thus God reproves Par'oh: עַד מָתַי מֵאַנְתָּ לֵעָנֹת מִפָּנָי. The criticism is leveled against his refusal to humble himself. By this stage, he is no longer capable of deciding to send out the Jewish People. His mind is no longer his own, his free choice has been removed; thus he is censured for failing to acknowledge this state of affairs and submit himself to God's will.

It is this trait which defines Par'oh as the personification of the evil inclination. As seen in the discussion between Antoninus and R. Yehudah HaNasi, the evil inclination is characterized by a strong resentment of restriction. Par'oh's virulent objection to the limitation of his power identifies him as negativity incarnate.

Total freedom of action is, paradoxically, a constraint to one's spiritual growth. Restrictions allow a person to attain the greatest spiritual heights, as they free him from the fetters of physicality and egotism which dominate this world.

The work *Shiurei Da'ath* expresses this idea as follows: פַּלֵּס מַעְגַּל רַגְלֶךָ — "Measure out the circle of your activity." The size of each person's circle is proportional to his spiritual standing. The greater he is, the smaller will be his circle. A lowly person needs a larger circle of outside interests to achieve self-satisfaction. The emptiness

---

24. *Shemoth* 9:27.
25. *Shemoth* 7:27.

within forces him to turn to external sources of fulfillment. The inner vacuum must somehow be filled; and so he turns to artificial sources to supply contentment. But physicality can never satisfy spiritual yearnings, and the person is thus forced to seek ever grander, ever more glorious external aids to fill the inner hollow. The area of his circle gradually increases. This is the force of the evil inclination at work, pressuring him to expand.

The individual of great stature requires only a small field of external activity to satisfy his inner self. His true contentment lies in the service of his Creator, and he is therefore not attracted to the pursuits of the outside world. A pulsating inner life leaves no vacuum to be filled with external substitutes. As R. Yehudah HaLevi expresses in his typical poetic style:

לוּ אֶחֱזֶה פָּנָיו בְּלִבִּי בָיְתָה לֹא שָׁאֲלוּ עֵינַי לְהַבִּיט חוּצָה.

*Would that I perceived Him in my heart; then my eyes would not seek elsewhere.*

# Bo

After witnessing the miracles and wonders of nine plagues, the Jewish People is about to experience the climax in the process of their redemption. At this juncture, they are given a very distinct set of instructions concerning the Pesach sacrifice.

**וְלָקְחוּ מִן הַדָּם וְנָתְנוּ עַל שְׁתֵּי הַמְּזוּזֹת וְעַל הַמַּשְׁקוֹף עַל הַבָּתִּים אֲשֶׁר יֹאכְלוּ אֹתוֹ בָּהֶם. וְאָכְלוּ אֶת הַבָּשָׂר בַּלַּיְלָה הַזֶּה צְלִי אֵשׁ וּמַצּוֹת עַל מְרֹרִים יֹאכְלֻהוּ... וְעָבַרְתִּי בְאֶרֶץ מִצְרַיִם בַּלַּיְלָה הַזֶּה וְהִכֵּיתִי כָל בְּכוֹר בְּאֶרֶץ מִצְרַיִם מֵאָדָם וְעַד בְּהֵמָה וּבְכָל אֱלֹהֵי מִצְרַיִם אֶעֱשֶׂה שְׁפָטִים אֲנִי ה'.**

*They shall take [some] of the blood and put [it] on the two doorposts and on the lintel of the houses where they will eat [the lamb]. They shall eat the meat on that night; they shall eat it roasted, with matzoth, [and] accompanied by bitter herbs.... I will pass through the land of Mitzrayim on that night and strike down every firstborn in the land of Mitzrayim, whether man or animal, and I will carry out acts of judgment against the gods of the Mitzrim — I, the Eternal.*[26]

Upon this last declaration of, "*I, the Eternal,*" Rashi makes the following comment:

**אֲנִי בְּעַצְמִי וְלֹא עַל יְדֵי שָׁלִיחַ.**

*I Myself and not through a messenger.*[27]

One of the points of emphasis in this climactic moment was that

26. *Shemoth* 12:7–12.
27. Rashi on *Shemoth* 12:12.

all the events would be performed by God Himself, and not through any agent or emissary. A later comment of Rashi further reinforces this idea:

**וְהָיָה הַדָּם לָכֶם לְאֹת עַל הַבָּתִּים אֲשֶׁר אַתֶּם שָׁם וְרָאִיתִי אֶת הַדָּם וּפָסַחְתִּי עֲלֵכֶם וְלֹא יִהְיֶה בָכֶם נֶגֶף לְמַשְׁחִית בְּהַכֹּתִי בְּאֶרֶץ מִצְרָיִם.**

*The blood will act for you as a sign on the houses where you are, [so that] I shall see the blood and skip over you, and there will be no destructive plague among you when I smite the land of Mitzrayim.*[28]

Rashi explains upon this verse that God would survey whether or not His children were engaged in the commanded deed, and accordingly would pass over them, withholding any suffering. Further, God's providence and supervision would be obvious to all, as even within one house, Egyptians and Jews would be distinguished from each other. A Jew in an Egyptian house would not perish, while an Egyptian who was seeking refuge in a Jewish house would find no reprieve.

Just a few verses later, however, an entirely different picture seems to be painted:

**וּלְקַחְתֶּם אֲגֻדַּת אֵזוֹב וּטְבַלְתֶּם בַּדָּם אֲשֶׁר בַּסַּף וְהִגַּעְתֶּם אֶל הַמַּשְׁקוֹף וְאֶל שְׁתֵּי הַמְּזוּזֹת מִן הַדָּם אֲשֶׁר בַּסָּף וְאַתֶּם לֹא תֵצְאוּ אִישׁ מִפֶּתַח בֵּיתוֹ עַד בֹּקֶר.**

*You shall then take a bundle of hyssop and dip [it] in the blood that is in the bowl, and touch [some] of the blood in the bowl to the lintel and to the two doorposts. And none of you may go out of the entrance of your houses until morning.*[29]

Rashi explains the reason for this final command:

וְאַתֶּם לֹא תֵצְאוּ – מַגִּיד שֶׁמֵּאַחַר שֶׁנִּתְּנָה רְשׁוּת לַמַּשְׁחִית לְחַבֵּל, אֵינוֹ מַבְחִין בֵּין צַדִּיק לְרָשָׁע וְלַיְלָה רְשׁוּת לַמְחַבְּלִים הִיא.

---

28. *Shemoth* 12:13.
29. *Shemoth* 12:22.

*After the destroying angel has been given permission to wreak its damage, it does not distinguish between the righteous or the wicked, and night is the domain of the angels of destruction.*[30]

The Children of Yisrael were therefore enjoined not to leave their houses, for if associated with Egyptians, they would not be spared the Egyptians' fate.

Initially the Torah emphasizes God's direct involvement in both the damnation of the Egyptians and the salvation of the Jewish People, however this latter information implies that punitive power was in fact transmitted to an agent. Rashi explains that while a Jew stayed safely within his own four walls, God Himself would distinguish between Jew and Gentile and save those within. However, upon leaving the house, the Jew would no longer be distinguished from his Egyptian neighbour, and both would be prey to the angel of destruction. What is the connection between the change of location and the transfer of supervision? Why does God's Hand protect the Jews in their houses, while an emissary is given dominion upon their exit?

Our Sages state: מְשַׁנֶּה מָקוֹם מְשַׁנֶּה מַזָּל, which roughly translated reads as, "A change of place engenders a change of fortune." In contrast to this statement is the famous adage: אֵין מַזָּל לְיִשְׂרָאֵל — "Israel exists on a realm in which the terms 'fortune' and 'destiny' are irrelevant."[31]

Considering the following statement will shed light upon the matter at hand.

הקב"ה גּוֹזֵר עַל הָאָדָם קֹדֶם שֶׁנּוֹצַר אִם חָכָם יִהְיֶה אוֹ שׁוֹטֶה. אִם גִּבּוֹר אוֹ חַלָּשׁ, בָּרִיא אוֹ חוֹלֶה, עָשִׁיר אוֹ עָנִי, וְרַק אִם צַדִּיק יִהְיֶה אוֹ רָשָׁע לֹא נִגְזַר מֵרֹאשׁ, כִּי זֶה תָּלוּי בִּבְחִירַת אָדָם עַצְמוֹ.

*Before one is formed, the Almighty decrees whether he will be clever or foolish, strong or weak, healthy or frail, rich or poor. Only whether the individual will be righteous or wicked*

30. Rashi *ad loc.*
31. *Shabbath* 156a.

*is not decreed, for this depends upon man's free will.*[32]

Rabbi Dessler elucidates this principle. Every individual has a unique role in implementing the purpose of creation. Each person's contribution is a vital cog in the intricate mechanism which is our world. However, for each man to fulfill his own mission, certain external conditions are required. For example, if one person's task in life is to head an institution of Torah learning, he will need to have received an education of quality, and have teachers and friends who will help him achieve this end. He will require the necessary books, and will need to live in a place of Torah learning. Another person may have the mission of fortifying Torah financially, and establishing Torah institutions. To fulfill his mission he will require material wealth. Whatever one's role in life might be, one is always given the external aids to enable him to carry out the task.

Parenthetically, herein lies the great folly of jealousy. Everyone receives possessions and qualities unique to him, as aids to his specific purpose. To be jealous is to see possessions divorced from purpose. One sees entities in their own right, rather than for what they are — merely extensions of an individual labouring in his Divine service. Furthermore, everyone receives exactly what he needs to fulfill his mission. To desire something other than that which one possesses is to desire irrelevancies.

Through a decision to change one's habitation, one's external tools, one can alter one's mission. An example of this would be a person in Russia, who spends his days disseminating Torah to the masses. As the financial situation becomes increasingly dire, the individual emigrates to America. Upon his move, he becomes very wealthy, and plays a crucial role in building up Torah institutions. His change of place has seen a change of tools of implementation and thus a change in his life's task. A new place can engender a new mission: מְשַׁנֶּה מָקוֹם מְשַׁנֶּה מַזָּל.

However, there are people who are not affected by external

32. *Michtav MeEliyahu,* Part One, p. 22.

circumstances and instead disregard and defy the circumstances in which they are placed. One famous example is Hillel.[33] Hillel stands as the yardstick against whom we are all measured on the day of judgment. In a rebuff of claims that we were unable to devote ourselves to Torah study due to financial pressures, the question will be forthcoming, "Were you as poor as Hillel?"

Hillel earned only one coin per day for his labour, half of which was used to enter the study hall while the other half had to suffice for all his family's expenditures, to provide them with all basic necessities. Upon one occasion, even this small coin was not earned, and Hillel was left without the means to pay for entrance to the study hall. Refusing to forgo the opportunity to hear words of Torah, Hillel climbed onto the roof to hear the holy words through the skylight. The incident is famous in its continuation: Hillel lay on the roof as snowflakes descended around him. He was discovered there, unconscious, the next morning, on the Sabbath day, when rays of morning light failed to enter the study hall and the scholars wondered at the darkness.

Although Hillel was placed in a situation which seemed to make the ideal course of action impossible, he refused to change his behaviour, instead defying the circumstances into which he was placed. Unable to enter the door, he would listen through the roof.

Another example of this attitude is evident in an opposite set of circumstances. The Talmud states that would anyone claim that he was unable to involve himself in Torah due to his many financial commitments and great wealth, he will be scrutinised against R. El'azar ben Chasim. R. El'azar inherited numerous villages and properties and owned a thousand ships. Yet R. El'azar contented himself with a small bag of provisions and traveled from place to place in his quest to learn Torah. His situation of wealth did not affect him or deter him from his desired course. He remained unaffected by his situation.

Rav Dessler explains that people regard nature at various levels. Some view nature as a mere illusion, knowing that it contains no

---

33. *Yoma* 35b.

inherent power at all. It is to this level that we all aspire, to be able to utter God's Name אֱלֹקִים in our prayers and truly believe that He is the בַּעַל הַכֹּחוֹת כֻּלָּם, the only source of all power.

A lower level is the perception that there are no inherent powers in nature, but that nature is a tool in God's Hand. Nature is compared to a pen used by a scribe to write a document. This level contains a flaw however, for use of a tool always denotes a deficiency. An intermediary is employed only when one is unable to achieve the desired result directly. By viewing nature as a pen in God's Hands, one is acknowledging the presence of the pen. Although nature is directed solely by the Almighty, "nature" per se does exist for one on this level; it is not merely the mirage of the higher level of perception. The difference between the two levels is fundamental: the difference between existence of nature and its non-existence, the difference between recognising a tool, an intermediary, and recognition of the Hand of God Himself.

R. Chanina ben Dosa made the famous statement:

מִי שֶׁאָמַר לַשֶּׁמֶן וְיִדְלֹק הוּא יֹאמַר לַחֹמֶץ וְיִדְלֹק.

*He Who declared that oil will burn will say the same to vinegar, and it will ignite.*[34]

There is nothing intrinsic to oil which effects its combustion. Oil burns only because of God's utterance that oil should burn. The "מִי שֶׁאָמַר" echoes בָּרוּךְ שֶׁאָמַר וְהָיָה הָעוֹלָם — "Blessed is He Who uttered and the world was." It is through God's constant utterance that the world endures. There is no other power but the Almighty. R. Chanina did not view the oil as the means God created through which things can burn. With such a perspective, vinegar would not suffice; oil is the means which is required. R. Chanina instead saw everything directly from the Almighty. To posit that God performs an action through a messenger is to recognise and thus attribute existence to a messenger.

---

34. *Ta'anith* 25a.

According to the natural pathway, a righteous individual would not be spared the ravages of an epidemic; he would suffer alongside his wicked contemporary. As stated by the *Chovoth HaLevavoth*, if one believes in nature, one is delivered into nature's hands. If one believes in an intermediary, one's life is dictated by the intermediary's course. If one does not recognise nature as having any implicit existence, however, but views everything as a direct action of God, one can be spared the illness and suffering.

Let us apply this to the circumstances in Egypt. The command to perform the Pesach sacrifice was fraught with danger. This was acknowledged by Par'oh himself, as the verses state:

> **וַיִּקְרָא פַּרְעֹה אֶל מֹשֶׁה וּלְאַהֲרֹן וַיֹּאמֶר לְכוּ זִבְחוּ לֵאלֹקֵיכֶם בָּאָרֶץ. וַיֹּאמֶר מֹשֶׁה לֹא נָכוֹן לַעֲשׂוֹת כֵּן כִּי תּוֹעֲבַת מִצְרַיִם נִזְבַּח לַה' אֱלֹקֵינוּ הֵן נִזְבַּח אֶת תּוֹעֲבַת מִצְרַיִם לְעֵינֵיהֶם וְלֹא יִסְקְלֻנוּ. דֶּרֶךְ שְׁלֹשֶׁת יָמִים נֵלֵךְ בַּמִּדְבָּר וְזָבַחְנוּ לַה' אֱלֹקֵינוּ כַּאֲשֶׁר יֹאמַר אֵלֵינוּ. וַיֹּאמֶר פַּרְעֹה אָנֹכִי אֲשַׁלַּח אֶתְכֶם וּזְבַחְתֶּם לַה' אֱלֹקֵיכֶם בַּמִּדְבָּר רַק הַרְחֵק לֹא תַרְחִיקוּ לָלֶכֶת הַעְתִּירוּ בַּעֲדִי.**
>
> *Par'oh called Moshe and Aharon and said [to them], "Go [and] sacrifice to your God [here] in the land. Moshe replied, "It [would] not be right to do so, for we shall sacrifice the Mitzrim's idol to the Eternal, our God. Now, [if] we would sacrifice the Mitzrim's idol before their eyes, would they not stone us?! We shall go on a three-day journey into the desert and there we will sacrifice to the Eternal, our God as He will [then] tell us." Par'oh said, "I shall let you go, [so that] you may sacrifice to the Eternal, your God, in the desert, but you must not go very far. Pray [right here] near me!"*[35]

Par'oh himself admitted the impossibility of offering sacrifices while in Egypt. The peril was of too great a magnitude, the jeopardy augmented by the requirement that the Jews seclude the lambs in their houses for four days, spread the blood of the slaughtered lamb upon their doorposts, and finally, roast the lamb, thus diffusing its odor throughout the land. The Egyptians would witness the entire

35. *Shemoth* 8:21–24.

procedure, and stone the Jewish People for this contemptuous treatment of their gods. The Children of Yisrael nevertheless pressed forth and fulfilled God's dictate. In response was God's statement:

**וְרָאִיתִי אֶת הַדָּם וּפָסַחְתִּי עֲלֵכֶם וְלֹא יִהְיֶה בָכֶם נֶגֶף לְמַשְׁחִית בְּהַכֹּתִי בְּאֶרֶץ מִצְרָיִם.**

*I shall see the blood and skip over you, and there will be no destructive plague among you when I smite the land of Mitzrayim.*[36]

Upon this, Rashi elaborates:

אֲנִי בְּעַצְמִי וְלֹא ע"י שָׁלִיחַ.

*I Myself, not through a messenger.*[37]

Further,

אָמַר הקב"ה נוֹתֵן אֲנִי אֶת עֵינַי לִרְאוֹת שֶׁאַתֶּם עֲסוּקִים בְּמִצְווֹתַי וּפוֹסֵחַ אֲנִי עֲלֵיכֶם.

God Himself will see the actions of the Jewish People, how, disregarding the extreme danger, they fulfill His command. He will then pass over the Jews' houses, saving them from destruction and distinguishing between the righteous and the wicked.

Fulfillment of their duty required a complete disregard for the physical danger to which the Jewish People were exposing themselves. It required a shattering of belief in the natural course of events. Upon the sublime level where everything is viewed as a direct action of the Almighty, they would consequently be saved from any ill, and could not be delivered into the hands of any malignant force. For the force, the intermediary, the agent, exists only inasmuch as one acknowledges its existence. But by leaving the house, a Jew would be delivered into the hands of the destructive force. He had left the doorposts upon which blood was smeared, the site of the Pesach sacrifice. It was no longer evident that he defied

36. *Shemoth* 12:12, 13.
37. Rashi *ad loc.*

the laws of nature, and he could thus be struck down according to the natural course of events.

It is commensurate with the amount of credence one attributes to nature that one is delivered into nature's hands. If one defies the circumstances into which one is placed, one can declare אֵין מַזָּל לְיִשְׂרָאֵל, that there is no "destiny" for Israel. For by placing oneself solely under the Almighty's jurisdiction, one rises above the natural course of events. It is when one sees an intermediary and adjusts one's actions accordingly, on account of circumstances, habitation, or situation, that the maxim of מְשַׁנֶּה מָקוֹם מְשַׁנֶּה מַזָּל is relevant. Seeing other factors apart from the Almighty renders one subject to these "other powers."

In our impoverished generation, we are very distant from the level of even viewing nature as a tool in God's Hands. It requires continuous contemplation to break through the deception painted by nature, and to internalise the conviction that everything is a direct result of God — He Who speaks and brings the world into being. Living as we do, constantly bombarded by perceptions of the natural world with its sequence of cause and effect, it requires effort, strength, and determination to break out of our self-made prison. Constant reiteration of the recognised truth, concentration in our prayers when we utter the word אֱלֹקֵינוּ, can teach us to perceive God as the only source of strength. Dispelling the mirage will bring about a revelation of miracles and wonders as we open ourselves to a personal and direct experience of God's guiding Hand.

# BESHALACH

AFTER THE MANNA is first bestowed upon the Jewish People, the following description is presented to us:

**וַתַּעַל שִׁכְבַת הַטָּל וְהִנֵּה עַל פְּנֵי הַמִּדְבָּר דַּק מְחֻסְפָּס דַּק כַּכְּפֹר עַל הָאָרֶץ. וַיִּרְאוּ בְנֵי יִשְׂרָאֵל וַיֹּאמְרוּ אִישׁ אֶל אָחִיו מָן הוּא כִּי לֹא יָדְעוּ מַה הוּא וַיֹּאמֶר מֹשֶׁה אֲלֵהֶם הוּא הַלֶּחֶם אֲשֶׁר נָתַן ה' לָכֶם לְאָכְלָה.**

*The layer of dew then rose, and there [all] over the desert, was an uncovered thin [layer], thin, and like frost on the ground. The Children of Yisrael saw [it], and each man said to the other, "It is a prepared food," for they did not know what it was. Moshe said to them, "It is the bread that the Eternal has given you to eat."*[38]

This phenomenon is commented upon in the Midrash on *Devarim.*

א"ר אִלְעַאי בְּשֵׁם ר' יוֹסֵי בֶּן זִמְרָה מִפְּנֵי מָה לֹא גִלָּה הקב"ה לְאַבְרָהָם אָבִינוּ שֶׁיִּתֵּן לְבָנָיו אֶת הַמָּן? א"ר אַבָּא כָּךְ הוּא דַּרְכָּן שֶׁל צַדִּיקִים, אוֹמְרִים מְעַט וְעוֹשִׂין הַרְבֵּה. ד"א מִפְּנֵי מָה לֹא גִלָּה אוֹתוֹ לָהֵן? שֶׁאִלּוּ גִלָּה אוֹתוֹ לָהֵן, הָיוּ יִשְׂרָאֵל אוֹמְרִים כְּבָר אָכַלְנוּ אוֹתוֹ עַל שֻׁלְחָנוֹ שֶׁל פַּרְעֹה.

*Why did God neglect to inform Avraham that his descendants would receive manna in the wilderness? Said R. Abba, "It is the manner of the righteous to say little and do much." [Thus God was reticent in speech yet magnanimous in action.] Another explanation: had [our forefathers] been informed of this phenomenon, the Jewish People in the desert would claim that they had enjoyed manna on a prior occasion, on the table of Par'oh.*[39]

---

38. *Shemoth* 16:14, 15.
39. *Devarim Rabbah* 1:11.

The *Mattenas Kehunah* explains concerning this last reason that, had this information been transmitted to the Jewish People in advance, they would have recognised and identified the substance when it appeared. But having received no prior warning of its descent, upon beholding the manna, the Jews were struck with the arresting scene and wondered as to the nature of the strange phenomenon.

The manna had to be something new. It is for this reason that Moshe failed to disclose the following information:

וַיְהִי בַּיּוֹם הַשִּׁשִּׁי לָקְטוּ לֶחֶם מִשְׁנֶה שְׁנֵי הָעֹמֶר לָאֶחָד וַיָּבֹאוּ כָּל נְשִׂיאֵי הָעֵדָה וַיַּגִּידוּ לְמֹשֶׁה. וַיֹּאמֶר אֲלֵהֶם הוּא אֲשֶׁר דִּבֶּר ה׳ שַׁבָּתוֹן שַׁבַּת קֹדֶשׁ לַה׳ מָחָר... הַנִּיחוּ לָכֶם לְמִשְׁמֶרֶת עַד הַבֹּקֶר... וְלֹא הִבְאִישׁ וְרִמָּה לֹא הָיְתָה בּוֹ. וַיֹּאמֶר מֹשֶׁה אִכְלֻהוּ הַיּוֹם כִּי שַׁבָּת הַיּוֹם לַה׳ הַיּוֹם לֹא תִמְצָאֻהוּ בַּשָּׂדֶה. שֵׁשֶׁת יָמִים תִּלְקְטֻהוּ וּבַיּוֹם הַשְּׁבִיעִי שַׁבָּת לֹא יִהְיֶה בּוֹ. וַיְהִי בַּיּוֹם הַשְּׁבִיעִי יָצְאוּ מִן הָעָם לִלְקֹט וְלֹא מָצָאוּ.

*It was on the sixth day [of the week] that they collected a double [amount of] bread, two omers for each one, and all the leaders of the community came and told Moshe. He said to them, "This is what the Eternal has spoken about: Tomorrow will be a [day of] complete cessation of work; a Sabbath of holiness to the Eternal...." It was on the seventh day that [some] of the people did go out to collect [manna], but they did not find [any].*[40]

Just a few verses later, Moshe is castigated by God for his failure to inform the people:

עַד אָנָה מֵאַנְתֶּם לִשְׁמֹר מִצְוֹתַי וְתוֹרֹתָי.

*Until when are you going to refuse to keep My commandments and My instructions?*[41]

Rashi explains the nature of Moshe's crime.

וַיָּבֹאוּ כָּל נְשִׂיאֵי הָעֵדָה וַיַּגִּידוּ לְמֹשֶׁה. שְׁאָלוּהוּ מַה הַיּוֹם מִיּוֹמַיִם. וּמִכָּאן יֵשׁ לִלְמֹד שֶׁעֲדַיִן לֹא הִגִּיד לָהֶם מֹשֶׁה פָּרָשַׁת שַׁבָּת שֶׁנִּצְטַוָּה

40. *Shemoth* 16:22–27.
41. *Shemoth* 16:28.

לוֹמַר לָהֶם בַּיּוֹם הַשִּׁשִּׁי וכו׳. עַד שֶׁשָּׁאֲלוּ אֶת זֹאת אָמַר לָהֶם הוּא אֲשֶׁר דִּבֶּר ה׳, שֶׁנִּצְטַוֵּיתִי לוֹמַר לָכֶם. וּלְכָךְ עֲנָשׁוֹ הַכָּתוּב שֶׁאָמַר לוֹ עַד אָנָה מֵאַנְתֶּם, וְלֹא הוֹצִיאוֹ מִן הַכְּלָל.

*"All the leaders of the community came and told Moshe." They asked him, "What is the difference between this day and other days?"*

*We derive from their question that Moshe had not yet told the people about the Sabbath. It was only when prompted by the chiefs' questions that Moshe declared, "This is what the Almighty said, and He commanded me to tell it over to you." Moshe is thus held accountable, and he is included in the general admonition of the people, for he had a part to play in their sin, by not informing them prior to the manna's appearance.*[42]

The Rashbam takes a different angle, however, and in his commentary he defends Moshe's actions:

וַיֹּאמֶר אֲלֵהֶם הוּא אֲשֶׁר דִּבֶּר ה׳. מִיּוֹם רִאשׁוֹן, וַאֲנִי לֹא הִגַּדְתִּי לָכֶם. וּמֹשֶׁה נִתְכַּוֵּן שֶׁיִּהְיוּ תְּמֵהִים כְּשֶׁיִּמְצְאוּ מִשְׁנֶה, לְהוֹדִיעַ לָהֶם עַתָּה כְּבוֹדוֹ שֶׁל יוֹם הַשַּׁבָּת.

*"This is what God spoke about." Moshe had known the information since the beginning of the week, and had withheld it, for he wanted the people to wonder at their find of a double portion. Thus the honour due to the Sabbath day would be made known to them.*[43]

Moshe wanted to utilise the element of surprise to make a deeper impression on the people. The above-quoted Midrash reinforces our argument that when something is new, when an element of surprise is present, a profound impression is made. That which one is expecting, or that which is familiar to a person, has much less impact and is thus much less effective.

---

42. Rashi *ad loc.*
43. Rashbam *ad loc.*

This principle is reiterated by an incident that is recorded in the Talmud.[44]

A Jew and a Gentile were walking together along a road, and the Gentile had difficulty keeping pace with the Jew, who was walking at considerable speed. The Gentile reminded the Jew about the destruction of the Temple. The Jew began to sigh, yet he still continued walking at a pace at which the Gentile lagged behind. The Gentile questioned the Jew: "Do you not say that a deep grief decreases a person's strength? Does this tragedy fail to affect you, considering that you can walk so fast?" The Jew replied that this rule applies only to a fresh piece of news. Hearing something which is already known does not affect a person to the same extent.

Our argument is thus intensified. It is something new and unexpected which makes the deepest impression upon a person.

However, the *Mesillath Yesharim* seems to indicate an entirely different pathway through which the deepest impression is made.

הַחִבּוּר הַזֶּה לֹא חִבַּרְתִּיו לְלַמֵּד לִבְנֵי אָדָם אֶת אֲשֶׁר לֹא יָדְעוּ. אֶלָּא לְהַזְכִּירָם אֶת הַיָּדוּעַ לָהֶם כְּבָר וּמְפֻרְסָם אֶצְלָם פִּרְסוּם גָּדוֹל. כִּי לֹא תִּמְצָא בְּרֹב דְּבָרַי אֶלָּא דְּבָרִים שֶׁרֹב בְּנֵי הָאָדָם יוֹדְעִים אוֹתָם וְלֹא מִסְתַּפְּקִים בָּהֶם כְּלָל. אֶלָּא שֶׁכְּפִי רֹב פִּרְסוּמָם וּכְנֶגֶד מַה שֶּׁאֲמִתָּתָם גְּלוּיָה לַכֹּל, כָּךְ הַהֶעְלֵם מֵהֶם מָצוּי מְאֹד וְהַשִּׁכְחָה רַבָּה. עַל כֵּן אֵין הַתּוֹעֶלֶת הַנִּלְקָט מִזֶּה הַסֵּפֶר יוֹצֵא מִן הַקְּרִיאָה בּוֹ פַּעַם אַחַת. כִּי כְּבָר אֶפְשָׁר שֶׁלֹּא יִמְצָא הַקּוֹרֵא בְּשִׂכְלוֹ חִדּוּשִׁים אַחַר קְרִיאָתוֹ שֶׁלֹּא הָיוּ בּוֹ לִפְנֵי קְרִיאָתוֹ אֶלָּא מְעַט. אֲבָל הַתּוֹעֶלֶת יוֹצֵא מִן הַחֲזָרָה עָלָיו וְהַהַתְמָדָה.

*This work was not written to teach people what they do not know, rather it is to remind them of that which they know and that which is well publicised and patently obvious. It is because the truth of these words is known unequivocally, and that these ideas are so manifest, that people tend to forget and neglect them. Thus, the purpose of this work is not realised when people read it just once, for upon one reading, no new ideas will be detected. The purpose of this work is realised*

44. *Kesuboth* 62a.

*when people repeatedly review what is written therein. It is only then that people will remember what they know, but forget. Through constant repetition, people will take heed of their duties, duties which are ignored, precisely because they are so well known.*[45]

The *Mesillath Yesharim* seems to be incongruous with our above-stated rule, that it is something new which makes an impression. He states that his work contains very few new ideas, and instead is composed mainly of things which are already known by people. However, he proposes that the impact will be made, the purpose will be realised, through continual repetition of that which is already known. If it is only something new which has an effect upon a person, why here does the *Mesillath Yesharim* state that it is only when something is repeated that it has maximum potency?

Let us digress to a comment of the Ramban concerning a prophecy experienced by Avraham.

**וַיֵּרָא ה' אֶל אַבְרָם וַיֹּאמֶר לְזַרְעֲךָ אֶתֵּן אֶת הָאָרֶץ הַזֹּאת וַיִּבֶן שָׁם מִזְבֵּחַ לַה' הַנִּרְאֶה אֵלָיו.**

*The Eternal appeared to Avram and said [to him], "I will give this land to your descendants." [Avram] then built an altar there to the Eternal Who had appeared to him.*[46]

The Ramban makes the following comment:

כִּי הוֹדָה לה' הַנִּכְבָּד וְזָבַח זֶבַח תּוֹדָה עַל שֶׁנִּרְאָה אֵלָיו. כִּי עַד הֵנָּה לֹא נִרְאָה אֵלָיו הַשֵּׁם וְלֹא נִתְוַדַּע אֵלָיו בְּמַרְאֶה וְלֹא בְּמַחֲזֶה, אֲבָל נֶאֱמַר לֵךְ לְךָ מֵאַרְצְךָ בַּחֲלוֹם הַלַּיְלָה אוֹ בְּרוּחַ הַקֹּדֶשׁ. וְיִתָּכֵן שֶׁיִּרְמֹז הַנִּרְאֶה אֵלָיו עַל סוֹד הַקָּרְבָּן.

*Avraham built an altar and brought thanksgiving offerings to God for having appeared to him. For until now God had not appeared to him, nor had He made Himself known visually. On prior occasions, the command, "Go for yourself from your*

---

45. *Mesillath Yesharim*, Introduction.
46. *Bereishith* 12:7.

*land," had been communicated through a dream or through Divine inspiration...*[47]

Rabbi Dessler explains the words of the Ramban.

סְגֻלָּתָם שֶׁל מַעֲשִׂים חִיצוֹנִיִּים הִיא לִקְבֹּעַ בַּלֵּב אֶת הַהַכָּרָה וְהַהִתְעוֹרְרוּת הָרוּחָנִית שֶׁהָאָדָם חָשׁ אוֹתָן. כִּי אִם לֹא יִקְבַּע אוֹתָן מִיָּד בְּמַעֲשֶׂה, עֲלוּלוֹת הֵן לְהִשָּׁאֵר רִגְשֵׁי סְרָק.

*It is external actions which fix and consolidate in the heart any intellectual recognition and spiritual inspiration that a person may experience. If one does not fix these things immediately in the form of a physical action, the inspiration is liable to bear no fruit and to remain barren.*[48]

It is not only that, unless brought to fruition, feelings of inspiration will dissipate. Any emotion or excitement which is not acted upon will be detrimental to a person. Our Sages compare one whose knowledge exceeds his actions to a tree with many branches and few roots. In the face of a strong wind, the tree could easily succumb. The more branches possessed by the tree, the more liable it is to fall. The extra branches do not add to the security of the tree; they only place it in an even more precarious position.

Avraham underwent a prophetic experience. He encountered transcendence. To thank God for this he brought a thanksgiving offering. He thus fixed his feelings of gratitude into a physical action. In this way, he shielded his fervor from becoming רִגְשֵׁי סְרָק, futile, abortive emotions. Avraham thus circumvented the danger to which a person is subject when emotions are aroused without bearing fruit in the physical world.

This principle is mentioned by the Ramban himself, just one verse earlier:[49] All decrees which are accompanied by a physical action will endure in the face of any eventuality. It was for this reason that prophets often performed a physical action with their prophecy.

47. Ramban *ad loc.*

48. *Michtav MeEliyahu,* Part Three, p.127.

49. Ramban on *Bereishith* 12:6.

An example of this is Yirmiyah, who after forecasting the downfall of Bavel, threw a stone into a river, thus physically depicting Bavel's downfall.

Hearing words of Torah can stimulate a person's emotions; new ideas make a profound imprint upon a person. Without anchoring the inspiration with a physical action, that which one heard not only does not bear fruit, it is detrimental to one's spiritual wellbeing. The initial acquisition of knowledge is termed וְיָדַעְתָּ הַיּוֹם: fulfillment of the injunction, "You shall know today."[50] The continuation of the verse: וַהֲשֵׁבֹתָ אֶל לְבָבֶךָ — "You shall impress it upon (literally, return it to) your heart," is the task then incumbent upon man. One must allow the words to permeate one's being and affect one's heart, one's very self. This is achieved through reviewing and meditating upon the information which has been acquired. It is only when considering the information again that one realises the inner changes and development which are incumbent upon oneself. One permanently acquires the knowledge as a result of the actions which stem from the initial comprehension.

When a person reviews that which has been gained, internal changes take place, such that he can no longer be considered the same person as the one who learned the information the first time. Thus we can understand the following:

הַיּוֹם הַזֶּה ה' אֱלֹקֶיךָ מְצַוְּךָ...

*Today the Eternal, your God, is commanding you.*[51]

Rashi defines the expression, "today":

בְּכָל יוֹם יִהְיוּ בְעֵינֶיךָ כַּחֲדָשִׁים כְּאִלּוּ בוֹ בַּיּוֹם נִצְטַוֵּיתָ עֲלֵיהֶם.

*Every day they should be in your eyes like new, as if you had been commanded them today.*[52]

Is the Torah, in this injunction, recommending self-deception?

---

50. *Devarim* 4:39.
51. *Devarim* 26:16.
52. Rashi *ad loc.*

It is axiomatic that the Torah is exclusively truth. How then can we understand this requirement?

Once a person has fixed an idea in his heart, he is no longer the same person as he was previously. Having actualized intellectual knowledge through spiritual labour, he has succeeded in transforming part of his inner being, undergoing a rebirth. Thus, to fulfill the need of constant freshness in one's spirituality, one must be constantly considering and implementing changes as a result of knowledge gained. Then, the commandments will truly be new every day, being fulfilled each day by a new individual. Since the person is new, another impression is made on him, unlike any ever made before, for it is novelty which creates the greatest impressions. The cycle continues: further repetition makes ever more profound impact, the knowledge being perpetually new, for the person himself is never static. It is through this method that we can embark upon a journey of unceasing growth.

The *Mesillath Yesharim* writes that the purpose of his work is realised only through repeated perusal. For iteration leads to an internalization of the knowledge, a fixing into one's heart. It is thus that one becomes a new person. The words can then be read again, and will again make a tremendous impression, for the words themselves are new, being read by a different person. The original inspiration will be transformed into a supply of fruit which is constantly being replenished. Mere excitement at hearing new Torah insights is insufficient, and could even be dangerous. Instead, continuous building and inner development is required, both of which result from the words which have been heard, and both of which generate a perpetual feeling of newness. May we merit to perpetually feel the sparkling freshness of Torah, through constant transformation of our personalities.

# YITHRO

THE MIDRASH INFORMS us of a struggle that occurred prior to the giving of the Torah to the Jewish People:

> וּמֹשֶׁה עָלָה אֶל הָאֱלקִים. בְּאוֹתָהּ שָׁעָה בִּקְשׁוּ מַלְאֲכֵי הַשָּׁרֵת לִפְגֹּעַ בְּמֹשֶׁה עָשָׂה לוֹ הקב"ה קְלַסְטֵירִין שֶׁל פָּנָיו שֶׁל מֹשֶׁה דּוֹמֶה לְאַבְרָהָם. אָמַר לָהֶם הקב"ה אִי אַתֶּם מִתְבַּיְּשִׁים הֵימֶנּוּ לֹא זֶהוּ שֶׁיְּרַדְתֶּם אֶצְלוֹ וַאֲכַלְתֶּם בְּתוֹךְ בֵּיתוֹ. אָמַר הקב"ה לְמֹשֶׁה לֹא נִתְּנָה לְךָ תּוֹרָה אֶלָּא בִּזְכוּת אַבְרָהָם שֶׁנֶּאֱמַר לָקַחְתָּ מַתָּנוֹת בָּאָדָם. וְאֵין אָדָם הָאָמוּר כָּאן אֶלָּא אַבְרָהָם שֶׁנֶּאֱמַר הָאָדָם הַגָּדוֹל בָּעֲנָקִים.
>
> *"And Moshe ascended to God." At that time [of the giving of the Torah], the angels sought to attack Moshe. God transformed Moshe's countenance to resemble the face of Avraham. God then said to the angels, "Are you not embarrassed before him? Did you not once descend and eat in his house?" God then said to Moshe, "The Torah was given to you only in the merit of Avraham..."*[53]

This cryptic Midrash will become clearer after we examine and reconcile two other *midrashim* which initially appear to contradict each other:

> הָאוֹמֵר שֶׁלֹּא אָכְלוּ הַמַּלְאָכִים אֵצֶל אַבְרָהָם לֹא אָמַר כְּלוּם. אֶלָּא בְּצִדְקָתוֹ שֶׁל אוֹתוֹ צַדִּיק וּבִשְׂכַר טֹרַח שֶׁהִטְרִיחַ פָּתַח לָהֶם הקב"ה פִּיהֶם וְאָכְלוּ שֶׁנֶּאֱמַר עֹמֵד עֲלֵיהֶם תַּחַת הָעֵץ וַיֹּאכֵלוּ.
>
> *One who claims that the angels did not eat while visiting Avraham is talking foolishness. Because of the righteousness of this tzaddik, and in the merit of his exertion in this mitzvah, God opened the angels' mouths, and they ate. Thus it states,*

---

53: *Shemoth Rabbah* 28:1.

*"...Standing over them under the tree, and they ate."*[54]

Just a few lines further, the Midrash seems to blatantly contradict itself:

וְהוּא עֹמֵד עֲלֵיהֶם תַּחַת הָעֵץ וַיֹּאכֵלוּ. לְעוֹלָם אַל יְשַׁנֶּה אָדָם מִמִּנְהַג הַמְּדִינָה שֶׁהֲרֵי מֹשֶׁה עָלָה לַמָּרוֹם וְלֹא אָכַל וְלֹא שָׁתָה וּמַלְאֲכֵי הַשָּׁרֵת יָרְדוּ לְמַטָּה וְאָכְלוּ וְשָׁתוּ. אוֹכְלִין וְשׁוֹתִין סַלְקָא דַעְתָּךְ?! אֶלָּא נִרְאִין כְּאִלּוּ אוֹכְלִין וְשׁוֹתִין.

*"...Standing over them under the tree, and they ate." A person should never differ from the practice of general society. We see that Moshe ascended to Heaven where he did not partake of food or drink. Conversely, we see that angels descended to earth where they ate and drank. Did they really eat and drink? They merely gave the appearance of eating and drinking.*

While on earth, and acting as the beneficiaries of Avraham's hospitality, did the angels eat and drink, or did they simply give the impression of eating and drinking, their celestial nature precluding ingestion of physical food?

Food is composed of two parts. While we swallow a physical, tangible entity, we are simultaneously ingesting that part of the food which is composed of spirituality. Thus the verse states:

**כִּי לֹא עַל הַלֶּחֶם לְבַדּוֹ יִחְיֶה הָאָדָם כִּי עַל כָּל מוֹצָא פִי ה׳ יִחְיֶה הָאָדָם.**

*Man does not live on bread alone, but man lives by whatever the Eternal decrees.*[55]

The ratio of physicality to spirituality present in food is dependent upon a crucial factor. To the extent that the food is sublimated for spiritual use will the food become primarily a spiritual, rather than a physical, entity. Consumption of such food will enhance a person's spiritual status, and our eating thus becomes elevated and distinct from the comparative consumption of fodder by beasts of the field.

---

54. *Yalkut Shimoni, Bereishith* 18.
55. *Devarim* 8:3.

Avraham possessed this ability to transform food from being mere physical sustenance into a spiritual entity. This was achieved through the *avodah*, the spiritual service, in which he laboured while the food was being prepared. The angels were thus able to eat. They ate, and yet they did not eat. They ate no physical food, but they did partake of the spiritual content which was dominant due to Avraham's preparations. The Midrash informs us of the incredible consequences of Avraham's exertion.

> לוּשִׁי וַעֲשִׂי עֻגוֹת. ר׳ יוֹנָה בְּשֵׁם ר׳ חָמָא בַּר חֲנִינָא הִיא מִדְבַּר סִין, הִיא מִדְבַּר אָלוּשׁ. מֵאֵיזֶה זְכוּת זָכוּ יִשְׂרָאֵל שֶׁנִּתַּן לָהֶם מָן בַּמִּדְבָּר. בִּזְכוּתוֹ שֶׁל אַבְרָהָם שֶׁאָמַר לוּשִׁי וַעֲשִׂי עֻגוֹת.
>
> *"Knead and make cakes." According to R. Yonah, in the name of R. Chama bar Chanina, it was the desert of Sin, the desert of Elush. By what merit was manna given to the Jewish People in the desert? In the merit of Avraham, who said, "Knead [in Hebrew, lushi] and make cakes."*[56]

The Jewish People received manna in a place named אָלוּשׁ, a name that indicates the merit that earned this Divine sustenance for them. It was due to Avraham's command to prepare sustenance for the angels who visited him.

Avraham elevated physical matter into spiritual nourishment. The manna, nourishment of an entirely spiritual nature, was thus bestowed in his merit. Further, it was this merit of Avraham that was pointed out by God to enable Moshe to take the Torah from Heaven and bring it into the realm of earth.

While ensconced on Mount Sinai, Moshe divorced himself from physicality. We are told: לֶחֶם לֹא אָכַלְתִּי וּמַיִם לֹא שָׁתִיתִי, Moshe abstained from food and drink. However, the Torah was not given to celestial beings. In order to bring the Torah down to this world, the merit of Avraham had to be invoked. The זְכוּת, the merit — or purity — that he transmitted to all subsequent generations, had to become manifest. The Torah is that which infuses every aspect of

56. *Bereishith Rabbah* 48:13.

our lives with spirituality. We are not required to live a monkish, ascetic existence; to eschew all physicality. Rather, it is our task to infuse everything in this physical world with spirituality, to return all that is corporeal to its Eternal source. Avraham demonstrated this ability, and it is in his merit that we received the Torah, and with it the ability to transform the world in which we live.

However, there is yet a further, deeper reason for the necessity of invoking Avraham's merit in order to receive the Torah. In the following passage we are presented with a description of an incident that transpired during the reign of King David:

**וַיִּקְרָא הַמֶּלֶךְ לַגִּבְעֹנִים וַיֹּאמֶר אֲלֵיהֶם וְהַגִּבְעֹנִים לֹא מִבְּנֵי יִשְׂרָאֵל הֵמָּה כִּי אִם מִיֶּתֶר הָאֱמֹרִי וּבְנֵי יִשְׂרָאֵל נִשְׁבְּעוּ לָהֶם וַיְבַקֵּשׁ שָׁאוּל לְהַכֹּתָם בְּקַנֹּאתוֹ לִבְנֵי יִשְׂרָאֵל וִיהוּדָה. וַיֹּאמֶר דָּוִד אֶל הַגִּבְעֹנִים מָה אֶעֱשֶׂה לָכֶם וּבַמָּה אֲכַפֵּר וּבָרְכוּ אֶת נַחֲלַת ה'.**[57]

During the reign of King David, the Givonim harboured resentment against the Jewish People over a certain matter. King David desired a means of placating the anger of the Givonim towards the Jewish People. In his attempt to appease them, he requested of them, וּבָרְכוּ אֶת נַחֲלַת ה' — "That you should bless the inheritance of God" [i.e., the Jewish nation], a phrase which is interpreted by Rashi as הִתְפַּלְלוּ עֲלֵיהֶם — "That you should pray for them." Why does Rashi suggest this alternate expression?

An incident recorded from the life of Rabbi Yisrael Salanter will aid our understanding of this subject. While traveling once by train, R. Yisrael was subjected to verbal abuse by a fellow passenger. When they arrived at their destination, the man who had been so rude to R. Yisrael discovered the identity of the person he had insulted. Shamefaced, the man sought out R. Yisrael to beg his forgiveness. R. Yisrael asked the man about his purpose in coming to the town, and received the reply that the man had been studying to become a ritual slaughterer, and had come there to be tested for certification, but had failed the examination. Upon hearing these words, R. Yisrael offered

57. *II Shemuel* 21:2, 3.

the man his own son-in-law as a study partner, to aid him through the rigorous demands of the test. The man then took the examination again and passed.

Returning to R. Yisrael, the man asked him why he had been so kind to him, particularly in light of the rude manner in which he had originally treated the Torah giant. R. Yisrael answered that he could have granted the man immediate forgiveness. However, some slight resentment would have remained in his heart. To expel any negative feelings which might have lingered, R. Yisrael exerted himself to act with *chessed*, loving kindness, towards the man. A feeling of closeness naturally ensued, facilitating a wholehearted forgiveness.

King David wanted the Givonim to fully forgive the Jewish People for any wrong which had been perpetrated against them. He realised, however, that true forgiveness can only be achieved by means of giving to the other person. Hence King David's request that the Givonim actively do something for the Jewish People. In this instance, the recommendation was that they bless the people. Required for a blessing, however, is a recipient. Further, a blessing possesses a potency affecting the subject of the blessing. The Givonim were a group of people with many dubious character traits, and King David wished to avoid any negative effects that could ensue from a blessing issuing from an impure source. ("Give me not your sting, nor your honey.") Thus we understand Rashi's substitution of the word הִתְפַּלְּלוּ, pray for them. Prayer for the Jewish People would be an act of giving to them, thus removing any traces of remaining animosity towards them. However, prayer does not need a recipient, thus the Jewish People would remain unaffected by the act of giving in which the Givonim would engage.

It is the act of giving that shatters the barriers between people and promotes a deep unity with others. This is illustrated further through the following incident:

תָּנוּ רַבָּנָן אַבְשָׁלוֹם בִּשְׂעָרוֹ מָרַד שֶׁנֶּאֱמַר וּכְאַבְשָׁלוֹם לֹא הָיָה אִישׁ יָפֶה בְּכָל יִשְׂרָאֵל... לְפִיכָךְ נִתְלָה בִּשְׂעָרוֹ שֶׁנֶּאֱמַר וַיִּקָּרֵא אַבְשָׁלוֹם לִפְנֵי עַבְדֵי דָוִד וְאַבְשָׁלוֹם רֹכֵב עַל הַפֶּרֶד וַיָּבֹא הַפֶּרֶד תַּחַת שׂוֹבֶךְ הָאֵלָה הַגְּדוֹלָה וַיֶּחֱזַק רֹאשׁוֹ בָאֵלָה וַיֻּתַּן בֵּין הַשָּׁמַיִם וּבֵין הָאָרֶץ וְהַפֶּרֶד אֲשֶׁר תַּחְתָּיו

עָבָר... תָּאנָא דְּבֵי רַבִּי יִשְׁמָעֵאל בְּאוֹתָהּ שָׁעָה נִבְקְעָה שְׁאוֹל מִתַּחְתָּיו. וַיִּרְגַּז הַמֶּלֶךְ וַיַּעַל עַל עֲלִיַּת הַשַּׁעַר וַיֵּבְךְּ וְכֹה אָמַר בְּלֶכְתּוֹ בְּנִי אַבְשָׁלוֹם בְּנִי בְנִי אַבְשָׁלוֹם וגו׳ הַנֵּי תְּמַנְיָא בְּנִי שִׁבְעָה דְּאַסְקֵיהּ מִשִּׁבְעָה מְדוֹרֵי גֵּיהִנָּם וְאִידָךְ אִיכָּא דְּאָמְרֵי דְּקָרִיב רֵישֵׁיהּ לְגַבֵּי גּוּפֵיהּ וְאִיכָּא דְּאָמְרֵי דְּאַתְיֵיהּ לְעָלְמָא דְּאָתֵי.

After his rebellion against his father David, Avshalom meets a bitter end. Avshalom possessed beautiful long hair, grown because of his status as a *nazir.*

> *...Riding on a mule, Avshalom passed under a tree, and his hair became entangled in the branches. Avshalom was unable to extricate himself, and was left dangling between Heaven and earth, as his mule continued without its burden. Suspended from the tree, Avshalom glimpsed Gehinnom opening beneath him.*
>
> *The King grew agitated, and began crying for his son. "My son! Avshalom! Avshalom, my son, my son!" David uttered the words, "My son!" seven times, which succeeded in raising Avshalom up from the seventh level of Gehinnom. The eighth "My son!" that he pronounced, according to one opinion, joined his head to his body. According to another opinion, the eighth utterance was sufficient to enable Avshalom to enter Gan Eden.*[58]

A philosophical question arises from consideration of the second opinion, which maintains that Avshalom was given a share in the next world upon the eighth utterance of "My son!" How can anyone bestow a share in the World to Come upon another? Everyone receives that which he deserves according to the labour undertaken in his own life. How could King David have given Avshalom a share in the World to Come?

Further, we are told that while suspended from the tree, and glimpsing the depths of Gehinnom, Avshalom engaged in repentance of his own volition. Why was his own repentance insufficient to save

---

58. *Yalkut Shimoni, Shemuel* 18.

him from entering Gehinnom?

While hanging by his hair, Avshalom purified himself from the sins committed between man and his Creator, and for these sins he attained forgiveness. However, there was still one barrier which precluded his entrance to Gan Eden. Avshalom had betrayed his father and rebelled against the monarchy, attempting to take the crown from David and place it on his own head. No repentance could completely eradicate this sin without wholehearted forgiveness on the part of King David. Avshalom, therefore, descended to Gehinnom. But through David's cries, in which he forgave his son in an ever deeper fashion, Avshalom slowly ascended from the depths to which he had plummeted. Once the barrier had been removed, Avshalom could enter Gan Eden through his own merits.

Thus we see the connection between the two achievements of the final cry of "My son!" A forgiveness of the calibre that David demonstrated did not stop at the seventh mention of "My son." David went further, entering the world of eight. Eight always denotes that which transcends the natural course of events, that which comes from a higher source. A superhuman forgiveness was required to extricate Avshalom from Gehinnom. This could only be achieved through an act of giving untainted by any personal interest. David engaged in such an act — a חֶסֶד שֶׁל אֱמֶת — that had the power to bring his son's body and head together. He thus removed any vestige of hurt from his heart, and allowed Avshalom to enter Gan Eden.

It is through giving that one achieves oneness with others, even uprooting schisms and contention between fellow men. It is giving which cultivates love. As Rabbi Samson Raphael Hirsch explains, אַהֲבָה, love, comes from the root letters הַב, meaning "to give."

However, giving to one's fellow has an effect which is even more profound. In the tangible, physical world in which we live, God's Presence is obscured. His Oneness is subject to contradictions, the most striking of which is man himself. אֱמֶת מַלְכֵּנוּ אֶפֶס זוּלָתוֹ: With these words we declare that nothing but God exists. Yet an utterance of this conviction involves "my" mind to think, "my" lips to articulate, "my" tongue to utter. There is an "I" involved, a self, a being. My own sense of self implies that there is something apart from God. There is ego, psyche. There is me. A feeling of selfhood is one of the deepest feelings within man. To lessen the contradiction to אֶפֶס זוּלָתוֹ, man is required to lessen his sense of self, and to the greatest extent possible, nullify himself before the Creator, thereby attaching himself to real existence.

Moshe said, מָה אָנוּ — "What are we?" concerning himself and Aharon, indicating that although reduced, some vestige of self remained. The bulk of the ego was diminished, yet some trace of "מָה" remained. Thus, the angels' complaint: מָה אֱנוֹשׁ כִּי תִזְכְּרֶנּוּ — "What is man that you should remember him?" They rejected the option of bestowing the Torah upon man, for man would always retain that trace of "what"; he would never be able to manifest Divine light in its fullness, the shadow of ego always preventing transparent vision.

Moshe's mission in Heaven was to counter their argument and succeed in bringing the Torah to the people on earth. It is for this reason that we find he adopted the countenance of Avraham, who demonstrated that special quality exclusive to humankind. This is elaborated upon by the Maharal in the following excerpt:

> כִּי הָאָדָם יֵשׁ לוֹ דְּבֵקוּת אֶל הש"י דִּכְתִיב וְאַתֶּם הַדְּבֵקִים בַּה' אֱלֹקֵיכֶם, וּמִדָּה זֹאת לֹא שַׁיָּךְ בַּמַּלְאָכִים. וּבֵאַרְנוּ דָּבָר זֶה בְּמָקוֹם אַחֵר כִּי הַדְּבִיקָה הִיא מִצַּד הָאַהֲבָה שֶׁבִּשְׁבִיל זֶה דָּבַק בּוֹ ית', וְלֹא שַׁיָּךְ אַהֲבָה בַּמַּלְאָכִים רַק יִרְאָה וּכְמוֹ שֶׁאָמַרְנוּ עוֹשִׂים בְּאֵימָה וּבְיִרְאָה רְצוֹן קוֹנֵיהֶם, אֲבָל הָאַהֲבָה לֹא תִמְצָא אֵצֶל הַמַּלְאָכִים. וּמִפְּנֵי כִּי הַקְּלִיטָה הִיא הַדְּבֵקוּת בְּמַה שֶׁקּוֹלֵט אוֹתוֹ וְדָבָר זֶה לֹא שַׁיָּךְ בַּמַּלְאָךְ.
>
> *It is only man who can achieve the level upon which he is considered to cleave to God, a status which is impossible to confer upon angels... for man alone has the quality of serving God with love. Angels serve God only through fear, as it is written "They do the will of their Creator with awe and trepidation." Angels have no connection to the quality of serving God with love.*[59]

---

59. *Chiddushei Aggadoth, Makkoth* 3, 4.

Angels are unable to serve God with love, for within their sphere of existence, no possibility of giving exists. The essence of the angel is his mission, he can not add or subtract; he carries out his mission in its entirety, but no more, no less. Inherent in love is the bestowing on others of more than one is obliged to do. In contrast, man has the possibility and the ability to engage in giving. Man lives within a society where each person is deficient until he receives from others. It follows that an ideal civilization must necessarily involve giving to one another. It is for this reason that love is created.

As explained, giving has not only the utilitarian value of creating a dynamic society, but contains a sublime value, as demonstrated by the following.

**אַחֲרֵי ה' אֱלֹקֵיכֶם תֵּלֵכוּ וְאֹתוֹ תִירָאוּ וְאֶת מִצְוֹתָיו תִּשְׁמֹרוּ וּבְקֹלוֹ תִשְׁמָעוּ וְאֹתוֹ תַעֲבֹדוּ וּבוֹ תִדְבָּקוּן.**

*You shall follow [the ways of] the Eternal, your God, and fear Him, and you shall keep His commandments, heed His voice, serve Him and adhere to [His ways].*[60]

The Gemara elaborates on this commandment of following His ways.

אַחֲרֵי ה' אֱלֹקֵיכֶם תֵּלֵכוּ. אָמַר ר' חָמָא בַּר חֲנִינָא מַאי דִּכְתִיב אַחֲרֵי ה' אֱלֹקֵיכֶם תֵּלֵכוּ, וְכִי אֶפְשָׁר לָאָדָם לְהַלֵּךְ אַחַר הַשְּׁכִינָה וַהֲלֹא כְּבָר נֶאֱמַר כִּי ה' אֱלֹקֶיךָ אֵשׁ אֹכְלָה הוּא. אֶלָּא לְהַלֵּךְ אַחַר מִדּוֹתָיו שֶׁל הקב"ה מָה הוּא מַלְבִּישׁ עֲרוּמִים אַף אַתָּה הַלְבֵּשׁ עֲרוּמִים, מָה הוּא בִּקֵּר חוֹלִים אַף אַתָּה בַּקֵּר חוֹלִים, מָה הוּא נִיחֵם אֲבֵלִים אַף אַתָּה נַחֵם אֲבֵלִים, מָה הוּא קָבַר מֵתִים, אַף אַתָּה קְבוֹר מֵתִים.

*"You shall follow the Eternal, your God..." Is it possible for man to walk after the Divine Presence? Is it not written that the Divine Presence is compared to a consuming fire? But the injunction to follow God means to imitate His ways. Just as God clothes the naked, so should you clothe the naked. Just as God visits the sick, so should you visit the sick. Just as God*

60. *Devarim* 13:5.

*comforts mourners, so should you comfort mourners. Just as God buries the dead, so should you bury the dead.*[61]

With these words we are enjoined to imitate God, particularly in the sphere of loving kindness. By giving of oneself to others, one achieves proximity to God. This has the further benefit of reducing the contradiction to God's Oneness that results from one's own sense of self. For man is naturally egocentric, and intensely feels his own presence as the centre of his universe. By giving to others, man reduces his sense of self, that which obscures the Uniqueness of God. By giving, man diffuses and uses his selfhood for the benefit of others; selflessness thus taking the place of ego.

The Yerushalmi depicts how this behaviour creates a feeling of solidarity and unity among all Jews. The parable is brought of a butcher, who, in the process of cutting meat, accidentally cuts his left hand with his right hand. Obviously, the left hand will not attempt to take revenge upon the right hand, for they are of one body.

At root level, the Jewish People are one. Herein lies the fallacy of revenge and dissension. Negative behaviour is directed to another limb of the same body. Intellectually, this comparison can be easily grasped. However, the route to an internalization of this idea lies in giving. Through giving, each person sees himself in the other, and the entire Jewish People can truly be compared to numerous limbs of one body. One's own personal interests, one's own sense of self is thus reduced, and the truth of אֶפֶס זוּלָתוֹ, that there is no existence apart from God, shines forth with clarity. Closeness to God can thus be attained.

Moshe said concerning himself that he was מָה — what? — indicating the presence of something, some shadow of self. Wresting the Torah away from the angels, he adopted the countenance of Avraham. He identified with the spiritual legacy which Avraham had bestowed, the quality of giving. For it is through this quality that man can receive a Torah which will generate a world dedicated

61. *Sotah* 14a.

only to the spiritual and sublime. It was thus that Moshe countered the angels' argument, and succeeded in bringing the Torah down to the Jewish People.

Standing at the foot of Mount Sinai, the Jewish People are described as being כְּאִישׁ אֶחָד בְּלֵב אֶחָד — "Like one man with one heart."[62] Giving to others, an outpouring of loving kindness, was what generated the "one man." Multifarious limbs became one body, unified in brotherhood. The "one heart," a unity of profundity, was produced through the common aspiration of the entire nation. All accepted the Torah; all accepted a life dedicated to service of God. A uniform purpose bound individuals together to form a nation, to form a society based upon giving, based upon attaining closeness with God. Let us clothe ourselves with the legacy of our forefathers, like one man with one heart.

62. Rashi on *Shemoth* 19:2.

# MISHPATIM

THIS WEEK'S PARASHAH contains the positive precept to lend money to those in need. Concerning this commandment the Midrash states the following:

> אִם כֶּסֶף תַּלְוֶה אֶת עַמִּי. הֲדָא הוּא דִכְתִיב יֵשׁ רָעָה חוֹלָה רָאִיתִי תַּחַת הַשָּׁמֶשׁ עֹשֶׁר שָׁמוּר לִבְעָלָיו לְרָעָתוֹ וְאָבַד הָעֹשֶׁר הַהוּא בְּעִנְיַן רָע. אַשְׁרֵי אָדָם שֶׁהוּא עוֹמֵד בְּנִסְיוֹנוֹ שֶׁאֵין בְּרִיָּה שֶׁאֵין הקב"ה מְנַסֶּה אוֹתָהּ. הֶעָשִׁיר מְנַסֵּהוּ אִם תְּהֵא יָדוֹ פְּתוּחָה לָעֲנִיִּים. וּמְנַסֶּה הֶעָנִי אִם יָכֹל לְקַבֵּל יִסּוּרִין וְאֵינוֹ כּוֹעֵס שֶׁנֶּאֱמַר וַעֲנִיִּים מְרוּדִים תָּבִיא בָּיִת. וְאִם עָמַד הֶעָשִׁיר בְּנִסְיוֹנוֹ וְעוֹשֶׂה צְדָקוֹת הֲרֵי הוּא אוֹכֵל מָמוֹנוֹ בעוה"ז וְהַקֶּרֶן קַיֶּמֶת לוֹ לעוה"ב והקב"ה מַצִּילוֹ מִדִּינָהּ שֶׁל גֵּיהִנָּם שֶׁנֶּאֱמַר אַשְׁרֵי מַשְׂכִּיל אֶל דָּל בְּיוֹם רָעָה יְמַלְּטֵהוּ ה'.

> *"When you lend money to My people" [Shemoth 22:24]. ...God tests all creatures. The rich He tests whether or not their hands will be open to provide for those in need. The poverty stricken are faced with the test of accepting their suffering without rancour.... If a rich person overcomes his challenge and passes the test, he will benefit both in this world and in the next, and God will save him from the judgment of Gehinnom. As it is written, "Fortunate is the one who helps a pauper, on the day of evil God will save him" [Tehillim 41:2].*[63]

The "day of evil" referred to here is the day of the Final Judgment. At the end of one's life, when one is brought to reckoning, the performance of a positive command has the potency to save one from Gehinnom. It follows that one who does not perform a positive commandment will not be saved from this fate.

---

63. *Shemoth Rabbah* 31:2.

An awesome principle is derived from this Midrash. Gehinnom is given not only to evil-doers and wicked individuals, but also to those who do not actively pursue the correct course of action, and fail to fulfill their spiritual potential. In this case, a man possessed money, the potential to give charity, and yet refrained from doing so. In the future, Gehinnom will be his lot. Let us elaborate upon this frightening principle.

Our Sages said that the world endures upon three forms of Divine worship. The first is the pulsating study of Torah, the second is *avodah*, the bringing of sacrificial offerings, and the third pillar is גְּמִילוּת חֲסָדִים, performing acts of kindness.[64] Today, we substitute prayer for offerings, and it is this which now constitutes the pillar of *avodah*, service.

The Maharal explains why the term *avodah* refers primarily to the act of bringing sacrifices by addressing the question of why sacrifices are brought. Obviously, God does not benefit from the offerings. To propose this is tantamount to heresy, for it implies deficiency instead of perfection; it supposes that God could, Heaven forbid, change in some way, from being "less satisfied" to "more satisfied." The Maharal explains, rather, that the act of bringing sacrifices is the act of dedicating oneself to God. In fact, the slaughtered animal is considered to be in place of man himself. Although one who brings sacrifices does not give up his own life, he does forfeit some of his money or material possessions, and this is considered as if he indeed consecrated a part of himself to the Almighty.

This is the explanation of the term *avodah*, service. A servant subjugates himself completely to his master. Money and self: all are dedicated to a higher authority. By offering sacrifices, we demonstrate our complete self-nullification in the face of our Master. All that we own is surrendered to Him. Thus it is called service; it is service we demonstrate in bringing sacrifices.

*Avodah* has a further feature, a corollary of the above-mentioned point. *Avodah* teaches us of the Unity of God, that there is none

---

64. *Pirkei Avoth* 1:2.

but Him. Any external entity that exists is a tangible denial of this axiom, for it negates His Oneness by implying that there is something apart from God. Rabbi Dessler elaborates upon the axiom, אֱמֶת מַלְכֵּנוּ אֶפֶס זוּלָתוֹ — "True is our King, there is none but Him." In this fundamental statement is contained a vital tenet of faith: the Unity of God. We declare that there is none but Him, for He is One and nothing besides Him can exist. Any "other" existence is precluded by His Unity. By bringing our money, we proclaim that all belongs to God in reality. Returning everything to its source and real existence, we testify to His Oneness.

Rabbi Dessler enumerates three main contradictions which we experience in this world which tarnish the gleaming clarity of God's Oneness:

1. An utterance of this conviction involves "my" mind to think, "my" lips to articulate, "my" tongue to utter. There is an "I" involved, a self, a being. My own sense of self, of אֲנָכִיּוּת, implies that there is something apart from God. There is ego, psyche; there is me. One's own person is the primary denial of God's Oneness.
2. Not only do we exist, we have a deep desire to preserve life, and to extend our existence *ad infinitum*. We yearn for eternity, for perpetuation of self, in essence seeking to maintain a constant denial of God's Oneness.
3. Man desires to amass wealth and possessions. He seeks to extend his own self through the power conferred upon him by his money. The existence of self, of an entity outside of God, is thus augmented. The darkness becomes ever more pervasive.

Corresponding to the denial engendered by these three points, we make a threefold statement in our recitation of the *Shema*, in our affirmation of God's Unity and Sovereignty. Here we avow to serve God in three ways:

בְּכָל לְבָבְךָ — With all your heart. We take the heart, seat of our personal desires, and pledge it to God. We nullify our own wishes, yielding the self in service of our Creator.

This is demonstrated in the following Midrash.

א"ר לֵוִי שִׁשָּׁה דְּבָרִים מְשַׁמְּשִׁין אֶת הָאָדָם. שְׁלֹשָׁה בִּרְשׁוּתוֹ וּשְׁלֹשָׁה אֵינָן בִּרְשׁוּתוֹ. הָעַיִן וְהָאֹזֶן וְהַחֹטֶם שֶׁלֹּא בִּרְשׁוּתוֹ. חָמֵי מַה דְּלָא בָּעֵי. שָׁמַע מַה דְּלָא בָּעֵי. מֵרִיחַ מַה דלָא בָּעֵי. הַפֶּה וְהַיָּד וְהָרֶגֶל בִּרְשׁוּתוֹ. אִין בָּעֵי הוּא לָעֵי בְּאוֹרָיְתָא אִין בָּעֵי לִשָּׁנָא בִּישָׁא אִין בָּעֵי מְחָרֵף וּמְגַדֵּף. הַיָּד אִין בָּעֵי הוּא עָבִיד מִצְוָתָא אִין בָּעֵי הוּא גָנִיב וְאִין בָּעֵי הוּא הוּא קָטִיל. הָרֶגֶל אִין בָּעֵי הוּא אָזִיל לְבָתֵּי טַרְטְסִיאוֹת וּלְבָתֵּי קִרְקְסֵיאוֹת. וְאִין בָּעֵי הוּא אָזִיל לְבָתֵּי כְּנֵסִיּוֹת וּלְבָתֵּי מִדְרָשׁוֹת. וּבְשָׁעָה שֶׁהוּא זוֹכֶה הקב"ה עוֹשֶׂה אוֹתָן שֶׁבִּרְשׁוּתוֹ שֶׁלֹּא בִּרְשׁוּתוֹ.

*Man is served by six different faculties, of which three are within his dominion and three are out of his control. The eye, ear, and nose are not in a person's control. One can witness sights which one does not want to see. One can hear that which one would prefer to avoid. One smells scents without a conscious decision to do so. However, the hands, the feet, and the mouth are within a person's control. The mouth can be used to utter words of Torah and holiness, or for evil speech and blasphemy. The hand can be a vital tool in the performance of mitzvoth, or can be employed in theft and robbery. One can walk with one's feet to theaters and circuses, or one can walk to shul and the study hall. The means for which a person utilises these faculties is within man's own free will and control. However, if man has special merit, God will transfer those limbs which are within his own dominion to being outside his control.*[65]

This Midrash teaches us that it is a זְכוּת, a merit, not to have control. This is because control is the companion and outcome of independence. A chosen course of action is born of a conscious decision, and one's sense of control, of self, is thereby fortified, thus further concealing the truth of אֶפֶס זוּלָתוֹ. A person feels that there is something apart from God, namely, oneself. Loss of control minimizes one's sense of self, one's feeling of independence, and

---

65. *Bereishith Rabbah* 67:3.

thus lessens the contradiction to אֶפֶס זוּלָתוֹ that one's own body and feelings present.

Although while we dwell in this transient world the contradictions will always exist, they can be minimized. The less we expand ourselves, in money, power, time, and ego, the more space can be permeated with truth. It is therefore a merit when things are outside of our own control.

וּבְכָל נַפְשְׁךָ — The yearning for Eternal life is the second contradiction to אֶפֶס זוּלָתוֹ. The antidote for this is contained in our Sages' explanation on these words: אֲפִילוּ הוּא נוֹטֵל אֶת נַפְשְׁךָ — "even if He takes your life." A Jew is prepared to sacrifice his very life in implementation of his Creator's will. The embodiment of this level of dedication was Rabbi Akiva, whose serenity in the midst of undergoing brutal torture by the Romans was marveled at by his students. Rabbi Akiva's reply: "I have been waiting my entire life to fulfill the mitzvah of serving God בְּכָל נַפְשְׁךָ — "with all your soul.' Now I have been given the opportunity; should I not rejoice?" For Rabbi Akiva, these two small words were pivotal. He hearkened to those familiar words which are verbalized each day. He removed the second means through which God's Unity is obscured.

וּבְכָל מְאֹדֶךָ — Our Sages say that this refers to מָמוֹנְךָ, one's material possessions. Transferring our material possessions into God's dominion rectifies the sense of expansion which added wealth and power confer upon a person. We reduce our sense of self, and lessen the shadow of darkness that we cast.

It is through these means that we declare שְׁמַע יִשְׂרָאֵל ה' אֱלֹקֵינוּ ה' אֶחָד, God is One; there is nothing but Him. Our Divine service consists of our efforts to lessen the contradictions to this truth, to reduce the self and thus raise the banner of the Almighty's absolute Kingship. We strive to constantly move nearer to the fulfillment of this sacred duty.

The Maharal elaborates on this theme in reference to the concept of sacrificial offerings.

> ...כִּי הַתְּמִידִים שֶׁצִּוָּה ה' יִתְבָּרֵךְ לְהוֹדִיעַ כִּי הָעוֹלָם הַזֶּה הוּא שָׁב וּמִתְקָרֵב אֶל ה' יִתְבָּרֵךְ וְאִם לֹא הָיָה שָׁב אֶל הַשי"ת לֹא הָיָה אֶל הָעוֹלָם

קִיּוּם בְּעַצְמוֹ, רַק שֶׁהוּא שָׁב אֶל השי״ת וְלֹא נִבְרָא הָעוֹלָם שֶׁיִּהְיֶה לְעַצְמוֹ... הָעוֹלָם הַזֶּה כְּמוֹ שֶׁהֻשְׁפַּע מִן השי״ת כָּךְ שָׁב אֶל עִלָּתוֹ כִּי הוּא תּוֹלֶה בְּעִלָּתוֹ וּבָזֶה הוּא שָׁב אֵלָיו יִתְבָּרֵךְ, וּלְפִיכָךְ יֵשׁ לָאָדָם לְהַקְרִיב קָרְבָּן אֶל השי״ת כִּי הַקָּרְבָּן הוּא הֲשָׁבָה וְהִתְקָרְבוּת אֶל השי״ת.[66]

Prayer was instituted in place of sacrifices, for in essence both forms of Divine worship perform the same function. Sacrifices were instituted to demonstrate to us that this world will all return to God. This Divine service expresses our role as עֲבָדִים, servants to the King. All that we have is His. Independent existence is inconceivable.

Were the world not to return to its source, it could have no continued existence. For physicality has no independent being, enduring only to the extent that it continuously receives existence from a higher Source. We say in our prayers that God is מְחַדֵּשׁ בְּטוּבוֹ בְּכָל יוֹם תָּמִיד מַעֲשֵׂה בְרֵאשִׁית, that He, in His goodness, continuously renews the cosmos. Creation *ex nihilo* was not a one-time event. Rather, it is the state of the world in which we live: a constant re-creation. Breaking a connection with God, therefore, is a fatal error. For, without His constant bestowal of life we cannot exist; severance of our relationship with Him is therefore cutting oneself off from life itself. When offering sacrifices, one brings one's possessions back to their source, back to life itself. We thus testify through our sacrifices that indeed, אֶפֶס זוּלָתוֹ. We emphatically declare that without God, there is nothing. There is no existence but Him.

The *Me'am Loez* on *Koheleth* elaborates upon this concept:

בּוֹטֵחַ בְּעָשְׁרוֹ הוּא יִפֹּל וְכֶעָלֶה צַדִּיקִים יִפְרָחוּ. שֶׁהַבּוֹטֵחַ בְּעָשְׁרוֹ וְלִבּוֹ מִתְגָּאֶה, לֹא רַק עָשְׁרוֹ יֵלֵךְ לְטִמְיוֹן אֶלָּא הוּא עַצְמוֹ יִפֹּל, וְלָכֵן נֶאֱמַר הוּא יִפֹּל. וּכְמַעֲשֶׂה שֶׁל אוֹתוֹ עָשִׁיר שֶׁהָיָה לְאֶחָד דִּין עִמּוֹ וְשָׁלַח רַב וְהִזְמִינוֹ לַדִּין. וְאָמַר, הַאִם נָאֶה לִי לֵילֵךְ וּלְהִתְדַּיֵּן עִם פְּלוֹנִי, שֶׁאֲפִלּוּ אִם יָבוֹאוּ עֲרָבִים עִם גְּמַלִּים לֹא יוּכְלוּ לִטְעֹן מַפְתְּחוֹת אוֹצְרוֹתַי. אָמַר רַב, לָמָּה הוּא מִתְגָּאֶה בְּמַה שֶּׁאֵינוֹ שֶׁלּוֹ. תָּבֹא מְאֵרָה בִּנְכָסָיו. וּמִיָּד יָצָא צַו מֵאֵת הַמַּלְכוּת שֶׁיָּחֳרַם הוּא וְכָל רְכוּשׁוֹ לַמֶּלֶךְ. בָּא לִפְנֵי רַב וְהִתְחַנֵּן בְּפָנָיו שֶׁיַּצִּיל אֶת נַפְשׁוֹ. הִתְפַּלֵּל עָלָיו וְנִצּוֹל. מִכָּאן רוֹאִים שֶׁהָעֹשֶׁר עָלוּל לְהַפִּיל אֶת בְּעָלָיו לְבוֹר שַׁחַת אִם הוּא מִתְגָּאֶה בּוֹ.

66. *Nethiv HaAvodah,* Ch. 3.

*The verse in Mishlei states, "One who places his trust in his wealth, he will fall..." This verse implies not merely that one's wealth is forfeited, but also that the owner of these riches himself will be destroyed through his pride. An illustration of this is found in the following incident: A wealthy man was summoned to court by Rav [the Torah leader of the period], concerning a monetary claim submitted by a simple Jew. The wealthy Jew declared, "Is it fitting that I should go and be judged against this nobody? Why, a caravan of camels couldn't even carry the keys to my storehouses!" Hearing this, Rav responded, "Why does he take pride in what does not belong to him? Let a curse come upon his possessions." Immediately, a royal edict was issued, confiscating the man's wealth and decreeing against his very life. Distraught, the man turned to Rav, who prayed on his behalf, whereupon he was saved. From this incident it is clear that wealth can cast one to the depths if it becomes a source of pride.*[67]

We can understand the lesson of this incident in light of the Maharal's elucidation of Gehinnom. He explains that one conception of Gehinnom is הֶעְדֵר, lack of existence. The common expression is that shrouds have no pockets; material possessions do not accompany a person on his final journey. In the next world, physicality is nothing — void, vain, empty. If one's life has been spent immersed in physicality, what can be waiting for him in the Eternal world? If one takes pride in one's wealth or possessions, attributing it all to himself and identifying closely with it, its inevitable dissipation when he reaches the reality, the World to Come, will mean the atrophy of one's very self. The only thing which grants a person Eternal existence is that which contains the seed of eternity therein. Mitzvoth, acts of kindness, charity, and Torah are all reality, and one who is involved in them will continue to live when the environment is one of reality. One bereft of spirituality bears nothingness. And this is what he is faced with in the world of truth. Nothingness, absence of existence,

67. *Me'am Loez, Koheleth* 5:13.

is one of the conceptions of Gehinnom.

We can now understand the Midrash cited at the beginning of this chapter, which implies that Gehinnom is received not only for deeds of evil, but also for abstention from good. Good deeds are what give a person Eternal existence, for true existence (closeness to God, the Source of all existence) is inherent within the action. When the day of reckoning comes, and a person, proud in his possession of material goods, has avoided becoming a generous beneficiary, he will be consigned to Gehinnom as a natural consequence of his behaviour. His money has thereby become an empty shell of nothingness, instead of a thing of eternity. His expansion of self, facilitated by his wealth, has heightened the contradiction to אֶפֶס זוּלָתוֹ. He has moved away from reality into oblivion. His money and material possessions have become a vacuum.

A nation-wide expression of עֲבָדוּת, service, occurred at this period of the year, when at the time of the Temple, each person donated half a shekel to fund the sacrificial offerings. Each person dedicated something that belonged to himself, taking a piece of "contradiction" and returning it to God. Instead of the expansion of self that material possessions engender, every coin became an expression of the Unity of God. בְּכָל מְאֹדֶךָ — with all your property — the antidote to a negation of God's Oneness, was here being implemented. The money was used for the *tamid* offering, the prototype sacrifice, and thus it was demonstrated how all belongs to the Almighty through the return of physicality to its Source.

Further, each individual did not bring a complete piece, but donated only half a coin. The message of incompleteness was being conveyed here. A person is never independent. The illusion of independence is the nothingness that money imbues in a person. Paradoxically, the sensation of being, of self, is that which results in void and nothingness. It is only by dedicating one's ego and one's possessions to eternity while in a life of transience that one can gain true existence. Self-negation causes being. Pride, the illusion of independence, severs one from the Source of life and true existence. The constant bestowal of life and blessing from the Source is thus lost. One's money and one's self become nothing, a hollow emptiness echoing through this world and the next.

Although this frightening prospect appears relevant only to one bestowed with material wealth, in reality it applies to one in possession of wealth of any description. One can be physically rich, in possession of strength and might. One can be endowed with influence and power. All gifts and qualities can be utilised for other people's good and for one's own Divine service. One thus translates that which would become ephemeral wisps of nothingness into something of reality, of eternity.

In connection to this the Meiri addresses the seemingly inappropriate juxtaposition of phrases in the verse: וְאָהַבְתָּ לְרֵעֲךָ כָּמוֹךָ אֲנִי ה׳ — "You shall love your fellow as yourself, I am God."[68] He explains that the greatest expression of one's love towards another person is to teach him אֲנִי ה׳, the existence of the Almighty. Enlightening others, revealing the sublime and beautiful purpose of our lives, is the greatest gift one can ever bestow. One in possession of spiritual wealth, one endowed with the ability to spread the light of Godliness, must utilise his riches. While possession of money places a person in a position of responsibility, spiritual currency places the same obligation upon a person. Failure to use this prosperity consigns one to the void of Gehinnom. Existence has been transformed to nothingness, potential life into a vacuum. The consequences of restraint are chilling.

Let us all expend every effort to translate riches of all types into eternity. Let us rid ourselves of a life and existence which are in reality void, and transform ourselves into the nothingness which is truly everything. It is then that the light shall shine.

---

68. *Vayikra* 19:18.

# TERUMAH

IN OUR PARASHAH we find the following instruction:

וְעָשׂוּ לִי מִקְדָּשׁ וְשָׁכַנְתִּי בְּתוֹכָם.

*They shall make a Sanctuary for Me [so that] I may dwell among them.*[69]

Seforno comments that this instruction from God was prompted by the Jewish People's sin in making the Golden Calf. It is a symptom, as it were, of the people's spiritual disease: before the sin, when they had worshipped God wholeheartedly, there had been no need for a fixed place of worship for Him to dwell in their midst. His Presence had been among them and over them, in all places and at all times. As we find earlier:

מִזְבַּח אֲדָמָה תַּעֲשֶׂה לִּי וְזָבַחְתָּ עָלָיו אֶת עֹלֹתֶיךָ... בְּכָל הַמָּקוֹם אֲשֶׁר אַזְכִּיר אֶת שְׁמִי אָבוֹא אֵלֶיךָ וּבֵרַכְתִּיךָ.

*An earthen altar you shall make for Me and you shall offer on it your burnt offerings... in every place where My Name is mentioned, I shall come to you and bless you.*[70]

All this had been before the people sinned in worshipping the Golden Calf. Afterwards, the manifestation of God's Presence was restricted, concentrated only in the *Mishkan* that the people had to build. Everything in the relationship between God and man became formalized, fixed, and limited in place, time, and manner of worship, in contrast to the rich all-abundance of His Presence with which Yisrael had formerly been blessed. The idyllic state of things, in

69. *Shemoth* 25:8, 9.
70. *Shemoth* 20:21.

which the whole of Yisrael was to be a nation of priests, a holy people rejoicing in the ever-available Presence of God, had been rejected by the people themselves in their creation of the Golden Calf. Let us discover, then, the essential element of sin that was involved in the Golden Calf, that necessitated the withdrawal of the Divine Presence from the world at large and its concentration in one particular place.

Our Sages inform us of a fundamental connection between the sin of the Golden Calf and the original sin of Adam. Thus by studying Adam's downfall, we may be able to gain insight into the essential flaw that underscored the sin of the Golden Calf.

> מִפְּנֵי מָה עוֹבְדֵי כּוֹכָבִים מְזוֹהֲמִין? שֶׁלֹּא עָמְדוּ עַל הַר סִינַי. שֶׁבְּשָׁעָה שֶׁבָּא הַנָּחָשׁ עַל חַוָּה הֵטִיל בָּהּ זוּהֲמָא. יִשְׂרָאֵל שֶׁעָמְדוּ עַל הַר סִינַי פָּסְקָה זֻהֲמָתָן. עוֹבְדֵי כּוֹכָבִים שֶׁלֹּא עָמְדוּ עַל הַר סִינַי לֹא פָּסְקָה זֻהֲמָתָן.
>
> *Why are the nations of the world tainted? Because they were not present at Mount Sinai. When the snake came to Chavah he injected her with impurity; when Yisrael stood at Mount Sinai, their impurity was dispelled, whereas the nations of the world did not stand at Mount Sinai, and their impurity was not dispelled.*[71]

Adam's sin caused a taint, an impurity, to be introduced into the world. The universal atmosphere, once entirely pure, was now sullied by sin, having an immediate effect on all creation. People, their ideas, and their behaviour, were all spiritually polluted.

However, with the gift of the Torah at Sinai, the Jewish nation were elevated to such high levels of sanctity that they were lifted above the realm of this toxic atmosphere, attaining the stature of Adam before the sin. It is for this reason that the Gemara states that the nations of the world are "impure," for they, unlike Yisrael, failed to raise themselves above the contamination, choosing to remain in their lives of corruption.

---

71. *Shabbath* 146a.

There is another Gemara which relates in a similar manner, that when Yisrael made their famous declaration of, "We will do and we will listen" at Mount Sinai,[72] 600,000 angels descended from Heaven and adorned each individual of the nation with two crowns. One crown corresponded to the declaration of נַעֲשֶׂה, "We will do," and one corresponded to נִשְׁמַע, "We will hear." However, when the Jewish People sinned with the Golden Calf, angels of destruction descended and removed the crowns.

These crowns hint to that level of spiritual perfection attained by the nation at Sinai. Their subsequent removal reveals to us that with the sin of the Golden Calf, the spiritual defilement initially brought into the world by Adam, once again found its place in the world. The level Yisrael achieved, equivalent to the level of Adam before the sin, was now lost. They once again became impure, albeit not to the same extent as previously.

The sin of the Golden Calf is thus seen to be, at root, a repetition of the quintessential sin: that of Adam. In time, worlds apart; in essence, one and the same. It remains to investigate the underlying cause of these two sins. And when this has been revealed, we must ask: is it at all possible to rise once again above the filth? Does Yisrael have a realistic hope of once again elevating themselves, individually and nationally, to the sublime level of Adam before the sin? Is there any means by which we can regain those crowns that were lost?

Our Sages reveal to us the clue. There is one channel through which we can obtain the precious crowns, and that is through proper observance of the Sabbath. Let us then analyse and gain insight as to how and why the Sabbath imbues a person with the holiness that he is lacking, how it aids him in scaling the heights of perfection.

כָּל הַמְעַנֵּג אֶת הַשַּׁבָּת נוֹתְנִין לוֹ נַחֲלָה בְּלִי מְצָרִים, שֶׁנֶּאֱמַר "אָז תִּתְעַנַּג עַל ה׳ וְהִרְכַּבְתִּיךָ עַל בָּמֳתֵי אָרֶץ וְהַאֲכַלְתִּיךָ נַחֲלַת יַעֲקֹב אָבִיךָ". לֹא כְּאַבְרָהָם שֶׁכָּתוּב בּוֹ "קוּם הִתְהַלֵּךְ בָּאָרֶץ לְאָרְכָּהּ וגו׳". וְלֹא כְּיִצְחָק שֶׁכָּתוּב בּוֹ "כִּי לְךָ וּלְזַרְעֲךָ אֶתֵּן אֶת כָּל הָאֲרָצֹת הָאֵל". אֶלָּא כְּיַעֲקֹב שֶׁכָּתוּב בּוֹ "וּפָרַצְתָּ יָמָּה וָקֵדְמָה וְצָפֹנָה וָנֶגְבָּה".

72. *Shemoth* 24:7.

*Whoever delights in the Sabbath will merit a portion without boundaries, as it states, "Then you will delight in God, and He will ride you on the heights of the land, and He will give you to eat the portion of your father Ya'akov." Not like the limited portion of Avraham, nor like the limited portion of Yitzchak, but like the portion of Ya'akov, who was promised [Bereishith 28:14], "You will expand to the west, east, north, and south."*[73]

There is a condition attached to this promise given to Ya'akov:

**אִם תָּשִׁיב מִשַּׁבָּת רַגְלֶךָ עֲשׂוֹת חֲפָצֶיךָ בְּיוֹם קָדְשִׁי וְקָרָאתָ לַשַּׁבָּת עֹנֶג לִקְדוֹשׁ ה' מְכֻבָּד וְכִבַּדְתּוֹ מֵעֲשׂוֹת דְּרָכֶיךָ מִמְּצוֹא חֶפְצְךָ וְדַבֵּר דָּבָר. אָז תִּתְעַנַּג עַל ה' וְהִרְכַּבְתִּיךָ עַל בָּמֳתֵי אָרֶץ וְהַאֲכַלְתִּיךָ נַחֲלַת יַעֲקֹב אָבִיךָ כִּי פִּי ה' דִּבֵּר.**

*If you restrain your foot because of the Sabbath, from performing your affairs on My holy day, and you call the Sabbath a delight... and you honour it by not pursuing your own affairs... then you will delight in God.... and I will give you to eat the heritage of Ya'akov our father.*[74]

The *Metsudath David* explains the various phrases used in describing the terms of the condition:

תָּשִׁיב מִשַּׁבָּת רַגְלֶךָ — Restraining one's foot. This refers to one who comes to the end of the *techum* — the 2000 cubit boundary beyond which it is forbidden to traverse — and does not walk any further, simply for the reason that it is forbidden to do so on the Sabbath.

עֲשׂוֹת חֲפָצֶיךָ — One refrains from doing weekday activities on the Sabbath that conflict with the laws pertaining to Sabbath observance.

מִמְּצוֹא חֶפְצְךָ וְדַבֵּר דָּבָר — One guards oneself from speaking forbidden speech on the Sabbath, such as the making of calculations or discussing business matters.

---

73. *Shabbath* 118a.
74. *Yeshayah* 58:13.

If these conditions are met, one deserves the unlimited reward of a "portion without boundary." The fulfillment of the condition on the part of the Sabbath observer corresponds to the reward given. One who restrains his walk, limits himself from doing forbidden activity, checks his speech; this person deserves an unlimited reward.

The limitation of the self results in an unlimited reward. This inversely proportional relationship is in fact only a manifestation of the original act of creation. The Malbim highlights this subtle but evident corollary.

"בְּרֵאשִׁית בָּרָא אֱלֹקִים..." הַיְנוּ שֶׁהֵנִיחַ מָקוֹם פָּנוּי שֶׁבּוֹ יַעַמְדוּ שָׁמַיִם וָאָרֶץ כָּל עוֹלָם ולפ"ז מַה שֶׁאָנוּ אוֹמְרִים שֶׁבָּרָא יֵשׁ מֵאַיִן הוּא לְפִי הַשָּׂגָתֵנוּ אֲבָל לְפִי הָאֱמֶת בָּא אַיִן מִיֵּשׁ כִּי הוּא הָיָה הָאֲמִתִּי הַנִּמְצָא הַמְּחֻיָּב הַמְּצִיאוּת.

*When creating the world, God, as it were, created a vacuum in which Heaven and earth could exist. Although we commonly say that creation was ex nihilo, "something" from "nothing," in reality, "nothing" was created from "something," for He was the Truly Existing One, the Positive Reality.*

One of the fundamental tenets of Judaism is that God, as Creator of the Universe and of all matter, transcends time and space. Time and space are attributes of matter; they belong to this physical realm. As God is non-corporeal, the very concept of time, age, and beginning do not apply to Him at all. As we say in our prayers: אֲדוֹן עוֹלָם אֲשֶׁר מָלַךְ בְּטֶרֶם כָּל יְצִיר נִבְרָא — "Master of the World, Who ruled before the existence of any creation." God was always in existence. In fact, God is "Existence" in the true sense of the word. The material world in which we live, being bound to time, does not truly and absolutely exist: A real existence can only be in a sphere which is above the limitations of the realm of time.

It follows then, that the comparison of our limited "existence" in this world to the Absolute and infinite existence of God, is like the comparison of "nothing" to "something." Absolute Existence and limited existence stand so far apart, they are on opposite ends of the spectrum. It is Infinity versus Nothing.

To demonstrate this concept mathematically, we can state that to divide any number by zero, the quotient would be infinity. To divide any number, however large, by infinity, the quotient would be zero. Our existence is similarly zero in relation to the infinite existence of God. We are אַיִן, "nothing," in comparison to the יֵשׁ, "something," of the מְחֻיַּב הַמְּצִיאוּת, Absolute Existence, i.e. God. Thus, as the Malbim said, the creation of a world by God, is not as we commonly describe: the creation of something from nothing, but is in fact more accurately the creation of nothing from something.

To envisage this idea pictorially, imagine a hall that is full of light. In the middle is a sphere that does not allow light to penetrate. The world in which we live is the sphere of "nothingness" through which no light passes. This "nothingness" was a creation that came about as a result of the withdrawal of Godly light from that space. Our world, our עוֹלָם, is a הֶעְלֵם, an obscurity or withdrawal; an אַיִן, an absence, void of the יֵשׁ, God's existence. The "existence" of a world then, is the absence of true Existence.

If one were at any point to increase the size of the sphere in the hall of light, one would simultaneously be decreasing the volume of light which fills the hall. Similarly, when one increases the void, the אַיִן of this world, one simultaneously decreases the real existence, the Godly light in this universe. And of course, the converse is true. The greater the צִמְצוּם, the decrease of the "absence of existence," the more Godly light, יֵשׁ, Absolute Existence, is allowed to penetrate.

Man has been endowed with the gift of free choice. He walks a tightrope, constantly faced with the decision of whether to follow his own, earthly desires, thereby expressing his own wishes, or whether to remain faithful to the will of "Him Who spoke and brought the world into being." Every act on the part of man in obedience to the word of God, is a negation of man himself, a dismissal of selfish ego. When man limits himself, like the reduction of the opaque sphere, he simultaneously allows the unlimited and Absolute Existence of God to fill the world. In contrast, every wrong choice that man makes increases the הֶעְלֵם, the vacuum, the absence of Godly existence in our plane.

Adam was placed in a world that was almost completely permeated with Godly light. The עוֹלָם, הֶעְלֵם on which he was placed, was a mere island of darkness surrounded by a sea of truth, the all pervading presence of the Absolute Existence. In Adam's perception there were no "grey areas." Everything was classified as either אֱמֶת or שֶׁקֶר, truth or falsehood, black or white, dark or light, wrong or right. This clarity limited the scope of his freedom of choice. In our terms, we could say that one who posited that two and two equals five, would immediately be classed as a fool. The correct answer is so evident, the truth so well known that such a statement would be immediately dismissed. For Adam, all falsehood was evident to this same degree. Such clarity in the knowledge of truth places man under the obligation to unhesitatingly reject the falsehood, to unfailingly choose the truth. In contrast, a clouded vision of the truth widens one's freedom of choice, as one now begins to consider other options as viable possibilities. This choice is only possible when one sees alternatives of good and evil in the relative terms of "better" and "worse," rather than the clarity of absolute truth versus absolute falsehood.

The word דַּעַת, knowledge, implies חִבּוּר, a merge or unification. As the verse states: וְהָאָדָם יָדַע אֶת חַוָּה אִשְׁתּוֹ — "And Adam knew Chavah, his wife," referring to the intimate union between them. The עֵץ הַדַּעַת טוֹב וָרָע, the Tree of the Knowledge of Good and Evil, represents an amalgamation of the forces of good and evil. Before Adam ate from this tree, he was in possession of a clarity that enabled him to differentiate plainly between truth and falsehood. The moment he ate from the tree, that clarity was lost. He was no longer able to classify things as completely good or completely bad. He moved over from a world in which all was black and white, into a sphere of thick, grey clouds, clouds that obscured his clarity of vision. The result: a wider freedom of choice.

Adam was in fact driven to sin out of an overwhelming desire for a greater freedom of choice. This desire stemmed from a desire to serve God better, which contained within it an element of rebellion, of ego. God issued the command not to eat from the Tree of Knowledge.

There was no positive action involved in fulfilling this command, merely abstention. Man was to do nothing. However, lying within this lack of activity is a nagging feeling that man's creation is for naught, that after all, he is accomplishing little on this planet. This feeling led the first man into an attempt to widen his freedom of choice by creating an arena wherein he could actively participate in effecting a revelation of God's Name, in increasing Godly light.

Adam wanted to express his personality through actively bringing about a revelation. This he tried to achieve by enlarging the sphere of הֶעְלֵם, by increasing the territory devoid of Godly presence, and thus simultaneously increasing his freedom of choice. From that point onwards he would be faced with a struggle to actively reject evil and choose its good counterpart.

The rectification of this sin was achieved when the Torah was given at Sinai. The underlying attitude behind the declaration of נַעֲשֶׂה וְנִשְׁמַע — "We will do and we will listen," is the yielding of one's freedom of choice. One unquestioningly accepts and commits oneself to act upon that acceptance, irrespective of whether it concurs with one's own understanding. Man submits his intellect, and in fact his very being, to the will of God.

Man is defined by his understanding, his freedom of choice, and therefore sacrifice of the self for what one understands to be true is indeed a noble act. However, the litmus test lies in man's ability to act when it defies his own understanding, when he cannot see the inherent goodness which lies within a particular act.

This was the level of submission attained by the nation only as they stood ready to accept the Torah upon themselves. Standing at the foot of Mount Sinai, the Jewish People negated themselves completely in the face of God's will. נַעֲשֶׂה וְנִשְׁמַע — We will do and only then try to understand. We do, without question. Our action is not out of our own choice or our own volition. It is not an expression of our finite "selves." This is true service of God: a total yielding of one's whole being — one's understanding, one's freedom of choice — to a Higher Power; a Power that transcends human understanding and perception.

This noble declaration was unfortunately short-lived. The Golden Calf was a step down from the total cleaving to God that the Jewish People experienced at Sinai; into nature, into cause and effect. The sin of the Golden Calf was a claim to right of ownership over one's own mind and judgment, an expression of one's own personality in an attempt to independently bring about a revelation of Godly light. The sin of the Golden Calf was thus an exact repetition of Adam's sin. The consequence: a Godly world polluted once again by the putrid egoism of man.

The only solution, the sole remedy of the sickly root that caused Adam's sin and the sin of the Golden Calf, is Shabbath. The Sabbath, with its laws of restraint and limitation, brings about the dissemination of the limitless light of God in the world, "a portion without boundaries."

In the narration of the earlier Gemara, describing how the lost crowns of נַעֲשֶׂה וְנִשְׁמַע are to be regained through the Sabbath, we find the addition of a seemingly insignificant detail:

נוֹתְנִין לוֹ נַחֲלָה בְּלִי מְצָרִים... "נַחֲלַת יַעֲקֹב אָבִיךָ". לֹא כְּאַבְרָהָם... וְלֹא כְּיִצְחָק... אֶלָּא כְּיַעֲקֹב.

*He will merit a portion without boundaries... "as your forefather Ya'akov"; not like Avraham, nor like Yitzchak, but like Ya'akov.*

The emphasis on Ya'akov concerning this issue remains to be understood. In an attempt to do so, let us examine the following words of Ya'akov himself.

**וַיֹּאמֶר יַעֲקֹב אֶל לָבָן הָבָה אֶת אִשְׁתִּי כִּי מָלְאוּ יָמָי וְאָבוֹאָה אֵלֶיהָ.**

*Ya'akov said to Lavan, "Give me my wife, for the allotted time has been fulfilled, so that I may come to her."*[75]

It seems strange that Ya'akov, our sublime Patriarch, should speak in a way that lacks all modesty, in a manner upon which Rashi

---

75. *Bereishith* 29:21.

comments that "even the lowest of the low would be ashamed to speak thus."

A similar absence of shame is seen in the dawn of history, before Adam and Chavah sinned by eating from the Tree of Knowledge. It is said about them, לֹא יִתְבֹּשָׁשׁוּ — "They were [totally] unashamed [of their nakedness]."[76] Is it not peculiar that Adam, the one fashioned by the very hands of the Almighty, as it were, should be so unashamed of his nakedness?

The answer, however, lies in the question itself. It was precisely because Adam and Ya'akov were of such lofty stature that they were not embarrassed to act in such a manner. Their shamelessness was a result of their purity and greatness.

Let us analyse:

Shame, בּוּשָׁה, rises from a feeling of contradiction between what one is and what one should be, the deed and the person's expectations of himself. It in fact results from the schism between the person's true, pure, inner essence, and the way it has been allowed to express itself. One who acts in an unfitting manner is possessed by an overwhelming feeling of shame which arises from man's realisation that he has betrayed his own inner Godly soul. Shame results from the amalgamation of good and evil which exists in the world, and within each individual. When one lives with absolute clarity of truth and falsehood, when the falsehood is clearly identifiable and easily rejected, falsehood remains alien to the person, and therefore no shame is felt.

Both Ya'akov and Adam, as he was before the sin, experienced no shame. Falsehood was totally foreign to them. They had no need to restrict themselves in order to allow God's light to shine through. It is only when freedom of choice is widened, as a result of sin, that one requires a measure of צִמְצוּם — limitation of the self — to allow a proliferation of Godly light.

When Adam ate from the Tree of Knowledge, God revealed the route to correction:

---

76. *Bereishith* 2:25.

**וַיַּעַשׂ ה' אֱלֹקִים לְאָדָם וּלְאִשְׁתּוֹ כָּתְנוֹת עוֹר וַיַּלְבִּשֵׁם.**

*God made for Adam and his wife coverings, and He clothed them.*[77]

After the sin, the attribute of shame is now in place. This is the idea behind clothes; the idea of covering oneself up, indicative of a degree of modesty as a result of the shame. This is the prescribed route for rectifying the sin. Boundaries are once again erected; limitations are once again put into place.

It is thus that we find that only after the sin of the Golden Calf, God chooses to manifest His presence in a *Mishkan*, in a place of defined parameters. God too, as it were, makes a physical limitation of Himself as a result of the sin.

A reward of נַחֲלָה בְּלִי מְצָרִים — "a portion without limitation," can now easily be understood as being ascribed specifically to Ya'akov. Ya'akov elevated himself to the level of Adam before the sin; he lived on a plane of נַחֲלָה בְּלִי מְצָרִים. For him, the light of God was unlimited. He lived with a clarity of absolute truth, and so to him, shame, בּוּשָׁה, did not apply. There is no question of how Ya'akov could speak with such a lack of modesty, for, on his level, embarrassment was not relevant. He had rejected and externalized evil to such an extent that from his perspective, all was viewed in terms of absolute sanctity.

With every צִמְצוּם, with every additional restriction that a person accepts upon himself in service of the Creator, he draws closer to the ultimate נַחֲלָה בְּלִי מְצָרִים, the portion without limitations. Let us transcend, and let us allow ourselves the boundless pleasure of נַחֲלָה בְּלִי מְצָרִים, the experience of a foretaste of the World to Come while yet living within the parameters of this finite world.

---

77. *Bereishith* 3:21.

# TETZAVEH

THIS PARASHAH ELABORATES upon the vestments made for the *Kohanim* for their service in the *Mishkan.*

**וְעָשִׂיתָ בִגְדֵי קֹדֶשׁ לְאַהֲרֹן אָחִיךָ לְכָבוֹד וּלְתִפְאָרֶת.**

*You shall make sacred garments for your brother, Aharon, for [his] honour and splendour.*[78]

The Ramban offers the following explanation:

לְכָבוֹד וּלְתִפְאָרֶת. שֶׁיִּהְיֶה נִכְבָּד וּמְפֹאָר בְּמַלְבּוּשִׁים נִכְבָּדִים וּמְפֹאָרִים כְּמוֹ שֶׁאָמַר הַכָּתוּב כְּחָתָן יְכַהֵן פְּאֵר כִּי אֵלֶּה הַבְּגָדִים לְבוּשֵׁי מַלְכוּת הֵן בִּדְמוּתָן יִלְבְּשׁוּ הַמְּלָכִים בִּזְמַן הַתּוֹרָה.

וְעַל דֶּרֶךְ הָאֱמֶת הוֹד לְכָבוֹד וְלַתִּפְאֶרֶת. יֹאמַר שֶׁיַּעֲשׂוּ בִּגְדֵי קֹדֶשׁ לְאַהֲרֹן לְשָׁרֵת בָּהֶם לִכְבוֹד הַשֵּׁם הַשּׁוֹכֵן בְּתוֹכָם וּלְתִפְאֶרֶת עֻזָּם, כִּדְכְתִיב כִּי תִפְאֶרֶת עֻזָּמוֹ אָתָּה....

וְהָיוּ הַבְּגָדִים צְרִיכִין עֲשִׂיָּה לִשְׁמָן, וְיִתָּכֵן שֶׁיִּהְיוּ צְרִיכִין כַּוָּנָה וְלָכֵן אָמַר וְאַתָּה תְּדַבֵּר אֶל כָּל חַכְמֵי לֵב אֲשֶׁר מִלֵּאתִיו רוּחַ חָכְמָה, שֶׁיָּבִינוּ מַה שֶּׁיַּעֲשׂוּ.[79]

The Ramban explains the significance of the priestly garments being sewn for כָּבוֹד וְתִפְאֶרֶת, "honour and splendour." The *Kohanim* wore royal garments as a reflection of their exalted status as courtiers of the King of kings. These opulent garments demonstrate the reverence in which the King is held, and pay homage to His exaltedness.

It was vital for the garments to be fashioned by individuals conferred with the title of חֲכַם לֵב, "wise-hearted," for the clothes had to be made with thoughts and lofty intentions that befitted their

---

78. *Shemoth* 28:2.

79. Ramban *ad loc.*

glorious purpose. The commentators on the Ramban elaborate:

לֹא הָיָה בָּהֶם תְּפִירָה אַחַת שֶׁלֹּא הָיָה רָמוּז בָּהּ תִּלֵּי תִּלִּים שֶׁל הֲלָכוֹת יְסוֹדוֹת מֻפְלָאִים בְּסֵתֶר הַתּוֹרָה.

*Every stitch involved mountains of laws and marvelous secrets of the Torah.*

It was for this reason that specifically חַכְמֵי לֵב, wise-hearted men, were required for the task.

Let us investigate the glory of God that was manifested in the garments. In particular, we will examine the significance of the *Urim VeTumim* in the breastplate, the supreme glory of the *Kohen Gadol*, the High Priest.

The breastplate was a vehicle of transmission of spiritual knowledge and guidance to the people, through the messages it delivered from God. These messages clarified the truth and revealed the correct course of action under particular circumstances. There were two stages in this process, which can be seen in the very name of the article.

1. אוּרִים (Illumination): The actual letters inscribed on the stones would light up to provide the answer to the question (hence the term אוּרִים derived from אוֹר, light).
2. תוּמִּים (Completion): The letters then required formatting in their correct order; a task which required Divine inspiration.

The necessity of both stages is demonstrated by Chanah, who was found by Eli, the *Kohen Gadol*, standing in the *Mishkan*, pouring out her heart to God.

**וְהָיָה כִּי הִרְבְּתָה לְהִתְפַּלֵּל לִפְנֵי ה׳ וְעֵלִי שֹׁמֵר אֶת פִּיהָ. וְחַנָּה הִיא מְדַבֶּרֶת עַל לִבָּהּ רַק שְׂפָתֶיהָ נָּעוֹת וְקוֹלָהּ לֹא יִשָּׁמֵעַ וַיַּחְשְׁבֶהָ עֵלִי לְשִׁכֹּרָה... וַתַּעַן חַנָּה וַתֹּאמֶר לֹא אֲדֹנִי...**

*Chanah was praying; her lips were moving, yet her voice could not be heard. Eli suspected her of drunkenness. She answered him, "It is not so, my master."*[80]

---

80. *I Shemuel* 1:13.

Rashi comments:

לֹא אֲדֹנִי — לֹא אָדוֹן אַתָּה בַּדָּבָר הַזֶּה. גִּלִּיתָ בְּעַצְמְךָ שֶׁאֵין רוּחַ הַקֹּדֶשׁ שׁוֹרָה עָלֶיךָ.

*"No, my master," [which could alternatively be read as, "Not my master"]. You are not a master over this thing. You have revealed with your accusation that you do not have Divine inspiration.*

The root of Eli's misjudgment lay in his inability to correctly arrange the order of the illuminated letters. Read in the correct order (with the help of Divine inspiration), the letters ש-כ-ר-ה would be rendered כְּשָׂרָה, like Sarah, a woman barren like our Matriarch Sarah. An alternative reading would be כְּשֵׁרָה, a proper woman. Eli mistakenly formatted the word as שִׁכֹּרָה, a drunken woman. His mistake demonstrated that he did not possess the necessary Divine inspiration for correct construction of the word.

The following passage of the Ramchal's *Da'ath Tevunoth* is relevant to understanding both the *Urim VeTumim* and *Megillath Esther*, although neither is mentioned explicitly herein.

חֶלְקֵי הַבְּרִיאָה הַזֹּאת, מִי שֶׁמַּבִּיט עֲלֵיהֶם לְפִי רְאוּת עֵינָיו, בַּתְּחִלָּה לֹא יִרְאֵם אֶלָּא עִנְיָנִים מְפֻזָּרִים וּמְפֹרָדִים. פֵּרוּשׁ: בִּלְתִּי מִתְקַשְּׁרִים כֻּלָּם אֶל תַּכְלִית אַחַת, אֶלָּא כָּל אֶחָד עִנְיָן מִפְּנֵי עַצְמוֹ, וְתַכְלִית מְיֻחָד נִשְׁלָם בְּעַצְמוֹ, בִּלְתִּי שֶׁיִּצְטָרֵךְ לַחֲבֵרוֹ. כִּי כָּל כָּךְ מִינִים בַּדּוֹמֵם, כָּל כָּךְ בַּצּוֹמְחִים, כָּל כָּךְ בְּבַעֲלֵי חַיִּים, אֵין בֵּינֵיהֶם קֶשֶׁר וְיַחַס שֶׁיִּצְטָרְכוּ לְהֵעָזֵר זֶה מִזֶּה, וְשֶׁיִּתְקַבְּצוּ לְתַכְלִית אַחַת, אֶלָּא כָּל אֶחָד נִבְרָא לְמַה שֶּׁנִּבְרָא וְעִנְיָנָיו מַשְׁלִימִים לְתַכְלִית הַמְכֻוָּן בּוֹ, לֹא יוֹתֵר.

... אַךְ מִי שֶׁיַּעֲמִיק בַּחָכְמָה יִמְצָא הֱיוֹת כָּל הַנִּמְצָאוֹת כֻּלָּם מִתְקַשְּׁרִים קֶשֶׁר גָּמוּר זֶה בְּזֶה, שֶׁכֻּלָּם צְרִיכִים לְהַשְׁלִים הָעִנְיָן שֶׁאֵלָיו כִּוְּנָה הַחָכְמָה הָעֶלְיוֹנָה בַּבְּרִיאָה, וְכֻלָּם מִתְקַבְּצִים לְתַכְלִית אַחַת שֶׁתְּנָאָיו רַבִּים וְסִדְרָם עָמֹק מְאֹד וְהֵם הֵם כָּל חֶלְקֵי הַבְּרִיאָה הָרַבִּים הָאֵלֶּה. הִנֵּה עַל כֵּן יִתְיַחֲסוּ כֻּלָּם אֵלֶּה לְאֵלֶּה בַּסֵּדֶר שֶׁרָצְתָה הַמַּחְשָׁבָה הָעֶלְיוֹנָה, וּמִכֻּלָּם יֵצֵא הַפְּרִי הַטּוֹב הָרָאוּי לָצֵאת מִן הַבְּרִיאָה. וְדָבָר זֶה כְּבָר אָמַרְתִּי עָמֹק הוּא, כִּי כָּאן הַחָכְמָה מִתְרַחֶבֶת וְהוֹלֶכֶת עַד אֵין תַּכְלִית, לָדַעַת פְּקֻדַּת כָּל הַנִּמְצָאוֹת, וּמַה הִגִּיעַ אֲלֵיהֶם בַּכַּוָּנָה הַכְּלָלִית

הַזֹּאת שֶׁזָּכַרְנוּ. וְרז"ל אָמְרוּ "כָּל מַה שֶּׁבָּרָא הקב"ה בְּעוֹלָמוֹ — לֹא בְּרָאוֹ אֶלָּא לִכְבוֹדוֹ."[81]

To paraphrase the above: At a glance, the world appears fragmented; every creation seems to exist in isolation, without any connection or relation to any other. Every thing seems a complete entity on its own, independent of all else to implement its purpose. There are an enormous number of inanimate objects, a vast amount of plant life, multitudes of animals and creations. We do not see how all are interlinked, how each requires all the others.

However, a higher perception reveals the presence of a profound unity connecting and encompassing all existence. Each entity is placed in the correct position to facilitate its interaction with every other creation, to achieve the ultimate mission of glorifying God's Name. Everything God made is for His glory; this is discernable only by perceiving the order and intricate symmetry in the universe. A prerequisite to beholding this glory, however, is, so to speak, the "arrangement" of the world in the correct order. Just as with the *Urim VeTumim*, the "message" of the world requires correct construction of the many disparate parts. And for this, one needs Divine inspiration.

An examination of the Ramchal's language reveals an echo of the Megillah. מְפֻזָּר וּמְפֹרָד — "Scattered and separate," were the words with which Haman described the situation of the Jews. וּמָה הִגִּיעַ אֲלֵיהֶם — "What happened to them," are the words used to describe the eventual consequences of the Purim story:

**עַל כֵּן קָרְאוּ לַיָּמִים הָאֵלֶּה פוּרִים עַל שֵׁם הַפּוּר עַל כֵּן עַל כָּל דִּבְרֵי הָאִגֶּרֶת הַזֹּאת וּמָה רָאוּ עַל כָּכָה וּמָה הִגִּיעַ אֲלֵיהֶם.**

*Therefore they called these days "Purim" because of the* פּוּר*, the lottery... and what happened to them.*[82]

Rashi comments:

**וּמָה הִגִּיעַ אֲלֵיהֶם — מָה רָאָה אֲחַשְׁוֵרוֹשׁ שֶׁמִּשְׁתַּמֵּשׁ בִּכְלֵי הַקֹּדֶשׁ וּמַה**

81. *Da'ath Tevunoth,* Section 128.
82. *Esther* 9:26.

הִגִּיעַ עֲלֵיהֶם שֶׁבָּא שָׂטָן וְרָקַד בֵּינֵיהֶם וְהָרַג אֶת וַשְׁתִּי. מָה רָאָה הָמָן שֶׁנִּתְקַנֵּא בְּמָרְדְּכַי וּמַה הִגִּיעַ אֵלָיו שֶׁתָּלוּ אוֹתוֹ וְאֶת בָּנָיו...[83]

At first glance, the Megillah seems to be a series of isolated events. Upon each of these events, the question, "Why did this happen?" could be asked. In fact, one insight on the word Purim relates it to the word פֵּרוּרִים, meaning crumbs. For a crumb by itself is insignificant. Yet a multitude of crumbs joined together form a slice of bread. Just as Divine inspiration was necessary to construct the letters of the *Urim VeTumim* in the correct order, Divine inspiration is required to correctly sequence the seemingly isolated events of this world.

The following incident is a striking illustration of this principle. In the early twentieth century, King Edward VIII of England wanted to marry Mrs. Wallis Simpson, a divorcée from America. The prospect of this marriage caused great furore amongst the population, and the government issued an ultimatum: leave the woman or abdicate the throne. In the course of a few days his decision to abdicate was publicised. And, just as at the time of Achashverosh no one understood how Vashti's death would affect the Jews, so here the significance to the Jews of Edward's decision was not yet apparent.

Thirty-six years later, in the course of Lord Bootheby's eulogy of Edward, the relevance of this incident became astoundingly clear. During the time that England was embroiled in this controversy over King Edward's marriage plans, Hitler was rising to power in Germany. Just one lone voice in Parliament saw Hitler as a real threat: Winston Churchill stood alone in his persistent calls for rearmament, in his cries to stunt the potential danger of this man called Hitler. Slowly, he was gaining a considerable following, forming a party which pressed for action to be taken.

It is only with hindsight that the relevance of this incident is perceived. In fact, in the case of the Megillah, it was only nine years after the event that the significance of Vashti's death became clear. In the Megillah, the phrase וַתִּכְתֹּב אֶסְתֵּר הַמַּלְכָּה — "And Esther

---

83. Rashi *ad loc.*

wrote," is written with an enlarged ת. The Maharal explains that this is indicative of the Divine inspiration required to write the Megillah. Only with Divine inspiration could the underlying unity and connection of the seemingly isolated events of nine years be seen.

The significance of the Ramchal's choice of words from the Megillah is now apparent. The Megillah: numerous different events which, when constructed in the correct order, form a majestic whole. Creation: a multitude of different parts which, when constructed in the correct order, reveal the majesty of the Almighty. How boundless is the wisdom required to put together the endless detail of this world — all forms of life — vegetation, animals, and all events occurring to all humanity! A breathtaking sanctification of God's Name is the result of this revelation.

Esther dispatched a command to the Sages, כִּתְבוּנִי לְדוֹרוֹת — "Write this down for future generations," for Purim's message is intended to uproot man's tendency to attribute events to random forces of nature. The Midrash[84] states that in the future, all festivals will be nullified, except for the festival of Purim. R. Yitzchak Hutner explains why Purim specifically will never pass away:

> ...כָּל הַמּוֹעֲדִים שֶׁהֵם זֵכֶר לִיצִיאַת מִצְרַיִם, לִכְשֶׁיָּבֹא הַיּוֹם אֲשֶׁר בּוֹ תִהְיֶה הַגְּאֻלָּה הָעֲתִידָה עִקָּר וּגְאֻלַּת מִצְרַיִם טָפֵל, וַהֲרֵי יֵשׁ בִּכְלָל מָאתַיִם מָנֶה, גַּם כָּל הַמּוֹעֲדִים יִתְכַּלְלוּ בְּאוֹר הַשֶּׁמֶשׁ שֶׁל הַגְּאֻלָּה. אֶלָּא דְּכָל זֶה הוּא בִּשְׁאָר הַמּוֹעֲדִים דִּיסוֹדָם הוּא הָאוֹר שֶׁל גְּאֻלַּת מִצְרַיִם. אֲבָל גְּאֻלָּה דְפוּרִים אֲשֶׁר עַל יָדָהּ כְּנֶסֶת יִשְׂרָאֵל לִמְדָה אֶת עַצְמָהּ לְהַכִּיר אֶת הֶ"אָנֹכִי" גַּם בַּחֹשֶׁךְ וּבַהֶסְתֵּר, בְּוַדַּאי שֶׁזֶּה יִשָּׁאֵר קִנְיַן עוֹלָם בְּנַפְשָׁהּ שֶׁל כְּנֶסֶת יִשְׂרָאֵל אֲפִלּוּ לְאַחַר שֶׁיַּעֲלֶה עַמּוּד הַשַּׁחַר.
>
> *...All the festivals which are a remembrance of the Exodus from Egypt will be eclipsed and included in the miracles of the Future Redemption. All the festivals will be included in the light of the future revelation. However, the redemption of Purim is unique in that it teaches the Jewish People to recognise the* אָנֹכִי*, the "I," [of* אָנֹכִי ה' אֱלֹקֶיךָ*, "I am the Lord your God"] in the darkness. This ability will remain an acquisition in the*

---

84. *Midrash Rabbah, Mishlei* 9.

*heart of the Jewish People, even after the sun [of redemption] rises.*[85]

In this spirit are we told, זָכוֹר אֵת אֲשֶׁר עָשָׂה לְךָ עֲמָלֵק בַּדֶּרֶךְ... אֲשֶׁר קָרְךָ בַּדֶּרֶךְ — "Remember what Amalek did to you.... when they met you by chance."[86] Amalek's ideology is contained in the word קָרְךָ, a chance encounter. Their essence is the conviction that everything happens by chance, nothing is connected. The world is an arbitrary place without purpose, design or designer. The victory over Amalek lies in the recognition of the order, the purpose, the design in the world.

The ability to discern the sequence of events was implanted in the heart of the Children of Yisrael at the time of Purim. It is an acquisition which will always remain. And this is the message of the priestly garments and the *Urim VeTumim*. They demonstrate the honour and glory of the master Designer, on seeing how every stitch in creation has a part to play, every detail is needed for every other detail, the perfectly constructed whole revealing the glory of the Almighty. A majestic yet simple structure.

This is the essence of the priestly garments. This is the significance of the *Urim VeTumim*. This is the meaning of Purim. This is the hallmark of a Jew.

---

85. *Pachad Yitzchak, Purim* 34.
86. *Devarim* 25:17, 18.

# KI THISA

WITH THE GIVING of the Torah at Mount Sinai, the world underwent a fundamental change, a change affecting all humanity until eternity. The Children of Yisrael attained the sublime level at which all internal evil, which was introduced into man with Adam's primordial sin, was expelled. Their spiritual essence, the beacon which was their souls, shone with incandescent illumination. However, the nation was unable to sustain this spiritual level. Thus followed the infamous episode in which the nation sinned with the Golden Calf. Upon his descent from the mountain, Moshe surveyed the scene of the nation dancing around a gleaming image, and decided to smash the two stone tablets which had been given to him by the Almighty Himself. He was then addressed by God, Who instructed him as follows:

**וַיֹּאמֶר ה' אֶל מֹשֶׁה פְּסָל לְךָ שְׁנֵי לֻחֹת אֲבָנִים כָּרִאשֹׁנִים וְכָתַבְתִּי עַל הַלֻּחֹת אֶת הַדְּבָרִים אֲשֶׁר הָיוּ עַל הַלֻּחֹת הָרִאשֹׁנִים אֲשֶׁר שִׁבַּרְתָּ.**

*The Eternal said to Moshe, "Carve out for yourself two stone tablets like the first ones, and I will inscribe upon the tablets the [same] words that were on the first tablets which you smashed."*[87]

Our Sages explain this command with the following parable:

פְּסָל לְךָ – אַתָּה שָׁבַרְתָּ הָרִאשׁוֹנִים, אַתָּה פְּסָל לְךָ אֲחֵרוֹת. מָשָׁל לְמֶלֶךְ שֶׁהָלַךְ לִמְדִינַת הַיָּם וְהֵנִיחַ אֲרוּסָתוֹ עִם הַשְּׁפָחוֹת, מִתּוֹךְ קִלְקוּל הַשְּׁפָחוֹת יָצָא עָלֶיהָ שֵׁם רַע, עָמַד שׁוֹשְׁבִינָהּ וְקָרַע כְּתֻבָּתָהּ, אָמַר אִם יֹאמַר הַמֶּלֶךְ לְהוֹרְגָהּ, אוֹמַר לוֹ עֲדַיִן אֵינָהּ אִשְׁתְּךָ, בָּדַק הַמֶּלֶךְ וּמָצָא

87. *Shemoth* 34:1.

שֶׁלֹּא הָיָה הַקִּלְקוּל אֶלָּא מִן הַשְּׁפָחוֹת, נִתְרַצָּה לָהּ, אָמַר לוֹ שׁוֹשְׁבִינָהּ, כְּתֹב לָהּ כְּתֻבָּה אַחֶרֶת שֶׁנִּקְרְעָה הָרִאשׁוֹנָה, אָמַר לוֹ הַמֶּלֶךְ, אַתָּה קָרַעְתָּ אוֹתָהּ, אַתָּה קְנֵה לְךָ נְיָר אַחֵר וַאֲנִי אֶכְתֹּב לָהּ בִּכְתַב יָדִי, כָּךְ הַמֶּלֶךְ, זֶה הקב"ה, הַשְּׁפָחוֹת אֵלּוּ עֵרֶב רַב, וְהַשּׁוֹשְׁבִין זֶה מֹשֶׁה, אֲרוּסָתוֹ שֶׁל הקב"ה אֵלּוּ יִשְׂרָאֵל, לְכָךְ נֶאֱמַר פְּסָל לְךָ.

*You broke the first tablets, thus you make the second set.*

*A parable is brought of a king who, required to journey to a foreign land, entrusted the woman whom he had betrothed to the care of maidservants.*

*The maidservants became corrupt, and because the woman was in their company, she too acquired a bad reputation.*

*An emissary of the king, who was charged with overseeing her, witnessed the events, and tore up the marriage contract. He reasoned that if the king would desire to put her to death for her alleged actions, he could be told that the woman was not yet his wife, and thus did not deserve the severity of this punishment.*

*The king returned and investigated the matter. He discovered that although the servants had become perverse, his betrothed one was innocent of any crime, and he was appeased. The emissary requested that the king write another document of marriage, for the first one had been torn up.*

*The king replied, "You tore up the document. You acquire new parchment and I will write in my own handwriting."*

*Thus was the situation with God, Who in our story is represented by the king. The maidservants correspond to the Mixed Multitude, the emissary corresponds to Moshe, and the betrothed one is the Jewish nation. God told Moshe to fashion the second set of tablets, the second marriage document, himself.*[88]

Contemplating this parable, we must understand what was the underlying gain in the emissary tearing up the marriage document?

Let us digress and examine a *Midrash Tanchuma*:

---

88. Rashi *ad loc.*

פְּסָל לְךָ. זֶה שֶׁאָמַר הַכָּתוּב חֲמַת מֶלֶךְ מַלְאֲכֵי מָוֶת וְאִישׁ חָכָם יְכַפְּרֶנָּה. חֲמַת מֶלֶךְ מַלְאֲכֵי מָוֶת, זֶה הקב"ה. שֶׁבְּשָׁעָה שֶׁעָשׂוּ אֶת הָעֵגֶל, נִזְדַּוְּגוּ לְמֹשֶׁה חֲמִשָּׁה מַלְאֲכֵי חַבָּלָה. כֵּיוָן שֶׁבִּקֵּשׁ רַחֲמִים וְהִזְכִּיר זְכוּת אָבוֹת נִסְתַּלְּקוּ מִמֶּנּוּ. כֵּיוָן שֶׁשָּׁבַר אֶת הַלּוּחוֹת, נִתְקָרְרָה דַּעְתּוֹ שֶׁל מֹשֶׁה.[89]

To paraphrase: The verse states in *Mishlei* that when the king is angry, he brings his messengers to deliver a fatal blow. The wise man, however, attains forgiveness for the deed, and thus removes these angels of death. The Almighty was angry with the Children of Yisrael when they sinned in the incident of the Golden Calf. He therefore dispatched five angels of destruction who sought to annihilate the nation. After Moshe pleaded for Heavenly mercy, and mentioned the merit of our forefathers, the angels departed. After he smashed the tablets, Moshe's anxiety abated.

Angels of destruction were loosed upon the Jewish People as a result of their sin. After Moshe prayed for them fervently, the angels were dispelled, and disaster was prevented. Moshe, however, then took the further step of smashing the two stone tablets, and it was only after this action that his mind was fully at rest. Why was the departure of the destructive angels not enough for Moshe? What lay in his further step of breaking the tablets? Further, what lies in the mention of our forefathers' merits that caused the angels of destruction to depart?

To answer these questions we will need to examine a principle borne out of the following interpretation of King David's psalm.

לְדָוִד ה' אוֹרִי וְיִשְׁעִי. רַבָּנָן פָּתְרֵי קַרְיָא בְּרֹאשׁ הַשָּׁנָה ויוה"כ בִּקְרֹב עָלַי מְרֵעִים אֵלּוּ שָׂרֵי עוֹבְדֵי אֱלִילִים, לֶאֱכֹל אֶת בְּשָׂרִי לְפִי שֶׁשָּׂרֵי עוֹבְדֵי אֱלִילִים מְקַטְרְגִים אֶת יִשְׂרָאֵל לִפְנֵי הקב"ה וְאוֹמְרִים אֵלּוּ עוֹבְדֵי אֱלִילִים וְאֵלּוּ עוֹבְדֵי אֱלִילִים אֵלּוּ מְגַלֵּי עֲרָיוֹת וְאֵלּוּ מְגַלֵּי עֲרָיוֹת אֵלּוּ שׁוֹפְכֵי דָמִים וְאֵלּוּ שׁוֹפְכֵי דָמִים אֵלּוּ יוֹרְדִים לְגֵיהִנָּם וְאֵלּוּ אֵינָם יוֹרְדִין, צָרַי וְאֹיְבַי לִי — אַתָּה מוֹצֵא מִנְיַן יְמוֹת הַחַמָּה שס"ה וּמִנְיַן הַשָּׂטָן שס"ד שֶׁכָּל יְמוֹת הַשָּׁנָה יֵשׁ לוֹ רְשׁוּת לְקַטְרֵג וּבְיוֹם הַכִּפּוּרִים אֵין לוֹ רְשׁוּת לְקַטְרֵג, אָמְרוּ יִשְׂרָאֵל לִפְנֵי הקב"ה אִם תַּחֲנֶה עָלַי מַחֲנֶה בְּזֹאת אֲנִי בוֹטֵחַ שֶׁהִבְטַחְתָּנוּ בְּתוֹרָתְךָ בְּזֹאת יָבֹא אַהֲרֹן אֶל הַקֹּדֶשׁ.

89. *Tanchuma*, *Ki Thisa* 30.

*"Of David. God is my light and my salvation..." [Tehillim 27]. Our Sages explain these verses in reference to the days of Rosh Hashanah and Yom Kippur. "The evildoers come near to me," refers to the spiritual representatives of the nations of the world. "To consume my flesh." The spiritual representatives accuse the Children of Yisrael before God, saying that just as the nations are idolaters, so the Children of Yisrael serve pagan gods. They claim that just as the nations fall prey to the temptations of immorality, so there are those amongst the Children of Yisrael who commit immoral deeds. Further, "Just as the nations murder, the Jews also spill blood. However, the Nations suffer in Gehinnom while the Jews will escape this fate." They question the fairness of this distinction.*

*There are 365 days in the solar year. The numerical value of the word* הַשָּׂטָן*, the Satan, is 364. This indicates that the Satan is given permission to accuse the Children of Yisrael for 364 days of the year. The single remaining day is Yom Kippur, on which Satan is powerless to accuse. The Children of Yisrael say in front of the Almighty, "If the nations of the world encamp against me, in this,* בְּזֹאת*, shall I trust." For, there is a promise in the Torah as follows:*[90] *"In this,* בְּזֹאת*, Aharon will go into the* קֹדֶשׁ*" [referring to Aharon's entrance into the Holy of Holies on Yom Kippur].*[91]

This entire extract seems enigmatic in the extreme. It appears that the Gentiles level a fair complaint: the preferential treatment that the Jews enjoy is undeserved. The Gentiles seem to be the subject of racial discrimination. How is their claim answered? Our Sages continue to inform us that the Jewish People can rely upon Yom Kippur, for on that day the Satan is unable to point his accusing finger and incriminate the people. This information seems only to augment the difficulty: how can this apparent favouritism be justified?

To understand this passage, we must call upon a concept concerning the nature of our essence as Jews. The Mishnah records the

90. *Vayikra* 16:3.
91. *Yalkut Shimoni, Tehillim*, 706.

following description of Avraham: וּנִיבְאָ סהֲרָבְאַ הסָּנַתְנְ תונויסָנְ הרָשָׁעֲ — "Our father Avraham was tested with ten trials."[92] In this sentence, the words "our father" seem to be redundant. Our Sages, however, explain the inclusion of this superfluous detail in a profound manner. The ten tests undergone by Avraham implanted a unique strength of character and spiritual potency within him, and these qualities were inherited by all of his descendants. These "spiritual genes" were crystallised and consolidated through the combined spiritual labour of Avraham, Yitzchak, and Ya'akov. This Mishnah then, which discusses Avraham's incredible moral fortitude in overcoming the ten tests, refers to Avraham in his capacity as a father, one who bequeaths to his children. Each member of the Jewish nation is a child of the forefathers, and has therefore inherited a unique soul. This is the Jewish *neshamah*, unique to our people, and subject to the envy of the nations. It is this soul that differentiates between the Children of Yisrael and the rest of the world. The concept of הַבְדָּלָה, distinction, is a constant reality for us in all its permutations: בֵּין קֹדֶשׁ לְחוֹל בֵּין אוֹר לְחֹשֶׁךְ בֵּין יִשְׂרָאֵל לָעַמִּים — "Between the sacred and the profane, between light and darkness, between Yisrael and the nations."

Our distinguishing feature, our uniqueness and separateness, lies in our *neshamah* and the spiritual strengths that were bequeathed to us by our forefathers. Although one can apply expressions of corruption and evil to the parts of our soul which are known as *nefesh* and *ruach*, these adjectives are never found in conjunction with the term *neshamah*. For the term *neshamah* denotes a part of the soul which is deeper, which constitutes part of the person's core and is impervious to evil. Negativity can besmirch both the *nefesh* and the *ruach*, but is unable to penetrate to the *neshamah*, one's essence. Thus we say each morning, אֱלֹקַי נְשָׁמָה שֶׁנָּתַתָּ בִּי טְהוֹרָה הִיא — "My God, the *neshamah* that you placed in me is pure." Despite the misdeeds of the previous day, despite how we stumbled and fell, we wake each morning and thank God for the pure soul that He gave us. Our sins

92. *Pirkei Avoth* 5:4.

are superficial, for the core of our soul remains pure. The statement of our Sages reflects this state: אַף עַל פִּי שֶׁחָטָא, יִשְׂרָאֵל הוּא[93]. Sin will never negate one's status as a Jew, for this identity stems from the depths of one's soul, a place that sin cannot touch.

External actions are subject to the scrutiny of God's attribute of strict justice and exactitude. Indeed, this is the only method that man can use to judge, for man, limited and corporeal, sees only that which is before him. God however, יִרְאֶה לַלֵּבָב — "sees the heart,"[94] discerning that which underlies one's deeds, evaluating actions in relation to one's personality, one's inner struggles and innate deficiencies.

When viewing actions with strict justice, looking only at the external deed, one can correctly register a complaint. A blatant and unjust inconsistency appears to be present. Both Gentiles and the Children of Yisrael commit the same crimes. The differing punishments seem a breach of justice.

With the mention of our forefathers' merits, however, the argument of the attribute of justice dissipates. For, when considering the purity and spiritual potential bequeathed to us by our forefathers, when arousing consideration of our spiritual core, accusation and strict justice are mitigated. Despite any misdeeds, our souls remain pure, and we cannot be incriminated. The *neshamah* has no connection to sin, and relating to its hallowed state removes any accusation. At the mention of our forefathers' merits and the strengths which they bequeathed, the angels of destruction depart. Their accusation has been repudiated.

For strict justice to be diminished, it is not enough merely to possess an inner purity: contact and identification with one's *neshamah* is required. One must be in touch with the purity within. On Yom Kippur, Aharon went to the inner recesses of the *Mishkan* to carry out the required service. He entered לִפְנֵי וְלִפְנִים, the innermost point of the *Mishkan*, the most sacred site on this earth. This site

---

93. *Sanhedrin* 44a.
94. *I Shemuel* 16:7.

was penetrated physically, and this is true also on a metaphysical level. Aharon, as representative of the entire people, entered the deepest place possible. He renewed contact with the Holy of Holies, with the depth of his Divinely bestowed soul. He entered a place where accusation is impotent, for purity abounds. He engaged in the process of repentance, the return journey to one's real self.

This lends us insight into the cryptic phenomenon of repentance. Logically, the rectification of deeds which have already been committed does not seem to make sense. A deed has been performed, an action done. How can this action be retrospectively negated? But with the understanding that repentance is the return to the לִפְנַי וְלִפְנִים, our innermost point, the answer becomes apparent. In the process of repentance, we reconnect ourselves to our innate purity. We identify with our essence of spirituality, with זְכוּת אָבוֹת, the merit, alternatively read as the purity, bequeathed to us by our fathers. In this place of unfettered light, sin casts no shadow. No accusation can be lodged, for no negativity is present, and culpability for former error vanishes. Real return has been effected, and one can no longer be punished for previous misdemeanors.

On Yom Kippur, the accusations of the nations of the world are rendered ineffectual. Although externally, similar crimes may be committed both by the Gentiles and by members of the Jewish nation, an equal punishment cannot be meted out, for the sin is of a totally different nature. The Children of Yisrael's sin is merely external, an ugly stain on an outer garment; a garment that can easily be discarded, a stain that can easily be removed. On Yom Kippur, Aharon enters לִפְנַי וְלִפְנִים and with this identification and reactivation of our core of purity, the accusation falls away. We are not subject to the same verdict as the nations of the world, for the purity and spiritual strength bestowed upon us by the forefathers, although at times latent, is nevertheless present within us, never sullied, never stained. The accusation is silenced. בְּזֹאת אֲנִי בוֹטֵחַ, I trust in "this," in the day in which Aharon, representative of the nation, makes the journey within.

The *Yalkut Shimoni* continues as follows:

וְעַתָּה יָרוּם רֹאשִׁי עַל אֹיְבַי סְבִיבוֹתַי, וּמִי הֵם אוֹיְבַי — עוֹבְדֵי אֱלִילִים, כֵּיוָן שֶׁעָשׂוּ יִשְׂרָאֵל אֶת הָעֵגֶל הָיוּ אוֹמְרִים אֵין לָהֶם תְּקוּמָה וְאֵינוֹ חוֹזֵר אֲלֵיהֶם לְעוֹלָם, כֵּיוָן שֶׁא"ל הקב"ה שֶׁיַּקְרִיבוּ לוֹ שֶׁנֶּאֱמַר שׁוֹר אוֹ כֶּבֶשׂ אוֹ עֵז מִיָּד נִגְלָה רֹאשָׁם.[95]

To paraphrase: When the Children of Yisrael sinned with the Golden Calf, the nations of the world thought that the Jewish nation would no longer endure; that after the performance of such a terrible deed the nation would be lost. God, however, commanded the people to sacrifice an ox, a sheep, or a goat. These instructions proved that the Children of Yisrael would indeed survive, and once again flourish.

To atone for their sin of worshipping a calf, the Almighty instructed the nation to sacrifice an ox, a mature calf. The people were given the opportunity to take the means with which they had sinned, and transform that very entity into a means of drawing close to God. The image of a calf, which previously acted as evidence for the prosecution against the nation, was changed into a defence of the Children of Yisrael. This metamorphosis from accusation to defence was viewed by the nations of the world with disbelief. For this is the underlying concept of repentance out of love, a concept that the Gentiles are not party to.

In this elevated form of repentance, God changes the transgression itself into a merit. The rationale for this is straightforward. When an errant Jew finally recognises the distance he has created between himself and his Creator, he longs to return, and thus engages in the repentance process. The distance itself becomes the incentive to return to the natural state of vibrant spirituality. Thus, the sin has become a springboard through which to renew the most important relationship in a person's life, and to identify ever more deeply with his inner being. Because of the positive outcome that stems from the transgression, God considers the transgression itself as a merit. Although the Gentiles can regret their sins, and change future actions, they lack the same pure root, and hence can never

---

95. *Yalkut Shimoni, Tehillim*, 707.

rectify wrongs already committed to the same extent.

The claim of the nations of the world has thus been answered. Taking into account the deep recesses of our souls, the Eternal purity bequeathed by our forefathers, the Children of Yisrael can never be indicted. There is always a place free of sin to which they can return. For this reason, the angels of destruction departed at the mention of the inherent purity within each Jew, the legacy of our forefathers.

Moshe's mind was not at rest, however, until he had taken the additional step of smashing the stone tablets. Although the essence of the Children of Yisrael is above reproach, an action of negativity had nevertheless been performed. The world had suffered a void of Godliness, a profanation of spirituality. A desecration of God's Name resulted from the sin. Blame for the external deed, for the desecration caused, could still be attributed to the Eternal Nation. It was this consideration that preyed upon Moshe's mind, and refused to give him peace, although the threat of destruction had been averted.

In an effort to rectify the desecration of God's Name, Moshe smashed the stone tablets. The extent of the desecration is dependent upon the degree of proximity to God. The closer one is, the more he is considered a representative of all that is good and pure. For one then to perpetrate an act of evil adds a severity to the crime which would otherwise not be present.

Herein lies the difference between one who is betrothed to her future husband, and one who is married. The Children of Yisrael, in their state of betrothal to the Almighty, had a relationship of less intensity than after the marriage was consummated. The distance was greater. The tablets, the marriage contract that signified the commencement of marriage proper, were smashed. The Children of Yisrael had to remain at the stage of betrothal. Thus we may understand the continuation of the above *Tanchuma*:

> אָמַר לוֹ הקב"ה לְמֹשֶׁה, הַמַּעֲשֶׂה יוֹכִיחַ, יָדַע שׁוֹר קֹנֵהוּ, אָמַר לוֹ הקב"ה לְאוֹתוֹ הָעֵגֶל מִי עָשָׂה אוֹתְךָ. אָמַר לוֹ, חֲמוֹר, הָעֵרֶב רַב שֶׁיָּצְאוּ עִם יִשְׂרָאֵל מִמִּצְרַיִם, שֶׁכָּתוּב בָּהֶם אֲשֶׁר בְּשַׂר חֲמוֹרִים בְּשָׂרָם. אָמַר לוֹ הקב"ה לֹא אָמַרְתִּי לְךָ לֵךְ רֵד כִּי שִׁחֵת עַמְּךָ אֲשֶׁר הֶעֱלֵיתָ מֵאֶרֶץ מִצְרַיִם, שֶׁהֵן עָשׂוּ אֶת הָעֵגֶל. אֲבָל עַמִּי לֹא עָשׂוּ, שֶׁנֶּאֱמַר יִשְׂרָאֵל לֹא

יָדַע, עַמִּי לֹא הִתְבּוֹנָן. מִיָּד קָפַץ מֹשֶׁה וְלִמֵּד סַנֵּגוֹרְיָא, ה' אֱלֹקִים אַל תַּשְׁחֵת עַמְּךָ וְנַחֲלָתְךָ אֲשֶׁר פָּדִיתָ בְּגָדְלֶךָ. עָמַד וְשָׁבַר אֶת הַלּוּחוֹת. כֵּיוָן שֶׁנִּתְרַצָּה לוֹ הקב"ה אָמַר לוֹ פְּסָל לְךָ שְׁנֵי לֻחֹת.

*God said to Moshe, "This act will bring out the truth — the ox knows its owner." God then asked the [Golden] Calf, "Who fashioned you?" The calf answered, "A donkey" (referring to the Mixed Multitude, who came out of Egypt with the Children of Yisrael and who are likened to a donkey).*

*God then addressed Moshe: "Descend, for the people whom you desired to bring out of Egypt have made this calf. The Children of Yisrael themselves however, all those whom I brought out, played no part in the sin, as it is written, 'Yisrael did not know, My people did not reflect [upon the deed].'" Immediately, Moshe arose and defended the people. "God, do not destroy the people whom in Your kindness You redeemed from Egypt." Moshe smashed the tablets. When God was appeased, He commanded Moshe to fashion a second set of tablets.*

The first set of tablets was fashioned by the Almighty. Their acceptance would have involved the eradication of the inner inclination towards evil, and the end of death in this world. The second tablets, however, were the handiwork of Moshe. They had less potency, and demonstrated the greater distance between the Children of Yisrael and the Almighty. By breaking the first set of tablets, and necessitating a second set, Moshe was effectively creating a distance between God and His people. Any subsequent desecration of God's glory was thus reduced, for once the intimate closeness was removed, the gravity of the betrayal was reduced. Had the betrothal become a marriage, a commitment on the level of the first set of tablets, the desecration perpetrated would have been too great, having been augmented by the closeness of the relationship. The Children of Yisrael would have justly deserved to suffer annihilation. Moshe's mind was not at rest until he tore up the marriage contract, until the stone tablets lay shattered upon the ground. The Jewish nation could now only become married to the Almighty on the level of the second tablets.

The emissary of the King protected the betrothed one. He tore up the contract, diminishing the treachery and allowing the continued survival of the King's beloved. The second marriage contract was made by the emissary, not by the King. It was on a level of less intensity than the first. Yet, although the closeness was reduced, it was a marriage that would last for eternity.

It is well known that the act of profaning God's Name is one of the hardest things for which to attain atonement. A desecration wreaks destruction upon the universe, and is a sin which requires the gravest of punishments. This desecration is magnified by closeness to Him; the treachery is augmented through the intimacy of the relationship. This is so whether the relationship is truly one of devotion, or whether this is only the impression given to an onlooker.

When living a life which accords with the dictates of Torah, and led by the guidance of our Torah Sages, an awesome responsibility is placed upon a person. The closer the person, the more profound the desecration. A person who exudes closeness to the Almighty must ensure that every action is a reflection and manifestation of the purity within. Any desecration that he might perpetrate is many times more severe than that caused by one at a distance. Conversely, the reward for sanctifying God's Name is many times greater than the punishment meted out for profanation. We are all created for the purpose of glorifying God's Name. Let us play our part in manifesting this glory in the world.

# VAYAKHEL

THIS PARASHAH DEALS with the construction of the *Mishkan*, and the gifts donated towards this edifice. The name of the *parashah* is from the *Hakhel*, the gathering together of the people to receive their instructions concerning this unique building project. This gathering was an essential prerequisite for the *Mishkan*'s construction. Let us investigate why this should be so.

Let us first elucidate a passage we find in relation to Moshe's breaking of the tablets of stone that he was given at Mount Sinai.

וַיֹּאמֶר ה' אֶל מֹשֶׁה פְּסָל לְךָ שְׁנֵי לֻחֹת אֲבָנִים כָּרִאשֹׁנִים... וַיַּשְׁכֵּם מֹשֶׁה בַבֹּקֶר וַיַּעַל אֶל הַר סִינַי כַּאֲשֶׁר צִוָּה ה' אֹתוֹ וַיִּקַּח בְּיָדוֹ שְׁנֵי לֻחֹת אֲבָנִים. וַיֵּרֶד ה' בֶּעָנָן וַיִּתְיַצֵּב עִמּוֹ שָׁם וַיִּקְרָא בְשֵׁם ה'. וַיַּעֲבֹר ה' עַל פָּנָיו וַיִּקְרָא ה' ה' אֵ-ל רַחוּם וְחַנּוּן אֶרֶךְ אַפַּיִם וְרַב חֶסֶד וֶאֱמֶת. נֹצֵר חֶסֶד לָאֲלָפִים נֹשֵׂא עָוֹן וָפֶשַׁע וְחַטָּאָה וְנַקֵּה לֹא יְנַקֶּה פֹּקֵד עֲוֹן אָבוֹת עַל בָּנִים וְעַל בְּנֵי בָנִים עַל שִׁלֵּשִׁים וְעַל רִבֵּעִים. וַיְמַהֵר מֹשֶׁה וַיִּקֹּד אַרְצָה וַיִּשְׁתָּחוּ.

*[Moshe] carved out two stone tablets like the first ones, [he] rose early the [next] morning and ascended Mount Sinai, just as the Eternal had commanded him, and he took the two stone tablets in his hand. The Eternal descended in the cloud and positioned Himself there with [Moshe], and [Moshe] called out the Eternal's Name... Moshe hurried and he bowed towards the ground and prostrated himself.*[96]

Rashi elaborates that as soon as Moshe heard God's proclamation, he bowed down. The Talmud questions this act of prostration:

מָה רָאָה מֹשֶׁה. א"ר חֲנִינָא בֶּן גַּמְלִיאֵל, אֶרֶךְ אַפַּיִם רָאָה.

---

96. *Shemoth* 34:4–8.

*What prompted Moshe to bow? R. Chanina ben Gamliel states that Moshe bowed when he heard the words* אֶרֶךְ אַפַּיִם*, that God is slow to anger.*[97]

The *Yalkut Shimoni* on *Tehillim* explains why gratitude was due particularly for this act of mercy.

רַבִּי הוּנָא אָמַר מָשָׁל לְמֶלֶךְ שֶׁכָּעַס עַל בְּנוֹ וּלְפָנָיו אֶבֶן גְּדוֹלָה וְנִשְׁבַּע שֶׁהוּא זוֹרֵק בּוֹ עַל בְּנוֹ, אָמַר הַמֶּלֶךְ אִם זוֹרְקוֹ אֲנִי עַל בְּנִי אֵין לוֹ חַיִּים, מֶה עָשָׂה כִּתְּתוֹ וַעֲשָׂאוֹ צְרוֹרוֹת קְטַנּוֹת וְהָיָה זוֹרֵק בּוֹ אֶחָד אֶחָד נִמְצָא לֹא הִזִּיק בְּנוֹ וְלֹא בִּטֵּל אֶת גְּזֵרָתוֹ.

*R. Huna brought a parable of a king who, angered by his son, swore to throw the great boulder that was in front of him, onto his son. Considering the matter, the king realised that were he to throw the stone upon his son, his son would die. The king therefore cut the boulder into pieces, producing many little stones, and pelted his son with them one by one. Thus, the king did not unduly harm his son, and at the same time did not annul his oath.*[98]

In a similar vein, God does not inflict us with the full force of punishment and justice that we deserve. He rather waits, and metes out retribution in a manner in which the punishment is much less painful for us.

From these words we derive a general principle that breaking a big thing into many parts has the effect of reducing its potency. The strength of a huge boulder is dramatically diminished when it is splintered into thousands of pebbles. Likewise, the impact of God's attribute of strict justice is minimized when it is fractured into many pieces.

This principle throws light on an astonishing incident in the book of *Bereishith*. Journeying to Lavan's house, Ya'akov encountered a gathering of shepherds idling by a well.

---

97. *Sanhedrin* 111a.
98. *Yalkut Shimoni, Tehillim* 635.

**וַיֹּאמֶר הֵן עוֹד הַיּוֹם גָּדוֹל לֹא עֵת הֵאָסֵף הַמִּקְנֶה הַשְׁקוּ הַצֹּאן וּלְכוּ רְעוּ. וַיֹּאמְרוּ לֹא נוּכַל עַד אֲשֶׁר יֵאָסְפוּ כָּל הָעֲדָרִים וְגָלְלוּ אֶת הָאֶבֶן מֵעַל פִּי הַבְּאֵר וְהִשְׁקִינוּ הַצֹּאן... וַיְהִי כַּאֲשֶׁר רָאָה יַעֲקֹב אֶת רָחֵל בַּת לָבָן אֲחִי אִמּוֹ וְאֶת צֹאן לָבָן אֲחִי אִמּוֹ וַיִּגַּשׁ יַעֲקֹב וַיָּגֶל אֶת הָאֶבֶן מֵעַל פִּי הַבְּאֵר וַיַּשְׁקְ אֶת צֹאן לָבָן אֲחִי אִמּוֹ.**

*And Ya'akov said, "Behold, the day is still young. It is not yet time to gather in the cattle. Water the sheep, and go out and shepherd them in the pasture." The shepherds replied, "We are unable to, for all the sheep and shepherds must first be gathered together. Then we will be able to roll the stone from the mouth of the well and give the cattle to drink." And it was, when Ya'akov saw Rachel, the daughter of Lavan, his mother's brother, and Lavan's sheep, Ya'akov approached the well, and he rolled the stone off the well and gave his uncle's sheep to drink.*[99]

Rashi elaborates upon this amazing feat of strength.

כְּאָדָם שֶׁמַּעֲבִיר אֶת הַפְּקָק מֵעַל פִּי צְלוֹחִית, לְהוֹדִיעֲךָ שֶׁכֹּחוֹ גָּדוֹל.

*Ya'akov rolled the stone. Like someone unstopping a cork from a bottle. We are thus informed of the greatness of Ya'akov's strength.*[100]

The combined effort of many shepherds was required to roll the stone from the well. How can we understand Ya'akov's ability to single-handedly remove such an obstacle?

Rabbi Chaim Shmuelevitz warns us against the erroneous belief that Ya'akov's capability lay in his physical prowess. Surely many shepherds acting together would be physically stronger than Ya'akov individually. In a liturgical poem inserted into our prayers for rain we describe this very incident in the following words: יִחַד לֵב וְגָל אֶבֶן מִפִּי בְּאֵר מָיִם — Ya'akov unified his heart and was thus able to roll the boulder from the well. It was a singularity of will which was the secret of Ya'akov's immense power. The heart is the seat of

99. *Bereishith* 29:7, 8, 10.
100. Rashi *ad loc.*

desires, and when a person's desires are multifarious, his strength is fractured. As we have seen, an entity united has a degree of power incomparable to that of the sum of many parts. A heart cut into pieces has a power which is disproportionately weaker than a heart conjoined.

The great strength which lies in unification is highlighted by Rabbi Dessler.

> קֹדֶם חֶטְאוֹ שֶׁל אדה"ר הָיוּ כָּל הַנְּשָׁמוֹת כְּלוּלוֹת בּוֹ, כַּיָּדוּעַ. וְאִלּוּ לֹא חָטְאוּ הָיָה רַק הוּא וְעֶזְרָתוֹ מַגִּיעִים לְתַכְלִית הַבְּרִיאָה, כִּי בְּהַגִּיעַ הַשַּׁבָּת כְּבָר הָיָה מַגִּיעַ העוה"ב. נִמְצָא דְּכָל תֹּכֶן הַבְּרִיאָה הָיָה כָּלוּל בּוֹ וְעֶזְרָתוֹ, וּבְיוֹם אֶחָד, וּבִבְחִירָה אַחַת, ע"י הַחֵטְא נִתְפָּרֵט תֹּכֶן הַבְּרִיאָה לִפְרָטִים הַרְבֵּה. תַּחַת יוֹם אֶחָד נִתְפָּרֵט זְמַן הָעֲבוֹדָה לְשֵׁשֶׁת אַלְפֵי שָׁנָה. תַּחַת אֶחָד, נִתְפָּרְטוּ בְּנֵי אָדָם הַבּוֹחֲרִים לְמִלְיוֹנִים וְדוֹרוֹת הַרְבֵּה. וְכֵן תַּחַת בְּחִירָה אַחַת שֶׁהָיְתָה רְאוּיָה לְגַלּוֹת כְּבוֹדוֹ יתֹ', עַד כְּדֵי לְהַגִּיעַ אֶל תַּכְלִית הַבְּרִיאָה, נִהְיוּ בְּחִירוֹת לִבְלִי מִסְפָּר בְּכָל אֶחָד מִבְּנֵי אָדָם.[101]

Prior to Adam's sin, all souls were centralised in him. The whole of mankind was concentrated in one man. Had they not sinned, he and Chavah would have achieved the purpose of the universe, and entered the era of Eternal Sabbath. Everything could have been achieved by him and Chavah in only one day, through one act of free choice. But after the sin, the world was shattered into numerous shards. Six thousand years were now required to fulfill the mission of one day. Now every person in every generation, thousands of millions of individuals, are required to do what could have been accomplished by a lone man. Adam had only one choice to make through which God's glory would be manifest. Now, the glory can only be manifest through the sum of every act of free choice which each person makes. It takes thousands of days, billions of people, each faced with a multitude of choices, to add up to one choice of Adam. When all is concentrated in one, the power is of mammoth proportions. In our range of experience, this phenomenon can be likened to the awesome power of the atom bomb. The entire process being

---

101. *Michtav MeEliyahu*, Part One, p. 244.

concentrated in just one atom, the emanating power is enormous.

Rabbi Dessler later expands on this idea, quoting Rabbi Moshe Cordovero:

> עֲבֵרוֹת שֶׁבֵּין אָדָם לַחֲבֵרוֹ אֵין יוה"כ מְכַפֵּר... וְהַטַּעַם לָזֶה, כִּי הַנְּשָׁמוֹת מִתְרָאוֹת לְפָנָיו בַּיּוֹם זֶה בְּסוֹד... שֹׁרֶשׁ אֶל הַנְּשָׁמוֹת, וְהַנְּשָׁמוֹת הַנִּכְנָעוֹת בִּתְשׁוּבָה הֵן מְעוֹרֶרֶת הַתְּשׁוּבָה הָעֶלְיוֹנָה... וְעַתָּה אִם יִמְצָא בֵּינוֹ לְבֵין חֲבֵרוֹ טִינָה הֲרֵי הוּא מַפְרִיד... הַשֹּׁרֶשׁ הָעֶלְיוֹן... וְאֵיךְ אֶפְשָׁר שֶׁיַּשְׁפִּיעַ עָלָיו אוֹר הַתְּשׁוּבָה וְהוּא מַפְרִיד בּוֹ ח"ו... וְהָעִנְיָן בַּזֶּה, כִּי סוֹד הַנְּשָׁמוֹת הוּא ס' רִבּוֹא... וּכְדֵי לְהַמְשִׁיךְ אוֹר עֶלְיוֹן צָרִיךְ ס' רִבּוֹא לֵב אֶחָד, כְּדֵי שֶׁיִּתְיַחֲדוּ בִּשְׁמָא קַדִּישָׁא עִילָאָה רַבְרְבָא דְּלָא שַׁרְיָא אֶלָּא בְּאַחְדוּת הַשָּׁלֵם כְּעִנְיָן שֶׁהוּא אֶחָד.
>
> *Yom Kippur does not afford a cleansing for sins committed between man and his fellow. The reason for this is that on Yom Kippur we penetrate to the pure root of each soul. If antagonism exists between two people, the people are separate, and thus separated from the single Source. Separation from the Source precludes repentance, which is given to a person from the Source. There are 600,000 souls which constitute the Jewish People (as seen at Mount Sinai, where 600,000 people were present). This multitude must all be connected to the single Source to facilitate the reception of Divinely bestowed light. Just as God is One, and we are to be attached to Him, we must also be bound into oneness.*[102]

Attachment to God can only mean similarity to Him, for it is impossible for mortal man to cleave to the Divine. This is the command of, מַה הוּא אַף אַתָּה — "What He does, so should you do." The obligation incumbent upon us is one of imitation. It follows that just as God is One, we, emulating this exclusivity, must also be one.

On this basis we can understand why an assembly of people was the vital prerequisite to construction of the *Mishkan*. The מִשְׁכָּן, *Mishkan*, was a place of שְׁכִינָה, a place where the Divine Presence could rest. A related word to this is שָׁכֵן, literally a neighbour, which

---

102. *Michtav MeEliyahu*, p. 264.

clearly indicates the nature of the *Mishkan*. It was a place where the immediacy of God was readily apparent, a place of intimacy between God and the Jewish People. As stated, closeness, in relation to the Almighty, can only mean similarity to Him. As God is One, unity was the demand upon the Jewish People; and indeed, in the depths of the soul, every Jew is connected to every other. We were all originally part of one man, Adam, and although we are physically separated, at root, we are inextricably bound. Sin separated us into a multitude of pebbles in place of the huge boulder. The strength previously present was dramatically reduced. Unifying the proliferation actuates an awesome potential of power to which we are all but oblivious.

Ya'akov unified his heart, and thus he could free the well from its obstruction like one removing a stopper from a bottle. Ya'akov's ability in the area of will also manifests itself in a second incident, which results in the merging of numerous moments of time.

**וַיַּעֲבֹד יַעֲקֹב בְּרָחֵל שֶׁבַע שָׁנִים וַיִּהְיוּ בְעֵינָיו כְּיָמִים אֲחָדִים...**

*Ya'akov worked for Rachel for seven years, and... they seemed to him like a few days.*[103]

Ya'akov's singularity of desire contracted time itself, causing many years to become a few days.

This phenomenon was demonstrated by Ya'akov yet again, this time in the realm of space. On his journeys, Ya'akov passed Mount Moriah and upon arrival at Charan, he came to the following realisation:

אֶפְשָׁר שֶׁעָבַרְתִּי עַל מָקוֹם שֶׁהִתְפַּלְּלוּ אֲבוֹתַי וְלֹא הִתְפַּלַּלְתִּי בּוֹ יָהֵב דַּעְתֵּיהּ לְמֶהֱדַר וְחָזַר עַד בֵּית אֵל וְקָפְצָה לוֹ הָאָרֶץ.[104]

Regretting having passed the place where his father and grandfather had prayed without stopping to pray at the site, Ya'akov resolved in his mind and unified his heart in desire to return to the

103. *Bereishith* 29:20.
104. Rashi on *Bereishith* 28:17.

hallowed place. Immediately he experienced קְפִיצַת הַדֶּרֶךְ, meaning, as Rashi explains, that the land "jumped" beneath his feet, bringing his desired destination towards him so that a journey of considerable length took a disproportionately short time. Furlongs and yards melted into oneness. Space, too, contracted in the face of Ya'akov's unity of desire, a unity producing strength and power one would never think possible.

Returning to the subject of the *Mishkan*, the *Ohr HaChaim* makes a fascinating comment in explanation of a grammatical anomaly:

**וַיַּעֲשׂוּ כָל חֲכַם לֵב בְּעֹשֵׂי הַמְּלָאכָה אֶת הַמִּשְׁכָּן עֶשֶׂר יְרִיעֹת שֵׁשׁ מָשְׁזָר וּתְכֵלֶת וְאַרְגָּמָן... מַעֲשֵׂה חֹשֵׁב עָשָׂה אֹתָם... וַיְחַבֵּר אֶת חֲמֵשׁ הַיְרִיעֹת... וַיַּעַשׂ לֻלְאֹת תְּכֵלֶת...**

*All the wise-hearted among the craftsmen made the Dwelling [cover out of] ten drapes [made of] twined linen, and aquamarine, purple and scarlet [wool]... and he attached five of the drapes one to another... he made aquamarine [wool] loops....*[105]

פֵּרוּשׁ הֲגַם שֶׁהָעוֹשִׂים רַבִּים הֵם אַף עַל פִּי כֵן הָיְתָה הַמְּלָאכָה נַעֲשֵׂית כְּאִלּוּ עֲשָׂאָהּ אָדָם אֶחָד. וְהַכַּוָּנָה בָּזֶה כִּי כְּשֶׁיַּעֲשׂוּ הַמְּלָאכָה רַבִּים עַל כָּל פָּנִים יִשְׁתַּנֶּה תֹּאַר מְלֶאכֶת זֶה מִזֶּה, וְלֹא תִדְמֶה לַמְּלָאכָה שֶׁיַּעֲשֶׂנָּה כֻּלָּהּ אֻמָּן אֶחָד. וְהִשְׁמִיעָנוּ הַכָּתוּב כִּי מְלֶאכֶת הַמִּשְׁכָּן שְׁלֵמָה הָיְתָה גַּם בִּבְחִינָה זוֹ. כִּי הַנּוֹתֵן חָכְמָה בָּהֵמָּה הִשְׁוָה אוֹתָם בְּהִתְבּוֹנְנוּת הַחָכְמָה, שָׁוָה וְדוֹמִים כֻּלָּם לְאִישׁ אֶחָד. וּלְדֶרֶךְ זֶה יִתְיַשֵּׁב טַעַם אוֹמְרוֹ בְּכָל פְּרָטֵי הַמַּעֲשִׂים לְשׁוֹן יָחִיד.[106]

To paraphrase: In describing the work involved in the *Mishkan*'s construction, the verse initially mentions that it was the product of many people's labour. All subsequent descriptions indicate that the *Mishkan* was constructed by only one person, the references being in the singular, not the plural form. Although many people were involved in the work, it was done in a manner in which one would

105. *Shemoth* 36:8.
106. *Ohr HaChaim ad loc.*

think it was through the hands of only one man. Usually, when numerous people work on a project, the effort of each individual is discernable. The individual style of each worker will be noticeable and distinct from any other person's contribution. However, in the case of the *Mishkan*, every person involved in the building was imbued with the same wisdom and skill. This resulted in the appearance of the entire edifice as the work of only one man. Thus, the verse repeatedly refers to the work that "he" did. The "he" can not refer to Betzal'el for he himself only constructed the Ark. However, the phrase shows us that its appearance was that it was the workmanship of one man.

We see from the above, that the unity of the *Mishkan* had to be manifest in the manner of its construction. If the work of the *Mishkan* had involved many parts, it would have been considered a labour of diversity and difference, and thus the שְׁכִינָה, the closeness to the One God, could never have been brought to rest on the edifice. Unity in all areas was the prerequisite for closeness to the One God. Thus the "וַיַּקְהֵל" was needed to animate strengths which would otherwise have been impossible to achieve.

In conjunction with our theme, the *Sefer Beith Ya'akov* states the following:

> כְּשֶׁיֵּשׁ הִתְחַבְּרוּת לִדְבַר קְדֻשָּׁה יָכֹל כָּל אֶחָד מֵהַכְּלָל לְשַׁנּוֹת וּלְהִתְגַּבֵּר עַל הַרְבֵּה בְּרֶגַע אֶחָד.
>
> *When people join together for a holy purpose, everyone is able to change, and overcome much in but one moment.*

When many people join together with a single-mindedness, with a unity of desire, the many pebbles are transformed into one large boulder, with a power incomparable to that of the sum of many stones.

An application of this idea is particularly relevant to those who are members of Torah institutions. If many people coalesce with the same goals and aspirations, incredible results can be effected. Soldering diverse personal wills into a common identity, dedicated to God, can have an awesome effect — comparable to the explosion of an atom bomb. Uniting, with "one heart," each individual will discover strengths in himself which he would never have envisioned as being possible. May we merit the unity of the וַיַּקְהֵל, becoming one as He is One, and thus allowing the Divine Presence to dwell among us.

# PIKUDEI

PARASHATH PIKUDEI DEALS with God's commandments concerning the construction of the *Mishkan*: a majestic structure whose physical features were to reflect its lofty purpose. Its construction thus required highly skilled craftsmen, proficient in multifarious varieties of work. Betzal'el was the individual selected to execute this grand project, with Oholiav at his side to aid him.

> אֵלֶּה פְקוּדֵי הַמִּשְׁכָּן מִשְׁכַּן הָעֵדֻת אֲשֶׁר פֻּקַּד עַל פִּי מֹשֶׁה עֲבֹדַת הַלְוִיִּם בְּיַד אִיתָמָר בֶּן אַהֲרֹן הַכֹּהֵן. וּבְצַלְאֵל בֶּן אוּרִי בֶן חוּר לְמַטֵּה יְהוּדָה עָשָׂה אֵת כָּל אֲשֶׁר צִוָּה ה' אֶת מֹשֶׁה. וְאִתּוֹ אָהֳלִיאָב בֶּן אֲחִיסָמָךְ לְמַטֵּה דָן חָרָשׁ וְחֹשֵׁב וְרֹקֵם בַּתְּכֵלֶת וּבָאַרְגָּמָן וּבְתוֹלַעַת הַשָּׁנִי וּבַשֵּׁשׁ.
>
> *These are the accountings of the Dwelling, the Dwelling of the testimony, that were calculated according to Moshe's instructions; [for] the work of the Leviyim, under the direction of Ithamar the son of Aharon the Priest. Betzal'el, the son of Uri, the son of Chur, of the tribe of Yehudah, carried out all that the Eternal had commanded Moshe. And with him [was] Oholiav, the son of Achisamach of the tribe of Dan, a craftsman and skilled weaver, and an embroiderer in aquamarine, purple and scarlet [wool], and in linen.*[107]

A stark contrast between the description of Betzal'el and that of Oholiav is here presented to us. Oholiav's talents are multifaceted; Scripture details every area in which he excels. Betzal'el, however, is awarded no such description. We are told simply that he "obeyed the word of God." The *Beith Yosef* offers the following cryptic words to account for this distinction.

---

107. *Shemoth* 38:21–23.

אֵצֶל בְּצַלְאֵל נֶאֱמַר הַכְּלָל וְאֵצֶל אָהֳלִיאָב בִּפְרָט. בִּיהוּדָה אַתְּוָן רְשִׁמִי חֲקִיקָן בּוֹ וְלָזֶה לֹא הָיָה צָרִיךְ לְהַבִּיט אֶל הַפְּרָטִים. אָהֳלִיאָב שֶׁבָּא מִשֵּׁבֶט דָּן מְאַסֵּף לְכָל הַמַּחֲנוֹת הָיָה צָרִיךְ לְהַבִּיט אֶל כָּל פְּרָט וּפְרָט.

He explains that Betzal'el originated from the tribe of Yehudah. Incorporated into the name Yehudah is the holy Name of the Almighty: יְהוּדָה contains the letters י-ה-ו-ה. For this reason, Betzal'el was not required to focus on details. Oholiav, however, traced his lineage to the tribe of Dan. The task of Dan was to act as a rear guard throughout the Children of Yisrael's travels through the Wilderness. Whenever it was time to decamp and move on, Dan would be the last to leave, and if anyone were to stray, or slip out of the Clouds of Glory, it was Dan's mission to gather them back into the camp. It was thus necessary for them to attend to every detail.

Let us investigate the meaning of this obscure explanation. To unlock the secret, we will need to turn to a Midrash on this *parashah.*

אָמַר הקב"ה לְיִשְׂרָאֵל: בְּשָׁעָה שֶׁעֲשִׂיתֶם אֶת הָעֵגֶל הִכְעַסְתֶּם אוֹתִי בְּ"אֵלֶּה אֱלֹהֶיךָ". עַכְשָׁו שֶׁעֲשִׂיתֶם הַמִּשְׁכָּן בְּ"אֵלֶּה" אֲנִי מִתְרַצֶּה לָכֶם. הֱוֵי "אֵלֶּה פְקוּדֵי הַמִּשְׁכָּן".

*God said to Yisrael, "At the time when you fashioned the Golden Calf, you angered Me with the word* אֵלֶּה, *saying* אֵלֶּה אֱלֹהֶיךָ יִשְׂרָאֵל *— 'These are your gods, Yisrael.' Now that you have made the Mishkan, and used the word* אֵלֶּה *in its construction, I have been appeased with the word* אֵלֶּה.*"*[108]

This Midrash is not concerned simply with wordplay or semantics. Both God's displeasure and His later appeasement hinged on this small word. What lies in the word אֵלֶּה, which renders it the source of such extreme reactions?

Rabbi Eliezer Kahn, in his work *Nachalath Eliezer*, connects this Midrash with a comment of Rashi on the portion of *Mishpatim.* The *parashah* begins with the words:

---

108. *Shemoth Rabbah* 51:8.

**וְאֵלֶּה הַמִּשְׁפָּטִים אֲשֶׁר תָּשִׂים לִפְנֵיהֶם.**

*And these are the laws that you shall present before them.*[109]

Rashi comments:

כָּל מָקוֹם שֶׁנֶּאֱמַר "אֵלֶּה" פָּסַל אֶת הָרִאשׁוֹנִים. "וְאֵלֶּה" מוֹסִיף עַל הָרִאשׁוֹנִים. מָה הָרִאשׁוֹנִים מִסִּינַי, אַף אֵלּוּ מִסִּינַי.

*Whenever the word* אֵלֶּה *is used, it marks a separation, a new start, detached from that which transpired beforehand. The word "*וְאֵלֶּה*," "and these," however, indicates a connection and addition to that which preceded.*[110]

The אֵלֶּה in our *parashah*, concerning the construction of the *Mishkan*, serves to isolate the subject from the preceding theme.

At that infamous moment in Jewish history, as the nation feverishly constructed the Golden Calf, "אֵלֶּה" was the cry of the people. "אֵלֶּה," as Rashi states, cuts one off from prior events. With their declaration of אֵלֶּה אֱלֹהֶיךָ יִשְׂרָאֵל the nation divorced themselves from all prior events.

אֵלֶּה — From the liberation of Egypt, they severed themselves.

אֵלֶּה — From the wondrous splitting of the Red Sea, they rent themselves.

אֵלֶּה — From the countless miracles through which they were sustained in the desert, they isolated themselves.

אֵלֶּה — From their inner fear of God, they separated themselves.

אֵלֶּה — From all these, the Children of Yisrael divorced themselves, estranging themselves from their benevolent Father, forsaking His plan of creation.

And then:

אֵלֶּה פְקוּדֵי הַמִּשְׁכָּן — The nation purged the evil from within themselves, cutting off any connection to the Golden Calf. They began a new chapter — the construction of the *Mishkan*. The *Mishkan* was prescribed by God to atone for the sin of the Golden Calf. In this

109. *Shemoth* 21:1.
110. Rashi *ad loc.*

instance, therefore, the word אֵלֶּה denotes a fresh start, a separation from all that transpired beforehand. With this word then, the nation atoned for their previous אֵלֶּה of negativity and sin.

Furthermore, the verse states, אֵלֶּה פְקוּדֵי הַמִּשְׁכָּן — "These are the accountings of the *Mishkan*." One who loves money counts coins one by one, for each has importance and value to him. Counting is thus the act of according importance to an entity. Every part of the *Mishkan* was detailed out, indicating a collective change in priority. The *Mishkan* was now of utmost importance to them; spirituality was now what they sought.

> אֵלֶּה כְּתִיב וְלֹא כְּתִיב וְאֵלֶּה. אֶלָּא דָּא אִיהוּ חֻשְׁבְּנָא דְּפָסִיל כָּל חֻשְׁבְּנִין דְּעָלְמָא, וְדָא אִתְקַיַּים יַתִּיר מִכֻּלְּהוּ. דִּבְהַאי אִתְקַיַּים מִשְׁכְּנָא וְלֹא בְּאַחֲרָא.
>
> אֵלֶּה *is written, not* וְאֵלֶּה*. This calculation overrode any other estimation. Any desires, any other wishes, were all severed with the construction of the Mishkan. Thus, this project effected atonement for the tumultuous events that preceded its construction.*[111]

This can be related to the famous accounting to which each person is subject when he is eventually summoned to a judgment of his life.

> אָמַר רָבָא, בְּשָׁעָה שֶׁמַּכְנִיסִין אָדָם לַדִּין, אוֹמְרִים לוֹ: קָבַעְתָּ עִתִּים לַתּוֹרָה?
>
> *When a man is brought to stand in judgment (at the end of his life), he will be asked, "Did you fix times for Torah study?"*[112]

The work *Beith Ya'akov* highlights the underlying meaning of this question.

> הַמְכֻוָּן בִּקְבִיעַת עִתִּים שֶׁזֶּה יִהְיֶה אֵצֶל הָאָדָם הָעִקָּר.

---

111. *Zohar* on *Pikudei*.
112. *Shabbath* 31a.

Not everyone has the opportunity to be constantly involved in Torah study. However, everyone, irrespective of his standing, is required to appoint specific times in which to engage in Torah study. Fixing a time is not merely a technical act; instead, it reflects on the entirety of one's spiritual development. It indicates that throughout one's life, Torah is that which is "fixed," which is given the highest position, all else revolving around it. One can spend one's day involved in business, in financial endeavours, yet if one accords paramount importance to that time, at the end of the day, in which he devotes time to Torah study, then he implicitly demonstrates the purpose and priority of his life. All else is viewed as transient in relation to his period of Torah study, which can never be compromised. He has thus prioritized his spirituality over everything that this world so tantalizingly offers.

The antithesis of this value is seen in Haman, the villain of the Purim story. At the zenith of his power, in his position as Prime Minister, he received an invitation by Queen Esther to join her and Achashverosh at a banquet.

**וַיְסַפֵּר לָהֶם הָמָן אֶת כְּבוֹד עָשְׁרוֹ וְרֹב בָּנָיו וְאֵת כָּל אֲשֶׁר גִּדְּלוֹ הַמֶּלֶךְ וְאֵת אֲשֶׁר נִשְּׂאוֹ עַל הַשָּׂרִים וְעַבְדֵי הַמֶּלֶךְ. וַיֹּאמֶר הָמָן אַף לֹא הֵבִיאָה אֶסְתֵּר הַמַּלְכָּה עִם הַמֶּלֶךְ אֶל הַמִּשְׁתֶּה אֲשֶׁר עָשָׂתָה כִּי אִם אוֹתִי וְגַם לְמָחָר אֲנִי קָרוּא לָהּ עִם הַמֶּלֶךְ.**

*Haman related the glory of his wealth, his numerous children, and his promotion over the princes and servants of the king, to his wife and children. Haman said, "Further, Esther has invited no one apart from me to the banquet which she is preparing. I have also been called to join her and the king tomorrow."*

On top of the world, there seems to be nothing more that Haman could wish for. Everything, all success and prosperity, lie in his domain. Yet, Haman continues:

**וְכָל זֶה אֵינֶנּוּ שֹׁוֶה לִי בְּכָל עֵת אֲשֶׁר אֲנִי רֹאֶה אֶת מָרְדֳּכַי הַיְּהוּדִי יוֹשֵׁב בְּשַׁעַר הַמֶּלֶךְ.**

*"And all this means nothing to me when I see Mordechai the Jew sitting at the entrance to the king's palace."*[113]

Our Sages highlight Haman's use of the word זֶה — "this."

וְכָל זֶה אֵינֶנּוּ שֹׁוֶה לִי. מְלַמֵּד שֶׁכָּל גְּנָזָיו שֶׁל אוֹתוֹ רָשָׁע חֲקוּקִין עַל לִבּוֹ. וּבְשָׁעָה שֶׁרוֹאֶה אֶת מָרְדְּכַי יוֹשֵׁב בְּשַׁעַר הַמֶּלֶךְ, אָמַר וְכָל זֶה אֵינֶנּוּ שֹׁוֶה לִי.

*From the expression, "All this means nothing to me," we learn that all the treasures of this evil man were engraved upon his heart. When he encountered Mordechai sitting at the king's gate, he said, "All this means nothing to me."*[114]

The term זֶה remains ambiguous if it does not overtly refer to a specific thing. זֶה must be used in conjunction with a signal, a sign, a pointing finger, for it to be meaningful. Passing by Mordechai, Haman was filled with venomous anger and hate, to the extent that his vast treasuries and power were rendered valueless. Expressing this feeling, Haman used the word זֶה. Although this word would normally be considered ambiguous, Haman's wealth was constantly the centre of his focus, "engraved upon his heart." He could declare, "and all this means nothing to me," with absolute clarity; it was obvious and unquestionable what he was referring to. For materialism, amassing riches, this was what dominated Haman's thoughts, and his whole life. His energies revolved around the pursuit of more and more wealth. It was this that was "engraved upon his heart."

The antithesis of Haman was Betzal'el. Betzal'el originated from the tribe of Yehudah, concerning whom it is written, אַתְוָן רִשְׁמִי חֲקִיקָן בּוֹ — "The Name of God was inscribed in his." Integrated into Yehudah's name is the Tetragrammaton. Pursuit of holiness was his essence; Godliness was weaved into the fabric of his being, an indelible stamp on his soul, on his heart. Thus, his whole interest, all of his desires, energy and focus were concentrated on one thing:

113. *Esther* 5:11–13.
114. *Megillah* 15b.

devotion to God. His every fibre was dedicated to Divine service. When Betzal'el uttered the word זֶה, it was clearly obvious to what he was referring. There was nothing else to which it could refer apart from spirituality, fulfillment of God's will. Indeed, the expression that Betzal'el acted "just as God commanded Moshe," is mentioned no less than eighteen times in this *parashah*. Betzal'el's exclusive desire was to fulfill God's will, and faithfully follow His command. While Haman's heart was engraved with a lust for physicality, on Betzal'el's heart, the Name of God was delicately chiseled.

Turning back to the distinction between Betzal'el and Oholiav, we can understand the words of the *Beith Yosef* through comparing the two prophets Yechezkel and Yeshayah. Both prophets merited a mystical vision of the Throne of Glory, and the Heavenly chariot, and both prophets recorded the awesome experience. Yet, there is a marked difference between their descriptions of this vision. While Yechezkel gives a long and detailed description of the Heavenly sight, Yeshayah's account consists of a mere three verses. This marked difference prompted our Sages' comment.

כָּל מַה שֶּׁרָאָה יְחֶזְקֵאל רָאָה יְשַׁעְיָה. יְחֶזְקֵאל לְמָה הוּא דוֹמֶה לְבֶן כְּפָר שֶׁרָאָה אֶת הַמֶּלֶךְ. יְשַׁעְיָה לְבֶן כְּרַךְ שֶׁרָאָה אֶת הַמֶּלֶךְ.[115]

We are urged not to err and think that Yechezkel attained a higher level of prophecy than did Yeshayah. We are told, "All that Yechezkel saw, Yeshayah saw." However, Yechezkel can be compared to a villager who, to his good fortune, caught a glimpse of the king. Yeshayah can be compared to an inhabitant of the capital city. Living in the king's vicinity, he is accustomed to catching sight of the king during his daily schedule. Encountering the king is commonplace, and will thus not elicit excitement, or a significant reaction. He will speak about it an offhand manner, mentioning the meeting in passing.

In contrast, the villager will enthuse about his experience to friends and family, describing every detail. The coach, the king's garb,

---

115. *Chaggigah* 13b.

posture, expression, and commands will all have been painstakingly committed to memory.

Our Sages elaborate: Yeshayah and his generation were on a greater spiritual plane than that of Yechezkel and his generation. Accustomed as they were to God's Presence, it was sufficient to report only the generality, the overall picture. Yechezkel was on a lower level; it was a rare occurrence to behold a vision of the Almighty. Therefore, every small detail was mentioned. The nearer one is to majesty, the closer the relationship, the less detail required.

Returning to the function of the tribe of Dan in the Wilderness as retrievers of those who strayed from the camp, we must understand that exclusion from the Clouds of Glory did not occur simply on a physical level, because some people walked at a slower pace than the rest of the camp. There was a deeper cause, a spiritual root. It was only those who had distanced themselves from Godliness, who were spiritually weak, who fell out of the protection of the Clouds of Glory. The mission of the tribe of Dan was to reintroduce these individuals into the camp by leading them along the path of self-development. For these people who were far away, the most effective method to achieve this was to elaborate upon details. The further away the person, the more information required to return him to the truth.

To illustrate this principle let us bring a parable. A man complaining of a certain ailment is advised to undergo serious and complicated surgery. The gravity of the situation is such that the man seeks a second opinion. Entering the doctor's office, he explains his situation, and tells the doctor about the entire procedure which has been recommended. After stating his opinion, the doctor is questioned closely by the patient. Everything from the prior anaesthetic to the pain relief and antibiotics administered after the operation is queried, and the patient elicits every detail possible from the doctor.

Let us contrast this with another scenario. The patient, anxious about a certain malady, desires to see a doctor. He investigates, and makes an appointment with a world-renowned specialist in the field, a doctor to whom all others defer. When the specialist recommends a certain course of action, it would not enter the patient's mind to seek a second opinion. He has no understanding of the procedure, yet he has such total faith in the competence and professionalism of the doctor that he is happy to blindly follow any instructions that the doctor might issue.

Betzal'el always did כַּאֲשֶׁר צִוָּה ה' אֶת מֹשֶׁה — "Just as God commanded Moshe." Filled with trust and total faith in the Almighty, it was unnecessary to delve into the reasons and details of the procedure. He was secure in the knowledge that he was executing the wishes of an omniscient, omnipotent God. One who is close to God will not need the many details, explanations, and rationale that must be presented when dealing with someone stationed lower on the ladder of spirituality.

Over the years, different prophets distilled the essence of man's Divine service in as few verses as possible. Chavakkuk succeeded in defining the one vital area which is the foundation of all of man's labour: וְצַדִּיק בֶּאֱמוּנָתוֹ יִחְיֶה — "A righteous man will live by his faith."[116] In condensing the Torah into this pithy statement, Chavakkuk was declaring that a Jew's very life is bound up with his belief in God. *Emunah* is that which is "engraved upon his heart" and forms the basis of his whole weltanschauung. All of life's vicissitudes, all events in the world, are viewed from a perspective of *emunah*, of absolute, unequivocal, unwavering faith. One whose *emunah* is etched upon his heart will constantly feel God's presence before him, in fulfillment of the dictum, שִׁוִּיתִי ה' לְנֶגְדִּי תָמִיד. His thoughts are constantly occupied with a desire to serve the Almighty more fully; Torah is the constant around which all other variables revolve.

Too often do people fall prey to the allure of this limited physical world. Their hearts resemble the heart of Haman, for it is materialism, the plans to augment one's fortune and supplement one's income, which occupy centre stage in their mind. Engraved upon the hearts of so many is desire for materialism, selfishness, and the futility of this transient world.

---

116. *Chavakkuk* 2:4.

Returning to Oholiav, we find that every detail of his role is mentioned. Originating from the tribe of Dan, he acquired enough information to attract those who had strayed from the correct path. Betzal'el was from the tribe of Yehudah; the name of God was "engraved upon his heart." His every thought was occupied with serving the Almighty, which he did with eagerness and wholesome simplicity. Anything that he was commanded to do, he willingly fulfilled.

To determine what is engraved upon our own hearts, we must scrutinise ourselves with unflinching honesty. What occupies our thoughts? Around which subjects are our conversations centred? Wherein lie our priorities? What is the source of our pleasure and happiness? Let us strive to obliterate any remnant of Haman, and instead cultivate the trait of Betzal'el. Let us make Torah the centre of our focus, and spirituality that which is "engraved upon our hearts."

# VAYIKRA

# VAYIKRA

THE BA'AL HATURIM makes a famous comment upon the letter *alef* in the first word of וַיִּקְרָא, our *parashah*:

> אָלֶ"ף דְּוַיִּקְרָא זְעִירָא. שֶׁמֹּשֶׁה הָיָה גָּדוֹל וְעָנָו לֹא רָצָה לִכְתֹּב אֶלָּא "וַיִּקֶר" לְשׁוֹן מִקְרֶה כְּאִלּוּ לֹא דִּבֵּר הקב"ה עִמּוֹ אֶלָּא בַּחֲלוֹם כְּדֶרֶךְ שֶׁנֶּאֱמַר בְּבִלְעָם כְּאִלּוּ לֹא נִרְאָה לוֹ ה' אֶלָּא בְּמִקְרֶה, וְאָמַר לוֹ הקב"ה לִכְתֹּב גַּם האל"ף וְשׁוּב אָמַר לוֹ מֹשֶׁה מֵחֲמַת רֹב עֲנָוָה שֶׁלֹּא יִכְתְּבֶנָּה אֶלָּא קְטַנָּה יוֹתֵר מִשְּׁאָר אלפי"ן שֶׁבַּתּוֹרָה וּכְתָבָהּ קְטַנָּה.
>
> *The letter alef in this word has a smaller appearance than all the other alefs in the Torah. Moshe had wanted to omit the letter completely, instead writing* וַיִּקֶר*, a term used when God appeared to Bilaam in a dream, denoting a chance encounter. God told him that he should write the alef; however, due to his great humility, Moshe pleaded for permission to write it smaller than the rest of the alefs in the Torah.*[1]

What is the underlying difference between וַיִּקֶר, to chance (the word Moshe originally wanted to write), and וַיִּקְרָא, to call?

An echo of the וַיִּקֶר, the happenstance, is discernable in the reading for *Parashath Zachor*, concerning the remembrance of Amalek:

> **זָכוֹר אֵת אֲשֶׁר עָשָׂה לְךָ עֲמָלֵק בַּדֶּרֶךְ בְּצֵאתְכֶם מִמִּצְרָיִם. אֲשֶׁר קָרְךָ בַּדֶּרֶךְ וַיְזַנֵּב בְּךָ כָּל הַנֶּחֱשָׁלִים אַחֲרֶיךָ וְאַתָּה עָיֵף וְיָגֵעַ וְלֹא יָרֵא אֱלֹקִים.**
>
> *Constantly remember what Amalek did to you on the way when you went out of Mitzrayim, that they encountered you on the way...*[2]

---

1. *Ba'al HaTurim* on *Vayikra* 1:1.
2. *Devarim* 25:17,18.

Rashi offers two explanations for the word קָרְךָ:

אֲשֶׁר קָרְךָ בַּדֶּרֶךְ – לְשׁוֹן מִקְרֶה. דָּבָר אַחֵר, לְשׁוֹן קֶרִי וְטֻמְאָה.

*The word* קָרְךָ *denotes a chance encounter, or alternatively can be interpreted as an expression of impurity.*[3]

To combat this impurity, we have the injunction of זָכוֹר — "Remember!" Memory is the life-giving elixir which will provide the antidote to אֲשֶׁר קָרְךָ בַּדֶּרֶךְ. The *Sefath Emeth* deals with the connection between memory and "coincidence":

וַיִּקָר לְשׁוֹן עֲרַאי הַיְנוּ שֶׁנִּפְרַשׁ וְנִכְרַת מֵהַשֹּׁרֶשׁ וכ"כ מהר"ל בְּאוֹר חָדָשׁ עִנְיַן עֲמָלֵק. אֲשֶׁר קָרְךָ שֶׁכֵּיוָן שֶׁהוּא מִתְנַגֵּד אֶל הָאֱמֶת. כמ"ש מִלְחָמָה לה' בַּעֲמָלֵק. א"כ אֵינוֹ בְּמַסְקָנָא. רַק בְּדֶרֶךְ מִקְרֶה כמ"ש שֶׁקֶר אֵין לוֹ רַגְלַיִם כו' עַיֵּן שָׁם דְּבָרִים נֶחְמָדִים.

*The word* וַיִּקָר *denotes chance, that which is divorced from its source. Thus did the Maharal write concerning Amalek in his work Ohr Chadash: Amalek opposed the truth, as it is written, "A war against God was the campaign of Amalek." No final conclusion was reached, this being only a matter of chance. As it is written, "Falsehood has no standing."*[4]

The *Sefath Emeth* thus praises the words of the Maharal, which to us are all but incomprehensible. How does it follow that "because Amalek fought against truth, he did not reach a final conclusion?" Further, how does this relate to the concept of chance?

Amalek is given the title of רֵאשִׁית גּוֹיִם — "First of the nations," by Bil'am.[5] There is a Midrash concerning this title in *Bereishith Rabbah.*

וַיֵּצֵא הָרִאשׁוֹן אַדְמוֹנִי. "אֲנִי רִאשׁוֹן וַאֲנִי אַחֲרוֹן". וּפוֹרֵעַ לָכֶם מִן הָרִאשׁוֹן זֶה עֵשָׂו דִּכְתִיב וַיֵּצֵא הָרִאשׁוֹן אַדְמוֹנִי. וּבוֹנֶה לָכֶם רִאשׁוֹן זֶה בֵּית הַמִּקְדָּשׁ דִּכְתִיב בֵּיהּ כִּסֵּא כָבוֹד מָרוֹם מֵרִאשׁוֹן וגו'. וְאָבִיא לָכֶם רִאשׁוֹן זֶה מֶלֶךְ הַמָּשִׁיחַ דִּכְתִיב בֵּיהּ רִאשׁוֹן לְצִיּוֹן הִנֵּה הִנָּם.

3. *Rashi ad loc.*
4. *Sefath Emeth on the Torah*, Part Two, p.165.
5. *Bemidbar* 24:20.

> *And the first one came ruddy. Says God, "I am the first and I am the last. I will punish them with the first, referring to Esav, as it says, 'and the first one came out red.' I will build for them a first, referring to the Temple concerning which is written, 'the glorious throne, elevated from the first.' I will bring them the first, referring to Mashiach, as it says, 'the first one of Zion.'"*[6]

One of the opening comments which Rashi makes in *Bereishith* deals with this theme of רֵאשִׁית, the first. Rashi here cites the principle that the world was created for the רֵאשִׁית, specifically for the Children of Yisrael and the Torah, which both march under this banner. A Midrash states that רֵאשִׁית also refers to the tithes which one must bring from one's possessions, to בִּכּוּרִים, the first of one's produce, and to חַלָּה, the first of one's dough. The world was created for these five things.

The explanation can be understood upon consideration of the underlying theme of these five. The sacred task of the Jewish People and of Torah is to take everything in this world and return it to its Source. This we must do in all areas of life, whether harvesting in the field or baking in the kitchen. All must be underscored by a realisation and intense feeling of the רֵאשִׁית, the Source from which all blessing and goodness is endowed. All must be related to the First Cause: the question מִי בָרָא אֵלֶּה — "Who created these?"[7] must be constantly on our lips as we view nature and the world at large in the context of its creation by God, the Source of all.

One who fails to ask the question of מִי בָרָא אֵלֶּה is left merely with the אֵלֶּה, the phenomena of the world as they appear superficially. This אֵלֶּה, this proliferation without First Cause, underscored the statement of the Jewish People at that infamous hour of the sin of the Golden Calf, where the cry rang out, אֵלֶּה אֱלֹהֶיךָ יִשְׂרָאֵל — "These are your gods, Yisrael."[8] It is our mission to add the query מִי to the אֵלֶּה, to question what lies behind the proliferation of the

6. *Bereishith Rabbah* 63:10.
7. *Yeshayah* 40:26.
8. *Shemoth* 32:4.

world. Indeed, the combination of the two words forms a permutation of the Name of God: אֱלֹקִים. Applying the correct question to the external vision leads one to the Almighty, Source of everything.

People resist taking things back to the source in an attempt to free themselves of obligation. Rabbi Dessler brings the example of a person who, reluctant to repay a debt, repeatedly pushes off appointments with his creditor. The constant delay and excuses, the constant pushing off of appointments, indicates that this person wants to avoid repaying his debt.

A parallel to such constant evasion is seen in today's society. The prevalent dogma is that man originated from apes, which evolved from more primitive organisms, which in turn evolved from even more primitive organisms until we reach the simplest amoeba, from which the entire multifarious animal (and human) kingdom are believed to have originated. The advanced scientists of today's futuristic world, however, do not question further, deeper. The single-celled amoeba has become the end point. Here, supposedly, lies the root of man's creation. Scientists thus designate the end point before reaching the end, never penetrating to the true Source of life itself.

When the spies brought back a slanderous report concerning the Land of Israel, the Jewish People cried, in their dashed hopes, נִתְּנָה רֹאשׁ — "Let us appoint a head (to return to Egypt)."[9] Rashi interprets these words as being לְשׁוֹן עֲבוֹדָה זָרָה, an expression of idolatry. The root of paganism is failing to discern the true רֹאשׁ, the true Source of everything in our lives. Paganism is the act of divorcing the mechanism from the Mechanic, Who stands just out of view. Paganism is the erroneous declaration of a רִאשׁוֹן while still very much in the middle, far from the true point of origin.

The Temple is called a true רִאשׁוֹן, for it is a structure whose purpose is to return people to the true source of all things. It is a place where the Divine Presence is manifest and felt, thus putting people back into contact with the truth. Mashiach, too, will be a conduit

9. *Bemidbar* 14:4.

through which the people will realise, מִי בָרָא אֵלֶּה. His coming will herald a newfound perspective as people begin to trace everything back to the Source.

Our world today is under the influence of Edom, concerning whom the Sages state: חָכְמָה בַּגּוֹיִם תַּאֲמִין[10]. One who claims that Edom possesses tremendous wisdom must be believed. Indeed, our world has been swamped by the dizzying influx of science and technology, both of which are advancing further with each passing day. Scientists become a רֵאשִׁית, with the apparent ability to do almost anything and a conviction in their own prowess. There is a נִתְּנָה רֹאשׁ, a cry of "Let us appoint a head," as they make themselves the רֵאשִׁית. Nothing is traced back to the first cause; the Hand of God is obscured behind the beguiling mask of nature and advancement.

The words of the Maharal, concerning the word מִקְרֶה, happenstance, that אֵינָהּ בַּמַּסְקָנָה — it lacks finality, conclusion — can now be understood. מִקְרֶה is that which stops in the middle, that which does not penetrate past the superficiality to reach the conclusion, the reality behind the illusion. It is this delusion that is nurtured by those who believe in a world of chance, a world which somehow, somewhere, came into being. They do not come to the First Cause; they lack a true conclusion.

This is what is meant by the statement שֶׁקֶר אֵין לוֹ רַגְלַיִם — "Falsehood has no standing."[11] The three letters which constitute the word שֶׁקֶר are all found at the end of the Hebrew alphabet. However, the final letter, the *tav*, is omitted. Although the message conveyed by these three letters reaches almost to the end, it never quite reaches the ultimate conclusion. Conversely, if we analyse the word truth, אֱמֶת, we see the word begins with an *alef*, the very first letter of the alphabet, continues with a *mem*, a letter which traces its course through the middle of the alphabet, and reaches the *tav*, the final letter, the completion and perfection of all. This beautiful demonstration in the actual words themselves reflects this abstract concept, for

10. *Eichah Rabbah* 2:17.
11. *Tikkunei Zohar* 425.

truth is the journey along a pathway leading to the ultimate recognition of אֲנִי רִאשׁוֹן וַאֲנִי אַחֲרוֹן — "I am the first and I am the last."

Falsehood is unable to endure, for no one, in the depths of their being, is genuinely convinced of a lie. *Emunah* is explained by Rabbi Dessler to denote honesty, and as such, is the only necessary ingredient for the recognition of the truth of creation and acknowledgement of the supremacy of God. The truth is present and discernable; it requires only a willingness to admit to one's perceptions.

The *Sefath Emeth*, in his elucidation of the command to remember Amalek, continues as follows:

> וְעִקַּר פֵּרוּשׁ זְכִירָה הוּא פְּנִימִיּוּת הַחִיּוּת מָקוֹם שֶׁאֵין שָׁם שִׁכְחָה. כֵּיוָן שֶׁהוּא עִקַּר הַחִיּוּת נִקְרָא זִכָּרוֹן. כמ"ש אַזְכָּרָתָהּ הוּא עִקָּר מְכֻוָּן וּמַהוּת הַדָּבָר. וְזֶהוּ מְחִיַּת עֲמָלֵק שֶׁלֹּא לַעֲשׂוֹת שׁוּם דָּבָר דֶּרֶךְ עֲרַאי רַק לִהְיוֹת דָּבוּק בְּשֹׁרֶשׁ הַחִיּוּת תָּמִיד כנ"ל.
>
> *Remembrance is the innermost point of life, the place where forgetfulness cannot exist. It is because it is the essence of one's life that it is called* זִכָּרוֹן*. The obliteration of Amalek is the rejection of performing any action in a manner of carelessness and thoughtlessness, in order that man develop a constant link to the Source of life.*

To understand this, let us turn to the words of Rabbi Dessler:

> הִנֵּנוּ סוֹבְרִים בְּטָעוּת, כִּי הַמַּחְשָׁבָה שֶׁשְּׁכַחְנוּהָ, כְּבָר אֵינֶנּוּ בָּנוּ. בֶּאֱמֶת קַיֶּמֶת תְּמוּנָתָהּ בְּמֹחֵנוּ, אֶלָּא שֶׁרְחוֹקָה הִיא מִנְּקֻדַּת הַהַכָּרָה. כְּשֶׁאָנוּ מִתְרַכְּזִים לִזְכֹּר הַמַּחְשָׁבָה הַשְּׁכוּחָה הִיא שָׁבָה אֶל הַכָּרָתֵנוּ. הַמִּדּוֹת וְהַכֹּחוֹת שֶׁעוֹבְדִים מִתַּחַת לְסַף הַכָּרַת הָאָדָם, הֵמָּה אֲשֶׁר יְקָרְבוּ אֶת הַמַּחְשָׁבוֹת לְהִזָּכֵר וַאֲשֶׁר יַרְחִיקוּן לְבִלְתִּי תִּזָּכַרְנָה. אָנוּ אֵינֶנּוּ מַבְחִינִים בְּשָׁרְשֵׁי וְאוֹפַנֵּי הַהַרְחָקָה הַהִיא, אֶלָּא קוֹרְאִים לָזֶה פָּשׁוּט — שִׁכְחָה.[12]

People erroneously believe that if one has forgotten something, the information has been lost. In truth, the information is still present; it is simply not being recalled. Everything is remembered; all that happens leaves an imprint on one's subconscious. However, one

---

12. *Michtav MeEliyahu*, Part One, p.129.

may encounter difficulties bringing it from the subconscious to one's active mind.

The principal of the Manchester Yeshiva, citing a story involving a woman who underwent an operation, brought an apt illustration of this idea. While under anaesthesia, the woman sang an Italian opera from start to finish. Upon awaking from the anaesthetic, the nurse questioned the woman on her obvious love of Italian opera. The woman denied any knowledge of opera, claiming that she had never seen a performance. Questioned further, the woman recalled that she had indeed, while in school, once been taken on a class trip to the opera. It was the arias from this performance that she had sung during the surgery. Although we may remain oblivious to the process, every single experience is filed away in our minds. When we exert ourselves, and think deeply, we will be able to retrieve these impressions. Superficial thinking precludes recollection, for retrieval is only possible through the means of deep and penetrating thought.

While in the womb, a fetus is taught the entire Torah. Upon birth, the child is touched upon the lips, and the information dissipates. What then is the purpose of teaching the child? Upon reflection, the answer is clear. Although nothing is recalled, nothing is forgotten. All knowledge imparted to the child is driven down deep into the subconscious at the moment of entry into this world. This ensures that the most profound thing in the child, and in every person, is the unadulterated truth. It is only the introduction of physicality and materialism that prevents the knowledge being readily accessible. Living life with an outlook of superficiality will prevent the truth from ever becoming manifest. However, the one who exerts himself to reach the root of his being, is one who lives in a manner of thought and profundity; one who lives a life of recollection.

מִלְחָמָה לַה' בַּעֲמָלֵק — A life of happenstance and coincidence is a life-long battle with truth. As explained by the *Sefath Emeth*, מִקְרֶה denotes severance from the Source. It is that which never reaches a final conclusion, that which never penetrates to the First Cause. It is a life of forgetfulness; a forgetfulness stemming from a refusal to recall, a refusal to search still deeper, to live a life of depth.

We are commanded to obliterate the name of Amalek. In this mitzvah, we are enjoined to view nothing as happenstance, but rather to come back to the First Cause of all. We are commanded to meditate deep within ourselves, and thus reach the conclusion that lies in our core. We must divest ourselves of viewing merely the superficial appearance and fathom the root of all.

Obliteration of Amalek, then, is rejection of superficiality, renunciation of a life of chance and coincidence. Obliteration of Amalek is a dismissal of the idolatry, the paganistic weltanschauung which refuses to reach a final conclusion, instead stopping in the middle and constructing an artificial רֵאשִׁית. It is a dismissal of the scientific frenzy in which the world currently finds itself. Obliteration of Amalek is a return of the אֲנִי רִאשׁוֹן וַאֲנִי אַחֲרוֹן — "I am the first and I am the last," of God Himself. We are called upon to live a life of remembrance, constantly recalling the impression, the truth that is present deep within.

Our Sages state:

> כָּל הָאוֹמֵר דָּבָר בְּשֵׁם אוֹמְרוֹ מֵבִיא גְאֻלָּה לָעוֹלָם.
>
> *Everyone who credits his words to the originator of the saying brings redemption to the world.*[13]

It is this trait that must be nurtured, the trait of returning things to their source, of acknowledging the beginning, and thereby bringing the Redemption. We must peer behind the mask and recognise the Source and First Cause of all. It is this fundamental lesson that the festival of Purim instills in the Jew. And, only once this lesson has been internalised, do we indeed experience redemption. Hence, Purim, penetration of the mask, is followed by Pesach, the festival of revelation and redemption.

May each of us merit to cultivate this trait inside ourselves, recognising the Source of all, and recalling the truth which lies within each one of us. May we thus merit the Ultimate Redemption, where the mask will be removed and all will recognise מִי בָרָא אֵלֶּה.

---

13. *Megillah* 15a.

# T'ZAV

IN THIS WEEK'S *parashah*, the *Kohanim* are instructed in the laws pertaining to the קָרְבָּן עוֹלָה, the burnt offering.

**וַיְדַבֵּר ה' אֶל מֹשֶׁה לֵּאמֹר. צַו אֶת אַהֲרֹן וְאֶת בָּנָיו לֵאמֹר זֹאת תּוֹרַת הָעֹלָה...**

*The Eternal spoke to Moshe saying, "Command Aharon and his sons, saying: this is the law of the burnt offering.*[14]

Rashi explains the significance of the word צַו, "command."

צַו אֶת אַהֲרֹן – אֵין צַו אֶלָּא לְשׁוֹן זֵרוּז מִיָּד וּלְדוֹרוֹת. אָמַר ר' שִׁמְעוֹן בְּיוֹתֵר צָרִיךְ הַכָּתוּב לְזָרֵז בְּמָקוֹם שֶׁיֵּשׁ בּוֹ חֶסְרוֹן כִּיס.

*The word "command" expresses encouragement for the performance of the mitzvah in the present and throughout the generations to come. R. Shimon said: the Torah urges one particularly in a situation which involves monetary loss.*[15]

Rabbi Dessler highlights the fact that the monetary loss involved in this sacrifice was simply that the *Kohanim* did not receive a small piece of meat, as the animal, in this case, was completely burned on the altar. Considering the seemingly insignificant value of the loss, the need for encouragement in this instance is surprising. Our curiosity is augmented when considering the subject of this encouragement, the chosen *Kohanim*, who are praised by our Sages for their trait of serving the Almighty with zeal and alacrity: כֹּהֲנִים זְרִיזִים הֵם. Further, we are reminded of the comments concerning the sublime intentions of the *Kohanim* when partaking of the sacrificial meat;

14. *Vayikra* 6:1, 2.
15. Rashi *ad loc.*

their very act of eating is described as effecting atonement for the entire nation. The necessity for the expression צַו — "command," therefore, with its implications of special encouragement, calls for explanation.

A second, seemingly unrelated, difficulty can be discerned in the various explanations given by our Sages concerning the motives of Esther in inviting Haman to her feast. One opinion appears enigmatic in the extreme: אָמַר ר' אֶלְעָזָר פַּחִים טָמְנָה לוֹ — "R. El'azar said, 'She set a trap for him.'"[16] In extending an invitation to Haman, Esther is said to have laid a trap for the archenemy of the Jews. To what kind of trap does R. El'azar refer?

Let us turn our attention to the infamous incident of the Spies, dispatched by the Jewish People on a mission to investigate the Land of Israel. Two of these spies were singled out for extra words of encouragement. One was Yehoshua, who at this juncture had the letter 'י added to his former name Hoshea, as Moshe prayed, יָ-ה יוֹשִׁיעֲךָ מֵעֲצַת מְרַגְּלִים — "May God save you from the bad advice of the spies."[17] The other recipient of this spiritual fortification was Kalev, concerning whom we are told the following:

וַיַּעֲלוּ בַנֶּגֶב וַיָּבֹא עַד חֶבְרוֹן...

*They went up through the south [of the land], and [Kalev] came as far as Chevron.*[18]

Rashi explains the grammatical difficulty in this sentence, the beginning of which is in the plural while the conclusion is in the singular form:

כָּלֵב לְבַדּוֹ הָלַךְ וְנִשְׁתַּטֵּחַ עַל קִבְרֵי אָבוֹת, שֶׁלֹּא יְהֵא נִיסַּת לַחֲבֵרָיו לִהְיוֹת בַּעֲצָתָם.

*Kalev alone went [to Chevron,] to pray at the burial sites of our forefathers, to plead that he not be entrapped with the*

16. *Megillah* 15a.
17. Rashi on *Bemidbar* 13:15.
18. *Bemidbar* 13:22.

*other spies and led into joining them in their evil report [concerning the Land].*[19]

Later we find that this town of Chevron was actually bequeathed to Kalev. It was because he alone, out of the twelve tribes, showed an appreciation for the site's inherent holiness that he later received this portion of land. Hence we see that through the medium of prayer, Kalev, too, received additional support as he embarked upon this mission. Why is it that specifically Kalev and Yehoshua receive greater assistance than the other spies?

Analysing some of the lengthy descriptions which deal with the sin of the spies, we find the following change of expression within the verses themselves. When the Jewish People traveled in the desert, the verse states:

וְנוֹעֲדוּ אֵלֶיךָ הַנְּשִׂיאִים רָאשֵׁי אַלְפֵי יִשְׂרָאֵל.

*...Then the leaders, the heads of the thousands of Yisrael, shall convene with you.*[20]

When the incident of the spies transpired, the verse states:

כֻּלָּם אֲנָשִׁים רָאשֵׁי בְנֵי יִשְׂרָאֵל הֵמָּה.

*They were all [great] men, the heads of the Children of Yisrael.*[21]

Here, instead of being referred to as "heads of thousands of Yisrael," they are referred to as being directly "heads of the Children of Yisrael." The Alshich explains that at this point particularly, when embarking upon a mission fraught with spiritual danger, the merit and spiritual strength of our forefathers had to be invoked. It was the ראש, the head — the spirit of the originator of each tribe, of each individual son of Yisrael — that accompanied the spies on their dangerous mission.

---

19. Rashi *ad loc.*
20. *Bemidbar* 10:4.
21. *Bemidbar* 13:2, 3.

Tracing the lineage of Yehoshua and Kalev, the Alshich highlights how these two individuals were in a much more vulnerable position than the rest of the tribes. Kalev descended from the tribe of Yehudah, and as such, was a carrier of Yehudah's spiritual strengths and weaknesses. When Yosef was sold, it was Yehudah who bore the responsibility of disclosing the news to his father Ya'akov. To this end, Yehudah had taken Yosef's special coat, and dipped it in blood to show to his father; thus leading Ya'akov to believe that Yosef had fallen prey to a wild beast. Yehudah had here used his tongue to utter words which were not completely true.

Cloaked in the spirit of the progenitor of his tribe, Kalev was aided by Yehudah, Yehudah who had within him some taint, some slight sullying of the power of speech. It was this very spirit that rendered Kalev vulnerable to participation in the incorrect speech concerning the Land of Israel. Hence, he required the extra fortification achieved through his prayer.

Despite this inherent weakness, Kalev stood straight and firm, refusing to stumble when faced with the challenge.

**וְעַבְדִּי כָלֵב עֵקֶב הָיְתָה רוּחַ אַחֶרֶת עִמּוֹ וַיְמַלֵּא אַחֲרָי...**

*But My servant, Kalev — since he [really] had a different, [hidden] motivation [literally, "spirit"] and followed Me wholeheartedly.*[22]

According to the Alshich, this "different spirit" would refer to Yehudah. Conquering innate deficiency, Kalev followed the ways of the Almighty wholeheartedly.

Now turning to Yehoshua, we trace his lineage back to Yosef. Yosef, too, is accused of the misuse of the faculty of speech in the slander he leveled against his brothers: הֵבִיא דִּבָּתָם רָע אֶל אֲבִיהֶם — "He brought a bad report to their father."[23] Yehoshua therefore, possessed the same inherent flaw as Kalev, and required the advocacy of Moshe to prevent him from stumbling.

---

22. *Bemidbar* 14:24.
23. *Bereishith* 37:2.

Yehoshua and Kalev were in greater danger than the rest of the spies, and therefore received extra encouragement and fortification to counteract their weakness. It is notable, however, that Yehoshua and Kalev were the only two of the whole contingent who did not return a bad report about the Land. To understand the moral fortitude they must have possessed in withstanding their trial, let us turn to another individual who displays similar exceptional strength.

In *Parashath Naso*, we encounter the *nazir*, one who has made a vow committing himself to an extra degree of separation from physical pleasures, to live a life on a higher spiritual plane. The verse states:

> **וַיְדַבֵּר ה' אֶל מֹשֶׁה לֵּאמֹר. דַּבֵּר אֶל בְּנֵי יִשְׂרָאֵל וְאָמַרְתָּ אֲלֵהֶם אִישׁ אוֹ אִשָּׁה כִּי יַפְלִא לִנְדֹּר נֶדֶר נָזִיר לְהַזִּיר לַה'. מִיַּיִן וְשֵׁכָר יַזִּיר חֹמֶץ יַיִן וְחֹמֶץ שֵׁכָר לֹא יִשְׁתֶּה וְכָל מִשְׁרַת עֲנָבִים לֹא יִשְׁתֶּה וַעֲנָבִים לַחִים וִיבֵשִׁים לֹא יֹאכֵל.**
>
> *The Eternal spoke to Moshe, saying, "Speak to the Children of Yisrael and you shall say to them: A man or woman who shall distinguish him — [or her]self by making a separation vow to separate himself [from wine] for [the sake of] the Eternal, shall separate himself from new and old wine, must not drink new-wine vinegar or old-wine vinegar, and must not drink any grape beverage nor eat fresh or dried grapes."*[24]

The *Ha'amek Davar* highlights the unusual expression of כִּי יַפְלִא — "who shall distinguish himself," literally, "who shall do wondrously."

> מַשְׁמָעוֹ שֶׁעוֹשֶׂה דְּבַר מִצְוָה, וְאֵינוֹ לְרָצוֹן לה', אִם לֹא בְּדֶרֶךְ פֶּלֶא שֶׁהַשָּׁעָה אוֹ הָעִנְיָן נָחוּץ לְכָךְ.
>
> *This phrase implies that the nazir is doing a mitzvah that is not desired by God, except in exceptional cases when the occasion or the situation requires it.*[25]

---

24. *Bemidbar* 6:1–3.
25. *Ha'amek Davar ad loc.*

In other words, unless there is an extraordinary circumstance, it is unwarranted to take upon oneself the praiseworthy restrictions of a Nazirite lifestyle. This vow is thus seen to be, paradoxically and wondrously, "a mitzvah which is not the will of God." The Talmud tells of a certain individual who did take on the Nazirite vow in an appropriate manner.

בָּא אָדָם אֶחָד מִן הַדָּרוֹם, וְרָאִיתִי שֶׁהוּא יְפֵה עֵינַיִם וְטוֹב רֹאִי וּקְוֻצּוֹתָיו סְדוּרוֹת לוֹ תַּלְתַּלִּים. אָמַרְתִּי לוֹ בְּנִי מָה רָאִיתָ לְהַשְׁחִית אֶת שְׂעָרְךָ זֶה הַנָּאֶה. אָמַר לִי, רוֹעֶה הָיִיתִי לְאַבָּא בְּעִירִי הָלַכְתִּי לְמַלְאוֹת מַיִם מִן הַמַּעְיָן וְנִסְתַּכַּלְתִּי בְּבָבוּאָה שֶׁלִּי, וּפָחַז עָלַי יִצְרִי, וּבִקֵּשׁ לְטוֹרְדֵנִי מִן הָעוֹלָם. אָמַרְתִּי לוֹ, רָשָׁע לָמָּה אַתָּה מִתְגָּאֶה בְּעוֹלָם שֶׁאֵינוֹ שֶׁלְּךָ, בְּמִי שֶׁהוּא עָתִיד לִהְיוֹת רִמָּה וְתוֹלֵעָה. הָעֲבוֹדָה שֶׁאֲגַלֵּחֲךָ לַשָּׁמַיִם. מִיָּד עֲמַדְתִּי וּנְשַׁקְתִּיו עַל רֹאשׁוֹ. אָמַרְתִּי לוֹ, בְּנִי כָּמוֹךָ יִרְבּוּ נוֹזְרֵי נְזִירוּת בְּיִשְׂרָאֵל. עָלֶיךָ הַכָּתוּב אוֹמֵר "אִישׁ כִּי יַפְלִא לִנְדֹּר נֶדֶר נָזִיר לְהַזִּיר לַה'".

*A man from the south once came to me [to Shimon the High Priest]. I saw that he was tall, with beautiful eyes and curling hair. He declared his wish to become a nazir. I said to him, "My son, why do you want to destroy your beautiful hair?"*

*He replied: "I was a shepherd for my father in my town, and I went to draw water from a spring. Catching a glimpse of my reflection in the water, I was struck by the beauty of my appearance. My evil inclination overcame me, seeking to fill me with pride at my handsome bearing, and thus drive me out of the world. I seized myself, saying, 'Why are you proud in a world that belongs not to you? Your end will be as lowly as worms! I will shave you [and dedicate you] to Heaven!'"*

*When I heard this I stood up, kissed him on the head, and said, "May there be many more nazirim like you in Israel!"*[26]

This Nazirite vow was taken in an effort to eliminate a certain element of pride, to remedy and atone for a subtle flaw the individual in question discerned in himself.

There is an elementary principle of our Sages which has bearing on our subject, which is that the reaction to a situation or an entity is

26. *Nedarim* 9b.

stronger than the original force of that entity or situation. One such example is that of Ruth and Orpah, two Moabite princesses who sought to forsake their opulent lifestyles and return with Naomi to the Land of Israel and join the Jewish People. Following strong messages of discouragement on the part of their mother-in-law, Naomi, the two sisters are distinguished by their opposite reactions. וַתִּשַּׁק עָרְפָּה לַחֲמוֹתָהּ וְרוּת דָּבְקָה בָּהּ — "Orpah kissed her mother-in-law, and Ruth clung to her."[27] At first glance it would seem that the act of kissing is one of lesser closeness than Ruth's act of clinging to her mother-in-law. However, an examination of the following comment of our Sages reveals a startling phenomenon:

> *The children of the one who kissed will fall into the hands of the children of the one who clung.*[28]

This statement refers to the fall of Goliath to David, the former a descendant of Orpah, the latter, a descendant of Ruth. The Maharal explains that this statement of our Sages does not denote a "tit-for-tat," as we would imagine, namely that the one who demonstrated a bond of weaker attachment will fall into the hands of the one who clung steadfast. Rather, just the converse: the kiss of Orpah was in fact a greater bond than the clinging of Ruth to Naomi. For Orpah to have had such a deep connection, and yet to have severed this link, aroused within her a profound reaction against that to which she was previously so connected. Once Orpah had turned her back on her mother-in-law, she fell to a level of moral depravity; an acute reaction to the previously enjoyed closeness.

In this light we can understand the statement:

> בִּמְקוֹם שֶׁבַּעֲלֵי תְּשׁוּבָה עוֹמְדִין צַדִּיקִים גְּמוּרִים אֵינָם עוֹמְדִין.
>
> *Even the perfectly righteous are unable to stand in the place in which penitents stand.*[29]

---

27. *Ruth* 1:14.
28. *Sotah* 42b.
29. *Berachoth* 34b.

A penitent has a certain superiority over even a completely righteous individual, for, having sinned, he experiences the reaction against the sin, a hatred for that evil unparalleled by one who has never experienced the darkness of night. It can be likened to two friends, who, on a visit to a relative, are offered some light refreshments. One at the outset refuses the proffered cake, while the other accepts a slice and, after one bite, rejects the remainder. Doubtlessly, the reaction which follows the initial acceptance is far more offensive than the rejection from the outset. The reaction against has a degree of potency unmatched by the original condition.

With this principle, let us return to discover the trap that Esther laid for Haman in inviting him to the feast. The Maharal, in his work on *Megillath Esther*, makes a profound observation.

> כַּאֲשֶׁר הָאָדָם הוּא בְּטוֹב וּבְשִׂמְחָה וּבְדַעְתּוֹ שֶׁהוּא שָׁלֵם וְאֵין לוֹ חִסָּרוֹן – אָז הוּא מוּכָן לְחִסָּרוֹן, לִהְיוֹת לוֹ נְפִילָה... אֲבָל אִם אֵין לוֹ הַשְׁלָמָה מוּכָן הוּא שֶׁיֻשְׁלַם.
>
> *When a person finds himself in a favourable situation, in which he is joyful and serene, in which he arrives at a feeling of self-perfection, then he is vulnerable to defect; it is then that he falls. But a feeling of imperfection breeds true perfection.*[30]

In explaining Esther's motives in inviting Haman to her feast, our Sages describe Esther as thereby, "heaping coals upon the head of Haman." The event of being singled out to attend Esther's banquet filled Haman with an overwhelming pride, to the extent that he publicised his news to all his beloved ones. Bestowed with an honour unparalleled by that accorded to anyone but the king, Haman was overtaken by an aura of self-contentment and placid complacency. These are the coals which the Sages describe as being heaped upon Haman's head. It was this feeling that formed the basis for the trap Esther laid for him. Completely satisfied with his lot, Haman was liable to the inevitable loss which this feeling engenders. "Pride comes before a fall." Complacency breeds deficiency.

---

30. *Ohr Chadash.*

This underlying theme can be traced through the subject of the Nazirite vow, in which an oath of special conduct is accepted upon oneself. One would only undertake an oath when one feels oneself in the position to fulfill the promise, and comply with all its stipulations. If one were lacking conviction in one's ability to adhere to the promise, one would be unable to make such a vow. And herein lies the pitfall: that belief in one's own moral fortitude, the satisfaction with one's spiritual ability to the extent that one feels confident in accepting extra restrictions upon oneself. These are feelings that engender a moral decline. Thus we find that a prerequisite for making such a vow is the existence of some factor that would prevent a fall due to self-confidence. כִּי יַפְלִא — there must be a special reason for the oath. It is only if the vow stems from a reaction against some evil that the underlying feelings will take on an intensity which would render one unlikely to fall. Hence, Shimon the High Priest lauded the *nazir* that came to him, his vow of *naziruth* resulting from a reaction to the evil inclination. Stemming from a reaction, an extra strength was present which would facilitate the fulfillment of the oath, preventing a fall due to overconfidence.

Returning to Yehoshua and Kalev, the Alshich explains the reason why, out of all of the spies, it was only these two who withstood the challenges they faced. Yehoshua and Kalev were highly conscious of the particular weakness and spiritual deficiency which they possessed due to their ancestry. The other tribes had confidence in the merit of their progenitors, a merit which accompanied them on their mission. On the other hand, the slight flaw in the faculty of speech stemming from Yehudah and Yosef inhibited their descendants, Yehoshua and Kalev, from relying upon the aid of their lineage, and acted as an incentive for extra exertion in this area. Feeling that they had a weakness to overcome, Yehoshua and Kalev mustered up moral courage, expelling any notion of complacency, and were thus saved from the fate of the other ten spies. It was because they sought additional encouragement and aid, that they achieved a level of perfection unattainable by those naturally nearer this level.

On the basis of this principle, Rabbi Dessler explains why extra encouragement was given to the *Kohanim*, concerning the paltry monetary loss which the burnt offering incurred:

> *The Kohanim were on such a high spiritual level that they did not feel the need to strengthen themselves, particularly in regard to this insignificant loss. However, it was just this feeling of satisfaction that was so perilous. No priest felt that he had to overcome a moral tussle to forgo the meat of the burnt offering. But it was precisely because of their stature that a thought, some subtle desire for the meat, could enter their minds. Their service might then be performed without the fullest degree of joy. Thus, even Aharon received this encouragement, for, as Rashi states, the extra stimulus was given* מִיָּד וּלְדוֹרוֹת*, for the contemporary generation of Aharon himself, as well as for subsequent generations.*[31]

Aharon is described as possessing an "absolute beauty," which refers to his freedom from any spiritual blemish. In this state of perfection, Aharon himself needed extra support, for the state of flawlessness is a precarious one indeed.

One of the most dire of spiritual dangers is the feeling of complacency, the feeling that one lacks blemish, the feeling of freedom from the slightest taint of sin or negative character trait. It is thus we find that upon departing from a place, one is blessed with the parting words לֵךְ לְשָׁלוֹם, rather than לֵךְ בְּשָׁלוֹם. One small letter has grave ramifications. In the blessing לֵךְ לְשָׁלוֹם, one wishes the other party that he continue in his journey *towards* perfection, that he be successful in his striving to reach ever higher. לֵךְ בְּשָׁלוֹם — "Go in peace," on the other hand, implies a journey in a state of completion, as though the individual has already reached his point of perfection. It is thus that in Scriptures we find this latter blessing is always followed by an account of the person's death. Once perfection has been reached, the gift of life, the opportunity to continue on the path of growth, becomes superfluous.

31. *Michtav MeEliyahu,* Part Three, p. 109.

The greatest peril is the feeling that one's spiritual labour has been successfully completed. Only when one clearly feels the extent of one's weakness and deficiencies, when one is aware of the areas in which improvement is necessary, can one truly be described as being firmly placed on the road to perfection.

# SHEMINI

THE WEEKS PRECEDING Pesach constitute distinct periods of time. The first landmark in the calendar is *Parashath Parah*, which is always the Sabbath immediately preceding *Parashath HaChodesh*, which marks the commencement of the new month and the second stage of the countdown to Pesach. A period of two weeks follows, leading up to the eve of Pesach and climaxing in the night of Pesach itself, that cataclysmic moment of our redemption. This three-week period is designated as a progressive process in our personal re-experience of the events of the Exodus. The topic of our discussion is the discovery of the specific spiritual labour in which we must engage during each of these stages.

Before embarking on this discussion, let us first consider a fundamental question that arises from the very fact that this period is dedicated to re-experiencing this historical occurrence. The following Gemara raises the question as to the necessity of both the affliction in Egypt and our subsequent redemption:

> מִפְּנֵי מָה נֶעֱנַשׁ אַבְרָהָם אָבִינוּ וְנִשְׁתַּעְבְּדוּ בָּנָיו לְמִצְרַיִם מָאתַיִם וְעֶשֶׂר שָׁנִים?
>
> *Why was Avraham punished through his descendants being enslaved for 210 years?*[32]

The Gemara puts forward several reasons concerning why the Jewish People had to endure the grueling slavery and affliction of Egypt. From the very subject matter of the Gemara's discussion, it appears logical to assume that had the specified causes never existed, the whole exile, and the subsequent Exodus, would not have

32. *Nedarim* 32a.

occurred. Our Sages implicitly inform us that there had to be some grounds for the suffering. This reasoning, however, raises a crucial difficulty, highlighted by the *Avnei Nezer*. The events of the Exodus are not recorded in the Torah merely as an historical account, but are seen on numerous occasions to be a founding principle of various fundamental precepts and ideas. The miracles and wonders of the Exodus demonstrated God's omnipotence, His system of reward and punishment, and His direct intervention in the lives of mankind. Due to this, we find many mitzvoth hinging upon the events of our redemption. The entire festival of Pesach, the mitzvah to tell the events of the Exodus to our children, Sabbath, Kiddush — numerous mitzvoth have the Exodus as one of the central themes. The difficulty is now striking; it would appear that were it not for the rise of the causes specified in the Gemara, many mitzvoth that are regarded as central to the Jewish faith would be obliterated from the face of religious observance! A whole array of mitzvoth commemorating this historic event would simply not exist.

The resolution to this observation lies in the following declaration of King David concerning the nature of these events, quoted and elaborated upon in the *Tanchuma*.

**לְכוּ וּרְאוּ מִפְעֲלוֹת אֱלקִים נוֹרָא עֲלִילָה עַל בְּנֵי אָדָם.**

*Come and behold the deeds of God; awesome are His pretexts towards mankind.*[33]

There are occasions when God calls upon a pretext to justify a particular retribution. The nature of such pretexts is described in the *Tanchuma* with the following allegory:

מָשָׁל לְמָה הַדָּבָר דּוֹמֶה לְמִי שֶׁמְּבַקֵּשׁ לְגָרֵשׁ אֶת אִשְׁתּוֹ כְּשֶׁבִּקֵּשׁ לֵילֵךְ לְבֵיתוֹ כָּתַב גֵּט, נִכְנַס לְבֵיתוֹ וְהַגֵּט בְּיָדוֹ, מְבַקֵּשׁ עֲלִילָה לִתְּנוֹ לָהּ. אָמַר לָהּ, מִזְגוּ לִי אֶת הַכּוֹס שֶׁאֶשְׁתֶּה. מָזְגָה לוֹ, כֵּיוָן שֶׁנָּטַל הַכּוֹס מִיָּדָהּ, אָמַר לָהּ הֲרֵי זֶה גִּטֵּךְ. אָמְרָה לוֹ מַה פִּשְׁעִי? אָמַר לָהּ צְאִי מִבֵּיתִי שֶׁמָּזַגְתְּ לִי כּוֹס פָּשׁוּר. אָמְרָה לוֹ כְּבָר הָיִיתָ יוֹדֵעַ שֶׁאֲנִי עֲתִידָה לִמְזֹג לְךָ כּוֹס פָּשׁוּר, שֶׁכָּתַבְתָּ הַגֵּט וֶהֱבֵיאתוֹ בְּיָדְךָ.

33. *Tehillim* 66:5.

*An individual who wished to divorce his wife wrote out a bill of divorce before he arrived home. Upon entering the house armed with the document, he sought an excuse for which to present it to his wife. The man instructed his wife to prepare him a hot drink. She complied. Upon taking the cup from her, the man handed her the bill of divorce. The woman challenged him, "What sin have I committed?" Replied the man, "I command you to leave my house for having prepared me a lukewarm beverage."*

*The woman retorted, "You must have had prior knowledge that I would do so, for you entered the house already armed with the document of divorce!"*[34]

Through the annals of our history, there have been several occurrences of punishment that are described aptly as a "bill of divorce." This description applies specifically to situations in which the consequences of a particular action were inevitable in Jewish history; that particular event had to occur. In these cases, the actual misdeed seems insignificant in relation to the gravity of the consequences; a bill of divorce seems to have been issued merely for the preparation of a lukewarm drink. However, the recorded misdeed serves as a pretext to bring about the unavoidable result.

An application of this principle is found in connection with the descent of Ya'akov and his family to Egypt. The continuation of the *Midrash Tanchuma* reads as follows.

וְאָמַר רַבִּי יוּדָן, הָיָה הקב"ה מְבַקֵּשׁ לְקַיֵּם גְּזֵרַת יָדֹעַ תֵּדַע, וְהֵבִיא עֲלִילָה לְכָל דְּבָרִים אֵלּוּ, כְּדֵי שֶׁיֹּאהַב יַעֲקֹב אֶת יוֹסֵף וְיִשְׂנְאוּהוּ אֶחָיו וְיִמְכְּרוּ אוֹתוֹ לַיִּשְׁמְעֵאלִים וְיוֹרִידוּהוּ לְמִצְרַיִם וְיִשְׁמַע יַעֲקֹב שֶׁיּוֹסֵף חַי בְּמִצְרַיִם וְיֵרֵד עִם הַשְּׁבָטִים וְיִשְׁתַּעְבְּדוּ שָׁם.

*God sought to effect the fulfillment of, "You shall surely know" [Bereishith 15:13 — the prediction of Egyptian slavery given to Avraham]. He thus organized a pretext for the series of events leading up to the enslavement: Ya'akov would favour*

34. *Tanchuma, Vayeshev* 4.

*Yosef, who in turn would be hated by his brothers and sold to the Yishma'elites, who would then bring him to Egypt. Ya'akov would then hear that Yosef was alive in Egypt and descend there with the tribes, who would be enslaved there.*

The Egyptian exile was an inevitability; an event in Jewish history which had to occur. Nevertheless, we have seen in the earlier *Tanchuma* that there is always a pretext upon which events of this nature are suspended. There must be some undesirable feature in the Jewish People, some taint or subtle flaw that must be expunged, which the experience must cleanse. It is to this flaw which our Sages refer when they question, "Why was Avraham punished that his descendents were enslaved for 210 years?" An impurity is found particularly amongst the Egyptians, and the process of bondage followed by physical and spiritual liberation would achieve this rectification. The nation's purity was achieved at the point of Exodus, when physical liberty reflected spiritual emancipation. Extrication from the external evil was a manifestation of the moral battle that was fought within every Jew. The festival of Pesach was established for all generations; however, this festival does not commemorate only the newfound national purity. Our annual celebration also transpires on a personal level, as we rejoice in our own individual moral freedom. We re-experience the process of breaking the attachment to the Egyptian nation, an attachment that lies within each one of us. This is the process of Divine service to which we referred earlier, in defining the four individual periods leading up to Pesach itself. We now return to examine the unique feature of each of these individual periods.

The first stage in this process is *Parashath Parah*, in connection to which we are presented with the overall picture of the rewards guaranteed to one who dedicates himself to the inner duties of the period ahead. *Parashath Parah* contains, in a microcosm, every subsequent stage of our freedom. This is symbolically seen in the description of the service which is to be performed upon the red heifer, whose purpose is to effect purification for one who has been in contact with the dead.

**וְלָקְחוּ לַטָּמֵא מֵעֲפַר שְׂרֵפַת הַחַטָּאת וְנָתַן עָלָיו מַיִם חַיִּים אֶל כֶּלִי.**

*They shall take for the impure person [some] of the ashes [from] the burning of the purifying [cow], and [someone] shall put spring water on [them], into a vessel.*[35]

The significance of this process is seen through two varying descriptions of our Sages as to the nature of the wicked. In one instance, our Sages comment רְשָׁעִים מְלֵאֵי חֲרָטוֹת הֵם — there is a category of sinners who continuously experience feelings of regret for their actions. Yet another description reads: רְשָׁעִים אַף בְּחַיֵּיהֶם קְרוּאִים מֵתִים, those who repeatedly sin are considered dead in their lifetimes, spiritually comatose, immune to twinges of guilt or conscience. This second classification of evildoers refers to the deteriorated state of the original category. In the first stages of descent, the sinner has at least some feelings towards the mitzvoth and hence his conscience elicits feelings of remorse for his actions. However, if he stubbornly refuses to heed these messages, he reaches a stage of spiritual death, a state in which he experiences no feelings of desire to follow the correct path.

This final stage is diametrically opposed to the manner in which the Torah enjoins us to observe mitzvoth, which is as follows:

**וּשְׁמַרְתֶּם אֶת חֻקֹּתַי וְאֶת מִשְׁפָּטַי אֲשֶׁר יַעֲשֶׂה אֹתָם הָאָדָם וָחַי בָּהֶם...**

*You shall keep My statutes and laws, which a person shall do and [thereby] live [eternally].*[36]

The *Chiddushei HaRim* comments that the phrase וָחַי בָּהֶם, “and thereby live,” is to be interpreted not as an independent commandment, but as a condition attached to the fulfillment of all the mitzvoth. This expression contains the enjoinder that our whole life, our entirety of self, must be invested into the action at hand. An element of vivacity, vitality, an outpouring of inner feeling and desire for the mitzvah, is seen not merely as an extra quality, but as an integral and

35. *Bemidbar* 19:17.
36. *Vayikra* 18:5.

essential part of its performance. It is for this reason that we have the law of הָעוֹסֵק בְּמִצְוָה פָּטוּר מִן הַמִּצְוָה, that one involved in the performance of a mitzvah is exempt from involvement in another mitzvah that might present itself. If the whole person is invested in the present obligation, there is nothing left with which to perform another commandment!

The achievement of this dimension is the secret contained within the *parashah* of the red heifer. Within each individual lie elements of this heifer — animalistic desires that drive a person to pursue the pleasures of this world. When we allow such a drive to determine an action that we take, we in fact strengthen its grip over us, and gradually such drives come to dominate us. The power of these desires and a desirable strength of feeling towards the mitzvoth, towards spirituality, are mutually exclusive. To the extent that we are pulled towards the material, our desire for spiritual gains is reduced. The key then, to attaining the level at which each of our mitzvoth is infused with the spirit of וָחַי בָּהֶם, is to slaughter our animalistic tendencies, thus freeing our entirety of self to be dedicated to spirituality.

*Parashath Parah* is the illustration of this road that leads towards ultimate freedom. The epitome of an animalistic lifestyle is Egypt, described as מִצְרִים שְׁטוּפֵי זִמָּה הֵם — "Egyptians are steeped in immorality." We were subjugated to this nation, indicating that wc too must have in some way contained an attachment to this material lifestyle, the reason for the pretext of our enslavement. Our personal re-experience of freedom can only be achieved when we commit ourselves to dissolving this attachment. And within this commitment lies the guarantee of the final stage in the process enacted upon the heifer, the וְנָתַן עָלָיו מַיִם חַיִּים אֶל כֶּלִי — "And someone shall put spring [living] water on [them], into a vessel," a stage at which we will find our vitality invested solely in the service of our Creator.

It is this path that lies ahead of us in these weeks preceding the Exodus from Egypt. *Parashath Parah* may be likened to the architect's plan for the edifice that we have the opportunity to erect during this period. But the building itself must be actualized in stages, from its foundation stone to the last brushstroke of the inner decor.

The intermediate stages leading to the ultimate goal of מַיִם חַיִּים אֶל כֶּלִי lie in the process of spiritual labour uniquely ascribed to each of the three periods that follow.

Another mention of these three periods is found in a paragraph near the beginning of the Haggadah. The topic of discussion is the time that the obligation to relate the events of the Exodus commences:

> יָכֹל מֵרֹאשׁ חֹדֶשׁ, תַּלְמוּד לוֹמַר בַּיּוֹם הַהוּא, אִי בַּיּוֹם הַהוּא יָכֹל מִבְּעוֹד יוֹם תַּלְמוּד לוֹמַר בַּעֲבוּר זֶה, בַּעֲבוּר זֶה לֹא אָמַרְתִּי אֶלָּא בְּשָׁעָה שֶׁיֵּשׁ מַצָּה וּמָרוֹר מֻנָּחִים לְפָנֶיךָ.
>
> *Perhaps the mitzvah commences from the beginning of the month. However, the verse states, "On that day," referring to the day of the Exodus. One might think that the mitzvah applies to the day of the eve of Pesach, when the Paschal sacrifice was offered. The Torah therefore uses the expression* בַּעֲבוּר זֶה *— "Because of this." "This" obviously refers to a tangible object placed before a person, in this case referring to the matzah and bitter herbs that must be eaten with the Paschal sacrifice on the night of the fifteenth of Nissan.*

The conclusion reached in the Haggadah is that the mitzvah of relating the story of the Exodus commences on the night of the fifteenth of Nissan. However, three periods of time emerge from the discussion, periods corresponding exactly with the three periods we set out earlier to investigate: Rosh Chodesh Nissan, of which the preceding Sabbath is *Parashath HaChodesh*, the eve of Pesach, and the actual night of Pesach.

A second set of three will throw light upon the subject of our investigation. This second set is found in the description of man as a composition of three basic faculties. Man is composed of his שֵׂכֶל, his intellect or understanding, his נֶפֶשׁ, the seat of his innermost feelings and desires, and finally, the ability to perform physical action, achieved with his גוּף, his body.

These three faculties are intimately connected with each time period detailed above. On the first day of Nissan, the faculty of שֵׂכֶל

is called into play. Our Sages enjoin us to begin delving into the laws and the underlying meaning of the festival two weeks beforehand. Rosh Chodesh falls two weeks before Pesach, and it is thus at this juncture that our intellect becomes involved with the ideas and themes of the festival. It is this which underlies the opinion of the Rabbis who posit: יָכֹל מֵראשׁ חֹדֶשׁ. Perhaps it is at this point, at the time when we begin occupying our minds with the Exodus, that the mitzvah of relating the Exodus begins.

Although the mind must become attuned to the Haggadah at this point, the actual mitzvah only applies upon the day on which the sacrifice is brought. This is the point at which man's נֶפֶשׁ is activated, as symbolized by the sprinkling of the animal's blood upon the altar. The significance of this performance is explained to us in the following manner:

> **כִּי נֶפֶשׁ הַבָּשָׂר בַּדָּם הִוא וַאֲנִי נְתַתִּיו לָכֶם עַל הַמִּזְבֵּחַ לְכַפֵּר עַל נַפְשֹׁתֵיכֶם כִּי הַדָּם הוּא בַּנֶּפֶשׁ יְכַפֵּר.**
>
> *The soul of the flesh is in the blood, and I have decreed it be placed upon the altar for you, to provide atonement for your soul, for it is the blood which atones for the soul.*[37]

Rashi explains the meaning of the verse:

> כִּי נֶפֶשׁ הַבָּשָׂר שֶׁל כָּל בְּרִיָּה בַּדָּם הִיא תְּלוּיָה וּלְפִיכָךְ נְתַתִּיו (עַל הַמִּזְבֵּחַ) לְכַפֵּר עַל נֶפֶשׁ הָאָדָם, תָּבוֹא נֶפֶשׁ וּתְכַפֵּר עַל נֶפֶשׁ.
>
> *For the life-force of the body is in [its] blood, and I have [therefore] given it to you [to offer] on the altar to make an atonement for your lives; let blood — through the life-force [that is in it] — atone for your lives.*[38]

The blood, in its capacity of the soul of the animal, is here said to atone for man's own soul. This refers to achieving atonement for man's incorrect feelings and emotions, which find root in his faculty of נֶפֶשׁ. Although previously his feelings may have been identified

---

37. *Vayikra* 17:11.
38. Rashi *ad loc.*

with those epitomized by Egyptian culture, on the eve of Pesach the individual discovers the real activation of the נֶפֶשׁ. After two weeks of intense intellectual occupation, and the subsequent implementation of his involvement, the individual finally feels that his strongest desires lie in fulfilling the commands of his Creator. After engaging himself for two weeks in the true meaning of freedom, freedom from enslavement to Egyptian culture, he is guaranteed to reach this praiseworthy level at the time of the sprinkling of the blood.

The labour in which we are involved reaches a crescendo on the night of Pesach, the time when we partake of the Paschal sacrifice, with its accompanying matzah and bitter herbs. At this juncture, even the faculty of גוף reaches its perfection; one's very body is infused with a spirit of holiness. This achievement is the underlying idea in the consumption of matzah. The matzah is made without leaven, leaven being a symbol of the evil inclination that rises up within man. The evil inclination has no grip over matzah, for it is a food without taste; no physical gratification is attached to its consumption. Thus, matzah acts as the paradigm of a food eaten solely for the sake of Heaven. This quality of the matzah, its use solely for spiritual ends, is one which we strive to infuse into every area of mundane life, in accordance with the dictum: בְּכָל דְּרָכֶיךָ דָעֵהוּ, the enjoinder to "know God in all your ways," elevating every area of our physical existence for spiritual ends.

Although this is an obligation upon every area of life, it is particularly in the realm of eating that we strive to reach perfection on the night of the Exodus. The first sin of mankind, when Adam partook of the fruit of the Tree of Knowledge, involved an act of eating. As such, the act of eating contains the root of all evil that consequently descended upon this world. Eating the bland, tasteless matzah on the night of Pesach thus detaches us from the source of all sin. It is for this reason that our Sages term matzah as "bread of healing," for this act of eating, performed with a true purity of intention, remedies all previous instances of physical indulgence. On this night, man is brought to realise that the purpose of food lies only in its capacity to provide necessary physical strength, which can then be ploughed into one's Divine service. At this point man is released from the Egyptian ideal of pursuit of worldly pleasures. This level achieved, the faculty of גוּף is brought to its perfection.

The Jewish nation was originally sent to Egypt to rectify a pretext, to break that connection to Egyptian characteristics. It is thus that for a period of two weeks, from Rosh Chodesh Nissan until the eve of Pesach, culminating in the night of Pesach itself, that we divest ourselves of all such material lusts and cravings. This is achieved through our intellectual contemplation concerning the meaning of the subservience, and the subsequent freedom from the pervasive grip of Egyptian culture. Fortified with this preparation, our נֶפֶשׁ finds affinity with the spiritual arena, and our appetite is aroused purely for the service of God. Our whole being now identifies solely with our elevated mission. And with the advent of the night of our ultimate freedom, we finally achieve the glorious promise of מַיִם חַיִּים אֶל כֶּלִי, when all physical involvement is directed completely towards spiritual gain. It is at this point that we have effectively fulfilled the obligation of this night, dictated to us by our Sages:

חַיָּב אָדָם לִרְאוֹת אֶת עַצְמוֹ כְּאִלּוּ הוּא יָצָא מִמִּצְרַיִם.

*Every person is obligated to see himself as if he personally was delivered from Egypt.*[39]

39. *Pesachim* 116b.

# TAZRIYA — METZORA

OUR SUBJECT IS profound, and has applications to every area of life. The verses in *Parashath Tazriya* state:

**וַיְדַבֵּר ה׳ אֶל מֹשֶׁה לֵּאמֹר: דַּבֵּר אֶל בְּנֵי יִשְׂרָאֵל לֵאמֹר אִשָּׁה כִּי תַזְרִיעַ וְיָלְדָה זָכָר וְטָמְאָה שִׁבְעַת יָמִים.**

*The Eternal spoke to Moshe saying: "Speak to the Children of Yisrael, saying [to them]: if a woman conceives, and gives birth to a male child, she will be impure for a seven-day period."*[40]

Rashi's comment on this verse touches upon a concept which is as profound as it is pivotal:

א"ר שִׂמְלַאי, כְּשֵׁם שֶׁיְּצִירָתוֹ שֶׁל אָדָם אַחַר בְּהֵמָה חַיָּה וְעוֹף בְּמַעֲשֵׂה בְרֵאשִׁית, כָּךְ תּוֹרָתוֹ נִתְפָּרְשָׁה אַחַר תּוֹרַת בְּהֵמָה חַיָּה וְעוֹף.

*As R. Simlai stated, just as man was created only after the creation of cattle, beasts, and fowl, so is the sequence of laws in the Torah, the laws pertaining to man coming after those pertaining to cattle, beasts, and fowl.*[41]

The laws regarding these animals are contained in the previous chapter, and it is only after they are mentioned that laws pertaining to man are listed. The Torah, then, parallels the sequence of Creation. The reason for the sequence of Creation is supplied by the Gemara:

תָּנוּ רַבָּנָן, אָדָם נִבְרָא בְּעֶרֶב שַׁבָּת. וּמִפְּנֵי מָה, שֶׁלֹּא יְהִיוּ הָאַפִּיקוֹרְסִים אוֹמְרִים שֻׁתָּף הָיָה לוֹ להקב"ה בְּמַעֲשֵׂה בְרֵאשִׁית.

40. *Vayikra* 12:1, 2.
41. Rashi *ad loc.*

> *Adam was created on the eve of the Sabbath, and why? To prevent heretics from claiming that God had a partner in the creation of the world.*[42]

The Maharal asks a penetrating question upon this idea. Man was created on the sixth day to prevent the misconception that he was God's partner in the act of Creation. Why were the angels, who were created on the second day, not subject to the same concern? Why would these celestial beings not be mistaken as partners in Creation?

Before answering this question, let us establish a principle elaborated upon by the Vilna Gaon:

> *"Everything that was, is, and ever will be is included in the Torah. This does not only refer to general events, but even to the most minute detail of every species, every single person, and every event that happens to a person from the day he was born until the day he dies. Information concerning every animal, beast, and living being, of every blade of grass and vegetation, and even of every inanimate object, are all included in the Torah."*

The root of this principle lies in the famous maxim from the *Zohar*: אִיסְתַּכַּל בְּאוֹרַיְתָא וּבָרָא עָלְמָא, God, as it were, looked into the Torah, and from the Torah created the world. The world in which we live, then, can be conceived of as Torah unfolding, being merely a crystallization and physical expression of everything contained therein. Torah being the blueprint of the world, everything in the world must perfectly parallel that which is contained in the Torah. Thus we understand the above-cited comment of Rashi, which states that the order of creation correlates to the order of the Torah. Understanding the nature of Torah's essence, we realise that it must necessarily be so.

This parallel, however, runs even deeper. Man is termed as an עוֹלָם קָטָן, a world in himself, a microcosm of a vast creation. Thus,

---

42. *Sanhedrin* 38a.

not only is there a correlation between Torah and the world, there is a correlation between man and the world. Evidence for this is found in the following Midrash.

אָמַר ר' בֶּרֶכְיָה וְרַבִּי חֶלְבּוֹ וְר' שְׁמוּאֵל בַּר נַחְמָן, בְּשָׁעָה שֶׁבָּרָא הקב"ה אָדָם הָרִאשׁוֹן מִסּוֹף הָעוֹלָם וְעַד סוֹפוֹ מְלֹא כָּל הָאָרֶץ כֻּלּוֹ בְּרָאוֹ מִן הַמִּזְרָח לַמַּעֲרָב מִנַּיִן שֶׁנֶּאֱמַר אָחוֹר וָקֶדֶם צַרְתָּנִי מִן הַצָּפוֹן לַדָּרוֹם מִנַּיִן שֶׁנֶּאֱמַר וּלְמִקְצֵה הַשָּׁמַיִם וְעַד קְצֵה הַשָּׁמַיִם.

*...The Almighty created Adam from all over the world, the entire world was filled with his creation. From east to west, as it says, "Later and before He created me." ["Later" refers to the west, the place of sunset, and "Earlier" refers to the east, place of sunrise.] From north to south, as it says, "From one end of the heavens to the other."*[43]

Adam, who was "created from the whole world," contained within his makeup the world's every element and dimension. The relationship between man and the physical creation is expounded upon in the *Avoth D'Rabbi Nathan.*

וְיָצַר בְּאָדָם כָּל מַה שֶּׁנִּבְרָא בְּעוֹלָמוֹ. חֳרָשִׁים בְּעוֹלָם חֳרָשִׁים בְּאָדָם זֶה שְׂעָרוֹת שֶׁל אָדָם... מַיִם מְלוּחוֹת בָּעוֹלָם מַיִם מְלוּחוֹת בָּאָדָם זֶהוּ דְּמָעוֹת שֶׁל עֵינַיִם.

*God formed in man all that He created in His world. The forests of the world is the hair of man. The saltwater in the world is the tears of man's eyes.*

The *Avoth D'Rabbi Nathan* continues, detailing how every facet of the world is found in man. We thus arrive at a simple equation: man is a microcosm of the world, which is in turn a physical manifestation of Torah. We can say that man, in his capacity of an עוֹלָם קָטָן, is a reflection of Torah.

The *Mesillath Yesharim* elaborates upon this concept, and in doing so establishes an awesome principle, one with ramifications upon every sphere of a person's life:

---

43. *Vayikra Rabbah* 14:1.

וְאִם תַּעֲמִיק עוֹד בָּעִנְיָן תִּרְאֶה כִּי הָעוֹלָם נִבְרָא לְשִׁמּוּשׁ הָאָדָם. אָמְנָם הִנֵּה הוּא עוֹמֵד בְּשִׁקּוּל גָּדוֹל. כִּי אִם הָאָדָם נִמְשָׁךְ אַחַר הָעוֹלָם וּמִתְרַחֵק מִבּוֹרְאוֹ, הִנֵּה הוּא מִתְקַלְקֵל וּמְקַלְקֵל הָעוֹלָם עִמּוֹ. וְאִם הוּא שׁוֹלֵט בְּעַצְמוֹ וְנִדְבַּק בְּבוֹרְאוֹ וּמִשְׁתַּמֵּשׁ מִן הָעוֹלָם רַק לִהְיוֹת לוֹ לְסִיּוּעַ לַעֲבוֹדַת בּוֹרְאוֹ הוּא מִתְעַלֶּה וְהָעוֹלָם עַצְמוֹ מִתְעַלֶּה עִמּוֹ. כִּי הִנֵּה עִלּוּי גָּדוֹל הוּא לַבְּרִיּוֹת כֻּלָּם בֶּהֱיוֹתָם מְשַׁמְּשֵׁי הָאָדָם הַשָּׁלֵם הַמְקֻדָּשׁ בִּקְדֻשָּׁתוֹ יִתְבָּרֵךְ.

*...The world was created for the use of man. Man, therefore, is stationed on a tightrope. If he strays after worldly desires, distancing himself from his Creator, he wreaks havoc on himself, and the world is destroyed with him. However, if man reigns over himself, cleaving to his Creator, using the world only as an implement to further spiritual growth, he strengthens the bond between himself and his Creator. Indeed, he elevates and sublimates the entire world with him. For all creatures are greatly uplifted when they serve the "Whole Man," who is sanctified with the holiness of the Blessed One.*[44]

Every one of man's actions carries ramifications which can either infuse the world with sanctity, or wreak cosmic damage. This idea is elaborated upon in the Midrash:

אִשָּׁה כִּי תַזְרִיעַ הֲדָא הוּא דִכְתִיב אָחוֹר וָקֶדֶם צַרְתָּנִי... אָמַר ר' יוֹחָנָן אִם זָכָה אָדָם נוֹחֵל שְׁנֵי עוֹלָמוֹת, הַזֶּה וְהַבָּא הֲדָא הוּא דִכְתִיב אָחוֹר וָקֶדֶם צַרְתָּנִי... וְאִם לָאו בָּא לִתֵּן דִּין וְחֶשְׁבּוֹן.

*...If man merits, he will inherit both this world and the next world...if he is not worthy, he will be called upon in judgment.*[45]

With these ideas, let us return to the Maharal's question and attempt to fathom the proffered answer. Man was created on the sixth day to prevent the misconception that he was a partner with God in the creation of the universe. We as yet fail to understand why this danger does not apply to the creation of the angels, which took place on the second day.

---

44. Chapter 1.
45. *Vayikra Rabbah* 14:1.

The answer: וְיָדוּעַ כִּי הַפּוֹעֵל שֶׁהוּא אֶחָד יָבוֹא מִמֶּנּוּ פְּעֻלָּה אַחַת — "As is known, a unified producer will issue a unified product."[46] Any object which is manufactured bears the stamp of the manufacturer. The article identifies the maker of the object; a definite parallel exists between creation and Creator. Applying this principle to the universe at large, the world is composed of two opposing elements: the עֶלְיוֹנִים, higher beings, and תַּחְתּוֹנִים, life on the lower realm. Both exist simultaneously, yet each element is exclusive. The existence of these two antithetical domains could lead one to conclude that there must be two creators, one of the lower world and one of the higher world. It is the creation of man that remedies this heretical philosophy, as is seen from an analysis of his makeup.

Fashioned from dust, yet infused with a spirit of Godliness, man himself is the ultimate paradox. The upper realm and the lower realm, soul and body, welded together form the being called man. Man's essence is the merging of these two opposite poles, the fusion of Heaven and earth. Man's very composition counters the philosophy propagated by the heretics. It is he who infuses the world of earthliness with the world of spirit, he who merges the upper and lower spheres into one.

We can now understand why it was necessary that man be fashioned on the sixth day. The pinnacle of creation, man steps onto the stage only when the orchestra is poised to play, when the characters have already received their scripts. It is only once the stage is set, when both the higher and lower elements are in place, that man can take his place in directing the performance, in engineering the interaction between the players, between the parts of the cosmos.

However, it was on the second day that the angels were created. In contrast to man, these celestial beings belong to one realm only. Their place is in Heaven, in the upper spheres, divorced from any connection to earthliness and physicality. Rather than negating the heretical notion of duplicity within creation, they intensify the idea, reinforcing the schism within the world by suggesting the existence

46. *Chiddushei Aggadoth.*

of two creators, one of spirituality and one of physicality. God's Oneness is proclaimed by one being alone: man. Only man demonstrates how all comes from One Creator, how the material world and the realm of spirit merge into one. The manufactured object, this world of oneness, points to an Almighty God, the One and Only.

It is for this reason that the original man was created as an individual. Adam, that primal being, stood alone. If a whole population had been fashioned, if the world had been full of inhabitants, the Oneness of God would have been obscured. The Unique Creator could not have been identified through the creation; diversity and multiplicity would instead be evident. A single man, encompassing and utilising every facet of the creation, proclaims and bears testimony to an omnipotent God. The philosophy propagated by heretics has thus been countered, exposed as a fallacy.

An application of this idea is found concerning the wicked individuals mentioned in the following Midrash.

> לְמָה נִדְמָה עֵשָׂו הָרָשָׁע, וֶאֱלִיפָז, וַעֲמָלֵק בְּנוֹ, וְיָרָבְעָם, וּנְבוּכַדְנֶצַּר, וְהָמָן הָאֲגָגִי? לְאֶחָד שֶׁמָּצָא כְּסוּת בַּדֶּרֶךְ, תְּפָשָׂהּ בְּיָדוֹ וְהִכְנִיס לְתוֹךְ הָעִיר וְהָיָה מַכְרִיז וְאוֹמֵר אֲבֵדָה זוֹ שֶׁל מִי. נִתְקַבְּצוּ כָּל בְּנֵי הָעִיר וְיָצְאוּ לִקְרָאתוֹ. אָמְרוּ רְאִיתֶם אִישׁ פְּלוֹנִי כַּמָּה צַדִּיק הוּא, כַּמָּה חָסִיד הוּא. מִיָּד עָמְדוּ וְעָשׂוּהוּ רֹאשׁ וְקָצִין עֲלֵיהֶם שָׁנָה, בִּשְׁתֵּי שָׁנִים וּבְשָׁלֹשׁ שָׁנִים בד' בה', עַד שֶׁהֶחֱרִיב אֶת כָּל הָעִיר כֻּלָּהּ לְכָךְ נִדְמוּ הָרְשָׁעִים.
>
> *To what can Esav, Elifaz, Amalek, Yerav'am, Nevuchadnetzar, and Haman the Aggagi be compared? To one who found a garment on the road. He took the garment, brought it into the city, and called out, "To whom does this lost garment belong?" The people of the city gathered together, and declared, "Look at this man. See how righteous he is, behold his piety!" Immediately, they appointed the man as head of the city. Within five years, the man had destroyed the entire city. To this are wicked people compared.*[47]

In this incident we gain a perspective on the good and righteous

---

47. *Yalkut Shimoni, Toldoth* 116.

deeds performed by people who are essentially evil. Ethical action, accomplishments of moral rectitude, can be, and evidently are, undertaken by corrupt and decadent individuals. However, there is a fundamental distinction between these deeds and the similar deeds of the righteous. The underlying motives of the wicked individual are evil ones. Their goodness can be compared to the man in the analogy of the Midrash, who performed a good deed to gain the people's confidence and subsequently abused the power which he had been granted. Goodness is used as a tool in the hands of the forces of evil, like dark shadows superimposed upon a beam of light.

One of the most profound abilities possessed by man is his power of חִיבּוּר, his ability to merge two opposing forces into one. But this can be achieved in two directions. The wicked individuals take Heaven, entering the world of spirit, to degrade and defile it, so that Heaven comes down to earth. The innate sanctity of the mitzvoth is abused, becoming sullied and stained.

Actions of the righteous, in contrast, elevate the physical world to Heavenly spheres; they take the material, the corporeal, and join it to the spiritual, the Eternal. The difference between the two will be evident only in the world of truth, upon the day of reckoning, when all deeds are examined, and all actions receive their due. On that day, the ultimate goal of man's actions, the realisation of the plan of the universe will come to light. "On that day will God be One and His name One."

Man, by utilising every disparate feature of this world solely for the purpose of sanctifying God's Name, demonstrates God's Majesty and Oneness. When he achieves unity between opposing forces in the world, man testifies to the existence of One Creator. Man alone bears this responsibility, which is simultaneously the ultimate privilege.

It is in this vein that Rabbi Chaim Volozhin explains the maxim, דַע מַה לְמַעְלָה מִמְּךָ, a dictum normally translated as, "Know what is above you." Rabbi Chaim Volozhin instead renders it, "Know what is above — it is from you." He thus expresses the principle that all of man's actions have profound and awesome effects in the world, the macrocosm of man, and in spheres far above the physical universe. Just one, seemingly insignificant action, can prompt the fanfare of coronation. God is declared King over the physical and the spiritual.

May we merit to continually express the essence of our humanity, taking earth and elevating it for the spiritual purpose of our lives.

# ACHAREI MOTH

THE VERSES IN this week's *parashah* state the following:

וַיְדַבֵּר ה׳ אֶל מֹשֶׁה לֵּאמֹר. דַּבֵּר אֶל בְּנֵי יִשְׂרָאֵל וְאָמַרְתָּ אֲלֵהֶם אֲנִי ה׳ אֱלֹקֵיכֶם. כְּמַעֲשֵׂה אֶרֶץ מִצְרַיִם אֲשֶׁר יְשַׁבְתֶּם בָּהּ לֹא תַעֲשׂוּ וּכְמַעֲשֵׂה אֶרֶץ כְּנַעַן אֲשֶׁר אֲנִי מֵבִיא אֶתְכֶם שָׁמָּה לֹא תַעֲשׂוּ וּבְחֻקֹּתֵיהֶם לֹא תֵלֵכוּ.

*The Eternal spoke to Moshe saying, "Speak to the Children of Yisrael and you shall say to them, 'I am the Eternal your God. You must not act in the [same] manner as [the people of] the land of Mitzrayim where you dwelled, nor may you act in the [same] manner as [the people of] the land of Canaan to where I am bringing you, and you must not follow their customs.'"*[48]

Rashi explains why specifically the countries of Egypt and Canaan are highlighted in the verse.

כְּמַעֲשֵׂה אֶרֶץ מִצְרַיִם. מַגִּיד שֶׁמַּעֲשֵׂיהֶם שֶׁל מִצְרִיִּים וְשֶׁל כְּנַעֲנִיִּים מְקֻלְקָלִים מִכָּל הָאֻמּוֹת, וְאוֹתוֹ מָקוֹם שֶׁיָּשְׁבוּ בוֹ יִשְׂרָאֵל מְקֻלְקָל מִן הַכֹּל.

*...This indicates that the behaviour of the Egyptians and Canaanites was more degenerate than that of any other nation. Further, the area [in Egypt] in which the Jewish People settled was more degenerate than any other area.*[49]

This Rashi can be traced back to the words of our Sages found in the *Sifra*. Our Sages derive from the words of the verse, כְּמַעֲשֵׂה

48. *Vayikra* 18:1–3.
49. Rashi *ad loc.*

אֶרֶץ מִצְרַיִם אֲשֶׁר יְשַׁבְתֶּם בָּהּ — "the same manner as the people of the land of Mitzrayim, where you dwelled," that it was the presence of the Children of Yisrael in Egypt that provided the catalyst for the moral depravity of the Egyptian nation. A similar derivation applies to the land of Canaan: it was the prospect of the Jewish settlement in the land that gave rise to the corruption of the Canaanite nation. The paradox is striking: the Chosen People of God, the "light unto all the nations," the shining beacon of Godliness and morality in this world, are seen as the underlying reason for an upsurge of immorality! We can further ask with regard to the land of Egypt: how is it possible that by merely living in the land, the Jewish People would have such a tremendously negative effect upon the inhabitants?

Let us examine the following Midrash, which expounds upon the verse under discussion.

> אָמַר ר' בֶּרֶכְיָה אָמַר הקב"ה לְמֹשֶׁה לֵךְ אֱמֹר לְיִשְׂרָאֵל כְּשֶׁהֱיִיתֶם בְּמִצְרַיִם הֱיִיתֶם דוֹמִין לְשׁוֹשַׁנָּה בֵּין הַחוֹחִים, עַכְשָׁו שֶׁאַתֶּם נִכְנָסִין לְאֶרֶץ כְּנַעַן הֱיוּ דוֹמִין לְשׁוֹשַׁנָּה בֵּין הַחוֹחִים וּתְנוּ דַעְתְּכֶם שֶׁלֹּא תַעֲשׂוּ לֹא כְּמַעֲשֶׂה אֵלּוּ וְלֹא כְּמַעֲשֵׂה אֵלּוּ. הֲדָא הוּא דִכְתִיב כְּמַעֲשֵׂה אֶרֶץ מִצְרַיִם. א"ר חֲנִינָה מָשָׁל לְמֶלֶךְ שֶׁהָיָה לוֹ בַּת יְחִידָה וְהִשְׁרָה אוֹתָהּ בְּמָבוֹי אֶחָד וְנִמְצְאוּ כֻּלָּן בַּעֲלֵי זְנוּת וּבַעֲלֵי כְשָׁפִים. א"ל בִּתִּי, תְּנִי דַעְתֵּךְ שֶׁלֹּא תַעֲשֶׂה לֹא כְּמַעֲשֶׂה אֵלּוּ וְלֹא כְּמַעֲשֵׂה אֵלּוּ. כָּךְ כְּשֶׁהָיוּ יִשְׂרָאֵל בְּמִצְרַיִם הָיוּ מִצְרִים בַּעֲלֵי זְנוּת וּבַעֲלֵי כְשָׁפִים שֶׁנֶּאֱמַר מֵרֹב זְנוּנֵי זוֹנָה טוֹבַת חֵן בַּעֲלַת כְּשָׁפִים. אָמַר לָהֶן הקב"ה בָּנַי הִזָּהֲרוּ שֶׁלֹּא תַעֲשׂוּ לֹא כְּמַעֲשֶׂה אֵלּוּ וְלֹא כְּמַעֲשֵׂה אֵלּוּ הֲדָא הוּא דִכְתִיב כְּמַעֲשֵׂה אֶרֶץ מִצְרַיִם.

*R. Berechya said, "God said to Moshe: Go and tell the Jewish People, When you were in Egypt, you were compared to a rose amongst thorns. Now that you are entering the land of Canaan, continue to be worthy of that title. Take precautions that you do not perform deeds similar to their deeds, as it says, You must not act in the [same] manner as [the people of] the land of Mitzrayim." R. Chanina likens this to a king who places his only daughter in an environment populated by immoral people and practitioners of witchcraft. He exhorts her not to follow in their ways. When the Jewish People were in*

*Egypt, the Egyptians indulged in immorality and witchcraft. God exhorted them, "My children, take heed that you imitate neither of their practices."*[50]

A striking question emerges from this analogy. If the king was so opposed to immoral practice, why did he place his daughter in an environment in which she would be subject to its allure? A parallel question can be directed at the real event: why did the Almighty exile His nation to places so perilous to their spiritual welfare?

Let us digress, and examine the obligation which is incumbent upon every Jew, to sacrifice his life to sanctify the Name of God.

**וְלֹא תְחַלְּלוּ אֶת שֵׁם קָדְשִׁי וְנִקְדַּשְׁתִּי בְּתוֹךְ בְּנֵי יִשְׂרָאֵל אֲנִי ה׳ מְקַדִּשְׁכֶם.**

*And you must not desecrate My Holy Name. I will be sanctified among the Children of Yisrael, [for] I am the Eternal Who sanctifies you.*[51]

Rashi explains the seeming tautology of these words.

וְלֹא תְחַלְּלוּ... מִמַּשְׁמַע שֶׁנֶּאֱמַר לֹא תְחַלְּלוּ. מַה תַּלְמוּד לוֹמַר וְנִקְדַּשְׁתִּי, מְסֹר עַצְמְךָ וְקַדֵּשׁ שְׁמִי. וּכְשֶׁהוּא מוֹסֵר אֶת עַצְמוֹ, יִמְסֹר עַל מְנָת לָמוּת, שֶׁכָּל הַמּוֹסֵר עַצְמוֹ עַל מְנַת הַנֵּס, אֵין עוֹשִׂין לוֹ נֵס.

*You must not desecrate. Since it states, "You must not desecrate," what does the verse teach with the words, "I will be sanctified?" It means: surrender your life, and sanctify My Name. And when he surrenders his life, it should be on the understanding that he might die. For, whoever sacrifices his life in anticipation of a miracle, a miracle is not performed for him.*[52]

At times, one must be prepared to sacrifice his very life, rather than bow to the demands placed upon him. In our daily recitation of the *Shema*, we make the statement, and iterate to ourselves: וְאָהַבְתָּ

50. *Vayikra Rabbah* 23:7.
51. *Vayikra* 22:32.
52. Rashi *ad loc.*

אֵת ה' אֱלֹקֶיךָ בְּכָל לְבָבְךָ וּבְכָל נַפְשְׁךָ. We declare our willingness to sacrifice our very lives on the basis of our love of God.

While undergoing brutal torture at the hands of the Romans, R. Akiva was seen to remain calm and serene. Amazed at his tranquility, his students asked how he could withstand the terrible suffering. R. Akiva's reply: "All my life I yearned for the opportunity to fulfill the commandment of loving God 'with all your soul,' which involves giving up one's very life out of love for one's Creator. Now that I have been presented with this opportunity, should I not rejoice?"

The annals of Jewish history are soaked with blood, that heroic blood of individuals and families who died rather than compromise their conviction and faith. Their lives, and their deaths, were a true sanctification of God's Name. When we, in our comfortable and respected positions, utter the words בְּכָל נַפְשְׁךָ, declaring that we will serve God with our very lives, there is one question which we must ask ourselves: would we too have the resolution, the moral fortitude to give up our lives to sanctify God's Name? Would we have that ability to be "a rose amongst thorns," girding ourselves with strength in the face of our oppressors?

The following rule, as expressed by Rabbi Zaitchek, might provide us with comfort.

הַהִתְנַגְּדוּת מְלַטֶּשֶׁת וּמְחַדֶּדֶת כֹּחוֹת הַנֶּפֶשׁ.

*Opposition sharpens one's spiritual strength.*[53]

A person is strengthened through the challenge of an opposing force. As mentioned in previous essays, the reaction against something is much stronger than an action before the situation arises. An example of this can be observed quite frequently in everyday life. When a child misbehaves, his mother may threaten to punish him, and at that time, the intense love she has for her child is temporarily forgotten. However, upon witnessing a stranger attack her child, the mother will furiously defend her child. The opposition which her child faces arouses the mother's love.

---

53. *Torath HaNefesh.*

To take this principle further, let us turn to the following story from the Talmud.[54]

Prior to his death, the following conversation took place between R. Yehoshua ben Chananya and the Sages. The Sages asked R. Yehoshua how they would counter the heretical arguments of the *Tzedukim* without his assistance. His answer: אָבְדָה עֵצָה מִבָּנִים נִסְרְחָה חָכְמָתָם — "When wisdom departs from the children (of Yisrael), their wisdom (that of the *Tzedukim*) departs."[55] With the death of R. Yehoshua ben Chananya, the Jewish People would be rendered bereft of the wisdom of this holy individual. This should not be cause for concern, however, because with the departure of his Torah wisdom, the knowledge and intellectual prowess of the *Tzedukim* would simultaneously decrease. The underlying purpose of their wisdom was to challenge the Jewish People, thus stimulating them to attain ever greater spiritual heights. This allowed the Jewish People an opportunity to overcome, to triumph, and thus to actualize latent strengths. If they had been unable to counter the provocation of the *Tzedukim*, there would be no constructive result from their heretical arguments, and so the Almighty would not orchestrate such a challenge.

This principle has both positive and negative manifestations. This is seen clearly in the following Midrash:

> א"ר לֵוִי אָמַר הקב"ה. בְּחֻרְבָּנָהּ הֶעֱמִידָה לִי צַדִּיקִים, וּבְבִנְיָנָהּ הֶעֱמִידָה לִי רְשָׁעִים. בְּחֻרְבָּנָהּ הֶעֱמִידָה לִי צַדִּיקִים — דָּנִיֵּאל וַחֲבוּרָתוֹ, מָרְדְּכַי וַחֲבוּרָתוֹ, עֶזְרָא וַחֲבוּרָתוֹ. בְּבִנְיָנָהּ הֶעֱמִידָה לִי רְשָׁעִים כְּגוֹן אָחָז וַחֲבוּרָתוֹ, מְנַשֶּׁה וַחֲבוּרָתוֹ, אָמוֹן וְסִיעָתוֹ. ר' אַבָּא ב"כ בְּשֵׁם ר' יוֹחָנָן עַל הָדָא דר' לֵוִי אָמַר "כִּי רַבִּים בְּנֵי שׁוֹמֵמָה מִבְּנֵי בְעוּלָה".
>
> *Said the Almighty, "The destruction of the Temple produced righteous individuals for Me, whereas its construction generated evildoers. After the Temple's destruction, there arose such personalities as Daniel, Mordechai, Ezra, and their contemporaries. When the Temple was standing, however, we find wicked people such as Achaz, Menashe, Ammon, and their*

54. *Chaggigah* 5b.
55. *Yirmiyah* 49:7.

*contemporaries." R. Abba said, "For the children of the desolate [Jerusalem] outnumber those of the inhabited [city]."*[56]

The destruction of the *Beith HaMikdash* generated a terrible and potent force of impurity in the world. It was precisely this factor, the reaction against evil, that caused the development of so many righteous people, individuals of such lofty standing.

Understanding this principle, we can now return to answer the question we previously presented, as to why God chose to exile the Jewish People to Egypt and Canaan, places of intense immorality and perversion.

As the Omniscient Creator of all, God knows the particular strengths and weaknesses, talents and deficiencies, of each individual. It is only God Who can place His people in a situation of danger, for it is only He Who knows that they will emerge not only unscathed, but positively strengthened through the experience. No human being may deliberately place himself in a situation jeopardous to his spirituality, for he cannot guarantee himself that he possesses the fortitude to withstand the challenges he will face. However, when God places His nation in Egypt, it draws out their hidden potential, allowing latent spirituality and strength to surface and be made manifest. It was ultimately for the benefit of His people that the Almighty exiled the Children of Yisrael to that dangerous territory, the "refinery" of Egypt.

Writing about this very subject, Rabbi Dessler explains the following dictum:

יָבוֹא עוֹבַדְיָה שֶׁדָּר בֵּין שְׁנֵי רְשָׁעִים וְלֹא לָמַד מִמַּעֲשֵׂיהֶם וְיִתְנַבֵּא עַל עֵשָׂו שֶׁדָּר בֵּין שְׁנֵי צַדִּיקִים וְלֹא לָמַד מִמַּעֲשֵׂיהֶם.

*Let Ovadiah, who lived among two wicked people [Achav and Izevel], without learning from their deeds, prophesy against Esav, who dwelled with two righteous people [Yitzchak and Rivkah], without learning from their deeds.*[57]

56. *Shir HaShirim Rabbah* 4:10.
57. *Sanhedrin* 39b.

Ya'akov's brother, Esav, sank so deeply into evil that Satan himself became his guardian angel, as seen in the famous wrestling match with Ya'akov. The very essence of his being was falsehood and wickedness. His offspring, Amalek, adopting his characteristics, initiated war against the Jewish People for no apparent reason. Amalek fought a spiritual battle, opposing the truth, the purpose, that the Jewish People represent. Amalek yearned to counteract and ultimately suppress and vanquish the sublime purpose of the cosmos. This burning hatred, directed against "God and His anointed," could only develop in a descendant of Esav — Esav who had experienced goodness and yet rejected it. The great and awesome deeds he had witnessed, the holy teachings the righteous ones tried to instill in him, only further hardened his obstinate resolve. He garbed himself in the spirit of defilement, a spirit which he then transmitted to his descendants. They in turn were infused with such a love of falsehood that they were driven to fight a suicidal battle to wipe out the Nation of Truth.

It is thus that we can understand the words of the *Sifra* quoted earlier. It was indeed the presence of the Jewish People in Egypt and Canaan that caused, and even necessitated, the corruption of these two nations. "Opposition sharpens one's spiritual strengths." For the Jewish People to develop and grow in the manner desired, they had to be faced with perversity and corruption.

Further, let us propose an answer to that question which we ask ourselves upon our recitation of the *Shema*. Do we indeed possess the strength to sacrifice our lives in sanctification of God's Name? True, in a normal situation, it might be a question left unanswered. However, were the opportunity to arise, each person would surely discover within himself the courage to forfeit his life for a higher ideal. The awesome trial with which he is faced serves to bring out the courage and determination latent within.

Applying this idea to contemporary society, one must be wary on two accounts. One who lives in an upright society, surrounded by moral and righteous individuals, is paradoxically in a situation of danger. As Rabbi Dessler writes, "Someone living in an environment inhabited by righteous individuals, who has chosen to follow the opposite path, will develop an overwhelming hatred for the ideals of the righteous, to a degree greater than one whose wickedness does not result from an exposure to true good." Those of us who are fortunate enough to reside in a place pulsating with Torah, with righteous examples to emulate, must indeed acknowledge and guard ourselves against this possible danger.

Conversely, with the steep moral decline of our age, we are in a position to react against the pervasive evil, and to develop our spirituality in a manner of extreme intensity. May we all merit to achieve that intensity of strength in the face of the ever declining society in which we live.

# KEDOSHIM

STRIVE FOR HOLINESS – this is the injunction at the beginning of our *parashah* and the aim encapsulating all of man's Divine service.

**וַיְדַבֵּר ה' אֶל מֹשֶׁה לֵּאמֹר. דַּבֵּר אֶל כָּל עֲדַת בְּנֵי יִשְׂרָאֵל וְאָמַרְתָּ אֲלֵהֶם קְדֹשִׁים תִּהְיוּ כִּי קָדוֹשׁ אֲנִי ה' אֱלֹקֵיכֶם.**

*The Eternal spoke to Moshe, saying, "Speak to the entire congregation of the Children of Yisrael, and you shall say to them, "You shall be holy, for I, the Eternal your God, am holy.'[58]"*

The verse emphasizes that this pivotal command was to be delivered to the "entire congregation of the Children of Yisrael," an unusually emphatic expression. Rashi explains:

מְלַמֵּד שֶׁנֶּאֶמְרָה פָּרָשָׁה זוֹ בְּהַקְהֵל, מִפְּנֵי שֶׁרֹב גּוּפֵי תוֹרָה תְּלוּיִין בָּהּ.

*This expression teaches us that this section of the Torah was delivered to a gathering of the whole congregation. This is because a majority of the essential elements of Torah are dependent upon it.*[59]

Rashi's comment raises an interesting question. Was not the entire Torah transmitted to the whole congregation? Was not every individual informed of his obligations as a member of the Jewish nation? If so, then why are we told of the communal transmission in this particular case? Let us examine the manner in which Torah was originally conveyed to the Children of Yisrael.

**וְאַחֲרֵי כֵן נִגְּשׁוּ כָּל בְּנֵי יִשְׂרָאֵל וַיְצַוֵּם אֵת כָּל אֲשֶׁר דִּבֶּר ה' אִתּוֹ בְּהַר סִינָי.**

---

58. *Vayikra* 19:1, 2.
59. Rashi *ad loc.*

*Afterwards all the Children of Yisrael would draw near, and [Moshe] would command them whatever the Eternal had spoken to him on Mount Sinai.*[60]

Rashi details the mechanics of this process:

אַחַר שֶׁלִּמֵּד לִזְקֵנִים, חוֹזֵר וּמְלַמֵּד הַפָּרָשָׁה אוֹ הַהֲלָכָה לְיִשְׂרָאֵל, תָּנוּ רַבָּנָן כֵּיצַד סֵדֶר הַמִּשְׁנָה? מֹשֶׁה הָיָה לוֹמֵד מִפִּי הַגְּבוּרָה. נִכְנַס אַהֲרֹן, שָׁנָה לוֹ מֹשֶׁה פִּרְקוֹ, נִסְתַּלֵּק אַהֲרֹן וְיָשַׁב לוֹ לִשְׂמֹאל מֹשֶׁה. נִכְנְסוּ בָּנָיו, שָׁנָה לָהֶם מֹשֶׁה פִּרְקָם, נִסְתַּלְּקוּ הֵם, יָשַׁב אֶלְעָזָר לִימִין מֹשֶׁה וְאִיתָמָר לִשְׂמֹאל אַהֲרֹן. נִכְנְסוּ זְקֵנִים, שָׁנָה לָהֶם מֹשֶׁה פִּרְקָם, נִסְתַּלְּקוּ זְקֵנִים יָשְׁבוּ לִצְדָדִין. נִכְנְסוּ כָּל הָעָם, שָׁנָה לָהֶם מֹשֶׁה פִּרְקָם, נִמְצָא בְּיַד כָּל הָעָם אֶחָד, בְּיַד הַזְּקֵנִים שְׁנַיִם, בְּיַד בְּנֵי אַהֲרֹן שְׁלשָׁה, בְּיַד אַהֲרֹן אַרְבָּעָה וכו'.

*After Moshe taught the Elders, he would teach the section of the law to Yisrael. Our Rabbis ask, "In what order was the teaching transmitted?" They explain:*

1. *Moshe would learn from God's Mouth.*
2. *Aharon would enter, and Moshe would teach him his chapter. Aharon would then remove himself, and sit on Moshe' left.*
3. *Aharon's sons would enter, and Moshe would teach them their chapter. El'azar would remove himself to a seat on Moshe' right, and Ithamar would sit at Aharon's left.*
4. *The Elders would enter, and Moshe would teach them their chapter. The Elders would then remove themselves and sit on the sides.*
5. *The whole congregation would enter, and Moshe would teach them their section of the law.*

*Thus, the entire congregation received one lesson in the chapter, the Elders heard two lessons, the sons of Aharon heard the lesson three times, Aharon heard the lesson four times, etc.*[61]

---

60. *Shemoth* 34:32.
61. Rashi *ad loc.*

Through this long narrative, we learn that every member of the Children of Yisrael was taught the Torah. What, therefore, is the significance of קְדֹשִׁים תִּהְיוּ — "You shall be holy," being said in front of the entire congregation? How does this differ from the usual manner of conveying the lessons of the Torah?

*Sifthei Chachamim*, a commentary on Rashi, offers two possible solutions:

1. Usually, a gathering of "all the nation" denotes that all the men were gathered. Concerning the mitzvah to "be holy," the women and children were also required to be present.
2. The Torah was normally taught to the people in sections; one portion was explained, followed by the next portion. However, *Parashath Kedoshim* was read to the people in one continuous speech.

The Maharal in his commentary to Rashi, *Gur Aryeh*, offers another distinction between the manner in which Torah was normally taught to the people, and the instance in our *parashah*:

> שֶׁלֹּא הָיוּ מְחֻיָּבִים שֶׁיָּבוֹאוּ כָּל יִשְׂרָאֵל, שֶׁאִם לֹא הָיָה לָהֶם פְּנַאי לֹא הָיוּ בָּאִים... אֲבָל בְּפָרָשָׁה הַזֹּאת הָיָה מַקְהִיל כָּל יִשְׂרָאֵל, וְהָיוּ צְרִיכִין לָבֹא.
>
> *For the reading of the Portion of Kedoshim, attendance was compulsory. Normally, the entire nation was not under obligation to attend the teaching sessions. However, for the gathering to hear the Portion of Kedoshim, all were required to be present.*[62]

The Malbim[63] explains why *Parashath Kedoshim* is of such primary importance, such significance that it necessitates the presence of the entire nation. He reiterates the words of Rashi, explaining that *Kedoshim* contains גּוּפֵי תוֹרָה — "The essentials of Torah." All were required to hear those "essentials," those vital parts of Torah. The Malbim continues to explain the meaning of this term, "גּוּפֵי תוֹרָה."

62. *Gur Aryeh* on *Vayikra* 19:1.
63. Malbim *ad loc.*

Just as every person is made up of a גוף and a נְשָׁמָה, a body and a soul, so every mitzvah is subject to this makeup. Every mitzvah involves a clearly defined physical action – the גוף of the mitzvah. However, the significance of each mitzvah is not confined to the tangible world. Each mitzvah also has a נְשָׁמָה, a spiritual effect in the higher worlds. Knowledge of the נְשָׁמָה of a mitzvah, understanding the profound changes it effects in the upper spheres, is the domain of the scholar. The "גוף" of each mitzvah, however, must be known by everyone, practiced by the entire congregation. It is for this reason that *Kedoshim* was said in front of a gathering of the entire congregation. The numerous mitzvoth that the *parashah* contains are vital knowledge for all; the men, women, and children are all required to be well-versed in these essential laws.

Referring back to our original verse, a further difficulty becomes evident. We are enjoined to pursue the goal of holiness for a specific reason – because God is holy. Let us investigate the significance of this rationale. To do so, we shall have to digress to a *mishnah* in *Pirkei Avoth.*

> רַבִּי חֲלַפְתָּא בֶּן דּוֹסָא אִישׁ כְּפַר חֲנַנְיָא אוֹמֵר עֲשָׂרָה שֶׁיּוֹשְׁבִין וְעוֹסְקִין בַּתּוֹרָה שְׁכִינָה שְׁרוּיָה בֵּינֵיהֶם שֶׁנֶּאֱמַר אֱלֹקִים נִצָּב בַּעֲדַת אֵ-ל. וּמִנַּיִן אֲפִלּוּ חֲמִשָּׁה שֶׁנֶּאֱמַר וַאֲגֻדָּתוֹ עַל אֶרֶץ יְסָדָהּ. וּמִנַּיִן אֲפִלּוּ שְׁלֹשָׁה שֶׁנֶּאֱמַר בְּקֶרֶב אֱלֹהִים יִשְׁפֹּט. וּמִנַּיִן אֲפִלּוּ שְׁנַיִם שֶׁנֶּאֱמַר אָז נִדְבְּרוּ יִרְאֵי ה' אִישׁ אֶל רֵעֵהוּ וַיַּקְשֵׁב ה' וַיִּשְׁמַע וגו'. וּמִנַּיִן אֲפִלּוּ אֶחָד שֶׁנֶּאֱמַר בְּכָל הַמָּקוֹם אֲשֶׁר אַזְכִּיר אֶת שְׁמִי אָבוֹא אֵלֶיךָ וּבֵרַכְתִּיךָ.
>
> *R. Chalafta ben Dosa of Kfar Chananya said: "If ten people sit together and engage in Torah study, the Divine Presence rests among them, as it states, 'God stands in an assembly of the Lord.'*
>
> *How do we know this even of five people? It states, 'He has established His gathering upon earth.'*
>
> *How do we know this even of three people? It states, 'In the midst of judges He will judge.'*
>
> *How do we know this even of two people? It states, 'Then the God-fearing people spoke, one man to his neighbour, and God listened and heard.'*

*How do we know that the Divine Presence rests on even one person? It states, 'In every place in which I cause My Name to be mentioned, I will come to you and bless you.'"*[64]

The question on this Mishnah stands out boldly: If God's Presence can be felt by even a solitary individual who involves himself in spirituality, why is it necessary to prove that the Divine Presence is felt when larger numbers of people are gathered together? Surely, if just one person can experience the *Shechinah*, it can be felt when ten people collectively are involved in Torah study! What then is the reason for the Mishnah's enumeration?

The *Eitz Yosef* explains that the answer can be found in an analysis of the proof texts used by the Mishnah. Various different expressions are employed to denote the manner in which God's Presence rests. In the verse referring to a person studying alone, we find the words אָבוֹא אֵלֶיךָ — "I will come to you." אָבוֹא is an expression denoting מִקְרֶה, a chance encounter. Concerning two people engaged in study, the expression is וַיַּקְשֵׁב ה' וַיִּשְׁמַע, which implies greater intent, and a more intense sensation of Godliness. The *Eitz Yosef* proves that as the number of people increases, their combined study causes God's Presence to be felt ever more strongly.

The Mishnah, in enumerating the various proofs for God's Presence, informs us of an important principle: there are degrees in which God's Presence can be felt. Ten people will feel God's presence more intensely than five people, and in turn, five people will have more awareness than three, two, or one. Further, a feeling of closeness to God, of the Divine Presence, is not inspired exclusively by Torah study. Any gathering that causes a sanctification of God's Name, will experience the Divine Presence. As it states in the Talmud, כָּל בֵּי עֲשָׂרָה שְׁכִינְתָּא שַׁרְיָא.[65]

We find that the Mishnah[66] elaborates on this theme. As Grace is recited at the end of each meal, the *Shechinah* is present even when

64. *Pirkei Avoth* 3:7.
65. *Sanhedrin* 39a.
66. *Berachoth* 7:3.

people sit down to dine. When three or more people are present at a meal, זִמּוּן, a formal invitation to begin the blessing, is recited. The format of this invitation depends on the number of people present. The invitation changes on occasions when ten, one hundred, one thousand or ten thousand people are present. It is apparent that the larger the group of people, the more the *Shechinah* can be felt.

Any gathering dedicated to spreading the light of spirituality in the world, will experience God's Presence. The larger the gathering, the more potent will be this feeling. It must be noted that God's Presence does not depart from His people, even when they are embroiled in sin.

**וְכִפֶּר עַל הַקֹּדֶשׁ מִטֻּמְאֹת בְּנֵי יִשְׂרָאֵל וּמִפִּשְׁעֵיהֶם לְכָל חַטֹּאתָם וְכֵן יַעֲשֶׂה לְאֹהֶל מוֹעֵד הַשֹּׁכֵן אִתָּם בְּתוֹךְ טֻמְאֹתָם.**

*He shall [thus] make an atonement for the [inner] Sanctuary from the defilements [caused by] the Children of Yisrael — from those done iniquitously [besides] all those done inadvertently. He shall then carry out the same [procedure] on [the partition of] the Tent of Meeting, [where the Divine Presence] dwells with [the Children of Yisrael] in the midst of their impurities.*[67]

Rashi's comment is both comforting and obligating:

אַף עַל פִּי שֶׁהֵם טְמֵאִים, שְׁכִינָה בֵּינֵיהֶם.

*Despite the fact that the people are impure, the Divine Presence resides among them.*[68]

God is always amongst us, although, due to our deadened spiritual state, this is at times indiscernible. Despite our number, despite our level of purity, despite our anaesthetized, comatose state, the *Shechinah* is constantly present.

If God's presence is amongst us even in our lowly state, one can conclude that at a gathering of the entire nation for the express

67. *Vayikra* 16:16.
68. Rashi *ad loc.*

purpose of sanctifying God's Name, a הַקְהֵל, gathering, of the nature described in our *parashah*, God's presence could be clearly felt by all.

The nature of this closeness between the Jewish nation and the Almighty is explained in the following parable brought by the Midrash.

ר׳ יודָן בְּשֵׁם ר׳ יִשְׁמָעֵאל בַּר נַחְמָן מָשָׁל לְמֶלֶךְ שֶׁהָיוּ לוֹ פְּרַקְסִין, וְהָיָה מְצַוֶּה אֶת עַבְדּוֹ וְאָמַר לוֹ קַפְּלוֹ וְנַעֲרוֹ, וְתֵן דַּעְתְּךָ עָלָיו. אָמַר לוֹ עַבְדּוֹ אֲדוֹנִי הַמֶּלֶךְ, מִכָּל פְּרַקְסִין שֶׁיֵּשׁ לְךָ אִי אַתָּה מְצַוֶּה אוֹתִי אֶלָּא עַל זֶה. אָמַר לוֹ שֶׁאֲנִי מַדְבִּיקוֹ לְגוּפִי. כָּךְ אָמַר מֹשֶׁה לִפְנֵי הַקָּדוֹשׁ בָּרוּךְ הוּא, רִבּוֹנוֹ שֶׁל עוֹלָם מִשִּׁבְעִים אֻמּוֹת אוֹתֵינְטִיאוֹת שֶׁיֵּשׁ לְךָ בְּעוֹלָמְךָ אִי אַתָּה מְצַוֶּה אוֹתִי אֶלָּא עַל יִשְׂרָאֵל, צַו אֶת בְּנֵי יִשְׂרָאֵל, דַּבֵּר אֶל בְּנֵי יִשְׂרָאֵל, אֱמֹר אֶל בְּנֵי יִשְׂרָאֵל. אָמַר לוֹ שֶׁהֵן דְּבוּקִין לִי, הֲדָא הוּא דִכְתִיב כִּי כַּאֲשֶׁר יִדְבַּק הָאֵזוֹר אֶל מָתְנֵי אִישׁ...

*A king had a vest. He charged his servant to wash it, fold it, and care for it.*

*Servant: "Your Majesty, of all the garments that you own, why are you commanding me only concerning this one?"*

*King: "This is the garment that lies closest to my body."*

*This was the question Moshe asked of the Almighty. "Master of the Universe, there are seventy nations in Your world. Why do You command me concerning only the Jewish nation [as it says], 'Command the Jewish People, speak to the Jewish People, say to the Jewish People, etc?'"*

*Replied the Almighty, "It is this nation that clings to Me," as it says, 'Just as a girdle clings to a man's loins....'"*[69]

The world is inhabited by seventy nations, each of which appears to be stronger and more powerful than the Jewish People. However, only the Jewish People are afforded special protection and closeness. For only the Jewish People cling to God.

As the following Midrash highlights, this unparalleled position brings not only privileges, but also obligations.

---

69. *Vayikra Rabbah* 2:4.

אָמַר ר' שְׁמוּאֵל בַּר נַחְמָן מָשָׁל לְכֹהֵן גָּדוֹל שֶׁהָיָה מְהַלֵּךְ בַּדֶּרֶךְ וְנִזְדַּמֵּן לוֹ חִלוֹנִי אֶחָד. אָמַר לוֹ אֵלֵךְ עִמְּךָ. אָמַר לוֹ בְּנִי כֹּהֵן אֲנִי וּבְדֶרֶךְ טָהוֹר אֲנִי מְהַלֵּךְ וְאֵין דַּרְכִּי לְהַלֵּךְ בֵּין הַקְּבָרוֹת, אִם אַתָּה הוֹלֵךְ עִמִּי מוּטָב, וְאִם לָאו סוֹף שֶׁאֲנִי מַנִּיחֲךָ וְהוֹלֵךְ לִי.

*R. Shemuel bar Nachman brought a parable of a High Priest who, walking on the way, encountered a person who was estranged from Torah and mitzvoth. This man asked to accompany the High Priest. The High Priest replied, "My son, I am a priest, and must walk on a road which is pure and undefiled. I may not step between gravestones. If you will travel with me, well and good. If not, I will eventually have to leave you and walk alone."*[70]

One of the recent Chassidic masters, the *Mei HaShiloach*, draws a similar analogy describing a king and his close friend. The king is forced to accompany the friend regardless of the journey's route or destination. The king thus implores his friend to take care concerning the places in which he walks. Having no choice but to follow, the king entreats his friend to avoid places that will cause him shame or embarrassment.

We, members of the Jewish People, are that "close friend" of the King of kings. The friendship is everlasting, Eternal, independent of our spiritual stature or whereabouts. An awesome responsibility is thus placed upon us: to maintain a standard appropriate for the company that is constantly present. As the verse states:

**כִּי ה' אֱלֹקֶיךָ מִתְהַלֵּךְ בְּקֶרֶב מַחֲנֶךָ לְהַצִּילְךָ וְלָתֵת אֹיְבֶיךָ לְפָנֶיךָ וְהָיָה מַחֲנֶיךָ קָדוֹשׁ וְלֹא יִרְאֶה בְךָ עֶרְוַת דָּבָר וְשָׁב מֵאַחֲרֶיךָ.**

*Since [the Presence of] the Eternal, your God, moves within your camp, so as to save you, and place your enemies before you, your camp shall be holy. And let [the Eternal] not see any sort of nakedness among you, that He [then] withdraw [His Divine Presence] from [among] you.*[71]

---

70. *Vayikra Rabbah* 24:7.
71. *Devarim* 23:15.

The Ibn Ezra[72] explains עֶרְוַת דָּבָר — "nakedness," to refer to either the realm of speech or of deed. Both one's words and actions must be appropriate in the presence of royalty. The Midrash[73] interprets the words homiletically, rendering עֶרְוַת דָּבָר as עֶרְוַת דִּבּוּר: it is thus taken as an injunction to avoid inappropriate speech. Underlying these interpretations is one common thread: God Himself is present amongst us. We must constantly pay homage to the royalty we find in our midst. This involves not only following the letter of the law with exactitude. There are many actions that are technically permitted, but nevertheless cannot be classified as actions of holiness. They fail to comply with the "spirit of the law," the striving for spirituality that must pervade the Jew's every thought, word, and deed. Faithfulness to the spirit of the law can be maintained when we are conscious of the presence of a respected superior, of one whom we desire to impress. If each one of us were cognizant of God's presence among us, many questionable incidents, many paltry deeds would be eradicated. For Who is among us? The *Yalkut Shimoni* describes the Almighty as being holy in every respect: שֶׁהוּא קָדוֹשׁ בְּכָל מִינֵי קְדֻשּׁוֹת — "He is holy with every kind of holiness."

As "close friends" of the King, we must maintain our dignity and nobility. We must act in a manner that befits our elevated status. God is amongst us — He will save us from our enemies, guard us and protect us. He constantly provides us with the gift of life, so that we can develop our spirituality, spreading the light of His Name. And then, in our journey onwards and upwards, we will feel His constant companionship and guidance.

72. Ibn Ezra *ad loc.*
73. *Vayikra Rabbah* 24:7.

# EMOR

ON OUR JOURNEY through the year, our path takes us through a number of festivals, which are detailed in this *parashah*. The period between Pesach and Shavuoth is one of intense spiritual labour, and is termed *Sefirath HaOmer*, literally "the counting of the *omer* (measure)." Let us uncover the underlying themes of this period. In the course of our voyage we will reveal a parallel between *Sefirath HaOmer* and the festival of Sukkoth.

> **וַיְדַבֵּר ה' אֶל מֹשֶׁה לֵּאמֹר. דַּבֵּר אֶל בְּנֵי יִשְׂרָאֵל וְאָמַרְתָּ אֲלֵהֶם כִּי תָבֹאוּ אֶל הָאָרֶץ אֲשֶׁר אֲנִי נֹתֵן לָכֶם וּקְצַרְתֶּם אֶת קְצִירָהּ וַהֲבֵאתֶם אֶת עֹמֶר רֵאשִׁית קְצִירְכֶם אֶל הַכֹּהֵן... וּסְפַרְתֶּם לָכֶם מִמָּחֳרַת הַשַּׁבָּת מִיּוֹם הֲבִיאֲכֶם אֶת עֹמֶר הַתְּנוּפָה שֶׁבַע שַׁבָּתוֹת תְּמִימֹת תִּהְיֶינָה. עַד מִמָּחֳרַת הַשַּׁבָּת הַשְּׁבִיעִת תִּסְפְּרוּ חֲמִשִּׁים יוֹם וְהִקְרַבְתֶּם מִנְחָה חֲדָשָׁה לַה'.**
>
> *The Eternal spoke to Moshe, saying, "Speak to the Children of Yisrael and you shall say to them: When you come to the land that I am giving to you and you reap its harvest, you shall bring to the priest an omer-measure of the first [grains] of your harvest... From the day after the [first] rest day [of Pesach], from the day you bring the omer-measure [for] the wave offering, [each of] you shall count for yourselves seven weeks, [these weeks] being complete. You shall count up to the day after the seventh week, [that day completing] fifty days, and [then] offer up a new meal offering [before] the Eternal.*[74]

Well established is the principle that the name given to an entity reflects its essence. To understand the essence of any festival, therefore, we would do well to analyse its term of reference. Turning to

---

74. *Vayikra* 23:9, 10, 15–16.

the period in time under examination, we can ask why the counting is called *Sefirath HaOmer*, *omer* referring to a specific measure of the harvest.

The Midrash elaborates upon the "*omer*" that is brought.

א"ר בֶּרֶכְיָה אָמַר הקב"ה לְמֹשֶׁה לֵךְ אֱמֹר לְיִשְׂרָאֵל כְּשֶׁהָיִיתִי נוֹתֵן לָכֶם אֶת הַמָּן הָיִיתִי נוֹתֵן עֹמֶר לְכָל אֶחָד וְאֶחָד מִכֶּם הֲדָא הוּא דִכְתִיב עֹמֶר לַגֻּלְגֹּלֶת וְעַכְשָׁו שֶׁאַתֶּם נוֹתְנִים לִי אֶת הָעֹמֶר אֵין לִי אֶלָּא עֹמֶר אֶחָד מִכֻּלְּכֶם וְלֹא עוֹד אֶלָּא שֶׁל שְׂעוֹרִים לְפִיכָךְ מֹשֶׁה מַזְהִיר אֶת יִשְׂרָאֵל וְאוֹמֵר לָהֶם וַהֲבֵאתֶם אֶת עֹמֶר.[75]

Moshe exhorted the Children of Yisrael to be particularly careful concerning the *omer* offering. For, in the desert, God gave an *omer*, a measure, of manna, to each individual every day. It is thus a symbol of God's great benevolence to His people. In contrast, the *omer* sacrifice offered by the Children of Yisrael is just one collective measure from the entire people. The required measure being so small, Moshe warned the people to exercise special vigilance to ensure its implementation. Let us discover the underlying significance of the *omer*, this measure.

The Ran, in his study of the subject of *Sefirath HaOmer*, writes the following:

בְּשָׁעָה שֶׁאָמַר לָהֶם מֹשֶׁה לְיִשְׂרָאֵל תַּעַבְדוּן אֶת הָאֱלֹקִים עַל הָהָר הַזֶּה אָמְרוּ לוֹ יִשְׂרָאֵל, מֹשֶׁה רַבֵּנוּ אֵימָתַי עֲבוֹדָה זוֹ? אָמַר לָהֶם לְסוֹף נ' יוֹם וְהָיוּ מוֹנִים כָּל אֶחָד וְאֶחָד לְעַצְמוֹ. מִכָּאן קָבְעוּ חֲכָמִים לִסְפִירַת הָעֹמֶר.

*When Moshe said to Yisrael, "You will serve the Almighty on this mountain," they said to him, "Moshe our teacher, when is this service to take place?"*

*"After fifty days," was the reply. Each individual counted the fifty days. From here, our Sages instituted Sefirath HaOmer, the counting of the omer.*[76]

This comment of our Sages requires explanation on a number of fronts.

75. *Vayikra Rabbah* 28:3.

76. Ran, end of *Pesachim*.

Firstly, when anticipating an event with excitement, it is clear that one normally counts down towards the awaited day, as demonstrated, for example, by the excited chant of schoolchildren, "Ten more days 'till we'll be free, out of this house of misery." When anticipating the giving of the Torah, however, instead of focusing on the days gone by, we are instructed to count upwards, a surprising thing indeed.

Perhaps we can understand this phenomenon by way of an analogy. Like a man counting gold coins, we only count that which has intrinsic value. Counting the days gone by shows that these days must contain intrinsic value. What then gives intrinsic value and special significance to these fifty days in particular?

The period begins with the night of the Exodus from Egypt, that cosmic night of redemption, on which the Children of Yisrael beheld מוֹרָא גָּדוֹל — "great awe," a transcendent revelation of overwhelming proportions. This revelation is evident in the plague of the night, of מַכַּת בְּכוֹרוֹת — the killing of the firstborn sons. In Jewish tradition, the firstborn is said to have a greater capacity for spirituality than the norm.

It is thus that the Egyptian firstborns had some perception of the revelation to which the rest of the nation was oblivious. This exposure to the sublime shattered their coarse, finite Egyptian vessels and resulted in their death. They could not continue living in the face of it. Such was the power and magnitude of this revelation!

From this vantage point of awesome light, the Children of Yisrael were plunged into darkness. But the memory of this experience remained, and inspired an anticipation for the forthcoming revelation of the giving of the Torah. That scene, too, was awesome in its proportions: Darkness. Fire. Thunder. Lightning. The piercing sound of the shofar growing increasingly louder. All this accumulated into the ultimate paradox: a palpable manifestation of Godliness.

When we examine the words of the Jewish People, however, it seems that they looked forward to the spiritual labour involved in receiving the Torah, תַּעַבְדוּן אֶת הָאֱלֹקִים עַל הָהָר הַזֶּה "You shall serve God on this mountain." How can this be understood?

A law in the construction of a *sukkah* has profound implications on our subject:

**בַּסֻּכֹּת תֵּשְׁבוּ שִׁבְעַת יָמִים כָּל הָאֶזְרָח בְּיִשְׂרָאֵל יֵשְׁבוּ בַּסֻּכֹּת.**

*You shall live in sukkoth (thatched-roof huts) for a seven-day period; all natives among Yisrael shall live in thatched-roof huts.*[77]

The Gemara provides the definition of this *sukkah*:

מַאי שְׁנָא גַּבֵּי סֻכָּה דְּתָנֵי פְּסוּלָה? ...וְרָבָא אָמַר מֵהָכָא "בַּסֻּכֹּת תֵּשְׁבוּ שִׁבְעַת יָמִים" אָמְרָה תוֹרָה כָּל שִׁבְעַת הַיָּמִים צֵא מִדִּירַת קֶבַע וְשֵׁב בְּדִירַת עֲרַאי, עַד עֶשְׂרִים אַמָּה אָדָם עוֹשֶׂה דִּירָתוֹ דִּירַת עֲרַאי, לְמַעְלָה מֵעֶשְׂרִים אַמָּה אֵין אָדָם עוֹשֶׂה דִּירָתוֹ דִּירַת עֲרַאי אֶלָּא דִּירַת קֶבַע.[78]

The Torah instructs us to leave our permanent dwelling and reside in a temporary abode. A booth higher than twenty *amoth* (armspans) is not considered temporary and thus does not qualify as a *sukkah.*

The emphasis, then, is seen to be on the temporary nature of the abode. However, the Talmud continues, informing us that a *sukkah* of iron walls is categorized as a *sukkah*, provided it is lower than twenty *amoth*. This law seems to directly contradict the underlying principle of a *sukkah*: that it be a dwelling which is temporary.

An interesting derivation is made by Rabbi Simcha Zissel:

הַמִּתְבָּאֵר כִּי תֵּכֶף אַחַר יוהכ"פ שֶׁשָּׁב בִּתְשׁוּבָה, צִוְּתָה הַתּוֹרָה לַעֲשׂוֹת מַעֲשֶׂה לְמַעַן יִתְחַזֵּק בְּרַעְיוֹן יוֹתֵר, כִּי אִי אֶפְשָׁר לַעֲמֹד בִּתְשׁוּבָתוֹ רַק כְּשֶׁיַּעֲשֶׂה הָעוֹלָם עֲרַאי וְלֹא קֶבַע. וְאָמְנָם לִהְיוֹת תָּמִיד כֵּן בְּמַעֲשֶׂה בְּפֹעַל, לֹא עָמְדוּ בָּזֶה רַק חֲסִידִים הָרִאשׁוֹנִים שֶׁעָשׂוּ מְלַאכְתָּם עֲרַאי וְתוֹרָתָם קֶבַע, מַה שֶּׁאֵין כֵּן כָּל הָעוֹלָם אֵין יְכוֹלִים לַעֲמֹד בָּזֶה, וַהֲרֵי מִצְוַת זְכִירַת יְשִׁיבַת סֻכָּה לְכָל הָעוֹלָם, ע"כ בָּאָה הַהֲלָכָה שֶׁיִּהְיֶה אֶפְשָׁר לַעֲשׂוֹת עֲרַאי, פי' שֶׁיִּשְׁמֹר אֶת כֹּחוֹתָיו שֶׁלֹּא יִתְקַלְקְלוּ ח"ו בְּאֹפֶן שֶׁיִּהְיֶה מֻכְרָח לַעֲשׂוֹת הָעוֹלָם קֶבַע תָּמִיד דַּוְקָא, וְרַק יַרְגִּיל עַצְמוֹ

77. *Vayikra* 23:42.

78. *Sukkah* 2a.

לִפְרָקִים לְהַיְכֹלֶת לַעֲשׂוֹת הָעוֹלָם עֲרַאי גַּם בְּמַעֲשֶׂה אִם יִרְצֶה לְעֵת מְצֹא כְּשֶׁנִּדְרָשׁ הָעִנְיָן. וְזֶהוּ מַה שֶּׁאָנוּ אוֹמְרִים שֶׁלְּכָל הַפָּחוֹת לַעֲשׂוֹת מְלָאכְתּוֹ עֲרַאי בְּמַחְשַׁבְתּוֹ, וְאֵין יָכֹל לִהְיוֹת זֹאת רַק בְּרֹב מַחְשַׁבְתּוֹ בְּעִיּוּן בְּהֶבֶל הָעוֹלָם, וּבַנֹּעַם הַנִּצְחִי בְּכַמּוּת וּבְאֵיכוּת, וְזֶהוּ קֹטֶב כַּוָּנַת מִצְוַת הַסֻּכָּה לְפִי דַּעַת רָבָא דקיי"ל כְּוָתֵיהּ.

*Immediately after Yom Kippur, when we have returned to the Almighty in repentance, the Torah commands us to take action to reinforce the high spiritual level attained. It is impossible to maintain a state of purity unless we view this world as transient. It was only the* חֲסִידִים הָרִאשׁוֹנִים*, the spiritual giants of old, who could live immersed in this world, yet transcend it:* מְלָאכְתָּם עֲרַאי וְתוֹרָתָם קֶבַע*. The world at large cannot constantly live with this clarity.*

*The mitzvah of sukkah is an aid for us to internalise the ephemeral nature of this world, (giving us the possibility of later drawing upon this knowledge as required).*[79]

A *sukkah* with iron walls, representing stability and strength, is kosher, provided it is less than twenty *amoth*, for it has the possibility of being merely a temporary building. However, a booth higher than twenty *amoth*, regardless of its construction material, is almost always a structure of permanent standing and is hence rendered unfit for the mitzvah.

Our homes are not built on such permanent foundations as we like to think. Nevertheless, it is not required of us to live in a temporary manner throughout the year. The crucial factor involved is that we have the possibility of living in such a manner; that our attachment to the world is not so strong that we are unable to break away from it. These short seven days in the year, during which we leave our comfortable homes, are enough to enable us to internalise this possibility of detachment from our belief in the permanence of this transient world. After seven days we can return to our homes, having acquired the knowledge that our lives in this world are like "a passing shadow."

---

79. *Chochmah U'Mussar*, Part Two, p. 174.

The profound lessons to be drawn from the above law must still be investigated further. First, however, let us turn to another law in the mitzvah of *sukkah*.

As seen in the Talmud,[80] a feature unique to the mitzvah of *sukkah* is the law that one who is in some way aggrieved by the mitzvah, termed a מְצְטַעֵר, is exempt from the commandment. For example, one who is cold or uncomfortable is permitted to re-enter his home. This stipulation is striking in that we find mention of it in no other connection. We do not find, for example, that one who is inconvenienced by donning *tefillin* is exempt from fulfilling that mitzvah. We neither find that one who is uncomfortable holding the four species is freed from his obligation. It is only with the mitzvah of *sukkah* that comfort is a requirement for the fulfillment of the obligation. Why is this so? What lies at the root of this distinction?

Still bearing the subject of *sukkah* in mind, let us now return to *Sefirath HaOmer*.

The forty-nine days counted culminate in the שְׁלֹשֶׁת יְמֵי הַגְבָּלָה, which, literally translated, means "three days of restriction." And herein lies the essence of *Sefirath HaOmer*. During these days we undergo an intensive program of self-improvement as preparation for receiving the Torah. *Pirkei Avoth* lists forty-eight elements of character perfection, each of which correspond to one day counted. Upon examination, many of these involve self-discipline and restriction. Examples are:

מִעוּט סְחוֹרָה — restricting one's involvement in business and finance.

מִעוּט תַּעֲנוּג — restricting the pleasures in which one would normally indulge.

מִעוּט שִׂיחָה — restricting one's speech; keeping check on idle chatter.

מִעוּט שְׂחוֹק — restricting one's frivolous behaviour.

שָׂמֵחַ בְּחֶלְקוֹ — being satisfied with the boundaries of one's present life.

---

80. *Sukkah* 28b.

מִתְרַחֵק מִן הַכָּבוֹד — restricting oneself to be happy with less recognition.

Every day of this period we scale new heights in self-restraint and restriction. We therefore accord importance and value to the days we have counted. We take pride in limiting the expansiveness of the physical and being satisfied with less. In labouring in this area we are in fact emulating the Almighty, for God Himself accepts the one, collective *omer*, given with love. He is מִסְתַּפֵּק, satisfied with little.

It is this trait which we imitate when we fill our temporary huts with beautiful vessels and ornaments, thus beautifying the *sukkah*. It seems incongruous to do this to a temporary dwelling! However, it is the very transience of the *sukkah* that we appreciate and seek to glorify.

An application of this idea lies in the law, quoted above, that one who is aggrieved in any way is exempt from this mitzvah. Any measure of distress, or resentment felt, defeats the lesson Sukkoth comes to teach us. This attachment to physicality, to the extent that one is distressed in its absence, precludes the freedom of spirit Sukkoth engenders. One who sits in a *sukkah* while being attached to materialism sits merely in an empty shell. We take pride in our recognition of the transience of the world, and our ability to implement this knowledge for seven days.

This same element of restriction is also seen in the period of *Sefirath HaOmer. Sefirath HaOmer* is Sukkoth revisited. When the refinement of character and the restrictions are valued, *Sefirath HaOmer* has been used to the full.

Our Sages encapsulate this in their statement,

> כָּל הַמְקַיֵּם אֶת הַתּוֹרָה מֵעֹנִי סוֹפוֹ לְקַיְּמָהּ מֵעֹשֶׁר.
>
> *One who fulfills Torah in poverty will come to fulfill it in wealth.*[81]

Through self-restriction one demonstrates the ability to live without materialism. Any physical entities subsequently attained

81. *Pirkei Avoth* 4:9.

will be dedicated solely to spiritual ends, for one has already rejected physicality for its own sake. Rabbeinu HaKadosh (Rabbi Yehudah HaNasi) personified this idea. Despite living in tremendous wealth, at the end of his life he was able to raise his hands heavenward and declare, "I have not had any self-gratification from my fortune."

A *sukkah* of twenty *amoth*, even with iron walls, is kosher, for despite the solidity of the structure, it has the possibility of being a temporary dwelling. One can live in a mansion and do so solely for spiritual ends if one possesses the innate ability to live and thrive in a ramshackle hut, if necessary. It is the pride taken in one's material restrictions, and the importance attributed to them, that allow a person to live a spiritual life even amidst luxury.

The period of restriction that is *Sefirath HaOmer* precedes the giving of the Torah. The Children of Yisrael anticipated the forthcoming spiritual labour of the day on which they were to "serve God on this mountain." The promise of awesome revelation was not the focus of their excitement. We can understand this further by bearing in mind that desire for external pleasures indicates an inner void, a lack of a wholesome inner life. When one contains everything within, external satisfaction is unnecessary, for no deficiency is felt.

*Sukkah* is not a mitzvah for one who is distressed. *Sukkah*, in essence, is the satisfaction which stems from a reduction of one's dependence on material possessions, one's satisfaction instead stemming from the feeling of inner completion. It is only when one's spirituality is primary that one appreciates restriction. Having acquired this quality we can re-enter our "permanent" homes. In other words, we can live with, for we have the possibility of living without.

Restriction of the physical allows the spiritual, one's inner aspirations, to surface. The Children of Yisrael experienced forty-nine days of restriction and self-restraint, bringing their inner desire to serve God to the fore. Through their divesting themselves of any physical desires, their pulsating core shone in its brightness. Their anticipation for the giving of the Torah thus stemmed from the longing to serve, not to experience the cosmic revelation.

It is thus that we can understand the name of the period — *Sefirath HaOmer*. Just one *omer* of manna was given per person, the minimum requirement for each day. This satisfaction with the minimum requirement is what we are seeking. Armed with this quality, we can accept the Torah in the true fashion.

# BEHAR

LAST WEEK'S PARASHAH informed us of the period of *Sefirath Ha-Omer*, the seven-week interval between Pesach and Shavuoth which is marked by each day's enumeration. The verses instruct us:

**וּסְפַרְתֶּם לָכֶם מִמָּחֳרַת הַשַּׁבָּת... שֶׁבַע שַׁבָּתוֹת תְּמִימֹת תִּהְיֶינָה. עַד מִמָּחֳרַת הַשַּׁבָּת הַשְּׁבִיעִת תִּסְפְּרוּ חֲמִשִּׁים יוֹם.**

*From the day after the [first] rest day [of Pesach]... [each of] you shall count for yourselves seven weeks, [these weeks] being complete. You shall count up to the day after the seventh week, [that day completing] fifty days....*[82]

A grammatical nuance in the verse is highlighted by the Talmud.

שֶׁתְּהֵא סְפִירָה לְכָל אֶחָד וְאֶחָד.

*"You" is written in the plural, for every individual has an obligation to count.*[83]

In our *parashah*, another enumeration is mentioned, this time in connection with the Jubilee year, the *Yovel*.

**וְסָפַרְתָּ לְךָ שֶׁבַע שַׁבְּתֹת שָׁנִים שֶׁבַע שָׁנִים שֶׁבַע פְּעָמִים וְהָיוּ לְךָ יְמֵי שֶׁבַע שַׁבְּתֹת הַשָּׁנִים תֵּשַׁע וְאַרְבָּעִים שָׁנָה. וְהַעֲבַרְתָּ שׁוֹפַר תְּרוּעָה בַּחֹדֶשׁ הַשְּׁבִעִי בֶּעָשׂוֹר לַחֹדֶשׁ בְּיוֹם הַכִּפֻּרִים תַּעֲבִירוּ שׁוֹפָר בְּכָל אַרְצְכֶם. וְקִדַּשְׁתֶּם אֵת שְׁנַת הַחֲמִשִּׁים שָׁנָה וּקְרָאתֶם דְּרוֹר בָּאָרֶץ לְכָל יֹשְׁבֶיהָ יוֹבֵל הִוא תִּהְיֶה לָכֶם...**

*You shall count for yourselves seven [cycles of] Sabbatical years, [being] seven times seven years, and [thus] the period*

82. *Vayikra* 23:15, 16.
83. *Menachoth* 65a.

*of the seven [cycles of] Sabbatical years will [total] for you forty-nine years. You shall then sound the wailing shofar in the seventh month, on the tenth of the month; on the Day of Atonement you shall sound the shofar throughout your land. You shall sanctify the [entire] year of the fiftieth year and proclaim freedom in the land for all its inhabitants...*[84]

The injunction to count the *Yovel* year is expressed in the singular form, from which our Sages derive that the obligation to count the years applies only to the High Court, the great *Beith Din*. Individuals must count days, while only the *Beith Din* record years. What lies in this distinction?

Let us turn to the following Midrash:

אִם בְּחֻקֹּתַי תֵּלֵכוּ. הֲדָא הוּא דִכְתִיב חִשַּׁבְתִּי דְרָכָי וָאָשִׁיבָה רַגְלַי אֶל עֵדֹתֶיךָ. אָמַר דָּוִד רבש"ע, בְּכָל יוֹם וְיוֹם הָיִיתִי מְחַשֵּׁב וְאוֹמֵר לְמָקוֹם פְּלוֹנִי וּלְבֵית דִּירָה פְּלוֹנִית אֲנִי הוֹלֵךְ, וְהָיוּ רַגְלַי מְבִיאוֹת אוֹתִי לְבָתֵּי כְּנֵסִיּוֹת וּלְבָתֵּי מִדְרָשׁוֹת. הֲדָא הוּא דִכְתִיב וָאָשִׁיבָה רַגְלַי אֶל עֵדֹתֶיךָ.

*"If you walk in my statutes." In connection with this the verse states, "I considered the ways in which I would go, but my feet carried me to Your statutes." King David stated, "Every day I decided to go to a specific place, to one person's home and another person's house. However, my feet brought me to Your synagogues and study halls." This is why it says, "My feet carried me to Your statutes."*[85]

The difficulty in this Midrash is striking. Did King David never decide to go to the synagogue or the study hall of his own accord? Did he not compose many psalms that express his yearning to come close to the Almighty through study and prayer? Did he not say,[86] "There is but one thing I seek from the Lord, for this do I long: to sit in the house of God all the days of my life"? Why, then, does the Midrash indicate that King David lacked this intent?

---

84. *Vayikra* 25:8–10.
85. *Vayikra Rabbah* 35:1.
86. *Tehillim* 27:4.

The days between Pesach and Shavuoth are punctuated not only by our counting the days that lead up to our receiving of the Torah, but also by a communal semi-mourning. It was in this time of year that a great tragedy befell the Jewish People: twenty-four thousand of Rabbi Akiva's students were struck down by a terrible plague. Our Sages reveal to us the reason for this tragedy: מִפְּנֵי שֶׁלֹּא נָהֲגוּ כָּבוֹד זֶה לָזֶה, they did not accord sufficient honour and respect to each other. It seems there was an impediment in this area, which made attribution of honour a difficult goal to achieve. What lies at the root of this difficulty?

To understand this topic, let us consider the following. Every single person is unique and special, differing from every other person alive: כְּשֵׁם שֶׁאֵין פַּרְצוּפֵיהֶם שָׁוִים זֶה לָזֶה כָּךְ אֵין דַּעְתָּם שָׁוָה — "Just as everyone has a different countenance, so everyone's temperament and character differs."[87] Every individual has a combination of qualities which cannot be found in any other person alive. Each person shines in a different area, achieving excellence in a field exclusive to him. This character development, however, contains a potential pitfall: One who has developed a trait to a high degree is extremely sensitive in this area, and will be unable to tolerate presence of the opposite trait in one's fellow. A person who excels in his generosity will become vexed when witnessing another person's miserliness. It is incompatible with the fabric of his being he has worked so hard to weave. This dissonance precludes a relationship of mutual respect and honour. One who is very particular to tell the absolute truth is unable to countenance those who are prone to exaggeration and hyperbole. Respect, in such instances, is hard to accord. Such is the case with any quality in which one specializes; one is sensitized to those who lack the trait, and particularly to those of the opposite temperament.

All of humankind being different, and each individual having a forte in a different area, we are left in a quandary. How can one give one's fellow the honour due to him? How can we rectify the area in

87. *Tanchuma, Pinchas* 10.

which the students of Rabbi Akiva stumbled?

Our question is fortified when we consider Rabbeinu Yonah's recommendation in his commentary on *Pirkei Avoth*. He enjoins every Jew to excel in one trait, lauding this achievement as greater than the attainment of mediocrity in all areas. But considering what happens when a person views another who fails where he excels, this would appear to be a recipe for schism and contention. How can the negative feelings which such achievement engenders be neutralized?

The period of *Sefirath HaOmer* is one of intense spiritual labour. During this time, each individual asserts himself, concentrating on self-perfection in preparation for Shavuoth, the day the Torah was bestowed upon mankind. The very word סְפִירָה contains the word סַפִּיר, a thing of purity. When we left Egypt, we were on the forty-ninth level of impurity. The next forty-nine days were for each individual to expiate corruption and perversion from his heart, and attain a sublime level of purity and wholesomeness. This cathartic process is to be undergone by every individual in this period of the year, as we ready ourselves for the day of revelation. Every day counted should mark the achievement of further purity, a higher level in one's field of excellence. Each person develops his personality, and thus further accentuates his own individuality. A danger is thereby generated: perfection in one's own field breeds intolerance of others who are not working in harmony with oneself, and who are not attaining the same sensitivities as oneself. It is thus that during the days of *Sefirath HaOmer*, the period marked by intense character building, there is a tendency to deny others the honour and respect which one would ordinarily accord.

A change of perspective is the cure for the potential malady. If one excels in a specific area, it must be that one's fellow excels in a different field. One must simply look for the other's area of greatness and focus upon the outstanding quality which one personally does not possess. One transfers one's concentration from viewing other people in light of one's own character traits to a perspective in which one sees other people in the context of their own expertise. One can then honour one's fellow for the perfection he has achieved.

The Midrash describes the manner in which Torah was given:

*How did the voice emanate from Mount Sinai when the Torah was given? Everyone experienced it according to his capacity. The elders heard according to what they could hear, the young people heard according to what they could hear, children and babies heard according to their ability, women according to their ability, and even Moshe himself according to his ability. Everyone heard a voice which he could bear. Each individual discerned what he was able to discern and absorb in this revelation.*[88]

Further:

ר׳ יוֹחָנָן אָמַר קוֹל אֶחָד נֶחְלַק לְשִׁבְעָה קוֹלוֹת, וְהֵם נֶחְלָקִים לְשִׁבְעִים לָשׁוֹן.

*R. Yochanan said that the voice was in fact one voice, however it was split into seven voices which then became seventy languages.*[89]

Seven is the largest prime number under ten, the largest number which still manifests as an entity in its own right. That is, seven is the biggest number without factors; it cannot be formed by multiplying two other numbers. Seven, therefore, indicates individuality, that which is not grouped together. The voice was split into seventy parts, seven multiplied by ten. Seven, the number of individuality, was multiplied by ten, the number of collectivity. The number ten indicates the affiliation of individuals to form a single entity. The whole has a value many times greater than the sum of its parts. Ten people form a *minyan* for prayer, with a potency disproportionate to ten individuals standing separately in prayer. A transformation of existence has occurred, not merely an assembly of disconnected beings.

Our character development must follow the pathway of seventy.

---

88. *Shemoth Rabbah* 5:9.
89. *Shemoth Rabbah* 28:4.

The seven must fuse with the ten. Not only must we exert ourselves in the development of our own person, we must recognise the qualities of others. Relating to the traits of other people connects us with the community as a whole. It is insufficient to focus exclusively on our own improvement. We must seek out, and pay homage to, the traits of our fellow. It is thus that we build a community of solidarity and brotherhood consisting of many people who have developed their individuality to an intense degree. Seven combines with ten to produce seventy.

At Mount Sinai, seventy voices were heard. Every voice was different, yet they are classed as one group. Perfection of one's own individuality is achieved only when one seeks the perfection of others.

With this principle we can comprehend the explanation of the Midrash concerning King David. Our Sages state, "If I am not for myself, who will be for me?"[90] Every person is unique, with his own personal mission, for which no other person can be substituted. Parallel to this, every hour in one's life has its own potential to be realised. Every moment of time is given for a specific purpose, generating our grave responsibility to utilise each moment to the full. "If not now, when?"[91] is the expression of this concept in the words of our Sages. If this moment is not exploited, no other moment can subrogate. Thus, each individual is responsible for the rectification of both his own person, and also the hours and days allotted for his spiritual endeavours.

The *Chiddushei HaRim* explains that, paradoxically, perfection on an individual level alone contains an inherent deficiency. As our Sages continue their maxim, "If I am only for myself, what is my worth?" Although one's individual toil is a necessary stage, which is fulfilled by the individual counting of *Sefirath HaOmer*, the process leading to completion requires each person to conquer an additional field. Each individual must align himself with the community, recognising the qualities of other people and using his own gifts.

90. *Pirkei Avoth* 1:14.
91. *Pirkei Avoth* 1:14.

King David sought initially to actualize his own individual potential. He attempted to go to מָקוֹם פְּלוֹנִי וּלְבֵית דִּירָה פְּלוֹנִית, specific and individual places. King David desired to attain ever greater heights in his own Divine service and personal spirituality. But the time came when he was directed to the places where the community gathers. His feet led him to the synagogue, the place where people gather together and seek direction in their capacity as a community. King David was duty-bound to guide the assembly of people, in place of his yearning to continue in his quest for personal perfection. He was bound to merge the seven with the ten, thus producing seventy, a level of perfection that would otherwise not be achieved.

Although each person is required to actively participate in and align himself with the community, the degree of prior self-development required can vary. A prime example in recent times is that of the Chazon Ish, a towering Torah personality revered around the world. His name is synonymous with intense, unrelenting labour in Torah study, and he was looked upon as the father of *yeshivoth* in the modern era. Yet, the Chazon Ish spent the first fifty years of his life secluded from the public eye, ensconced in his own world of scholarship. When the time came for him to be revealed to the world, the Chazon Ish became intimately involved in all the affairs of the community, and devoted himself to all that was required of him by the Jewish nation.

The pathway begins as a personal one. Each individual perfects his avenue of Divine service. Initially, it is incumbent upon every single person to perform the mitzvah of *Sefirath HaOmer*, using each single day to develop his singularity. Each element and detail is thus attended to, culminating in the perfection of every part of the whole. The obligation now shifts to the whole itself.

In our *parashah* we are enjoined to count the years. We no longer count individual days, we turn our attention to each year, to compete entities. These years are counted by the great *Beith Din*, one institution, with the interests of the community at the fore. Seven thus merges with ten, resulting in the higher perfection of seventy. It is fascinating to note that this great *Beith Din*, the institution which presided over the nation in its entirety, consisted of seventy members!

Our *Sefirath HaOmer* cannot be the counting of only days. It was this emphasis on individuality which proved fatal for thousands of Rabbi Akiva's students. Cultivation of individuality must be followed by ploughing one's gifts into the community. Days are followed by the enumeration of years, an emphasis on congregation and collectivity.

Standing at the foot of Mount Sinai, the Jewish People are described as being "like one man with one heart." This unity is only possible through recognition of the qualities of other people while concurrently achieving self-perfection. The seven weeks of seven days which constitute the period of *Sefirath HaOmer* thus culminate. The counting of each individual, each person's own perfection, is fused with the perfection of the nation as a whole, thus allowing the declaration of, "We will do and we will listen," to resound through the eons of time.

# BECHUKOTHAI

THIS WEEK'S PARASHAH contains the famed blessings and curses to which the Jewish People are subject, in accordance with their behaviour. The opening of the admonition reads as follows:

> וְאִם בְּחֻקֹּתַי תִּמְאָסוּ וְאִם אֶת מִשְׁפָּטַי תִּגְעַל נַפְשְׁכֶם לְבִלְתִּי עֲשׂוֹת אֶת כָּל מִצְוֹתַי לְהַפְרְכֶם אֶת בְּרִיתִי.
>
> *And if you then [even] despise [those who observe] My statutes and utterly reject those who interpret My laws, [such that you] prevent all My commandments from being carried out, [thereby] nullifying My covenant.*[92]

According to the interpretation of the Seforno, this verse would be translated as follows:

> וְאִם בְּחֻקֹּתַי תִּמְאָסוּ. שֶׁלֹּא בִּלְבַד תְּבַטְּלוּם אֲבָל תִּמְאֲסוּ בָם. וְאִם אֶת מִשְׁפָּטַי תִּגְעַל נַפְשְׁכֶם. תִּגְעַל אוֹתָם כְּמוֹ שֶׁמֵּקִיא אָדָם בְּכַוָּנָה מַסְכֶּמֶת, מִבְּלִי אֵין דֶּרֶךְ לִמְאֹס אוֹתָם בִּהְיוֹת טַעְמָם נוֹדָע וְהָגוּן.[93]
>
> וְאִם בְּחֻקֹּתַי תִּמְאָסוּ — *If you not only disobey my statutes, but are disgusted by them.* וְאִם אֶת מִשְׁפָּטַי תִּגְעַל נַפְשְׁכֶם — *If you reject them, like a person who deliberately vomits, without any reason to be sickened by them, since they are known to be good.*

The term מוֹאֵס applies to *chukim*, statutes — laws which are beyond human comprehension. Due to a lack of understanding, one finds this genre of laws despicable. The term תִּגְעַל applies particularly to *mishpatim*, laws that man is able to understand, often related

---

92. *Vayikra* 26:15.
93. Seforno *ad loc.*

to maintaining the infrastructure of society. The word תִּגְעַל implies an artificial rejection, similar to the practice among the Romans of intentionally vomiting their food so that they could indulge further in physical gratification. One who loathes *mishpatim*, laws which are usually palatable and agreeable, does so artificially, as a result of his own will.

As the retribution continues, and we are informed of the devastating consequences of defying God's will, a reversed phraseology is used in relation to these two types of commandments.

**וְהָאָרֶץ תֵּעָזֵב מֵהֶם וְתִרֶץ אֶת שַׁבְּתֹתֶיהָ בָּהְשַׁמָּה מֵהֶם וְהֵם יִרְצוּ אֶת עֲוֹנָם יַעַן וּבְיַעַן בְּמִשְׁפָּטַי מָאָסוּ וְאֶת חֻקֹּתַי גָּעֲלָה נַפְשָׁם.**

*But the land will be left abandoned of [its people], and will appease [God's anger on account of] its [unobserved] Sabbatical years while it lies desolate of [its people], and they will gain appeasement for their transgressions. This is redress [for that] they despised My laws, and redress [for that] they utterly rejected My statutes.*[94]

In this case, the *chukim*, laws which man is unable to understand, are described as גָּעֲלָה נַפְשָׁם — "loathsome" while the *mishpatim* are termed as מָאָסוּ — "despicable." The *chukim* in this case are described in the term implying an intentional hatred; they are artificially spewed out and rejected. The palatable *mishpatim*, however, have the word מוֹאֵס applied to them, implying that they are intolerable by their very nature. This interpretation is the reverse of that presented above. How can this discrepancy be resolved?

Rabbi Simcha Zissel[95] explains the psychological state of man at the time of his performance of *chukim*, commandments which cannot be understood by limited human intellect.

*When one is involved in injunctions which one does not understand, a deep love and ardour is often experienced. An example of this principle is the recitation of the service performed in the*

94. *Vayikra* 26:43–44.
95. *Ohr Rashaz*, Part Three, p. 178.

*Temple which is said on Yom Kippur. People lack an understanding of the basic meaning of the procedure, with its many details and enigmatic rites, yet the words are uttered with profound devotion and enthusiasm. People accept their lack of understanding, content with the knowledge that comprehension is beyond the scope of human intellect, and comfortable with the realisation that many mysteries and holy secrets lie in the command.*

This excitement and devotion is not generated to the same degree by *mishpatim*. People believe that they know the underlying reason for these commands, and understand what lies therein. The injunctions against theft and murder accord with basic human understanding and moral sentiment. When fulfilling these dictates, therefore, this burning zeal to serve God is often absent. It is much easier to inject deeds with joy and devotion when one knows that unfathomable depths lie in the command.

An incident in Scriptures provides support for the position of Rabbi Simcha Zissel:

Naaman was the venerated general of the army of Aram, a person of utmost importance. He contracted leprosy. During a war against Israel, his army captured a young Jewish girl, who served Naaman's wife. The maidservant advised her mistress that Naaman seek counsel from a prophet to rid himself of his malady. The King of Aram subsequently dispatched Naaman to the Land of Israel in search of a cure. Naaman arrived in the Land of Israel with his entourage, and stood at the entrance of Elisha the prophet's house. Elisha sent a messenger to Naaman, who instructed him to immerse himself in the Jordon river seven times to ensure the cure of his leprosy.

Naaman became very upset. "I thought the prophet would come out and stand and call out in God's Name. I thought he would wave his hands in the air and thus would the leprosy vanish. There are better rivers in Damascus! If I will be cured by dipping in a river, I could do so in the waters of Damascus." Naaman departed in anger.[96]

---

96. *II Melachim* 5:1–12.

Had the prophet approached Naaman and performed a mysterious ritual or a sacramental procedure, Naaman would have been satisfied. It was the banality of the cure which led to his agitation. Thus we see how people are much more accepting of something which they are unable to understand, and will carry out cryptic instructions and procedures much more readily than those which are more simplistic in nature.

Rabbi Simcha Zissel observes that acts which are not understood are performed with more devotion than acts which are comprehended on some level. This seems incongruous with the explanation of the Seforno that people perform *mishpatim* with more satisfaction.

It is incumbent upon man to recognise that just as *chukim* are Divine decrees, with impenetrable depth, so are *mishpatim* dictates of the Almighty, and thus also contain profundities which human intellect is unable to plumb. Upon this realisation, one will be able to invest both deeds which seem comprehensible, and deeds which are by their very nature esoteric and mysterious, with an equal level of devotion and love. Acceptance of the mitzvoth that one can grasp on some level will follow, an acceptance permeated with sincere joy.

This principle seems to be contradicted, however, by the explanation of the *Sefath Emeth* on the following Midrash:

אִם בְּחֻקֹּתַי תֵּלֵכוּ. הֲדָא הוּא דִכְתִיב חִשַּׁבְתִּי דְרָכָי וָאָשִׁיבָה רַגְלַי אֶל עֵדֹתֶיךָ. אָמַר דָּוִד רבש"ע, בְּכָל יוֹם וְיוֹם הָיִיתִי מְחַשֵּׁב וְאוֹמֵר לְמָקוֹם פְּלוֹנִי וּלְבֵית דִּירָה פְּלוֹנִית אֲנִי הוֹלֵךְ, וְהָיוּ רַגְלַי מְבִיאוֹת אוֹתִי לְבָתֵּי כְּנֵסִיּוֹת וּלְבָתֵּי מִדְרָשׁוֹת. הֲדָא הוּא דִכְתִיב וָאָשִׁיבָה רַגְלַי אֶל עֵדֹתֶיךָ.

*"If you walk in My statutes." In connection with this the verse states, "I considered the ways in which I would go, but my feet carried me to Your statutes." King David stated, "Every day I decided to go to a specific place, to one person's home and another person's house. However, my feet brought me to Your synagogues and study halls." This is why it says, "My feet carried me to Your statutes."*[97]

97. *Vayikra Rabbah* 35:1.

The *Sefath Emeth* expounds that King David's statement indicates nullification of one's own intellectual capacity and thoughts to the ultimate wisdom of the Almighty. This is achieved by first, חִשַּׁבְתִּי דְרָכָי — "I considered the ways," intimating initial use of one's own mind. This is followed by the automatic gravitation of King David's footsteps towards the study hall. No thought was involved in this action; he could instead follow God's dictates free of the need to follow his own reckoning. A two-stage process is here being presented to us. The first stage involves use of one's own mind, which will lead to the second stage, at which point one's own intellect is negated in the face of infinite wisdom.

*Mishpatim*, we learn in this Midrash, precede *chukim*, actions without understanding. King David's actions originally following his own considerations can be classed as *mishpatim*. Following these were actions with the same underlying self-abnegation as *chukim*. This sequence accords with the original comment of the Seforno, but is incongruous with the observation of Rabbi Simcha Zissel, who maintains that ardour is generated through *chukim*, which are beyond human grasp.

The following Midrash will aid us in penetrating the superficial confusion to reach some conclusion.

> וְאֵלֶּה הַמִּשְׁפָּטִים. מַה כְּתִיב לְמַעְלָה מִן הַפָּרָשָׁה וְשָׁפְטוּ אֶת הָעָם בְּכָל עֵת. וְאָמַר כָּאן וְאֵלֶּה הַמִּשְׁפָּטִים וְהַדִּבְּרוֹת בָּאֶמְצַע. מָשָׁל לְמַטְרוֹנָה שֶׁהָיְתָה מְהַלֶּכֶת וְהַזַּיִן מִכָּאן וְהַזַּיִן מִכָּאן וְהִיא בָּאֶמְצַע. כָּךְ הַתּוֹרָה דִּינִין מִלְּפָנֶיהָ וְדִינִין מֵאֲחוֹרֶיהָ וְהִיא בָּאֶמְצַע.
>
> *In the book of Shemoth, a progression is found. Initially, we are informed of mishpatim. Following this are the Ten Commandments, after which we find recorded further mishpatim. This can be compared to a queen walking in a procession. She is protected by bodyguards who are both in front and behind, while she is situated in the middle. So with the Torah. Mishpatim are both before and after, with other laws in the middle.*[98]

---

98. *Shemoth Rabbah* 30:3.

It appears from the Midrash that the *chukim* require protection. Indeed, Rashi highlights this very idea.

זֹאת חֻקַּת הַתּוֹרָה. לְפִי שֶׁהַשָּׂטָן וְאוּמּוֹת הָעוֹלָם מוֹנִין אֶת יִשְׂרָאֵל לוֹמַר מָה הַמִּצְוָה הַזֹּאת. וּמַה טַּעַם יֵשׁ בָּהּ. לְפִיכָךְ כָּתַב בָּהּ חֻקָּה. גְּזֵרָה הִיא מִלְּפָנַי וְאֵין לְךָ רְשׁוּת לְהַרְהֵר אַחֲרֶיהָ.

*"This is the statute of the Torah." The Satan and the nations of the world taunt the Jewish People: "What is this commandment? What reason is there for your action?" This is why this genre of mitzvoth are termed chukim, statutes. They are decrees of the Almighty, and must be performed without understanding.*[99]

It is the *chukim* which are vulnerable to attack, which require a defence. As seen in the Midrash, it is the *mishpatim* which provide their shield. When one contemplates the *mishpatim*, their judiciousness, wisdom, and goodness are clearly evident. Seeing that the *chukim* originate from the same Source, it follows that all the wisdom and goodness which are co ntained in the *mishpatim* are also present in the *chukim*, albeit not as readily apparent to us with our frail human intelligence. The sagacity of *mishpatim* substantiate the hidden enlightenment of the *chukim*.

A demonstration of this phenomenon can be observed in a game of chess. An amateur is pitted against the world's chess champion. The champion moves a piece, facilitating an easy capture by the amateur. Being on his guard, the amateur considers the repercussions of taking the piece. After much consideration, the amateur might work out the sequence of moves which would follow the capture, and conclude that the end would be his defeat. Alternatively, the amateur could spend a long time considering why the piece has been made available by the champion for him to take, but could be unable to reach any conclusion, or have any idea as to the champion's strategy. The amateur will then immediately surmise that much more lies in the move than he is able to comprehend. His esteem for the

---

99. Rashi on *Bemidbar* 19:2.

champion grows inestimably, much more than if he were able to deduce the careful reasoning behind his opponent's move.

Another example of this attitude is evident in the response of a man who was present at a lecture delivered by Rabbi Dessler. After effusively praising the lecture, the man admitted that he had not understood the content of the presentation. In fact, it was his inability to understand that raised his opinion of the lecture. One who is unable to understand realises how much more there is to understand.

It is from this perspective that the *chukim*, which were formerly seen to draw protection from the fathomable laws, are now seen to enhance one's appreciation of these very *mishpatim*! Since both stem from the ultimate "Mastermind," it follows that the *mishpatim* themselves must contain an element of *chukim*. Even actions and deeds which lie within human understanding, stemming from a Divine Source, must contain infinite wisdom and depth. It is thus that one comes to perform *mishpatim* with the same ardour as *chukim*, as posited by Rabbi Simcha Zissel.

Returning to the opening of our *parashah*, the Seforno highlighted the terminology applied to the *chukim* and *mishpatim. Chukim* were termed as naturally repellent, while *mishpatim* were artificially rejected, their palatable qualities being spurned. The Seforno is obviously referring to a state where one is still involved in the initial stages, where *chukim* are only appreciated on the basis of *mishpatim* which accord with human understanding. The *Sefath Emeth* also refers to this state in his explanation of how King David first considered his actions, and then nullified his own intellect before God's will.

At a later stage, one is inspired by the enigmatic nature of the *chukim*, as Rabbi Simcha Zissel describes, and carries them out with an enthusiasm and love that is enhanced by their mysterious nature. This in turn engenders the performance of *mishpatim* with a new ardour, as one gains a consciousness that *mishpatim*, too, as commands of the Almighty, contain profundities totally removed from human intelligence or intellectual capacity. *Mishpatim* will then be infused with love, as one recognises one's own puny standing in relation to all areas of Torah. It is to this that the second verse in the admonition refers, in describing the artificial rejection of the *chukim*, as opposed to the *mishpatim*. The incongruity of the verses has thus been resolved.

The ability to recognise the element of *chukim* even in *mishpatim* is a fundamental requirement in all areas of Torah. After studying a certain area of Torah, or becoming acquainted with various attitudes or insights, there is a danger that a person will develop a feeling of self-satisfaction. Proud of his accomplishments and intellectual acumen, the individual could feel that he has mastered a certain subject. The underlying error in these feelings is a grave one. Torah, by its very definition a transcendent wisdom, can never be completely understood. There will always remain unplumbed depths, unfathomable areas, and endless profundity, both in subjects which by their very nature are enigmatic, and in areas which appear deceptively simple. The accounts which we read in the Torah and in Scriptures must be regarded not as fairy tales and legends, but as sublime and holy enlightenment, impenetrable by our finite human minds.

Our Sages inform us of a law that the Torah must always be held while clothed by a cover. The Maharal explains the significance underlying this law. The Torah must always be regarded as clothed, its essence covered as by a garment. One must never believe that the understanding one has attained is a mastery of Torah; one must regard one's knowledge as still in the realm of a garment. For there is always something beneath, beyond, which is as yet unknown and undiscovered.

This knowledge should generate a deep joy and satisfaction in performing the mitzvoth. Every action, whether understood superficially or whether cloaked in mystery, has a potency to which we are oblivious. Every mitzvah, as a command of the infinite Almighty, is an incandescent expression of God's glory. The greatness of the deed is precisely because it is incomprehensible to the human mind. This appreciation will imbue every action with renewed devotion and ardour. Our love and appreciation for Torah is then transferred, bringing us to a level which facilitates fulfillment of a command which is demanding in the extreme, the obligation of אַהֲבַת ה', love of God. Loving the Torah brings us to love Him Who bequeathed the Torah to the Jewish People, thus fulfilling the injunction of, "You shall love the Lord your God with all your heart." Let us approach the day of the giving of the Torah with anticipation and fervor, readying ourselves to accept the unlimited Torah from Him Who in His infinite wisdom and love bestows it upon us.

# BEMIDBAR

# BEMIDBAR

COUNTING IS NOT merely a technical act to determine the number of the population. It is an act rich with spiritual significance, as our *parashah* demonstrates.

**וַיְדַבֵּר ה' אֶל מֹשֶׁה בְּמִדְבַּר סִינַי... שְׂאוּ אֶת רֹאשׁ כָּל עֲדַת בְּנֵי יִשְׂרָאֵל לְמִשְׁפְּחֹתָם לְבֵית אֲבֹתָם בְּמִסְפַּר שֵׁמוֹת כָּל זָכָר לְגֻלְגְּלֹתָם.**

*The Eternal spoke to Moshe in the Sinai desert... Calculate the total number of the entire community of the Children of Yisrael, by their family [groupings], following their fathers' lineage; every male [shall be counted] by a head count, according the number of names.*[1]

Upon these opening words of the book of *Bemidbar*, the *Ba'al HaTurim* makes the following observation.

בְּמִדְבַּר סִינַי — לְעֵיל מִינֵהּ כְּתִיב אֵלֶּה הַמִּצְוֹת וְסָמִיךְ לֵיהּ בְּמִדְבַּר סִינַי. לוֹמַר אִם אֵין אָדָם מֵשִׂים עַצְמוֹ כְּמִדְבָּר אֵינוֹ יָכֹל לֵידַע תּוֹרָה וּמִצְוֹת.

*At the end of the book of Vayikra it is written, "These are the commandments..." Immediately following this, at the opening of the book of Bemidbar are the words, "In the Sinai desert." This teaches us that if a person does not make himself like a desert, he can not properly know Torah and perform mitzvoth.*[2]

A prerequisite for receiving Torah is self-abnegation, nullification of one's personal desires such that the self becomes comparable to a desert — a desolate, ownerless place. This idea is found

1. *Bemidbar* 1:1–2.
2. *Ba'al HaTurim ad loc.*

in our prayers, where we state, וְנַפְשִׁי כֶּעָפָר לַכֹּל תִּהְיֶה, פְּתַח לִבִּי בְּתוֹרָתֶךָ — "Let my soul be like dust to all; open my heart to Your Torah." If one takes on the characteristic of dust, diminishing one's self, one's heart becomes receptive to Torah. The vital factor then, to enable us to receive Torah, is the slaughter of one's personal ego and desires.

On this verse, Rashi makes the following comment:

מִתּוֹךְ חִבָּתָן לְפָנָיו, מוֹנֶה אוֹתָם כָּל שָׁעָה, כְּשֶׁיָּצְאוּ מִמִּצְרַיִם מְנָאָן, וּכְשֶׁנָּפְלוּ בָּעֵגֶל מְנָאָן לֵידַע מִנְיַן הַנּוֹתָרִים, כְּשֶׁבָּא לְהַשְׁרוֹת שְׁכִינָתוֹ עֲלֵיהֶם מְנָאָם, בְּאֶחָד בְּנִיסָן הוּקַם הַמִּשְׁכָּן, וּבְאֶחָד בְּאִיָּיר מְנָאָם.

*God repeatedly counted the people due to His love for them. At every opportunity they were counted: when they went out of Egypt He counted them, when they fell at the sin of the Golden Calf He counted them, when He came to manifest His Divine Presence He counted them. On the first of Nissan the Mishkan [Tabernacle] was erected, and on the first of Iyar He counted them.*[3]

Enumeration then, is an expression of endearment, similar to the habit of a miser who constantly counts his cherished money.

In relation to this theme, the Ramban cites a Midrash.

שְׂאוּ אֶת רֹאשׁ כָּל עֲדַת בְּנֵי יִשְׂרָאֵל. אֵין שְׂאוּ אֶלָּא לְשׁוֹן גְּדֻלָּה, כְּמוֹ דִּכְתִיב יִשָּׂא פַרְעֹה אֶת רֹאשְׁךָ וֶהֱשִׁיבְךָ עַל כַּנֶּךָ. אָמַר הקב"ה לְיִשְׂרָאֵל, נָתַתִּי לָכֶם תְּלוּי רֹאשׁ וְדִמִּיתִי אֶתְכֶם לִי, כְּשֵׁם שֶׁיֵּשׁ לִי תְּלוּי רֹאשׁ עַל כָּל בָּאֵי עוֹלָם שֶׁנֶּאֱמַר לְךָ ה' הַמַּמְלָכָה וְהַמִּתְנַשֵּׂא לְכֹל לְרֹאשׁ, אַף לָכֶם עָשִׂיתִי תְּלוּי רֹאשׁ, שֶׁנֶּאֱמַר שְׂאוּ אֶת רֹאשׁ כָּל עֲדַת בְּנֵי יִשְׂרָאֵל, לְקַיֵּם מַה שֶּׁנֶּאֱמַר וַיָּרֶם קֶרֶן לְעַמּוֹ.[4]

The Midrash interprets the word שְׂאוּ to indicate not only the counting of the people, but also an elevation to a high position. This is the word used by Par'oh when reinstating the condemned butler to his original position. Counting the people, then, makes the people great, raising them to a level of increased importance.

---

3. Rashi on *Bemidbar* 1:2.
4. Ramban *ad loc*.

The Seforno reinforces this idea, in his explanation of the words בְּמִסְפַּר שֵׁמוֹת — "The number of their names."

כִּי הָיָה אָז כָּל אֶחָד מֵאוֹתוֹ הַדּוֹר נֶחְשַׁב בִּשְׁמוֹ הַמּוֹרֶה עַל צוּרָתוֹ הָאִישִׁית, לְמַעֲלָתָם.

*The greatness of the generation was such that each individual was counted, not only as a unit, but also by a name. The individual names were an indication of each person's singularity and personal importance.*[5]

Both the Seforno and the Ramban highlight the importance and greatness of the generation, discerned through their enumeration. How can this be reconciled with the recommendation to reduce oneself in order to receive Torah? Should the attitude to our personal standing be one of humility and submissiveness, or recognition of our greatness?

The Hebrew terms for counting, מִנְיָן and פָּקַד, contain a duality. For example, we find the following uses of the verb פָּקַד:

**מִבֶּן עֶשְׂרִים שָׁנָה וָמַעְלָה... תִּפְקְדוּ אֹתָם.**

*From twenty years and upwards shall you count them.*[6]

**עַל פִּי אַהֲרֹן וּבָנָיו תִּהְיֶה כָּל עֲבֹדַת בְּנֵי הַגֵּרְשֻׁנִּי לְכָל מַשָּׂאָם וּלְכֹל עֲבֹדָתָם וּפְקַדְתֶּם עֲלֵהֶם בְּמִשְׁמֶרֶת אֵת כָּל מַשָּׂאָם.**

*All the work of the sons of the Gershuni shall be according to Aharon's and his sons' instructions... you shall delegate to them all the things they are to carry...*[7]

Not only does the word פָּקַד mean to count, it is also used in various contexts to indicate appointment to a high position, and the delegation of each individual's task and mission. When Moshe wanted to transfer the mantle of leadership to Yehoshua, his words were: יִפְקֹד ה' אֱלֹקֵי הָרוּחֹת — "May the Eternal, God of all people's characters,

5. Seforno *ad loc.*
6. *Bemidbar* 1:3.
7. *Bemidbar* 4:27.

appoint a man..."[8] Thus, the word פָּקַד also means the specification of a person's role in life.

This idea is also seen in the use of the verb לִמְנוֹת. Bil'am, while recounting the praise of the Jewish People, said, מִי מָנָה עֲפַר יַעֲקֹב וּמִסְפָּר אֶת רֹבַע יִשְׂרָאֵל — "Who can count the infants of Ya'akov who are [as numerous as] dust, or the number of a quarter of Yisrael?"[9] The verb is also found in *Daniel*:

> וַיֹּאמֶר דָּנִיֵּאל אֶל הַמֶּלְצַר אֲשֶׁר מִנָּה שַׂר הַסָּרִיסִים עַל דָּנִיֵּאל חֲנַנְיָה מִישָׁאֵל וַעֲזַרְיָה.[10]

Here, the word indicates appointing a person to a position.

These two words, then, mean both "to count," and "to provide someone with a mission." Let us investigate the intrinsic connection between the two meanings of these words.

It is clear that counting attaches importance to an entity. A clear manifestation of this is seen in the law that an entity is always subordinate to sixty times its amount. Particularly relevant to the laws of *kashruth*, the law applies to situations where an entity accidentally falls into some food, thereby rendering it unfit to eat. If the foreign entity, e.g. a drop of milk, is less than one-sixtieth in volume than the original item, e.g. a pot of meat, then that which fell in is considered nullified in relation to the larger item, and the entire mixture is permitted. However, this law does not apply to an entity which by its nature is counted as an individual unit, as this cannot be considered as subordinate to the larger item. For items reckoned individually always retain their own identity: דָּבָר שֶׁבְּמִנְיָן לֹא בָטֵל. That which is counted has an inherent importance. For example, one would never ask for one pea; one always buys them in bulk. However, one could ask for a dozen eggs, which shows that each egg retains its own identity.

Importance brings obligation and responsibility in its wake. He who has more importance has been endowed with a greater mission

8. *Bemidbar* 27:16.
9. *Bemidbar* 23:10.
10. *Daniel* 1:11.

in life which he is required to fulfill. A person cognizant of his importance will concurrently be filled with anxiety lest he has failed to utilise all of his gifts to the correct end. In this light we can understand the story told of a certain brilliant individual, who, following his immediate response to a halachic question, broke down in tears. The sharpness he had demonstrated in his quick reply highlighted his tremendous ability. On this account he cried, awed by the great expectations which the Almighty doubtlessly had of him.

Now that we have seen how a mission results from man's importance, we can understand the duality inherent in the two verbs we have been discussing. It is enumeration that gives each person his importance, and thus his task in this world. No wonder that the words מִנְיָן and פָּקַד have the double meaning of "to count" and "to appoint"; counting is an expression of appointment to mission.

This principle can be seen clearly in the earlier explanation of Rashi, wherein he enumerated the various occasions upon which the Almighty counted the Jewish People. God counted them upon their departure from Egypt — for the journey from Egypt involved awesome wonders and miracles, the likes of which had never been witnessed. Once having experienced sights of this nature, greater service was incumbent upon them. They were now endowed with a new mission.

The Almighty counted the Jewish People after the sin of the Golden Calf. He counted individuals who had witnessed the devastation born out of sin, the death that results from disobeying God's word. The Jewish People now possessed a depth of realisation that placed added demands upon them. A new charge lay upon the survivors; hence they were counted again.

When God manifested His Divine Presence on the occasion of the establishment of the *Mishkan*, He counted His nation once again. The people now had an intimate connection to the Divine Presence. More was expected of them; the level of their previous service was no longer sufficient. The counting thus brought a greater task to the people.

Another counting is detailed in our *parashah*: the calculation of the tribe of Levi.

**וְהַלְוִיִּם לְמַטֵּה אֲבֹתָם לֹא הָתְפָּקְדוּ בְּתוֹכָם. וַיְדַבֵּר ה' אֶל מֹשֶׁה לֵּאמֹר. אַךְ אֶת מַטֵּה לֵוִי לֹא תִפְקֹד וְאֶת רֹאשָׁם לֹא תִשָּׂא בְּתוֹךְ בְּנֵי יִשְׂרָאֵל.**

*The Leviyim, however, according to their ancestral tribe, did not have themselves counted among them. The Eternal then spoke to Moshe, saying, "However, the tribe of Levi you must not count, nor calculate their total number among the [rest of] the Children of Yisrael."*[11]

The hallowed task of the tribe of Levi, a tribe dedicated to service of the Almighty and thus elevated above the rest of the people, necessitated a separate counting.

א"ר פִּנְחָס בַּר אִידִי מַה כְּתִיב בְּרֹאשׁ הַסֵּפֶר שְׂאוּ אֶת רֹאשׁ כָּל עֲדַת בְּנֵי יִשְׂרָאֵל. רוֹמֵם אֶת רֹאשׁ, גַּדֵּל אֶת רֹאשׁ לֹא נֶאֱמַר אֶלָּא שְׂאוּ אֶת רֹאשׁ. כְּאָדָם הָאוֹמֵר לְקוּסְטִנַר סַב רֵישֵׁהּ דִּפְלָן כָּךְ נָתַן רֶמֶז, לָמָּה שְׂאוּ אֶת רֹאשׁ, שֶׁאִם יִזְכּוּ, יַעֲלוּ לִגְדֻלָּה כמ"ד יִשָּׂא פַּרְעֹה אֶת רֹאשְׁךָ וֶהֱשִׁיבְךָ עַל כַּנֶּךָ. אִם לֹא יִזְכּוּ, יָמוּתוּ כֻּלָּם כְּמָה דְתֵימָא יִשָּׂא פַּרְעֹה אֶת רֹאשְׁךָ מֵעָלֶיךָ וְתָלָה אוֹתְךָ עַל עֵץ. וְהָיָה גָּלוּי לִפְנֵי הַמָּקוֹם שֶׁיָּמוּתוּ כֻּלָּם בַּמִּדְבָּר וְיִנָּטְלוּ רָאשֵׁיהֶן, לְפִיכָךְ אָמַר הקב"ה לְמֹשֶׁה אַךְ אֶת מַטֵּה לֵוִי וגו'. בְּתוֹךְ בְּנֵי יִשְׂרָאֵל אֵין אַתָּה מוֹנֶה אוֹתָן אֲבָל לְעַצְמָן מְנֵה אוֹתָן. לָמָּה אָמַר הקב"ה אִם נִמְנָה שֵׁבֶט לֵוִי עִם יִשְׂרָאֵל וּמִתְעָרֵב עִמָּהֶם בָּא מַלְאַךְ הַמָּוֶת לַהֲרֹג אֶת יִשְׂרָאֵל וְהַגְּזֵרָה יוֹצֵאת עֲלֵיהֶם שֶׁלֹּא יִכָּנְסוּ לָאָרֶץ אֶלָּא מֵתִים בַּמִּדְבָּר שֶׁנֶּאֱמַר בַּמִּדְבָּר הַזֶּה יִפְּלוּ פִגְרֵיכֶם וְכָל פְּקֻדֵיכֶם לְכָל מִסְפַּרְכֶם וְהוּא מוֹצֵא לְשִׁבְטוֹ שֶׁל לֵוִי מְעֹרָב עִמָּהֶם וְהֵם מִתְעָרְבִים עִם יִשְׂרָאֵל לָמוּת. לְפִיכָךְ לֹא מָנָה אוֹתָם עִם יִשְׂרָאֵל אֶלָּא הִפְרִישָׁם בַּמִּנְיָן. וּלְכָךְ אַף בַּלָּשׁוֹן שֶׁכָּתוּב בָּהֶן בְּיִשְׂרָאֵל שְׂאוּ אֶת רֹאשׁ לֹא נֶאֱמַר בָּהֶם אֶלָּא פְּקֹד אֶת בְּנֵי לֵוִי.[12]

To paraphrase the Midrash: The expression שְׂאוּ אֶת רֹאשׁ literally means to lift up their heads. This expression is reminiscent of an executioner, who "lifts off" the head of the one he is executing. Why is an expression of elevation, or one implying an increased importance, not used instead? Contained in the expression used here are in fact two nuances. "Lift up their heads," for if they merit, they will

11. *Bemidbar* 1:47–49.
12. *Bemidbar Rabbah* 1:9.

become great, just as it is written, "And Par'oh lifted up your head, and reinstated you to your position." If they do not merit, they will all die, as it is written, "Par'oh will lift off your head from you, and you shall be hanged on a tree."

The Almighty knew that the rest of the Jewish People would perish in the wilderness, their heads separated from their bodies. The tribe of Levi was singled out, and was not reckoned with the rest of the nation. The Almighty stated that were the tribe of Levi to be amalgamated with the other tribes, the Angel of Death would include Levi in the edict against the rest of the Jewish People. Levi, too, would be doomed to die in the desert, sin precluding entrance to the Land of Israel. Levi had to maintain a separation, an individual identity, remaining apart from the rest of the Jewish People. They were counted alone.

One with a distinct mission in life cannot be reckoned with others who have been given a different task to perform. The tribe of Levi was given the job of transporting the *Mishkan*, and the ark in which were kept the tablets of stone. Equating themselves with other tribes would, in their case, have been incorrect. A person of greater standing must be cognizant of his status, and not reduce himself to the level of the masses. The tribe of Levi, imbued with a greater sanctity than the rest of the nation, and thus bestowed with a more eminent task than any other, had to retain their distinctiveness.

Returning to the original question, let us examine the following Midrash in an attempt to resolve the conflict:

מִי יִתְּנֵנִי בַמִּדְבָּר מְלוֹן אֹרְחִים וְאֶעֶזְבָה אֶת עַמִּי וגו' הֵיכָן שֶׁהָיִיתִי מִתְקַלֵּס שֶׁנֶּאֱמַר יִשְׂאוּ מִדְבָּר וְעָרָיו חֲצֵרִים תֵּשֵׁב קֵדָר יָרֹנּוּ יֹשְׁבֵי סֶלַע. לְנָשִׂיא שֶׁכָּנַס לַמְּדִינָה וְרָאוּ אוֹתוֹ בְּנֵי הַמְּדִינָה וּבָרְחוּ. נִכְנַס לִשְׁנִיָּה וּבָרְחוּ מִלְּפָנָיו. נִכְנַס לְעִיר חֲרֵבָה וְקִדְּמוּ אוֹתוֹ וְהָיוּ מְקַלְּסִין אוֹתוֹ. אָמַר הַנָּשִׂיא זוֹ הָעִיר טוֹבָה הִיא מִכָּל הַמְּדִינוֹת, כָּאן אֲנִי בוֹנֶה כֵּס נָאֶה וְכָאן אֲנִי דָר. כָּךְ כְּשֶׁבָּא הקב"ה לַיָּם בָּרַח מִלְּפָנָיו שֶׁנֶּאֱמַר הַיָּם רָאָה וַיָּנֹס. וְכֵן הֶהָרִים רָקְדוּ כְאֵילִים. בָּא בַמִּדְבָּר חֲרֵבָה קִדְּמָה אוֹתוֹ וְקִלְּסָה אוֹתוֹ, שֶׁנֶּאֱמַר יִשְׂאוּ מִדְבָּר וְעָרָיו חֲצֵרִים תֵּשֵׁב קֵדָר יָרֹנּוּ יֹשְׁבֵי סֶלַע. אָמַר זוֹ הָעִיר טוֹבָה לִי מִכָּל הַמְּדִינוֹת בּוֹ אֲנִי בוֹנֶה כְּנֵסִיָּה וְדָר בְּתוֹכָהּ. הִתְחִילוּ שְׂמֵחִים שהקב"ה דָּר בְּתוֹכָן שֶׁנֶּאֱמַר יְשֻׂשׂוּם מִדְבָּר וְצִיָּה.

> *The Almighty said, "Who will place Me in a desert? Who will station Me in a place where I may abide, that I may forsake My people? I am praised in the desert." The situation can be compared to a prince who entered his kingdom, whereupon all who saw him fled from before him. He entered another state, where again the people fled from before his eyes. Finally, the prince entered a ruined city, and the inhabitants met him and began praising him. Thereupon, the prince declared that he preferred this town to any other, and it was here that he would establish his throne. It was in this place of ruins that he would dwell.*
>
> *God encountered the sea, which fled from before Him. He met the hills, which danced away as rams. God then came to a desolate wilderness, and there He was praised. God then declared that it was this place of ruins which was preferred above all the states. It was in this place tha g, filled with joy at the prospect that the Almighty would dwell amongst them.*[13]

Those cities which had already been built, where civilization was already established, did not welcome the prince. In such a place, a feeling of satisfaction prevails. An infrastructure has already been accepted, and the prince is not required. No void is present which they seek to fill, thus they fail to acknowledge the presence of a prince who is able to found a coherent system of government. It is only when there is a lack of established protocol that a state will welcome a visiting prince and praise him, desiring that he lead them in the establishment of their country.

When one feels one's past is in ruins, when one's yesterday is derelict, one looks to the future with an attitude of hope and receptiveness. Future changes are excitedly anticipated. However, when one recalls one's past with a smug satisfaction at one's previous achievements, one faces but one thing: stagnation. It is only when one considers one's past as insignificant, and even deleterious, that one faces a tomorrow of change and growth.

---

13. *Bemidbar Rabbah* 1:2.

Each person must view himself as standing on a frontier; past behind him, and future ahead. In the perspective of the past, one must consider one's achievements as insignificant. מָה אָנוּ? מֶה חַיֵּינוּ? מַה צִּדְקוֹתֵינוּ? — "What are we? What is our life? What is our righteousness?" These piercing questions from our prayers must shake each person out of his slumber. Our past must be considered as a wilderness, barren and desolate. This attitude, however, must be accompanied by a strong recognition of the future, of the seeds which at present lie dormant beneath the sand. It is through negating past fulfillment that one can truly build the future. And that future is a thing of wonder, of enormity, of potential unlimited.

The *Chovoth HaLevavoth* applies this idea to the study of Torah:

> רָאוּי לְךָ לְהַתְחִיל בְּעֵת חֹזֶק שִׂכְלְךָ וְהַכָּרָתְךָ לְעַיֵּן בְּסֵפֶר תּוֹרַת הָאֱלֹקִים וְסִפְרֵי נְבִיאִים כְּמִי שֶׁלֹּא לָמַד מֵהֶם... וְכֵן תַּעֲשֶׂה בְּדִבְרֵי חֲכָמִים.
>
> *When one's intellect is developing, and one begins investigating the books of the Torah and the prophets, one should read them as if one has never learned them before. So one should do with all works of the Sages.*

Before embarking on the journey in search of knowledge and wisdom, one must consider oneself as a desert. Through negation of one's past intellectual achievements, one will be able to learn Torah on a much higher level. Once one is willing to uproot preconceived ideas, one is receptive to change and new intellectual awareness, and can thus absorb words of holiness, understanding them as they should be grasped. The past is nullified; and the future is thereby elevated.

The future is life's mission. It will only become great if one does not rely upon the past. The gift of Torah, the ultimate exaltation and transformation of one's life, was given in the desert. For it is only when one makes oneself as dust that one's heart is open to receive Torah.

In conjunction with this is the insight on the Mishnah in *Pirkei Avoth.*

הוּא הָיָה אוֹמֵר, חָבִיב אָדָם שֶׁנִּבְרָא בְּצֶלֶם. חִבָּה יְתֵרָה נוֹדַעַת לוֹ שֶׁנִּבְרָא בְּצֶלֶם שֶׁנֶּאֱמַר כִּי בְּצֶלֶם אֱלקִים עָשָׂה אֶת הָאָדָם. חֲבִיבִין יִשְׂרָאֵל שֶׁנִּקְרְאוּ בָנִים לַמָּקוֹם חִבָּה יְתֵרָה נוֹדַעַת לָהֶם שֶׁנִּקְרְאוּ בָנִים לַמָּקוֹם שֶׁנֶּאֱמַר בָּנִים אַתֶּם לה׳ אֱלקֵיכֶם. חֲבִיבִין יִשְׂרָאֵל שֶׁנִּתַּן לָהֶם כְּלִי חֶמְדָּה. חִבָּה יְתֵרָה נוֹדַעַת לָהֶם שֶׁנִּתַּן לָהֶם כְּלִי חֶמְדָּה שֶׁבּוֹ נִבְרָא הָעוֹלָם שֶׁנֶּאֱמַר כִּי לֶקַח טוֹב נָתַתִּי לָכֶם תּוֹרָתִי אַל תַּעֲזֹבוּ.

*Man is dear to the Almighty, for he is created in His image. A greater love lies in that he is informed that he is created in the Divine image, as is said, "For in the image of God He made man." How dear are Yisrael that they are called "children of the Almighty." A greater love lies in that they are informed of this, as is written, "You are children of the Almighty." The Jewish People are so dear, they are given this beautiful tool, the Torah. A greater love lies in that they are informed of this... as is written, "For a goodly portion I have given you — My Torah — do not forsake it."*[14]

This Mishnah informs us of the tremendous potential latent within. Momentous achievements are possible, for man is created בְּצֶלֶם אֱלקִים, in the image of God, with the ability to imitate His holy ways. Our relationship to the Almighty is as of a child to a father. We have the potential to develop a relationship of such a depth of love that it can be compared to the intense tie between father and son. We have been bestowed with a Torah, with a goodly portion, through which all this can be achieved. Our potential achievements are awesome; inherent capacity to achieve greatness is possessed by all. The past achievements, however, must be disregarded, rendered as the barren nothingness of a desert. All depends upon the future, and the recognition of the challenges which remain to be conquered. It is through this attitude that one's spiritual progress will continue on an upward gradient.

Let us conclude with the examination of one more counting of the people. After the immorality of the Jewish People in Shittim, a plague ravaged the nation.

---

14. *Pirkei Avoth* 3:18.

**וַיְהִי אַחֲרֵי הַמַּגֵּפָה וַיֹּאמֶר ה' אֶל מֹשֶׁה וְאֶל אֶלְעָזָר בֶּן אַהֲרֹן הַכֹּהֵן לֵאמֹר. שְׂאוּ אֶת רֹאשׁ כָּל עֲדַת בְּנֵי יִשְׂרָאֵל מִבֶּן עֶשְׂרִים שָׁנָה וָמַעְלָה לְבֵית אֲבֹתָם כָּל יֹצֵא צָבָא בְּיִשְׂרָאֵל.**

*It was after the plague, and the Eternal said to Moshe, and to El'azar, the son of Aharon the Priest, [for them] to say [to the Children of Yisrael], "Calculate the total number of the whole community of the Children of Yisrael..."*[15]

Upon this verse, Rashi makes the following comment:

מָשָׁל לְרוֹעֶה, שֶׁנִּכְנְסוּ זְאֵבִים לְתוֹךְ עֶדְרוֹ וְהָרְגוּ בָּהֶן, וְהוּא מוֹנֶה אוֹתָן, לֵידַע מִנְיַן הַנּוֹתָרוֹת.

*A comparison can be made to a shepherd, who, wolves having attacked his flock, counted the number of remaining sheep.*[16]

Those who remain after a plague, after destruction, are counted again. Survivors are imbued with a special mission.

Just sixty years ago, there was a terrible מַגֵּפָה, plague, that swept through the Jewish nation, ravaging all in its path. Millions of our brethren underwent brutal torture and inconceivable suffering. Six million of our brethren perished. We are the brand saved from the flames. We are the survivors. Survivors are counted. They are bestowed with a special mission.

A mission is dependent upon one's importance. Those who merited seeing a manifestation of the Divine Presence were reckoned again, an indication of their elevated status. Having experienced a closeness to holiness unbeknown to many, their standing was altered. Those exposed to Torah teachings in our generation, those who merit an upbringing based upon the unshakeable foundations of Eternal truth, are bestowed with a task of higher calibre than the charge of the masses.

Past achievements must be viewed as inconsequential. One must instead consider one's role in life, and the position which one

---

15. *Bemidbar* 26:1, 2.
16. Rashi *ad loc.*

has assumed upon the path of history. And then, as one turns to the future, one must see it beckoning him to potential greatness. We tread the path through the means of the "beautiful tool," the Torah bequeathed to us. A relationship of profound love connects the Jew to his Creator. Image of God within, the Jew can move worlds. The capacity for greatness lies within our very beings. Negating past achievements, let us look to the future and build. Build majesty, and build greatness.

# NASO

IN THIS PARASHAH, the blessings bestowed upon the people are recounted:

וַיְדַבֵּר ה' אֶל מֹשֶׁה לֵּאמֹר. דַּבֵּר אֶל אַהֲרֹן וְאֶל בָּנָיו לֵאמֹר כֹּה תְבָרֲכוּ אֶת בְּנֵי יִשְׂרָאֵל אָמוֹר לָהֶם. יְבָרֶכְךָ ה' וְיִשְׁמְרֶךָ. יָאֵר ה' פָּנָיו אֵלֶיךָ וִיחֻנֶּךָּ. יִשָּׂא ה' פָּנָיו אֵלֶיךָ וְיָשֵׂם לְךָ שָׁלוֹם. וְשָׂמוּ אֶת שְׁמִי עַל בְּנֵי יִשְׂרָאֵל וַאֲנִי אֲבָרֲכֵם.

*The Eternal spoke to Moshe, saying, "Speak to Aharon and his sons saying [to them], 'So shall you bless the Children of Yisrael, saying to them:*

*May the Eternal bless you and protect you.*

*May the Eternal show Himself to you in a shining, [friendly] image and favour you.*

*May the Eternal give you special consideration and grant you peace.'*

*They shall bestow [their blessing] upon the Children of Yisrael [with] My Name, and I, Myself, will bless them."*[17]

Thus did the *Kohanim* direct the Almighty's blessing to the people. It is concerning this blessing that our Sages state:

תָּאנָא, כֹּהֵן דְּבָעֵי לְפָרְסָא יָדוֹי בָּעֵי דְיִתּוֹסַף קְדֻשָּׁה עַל קְדֻשָּׁה דִילֵהּ. דְּבָעֵי לְקַדְּשָׁא יָדוֹי עַל יְדָא דְקַדִישָׁא. מָאן יְדָא דְקַדִישָׁא? דָּא לֵיוָאֵי.

*A Kohen must purify and sanctify his hands through one who is holy, before blessing the people. Who is one who is holy? A Levite.*[18]

---

17. *Bemidbar* 6:22.
18. *Zohar Naso*, 156:1.

Before blessing the people, the *Kohanim* require an added dimension of sanctity which is supplied by the Levites (*Leviyim*). What is the significance of this requirement?

The Jewish People had been blessed once prior to this occasion, after the inauguration ceremony of the *Mishkan*. There the verse states:

**וַיִּשָּׂא אַהֲרֹן אֶת יָדָו אֶל הָעָם וַיְבָרְכֵם...**

*Aharon then raised his hands towards the people and blessed them.*[19]

The Ramban highlights an interesting point.

וְאִם כֵּן, יִהְיֶה פָּרָשַׁת "דַּבֵּר אֶל אַהֲרֹן וְאֶל בָּנָיו לֵאמֹר כֹּה תְבָרְכוּ..." שֶׁבְּחֻמָּשׁ הַפְּקוּדִים מֻקְדֶּמֶת לָזֶה. וְאוּלַי כֵּן הוּא, כִּי יִסְמֹךְ לְמַה שֶּׁנֶּאֱמַר שָׁם: "וַיְהִי בְּיוֹם כַּלּוֹת מֹשֶׁה לְהָקִים אֶת הַמִּשְׁכָּן".

וְיִתָּכֵן לוֹמַר, כִּי אַהֲרֹן פָּרַשׂ כַּפָּיו הַשָּׁמַיִם וּבֵרַךְ אֶת הָעָם כַּאֲשֶׁר עָשָׂה שְׁלֹמֹה, שֶׁנֶּאֱמַר "וַיְבָרֶךְ אֵת כָּל קְהַל יִשְׂרָאֵל ... וַיַּעֲמֹד שְׁלֹמֹה לִפְנֵי מִזְבַּח ה'... וַיִּפְרֹשׂ כַּפָּיו הַשָּׁמָיִם..."[20]

The Ramban notices a discrepancy in the chronology of events. For the commandment to bless the people is only given much later, in our *parashah* of *Naso*. And yet we find that Aharon's blessing to the people is mentioned earlier, in *Parashath Shemini*. The Ramban therefore concludes that the command to bless the people actually occurred before Aharon's inauguration blessing, albeit chronologically out of place.

The Ramban continues to describe how Aharon raised his hands heavenward and blessed the people, in a manner comparable to King Shlomo's blessing of the people which occurred centuries later in the dedication of the Temple. After the inauguration ceremony of the *Mishkan*, Aharon blessed them of his own volition, thus the verse does not state that Aharon did so upon the command of Moshe.

Indeed, our Sages state:

---

19. *Vayikra* 9:22.
20. Ramban *ad loc*.

וְיִשָּׂא אַהֲרֹן אֶת יָדָיו. יָדָיו הֲוֵי זָקְפִין בְּלֹא טֹרַח, וְאִזְדַּקְפִין אִינְהוּ מִגַּרְמַיְיהוּ.

*Aharon's hands moved effortlessly. It was as if Aharon's body acted of its own accord.*

We find another instance in this *parashah* where people acted of their own volition, without prior commandment:

**וַיַּקְרִיבוּ הַנְּשִׂאִים אֵת חֲנֻכַּת הַמִּזְבֵּחַ בְּיוֹם הִמָּשַׁח אֹתוֹ וַיַּקְרִיבוּ הַנְּשִׂיאִם אֶת קָרְבָּנָם לִפְנֵי הַמִּזְבֵּחַ.**

*The leaders then brought the dedication [offerings] of the altar on the day it was anointed, and the leaders brought their offerings near, before the altar.*[21]

Uncharacteristically, the Torah elaborates extensively concerning these sacrifices.

**בַּיּוֹם הַשֵּׁנִי הִקְרִיב נְתַנְאֵל בֶּן צוּעָר נְשִׂיא יִשָּׂשכָר. הִקְרִב אֶת קָרְבָּנוֹ...**

*On the second day, Nethan'el the son of Tzu'ar, the leader of [the tribe of] Yissachar, brought [his offering]. He brought as his offering....*[22]

רש"י – וּמַהוּ הִקְרִיב הִקְרִב ב' פְּעָמִים? שֶׁבִּשְׁבִיל ב' דְּבָרִים זָכָה לְהַקְרִיב שֵׁנִי לַשְּׁבָטִים. אַחַת – שֶׁהָיוּ יוֹדְעִים בַּתּוֹרָה שֶׁנֶּאֱמַר וּמִבְּנֵי יִשָּׂשכָר יוֹדְעֵי בִינָה לָעִתִּים, וְאַחַת – שֶׁהֵם נָתְנוּ עֵצָה לַנְּשִׂיאִים לְהִתְנַדֵּב קָרְבָּנוֹת הַלָּלוּ. וּבִיסוֹדוֹ שֶׁל ר' מֹשֶׁה הַדַּרְשָׁן מָצָאתִי, אָמַר ר' פִּינְחָס בֶּן יָאִיר, נְתַנְאֵל בֶּן צוּעָר הִשִּׂיאָן עֵצָה זוֹ.

*Rashi — The word* הִקְרִיב*, "he brought," is mentioned twice with reference to Yissachar. Why is there this disparity between Yissachar and the other tribes?*

*The distinction was for two reasons:*

*1. They were knowledgeable in Torah.*

*2. They advised the princes to volunteer these offerings.*[23]

---

21. *Bemidbar* 7:10.

22. *Bemidbar* 7:18–19.

23. Rashi *ad loc.*

Rashi continues, citing R. Pinchas ben Yair, who states that it was Nethan'el ben Tzu'ar who supplied the princes with the idea to bring these offerings.

Drawing from these two occasions of Aharon's blessing, and the sacrifices of the princes, we can discern four different levels through which man can be inspired to the service of God:

1. The action is a direct result of God's command. An example of this category would be the blessing bestowed upon the people by the *Kohanim.*
2. The individual acts upon the advice of another. It was at this level that the princes acted; they listened to Nethan'el ben Tzu'ar, who advised them to bring offerings for the dedication of the altar.
3. One is aroused to act of one's own volition. This we see in Aharon's blessing to the people at the inauguration ceremony without specific command. The same level of service was adopted by the people of Yissachar who advised the princes to bring the offerings for the dedication of the *Mishkan.*
4. At its highest level, the body automatically fulfils God's will. Aharon's hands lifted of their own accord to bless the people during the inauguration ceremony.

These four categories are each rungs on the ladder of Divine service. At the base of the ladder are those deeds commanded by God. It is these actions which provide a firm foundation from which to ascend to the lofty heights at which one's very body is attuned to one's spiritual exertion. At this advanced stage the body performs the Almighty's will automatically, as metal gravitates towards a magnet, as an object is pulled, by force of gravity, towards earth. Upon the first rung of the ladder, a person remains stable and secure in its firm hold. The second rung, too, has a steadiness which enables us to stand upon this higher rung without fear. However, there is a danger which lies inherent in the two loftiest of levels. This is seen in Moshe's warning to the people on that awesome day upon which the *Mishkan* was inaugurated.

**וַיֹּאמֶר מֹשֶׁה זֶה הַדָּבָר אֲשֶׁר צִוָּה ה' תַּעֲשׂוּ וְיֵרָא אֲלֵיכֶם כְּבוֹד ה'.**

*Moshe then said, "This is the procedure that the Eternal has commanded you [to] do, and the Glory of the Eternal will [then] be revealed to you."*[24]

The *Ha'amek Davar* explains this verse.

זֶה הַפָּסוּק אוֹמֵר דִּרְשׁוּנִי שֶׁהֲרֵי כְּבָר עָשׂוּ מַה שֶּׁעֲלֵיהֶם וְהֵבִיאוּ הַכֹּל אֶל פְּנֵי אֹהֶל מוֹעֵד וּמַה לָּהֶם לַעֲשׂוֹת עוֹד?... וְהָעִנְיָן דִּכְבָר הָיָה בִּימֵי מֹשֶׁה כַּתּוֹת בְּיִשְׂרָאֵל שֶׁהָיוּ לְהוּטִים אַחַר אַהֲבַת ה' אֲבָל לֹא עַל יְדֵי גְּבוּלִים שֶׁהִגְבִּילָה תּוֹרָה. וְכַאֲשֶׁר יְבֹאַר בְּאֹרֶךְ בפ' קֹרַח שֶׁזֶּה הָיָה עִקַּר הַחֵטְא שֶׁל ר"ן אֲנָשִׁים שֶׁהָיוּ צַדִּיקִים גְּמוּרִים וְחָטְאוּ בְּנַפְשׁוֹתָם בְּמַה שֶּׁמָּסְרוּ עַצְמָם לְמִיתָה עַל יְדֵי תְּשׁוּקָה קְדוֹשָׁה זוֹ לְהַשִּׂיג אַהֲבַת ה' עַל יְדֵי הַקְּטֹרֶת אע"ג שֶׁלֹּא יִהְיֶה לְרָצוֹן לְפִי דֶּרֶךְ הַתּוֹרָה... בִּשְׁבִיל זֶה אָמַר מֹשֶׁה לְיִשְׂרָאֵל כִּי לֹא כֵן הַדָּבָר. אֶלָּא אוֹתוֹ יֵצֶר הָרַע הַעֲבִירוּ מִלִּבְּכֶם שֶׁגַּם זֶה הַתְּשׁוּקָה אע"ג שֶׁהִיא לְהַשִּׂיג אַהֲבַת ה' בִּקְדֻשָּׁה, מִכָּל מָקוֹם אִם הִיא לֹא בַּדֶּרֶךְ שֶׁעָלָה עַל רְצוֹנוֹ יתֿ' אֵינוֹ אֶלָּא דֶּרֶךְ יֵצֶר הָרַע לְהַטְעוֹת וּלְהַתְעוֹת דַּעַת גְּדוֹלֵי יִשְׂרָאֵל בְּזוֹ הַתְּשׁוּקָה.[25]

In the above-quoted verse, Moshe exhorts the Jewish People to fulfill the will of God. However, the Jewish People having already performed the deed, the words appear redundant. Placing ourselves in the situation of the time lends us a better understanding of the issue.

As the *Ha'amek Davar* explains, there were sections of the Jewish People in that generation who yearned for spirituality, longed for closeness to God. The hazard that lies in this deep yearning however, is the danger of breaking the clearly defined boundaries prescribed by the Torah, in an attempt to reach ever closer to the Divine Source. Such was the mistake of the 250 followers of Korach, who though their deepest desire lay in the attainment of holiness, were driven by these emotions to break beyond the restrictions of the law. It was thus that they approached the altar with incense, a service permitted to the *Kohanim* alone. They disregarded the boundaries imposed by

---

24. *Vayikra* 9:6.
25. *Ha'amek Davar ad loc.*

the Torah, leading to the infamous consequences which Korach and his followers suffered.

Although immediate and spontaneous closeness to the Almighty is desirable, it must be guided by set laws to which we are bound. We must adhere to the "map" of the Almighty. There are roads which we must follow, although we might crave to bypass the highways and instead investigate the meandering lanes which seem to lead to a much longed-for destination. Ultimately, however, we must realise that any persuasion to reach the destination along a different route is merely the guise of the evil inclination, who aims to deceive and corrupt.

This quality of absolute and unwavering adherence, then, is the message delivered by Moshe himself on the day of inauguration. And in fact, we see the implementation of this vital principle time and again in the dedication of the altar:

**וַיַּקְרִיבוּ נְשִׂיאֵי יִשְׂרָאֵל... וַיָּבִיאוּ אֶת קָרְבָּנָם לִפְנֵי ה'... וַיַּקְרִיבוּ אוֹתָם לִפְנֵי הַמִּשְׁכָּן.**

*The leaders of Yisrael brought... they brought their offering before the Eternal... and brought them up to the front of the Dwelling.*[26]

רש"י — וַיַּקְרִיבוּ אוֹתָם לִפְנֵי הַמִּשְׁכָּן. שֶׁלֹּא קִבֵּל מֹשֶׁה מִיָּדָם עַד שֶׁנֶּאֱמַר לוֹ מִפִּי הַמָּקוֹם.[27]

Rashi explains the seemingly unnecessary phrase, "and they brought them up to the front of the Dwelling," as implying that Moshe obtained permission from God before accepting the sacrifices from the princes' hands.

As we read further:

**וַיֹּאמֶר ה' אֶל מֹשֶׁה לֵּאמֹר. קַח מֵאִתָּם וְהָיוּ לַעֲבֹד אֶת עֲבֹדַת אֹהֶל מוֹעֵד...**

26. *Bemidbar* 7:2, 3.
27. Rashi *ad loc.*

*The Eternal then said to Moshe, to [inform the leaders], "Accept [these gifts] from them and let them be used in the service in the Tent of Meeting."*[28]

Similarly:

**וַיֹּאמֶר ה' אֶל מֹשֶׁה נָשִׂיא אֶחָד לַיּוֹם... יַקְרִיבוּ אֶת קָרְבָּנָם לַחֲנֻכַּת הַמִּזְבֵּחַ.**

*The Eternal then said to Moshe, "[The leaders] shall bring their offerings for the dedication of the altar, one leader for each day."*[29]

In all of these cases, a specific command was given by the Almighty. It was only after this instruction that Moshe accepted the donations and offerings of the princes. Sentiments may be lofty indeed, however without specific instruction to channel the feelings, the emotions can manifest in a manner actually antithetical to God's will.

It is this theme which runs through the preparations for the priestly blessings: the Levites washed the hands of the *Kohanim*, thus purifying them. To understand the significance of this action, we must learn of the essential nature of a *Kohen*. What is a *Kohen*? Wherein lies his special quality?

The key to this concept lies in the blessing to the tribe of Levi, in which the bearer of the *Urim VeTumim*, himself of Levite descent, is described in the words, תֻּמֶּיךָ וְאוּרֶיךָ לְאִישׁ חֲסִידֶךָ — "[You have given] Your *Urim VeTumim* to Your pious one."[30] Here, the quality of the Levi is defined specifically as that of an אִישׁ חֶסֶד, one endowed with the quality of loving kindness and expansiveness. This quality is comparable to water bubbling up from an underground spring. Reaching the surface, it is released under enormous pressure. The water sprays in all directions, depositing sparkling droplets upon the

---

28. *Bemidbar* 7:4, 5.
29. *Bemidbar* 7:11.
30. *Devarim* 33:8.

surrounding area. The spring continues to flow, yet it is possible for weeds to sprout in place of flowers. Thus the quality of חֶסֶד, an outpouring of giving and expansiveness, contains a great danger: that of giving in instances when the Torah does not command us to give. That of giving against the will of God. Such expansiveness, with its benefits and dangers, is the domain of the *Kohen*.

A second quality of Levi can be discerned from the incident of the sin of the Golden Calf. There it was the tribe of Levi alone who responded to the cry of מִי לה' אֵלָי, who stood, prepared to fight for God, for goodness, against the evil of sin. They were seen to adhere to strict justice and exactitude, to possess an eagerness to fulfill the word of God in every detail. This quality is reflected in the praise they received from Moshe in the selfsame blessing from which we quoted above.

> **הָאֹמֵר לְאָבִיו וּלְאִמּוֹ לֹא רְאִיתִיו וְאֶת אֶחָיו לֹא הִכִּיר וְאֶת בָּנָו לֹא יָדָע כִּי שָׁמְרוּ אִמְרָתֶךָ וּבְרִיתְךָ יִנְצֹרוּ.**
>
> *...who said about [the] father [of] his mother, "I did not see [my relationship to] him," and who did not recognise his [maternal] brother or know his [grand]sons; for they kept Your pronouncement and observed Your covenant.*[31]

The Levites demonstrated rigidity; they remained unwavering and unaffected by personal sentiments in ensuring that justice against offenders was executed. They wiped out every sinner, regardless of familial affiliations, in an effort to uproot a profanation of the Divine Name.

The Levites washed the hands of the *Kohanim*, thereby increasing their level of sanctity. The exactitude and upright quality of the Levites merged with the expansiveness and aspirations of the *Kohanim*, thus producing holiness and beauty. The boundaries set by the Levites provided the framework in which to channel the lofty feelings and ideals of the *Kohen*. It is when these two elements fuse that we are guaranteed the correct and fitting intentions for blessing

31. *Devarim* 33:9.

the people in an outpouring of love.

The scaling of the ladder of Divine service must be one of steady ascent. One must first be firm in the initial rungs, following the word of God with precision, exactitude, and wholesomeness. Only then can we cautiously ascend to the third level, and the fourth, eventually reaching the lofty heights where one's very body is attuned to the Divine will. The spring flows forth. Channeled, it irrigates the surrounding land, producing only the true flowers of spiritual growth.

# BEHA'ALOTHCHA

IN THIS PARASHAH, we are presented with the words spoken by Miriam and Aharon against their brother Moshe, words which were later criticised by God.

> **וַיֹּאמְרוּ הֲרַק אַךְ בְּמֹשֶׁה דִּבֶּר ה' הֲלֹא גַּם בָּנוּ דִבֵּר וַיִּשְׁמַע ה'. וְהָאִישׁ מֹשֶׁה עָנָו מְאֹד מִכֹּל הָאָדָם אֲשֶׁר עַל פְּנֵי הָאֲדָמָה...פֶּה אֶל פֶּה אֲדַבֶּר בּוֹ וּמַרְאֶה וְלֹא בְחִידֹת וּתְמֻנַת ה' יַבִּיט וּמַדּוּעַ לֹא יְרֵאתֶם לְדַבֵּר בְּעַבְדִּי בְמֹשֶׁה.**
>
> *They said, "Was it only with Moshe that the Eternal spoke alone? Did He not also speak with us?" Now the [great] man, Moshe, was extremely humble; [even] more than all the people on the face of the earth... [The Eternal said to them]... "I speak to him face to face, lucidly and not in riddles, and he perceives the Eternal's image. So why were you not afraid to speak against My servant, against Moshe?"*[32]

In the above extract, two terms of description are applied to Moshe: "the humble one" and "servant." These two qualities are intrinsically related. In the course of our essay, we will examine the link between these two titles.

The qualifications necessary to receive prophecy are derived from the prototype prophet, our teacher Moshe. The Gemara enumerates these qualifications:

> א"ר יוֹחָנָן אֵין הקב"ה מַשְׁרֶה שְׁכִינָתוֹ אֶלָּא עַל גִּבּוֹר וְעָשִׁיר וְחָכָם וְעָנָו וְכֻלָּן מִמֹּשֶׁה. גִּבּוֹר – דִּכְתִיב... וָאֶתְפֹּשׂ בִּשְׁנֵי הַלֻּחֹת וָאַשְׁלִכֵם מֵעַל שְׁתֵּי יָדָי וָאֲשַׁבְּרֵם... עָשִׁיר – פְּסָל לְךָ, פְּסוֹלְתָן שֶׁלְּךָ יְהֵא. חָכָם – רַב

32. *Bemidbar* 12:2–3, 6–8.

וּשְׁמוּאֵל דְּאָמְרֵי תַּרְוַיְהוּ חֲמִשִּׁים שַׁעֲרֵי בִינָה נִבְרְאוּ בָּעוֹלָם וְכֻלָּם נִתְּנוּ לְמֹשֶׁה חָסֵר אַחַת שֶׁנֶּאֱמַר וּתְחַסְּרֵהוּ מְעַט מֵאלקים. עָנָו — דִּכְתִיב וְהָאִישׁ מֹשֶׁה עָנָו מְאֹד.

*Said R. Yochanan: "God does not rest His Divine Presence upon a person (referring to the bestowal of prophecy) unless he is physically strong, rich, wise, and humble. All these requirements are derived from Moshe. His physical prowess is evident from his ability to smash the heavy stone tablets. His wealth is evident from the verse, 'Carve out for yourself' — the chips [from the precious stone tablets that Moshe carved out] shall be yours. His wisdom is explained by Rav and Shemuel: Moshe had access to forty-nine levels of transcendent wisdom. From our parashah we see his humility in the description, 'The [great] man, Moshe, was extremely humble.'"*[33]

A problem arises with these enumerated qualifications when we contrast them with another dictum of our Sages, as quoted by Rabbi Dessler in *Michtav MeEliyahu.*

לָמַדְנוּ בַּגְּמָרָא הָרוֹצֶה שֶׁיַּחְכִּים יַדְרִים, וְשֶׁיַּעֲשִׁיר יַצְפִּין וְסִימָנְךָ מְנוֹרָה בַּדָּרוֹם וְשֻׁלְחָן בַּצָּפוֹן וְרָאִיתִי לָרַב נַחְמָן מִבְּרֶסְלַב ז"ל שֶׁהִקְשָׁה שֶׁלִּכְאוֹרָה מַשְׁמַע מִכָּאן שֶׁאִי אֶפְשָׁר לָאָדָם לִהְיוֹת חָכָם בַּתּוֹרָה וְגַם עָשִׁיר, כִּי הַפּוֹנֶה לַדָּרוֹם אֵינוֹ יָכֹל לִפְנוֹת גַּם לַצָּפוֹן, וְנִרְאֶה שֶׁלַּחָכְמָה וְלָעֹשֶׁר מְקוֹמוֹת מְחֻלָּקִים, אֲבָל קָשֶׁה הֲרֵי מָצָאנוּ כַּמָּה גְּדוֹלִים שֶׁהָיוּ לָהֶם תּוֹרָה וּגְדֻלָּה בְּמָקוֹם אֶחָד. וְתֵרֵץ שֶׁזֶּה עַל יְדֵי עֲנָוָה, שֶׁאָז אֵין לוֹ מָקוֹם.

*One who desires wisdom should turn towards the south (when standing in prayer). One who desires wealth should similarly angle himself slightly towards the north. For, the Menorah, symbol of wisdom was positioned in the south, and the Shulchan upon which was placed the Lechem HaPanim, symbolising material well-being, was positioned in the north.*[34]

---

33. *Nedarim* 38a.
34. *Michtav MeEliyahu*, Part Four, p.23.

The statement is striking when we note that the simultaneous achievement of both physical positions (north and south) is impossible. If one is turning north, one is facing away from the south, and similarly in the converse. This reflects the spiritual realm, where the attainment of materialistic desires and the yearning to achieve closeness to the Creator are mutually exclusive wishes. Inasmuch as one is pulled towards one direction, one is removed from the other.

If the possession of wealth precludes attainment of wisdom, and conversely, if the attainment of wisdom involves a renunciation of material possessions, how can prophecy require possession of both of these gifts? The problem is augmented when we consider the many individuals throughout our history who possessed Torah and wealth concurrently. How can these polar opposites coexist in harmony?

This question was originally raised by Rabbi Nachman of Breslov, who supplied the following cryptic answer: The simultaneous possession is possible with עֲנָוָה, the trait of humility. For, as he continues, "A person with humility does not have a place."

R. Nachman's answer obviously requires further explanation. In the course of our investigation, we will have to resolve a difficulty in the following Midrash:

וְכֵן יִרְמְיָה אוֹמֵר כֹּה אָמַר ה׳ אַל יִתְהַלֵּל חָכָם בְּחָכְמָתוֹ וְאַל יִתְהַלֵּל הַגִּבּוֹר בִּגְבוּרָתוֹ אַל יִתְהַלֵּל עָשִׁיר בְּעָשְׁרוֹ. כִּי אִם בְּזֹאת יִתְהַלֵּל וגו׳. וּמַתָּנוֹת אֵלוּ בִּזְמַן שֶׁאֵינָן בָּאִין מִן הקב"ה סוֹפָן לְהִפָּסֵק מִמֶּנּוּ. שָׁנוּ רַבּוֹתֵינוּ שְׁנֵי חֲכָמִים עָמְדוּ בָּעוֹלָם אֶחָד מִיִּשְׂרָאֵל וְאֶחָד מֵאוּמוֹת הָעוֹלָם. אֲחִיתֹפֶל מִיִּשְׂרָאֵל וּבִלְעָם מֵאוּמוֹת הָעוֹלָם וּשְׁנֵיהֶם נֶאֶבְדוּ מִן הָעוֹלָם. וְכֵן שְׁנֵי גִּבּוֹרִים עָמְדוּ בָּעוֹלָם אֶחָד מִיִּשְׂרָאֵל וְאֶחָד מֵאוּמוֹת הָעוֹלָם. שִׁמְשׁוֹן מִיִּשְׂרָאֵל וְגָלְיָת מֵאוּמוֹת הָעוֹלָם וּשְׁנֵיהֶם נֶאֶבְדוּ מִן הָעוֹלָם. וְכֵן שְׁנֵי עֲשִׁירִים עָמְדוּ בָּעוֹלָם אֶחָד מִיִּשְׂרָאֵל וְאֶחָד מֵאוּמוֹת הָעוֹלָם. קֹרַח מִיִּשְׂרָאֵל וְהָמָן מֵאוּמוֹת הָעוֹלָם וּשְׁנֵיהֶם נֶאֶבְדוּ מִן הָעוֹלָם. לָמָּה? שֶׁלֹּא הָיָה מַתְּנָתָן מִן הקב"ה אֶלָּא חוֹטְפִין אוֹתָן לָהֶם.

*The prophet Yirmiyah said, "So says the Lord: A wise man should not exult in his wisdom, a strong man should not exult in his prowess, a wealthy man should not exult in his wealth." These gifts, when they do not originate from God, will depart from the person. Our Sages learned: there were two wise people in the world, Achitophel from Yisrael, and Bil'am from the nations of the world. They both perished from the face of the earth. There were two mighty people in the world, Shimshon from Yisrael and Goliath from the nations of the world. Both perished from the face of the earth. There were two wealthy people in the world: Korach from Yisrael, and Haman from the nations of the world. Both perished from the face of the earth. Why were all these people destroyed? Because their gifts were not from the Almighty, but were instead snatched for themselves.*[35]

The problem in this Midrash is glaringly obvious. Our Sages have here explained that gifts that are not from God are merely transitory, and will fade away. Is it possible, then, to receive gifts (or indeed anything) that are not from God, the Source of all bounty?

This difficulty is augmented in light of the Gemara which states that before every child is born, it is decreed whether he will be clever or foolish, rich or poor. These gifts are thus determined for the individual before the time of birth. If one were decreed to be a fool, no exertion or "snatching" in the world would help one gain wisdom. What then is this "snatching" to which the Sages refer?

The following enigmatic *Tanchuma* relates to the above Midrash.

וָאֲמַלֵּא אֹתוֹ רוּחַ אֱלֹקִים בְּחָכְמָה שֶׁכְּבָר הָיְתָה בּוֹ חָכְמָה לְמֶדְךָ שֶׁאֵין הקב"ה מְמַלֵּא חָכְמָה אֶלָּא לְמִי שֶׁיֵּשׁ בּוֹ כְּבָר. מַטְרוֹנָה אַחַת שָׁאֲלָה אֶת ר"י בַּר חֲלַפְתָּא מַהוּ שֶׁכָּתַב יָהֵב חָכְמְתָא לְחַכִּימִין, לַטִּפְּשִׁים הָיָה צָרִיךְ לוֹמַר. א"ל בִּתִּי אִם יָבוֹאוּ אֶצְלֵךְ שְׁנַיִם אֶחָד עָנִי וְאֶחָד עָשִׁיר וְהֵן צְרִיכִין לִלְוֹת מִמֵּךְ לְאֵיזֶה מֵהֶם אַתְּ מַלְוָה? אָמְרָה לוֹ לֶעָשִׁיר. א"ל לָמָּה? אָמַר לוֹ שֶׁאִם יֶחְסַר יִהְיֶה לוֹ מָמוֹן שֶׁיִּפְרַע אֲבָל עָנִי אִם יְאַבֵּד מְעוֹתַי מֵהֵיכָן יִפְרַע? א"ל יִשְׁמְעוּ אָזְנַיִךְ מַה שֶּׁפִּיךְ מְדַבֵּר, כָּךְ אִם הָיָה הקב"ה נוֹתֵן חָכְמָה לַטִּפְּשִׁים הָיוּ יוֹשְׁבִין בְּבָתֵּי כִסְאוֹת וּבִמְבוֹאוֹת מְטֻנָּפוֹת וּבְבָתֵּי מֶרְחֲצָאוֹת וְאֵין מִתְעַסְּקִין בָּהּ.

35. *Bemidbar Rabbah* 22:6.

*The Almighty bestowed Betzal'el with wisdom only because Betzal'el already possessed wisdom. This teaches us that a person is bestowed with wisdom only if he already possesses some wisdom.*

*A princess asked Rabbi Yosi ben Chalafta about the verse in Daniel which states, "He gives wisdom to those who have wisdom." Surely wisdom should be given to foolish people, rather than to those who already possess wisdom?*

*His reply: "My daughter, if a rich person and a poor person both approached you for a loan, to whom would you lend money?"*

*"To the rich person."*

*"Why?"*

*"If he cannot presently repay the loan, he will eventually find the means to do so. Thus, lending to a rich person ensures the security of my money. Were I to lend to a poor person, there would be no guarantee that my money would be returned to me."*

*R. Yosi then told the princess, "Let your ears hearken to the utterance of your lips! If God were to give wisdom to fools, they would sit in unclean places (where it is forbidden to think Torah thoughts), and misuse the wisdom. If wisdom is bestowed upon wise people, they will utilise the wisdom in the correct manner. Therefore, God bestows wisdom only upon one who is already in possession of wisdom."*[36]

Rabbi Lazer Kahn highlighted a discrepancy in this Midrash. An analogy concerning *lending* money is used to answer a question concerning the *gift* of wisdom. Thus, the answer does not seem to address the question posed. Further, were one to find oneself in a position of giving, rather than lending money, it would be preferable to give money to the poor man, not the rich person. Of what relevance is a scenario concerning the lending of money?

The fundamental principle that we must derive from the Midrash

---

36. *Tanchuma, Vayakhel* 2.

is as follows. That which is bequeathed to us from Heaven, that bounty which we receive as a result of God's kindness, is not to be viewed as a gift, which has passed into the ownership of the recipient. It is all to be seen as a mere loan from the Almighty, as a tool to be utilised in our spiritual development. This perspective can be understood from the following analogy. If one receives a present from a donor who attaches numerous stipulations concerning the gift's correct usage, one could not claim true dominion or ownership over the gift. For example, if one were to receive a book that is to be read only in certain places, during specific times, that may not be lent to others, nor be mishandled in any way, one would not be said to possess full ownership of the book. Complete ownership of an article by definition must involve the freedom of its use in any way desired. An act of acquisition is actually an extension of power over the article, the licence to wield the gift both positively and negatively, in both a constructive and destructive fashion.

The gifts that we receive from Heaven, therefore, cannot be truly classified as gifts. The Donor Himself places certain restrictions upon these so-called gifts. We are bequeathed wealth to be used not for indulgence in physicality, nor for satisfaction of materialistic urges. It is rather to be used solely for spiritual ends. We are granted wisdom, not to revel in futile intellectual acrobatics, nor to delve into prohibited studies, and definitely not to devise methods by which to cheat in business. Wisdom is to be used for the furtherance of Torah study. We are entrusted with physical prowess and good health, not to feel the "strength and might of my hand," but to be used for the furtherance of Godly ideals. Each "gift" bestowed upon us comes with a detailed instruction manual, containing many conditions and stipulations which we are bound to follow. Can we thus claim to have true ownership of these attributes? Surely our personal power cannot be said to have been extended over these gifts; if anything, egoistic desires are curtailed through the ownership. That which we receive is given for a purpose; and it is for this goal alone that they are to be used. Thus, "gifts" from Heaven cannot properly be called gifts at all; rather they fall into the category of generous loans which can be fully enjoyed only through strict adherence to the attached stipulations.

With this, we can understand the words of the above Midrash. God gives wisdom to those who already possess it. The prerequisite wisdom refers to the knowledge and realisation that money and resources are sent from Heaven as loans. With this perspective, people will comply with the regulations of the loan, using it only in its correct time and application. Such people will act as faithful guardians of whatever is lent them, and as such can be entrusted with additional currency: money, physical prowess, or intellectual excellence.

Returning to the verse quoted earlier in the Midrash, which described the "snatching" of gifts from God, an extra nuance can now be discerned in the words themselves.

**כֹּה אָמַר ה' אַל יִתְהַלֵּל חָכָם בְּחָכְמָתוֹ וְאַל יִתְהַלֵּל הַגִּבּוֹר בִּגְבוּרָתוֹ אַל יִתְהַלֵּל עָשִׁיר בְּעָשְׁרוֹ...**

*So says the Lord: A wise man should not exult in his wisdom, a strong man should not exult in his prowess, a wealthy man should not exult in his wealth.*[37]

The stress here is placed on the personal ownership of the gifts: his wisdom, his prowess, his wealth. The acumen of the wise person is not his own — it does not belong to him in the sense of full ownership. There is no room for pride in one's wisdom; it does not belong to him. Similarly with regard to wealth or physical prowess: bounty is bestowed upon man for one purpose alone — the service of God. Thus, they will only be granted to those who have the wisdom to utilise these gifts in the manner which God intends.

Having established this idea, let us return to the original question. Moshe is termed as both "My servant" and as "the humble one." These are not two separate characteristics; rather it is clear that these qualities are intrinsically linked. The connection is explained by Rabbi Dessler in the continuation of the essay we quoted earlier:

37. *Yirmiyah* 9:22.

בֵּאוּר דְּבָרָיו ז"ל שֶׁאִי אֶפְשָׁר שֶׁתְּהֵא לוֹ חָכְמָה, וְשֶׁתְּהֵא לוֹ עֹשֶׁר גַּם כֵּן, כִּי כָּל זְמַן שֶׁמַּשִּׂיג שֶׁהַחָכְמָה אוֹ הָעֹשֶׁר שֶׁלּוֹ, הֲרֵי זֶה בִּבְחִינַת מָקוֹם, שֶׁהֲרֵי בָּזֶה עוֹשֶׂה רְשׁוּת לְעַצְמוֹ, וְאָז אִי אֶפְשָׁר לָתֵת לוֹ שְׁתֵּיהֶן. וְלָמָּה כִּי כָּל מַה שֶּׁנּוֹתְנִים לָאָדָם בָּעוֹלָם הַזֶּה, בֵּין חָכְמָה בֵּין עֹשֶׁר, הֲרֵי זֶה נִסָּיוֹן עֲבוּרוֹ, לִרְאוֹת אִם יִתְגָּאֶה בּוֹ וִיטְלֶנּוּ לְעַצְמוֹ אוֹ יִשְׁתַּמֵּשׁ בּוֹ לַעֲבוֹדַת ה'. וְלֹא הֲרֵי נִסְיוֹן הָעֹשֶׁר כַּהֲרֵי נִסְיוֹן הַחָכְמָה, וְאֵין נוֹתְנִים לָאָדָם עֲבוֹדָה כֹּה קָשָׁה שֶׁל שְׁנֵי נִסְיוֹנוֹת כְּאֶחָד. אֲבָל מִי שֶׁכְּבָר הִתְרוֹמֵם לְמַעְלָה מִנִּסְיוֹנוֹת אֵלּוּ וְעָלָה לְדַרְגָּה שֶׁל עֲנָוָה, שֶׁהַכֹּל אֶצְלוֹ רַק עַבְדוּת וְלֹא בַּעֲלוּת כנ"ל, עָנָו כָּזֶה אֵין לוֹ בְּחִינַת מָקוֹם כִּי אֵינוֹ עוֹשֶׂה רְשׁוּת וּתְחוּם לְעַצְמוֹ כְּלָל — אֶצְלוֹ יִתָּכֵן שֶׁיִּהְיוּ לוֹ תּוֹרָה וּגְדוּלָּה בְּיַחַד.

The possession of any of these qualities presents a constant trial to man. Money presents the challenge of how it will be used: in pursuit of personal desires or in dedication to spirituality? The wealthy individual may feel that he has complete and unfettered ownership, and that the money is in his own domain, his own מָקוֹם. As such, the Sages have predicted that the money will elusively slip through his fingers, for this was not the reason for which the wealth was bestowed. When used as a loan, credit can be extended — for months, years, and decades. Utilised for the correct purpose, the loan need never be recalled.

Intellectual acumen presents a similar challenge, that of gift versus loan. If "snatched" as a gift, it will fade away. The one who relinquishes his feeling of ownership and power, however, will emerge triumphant from the battlefield, and only then will the loan continue to be extended.

Man, for all his frailty, is only presented with challenges that he is capable of overcoming. The challenges presented by the simultaneous possession of wealth and wisdom are, under normal circumstances, beyond the capacity of man to contend with. He would inevitably fall, ensnared in the trap of pride, and come to view these resources as if they truly belonged to him. Thus, in His infinite kindness, God does not normally confer both gifts upon man at once.

There is one exception, however, that which we defined earlier in the words of R. Nachman of Breslov: there must be no מָקוֹם. Possession of both these gifts hinges upon the manner in which they will be used. If one relinquishes ownership, diminishing one's feeling of power; if one indeed withdraws from any מָקוֹם, any feeling of domain, then man can be bestowed with both wealth and wisdom. The blessings will not be abused; they will not be snatched for one's own selfish ends. Being only tools in one's Divine service, all gifts can be magnanimously granted. With the ingredient of humility, not taking personal pride in one's acumen and prowess, these gifts can be perpetuated.

Turning to the laws of a servant, we can discern a parallel between the servant and a humble person. In defining the status of a servant's property, the Gemara states: מַה שֶּׁקָּנָה עֶבֶד קָנָה רַבּוֹ — "The acquisitions of a servant are the acquisitions of his master." A servant is one who, in the face of his master, is divested of all identity. He has no ownership; he has no domain, no מָקוֹם. Everything he has, all resources with which he is bequeathed, are for the work he undertakes for his master.

Moshe was called "My servant,"; he earned the title of "the most humble of all men." He could be granted the whole array of Heavenly gifts, for he would snatch nothing for himself, but return all to the Almighty. It was thus that Moshe merited wealth, physical strength, and intellect simultaneously.

As servants of the ultimate Master, we too have no independent identity. All that we have is solely to enhance and intensify our Divine service and spiritual strivings. No ego or sense of self is superimposed upon our possessions; instead, all is for the "Boss." The *Ba'alei Mussar* state that the root of all negativity is pride. A haughty person casts off the responsibility that has been placed on his shoulders, and misuses Heavenly blessing for his own ends. Every resource brings obligation in its wake; it has been bestowed for the furtherance of spirituality, and one must remain faithful to this intention, utilising all of one's gifts in one's Divine service. It is when we merit the title of "servant," when every blessing is used to the full, when every gift is viewed as a loan, that one can merit wealth, physical well-being, wisdom, and indeed every blessing, from the ultimate Master.

# SHELACH

OUR PARASHAH BOTH opens and concludes with reference to spies. At the conclusion of the *parashah*, we read the following:

**וְהָיָה לָכֶם לְצִיצִת וּרְאִיתֶם אֹתוֹ וּזְכַרְתֶּם אֶת כָּל מִצְוֹת ה׳ וַעֲשִׂיתֶם אֹתָם וְלֹא תָתוּרוּ אַחֲרֵי לְבַבְכֶם וְאַחֲרֵי עֵינֵיכֶם אֲשֶׁר אַתֶּם זֹנִים אַחֲרֵיהֶם.**

*...They shall be for you as tassels, [so that] you see them... and you must not be searching, following your heart or your eyes, after which you [tend to] stray.*[38]

Rashi comments upon the expression וְלֹא תָתוּרוּ — "And you must not be searching."

כְּמוֹ מִתּוּר הָאָרֶץ. הַלֵּב וְהָעֵינַיִם הֵם מְרַגְּלִים לַגּוּף, וּמְסַרְסְרִים לוֹ אֶת הָעֲבֵרוֹת, הָעַיִן רוֹאָה וְהַלֵּב חוֹמֵד וְהַגּוּף עוֹשֶׂה אֶת הָעֲבֵרוֹת.

*This expression is related to that used in conjunction with, "spying out the land." The heart and the eyes are spies for the body, the agents which lead a person to sin. The eye sees, the heart desires, and the body performs the sin.*[39]

A discrepancy can be discerned between the words of the verse and the explanation of Rashi. Rashi enumerates the stages through which one is brought to sin as follows: The first stage in the process leading to sin is one's vision. This prompts the heart's desire, which in turn leads the body to execute the deed. Vision then, followed by the desire of the heart, initiates the course of action. In contrast, the verse first mentions the heart, and then mentions the eyes. What is the significance of Rashi's change of order?

---

38. *Bemidbar* 15:39.
39. Rashi *ad loc.*

The *Sifrei* records the following debate upon this verse:

ד"א וְלֹא תָתוּרוּ אַחֲרֵי לְבַבְכֶם. מַגִּיד שֶׁהָעֵינַיִם הוֹלְכִים אַחַר הַלֵּב. אוֹ הַלֵּב אַחֲרֵי הָעֵינַיִם. אָמַרְתָּ וְכִי יֵשׁ סוּמָא שֶׁעוֹשֶׂה כָּל תּוֹעֵבוֹת שֶׁבָּעוֹלָם הָא מַה ת"ל וְלֹא תָתוּרוּ אַחֲרֵי לְבַבְכֶם מַגִּיד שֶׁהָעֵינַיִם הוֹלְכִים אַחַר הַלֵּב.

*Our Sages discuss the meaning of the injunction, "Do not be searching, following your heart." Does this mean that the eyes follow the wishes of the heart? Or, could it be that the desires of one's heart follow one's vision?*

*Is it not possible for a blind man to indulge in all manner of sin? If the heart desires only what the eyes see, how would this be possible? It therefore cannot be that the heart desires only what the eyes see. Hence, the verse states, "and you must not be searching, following your heart," to teach us that one's eyes follow the yearnings of one's heart.*[40]

One's sight follows the inclination of one's heart. The heart, then, must begin the process leading to sin. To understand the profundities contained within this dispute, we will need to examine a Midrash upon this verse.

וְלֹא תָתוּרוּ אַחֲרֵי לְבַבְכֶם. הַלֵּב וְהָעֵינַיִם הֵם סַרְסוּרִין לַגּוּף שֶׁהֵם מְזַנִּין אֶת הַגּוּף לְמַעַן תִּזְכְּרוּ וַעֲשִׂיתֶם אֶת כָּל מִצְוֹתָי. מָשָׁל לְאֶחָד מֻשְׁלָךְ לְתוֹךְ הַמַּיִם. הוֹשִׁיט הַקַּבַּרְנִיט אֶת הַחֶבֶל וא"ל תְּפֹשׂ חֶבֶל זֶה בְּיָדְךָ וְאַל תְּנִיחֵהוּ שֶׁאִם תְּנִיחֵהוּ אֵין לְךָ חַיִּים. אַף כָּךְ א"ל הקב"ה לְיִשְׂרָאֵל כ"ז שֶׁאַתֶּם מְדֻבָּקִין בַּמִּצְוֹת "וְאַתֶּם הַדְּבֵקִים בה' אֱלֹקֵיכֶם חַיִּים כֻּלְּכֶם הַיּוֹם." כה"א "הַחֲזֵק בַּמּוּסָר אַל תֶּרֶף נִצְּרֶהָ כִּי הִיא חַיֶּיךָ".

*Tzitzith are worn as a remembrance of all the mitzvoth. The parable is brought of a man, drowning in the ocean's waves. The captain of the ship cast a rope to the floundering man, and ordered, "Grasp the rope, and do not let it go. If you let it go, you will die." So the Almighty said to the Jewish People. "The entire time you cling to the mitzvoth, you will live, as is written, 'And you, who cleave to God, are alive today.' Similarly,*

40. Sifrei *ad loc.*

*it is stated in Mishlei, 'Hold on to mussar; do not release it. Guard it; for it is your life.'"*[41]

*Tzitzith* is thus compared to a rope cast out to a drowning man. Life, or death, is dependent upon this cord. The pivotal nature of *tzitzith* is reminiscent of the ultimatum delivered to the Jewish People at Mount Sinai.

אִם אַתֶּם מְקַבְּלִים הַתּוֹרָה מוּטָב. וְאִם לָאו שָׁם תְּהֵא קְבוּרַתְכֶם.

*If you will accept Torah, well and good. If you refuse, there shall you be buried.*[42]

Torah is the key to Eternal life; failure to observe its commands is not considered merely as a state of neutrality. Rather, rejection of Torah consigns one to death.

Thus we find:

**אֲנִי ה' אֱלֹקֵיכֶם אֲשֶׁר הוֹצֵאתִי אֶתְכֶם מֵאֶרֶץ מִצְרַיִם לִהְיוֹת לָכֶם לֵאלֹקִים, אֲנִי ה' אֱלֹקֵיכֶם.**

*I am the Eternal, your God, Who took you out of the land of Mitzrayim, to act for you as God; I am the Eternal, your God.*[43]

Rashi elaborates upon these words:

שֶׁלֹּא יֹאמְרוּ יִשְׂרָאֵל מִפְּנֵי מָה אָמַר הַמָּקוֹם, לֹא שֶׁנַּעֲשָׂה וְנִטֹּל שָׂכָר, אָנוּ לֹא עוֹשִׂים וְלֹא נוֹטְלִים שָׂכָר, עַל כָּרְחֲכֶם אֲנִי מַלְכְּכֶם. וְכֵן הוּא אוֹמֵר אִם לֹא בְּיָד חֲזָקָה וגו' אֶמְלֹךְ עֲלֵיכֶם.

*This is to counter the argument of those who make the following rationale:*

*"We are commanded to perform the mitzvoth, and will receive reward for our deeds. Let us not perform the actions, and we will not receive the reward."*

*The response: God is our King, independent of one's individual will. God rules over us with a strong Hand.*[44]

---

41. *Bemidbar Rabbah* 17:9.
42. *Shabbath* 88a.
43. *Bemidbar* 15:41.
44. Rashi *ad loc.*

Desisting from fulfilling the dictates of the Torah is not a legitimate pathway. That which is not positively good, that which is not pulsating with life, does not remain in a state of limbo, but rather, is cast into the throes of destruction and death. Without grasping the rope, the stormy waves and fierce undercurrent drag one under the water.

The comparison of the mitzvoth to a rope is apt indeed, as it contains a further analogy. One who shakes a rope at one end sends ripples down the entire length of the cord, thus affecting the other end of the rope. The *Tosefoth Chaim* states that קְדֻשָּׁה, sanctity, comes to a person כְּשַׁלְשֶׁלֶת וְחֶבֶל, like a chain or a rope.

> עִנְיַן הִתְעוֹרְרוּת הַקְדֻשָּׁה הוּא עַל דֶּרֶךְ שֶׁהוּא עִם נִשְׁמָתוֹ כְּשַׁלְשֶׁלֶת וְחֶבֶל גְּדוֹלָה נוֹעֲצָה וּתְחוּבָה בְּקָצֶה אֶחָד לְמַטָּה וְקָצֶה הַשֵּׁנִי נָעוּץ וְתָחוּב וּמְקֻשָּׁר בְּרוּם הָעוֹלָמוֹת בְּשֹׁרֶשׁ הַשָּׁרָשִׁים שֶׁמִּצַּד זֶה כְּשֶׁיִּתְנוֹעֵעַ הַחֶבֶל בַּקָּצֶה הַתַּחְתּוֹן לְמַטָּה עַל כָּרְחָךְ יִתְנַעְנְעוּ כָּל חֶלְקֵי הַחֶבֶל עַד לְמַעְלָה שֹׁרֶשׁ הַשָּׁרָשִׁים כְּמוֹ כֵן ג״כ כְּשֶׁהוּא מִתְפַּלֵּל בְּכַוָּנָה מְעוֹרֵר הַקְּדֻשָּׁה דְּשָׁם כִּמְשַׁל הַשַּׁלְשֶׁלֶת.[45]

The top of the rope is bound up with the most lofty and sublime of all the worlds which exist. When the rope is moved at the bottom, the oscillations travel to the top of the rope. An example of this process is wholehearted prayer, which animates the קְדֻשָּׁה of many worlds.

Surrounding planet Earth are millions and millions of stars and planets, each taking their place in galaxies beyond our own. Each star is thousands of light years away, and is of proportions that are unimaginable. Staring out at the night sky, we ponder the purpose of the canopy above our heads. Everything physical is a reflection and crystallisation of a spiritual reality. In the spiritual realm, the number of worlds which exist is innumerable. This provides a hint pertaining to the potency of man's actions. Every deed of mortal, corporeal man affects every one of these worlds. Every action shakes the rope that begins in this world; its ripples traverse the spiritual spheres.

---

45. *Tosefoth Chaim* on *Chayei Adam*, *Hilchoth Tefillah*, Section 20.

The awesome impact of every deed hinges upon one vital factor. The action must be performed with exactitude; one must meticulously fulfill every condition and stipulation attached to the particular mitzvah in which one is engaged. The length of the *tzitzith* string must comply with requirements laid down by our Sages. The knots upon the cord must mirror the specifications of halachah.

Rabbi Dessler illustrates the pivotal nature of this principle with the following parable. The setting: a German village, overrun by Russian soldiers during the First World War. For the first time, primitive Russian soldiers are exposed to German technological advancements. The Russian soldier sees how, by simply turning a tap in a wall, a stream of water gushes forth. Seeking to alleviate the laborious drudgery involved in hoisting water up from a well, the Russian soldier detaches a tap from the wall and adds it to the booty with which he will return home. Excitedly showing off his prize upon his arrival in Russia, the soldier attaches the tap to the wall, and turns the faucet. Of course, nothing issues forth from the tap.

Simply attaching a tap to a wall is a futile activity. Behind the tap there are numerous pipes and complex plumbing; an entire system hidden from sight. Without this infrastructure, no water is forthcoming. Wearing *tzitzith* without knots, *tzitzith* of the incorrect color or material, can be compared to attempting to insert a tap into a brick wall. The numerous details and stipulations, the plumbing system, must all be present and in place for the life-giving liquid to flow. Only if all the details of a mitzvah are in place is one firmly gripping the end of this rope, a rope leading to the heights of Heaven.

Returning to our original subject, the *Sifrei* explains the phrase, אַחֲרֵי לְבַבְכֶם וְאַחֲרֵי עֵינֵיכֶם — "After your heart and after your eyes," to mean that all depends upon the yearnings of one's heart. Even a blind man is able, therefore, to transgress. Rashi's comment, however, presents a different picture — the heart following the eyes along the road to sin. The two opinions can be reconciled in light of the following insight:

The visions one perceives stem from one's heart. In both its negative and positive manifestations, it is the heart that determines the sights one will encounter. Let us investigate this further.

וּרְאִיתֶם אֹתוֹ. תַּנֵּי בְּשֵׁם ר׳ מֵאִיר, וּרְאִיתֶם אוֹתָם אֵין כְּתִיב כָּאן, אֶלָּא וּרְאִיתֶם אֹתוֹ. מַגִּיד שֶׁכָּל הַמְקַיֵּם מִצְוַת צִיצִית כְּאִלּוּ מְקַבֵּל פְּנֵי שְׁכִינָה. מַגִּיד שֶׁהַתְּכֵלֶת דּוֹמָה לַיָּם, וְהַיָּם לָעֲשָׂבִים, וַעֲשָׂבִים לָרָקִיעַ וְרָקִיעַ לְכִסֵּא הַכָּבוֹד.

*R. Meir highlights a grammatical discrepancy in the above phrase,* וּרְאִיתֶם אֹתוֹ *— "and you shall see Him." The singular form is here used, not the expected* וּרְאִיתֶם אוֹתָם *— "and you shall see them" [referring to mitzvoth]. An important lesson is hereby being conveyed: one who fulfills this commandment is considered to have received the Divine Presence.*[46]

The blue thread of *tzitzith* is reminiscent of the sea, which reminds one of the vegetation, and one is in turn reminded of the heavens and the Throne of Glory. Thus will one "behold" the Divine Presence.

There is one stipulation which is critical to the effectiveness of this line of association. An indomitable desire to achieve closeness with the Almighty must pulsate within. It is our forefather Avraham who taught us this lesson when he emerged victorious from the war against the Four Kings. Concerning the spoils, Avraham made an emphatic declaration, addressing the King of Sedom:

**אִם מִחוּט וְעַד שְׂרוֹךְ נַעַל וְאִם אֶקַּח מִכָּל אֲשֶׁר לָךְ וְלֹא תֹאמַר אֲנִי הֶעֱשַׁרְתִּי אֶת אַבְרָם.**

*[I will not keep] even a thread or shoelace, nor will I take anything of yours, [so that] so you will not [be able to] say, "I made Avram rich."*[47]

We see the consequences of Avraham's behaviour:

דָּרַשׁ רָבָא בִּשְׂכַר שֶׁאָמַר אַבְרָהָם אָבִינוּ אִם מִחוּט וְעַד שְׂרוֹךְ נַעַל זָכוּ בָּנָיו לב׳ מִצְווֹת, חוּט שֶׁל תְּכֵלֶת וּרְצוּעָה שֶׁל תְּפִלִּין.

46. *Yerushalmi Berachoth* 1:5, 2.
47. *Bereishith* 14:23.

*In the merit of Avraham's refusal to benefit from even a thread or shoelace, his descendants merited the mitzvoth of tzitzith and tefillin.*[48]

As explained above, the power of association contained within the *tzitzith* is only effective for one who is anxious to become close to the Almighty. One who eagerly awaits a guest will associate even the sound of the wind clanging the garden gate with the guest's arrival. One who yearns for closeness to God will develop a pathway of association to the extent that even the blue thread of the *tzitzith* reminds him of his Creator. Avraham refused the riches offered to him by the King of Sedom. It was his renunciation of materialism which indicates his intense desire to attain closeness to God.

Our Sages write that when standing in prayer, one who desires wisdom should turn south. One who yearns for riches should turn north. It is noteworthy that the attainment of both these geographical positions simultaneously is impossible. If one is turning north, one is facing away from the south, and vice versa. In the spiritual realm too, materialistic desires and the yearning to achieve closeness with one's Creator are mutually exclusive wishes. As much as one is pulled in one direction, one is removed from the other. Avraham said, not even a thread or a shoelace. His rejection of material goods demonstrates that his yearning was directed solely towards spiritual riches. He showed himself as a dedicated servant of the Almighty. Had he been involved in the physical world for its own sake, the blue thread, *techeleth*, would be ineffectual, for the relevant associations would not be entertained. However, after demonstrating the spiritual focus of his life, Avraham revealed himself as a fitting candidate to be the recipient of this mitzvah.

Every member of our nation possesses an innate purity. Latent spiritual strengths are within each Jew, resulting from the incredible stature and discipline of our forefathers. זְכוּת אָבוֹת, the merit of our forefathers, can be invoked in a plea for Heavenly mercy, due to our own spiritual potential and ability to raise ourselves to incredible

48. *Sotah* 17a.

heights, regardless of our present lowly station. There have been times in our history, however, when the Jewish People have been so entrenched in sin that this spiritual potential has been paralyzed, almost to the point of inaccessibility. At this point, one needs an external stimulation to pierce through the mire which has encrusted the heart, and thereby reanimate the strengths which lie dormant.

Fulfillment of mitzvoth with care and exactitude acts as an arrow; penetrating the external crust and releasing the abundant goodness within. Every action which man performs as a result of God's command engenders an increased closeness to Him. Accompanying the Almighty through one's deeds breeds increased contact with one's inner core of Godliness.

However, a prerequisite for this course of behaviour is the direction of one's vision. As Rashi describes, הָעַיִן רוֹאָה — "the eye sees." It glimpses an opportunity to fulfill a mitzvah, and only then does the action follow. Performance of this action bestirs the heart, rousing one's deepest desires and loftiest aspirations. Finally we reach the stage of וְהַלֵּב חוֹמֵד — "the heart desires."

Once this point is attained, once the purity inherent in the Jew has come once again to the fore, the process reverses its course. This is the order prescribed by the *Sifrei*, and by the verse itself. The heart, now animated, assumes the role of directing the vision of the eyes. One's sight will now exclusively be focused upon the correct things. The words, וְלֹא תָתוּרוּ אַחֲרֵי לְבַבְכֶם וְאַחֲרֵי עֵינֵיכֶם, can now be rendered, "and you will not stray after your heart and after your eyes."

The *tzitzith*, when donned, provide a man with profound aid in spiritual growth. Through adhering to every halachic detail of the mitzvah, the sin which encrusts man's heart can be penetrated, leaving him with unadulterated life, untainted purity throbbing within. His true yearnings have been determined, and with this clarity, the blue color of the *techeleth* will prompt him to attain heights in the service of God. The correct line of association will be entertained; the knock at the door is the only sound for which he longs.

As long as man retains his state of purity, it would be accurate to state, אַחֲרֵי לְבַבְכֶם וְאַחֲרֵי עֵינֵיכֶם — "after your heart and after your eyes," in that order. It is only resulting from a defective or negative desire that one falls into the trap of sin. When in that state of impurity, a process of "the eye sees and the heart desires," is required, by which positive external vision — catching sight of the chance to perform a mitzvah — provides the impetus for the heart to regain sensitivity.

Here we see the effects of vision to be life-giving. But vision can also propel a person further down a slippery slope which he has begun descending. Once the pure light of the heart is already obscured by grasping shadows, the darkness can easily be magnified. Negative sights have the ability to awaken the perverseness which man may possess, thus thickening the shell which is developing around, and obscuring his innate goodness.

There is no person in this world who is completely embroiled in sin, as there is no person in the world who is unimpeachable in his actions. Lying within each person is both light and dark, both good and evil. Sight has the power to activate either one of these two elements. The consequences of this stimulation are awesome, rippling up the rope, and affecting every spiritual sphere. Putrid night — death — could result. Alternatively, an incandescent light, and life, could result from one's action. One could be dragged under the waves, or one could be hauled into safety's grasp. All hangs upon the rope; all depends upon where one chooses to direct his eyes.

In today's society, we are constantly being bombarded by sights antithetical to Torah values. We are in possession of eyes which scout, spy, and discern that which is present around us. The outer evil is potent in arousing the negativity that lies within a person, stimulating a desire for that which is incorrect, rendering the body as the agent to perpetrate sin.

Guarding one's eyes from negativity is thus a vital area of exertion in one's Divine service. The faculty of vision should rather be nurtured in its positive manifestation. Reading Torah works, studying words of holiness, observing people of spiritual greatness; all these penetrate the crust of the heart, and arouse a true desire: the desire for truth. In turn, our sight will follow our wishes, leading to the ultimate וּרְאִיתֶם אֹתוֹ, as we behold the light of goodness, of spirituality, of the Divine Presence.

The greater the danger of falling in this area, the greater the reward received for the measures taken against stumbling. The preservation of pure sight in a generation such as the one in which we live has unimaginable repercussions. One good action influences innumerable spiritual spheres, as the ripples, initiated below, travel along the rope reaching the highest realm. Grasping this cord, clinging to it with all one's strength, shields one from the fierce waves of the ocean, which constantly threaten to engulf a person. Clinging to this cord bestows one with life.

The cord of the *tzitzith*, fashioned according to the hallowed words of our Sages, provides us with real sight. We clutch the cord, and the goodness it arouses within leads us on the avenue to real existence. Our yearning is for perfection, for wholesome fulfillment of the Torah's requirements. We thus merit that which is immeasurable, that which is outside our realm of experience. We merit the vision of ultimate perfection.

# Korach

Evident in this *parashah* is the devastating result of conflict. It remains to be discovered, however, why such harsh consequences are appropriate for the apparently minor crime of arguing with one's fellow.

Let us recall the incident to which we are referring:

**וַיֵּעָלוּ מֵעַל מִשְׁכַּן קֹרַח דָּתָן וַאֲבִירָם מִסָּבִיב וְדָתָן וַאֲבִירָם יָצְאוּ נִצָּבִים פֶּתַח אָהֳלֵיהֶם וּנְשֵׁיהֶם וּבְנֵיהֶם וְטַפָּם... וַתִּפְתַּח הָאָרֶץ אֶת פִּיהָ וַתִּבְלַע אֹתָם וְאֶת בָּתֵּיהֶם וְאֵת כָּל הָאָדָם אֲשֶׁר לְקֹרַח וְאֵת כָּל הָרְכוּשׁ.**

*They withdrew from next to the dwellings of Korach, Dathan and Aviram, all around, and Dathan and Aviram had come out, standing [defiantly] at the entrance of their tents, with their wives, children and infants... The earth opened its mouth and swallowed them and their households, as well as all the people who belonged to Korach['s household], and all [their] property.*[49]

Rashi questions the seemingly unfair suffering of innocent victims which this punishment entailed:

וּנְשֵׁיהֶם וּבְנֵיהֶם וְטַפָּם. בָּא וּרְאֵה כַּמָּה קָשָׁה הַמַּחֲלֹקֶת, שֶׁהֲרֵי בָּתֵּי דִּין שֶׁל מַטָּה אֵין עוֹנְשִׁין אֶלָּא עַד שֶׁיָּבִיא שְׁתֵּי שְׂעָרוֹת, וּבֵית דִּין שֶׁל מַעְלָה עַד עֶשְׂרִים שָׁנָה, וְכָאן אָבְדוּ אַף יוֹנְקֵי שָׁדַיִם.

*Come and consider the severity of dispute. An earthly court does not punish until one has reached the age of twelve or thirteen, and the Heavenly court does not punish until the transgressor reaches the age of twenty. Yet in this instance even babies perished.*[50]

---

49. *Bemidbar* 16:27–32.
50. Rashi *ad loc.*

Thus Rashi attributes the suffering and punishment of the wives and children who were uninvolved in the crime to the gravity of the dispute. Yet the question remains: why were innocent children punished because their fathers kindled this destructive fire?

Rabbi Chaim Shmuelevitz addresses this question with a principle born out of a verse in *Devarim*.

**פֶּן יֵשׁ בָּכֶם שֹׁרֶשׁ פֹּרֶה רֹאשׁ וְלַעֲנָה.**

*Perhaps there is amongst you a root sprouting gall and wormwood.*[51]

רמב"ן — אוֹ פֶּן יֵשׁ בָּכֶם שֹׁרֶשׁ רַע שֶׁיִּפְרֶה וְיִשְׂגֶּה וּבַיָּמִים הַבָּאִים יוֹצִיא פְּרָחִים רָעִים וְיַצְמִיחַ מְרוֹרוֹת וְזֶה עַל אֲשֶׁר אֵינֶנּוּ פֹּה הַיּוֹם כִּי הָאָב שֹׁרֶשׁ וְהַבֵּן נֶצֶר מִשָּׁרָשָׁיו יִפְרֶה.[52]

To paraphrase the Ramban:

*A bad root matures and eventually bitter and evil buds develop. A father is the root and a child, whether good or bad, is the inevitable result of the seed planted.*

There are many sins one can commit where the children are not punished for their parents' deeds. However, כַּמָּה קָשָׁה הַמַּחֲלֹקֶת — contention is the notable exception. For something lies at the root of strife which incontrovertibly leads to the sprouting of "gall and wormwood" in subsequent generations. Thus, even babies were involved in the terrible punishment of Korach and his congregation. In what way does the sin of dispute differ from other transgressions? Why must later generations necessarily be affected?

In an attempt to glimpse just some of the unfathomable depths of this topic, we must study the explanation of the Maharal on the following *mishnah*.

הִלֵּל וְשַׁמַּאי קִבְּלוּ מֵהֶם. הִלֵּל אוֹמֵר הֱוֵי מִתַּלְמִידָיו שֶׁל אַהֲרֹן, אוֹהֵב שָׁלוֹם וְרוֹדֵף שָׁלוֹם אוֹהֵב אֶת הַבְּרִיּוֹת וּמְקָרְבָן לַתּוֹרָה.

51. *Devarim* 29:17.
52. Ramban *ad loc*.

*Hillel used to say, "Be of the disciples of Aharon; love peace and pursue it...."*[53]

מהר"ל — הִלֵּל וְשַׁמַּאי קִבְּלוּ מֵהֶם. אֵלּוּ הֵם הַזּוּג הַחֲמִישִׁי בָּאוּ לְלַמֵּד מוּסָר עַל עִקָּר גָּדוֹל. כִּי הָעוֹלָם הַזֶּה מְסֻגָּל לְמַחֲלֹקֶת בְּיוֹתֵר מִכָּל הַדְּבָרִים שֶׁבָּעוֹלָם. כִּי זֶה עִנְיַן העוה"ז שֶׁהוּא עוֹלַם הַפֵּרוּד וְהַחִלּוּק, לְכָךְ הַמַּחֲלֹקֶת רָגִיל בָּעוֹלָם. וְדָבָר זֶה תּוּכַל לְהָבִין כִּי בְּאוֹתוֹ יוֹם שֶׁנִּבְרָא הָעוֹלָם בָּא הַמַּחֲלֹקֶת לְעוֹלָם מִן קַיִן וְהֶבֶל, שֶׁמִּזֶּה תִּרְאֶה כִּי הַמַּחֲלֹקֶת מְסֻגָּל לָעוֹלָם הַזֶּה, בַּעֲבוּר כִּי העוה"ז הוּא עוֹלַם הַחִלּוּק וְהַפֵּרוּד.

*Dissension is a feature of this earthly world. This world, by its very nature, is a place of division and dissension, and it is for this reason that friction is so prevalent. This is demonstrated at the very beginning of time, where the devastation caused by argument is manifest in the feud between Kayin and Hevel. This primordial conflict is an expression of the divisive nature of this world.*[54]

The Maharal continues, explaining why this world must by nature be prone to schism.

*We are exhorted to "love peace" and "pursue peace." "Loving peace" refers to the prevention of argument. "Pursuing peace" involves exerting oneself and pursuing after peace once one has become embroiled in argument. For when one becomes involved in a feud, it automatically distances one from his fellow. When one is distant from something, it is necessary to actively run after it to obtain the desired goal.*

*The ability to restore peace is so characteristic of* קְדֻשָּׁה*, holiness, that* שָׁלוֹם*, peace, is one of God's Names. Since* קְדֻשָּׁה *lies in the spiritual realm, outside the constraints of time, peacemaking must be undertaken with instant pursuit as befits this spiritual endeavour.*

*Just as we are exhorted not to allow matzah,* מַצָּה*, to leaven, so our Sages warn against allowing our mitzvoth,* מִצְוֹת*, to become affected by the passage of time. A mitzvah*

53. *Pirkei Avoth* 1:12.
54. *Derech Chaim* 1:12.

*is essentially a sublime and Godly thing; it should therefore not be tethered to this lowly, time-bound world, but should be performed in the smallest amount of time possible. Therefore we pursue peace in a quick action that transcends time. It is this concept of underlying spiritual unity that lies at the root of the idea of* שָׁלוֹם.

Let us turn to *Bereishith* to try and fathom the words of the Maharal:

**וַיֹּאמֶר אֱלֹקִים יְהִי מְאֹרֹת בִּרְקִיעַ הַשָּׁמַיִם לְהַבְדִּיל בֵּין הַיּוֹם וּבֵין הַלָּיְלָה...**

*God said, "[The] luminaries shall be positioned in the sky of the heavens to separate between day and night."*[55]

רש"י — יְהִי מְאֹרֹת. מִיּוֹם רִאשׁוֹן נִבְרְאוּ וּבָרְבִיעִי צִוָּה עֲלֵיהֶם לְהִתָּלוֹת בָּרָקִיעַ וְכֵן כָּל תּוֹלְדוֹת שָׁמַיִם וָאָרֶץ נִבְרְאוּ מִיּוֹם רִאשׁוֹן וְכָל אֶחָד וְאֶחָד נִקְבַּע בַּיּוֹם שֶׁנִּגְזַר עָלָיו.[56]

Rashi explains that everything was created in potential on the first day. Each creation was then given its own specific place on the day decreed. For example, the luminaries were created upon the advent of the first utterance, "בְּרֵאשִׁית." However, they only became manifest in the world on the fourth day.

Before Creation, everything was a unified oneness. With the advent of the world and Creation, with the advent of time, the world was divided into ordered parts: day one, day two, etc. Time necessarily shattered unity. Past, present, future — time is the division into sections and subsections. Now, in a world of minutes and hours, division reigns supreme. Divisiveness and schism are thus inextricably bound to the essence of the world. One aspect of the ultimate Oneness of the Almighty is described as לְמַעְלָה מִן הַזְּמַן — God transcends time; He must transcend time. Time is a creation, God the Creator.

---

55. *Bereishith* 1:14.
56. Rashi *ad loc.*

Rabbi Dessler illustrated this idea with a graphic parable. A map of the world is hanging on the wall, obscured by a piece of cardboard. A small hole has been punched in the cardboard. Moving the cardboard along the map from right to left changes the position of the hole and allows various cities to move into view: Delhi, Jerusalem, New York, San Francisco. Each city is seen in isolation, and the card is then moved on to the next city, sequentially, as we move along the map from right to left. Remove the card, uncover the map, and everything is seen simultaneously. There is no first, there is no last. There just is. There are no parts; all is a unified oneness.

As earthly beings, we live within the constraints of time. Like the sequence of cities seen on the map, we see moment of existence after moment of existence after moment of existence. We see the world, and time as an intrinsic part of that world. We do not perceive a unified whole, but many parts following one after the other at great speed.

God, however, sees the world without the cardboard covering. Everything is viewed simultaneously, rendering past and future, before and after, irrelevant. From a transcendent perspective, the world is a continuous unity.

Everything in the physical world is naturally drawn after that feature intrinsic to the world: time. A mitzvah performed slowly and laboriously is a deed performed in the physical realm and as such, it is confined to the world of physicality. Conversely, to perform a commandment with zeal and alacrity is to connect with the spiritual realm which operates on a level above time. Thus we can understand the Rabbinic dictum: מִצְוָה הַבָּאָה לְיָדְךָ אַל תַּחְמִיצֶנָּה — "If a mitzvah comes your way do not tarry in its performance (literally, do not let it become leaven)." For spiritual nourishment reflects physical substance. A delay in the preparation of matzah, מַצָּה, causes an expansion of the physical, rendering it invalid. So too when a mitzvah, מִצְוָה, is delayed, it expands into the physical realm, no longer connecting the performer with the spiritual world he strives to reach.

This world then, is inherently divided into factions, sections, and parts. The seeds with which this world is sown are the essence of strife; schism is the fabric of the universe. The opposite of this is unity or שָׁלוֹם — "peace" which, at root, is the other side of the same coin. No wonder then that one of God's Names is שָׁלוֹם. The more unified an entity, the more harmonious its existence, the closer it is to the spiritual world, to God's infinite Oneness.

It is our lofty task to assemble the pieces, to unify the factions, to live within time's finite subsections yet raise ourselves and our deeds to the level of timeless harmony. It is this which brings the entire world close to the ultimate Oneness of God.

We find in our *parashah*:

**זֹאת עֲשׂוּ קְחוּ לָכֶם מַחְתּוֹת קֹרַח וְכָל עֲדָתוֹ.**

*[So now] do this: Korach and all his group — take for yourselves firepans.*[57]

רש"י — מָה רָאָה לוֹמַר לָהֶם כָּךְ? אָמַר לָהֶם: בְּדַרְכֵי הַגּוֹיִים יֵשׁ נִימוּסִים הַרְבֵּה וְכוּמָרִים הַרְבֵּה וְאֵין כֻּלָּם מִתְקַבְּצִים בְּבַיִת אֶחָד. אָנוּ אֵין לָנוּ אֶלָּא ה' אֶחָד, וְתוֹרָה אַחַת, וּמִזְבֵּחַ אֶחָד, וְכֹהֵן גָּדוֹל אֶחָד. וְאַתֶּם ר"נ אִישׁ מְבַקְשִׁים כְּהֻנָּה גְדוֹלָה?[58]

"What was Moshe's rationale in saying this to them?" Rashi asks. In other words, why was this specific test performed to determine whether or not Korach was correct in his claim to High Priesthood? He answers: Moshe told them that among the ways of the other nations there are many rites and numerous clergymen, who do not all gather together in one place of worship. In contrast, we have but one God, one Ark, one Torah, one altar, and one *Kohen Gadol*. Yet in this instance 250 men are seeking this office!

Korach and his congregation failed to understand that unity is the fulcrum upon which rests all of man's Divine service. It is all the numerous commandments and laws together which form one perfect, coherent system. Every component is vital — to achieve a perfect whole, not as an end in itself.

---

57. *Bemidbar* 16:6.
58. Rashi *ad loc.*

This is highlighted by the Maharal as he describes Aharon's unique role.

> *There was only one High Priest, and it was his task to connect and unite the people until they were one unified nation. It is thus fitting that Aharon was one who pursued peace, and mediated between dissenting parties: his task was to join the people together. A corollary of this was his subsequent drawing the people near to the Almighty through the sacrificial services.*

The seemingly irrelevant phrase in our *mishnah*, "Be of the disciples of Aharon," is elucidated as we consider the implications of being a student of the premier peacemaker.

We also understand the severity of dispute and its inevitable place in the world. Dissension was the vital ingredient in the recipe of creation; it is the essence of the physical world. As such, it diametrically opposes our spiritual calling to unify every part of the world and our lives. By its very nature, this world is one of disparate parts and everything contained therein is pulled apart from all directions, splintered into tantalising shards. When this divisive root entwines itself around one's heart, a person's children and all their descendants will inevitably be affected. Being part of this world, they will have to endure the physicality that has already began to sprout.

The foundation of our spiritual struggle is to stand against the dissension which lies at the foundation of the world. Thus we can understand why וְאָהַבְתָּ לְרֵעֲךָ כָּמוֹךָ, loving one's fellow as oneself, is a כְּלָל גָּדוֹל, a "cardinal rule" of the Torah that includes all of one's spiritual work.

The Maharal continues most beautifully.

> וּכְמוֹ שֶׁהָיָה אַהֲרֹן עוֹבֵד עֲבוֹדַת יִשְׂרָאֵל לְהָבִיא הַטּוֹב עַל יְדֵי הַקָּרְבָּנוֹת, וְלֹא יָבִיא טוֹב לְאֶחָד רַק עַל יְדֵי מִי שֶׁהוּא אוֹהֵב אוֹתוֹ וּמְבַקֵּשׁ טוֹבָתוֹ. וּלְפִיכָךְ אַהֲרֹן בְּוַדַּאי אוֹהֵב אֶת יִשְׂרָאֵל. וְעוֹד, אֵיךְ יִהְיֶה מְקַשֵּׁר וּמְחַבֵּר אֶת הַבְּרִיּוֹת עַד שֶׁהֵם עַם אֶחָד אִם הוּא בְּעַצְמוֹ אֵינוֹ מְקֻשָּׁר עִמָּהֶם עַד שֶׁיִּהְיֶה אוֹהֵב אֶת הַבְּרִיּוֹת?

> *And similarly, we see that Aharon performed the sacrificial service on behalf of Yisrael, to bring good to them through the sacrifices, and good will only be brought about to a person through someone who loves him and is seeking his benefit. And therefore Aharon may certainly be called a lover of Yisrael. More than this, how could he bring people together and unite them into one nation if he himself were not bound to them to the point of loving them all?*

Korach wanted to be a High Priest, yet he failed to understand the implications of this role. He was correct in one respect however: we must all become High Priests, it being our sacred task to connect with our fellow man, seeking only his good. It is thus that we will unite numerous disparate individuals into a whole — called "nation." It is thus that we will take "nation" and go on to unify all the physical features of the world by bringing them to their spiritual goal. It is thus that we will together take a flying leap into utopia, into a world of peace that lies above the dimension of time.

# CHUKATH

MOSHE'S ACT OF hitting, instead of speaking to, a rock, done for the purpose of prompting a flow of water to issue forth, might seem an insignificant aberration from God's command. The punishment for this deed seems disproportionate to the misdemeanor — Moshe is now fated to die without leading his flock into the Promised Land. The commentators suggest a number of different approaches through which we can understand the gravity of Moshe's deviation.

**וְלֹא הָיָה מַיִם לָעֵדָה... וַיָּרֶב הָעָם עִם מֹשֶׁה... וַיְדַבֵּר ה' אֶל מֹשֶׁה... קַח אֶת הַמַּטֶּה... וְדִבַּרְתֶּם אֶל הַסֶּלַע לְעֵינֵיהֶם וְנָתַן מֵימָיו... וַיִּקַּח מֹשֶׁה אֶת הַמַּטֶּה... וַיַּקְהִלוּ מֹשֶׁה וְאַהֲרֹן אֶת הַקָּהָל אֶל פְּנֵי הַסָּלַע וַיֹּאמֶר לָהֶם שִׁמְעוּ נָא הַמֹּרִים הֲמִן הַסֶּלַע הַזֶּה נוֹצִיא לָכֶם מָיִם. וַיָּרֶם מֹשֶׁה אֶת יָדוֹ וַיַּךְ אֶת הַסֶּלַע בְּמַטֵּהוּ פַּעֲמָיִם וַיֵּצְאוּ מַיִם רַבִּים וַתֵּשְׁתְּ הָעֵדָה וּבְעִירָם. וַיֹּאמֶר ה' אֶל מֹשֶׁה וְאֶל אַהֲרֹן יַעַן לֹא הֶאֱמַנְתֶּם בִּי לְהַקְדִּישֵׁנִי לְעֵינֵי בְּנֵי יִשְׂרָאֵל לָכֵן לֹא תָבִיאוּ אֶת הַקָּהָל הַזֶּה אֶל הָאָרֶץ אֲשֶׁר נָתַתִּי לָהֶם.**

*But [then] there was no water for the community, so they congregated against Moshe and Aharon. The people quarreled with Moshe... The Eternal then spoke to Moshe saying, "Take the staff and assemble the community — you [together] with Aharon, your brother -- and you shall speak to the rock in full view of [the people] and it will produce its water..." Moshe took the staff from [its place] before the Eternal, just as He had commanded him. Moshe and Aharon then assembled the congregation in front of the rock, and [Moshe] said to them, "Listen now, you fools! From this rock shall we bring forth water for you?!" Moshe then raised his hand and struck the rock twice with his staff. A great amount of water came out, and the community drank, and their animals [as well].*

*The Eternal then said to Moshe and Aharon, "Because you*

*did not believe in Me [and did not] sanctify Me in full view of the Children of Yisrael, you will therefore not bring this congregation to the land that I have given to them."*[59]

Reading this account of events, it is difficult to identify the sin which Moshe perpetrated. Rashi explains that the fault lay in Moshe's disobedience of God's word. Commanded to speak to the rock, he had no right to lift his staff and deliver a blow. Through this action, a sanctification of God's Name was forestalled. For, were the people to have received water through an act of speech, a moral lesson would have been conveyed to the Children of Yisrael. The nation would have witnessed an object performing its Creator's will voluntarily; threats and physical force rendered unnecessary. This lesson could have been extrapolated and applied to themselves, each person meditating on how his Creator's will should ideally be performed — not as a response to threats or violence, but with a willingness to obey even spoken commands. The potential for this heightened spiritual awareness was aborted upon the impact of staff on stone.

The Rambam takes a different stance to that of Rashi, suggesting that the sin lay in Moshe's exclamation of displeasure, and the derogatory term he applied to the Jewish People: "Listen now, you fools!"

Rabbeinu Chananel highlights a grammatical nuance which, in his view, encapsulates Moshe's sin. נוֹצִיא לָכֶם מָיִם — "Shall we bring forth water." With these words, Moshe suggests that he has some power through which water will be forthcoming. In a subtle way, Moshe attributes some strength to himself, somewhat equating himself with God, Who alone has the power to perform miracles and wonders.

Moshe hit the rock not once but twice. It is this action which the Ramban underlines as being Moshe's misdemeanor.

Let us recall a fundamental principle of Rav Dessler's which will guide us in elucidating this enigmatic episode. A multitude of different hues emanate from a single white light. Each color reveals

---

59. *Bemidbar* 20:2–3, 7, 9–12.

another dimension of the original white, for all were originally contained therein. To divorce the individual color from other colors would be to confine the all-encompassing white, failing to reveal all that the white contains, the multifarious hues therein. Similarly, taking each explanation divorced from every other confines the ultimate truth, not leading one to a full explanation, not leading one to discover the underlying white light from which every subtle tint emanates. To reach the fundamental truth, each piece of the jigsaw must be related to every other, thus completing the overall picture. Each explanation thus reveals another facet of one panorama, of one truth. Utilising this principle, let us construct the broader picture through a closer examination of the explanations recounted above.

The Ramban posits that Moshe's sin lay in hitting the rock twice:

> וְהָאֱמֶת כִּי הָעִנְיָן סוֹד גָּדוֹל מִסִּתְרֵי הַתּוֹרָה. כִּי בָּרִאשׁוֹנָה אָמַר לוֹ הִנְנִי עוֹמֵד לְפָנֶיךָ שָּׁם עַל הַצּוּר בְּחוֹרֵב, וְהִכִּיתָ בַצּוּר. יֹאמַר כִּי שְׁמוֹ הַגָּדוֹל עַל הַצּוּר בְּחוֹרֵב שֶׁהוּא כְּבוֹד ה' הָאֵשׁ הָאוֹכֶלֶת בְּרֹאשׁ הָהָר. וּבַעֲבוּר כֵּן לֹא הִכָּה אֶלָּא פַּעַם אַחַת וְיָצְאוּ מַיִם רַבִּים. אֲבָל בְּכָאן לֹא פֵּרֵשׁ לוֹ כֵּן וְהִסְכִּימוּ שְׁנֵיהֶם לְהַכּוֹת בַּצּוּר פַּעֲמַיִם. וְהִנֵּה זֶה חֵטְא. וְעַל כֵּן אָמַר לֹא הֶאֱמַנְתֶּם בִּי לָשׂוּם אֱמוּנָה בִּשְׁמִי. וּבָאֱמוּנָה יֵעָשֶׂה הַנֵּס.[60]

To paraphrase:

> *This matter contains great secrets. Originally, while at Chorev [Mount Sinai], the people requested water, and Moshe was instructed to hit the rock, a rock upon which was manifest the glory of God. Moshe hit the rock once, and an abundance of water issued forth. In our incident, Moshe was not informed of how many times he should strike the rock. Moshe and Aharon therefore concluded that they should hit the rock twice. This was their sin — they lacked complete faith in God, for had they had complete faith, a miracle would have transpired.*

Rabbi Bloch of the Telshe Yeshiva, explains this comment in his work *Shiurei Da'ath*. Water, streaming from a rock after one blow,

---

60. Ramban on *Bemidbar* 20:1.

will be recognised as the result of a miracle. In contrast, if a rock is struck twice, and only then does water gush forth, one is more inclined to believe that the force in hitting the rock was the cause of the life-sustaining flow. The miracle is thought to have been prompted by an outside factor, through the impact of staff upon stone.

With the following explanation of the Seforno, a new perspective of all of the above approaches to this incident is gained. In his explanation, Seforno delineates three categories of miracles.

> הא׳ הוּא נֵס נִסְתָּר, כְּמוֹ יְרִידַת הַמָּטָר וְהַהִמָּלֵט מִן הַחֳלָאִים וּמִן הַצָּרוֹת. וְזֶה הַמִּין מִן הַנִּסִּים יַשִּׂיגוּהוּ הַצַּדִּיקִים בִּתְפִלָּתָם כְּעִנְיַן "וַיִּתְפַּלֵּל אַבְרָהָם אֶל הָאֱלקִים וַיִּרְפָּא אֱלקִים אֶת אֲבִימֶלֶךְ", וְכֵן "וַיִּתְפַּלֵּל מֹשֶׁה בְּעַד הָעָם".
>
> והב׳ הוּא נֵס נִגְלֶה, לֹא יוּכַל הַטֶּבַע לַעֲשׂוֹתוֹ בְּאוֹתוֹ הָאֹפֶן. אֲבָל יַעֲשֵׂהוּ אַחַר תְּנוּעוֹת רַבּוֹת בְּמֶשֶׁךְ זְמַן. וְזֶה הַמִּין מִן הַנִּסִּים יַעֲשֵׂהוּ הַקֵּל יִת׳ עַל יְדֵי עֲבָדָיו עִם הַקְדָּמַת אֵיזוֹ תְּנוּעָה מְסֻדֶּרֶת מֵאִתּוֹ כְּעִנְיַן "הַשְׁלִיכֵהוּ אַרְצָה", "הָרֵם אֶת מַטְּךָ וְהִכִּיתָ בַצּוּר", "יְרֵה וַיּוֹר" וְזוּלָתָם.
>
> והג׳ הוּא מִין מִן הַנִּסִּים שֶׁלֹּא יוּכַל הַטֶּבַע לַעֲשׂוֹתוֹ בְּשׁוּם אֹפֶן, וְזֶה הַמִּין יַעֲשֶׂה הַקֵּל יִת׳ עַל יְדֵי עֲבָדָיו בְּדִבּוּר בִּלְבַד שֶׁהִיא פְּעֻלָּה שִׂכְלִית וְיוֹתֵר נִכְבֶּדֶת מִשְּׁאָר תְּנוּעוֹתָיו הַגַּשְׁמִיּוֹת. כְּמוֹ שֶׁהָיָה הָעִנְיָן בִּפְתִיחַת פִּי הָאָרֶץ כְּאָמְרוֹ "וַיְהִי כְּכַלּוֹתוֹ לְדַבֵּר וַתִּבָּקַע הָאֲדָמָה."[61]

To paraphrase:

*The first class of miracle is termed as hidden miracles. An example of this is rainfall, which appears to be a natural process, with no relation to prayer. Similarly, being cured of a malady can be viewed as a natural course of events, ignoring the fact that it is God Who is the True Healer.*

*The second type of miracle is clearly recognizable as such, not being obscured as in the previous category. However, this miracle will occur only after certain actions have been performed. An example of this type of miracle is found where Moshe's staff was transformed into a serpent — something which occurred only after Moshe had thrown it on the ground.*

---

61. Seforno on *Bemidbar* 20:8.

*Similarly Elisha, when performing the miracle of resuscitating a dead child, performed extensive actions resembling a normal method of resuscitation as precursor to the actual miracle.*

*The third type of miracle is open and manifest to all and is not preceded by any actions. Prior to its performance, however, an agent must speak.*

Among the three categories, a fundamental distinction can be discerned. When a miracle is obscured by the mask of nature, the onlookers do not recognise the miracle that has taken place, being unworthy of experiencing an open miracle. When a miracle is preceded by a physical action, the onlookers behold not only the greatness of the miracle, but they view the agent with an added awe and reverence, believing that the agent played some part in the extraordinary event. God desired that the water required at this point result from the third, not the second type of miracle. In this third case, no action is performed by the agent, and the people are awed directly by the greatness of God. If the water had resulted from the third type of miracle, the people would have been impressed by Him Who sent Moshe, Moshe himself having almost no part in the miracle. No additional respect for Moshe would be incumbent upon the nation as a result of the third type of miracle.

The Seforno elaborates, applying his principle to our incident. He states that Moshe and Aharon lacked complete conviction in the worthiness of the people to experience the third type of miracle, where no action at all is involved. The people had previously expressed their dissatisfaction with their station in the wilderness, and had expressed a yearning to return to the stagnant, putrid waters of Egypt. Moshe exclaimed, "Listen now, you fools!" He calculated that the people, having expressed this reprehensible desire, were not on a sufficiently high spiritual station to enable them to behold a miracle of this sublime nature. A recognition of the second type of miracle, one involving prior physical action, and the illusion that there is some power which is possessed by the agent, was congruous with their moral position. Some obscurity was required, a haziness to dim the sharp clarity and shining brilliance of an open miracle. Moshe hit the rock twice, creating the illusion that some part was played by the agent. However, for downgrading the clarity of the miracle, Moshe and Aharon were chastised by God, Who desired that the fuller sanctification of His Name be made, and that an unobscured miracle be performed.

The following illustration should serve to clarify this idea. A picture needs to be secured upon a wall with eight nails. A person enters a large room, the picture positioned on the opposite wall. The man taps the wall, and miraculously, the picture on the opposite wall is secured by the eight nails which are suddenly driven into the wall. A miracle! The whole happening is so supernatural, that whether a tap or a bang are employed by the person is irrelevant. A second scenario: The picture is waiting to be secured upon the wall by the eight nails. The man approaches the picture and bangs just one nail. Wondrously, all eight nails suddenly secure the picture firmly in place. The event is hailed as a marvel. But if the nail were struck twice with a hammer, the supernatural character of the event would be obscured to some degree. One could postulate that the picture was secured through the effective hitting of a nail. The physical action performed is thought to have some bearing on the event.

Through the explanation of the Seforno, the pieces already begin falling into place. Rashi's view, that Moshe's sin lay in striking instead of speaking to the rock, can now be comprehended with added profundity. With this action, Moshe changed the nature of the miracle, placing it into the second category of miracles (as detailed above), instead of the third. This fundamental change was effected due to Moshe's low estimation of the nation's spiritual standing.

The words, "Listen now, you fools," are highlighted by the Rambam as the cause of Moshe's punishment. Feeling that the higher class of miracle would not accord with the nation's spiritual level, Moshe reduced the event's overtly supernatural character and hit the rock, thus preceding the open miracle with a physical action. The view of the Rambam can thus be understood in conjunction with the words of Rashi.

Rabbeinu Chananel provides an additional dimension to the picture we are forming. נוֹצִיא לָכֶם מָיִם — "shall we bring forth water." Moshe here attributes to himself some power to produce water. Moshe played an active part in the miracle, in a manner deemed inappropriate by the Almighty. An allusion to this interpretation can be found in the words of the Seforno, as he describes the second category of miracles, in which an agent's actions precede the performance of a miracle.

The Ramban's interpretation, that Moshe's sin lay in hitting the rock twice, is but another hue emanating from the one white light. Hitting something twice, as opposed to once, leads one to believe that the actions of the agent have some bearing on the final outcome, thus cloaking the clarity of the miracle.

All four interpretations lie in the words of the Seforno; each, however, must be meditated upon with profundity, so that the complete picture is evident, so that the light is not reduced and confined. Until the complete picture is assembled, each opinion represents only part of the truth, only a shard of the true, magnificent construction.

At Chorev, Moshe hit the rock but once, as he was commanded, for the "glory of God" was manifest clearly on the rock. The nation, in possession of a superior capacity to behold spirituality, did not require the rock to be hit twice, nor did they deserve the title of "fools." An agent's participation was rendered superfluous. A tap on the wall at one side of the room was sufficient to drive eight nails into position, securing a picture suspended on the other side of the room.

It was because of his actions in the incident in our *parashah*, that Moshe was precluded from leading his flock into the Land of Israel. A distinction between the level of Moshe's leadership and the level upon which Yehoshua led the people while in the Promised Land, is clear from the following verses:

**וַיְהִי בִּהְיוֹת יְהוֹשֻׁעַ בִּירִיחוֹ וַיִּשָּׂא עֵינָיו וַיַּרְא וְהִנֵּה אִישׁ עֹמֵד לְנֶגְדּוֹ וְחַרְבּוֹ שְׁלוּפָה בְּיָדוֹ... וַיֹּאמֶר לֹא כִּי אֲנִי שַׂר צְבָא ה' עַתָּה בָאתִי וַיִּפֹּל יְהוֹשֻׁעַ אֶל פָּנָיו אַרְצָה וַיִּשְׁתָּחוּ וַיֹּאמֶר לוֹ מָה אֲדֹנִי מְדַבֵּר אֶל עַבְדּוֹ.**

*And it was, when Yehoshua was in Yericho, he lifted up his eyes and he saw, and behold, a man [in reality an angel] was standing opposite him, a drawn sword in his hand. And he said, "I am the prince of God's army, now have I come. Yehoshua fell upon his face, to the ground, and prostrated himself. He then asked [the angel], "What does my master tell his servant [to do]?"*[62]

רש"י — עַתָּה בָאתִי. לְעֶזְרָתְךָ. שֶׁאֵין אָדָם יָכוֹל לְהִלָּחֵם עָלֶיהָ וּלְתוֹפְשָׂהּ לְהַפִּיל הַחוֹמָה. אֲבָל בִּימֵי מֹשֶׁה רַבְּךָ בָּאתִי וְלֹא חָפֵץ בִּי, שֶׁנֶּאֱמַר "אִם אֵין פָּנֶיךָ הוֹלְכִים...".

*Now have I come: to help you... I came in the days of Moshe your teacher, and he did not desire me, as it says, "Unless You come Yourself...".*[63]

The incident to which the angel refers is recounted in *Shemoth:*

**וַיֹּאמַר פָּנַי יֵלֵכוּ וַהֲנִחֹתִי לָךְ. וַיֹּאמֶר אֵלָיו אִם אֵין פָּנֶיךָ הֹלְכִים אַל תַּעֲלֵנוּ מִזֶּה.**

*And He said, "My presence will accompany you."*
*And he (Moshe) said to Him (God), "Unless You come Yourself, do not bring us out of the wilderness."*[64]

Rashi elaborates:

לֹא אֶשְׁלַח עוֹד מַלְאָךְ אֲנִי בְּעַצְמִי אֵלֵךְ כְּמוֹ וּפָנֶיךָ הוֹלְכִים בְּקֶרֶב. וַיֹּאמֶר אֵלָיו — בָּזוֹ אֲנִי חָפֵץ כִּי ע"י מַלְאָךְ אַל תַּעֲלֵנוּ מִזֶּה.

*"I will not send an angel with you. I Myself will go..." And [Moshe] answered, "This do I desire — for if it will be through a messenger, do not take us out.*[65]

Moshe eschewed guidance through a messenger, requesting the direct supervision of the Almighty, and exclusively God's constant guidance. In contrast, Yehoshua accepted the aid which the angel

62. *Yehoshua* 5:13, 14.
63. Rashi *ad loc.*
64. *Shemoth* 33:14, 15.
65. Rashi *ad loc.*

offered, a level once removed from that which Moshe enjoyed. The guidance of Moshe can be said to mirror miracles which are prompted by speech; Yehoshua's leadership corresponded to the class of miracles which are preceded by physical action. Moshe spurned the possibility of seeing any power, even that of an angel, beside the all-encompassing might of the Creator.

However, in his action of hitting the rock, Moshe himself engineered a situation where an intermediary could be credited with playing some part in the unfolding events. His action, in his capacity as an agent, obscured God's direct guiding hand. Previously, Moshe had adamantly refused to lead the people on this lower level. It was after this incident, then, after hitting the rock twice and involving the illusory power of an agent in the performance of a miracle, that Moshe could no longer lead the people. His refusal to countenance any intermediary between God and the Jewish People excluded even him from acting as a mediator. It was Yehoshua, who agreed to the lower level of having an angel as an intermediary, who led the Jewish People over the Jordan into the Promised Land.

The power of messengers and intermediaries is illusory, and we, in our present-day society, must integrate this knowledge into our lives and attitudes. From our lowly perspective, we imagine that it is the agent, the doctor, who holds the key to health, not the True Healer. A humorous, yet penetrating, anecdote is told of a man who, childless for many years, approached a *rebbe* for a blessing. Unsatisfied with merely going to one *rebbe*, the man approached a second personality, asking him, too, to pray that he should be blessed with a child. During the course of the year, the man was indeed blessed with a child. Upon hearing the joyous news, the *chassidim* of each *rebbe* entered into a heated dispute, each group of *chassidim* believed that the child was bestowed because of the blessings of their leader. A Torah giant was consulted, someone whom the *chassidim* hoped would determine which *rebbe*'s blessing had borne fruit. The answer given was terse: "The man was given a child because of the blessing of the Almighty. Unfortunately, however, the Almighty does not have any *chassidim*!"

It is incumbent upon us to trace everything back to the One Source, discerning the Sender of the messenger, He Who is behind the agent. Although the presence of an agent may be necessary, the true Source of all blessing, of health, livelihood, and salvation, should never be obscured. May we merit to always behold the salvation of the Almighty, in its sparkling, gleaming clarity.

# BALAK

MOSHE WAS THE greatest of prophets — his ability to constantly speak to God was paralleled only by the evil Bil'am, who could request an audience with God at whim. Who was Bil'am? What was his evil philosophy? And how is it countered by the Jewish People?

**וַיָּקָם בִּלְעָם בַּבֹּקֶר וַיַּחֲבֹשׁ אֶת אֲתֹנוֹ וַיֵּלֶךְ עִם שָׂרֵי מוֹאָב. וַיִּחַר אַף אֱלֹקִים כִּי הוֹלֵךְ הוּא וַיִּתְיַצֵּב מַלְאַךְ ה' בַּדֶּרֶךְ לְשָׂטָן לוֹ וְהוּא רֹכֵב עַל אֲתֹנוֹ וּשְׁנֵי נְעָרָיו עִמּוֹ. וַתֵּרֶא הָאָתוֹן אֶת מַלְאַךְ ה' נִצָּב בַּדֶּרֶךְ וְחַרְבּוֹ שְׁלוּפָה בְּיָדוֹ וַתֵּט הָאָתוֹן מִן הַדֶּרֶךְ וַתֵּלֶךְ בַּשָּׂדֶה וַיַּךְ בִּלְעָם אֶת הָאָתוֹן לְהַטֹּתָהּ הַדָּרֶךְ.**

*Bil'am got up the [next] morning, saddled his she-donkey, and went with the nobles of Mo'av. God's rage was aroused because he was going [willingly], so an angel of the Eternal stood himself in the road to obstruct him; and he was riding on his she-donkey and his two lads were with him. The she-donkey saw the angel of the Eternal standing in the road with a drawn sword in his hand, so the she-donkey turned off the road and went into the field. Bil'am then hit the she-donkey to turn it [back] onto the road.*[66]

This incident occurred not just once. An angel appcared to Bil'am's donkey three times in the course of this journey. Rashi, who points out that three is not merely an arbitrary number, but carries profound significance, highlights this fact:

מָה רָאָה לַעֲמֹד בִּשְׁלֹשָׁה מְקוֹמוֹת? סִימָנֵי אָבוֹת הֶרְאָהוּ.

*Why did the angel stand in those three places? He showed him signs of the Patriarchs.*[67]

66. *Bemidbar* 22:21–23.

67. Rashi on *Bemidbar* 22:26.

Upon a cursory reading, the parallel seems to be appropriate; the mathematics is correct. However, analysing this statement on a deeper level, we remain perplexed. There must be some intrinsic connection between the Patriarchs and Bil'am's mission. In the course of this essay, we will investigate the depth of this parallel.

The story goes on. Bil'am repeatedly hits his donkey, until the donkey itself berates his master:

**וַיִּפְתַּח ה' אֶת פִּי הָאָתוֹן וַתֹּאמֶר לְבִלְעָם מֶה עָשִׂיתִי לְךָ כִּי הִכִּיתַנִי זֶה שָׁלֹשׁ רְגָלִים.**

*The Eternal then gave the she-donkey the power of speech and it said to Bil'am, "What have I done to you that you hit me on these three occasions?"*[68]

A close look at the text reveals something unusual. The word "פְּעָמִים," the expression most commonly used to mean "times," is replaced here by the word רְגָלִים, which also means "feet." Rashi explains the significance of this change:

רָמַז לוֹ: אַתָּה מְבַקֵּשׁ לַעֲקֹר אֻמָּה הַחוֹגֶגֶת שָׁלֹשׁ רְגָלִים בַּשָּׁנָה.

*The donkey hinted to him: Do you want to uproot a nation that rejoices at the three foot-festivals?*[69]

The donkey berates Bil'am, emphasizing the futility of attacking a nation which ascends to Jerusalem on foot three times a year, upon each of the major festivals. It seems that it is this mitzvah of making a pilgrimage to Jerusalem that affords the Jewish People special protection, shielding them from Bil'am's curses. Why is this particular mitzvah selected as the one whose merit will save the Jewish People from potential disaster?

Returning to the connection between Bil'am and the Patriarchs, we see that the parallel can be traced throughout the episode. Indeed, this is referred to by Bil'am himself. Although Bil'am, wielding much power and prestige, possessed many servants and underlings,

---

68. *Bemidbar* 22:28.

69. Rashi *ad loc.*

he insisted on preparing for this journey himself. The verse states, וַיַּחֲבֹשׁ אֶת אֲתֹנוֹ — "And he saddled his donkey." In his enthusiasm to curse the Jewish People, he delegated the task of saddling his donkey to no other, retaining the job for himself. This course of action demonstrates a profound truth, highlighted by our Sages.

מִכָּאן שֶׁהַשִּׂנְאָה מְקַלְקֶלֶת אֶת הַשּׁוּרָה, שֶׁחָבַשׁ הוּא בְּעַצְמוֹ. אָמַר הקב"ה, רָשָׁע, כְּבָר קְדָמְךָ אַבְרָהָם אֲבִיהֶם שֶׁנֶּאֱמַר וַיַּשְׁכֵּם אַבְרָהָם בַּבֹּקֶר וַיַּחֲבֹשׁ אֶת חֲמוֹרוֹ.

*From the fact that Bil'am personally saddled his donkey, we see that hatred defies logic. The Almighty said, "Wicked one, you have already been preceded by Avraham, of whom it is written, "Avraham arose early in the morning and saddled his donkey."*[70]

In the description of Bil'am's actions we hear an echo of the actions of Avraham. Centuries earlier, embarking on the famous mission to sacrifice his only son, Avraham arose early, enthusiastic to fulfill the will of His Creator, and personally saddled his donkey. Now Bil'am shows the same intense resolution in perpetrating his evil task.

Another correlation between Bil'am and Avraham is found in *Pirkei Avoth*. The Mishnah states:

כָּל מִי שֶׁיֵּשׁ בּוֹ שְׁלֹשָׁה דְבָרִים הַלָּלוּ הוּא מִתַּלְמִידָיו שֶׁל אַבְרָהָם אָבִינוּ, וּשְׁלֹשָׁה דְּבָרִים אֲחֵרִים הוּא מִתַּלְמִידָיו שֶׁל בִּלְעָם הָרָשָׁע...

*Whoever possesses these three virtues is of the disciples of our forefather Avraham, and [whoever possesses] these three opposite characteristics is of the followers of the wicked Bil'am.*[71]

Again we see how Avraham and Bil'am somehow stand directly opposed to each other. The ideology of Bil'am is the antithesis of the goodness epitomized by Avraham. Not only must we delve into these opposing personalities, we must also elucidate a difficulty in

70. Rashi on 22:21.
71. *Pirkei Avoth* 5:22.

the above Mishnah. The Mishnah does not directly contrast Avraham and Bil'am; instead it makes a comparison between Avraham and Bil'am's disciples. What lies behind this emphasis on disciples?

After a bizarre and eventful journey, Bil'am arrives at his destination. Before attempting to curse the Jewish People, however, Bil'am erects seven altars. This was not only a (paradoxical) plea for Divine assistance, but it also contained a hidden agenda.

שִׁבְעָה מִזְבְּחוֹת עָרַכְתִּי אֵין כְּתִיב כָּאן אֶלָּא אֶת שִׁבְעַת הַמִּזְבְּחֹת. אָמַר לְפָנָיו, אֲבוֹתֵיהֶם שֶׁל אֵלּוּ בָּנוּ לְפָנֶיךָ שִׁבְעָה מִזְבְּחוֹת, וַאֲנִי עָרַכְתִּי כְּנֶגֶד כֻּלָּן. אַבְרָהָם בָּנָה אַרְבָּעָה... וְיִצְחָק בָּנָה אֶחָד... וְיַעֲקֹב בָּנָה שְׁתַּיִם.

*Instead of, "I erected seven altars," the expression, "these seven altars" is used. Bil'am said, "The ancestors of the Jewish People erected seven altars (for Your glory), and I erected seven altars to counter theirs. Avraham built four... Yitzchak built one... Ya'akov built two.*[72]

Through our Sages' words, we can extend the above comparison. Not only do we see Bil'am as the antithesis of Avraham, but by building seven altars, he seems to stand against all three of our sublime Patriarchs.

The Talmud relates that our Sages originally wanted to include the *parashah* of Balak in our twice-daily recitation of the *Shema*, the fundamental declaration of our belief and allegiance to God. This was prompted by the pivotal nature of the verse:

**הֶן עָם כְּלָבִיא יָקוּם וְכַאֲרִי יִתְנַשָּׂא.**

*Here is a people that rises like a lioness, and like a lion, raises itself.*[73]

Rashi explains the underlying meaning of this enigmatic praise of the Children of Yisrael.

כְּשֶׁהֵן עוֹמְדִין מִשְּׁנָתָם שַׁחֲרִית, הֵן מִתְגַּבְּרִין כְּלָבִיא וְכַאֲרִי, לַחְטֹף אֶת הַמִּצְוֹות, לִלְבֹּשׁ צִיצִית לִקְרֹא אֶת שְׁמַע, וּלְהָנִיחַ תְּפִלִּין.

---

72. Rashi on *Bemidbar* 23:4.
73. *Bemidbar* 23:24.

*When they rise in the morning from sleeping, they strengthen themselves like a lioness and a lion, to eagerly snatch mitzvoth — to don tzitzith, to recite the Shema, and to put on tefillin.*[74]

To understand this praise, and its connection to Bil'am, in greater depth, we must first establish a fundamental principle.

Moshe is famed as the greatest of all prophets. His spiritual level was such that he was constantly able to receive prophecy, and could communicate directly with God. In Moshe, the Children of Yisrael enjoyed a formidable leader, one who could gently guide the people along the correct path, a path that was lofty indeed. A complaint, however, could arise; a challenge, a claim of injustice: The nations of the world could protest that if they too had been led by such a leader, if they too had been guided by a shepherd of such calibre, surely they would also have fulfilled God's will. The nations could claim that they had simply been deprived of such an opportunity.

The *Tanchuma* deals with this question, and in doing so quotes a verse in *Devarim*:

הַצּוּר תָּמִים פָּעֳלוֹ כִּי כָל דְּרָכָיו מִשְׁפָּט...

*[Though He is] the Rock, His actions are perfect, for all His ways are just.*[75]

God, being absolutely perfect, could never commit an injustice. All his actions are, by definition, flawless. However, the Almighty wanted to prevent any suspicion on the part of the nations that they had been subject to discrimination, that they been treated unfairly. They thus received the same spiritual opportunities as the Jewish People. Just as the Jewish People merited a leader of the calibre of Moshe, the nations of the world had Bil'am, one who could receive Divine communication at will. For the nations, however, this experiment soon backfired. While a Jewish leader spurs his flock on to spiritual growth, the prophets of the nations, immersed in filth and impurity, eventually lead their followers into the suffering of Divine retribution.

---

74. Rashi *ad loc.*
75. *Devarim* 32:4.

The *Tanchuma* thus informs us of the purpose of this episode, the moral lessons and outlook to be gleaned from this story. From the story of Bil'am we learn of the destruction that the prophets of the nations wreaked, and we understand why God removed His spirit from them.

Bil'am himself raised a question concerning the role of the nations of the world. The *Tanchuma* paraphrases the thrust of Bil'am's ideology:

לֹא נָאֶה לְךָ שֶׁתְּהֵא נֶעֱבָד מִשִּׁבְעִים אֻמּוֹת וְלֹא מִן אֻמָּה אַחַת?

*Would it not be preferable for You to be served by seventy nations, rather than just by one nation?*[76]

It is this question that underlies so many of Bil'am's actions. His philosophy: perfect closeness to God lies not only in the dominion of the Jewish People. In an attempt to prove his ideology, Bil'am repeatedly imitated the actions of our holy Patriarchs. He constructed seven altars, covertly declaring that he could achieve the same as, and be considered equal to, the three Patriarchs. Specifically, he sought to be the counterpart of Avraham, a personality who was the root and very foundation of the Jewish People. He arose early, he saddled his own donkey — his external actions can indeed be compared to those of Avraham. Both were individuals of tremendous spiritual power, both performed the same deeds — wherein lies the real difference between the two?

Analysing the actions of these two personalities more closely, we find that the essential distinction between Avraham and Bil'am is subtly indicated in the text itself. Avraham is described as riding עַל הַחֲמוֹר, upon the donkey, a phrase suggesting a certain dominance and rulership. The Maharal finds in the חֲמוֹר, the donkey, a symbol of materialism — חֲמְרִיּוּת, the donkey being an animal that can be said to harbour a certain obsession with physical pleasure. A new depth is thus seen in the words. Avraham saddled his donkey; he bridled materialism, harnessing it only for spirituality. This phrase is

76. *Tanchuma*, *Ha'azinu* 5.

not found concerning Bil'am, who instead of dominating and mastering this world, was gradually dragged into materialism's quagmire, into the quicksand of physicality.

On a universal level, Bil'am and Avraham can again be pitted against each other: Avraham representing the Children of Yisrael, a people dedicated to holiness and spirituality, Bil'am representing the gentile nations. The shining light of genuineness, the faithful expression of a rich inner life; these are the domain of the Jew. While Jew and non-Jew alike, while both Avraham and Bil'am, can perform the external action, the deed of the non-Jew lacks a quality that the Jew's action contains. A Jew's action is invested with purity, with the burning desire to constantly grow nearer to God, to fulfill His will. This rich inner life is a cherished inheritance, one bequeathed to us by our forefathers. A Jew's actions are performed with purity, for we possess a purity that our Patriarchs implanted within — זְכוּת הָאָבוֹת. Lacking this inner purity, a non-Jew's actions belong to the external realm, and are limited to the superficial world in which we live.

The *Avnei Nezer* puts the comparison between Jew and non-Jew into yet sharper focus. He explains that closeness to God, fulfillment of the purpose of the universe, is the basic desire of Jew and non-Jew alike. For the Jew, however, this yearning lies at the core of his being. He is therefore willing to inconvenience himself, to exert himself; he finds happiness in sacrificing himself and his possessions for the sake of God, and in the fulfillment of His will. Such intent is not necessarily readily observable. Even if its presence is noted, it is only God Who knows "the hidden secrets of the heart." Devotion could be merely a charade, a superficial show of righteousness. Outer actions can be devoid of inner content — shells, empty of true conviction and love. The truth, however, the real intentions behind one's deeds, is evident upon observing that which has been transmitted to the next generation, to children and disciples. It is children and students who are notoriously gifted with the ability to discern the true intent behind each action. It is they who choose, on the basis of their teacher's example, whether to follow in his footsteps, or reject his teachings.

כָּל מִי שֶׁיֵּשׁ בּוֹ שְׁלֹשָׁה דְּבָרִים הַלָּלוּ הוּא מִתַּלְמִידָיו שֶׁל אַבְרָהָם אָבִינוּ, וּשְׁלֹשָׁה דְּבָרִים אֲחֵרִים הוּא מִתַּלְמִידָיו שֶׁל בִּלְעָם הָרָשָׁע...

*Whoever possesses these three virtues is of the disciples of our forefather Avraham, and [whoever possesses] these three opposite characteristics is of the followers of the wicked Bil'am.*

Externally, Avraham and Bil'am both performed the same actions. The difference between them is the difference between Jew and gentile, the difference between a deed rich with inner depth, and an action that is merely an empty husk. And how can this difference be most readily observed? By examining the students of these two schools of thought, by observing how each personality's values are transmitted to the next generation.

Closeness to God is the aim of Jew and non-Jew alike. It is the expression of this desire that marks the divergence between the two. The Jew's will permeating his very being, he is willing to undergo inconvenience, suffering, and even death to uphold his belief. In contrast, possessing a comparatively superficial desire, the gentiles will serve only in situations that they deem appropriate, only at times in which service will not interrupt their set routine. Their aspiration can be likened to one who yearns to complete the study of the entire Talmud. For this mammoth task, he allows himself just one night — but on this night, he also wishes to have a good sleep!

Attaining closeness to God is a lifetime's work, a goal that takes constant effort, constant self-evaluation and improvement, to attain. While the gentiles desire the end result, they remain unwilling to expend the necessary effort; they desire the destination, while spurning the journey's exertion. The task of a Jew is to walk the path, follow its meandering lanes, even tolerating the sharp rocks on uneven ground — and to do this with a deep joy, for his eye is constantly focused on the glorious destination.

A manifestation of the lofty nature of the Jewish soul can be seen in the fulfillment of one particular mitzvah: the thrice-annual pilgrimage to Jerusalem. Every man is required to ascend to Jerusalem for each of the three foot-festivals: Pesach, Shavuoth and Sukkoth. When the Temple stood, the Jews thus left their homes and possessions vulnerable to attack by the surrounding enemies.

**וְלֹא יַחְמֹד אִישׁ אֶת אַרְצְךָ בַּעֲלֹתְךָ לֵרָאוֹת אֶת פְּנֵי ה' אֱלֹקֶיךָ שָׁלֹשׁ פְּעָמִים בַּשָּׁנָה.**

*No man shall covet your land when you ascend to see the Presence of God, three times a year.*[77]

This was their only comfort — the Almighty's promise that He would protect their homes and families, and prevent any attack by a foreign ruler. If we examine the manner in which the Jewish People performed this mitzvah, an interesting phenomenon is seen. Although we might expect that the pilgrims would leave their homes reluctantly, and indeed, that the weaker sector of society would fail to fulfill this obligation, history proves otherwise. The *Shem MiShemuel*, analysing Rashi's turn of phrase, highlights that the Children of Yisrael in fact fulfilled this mitzvah with great joy. **חוֹגְגִים ג' רְגָלִים** is Rashi's expression, the word **חוֹגְגִים** relating to the root **חַג** – which denotes celebration. This was another opportunity for the Jewish nation to implement God's will, to demonstrate their devotion and appreciation towards their Master — a nation that "like a lion, raises itself," at all times prepared, at all times ready, to bring spirituality into the world, to fill the universe with Heavenly light.

Not only are we always poised to obey God's command; we actively give thanks for the opportunity to do so. Upon rising in the morning, we say,

בָּרוּךְ אַתָּה ה'... אֲשֶׁר נָתַן לַשֶּׂכְוִי בִינָה לְהַבְחִין בֵּין יוֹם וּבֵין לָיְלָה.

*Blessed are You, O God... Who gives the rooster the understanding to discern between day and night.*

As the sun's rays slowly appear over the horizon, the rooster crows, summoning us to begin a new day. For this wake-up call, we thank God, for it enables us to begin a day rich with potential, with

---

77. *Shemoth* 34:24.

spirituality, with Torah and mitzvoth. We continue, thanking the Almighty for the ability to walk, for the gift of vision, for the privilege of being part of the Jewish nation. We appreciate both the opportunity and the resources that we are given to enable us to serve God.

With each footstep on the thrice-yearly pilgrimage to Jerusalem, the distinction between Jew and gentile was more clearly delineated. The inner purity invested in us by Avraham, Yitzchak, and Ya'akov manifests in our sincere joy, our genuine happiness, in performing mitzvoth. "Our desire is to perform Your desire."[78] It is this aspiration that lies at the core of the Jew's being. And it is this aspiration that was apparent as our people left their homes and possessions and joyously traveled the long path to Jerusalem to serve God with exultation.

78. *Berachoth* 15b.

# PINCHAS

AN ACT OF IMMORALITY has been committed by Kozbi and Zimri. Unwilling to tolerate this breach in the sanctity of Yisrael, Pinchas takes action against the sinners. For this, he is praised:

**פִּינְחָס בֶּן אֶלְעָזָר בֶּן אַהֲרֹן הַכֹּהֵן הֵשִׁיב אֶת חֲמָתִי מֵעַל בְּנֵי יִשְׂרָאֵל בְּקַנְאוֹ אֶת קִנְאָתִי בְּתוֹכָם וְלֹא כִלִּיתִי אֶת בְּנֵי יִשְׂרָאֵל בְּקִנְאָתִי.**

*Pinchas, the son of El'azar, the son of Aharon the Priest, caused My anger to be withdrawn from against the Children of Yisrael by his acting zealously among them with the [same] zealous anger [that was fitting for Me to show], and I [therefore] did not wipe out the Children of Yisrael with the zealous anger [that I would have shown].*[79]

Let us recall the details of this incident:

**וַיַּרְא פִּינְחָס בֶּן אֶלְעָזָר בֶּן אַהֲרֹן הַכֹּהֵן וַיָּקָם מִתּוֹךְ הָעֵדָה וַיִּקַּח רֹמַח בְּיָדוֹ.**

*Pinchas, the son of El'azar, the son of Aharon the Priest, saw [what was happening], so he arose from the midst of the congregation and he took a spear in his hand.*[80]

Rashi elucidates:

וַיַּרְא פִּינְחָס. רָאָה מַעֲשֶׂה וְנִזְכַּר הֲלָכָה. אָמַר לוֹ לְמֹשֶׁה מְקֻבְּלַנִי מִמְּךָ — הַבּוֹעֵל אֲרַמִּית, קַנָּאִין פּוֹגְעִין בּוֹ. אָמַר לוֹ קַרְיָנָא דְאִגַּרְתָּא אִיהוּ לֶהֱוֵי פַּרְוַנְקָא. מִיָּד וַיִּקַּח רֹמַח בְּיָדוֹ וגו'.

*"Pinchas saw." He saw the incident and recalled the relevant halachah. He said to Moshe, "I learned from you that one who*

79. *Bemidbar* 25:11.
80. *Bemidbar* 25:7.

*commits immorality with an Aramite woman can be killed by one who is overcome by zealousness."*

*Moshe's reply: "The one who reads the letter can implement it."*

*Immediately (we read), "and he took a spear in his hand."*[81]

In this manner, Pinchas delivered the due punishment to the sinners. Pinchas took a spear and with it, killed Kozbi and Zimri in one blow. This punishment, however, is in the category of הֲלָכָה וְאֵין מוֹרִין כן — "A halachah which is not formally ruled."[82] In this particular case, the Torah legislates that one who is overcome by zealousness at the sight of a heinous crime, can take the law into his own hands, as it were, and, within the prescribed halachic guidelines, kill the two people involved. However, were the case to be taken to court, this punishment could not be executed, for both a warning and the testimony of two witnesses are required before the death penalty can usually be issued. Nevertheless, Pinchas accrued tremendous reward for his action.

The general principle in all of Torah is גָדוֹל הַמְצֻוֶּה וְעוֹשֶׂה מִמִּי שֶׁאֵינוֹ מְצֻוֶּה וְעוֹשֶׂה — "Greater is the one who is commanded and fulfills, than one who performs mitzvoth voluntarily."[83] The case at hand appears to be an exception to this principle. Pinchas' merit was precisely because he was not commanded to punish the evildoers. In fact, were Pinchas to have consulted with the *Beith Din*, they would not have advised to him to kill the sinners, for the formal legal procedure would instead have had to be implemented. As stated above, no punishment could have been executed because the presence of two witnesses, and the prerequisite warning, was missing in this situation. It appears that this incident is unusual in that a voluntary, spontaneous act of zealousness is the only avenue through which a punishment could be implemented. Why did Pinchas receive such bountiful reward for an action which he was not commanded to perform?

---

81. Rashi *ad loc.*
82. *Sanhedrin* 82a.
83. *Kiddushin* 31a.

Immediately after the incident, we read the following:

**וַיְדַבֵּר ה' אֶל מֹשֶׁה לֵּאמֹר. צָרוֹר אֶת הַמִּדְיָנִים וְהִכִּיתֶם אוֹתָם. כִּי צֹרְרִים הֵם לָכֶם בְּנִכְלֵיהֶם אֲשֶׁר נִכְּלוּ לָכֶם עַל דְּבַר פְּעוֹר וְעַל דְּבַר כָּזְבִּי בַּת נְשִׂיא מִדְיָן אֲחֹתָם הַמֻּכָּה בְיוֹם הַמַּגֵּפָה עַל דְּבַר פְּעוֹר.**

*The Eternal then spoke to Moshe saying, "Be [constantly] harassing the Midyanim, and [then] you shall smite them. For they harassed you through [the] intrigues that they conspired against you for the matter of Pe'or, and [wish to harass you] on account of their sister, Kozbi the daughter of the leader of Midyan, who was slain on the day of the plague because of the matter of Pe'or."*[84]

This moral crusade is further detailed in *Parashath Mattoth.*

**וַיְדַבֵּר ה' אֶל מֹשֶׁה לֵּאמֹר. נְקֹם נִקְמַת בְּנֵי יִשְׂרָאֵל מֵאֵת הַמִּדְיָנִים אַחַר תֵּאָסֵף אֶל עַמֶּיךָ... וַיִּשְׁלַח אֹתָם מֹשֶׁה אֶלֶף לַמַּטֶּה לַצָּבָא אֹתָם וְאֶת פִּינְחָס בֶּן אֶלְעָזָר הַכֹּהֵן לַצָּבָא וּכְלֵי הַקֹּדֶשׁ וַחֲצֹצְרוֹת הַתְּרוּעָה בְּיָדוֹ.**

*The Eternal spoke to Moshe, saying, "Exact the revenge of the Children of Yisrael from the Midyanim; after that, you will be gathered unto your people." ...Moshe then sent them to the army, a thousand [men] for each tribe, them [together] with Pinchas, the son of El'azar the Priest, to the army, and the Sanctuary vessels and the wailing trumpets with him.*[85]

Rashi questions:

וּמִפְּנֵי מָה הָלַךְ פִּינְחָס וְלֹא הָלַךְ אֶלְעָזָר? אָמַר הקב"ה מִי שֶׁהִתְחִיל בַּמִּצְוָה, שֶׁהָרַג כָּזְבִּי בַּת צוּר, יִגְמֹר.

*Why did Pinchas, not El'azar, lead the troops into war? Said the Almighty, "He who began the deed, by killing Kozbi the daughter of Tzur, shall complete the deed [by waging war against the Midianites]."*[86]

84. *Bemidbar* 25:16–18.
85. *Bemidbar* 31:1–2, 6.
86. Rashi *ad loc.*

Due to the decadent nature of the Midianite nation, we are commanded to wage war against them, thus opposing them on both a spiritual and physical level. Rashi highlights that although this is the appropriate behaviour when dealing with Midian, a different course must be pursued when dealing with the nation of Mo'av. As Rashi states:

מֵאֵת הַמִּדְיָנִים, וְלֹא מֵאֵת הַמּוֹאָבִים. שֶׁהַמּוֹאָבִים נִכְנְסוּ לַדָּבָר מֵחֲמַת יִרְאָה שֶׁהָיוּ יְרֵאִים מֵהֶם שֶׁהָיוּ שׁוֹלְלִים אוֹתָם, שֶׁלֹּא נֶאֱמַר אֶלָּא וְאַל תִּתְגָּר בָּם מִלְחָמָה. אֲבָל מִדְיָנִים נִתְעַבְּרוּ עַל רִיב לֹא לָהֶם.[87]

War was waged against the Midianites, but not against the Moabites. For the Moabites' animosity towards the Children of Yisrael stemmed from their fear of our nation. Mo'av's war against the Jews was thus prompted by a justifiable motive, and they cannot be censured for their hostility. Therefore, war against Mo'av, unlike Midian, is prohibited. In contrast, Midian had no real motive for attacking the Children of Yisrael. Their war was prompted simply by a hatemongering national personality, and specifically a base hatred of the Jewish nation. The Midianites interfered in a quarrel that was not theirs, thereby demonstrating their love of enmity of any kind. Due to this national corruption, they are dealt with in a more severe manner than Mo'av, and we are commanded to wage war against them.

We find a distinction not only in the manner of dealing with Midian as opposed to Mo'av, but also in the correct course of action against Ammon as opposed to Mo'av. This is detailed in *Devarim*:

**וַיֹּאמֶר ה' אֵלַי אַל תָּצַר אֶת מוֹאָב וְאַל תִּתְגָּר בָּם מִלְחָמָה כִּי לֹא אֶתֵּן לְךָ מֵאַרְצוֹ יְרֻשָּׁה כִּי לִבְנֵי לוֹט נָתַתִּי אֶת עָר יְרֻשָּׁה.**

*The Eternal then said to me, "Do not harass the Mo'avim and do not incite them to war, for I will not give you any of their land as an inheritance...."*[88]

Several verses later, we read:

87. Rashi on *Bemidbar* 31:2.
88. *Devarim* 2:9.

**וְקָרַבְתָּ מוּל בְּנֵי עַמּוֹן אַל תְּצֻרֵם וְאַל תִּתְגָּר בָּם כִּי לֹא אֶתֵּן מֵאֶרֶץ בְּנֵי עַמּוֹן לְךָ יְרֻשָּׁה כִּי לִבְנֵי לוֹט נְתַתִּיהָ יְרֻשָּׁה...**

*You will then draw near [to be] facing the Children of Ammon. Do not harass them, and do not intimidate them, for I will not give you any of the land of the Children of Ammon as an inheritance....*[89]

Rashi highlights the different responses required towards Ammon and Mo'av:

לֹא אָסַר לָהֶם עַל מוֹאָב אֶלָּא מִלְחָמָה, אֲבָל מְיָרְאִים הָיוּ אוֹתָם, וְנִרְאִים לָהֶם כְּשֶׁהֵם מְזֻיָּנִים. לְפִיכָךְ כְּתִיב וַיָּגָר מוֹאָב מִפְּנֵי הָעָם, שֶׁהָיוּ שׁוֹלְלִים וּבוֹזְזִים אוֹתָם. אֲבָל בִּבְנֵי עַמּוֹן נֶאֱמַר וְאַל תִּתְגָּר בָּם, שׁוּם גֵּרוּי. בִּשְׂכַר צְנִיעוּת אִמָּם שֶׁלֹּא פִּרְסְמָה עַל אָבִיהָ, כְּמוֹ שֶׁעָשְׂתָה הַבְּכִירָה שֶׁקָּרְאָה שֵׁם בְּנָהּ מוֹאָב.

*God forbade engaging Mo'av in war. However, it is permissible to intimidate them.*

*It is forbidden to take any action at all against Ammon, because of the modesty of the nation's predecessor. Ammon and Mo'av were products of the illicit union between Lot and his daughters. The progenitor of Mo'av publicised this act, in naming her son "Mo'av," literally, "from the father." The mother of Ammon did not publicise this fact, and thus deserves reward.*[90]

The ancestress of Ammon demonstrated a degree of refinement and modesty that was lacking in the progenitor of Mo'av. Due to this, there are differences in the behaviour required of the Jewish People towards each nation. Unlike Mo'av, Ammon may not even be intimidated or scared by the Jewish People.

The Maharal elaborates upon this theme. The younger daughter of Lot did not reveal the origin of her son, thereby demonstrating some degree of modesty. This refinement conceptually and spiritually affiliated her offspring, Ammon, with the Jewish People, for

---

89. *Devarim* 2:19.
90. Rashi on *Devarim* 2:9.

modesty and internality is one of the central qualities of the Children of Yisrael. Due to this similarity, a different course of behaviour is prescribed towards Ammon. The Jewish People are prohibited from even inciting or intimidating them in any way.

And thus, we learn the Jewish concept of war. In Jewish thought, war is not merely the sound of trumpets and the thundering of hooves, as each side vies for the glory of being the victor. Instead, war is the clash between two parties or ideologies that are essentially antithetical. When the two parties are similar in some way, battle is inappropriate, and must be prevented, and even litigated against. The extent to which one is permitted or prohibited from waging war depends upon the degree of similarity between the two nations.

As Ammon is, to some extent, similar to the Jewish People, we may not oppose them in battle. In contrast, it appears that Midian is the nation which is furthest away from Yisrael, the opposite of all Yisrael's ideology. Therefore we are commanded to fight against them.

We can thus discern three levels of war:

1. Ammon — we are commanded against even inciting or intimidating them.
2. Mo'av — we are forbidden to wage war against them, but permitted to frighten them.
3. Midian — we are commanded to engage in war against them.

While the Torah prescribes very specific guidelines concerning potential battle against Ammon and Mo'av, there is also a prohibition against any member of these nations converting to Judaism. The verse states, "Let no Moabite or Ammonite (ever) enter the congregation of God."[91] We will return to this point, and the reason for it, below. Before doing so, it is instructive to turn to the course of behaviour prescribed towards two other nations, Edom and Egypt.

**לֹא תְתַעֵב אֲדֹמִי כִּי אָחִיךָ הוּא לֹא תְתַעֵב מִצְרִי כִּי גֵר הָיִיתָ בְאַרְצוֹ. בָּנִים אֲשֶׁר יִוָּלְדוּ לָהֶם דּוֹר שְׁלִישִׁי יָבֹא לָהֶם בִּקְהַל ה'.**

---

91. *Devarim* 23:4.

*Do not despise the Edomite, for he is your brother. Do not despise the Egyptian, for you were strangers in his land. After the third generation, they may enter God's congregation.*[92]

Rashi highlights an important lesson to be learned from this command:

בָּנִים אֲשֶׁר יִוָּלְדוּ... הָא לָמַדְתָּ שֶׁהַמַּחְטִיא לָאָדָם, קָשֶׁה לוֹ מִן הַהוֹרְגוֹ, שֶׁהַהוֹרְגוֹ הוֹרְגוֹ בָּעוֹלָם הַזֶּה, וְהַמַּחְטִיאוֹ מוֹצִיאוֹ מִן הָעוֹלָם הַזֶּה וּמִן הָעוֹלָם הַבָּא, לְפִיכָךְ אֱדוֹם שֶׁקִּדְּמָם בַּחֶרֶב לֹא נִתְעָב, וְכֵן מִצְרִים שֶׁטִּבְּעוּם, וְאֵלּוּ שֶׁהֶחְטִיאוּם נִתְעֲבוּ.

*From here we learn that to cause someone to sin is worse than killing him. One who murders removes a person only from this world. One who causes a person to sin drives him from both this world and the World to Come. Therefore, Edom, who physically attacked the Jewish People, is not despised, as is true for the Egyptians, who drowned the baby boys. However, the nations that caused the Children of Yisrael to sin [thus opposing them on a spiritual, not only a physical plane], are subject to our animosity.*[93]

Edom and Egypt, unlike Ammon and Mo'av, are permitted to join the Jewish People. For, Edom and Egypt, unlike Ammon and Mo'av, simply obstructed the Children of Yisrael on a physical level. Ammon and Mo'av, however, attempted to thwart the Jewish People's spirituality. This is viewed in a much more severe manner than straightforward physical opposition.

Rabbi Leib Chasman elaborates on why causing another to sin is viewed with such harshness. He explains that although a person may commit innumerable sins, his basic character may still be wholesome. The sin does not necessarily indicate that this is a corrupt and perverted personality. The person is simply weak, having been swayed by the guile of his evil inclination, or the dazzling temptation that has blinded him. Thus, when he involves himself in

---

92. *Devarim* 23:8–9.
93. Rashi *ad loc.*

the process of repentance, he is able to return to his original, basic state of purity. Not so with one who causes others to sin. He has no inclination to follow; there are no potential benefits to be reaped by committing the sin. No temptation is being indulged, nor is any pleasure gained. We witness only a corrupt and decadent personality at work, one who simply desires to revolt against God, and spread evil in the world.

Ammon and Mo'av's sole desire was to cause the Jewish People to fall into sin. This was demonstrated in the incident at Shittim, in which the Children of Yisrael were lured into idolatry and immorality. Thus, they are considered inferior to Edom and Egypt, who waged only a physical battle against the Jewish nation. This action of Ammon and Mo'av forever precludes them from becoming part of God's nation. For, the mission of the Jewish People is to attain closeness with God. Deliberately spreading evil in the world, Ammon and Mo'av spurned this purpose. Having once tried to extinguish the light of the Jewish soul, they can never merit possession of this beacon.

We can still discern a distinction, however, between Ammon and Mo'av, and Midian. Ammon and Mo'av originally pitted themselves against the Jewish People due to their fear. Intimidated, they sought to destroy us, and attempted to do this on a spiritual level. In contrast, Midian simply joined in a quarrel that was not their concern, having no reason, no real motive to engage the Jewish People in battle. We can classify them as having a greater degree of corruption than even Ammon and Mo'av. The command against Midian is harsher than against either Ammon or Mo'av — we must wage war against them.

From our examination of these nations, we can discern three levels of sin:

1. One who sins out of weakness.
2. One who causes others to sin due to an initially legitimate motive (Ammon and Mo'av).
3. One who causes others to sin due to a corrupt personality (Midian).

In contrast, we find various manners in which one can perform mitzvoth. Good deeds can be performed for many reasons other than personal conviction. One's mitzvoth can stem from peer pressure, from the demands of society. They can be merely a hollow imitation of other's deeds, or the lingering remnants of a childhood education. This is termed as מִצְוַת אֲנָשִׁים מְלֻמָּדָה, mitzvoth performed by rote. Or, having some conception of Gehinnom, termed by Western culture as Hell, one can perform good deeds to avoid this frightening fate; one's service stems from יִרְאַת הָעֹנֶשׁ, fear of punishment. These are not ultimate levels of Divine service; they do not indicate a heart yearning for Godliness.

However, one who encourages others to perform mitzvoth, to direct their lives towards the Divine, does not do so out of imitation or fear. Causing others to do mitzvoth is the result of a pure heart, one's motivation simply a true desire to sanctify God's Name in the world.

Indeed, the manner by which to fulfill the command to love God is expressed by our Sages as follows: שֶׁיְּהֵא שֵׁם שָׁמַיִם מִתְאַהֵב עַל יָדְךָ — "Let God be beloved through you."[94] Merely professing to love God is not sufficient. We are enjoined to spread love of God through the nation. For this is what indicates genuine dedication — doing something that is not induced by society, and not motivated by fear of punishment. Spreading love of God through the nation is the antithesis of Midian, Ammon and Mo'av, who sought to blanket the world with darkness and obscurity.

The zealousness Pinchas demonstrated was not motivated by societal pressure, by fear of punishment, by desire for honour and glory. Rather, he sought to avenge those whom God wanted to avenge, not to fulfill a personal vendetta — בְּקַנְאוֹ אֶת קִנְאָתִי. His burning love of God meant that he was unable to tolerate any infringement of God's will. He wanted only to accrue merit for the Jewish nation, and he removed that which opposed this aim, not for any personal satisfaction, but only because of his love of God, his pure heart.

---

94. *Yoma* 86a.

Marching into battle against the Midianites, Pinchas was stationed at the head of the army. As explained earlier by the Maharal, war is fought against conceptual opposites, and it is thus appropriate that Pinchas, one whose inner desire was to sanctify God's Name in the world, should be the foil to the Midianites, who lured the Jewish nation into sin. Midian, those who, without compulsion, spread evil in the world, faced Pinchas who, without compulsion, sought to fill the world with goodness.

The bountiful reward that Pinchas received resulted from an action which he was not commanded to implement. It was necessarily so, for his action must stem solely from a pure heart, with no other motive apart from love of God.

Our Sages inform us that one who performs a mitzvah is rewarded in a manner that far outweighs any penalty that could be incurred by failing to fulfill it. Considering the harsh punishment meted out to Ammon, Mo'av and Midian, we glean some inkling of the tremendous reward bestowed upon those who influence and help others to do mitzvoth. Teaching children, encouraging those who are new to Torah observance, setting an unimpeachable example; all these are ways through which we can help others develop their spirituality, ways through which "the name of God will become beloved through you." And in doing so, as Pinchas was endowed with an Eternal covenant of peace, so we will be endowed with bountiful reward.

# MATTOTH

THE JEW'S MISSION is to remain a flagship of unbending values in a society in which truth is not only unfashionable; it is almost completely obscured in a sea of relativism. This timeless lesson is taught to us in this *parashah*:

> **וַיְדַבֵּר ה' אֶל מֹשֶׁה לֵּאמֹר. נְקֹם נִקְמַת בְּנֵי יִשְׂרָאֵל מֵאֵת הַמִּדְיָנִים... וַיְדַבֵּר מֹשֶׁה אֶל הָעָם לֵאמֹר... אֶלֶף לַמַּטֶּה אֶלֶף לַמַּטֶּה לְכֹל מַטּוֹת יִשְׂרָאֵל תִּשְׁלְחוּ לַצָּבָא. וַיִּשְׁלַח אֹתָם מֹשֶׁה אֶלֶף לַמַּטֶּה לַצָּבָא אֹתָם וְאֶת פִּינְחָס בֶּן אֶלְעָזָר הַכֹּהֵן...**
>
> *The Eternal spoke to Moshe, saying, "Exact the revenge of the Children of Yisrael from the Midyanim..." Moshe then spoke to the people, saying... "You shall send to the army a thousand [men] for each tribe." Moshe then sent them to the army, a thousand [men] for each tribe; [together] with Pinchas the son of E'lazar the Priest....*[95]

Rashi focuses on the fact that Pinchas was the personality who led the troops into battle:

> אֹתָם וְאֶת פִּינְחָס. מַגִּיד שֶׁהָיָה פִּינְחָס שָׁקוּל כְּנֶגֶד כֻּלָּם. וּמִפְּנֵי מָה הָלַךְ פִּינְחָס וְלֹא הָלַךְ אֶלְעָזָר? אָמַר הקב"ה מִי שֶׁהִתְחִיל בַּמִּצְוָה שֶׁהָרַג כָּזְבִּי בַּת צוּר יִגְמֹר. ד"א שֶׁהָלַךְ לִנְקֹם נִקְמַת יוֹסֵף אֲבִי אִמּוֹ שֶׁנֶּאֱמַר וְהַמְּדָנִים מָכְרוּ אוֹתוֹ.
>
> *...This tells us that Pinchas was considered equivalent to all the people. Why did Pinchas, not El'azar, lead the troops into war? Said the Almighty, "He who began the deed, by killing Kozbi the daughter of Tzur [a Midianite princess], shall complete the deed." An alternative explanation: he went to avenge*

95. *Bemidbar* 31:1–2, 4, 6.

*what happened to Yosef, his ancestor, as it states, "and the Midianites sold him."*[96]

Let us clarify the meaning of Rashi's second explanation. To do so, we must consider the infamous selling of Yosef, as recorded in *Bereishith*.

**וַיֹּאמֶר יְהוּדָה אֶל אֶחָיו מַה בֶּצַע כִּי נַהֲרֹג אֶת אָחִינוּ וְכִסִּינוּ אֶת דָּמוֹ. לְכוּ וְנִמְכְּרֶנּוּ לַיִּשְׁמְעֵאלִים וְיָדֵנוּ אַל תְּהִי בוֹ כִּי אָחִינוּ בְשָׂרֵנוּ הוּא וַיִּשְׁמְעוּ אֶחָיו. וַיַּעַבְרוּ אֲנָשִׁים מִדְיָנִים סֹחֲרִים וַיִּמְשְׁכוּ וַיַּעֲלוּ אֶת יוֹסֵף מִן הַבּוֹר וַיִּמְכְּרוּ אֶת יוֹסֵף לַיִּשְׁמְעֵאלִים בְּעֶשְׂרִים כָּסֶף וַיָּבִיאוּ אֶת יוֹסֵף מִצְרָיְמָה.**

*Yehudah said to his brothers, "What do we gain if we kill our brother and cover up his death? Come, let us sell him to the Yishme'elim and not [actually] harm him, for he is our brother, our flesh [and blood]." His brothers heeded [his words]. [Meanwhile], Midyani merchants passed by, and [the brothers] hauled Yosef up from the pit and sold Yosef to the Yishme'elim for twenty silver pieces, and they brought Yosef to Mitzrayim.*[97]

The verses in this extract seem ambiguous, littered with irrelevant references. Why mention an encounter with the Midianites if Yosef was in fact sold to the Yishma'elites, as was originally intended? Rashi explains:

**וַיִּמְשְׁכוּ. בְּנֵי יַעֲקֹב אֶת יוֹסֵף מִן הַבּוֹר וַיִּמְכְּרוּהוּ לַיִּשְׁמְעֵאלִים וְהַיִּשְׁמְעֵאלִים לַמִּדְיָנִים וְהַמִּדְיָנִים לַמִּצְרִים.**

*The sons of Ya'akov lifted Yosef from the pit, and sold him to the Yishma'elites. The Yishma'elites sold him to the Midianites, and the Midianites to the Egyptians.*[98]

Yosef, then, was not sold just once. On his journey to Egypt, he changed hands a number of times.

The Avnei Nezer questions the relevance of this incident to the

96. Rashi *ad loc.*
97. *Bereishith* 37:26–28.
98. Rashi *ad loc.*

battle against the Midianites that took place many hundreds of years later. Why was Pinchas sent to avenge his forefather after such a long interval? Further, the Midianites referred to in the Yosef story were merchants, interested in buying and selling items and profiting from their business. What great sin did they commit in innocently buying Yosef?

Let us digress and elaborate upon an important lesson taught to us by the manna.

**וַיֹּאכְלוּ מֵעֲבוּר הָאָרֶץ מִמָּחֳרַת הַפֶּסַח מַצּוֹת וְקָלוּי בְּעֶצֶם הַיּוֹם הַזֶּה. וַיִּשְׁבֹּת הַמָּן מִמָּחֳרָת בְּאָכְלָם מֵעֲבוּר הָאָרֶץ וְלֹא הָיָה עוֹד לִבְנֵי יִשְׂרָאֵל מָן...**

*They ate of the produce of the land, from the day after Pesach, matzoth and corn. From the day they started eating from the produce of the land, the manna ceased, and the Jewish People no longer ate manna.*[99]

From this account, a mathematical difficulty arises concerning the length of time during which the Jewish People enjoyed the manna. Rashi elaborates:

מִמָּחֳרַת הַפֶּסַח. יוֹם הֲנָפַת הָעֹמֶר, שֶׁהִקְרִיבוּ עֹמֶר תְּחִלָּה. ומז׳ בַּאֲדָר שֶׁמֵּת מֹשֶׁה שֶׁפָּסַק הַמָּן הָיוּ מִסְתַּפְּקִין עַד עַכְשָׁו מִמָּן שֶׁבִּכְלֵיהֶם שֶׁלָּקְטוּ בְּשִׁבְעָה בַּאֲדָר, שֶׁנֶּאֱמַר אֶת הַמָּן אָכְלוּ אַרְבָּעִים שָׁנָה. וַהֲלֹא אַרְבָּעִים שָׁנָה חָסֵר ל׳ יוֹם, שֶׁהֲרֵי תְּחִלַּת יְרִידַת הַמָּן בט״ו בְּאִיָּר? אֱמֹר מֵעַתָּה בַּחֲרָרָה שֶׁהוֹצִיאוּ יִשְׂרָאֵל מִמִּצְרַיִם טָעֲמוּ טַעַם מָן.

*From after Pesach. This means from the time that the omer offering was waved (and brought up to God). The manna actually stopped falling on the seventh of Adar, when Moshe died. The manna that they gathered on the seventh of Adar sufficed until this day (the fifteenth of Nissan), as it says, "They ate manna for forty years."*[100]

However, although they stopped eating manna on the fifteenth of

99. *Yehoshua* 5:11, 12.
100. Rashi *ad loc.*

Nissan, forty years earlier the Children of Yisrael only started eating manna on the fifteenth of Iyar. As Rashi goes on to say, this leaves the calculation thirty days short of forty years. How can we reconcile this with the verse that states that the Children of Yisrael ate manna for forty years?

We can reconcile the difference, Rashi explains, through the fact that for thirty days during the first year in the desert, from the fifteenth of Nissan until the fifteenth of Iyar, the matzah that they ate had the taste of manna.

Rashi's comment serves not only to solve a technical difficulty; it provides us with an important principle relevant to our spiritual development. The shift from matzah to manna occurred gradually; the transition was a gentle one. God gave His people a chance to accustom themselves to the taste of manna, before presenting them with it in its physical form. Gradual modification should be the hallmark of spiritual growth. God does not demand of His children to leap up to towering heights; rather, we are recommended to scale the ladder leading to greatness at a steady pace.

Another example of a measured alteration occurred in the changeover from eating exclusively manna to eating the natural produce of the Land of Israel, with all its accompanying spiritual implications. This was not merely a culinary metamorphosis; the change in food symbolizes the difference in their whole manner of living.

While in the desert, the Children of Yisrael constantly and explicitly saw God's Hand before their eyes. Miracles were an everyday occurrence, and the mask of nature was clearly just an illusion. Crossing the border into the Land of Israel, a whole new type of Divine service was required of the people. They now had to enter the world of nature, of cause and effect, the world in which God's hand is obscured, and penetrate through the world's system to perceive the Designer. They had to step down from a life of open miracles, and enter a world in which daily miracles — sunrise, budding blossoms, chirping birds — appear to be simply the manner in which the world runs. They changed from eating the supernatural manna, to consuming food made from the produce of the earth, bread baked through the "sweat of the brow." However, once again, the Jewish People were slowly weaned off the manna — when they first entered the Land, their food continued to taste like manna. This was symbolic of the nature of the change in their entire lifestyle: all was done slowly, stage-by-stage, until the people could accustom themselves to it. Man's elevation is painless and manageable when it occurs gradually.

This principle also has a negative manifestation. Just as man's growth must occur in stages, man's descent will also occur in stages. Gradual deterioration is particularly perilous, for this is the manner in which man can most easily fall. Our Sages teach us this principle through the following:

> הַמְקָרֵעַ בְּגָדָיו בַּחֲמָתוֹ וְהַמְשַׁבֵּר כֵּלָיו בַּחֲמָתוֹ וְהַמְפַזֵּר מְעוֹתָיו בַּחֲמָתוֹ יְהֵא בְעֵינֶיךָ כְּעוֹבֵד עֲבוֹדָה זָרָה. שֶׁכָּךְ אֻמָּנוּתוֹ שֶׁל יֵצֶר הָרַע. הַיּוֹם אוֹמֵר לוֹ עֲשֵׂה כָּךְ וּלְמָחָר אוֹמֵר לוֹ עֲשֵׂה כָּךְ, עַד שֶׁאוֹמֵר לוֹ עֲבֹד עֲבוֹדָה זָרָה, וְהוֹלֵךְ וְעוֹבֵד.
>
> *One who, in anger, tears his clothes, or smashes a utensil, or tips out a bag of money and scatters it on the ground, should be viewed as an idolater. For the evil inclination works in this way: today it tells you to do one thing. The next day, it tells you to do something else. Finally, it will tell you to serve idols, and, having heeded the previous instructions, you will listen to its persuasions, serving the false god.*[101]

One can fall very easily when one does so in stages; by compromising first on a small thing, one can eventually come to transgress a cardinal sin.

Let us now turn back to the sale of Yosef, and examine a Midrash describing the event.

> וְהַמִּדְיָנִים מָכְרוּ אוֹתוֹ וגו׳. כַּמָּה אוֹנִיּוֹת נִכְתְּבוּ לוֹ? ר׳ יוּדָן אָמַר אַרְבָּעָה. אֶחָיו לַיִּשְׁמְעֵאלִים, וְיִשְׁמְעֵאלִים לַסּוֹחֲרִים, וְסוֹחֲרִים לַמִּדְיָנִים וּמִדְיָנִים מָכְרוּ אוֹתוֹ אֶל מִצְרָיִם.

---

101. *Shabbath* 105b.

*How many sale documents were written regarding Yosef? Four: his brothers to the Yishma'elites, the Yishma'elites to the peddlers, the peddlers to the Midianites, and the Midianites sold him to Egypt.*[102]

The Maharal[103] explains the significance of the manner in which Yosef changed hands.

*An entity does not travel from one domain to another domain without an interface. There must be a gradual change, as the entity passes through many domains. In this case, we see that Yosef was sold four times, making a gradual transition from the domain of his brothers to the domain of Egypt. He was first sold by his brothers his own flesh and blood. He was delivered into the hands of the Ishmaelites who, also descending from Avraham, had some kinship with Yosef, albeit more distant than his brothers. The Ishmaelites brought Yosef down to Egypt, appropriate because of their close affiliation with Egypt, their ancestor Hagar being an Egyptian princess... After the Ishmaelites, Yosef was sold into the hands of the peddlers, who despite their Midianite origin, are not considered as such, as their idea was simply to sell Yosef to an interested purchaser. After this, Yosef was sold to the Midianites, who in turn sold him to Egypt. We see that God orchestrated a gradual transition, from Yosef being in the hands of his brothers to arriving as a slave in Egypt.*

Something about the national character of Egypt, the culture into which Yosef was entering, is learned through the following exchange:

**וַיִּקְרָא פַרְעֹה לְאַבְרָם וַיֹּאמֶר... לָמָה אָמַרְתָּ אֲחֹתִי הִוא וָאֶקַּח אֹתָהּ לִי לְאִשָּׁה וְעַתָּה הִנֵּה אִשְׁתְּךָ קַח וָלֵךְ.**

*Par'oh summoned Avram and said to him, "...Why did you say, 'She is my sister,' and I [therefore] took her for myself as a*

102. *Bereishith Rabbah* 84:22.
103. *Gur Aryeh, Bereishith* 25:28.

*wife? So now, here is your wife — take [her] and go!"*[104]

Fearful for his life, Avraham, on his sojourn in Egypt, had declared that Sarah was in fact his sister. His plan backfired, however, as Par'oh took her to his palace and married her. When he was struck with a plague as a consequence of his actions, Par'oh realised the truth, and immediately expelled Avraham from the country. Rashi contrasts Par'oh's reaction with the reaction of Avimelech, another king with whom a similar incident occurred.

קַח וָלֵךְ. לֹא כַּאֲבִימֶלֶךְ שֶׁאָמַר לוֹ הִנֵּה אַרְצִי לְפָנֶיךָ, אֶלָּא אָמַר לוֹ לֵךְ וְאַל תַּעֲמֹד, שֶׁהַמִּצְרִים שְׁטוּפֵי זִמָּה הֵם שֶׁנֶּאֱמַר וְזִרְמַת סוּסִים זִרְמָתָם.

*Take [her] and go! Not like Avimelech who said, "Behold my land is before you" [allowing Avraham to stay in the country], but Par'oh instructed Avraham not to delay, for the Egyptians were embroiled in immorality.*[105]

Par'oh recognised the dominant characteristic of his country: perversion and immorality. For Avraham's own safety Par'oh advised him to move elsewhere. And now, this was the country into which Yosef entered, a land steeped in debauchery. And here Yosef faced his tremendous trial with the wife of his master Potiphar. Yosef was commanded to face this particular evil, wrestle with it, and triumph. This he did, and in doing so earned the title צַדִּיק יְסוֹד עוֹלָם — "A righteous man who is the foundation of the world." Yosef was dropped, level by level, into a place that opposed spirituality. Yosef's mission was to battle the pervasive compromise, remaining a symbol of stubborn, unbending truth.

This battle against gradually corroding values was also fought by Moshe when he was in Egypt. When Par'oh heard the warning concerning the imminent plague of locusts, he acted as follows:

**וַיּוּשַׁב אֶת מֹשֶׁה וְאֶת אַהֲרֹן אֶל פַּרְעֹה וַיֹּאמֶר אֲלֵהֶם לְכוּ עִבְדוּ אֶת ה'**

---

104. *Bereishith* 12:18–19.
105. Rashi *ad loc.*

**אֱלֹקֵיכֶם מִי וָמִי הַהֹלְכִים. וַיֹּאמֶר מֹשֶׁה בִּנְעָרֵינוּ וּבִזְקֵנֵינוּ נֵלֵךְ בְּבָנֵינוּ וּבִבְנוֹתֵנוּ בְּצֹאנֵנוּ וּבִבְקָרֵנוּ נֵלֵךְ כִּי חַג ה' לָנוּ. וַיֹּאמֶר אֲלֵהֶם... לֹא כֵן לְכוּ נָא הַגְּבָרִים וְעִבְדוּ אֶת ה' כִּי אֹתָהּ אַתֶּם מְבַקְשִׁים וַיְגָרֶשׁ אֹתָם מֵאֵת פְּנֵי פַרְעֹה.**

*So Moshe, with Aharon, was brought back to Par'oh, and he said to them, "Go [and] serve the Eternal, your God. Who exactly is going?"*

*Moshe answered, "We will go with our youth and with our elderly. [Even] with our sons and our daughters [and] with our sheep, goats and cattle we will go, for it is a festival to the Eternal for us."*

*[Par'oh] said to them, "...This will not be. [Only] the men shall now go and serve the Eternal, for that is what you [have been] asking for." [He] then drove them out of Par'oh's presence.*[106]

In this exchange, it remains unclear exactly who drove Moshe and Aharon from the palace. This is highlighted by Rashi:

וַיְגָרֶשׁ אֹתָם. הֲרֵי זֶה לָשׁוֹן קָצָר, וְלֹא פֵּרֵשׁ מִי הַמְגָרֵשׁ.

*[He] then drove them out. This is an elliptical phrase; the identity of who drove them out is not specified.*[107]

Rabbi Dessler questions the reason why the Torah, precise in every word, here uses an ambiguous expression. He concludes that the Torah is teaching us that the identity of person who expelled them, and the manner in which it was done, are entirely irrelevant. The Torah instead wants to emphasize that Moshe and Aharon were somehow forced out of the palace. In this exchange, Par'oh would not allow the entire nation to leave, but granted permission to the menfolk alone. The minute that Moshe heard this, he and Aharon left the palace. For Moshe had perceived a strategy of compromise, the gentle lowering of his expectations. Moshe understood the dangerous allure of this strategy, and instead of attempting to negotiate, he

---

106. *Shemoth* 10:8–11.
107. Rashi *ad loc.*

fought it by remaining rigid in his request, and simply exiting the palace. The point that is focused upon here by the Torah, is not by whom, or the manner in which, Moshe was driven out of the palace. Relevant to us is the fact that Moshe adamantly refused to be party to a compromise in his Divine service.

Returning to our original difficulty, Rashi brings two reasons why Pinchas led the troops into battle against Midian. Pinchas was the one who began the war against Midian by killing Kozbi; therefore, he is assigned the task of completing this mission. Further, Pinchas was a descendant of Yosef,[108] who was sold to Egypt via the Midianites. Pinchas thus leads the troops to avenge the injustice done to his ancestor, many generations beforehand. Although on a cursory reading the reasons appear unrelated, in reality they are complementary.

Midian was so successful in their attempt to seduce the Children of Yisrael precisely because of their closeness to our people, descending from the union between Avraham and Keturah. It was specifically because of this feeling of kinship with Midian, that the Jewish People were susceptible to their influence. This feeling caused the Jewish People to bridge the irrevocable gap between the holiness and spirituality of the Children of Yisrael, and the corruption of the Midianites, and compromise themselves. The personality most appropriate to battle the Midianites, who symbolize a slow but insidious lowering of personal values, was Pinchas, who represents unbending truth. When he witnessed the breach of Jewish sanctity caused by Zimri's immoral act, Pinchas was the personality who administered a swift punishment, courageously battling Midian's evil strategy of gradual corruption. In the continuation of his agenda, Pinchas avenged the injustice perpetrated against his ancestor.

Midian's strategy is not only that of an individual nation, it is one of the main techniques employed by the evil inclination. A person is persuaded to make some small compromise, one which to him appears insignificant. However, this chink can lead to a fatal flaw in

---

108. See *Baba Bathra* 109b–110a.

a person's armour. Although one particular issue may seem trivial, it is the first step on a slippery downward path. When faced with this temptation, the only effective solution is וַיְגָרֶשׁ, to expel the notion completely. For it is the mission of each Jew to remain a bulwark of truth and values, despite the strong winds that threaten to move him.

# MASSEI

IN ALL, THE JEWISH People made forty-two journeys through the barren desert. The prophet Yirmiyah reviews this period with the following famous words.

**זָכַרְתִּי לָךְ חֶסֶד נְעוּרַיִךְ אַהֲבַת כְּלוּלֹתָיִךְ לֶכְתֵּךְ אַחֲרַי בַּמִּדְבָּר בְּאֶרֶץ לֹא זְרוּעָה.**

*I remember the kindness of your youth, the love of your bridal days, that you followed Me into the wilderness, to a land where nothing grows.*[109]

The verses elaborate upon the manner in which the Children of Yisrael journeyed:

**עַל פִּי ה' יִסְעוּ בְּנֵי יִשְׂרָאֵל וְעַל פִּי ה' יַחֲנוּ כָּל יְמֵי אֲשֶׁר יִשְׁכֹּן הֶעָנָן עַל הַמִּשְׁכָּן יַחֲנוּ. וּבְהַאֲרִיךְ הֶעָנָן עַל הַמִּשְׁכָּן יָמִים רַבִּים וְשָׁמְרוּ בְנֵי יִשְׂרָאֵל אֶת מִשְׁמֶרֶת ה' וְלֹא יִסָּעוּ.**

*On the Eternal's instructions the Children of Yisrael would travel; and on the Eternal's instructions they would camp; the whole time that the cloud stayed over the Dwelling they would remain encamped. And when the cloud stayed a long time over the Dwelling, the Children of Yisrael would keep the Eternal's restriction and not travel.*[110]

The Ramban[111] presents us with various scenarios, to depict the difficulty involved in fulfilling this command:

*The cloud could rest for many days on the Mishkan in a place*

---

109. *Yirmiyah* 2:2.
110. *Bemidbar* 9:18, 19.
111. Ramban *ad loc.*

*that the nation did not think was a good site. Although they strongly wished to depart, they would not transgress the will of God, and they encamped, not moving from the place. Further, the people could have already been traveling for two or three days, and be weary and tired from the journey. Yet, if the cloud traveled, the Jewish People followed. It could be that the cloud rested for just one night, after which the people were required to continue on their travels.*

*Even harder was when the people traveled through the night, arriving at a certain spot in the morning. They stayed there for that day and night, and in the morning, they once again set off. When this happened, it was more of a strain than if the people rested only one day or one night. For, thinking that they would stay in the place for a while, the nation began unloading their carts and unpacking their belongings. When the cloud then arose, signifying that they were to travel on, they faithfully began packing up once again, although they had not even sufficient time to prepare for the journey.*

The praise of the Jewish People, recorded by Yirmiyah, was deservedly given. The Jewish People endured much travail on their wanderings in the desert, and yet they remained steadfastly loyal to the will of God.

While we hear the praise of the Jewish People, Scripture presents us with a less than perfect picture of the nation:

**וַיְהִי הָעָם כְּמִתְאֹנְנִים רַע בְּאָזְנֵי ה'.**

*The people were like complainers in the eyes of God.*[112]

On this incident, we read the Ramban's comment:

וְהַנָּכוֹן בְּעֵינַי כִּי כַּאֲשֶׁר נִתְרַחֲקוּ מֵהַר סִינַי שֶׁהָיָה קָרוֹב לַיִּשּׁוּב וּבָאוּ בְּתוֹךְ הַמִּדְבָּר הַגָּדוֹל וְהַנּוֹרָא, בַּמַּסָּע הָרִאשׁוֹן הָיוּ מִצְטַעֲרִים בְּעַצְמָם לֵאמֹר: מַה נַּעֲשֶׂה וְאֵיךְ נִחְיֶה בַּמִּדְבָּר הַזֶּה וּמַה נֹּאכַל וּמַה נִּשְׁתֶּה וְאֵיךְ נִסְבֹּל הֶעָמָל וְהָעִנּוּי וּמָתַי נֵצֵא מִמֶּנּוּ... לְשׁוֹן כּוֹאֵב וּמִצְטַעֵר עַל עַצְמוֹ...

112. *Bemidbar* 11:1.

וְהָיָה רַע בְּעֵינֵי ה'. שֶׁהָיָה לָהֶם לָלֶכֶת אַחֲרָיו בְּשִׂמְחָה וּבְטוּב לֵבָב מֵרֹב כָּל טוֹבָה אֲשֶׁר נָתַן לָהֶם. וְהֵם הָיוּ כַּאֲנוּסִים וּמֻכְרָחִים, מִתְאוֹנְנִים וּמִתְרַעֲמִים עַל עִנְיָנָם.

*When the Jewish People traveled away from Mount Sinai, i.e. from civilization, and came into the great and awesome desert, they were initially very distressed. "How can we live in this wilderness? What shall we eat and drink? How will we bear the exertion and discomfort? When will we leave it?" These questions of distress angered the Almighty, for they were meant to come into the desert in a joyous state, happy with the boundless goodness that God had bestowed upon them. Yet, the Jewish People entered the desert as if they were forced to do so, and had complaints over the situation.*[113]

Two diametrically contrasting pictures are being painted for us. On the one hand, the Children of Yisrael are praised for the manner in which they blindly followed God into a "barren land." Yet, they are also criticised for their disgruntlement when faced with the harsh conditions. In light of these two portraits, how should we view the travels of the Jewish People in the desert?

From the moment he is born, man embarks on a journey: the journey through life. The path is not always smooth; it may contain many rocks and uneven stretches, it may bend and meander instead of taking a straight route. One such "rock," one challenge that the traveler might face could be *Shemittah*, fulfilling the injunction to leave one's land fallow for the entire seventh year. The Midrash vividly depicts the challenge involved in observing this mitzvah:

גִּבּוֹרֵי כֹחַ עוֹשֵׂי דְבָרוֹ. אָמַר ר' יִצְחָק: בְּשׁוֹמְרֵי שְׁבִיעִית הַכָּתוּב מְדַבֵּר. בְּנֹהַג שֶׁבָּעוֹלָם אָדָם עוֹשֶׂה מִצְוָה לְיוֹם אֶחָד, לְשַׁבָּת אַחַת, לְחֹדֶשׁ אֶחָד. שֶׁמָּא לִשְׁאָר יְמוֹת הַשָּׁנָה? וְדֵין חֲמֵי חַקְלֵהּ בַּיְרָא כַּרְמֵהּ בַּיְרָא, וְיָהֲבֵי אַרְנוֹנָא וְשָׁתִיק. יֵשׁ לְךָ גִּבּוֹר גָּדוֹל מִזֶּה?

*"Valiant ones who do His word." R. Yitzchak said, "This refers to those who observe the Shemittah year." Normally, a person*

113. Ramban *ad loc.*

> *will do a mitzvah and overcome his inclination for one day. He might even fulfill the mitzvah for one week, or one month. However, can he manage to overcome the challenge for an entire year? Yet, those who keep Shemittah see their fields and vineyards laid waste, thistles and briars covering the ground. Further, they are still required to pay government tax for their fields. Yet, these people are silent. Can there be one possessing more strength than this?*[114]

The silence of these people does not denote a grudging acceptance. It denotes a tranquil heart, content to fulfill God's word, despite the sacrifice this entails, despite the length of time which is involved.

There is one mitigating factor here, however: the challenge is anticipated from the outset. When one has prior warning of a difficulty, one has the opportunity to mentally prepare oneself to face the test. One can arouse one's determination and resolve not to fall prey to temptation. When one does not receive a warning, the difficulty of the challenge is intensified.

There is another type of rock upon life's path, another type of difficulty which one might encounter. The prime example of one subject to this kind of challenge is our Patriarch Ya'akov. Our sublime and holy forefather spent his time ensconced in the tents of Torah study. This, until he followed his mother Rivkah's command, and took the blessings that Esav felt were his. From this time onwards, Ya'akov was thrust, without respite, from difficulty to difficulty. He first had to flee from the wrath of his brother Esav, who sought to kill him. On his journey, he was terrorized by Elifaz, grandson of Esav, who stripped him of his possessions, leaving him with only the clothes he was wearing. Arriving at the house of his uncle, Lavan, Ya'akov had to undergo more difficulties in his dealings with the prototype fraudster. After the seven years of tireless work demanded of him by Lavan in exchange for the privilege of marrying his daughter Rachel, Ya'akov was deceived and instead given Leah as

---

114. *Vayikra Rabbah* 1:1.

a wife. Ya'akov was required to work seven more years for Rachel, after which, when he finally wanted to leave Lavan's house with his family, he was tricked once more, this time concerning his wages. Escaping from his uncle's house without his knowledge, Ya'akov once more encountered his old enemy, Esav. Even after emerging victorious from the battle, Ya'akov still had further trials to endure. His daughter Dinah was defiled, and his beloved son Yosef was believed dead, causing Ya'akov to mourn for him for twenty-two years. A tyrannical Egyptian ruler then held Shimon captive, and it is impossible for us to fathom Ya'akov's emotions when he learned that the despot also sought his youngest son, Binyamin.

An overview of Ya'akov's life, then, shows his courageous battle, his constant fight against the circumstances into which he was placed. But what led to all of his travail? What was the catalyst for his life of tribulation? To answer these questions we will need to turn back to the episode of the blessings. Considering the personality and the individual mission of his two sons, Yitzchak had designated the blessings for Esav. His wife Rivkah, however, received a prophecy that these blessings were destined for Ya'akov. She thus commanded her son to deceive his father (who was blind) into thinking that he was in fact Esav. With a leaden heart, Ya'akov, who excelled in the quality of absolute truthfulness, fulfilled the words of the prophecy, and heeded his mother's command. From that time onwards, Ya'akov was beset with anguish, facing ordeal after ordeal, until at the end of his life he could state, "I have not been tranquil, I have had no quiet, and I have had no rest."

Rabbi Yerucham Levovitz classes this type of experience as one more difficult than that facing the valiant farmers who observe the *Shemittah* year. He observes that sometimes a person faces ordeals after he has performed some good action. Particularly after a person has intended to "give pleasure" to the Creator, he can be beset with harrowing torment. The difficulty of this challenge lies in the fact that it is completely unexpected. It is precisely because one has chosen the correct path, the path of righteousness, that he is suffering. It was because Ya'akov obeyed God's prophecy, and listened to his mother's command, that he was assailed with anguish.

Another example of this is the life of Ruth, the Moabite princess who converted to Judaism.

**וּשְׁתֵּי כַלֹּתֶיהָ עִמָּהּ וַתֵּלַכְנָה בַדֶּרֶךְ לָשׁוּב אֶל אֶרֶץ יְהוּדָה.... וַתֹּאמֶר נָעֳמִי שֹׁבְנָה בְנֹתַי לָמָּה תֵלַכְנָה עִמִּי הַעוֹד לִי בָנִים בְּמֵעַי וְהָיוּ לָכֶם לַאֲנָשִׁים... כִּי אָמַרְתִּי יֶשׁ לִי תִקְוָה גַּם הָיִיתִי הַלַּיְלָה לְאִישׁ וְגַם יָלַדְתִּי בָנִים. הֲלָהֵן תְּשַׂבֵּרְנָה עַד אֲשֶׁר יִגְדָּלוּ הֲלָהֵן תֵּעָגֵנָה לְבִלְתִּי הֱיוֹת לְאִישׁ, אַל בְּנֹתַי...**

*...Her two daughters-in-law [were] with her, and they went on the way to return to the land of Yehudah. Naomi said, "Return, my daughters! Why do you come with me? Do I have more children inside me to give you as husbands? Even were I tonight with a man, and conceived, and gave birth to sons, would you enchain yourselves until they grew up?"*[115]

Naomi's entreaty moved Orpah, who indeed returned to Mo'av. Ruth, however, clung to Naomi, despite the image of a future life of poverty and degradation that Naomi so vividly painted. Her initial resolve that she would accompany Naomi, and return with her, did not waver, despite both the picture of future suffering and the pleadings of her mother-in-law. Faithful to her word, we find that when the two widows encountered hardship, Ruth did not turn her back on Naomi and travel to her homeland; she refused to return to the royal home from which she had originated. Instead, she cast off any inhibitions, and joined Naomi fully and wholeheartedly in her life of abject poverty, unashamedly pleading for permission to go to the fields and gather some sheaves of grain, an activity reserved for the poorest individuals. Again, we see how a choice of righteousness led to a life of suffering.

Turning back to the criticism leveled at the Jewish People while they were in the desert, let us analyse the words of the verse more closely. It states, "The people were like complainers." It is obvious that the people did not actually complain, but that their behaviour nevertheless hinted at some inner dissatisfaction with their lot, some

---

115. *Ruth* 1:7–13.

hidden protest. The consequence:

וַיִּשְׁמַע ה' וַיִּחַר אַפּוֹ וַתִּבְעַר בָּם אֵשׁ ה' וַתֹּאכַל בִּקְצֵה הַמַּחֲנֶה.

*The Eternal heard [this] and became angry, and the Eternal's fire blazed among them and consumed [those] at the extremity of the camp.*[116]

Rashi explains that the phrase "the extremity of the camp" refers to those people who, spiritually, were on the fringes.

בַּמּוּקְצִין שֶׁבָּהֶם לִשְׁפְלוּת, אֵלּוּ עֵרֶב רַב.

*(The fire consumed) those who were lowest in stature, namely the Mixed Multitude.*[117]

If the Children of Yisrael had traveled with a genuine joy that permeated their beings, if they had recognised the good that God bestowed upon them, then the desire to follow God into the wilderness would have infused the entire camp, including the Mixed Multitude. The nation did not regret or lose their earlier resolve to fulfill the command of the Almighty and travel into the desert. They staunchly followed the pillar of cloud by day, and the pillar of fire that led them by night, on the arduous journey described to us by the Ramban. They fulfilled God's word, and served Him with loyalty. Yet, in their heart of hearts, the people were considered "like complainers." Their joy was not full, their trust not complete.

From time to time, we, in our present-day lives, are called upon to sacrifice some of our worldly comforts, and to follow God "into a wilderness, in which nothing grows." We journey with the knowledge that challenges and ordeals are likely to cross our path. We must fortify ourselves in anticipation of these challenges, and confront them joyously, triumphantly, even when the situation threatens to overwhelm us. Most important, we must not harbour any inner complaints against the Almighty, for His ultimate plan is unknown to us, and His goal is unfathomable to the greatest mind.

---

116. *Bemidbar* 11:1.
117. Rashi *ad loc.*

"And I said in my tranquillity, I will never falter."[118] The Psalmist here reveals a secret attitude that is so ubiquitous, and yet so dangerous. During times of prosperity, no man of fortune believes that his wealth will one day dissipate. A man of health is unable to believe that his strength will eventually wane. However, life is filled with vicissitude; the "wheel of fortune" continues to turn, and each person goes through times of both joy and sorrow. The person whose life is guided by Torah will follow his chosen path with conviction despite all eventualities. He will be prepared to bear hardship with a heart of serenity, and continue his journey, step by step, as he travels "according to the word of God."

118. *Tehillim* 30:7.

# DEVARIM

# DEVARIM

THE KEY TO EFFECTIVE reproach is not simply to mount a moral high horse, but rather to consider the position, attitudes, and emotions of the person whom one is addressing. It is through understanding and appealing to the other party that one's criticism will be constructive. And it is this which marks the difference between the book of *Devarim* and the rest of the Torah. The first four books are the sublime word of God transmitted to the people and are written from a Heavenly perspective. The Jewish People must strive towards this truth, must constantly forge ahead in an attempt to gain an intellectual understanding, and an emotional grasp, of the Torah's words. The book of *Devarim*, however, is written "מִצַּד הַמְקַבֵּל," from the perspective of the recipient. It is more accessible, closer to the spiritual level of the people, and this change of style is specifically because it is a book preoccupied with reproach. Moshe's castigation is intended to be accepted, to be recognised as being for the good of the people. It is thus written in a manner which the people can relate to; their eyes are opened to their faults and the manner in which they can improve. It is this theme of reproach that is the basis of this essay.

**אֵלֶּה הַדְּבָרִים אֲשֶׁר דִּבֶּר מֹשֶׁה אֶל כָּל יִשְׂרָאֵל בְּעֵבֶר הַיַּרְדֵּן בַּמִּדְבָּר בָּעֲרָבָה מוֹל סוּף בֵּין פָּארָן וּבֵין תֹּפֶל וְלָבָן וַחֲצֵרֹת וְדִי זָהָב. אַחַד עָשָׂר יוֹם מֵחֹרֵב דֶּרֶךְ הַר שֵׂעִיר עַד קָדֵשׁ בַּרְנֵעַ. וַיְהִי בְּאַרְבָּעִים שָׁנָה בְּעַשְׁתֵּי עָשָׂר חֹדֶשׁ בְּאֶחָד לַחֹדֶשׁ דִּבֶּר מֹשֶׁה אֶל בְּנֵי יִשְׂרָאֵל כְּכֹל אֲשֶׁר צִוָּה ה' אֹתוֹ אֲלֵהֶם.**

*These are the words that Moshe spoke to all Yisrael on the opposite side of the Yarden, in the desert, in the plains, [and] opposite the [Sea of] Reeds, between Paran and Tophel and Lavan, and Chatzeros and Di-Zahav; an eleven-day [journey] from Chorev, by way of Mount Seir to Kadesh Barnea. It was in the fortieth year, in the eleventh month, on the first of the month, that Moshe told the Children of Yisrael everything that the Eternal had commanded him concerning them.*[1]

The verse contains a highly detailed description of the Jewish People's location at this point. Rashi brings a reason for this. He explains that the names of the places carry a hint to various sins that the Children of Yisrael committed.

בַּמִּדְבָּר — בִּשְׁבִיל מַה שֶׁהִכְעִיסוּהוּ בַּמִּדְבָּר שֶׁאָמְרוּ מִי יִתֵּן מֻתֵנוּ וגו'.

בָּעֲרָבָה — בִּשְׁבִיל הָעֲרָבָה שֶׁחָטְאוּ בְּבַעַל פְּעוֹר בַּשִּׁטִּים בְּעַרְבוֹת מוֹאָב.

מוֹל סוּף — עַל מַה שֶּׁהִמְרוּ בְּיַם סוּף בְּבוֹאָם לְיַם סוּף שֶׁאָמְרוּ הֲמִבְּלִי אֵין קְבָרִים בְּמִצְרַיִם וְכֵן בְּנָסְעָם מִתּוֹךְ הַיָּם שֶׁנֶּאֱמַר וַיַּמְרוּ עַל יָם בְּיַם סוּף.

*In the desert — Because of that by which they angered Him in the desert, for they said, "Would that we had died..."*

*In the plains — Because of the plains, for they sinned regarding Ba'al Pe'or in Shittim, which is situated in the Plains of Mo'av.*

*Opposite the [Sea of] Reeds — Over their having rebelled at the Sea of Reeds. When they arrived at the Sea of Reeds, they said, "Are there not enough graves in Egypt [that you took us to die in the desert]?"*[2]

Rashi continues, detailing how each geographical spot mentioned by Moshe in fact alludes to a sin that either took place there, or that can be connected to the name of the place. Lavan hints to their complaints and ingratitude concerning the manna, which was *lavan*, or white, in color. Di-Zahav alludes to the sin of the Golden Calf, that was fashioned out of the abundant *zahav*, or gold, that the people possessed. Subtle hints reminded the Jewish People of their transgressions; sins were not recalled explicitly. The reason for this is the same reason underlying the timing of Moshe's speech:

---

1. *Devarim* 1:1–3.
2. Rashi *ad loc.*

מְלַמֵּד שֶׁלֹּא הוֹכִיחָן אֶלָּא סָמוּךְ לַמִּיתָה.

*This teaches that Moshe rebuked the people only prior to his death.*[3]

This timing was deliberate, and its purpose was more than just to give additional portent to his words. Were Moshe to have rebuked the people at any point during his life, having to face him in the future, the nation might be overcome by a sense of shame. To avoid inflicting such embarrassment on God's people, Moshe waited until his final hours in this world to deliver his reproach. In fact, the source for this behaviour is to be found many years earlier. It is learned from Ya'akov, whose poetic deathbed rebuke to the twelve tribes is well-known. Ya'akov specifically chose this moment to direct and guide his sons along the correct path, to channel their individual personalities into the correct expression. He did not give his rebuke earlier, for he did not want to cause his sons shame on future occasions.

Considering this passage, the Maharal asks why the Jewish People's transgressions are not listed in chronological order, in the manner that one would expect. He states:

לָמָּה שִׁנָּה סֵדֶר הַחֲטָאִים שֶׁלָּהֶם, שֶׁאֵין מְסַפֵּר אוֹתָן כְּסֵדֶר? וְיֵשׁ לְתָרֵץ, שֶׁאֵינוֹ מוֹנֶה אוֹתָן כְּסֵדֶר כְּדֵי לְהַעֲלִים הַתּוֹכָחָה, שֶׁהֲרֵי אִלּוּ הָיָה מְסַפֵּר הַחֵטְא כְּסֵדֶר, הָיָה יוֹתֵר מְפֻרְסָם וְנִגְלֶה וְהַכָּתוּב בִּקֵּשׁ לְהַסְתִּיר, וְלֹא לְפַרְסֵם.

*Why did he change the order of their sins, recounting them in a different sequence? He did not recount them in sequence in order to somewhat conceal the rebuke. Were he to have recounted them chronologically, the sins would have been publicised and revealed.*[4]

A glimpse of Moshe's sensitivity towards his flock is hereby gleaned. Not only did he only begin his rebuke towards the Jewish People immediately prior to his death, his very mention of their sins

---

3. Rashi *ad loc.*

4. *Gur Aryeh* 1:3.

is in a most subtle and concealed manner.

Another leader of the Jewish People, the prophet Yeshayah, lived in a period in which the Jewish People were morally at a low ebb. His task was to chastise them, inspiring them to repentance. Yet, the techniques Yeshayah employed are strikingly different from those of Moshe. We read:

> יָדַע שׁוֹר קֹנֵהוּ וַחֲמוֹר אֵבוּס בְּעָלָיו יִשְׂרָאֵל לֹא יָדַע עַמִּי לֹא הִתְבּוֹנָן.
>
> *An ox knows his owner, and an ass his master's trough. Yisrael does not know; My people do not contemplate.*[5]

With these words, Yeshayah condemns the people as being on an inferior level to animals. While beasts instinctively know their owners, recognising the source of goodness they receive, Yisrael remains blind to their Master, to the endless source of goodness. Blind, numb, insensitive to a higher authority, the people recklessly continue along the path of corruption. And Yeshayah chastises the people, rebuking them for their witlessness. His rebuke is couched in the harshest of terms; Yeshayah's intent is unambiguous. But what of Yeshayah's sensitivity to the people? What of carefully guarding oneself against shaming one's fellow Jew? Why did Yeshayah not learn the lesson that Moshe (and Ya'akov) taught humanity?

This question can be directed not only to Yeshayah. The Torah itself seems to require humiliation of the worst kind in certain instances. One who incurs the punishment of מַלְקוּת, lashes, is struck with a very specific whip. It must be made up of two tongues of donkey's hide. The reason: to impress upon the sinner that he has descended to a level at which even a donkey is his superior. Imagining the emotions of the sinner at his time of punishment, we can envision the overriding humiliation of the experience. With each crack of the whip, the dignity of his very humanity is stripped away. How can we understand this punishment, one that is prescribed by the Torah itself? Are we in fact meant to disregard human pride, ignoring another's shame?

---

5. *Yeshayah* 1:3.

To answer these questions we must turn to a later episode in our *parashah*. Moshe reviews the overhaul of Yisrael's legal system. Initially, Moshe judged all legal cases alone. However, upon the advice of his father-in-law, Yithro, he appointed deputies to assist him in the onerous task.

> **אֵיכָה אֶשָּׂא לְבַדִּי טָרְחֲכֶם וּמַשַּׂאֲכֶם וְרִיבְכֶם. הָבוּ לָכֶם אֲנָשִׁים חֲכָמִים וּנְבֹנִים וִידֻעִים לְשִׁבְטֵיכֶם וַאֲשִׂימֵם בְּרָאשֵׁיכֶם. וַתַּעֲנוּ אֹתִי וַתֹּאמְרוּ טוֹב הַדָּבָר אֲשֶׁר דִּבַּרְתָּ לַעֲשׂוֹת. וָאֶקַּח אֶת רָאשֵׁי שִׁבְטֵיכֶם אֲנָשִׁים חֲכָמִים וִידֻעִים וָאֶתֵּן אֹתָם רָאשִׁים עֲלֵיכֶם שָׂרֵי אֲלָפִים וְשָׂרֵי מֵאוֹת וְשָׂרֵי חֲמִשִּׁים וְשָׂרֵי עֲשָׂרֹת וְשֹׁטְרִים לְשִׁבְטֵיכֶם.**
>
> *Oh! How can I alone bear your irksomeness, your grievances and your quarrels? Come [and choose] for yourselves [righteous], wise and intelligent men, well known by your [respective] tribes, and I shall appoint them as your leaders. You answered me and said, "The thing which you said to do is good." I then took the heads of your tribes — [righteous], wise and well-known men — and appointed them [as] leaders over you: officers of thousands, officers of hundreds, officers of fifties, and officers of tens, and [I appointed] policemen for your tribes.*[6]

The Jewish People accepted this legal revolution readily. When we consider this account in its context, however, a question arises. What is the point of connection between it, and the overarching theme of the book of *Devarim*, namely, rebuke of the Jewish People?

Upon close examination of the text, a further difficulty arises. Yithro advised Moshe to appoint men who were, "wise, intelligent, and well-known." However, reading the account of the judges' appointment, we are told only that they were "wise and well-known." The third virtue of בִּינָה, intelligence or understanding, seems to be missing; it appears that the judges lacked this quality.

To pinpoint the difference between one who is wise, a חָכָם, and

---

6. *Devarim* 1:12–15.

one who possesses intelligence, a נָבוֹן, we must turn to a parable brought by Rashi. Rashi describes two kinds of bankers. Both scrupulously fulfill their job description, opening accounts, dispensing financial advice, and making transactions. When they are occupied, there is nothing to distinguish between them. It is when customers are slow in coming that the difference between them can be discerned. One banker sits idle, listlessly staring into space as the minutes tick past. The other banker uses this time to make his own private transactions. A חָכָם is one who receives, learns and understands the information that he is taught. A נָבוֹן, one with intelligence, goes a step further. The נָבוֹן takes the knowledge and develops it; through contemplation he nurtures his own approach, his own related ideas, injecting his own creativity into the basic principles.

Moshe failed to appoint נְבוֹנִים, for the nation as a whole was deficient in this area. And this is the implicit reprimand in the account of the new legal system; this is why this account is placed in the book of *Devarim*, within the reproach delivered by Moshe.

Rashi gives a reason as to why the nation so readily accepted judges other than Moshe.

> *The people twisted the situation to their own advantage. It would have been appropriate for them to respond negatively to the suggestion, saying, "Our teacher Moshe, from whom is it better to learn, from you or from your students?" However, the nation was secretly gleeful. "Now that a number of judges have been appointed over us, we will be able to bring the judges gifts, in the hope that they will be favourably disposed towards us."*[7]

It is imperative to note that this is not a fault that can be understood in reference to our lowly stature. The generation of the desert was on a spiritual level higher than we can begin to comprehend; they experienced, firsthand, the revelation of God. With their own eyes they beheld the miracles and wonders of the Exodus. This was

---

7. Rashi on *Devarim* 1:14.

the דּוֹר דֵּעָה — "Generation of Knowledge" — who obtained absolute clarity in areas that many in our generation do not even know are obscured. They were not, Heaven forbid, low, crooked people, simply seeking to pervert the course of justice for their own ends.

Yet, some fault lay within. There was some leaning, some inclination for which the Jewish People were censured. And because of this bias, which they subconsciously chose to ignore, the people were eager to accept Yithro's suggestion to decentralise the legal protocol.

Although on a purely intellectual level, Yithro's suggestion was a logical one, it nevertheless failed to take the suprarational into account. It failed to recognise the enormous significance of being judged by Moshe himself. Yithro's suggestion was cast into the hands of the people. Acceptance would entail revolution, dismissal would herald Moshe's uniqueness as the nation's judge. The nation's response? Acceptance.

"Why?" we may ask. "Why did the people fail to appreciate Moshe's direct leadership?" The answer to this question applies to the foundation of our Divine service. The fault of the people did not lie in a lack of appreciation. Instead, it lay in a lack of contemplation. They failed to consider the outcome of an indirect leadership. This stemmed from another deficiency: the nation failed to discern the hidden bias that prompted them to accept Yithro's suggestion. They did not scrutinise their psyches to discern their secret motives. They did not explore and meditate on the labyrinth of their hearts, instead satisfying themselves with a superficial understanding. And so, they forfeited the right to the title נְבוֹנִים — "Intelligent ones," ones who contemplate. It was impossible for Moshe to meet Yithro's prescription for the judges, for the people as a whole were deficient.

As mentioned above, this generation was given the title of the דּוֹר דֵּעָה — "Generation of Knowledge." דֵּעָה carries other implications, however, and throughout Scripture, its use implies חִבּוּר, profound bonding, a joining of two things. "דַּעַת" is a level of knowledge in which the intellectual, external information has been internalised and joined with one's very self. Or, as we find in *Bereishith,* וְהָאָדָם יָדַע

אֶת חַוָּה אִשְׁתּוֹ — "And the man knew his wife."[8] In this context, דַּעַת is used to denote the intimate bonding of man and wife. The generation of the desert was one of דַּעַת — they knew God, and were welded to Him and His will. Real attachment to someone or something will dominate one's mind, one's thoughts. Any slight, and even obscure, association will bring to mind that person or object. And, so with the Jewish People; so attached were they to God and His Torah that any slight association, any hint, would be related to the Almighty. Every small occurrence was felt to have bearing on their Divine service, which was being constantly beautified. Thus, Moshe's rebuke, despite its subtlety, was understood and internalised by the people. The mere hint of rebuke could prompt genuine repentance.

Turning to the era in which Yeshayah lived, the people had a rather different description. No longer called a "Generation of Knowledge," their behaviour instead called for the words, "My people do not contemplate." The people failed to think, to connect everything to their Divine service. Thus, a rebuke like the one delivered by Moshe would have been futile. An open rebuke, one in which the nation's faults were painfully apparent, was required, as it was the only manner of castigation that would be effective. Thus, even at the expense of embarrassment, Yeshayah was required to redirect the people along the correct path. Similarly, subtle hints will not be effective for a transgressor who incurs lashing. Only a direct message, only being struck with tongues of donkey hide, will awaken him from his spiritual slumber.

In connection to our theme, we find a verse in *Yirmiyah*:

**שִׁמְעוּ דְבַר ה' בֵּית יַעֲקֹב.**

*Listen to the word of God, O house of Ya'akov!*[9]

Our Sages, in the *Yalkut Shimoni*, elaborate on these words:

**שִׁמְעוּ דִּבְרֵי נְבוּאָה עַד שֶׁלֹּא תִּשְׁמְעוּ תּוֹכֵחוֹת. שִׁמְעוּ דִּבְרֵי תּוֹכֵחוֹת עַד שֶׁלֹּא תִּשְׁמְעוּ קִנְטוּרִין. שִׁמְעוּ דִּבְרֵי קִנְטוּרִין עַד שֶׁלֹּא תִּשְׁמְעוּ קַל**

8. *Bereishith* 4:1.
9. *Yirmiyah* 2:4.

קַרְנָא מַשְׁרוֹקִיתָא. שִׁמְעוּ בָּאָרֶץ עַד שֶׁלֹּא תִּשְׁמְעוּ בְּחוּץ לָאָרֶץ. שִׁמְעוּ חַיִּים עַד שֶׁלֹּא תִּשְׁמְעוּן מֵתִים.

*Listen to words of prophecy before you are forced to listen to words of rebuke.*

*Listen to words of rebuke before you are forced to listen to the sound of punishment.*

*Listen to the sound of punishment before you are forced to listen to the sound of war.*

*Listen in the Land of Israel before you are forced to listen outside the holy Land.*

*Listen while you are alive before you are forced to listen from the dead.*[10]

Our Sages here warn us to listen to, and heed, the rebuke that is delivered. We must incline our ears to even the slightest hint of rebuke, thus preventing the sharp words that must be delivered to insensitive ears. Our nation has endured untold suffering, starting from the time of the destruction of the Temple and continuing throughout the ages, until the most recent tragedy, the destruction of European Jewry in the Second World War. Considering the lessons that history teaches, meditating on the events of the past, will yield fruit, lessons that we must apply to our lives. It is only by internalising these lessons that we can prevent another tragedy from occurring, pre-empting the need for God to send us yet another reminder to follow His will and to wholeheartedly observe His laws. We must follow the generation of Moshe, meditating on, contemplating, and heeding the hints that God sends us, in an attempt to constantly beautify our Divine service.

10. *Yalkut Shimoni, Yirmiyah* 264.

# VA'ETHCHANAN

**שְׁמַע יִשְׂרָאֵל ה' אֱלֹקֵינוּ ה' אֶחָד.**

*Listen, Yisrael! The Eternal is our God, the Eternal is One.*[11]

It is this declaration that parents impress upon their children from an early age. It is with this utterance that the smoldering spark of a Jewish soul can once again be ignited. It is with this proclamation that thousands upon thousands of Jews have met their deaths.

In our *parashah*, and indeed in our prayers, this epithet precedes the command to love God. However, our Sages trace it back to the twelve tribes, who made this declaration in an attempt to assuage Ya'akov's fears.

וַיִּקְרָא יַעֲקֹב אֶל בָּנָיו וַיֹּאמֶר הֵאָסְפוּ וְאַגִּידָה לָכֶם. בִּקֵּשׁ יַעֲקֹב לְגַלּוֹת לְבָנָיו קֵץ הַיָּמִין וְנִסְתַּלְּקָה מִמֶּנּוּ שְׁכִינָה. אָמַר שֶׁמָּא ח"ו יֵשׁ בְּמִטָּתִי פְּסוּל? כְּאַבְרָהָם שֶׁיָּצָא מִמֶּנּוּ יִשְׁמָעֵאל, וְאָבִי יִצְחָק שֶׁיָּצָא מִמֶּנּוּ עֵשָׂו? אָמְרוּ לוֹ בָּנָיו שְׁמַע יִשְׂרָאֵל ה' אֱלֹקֵינוּ ה' אֶחָד. כְּשֵׁם שֶׁאֵין בְּלִבְּךָ אֶלָּא אֶחָד, כָּךְ אֵין בְּלִבֵּנוּ אֶלָּא אֶחָד. בְּאוֹתָהּ שָׁעָה פָּתַח יַעֲקֹב אָבִינוּ וְאָמַר בָּרוּךְ שֵׁם כְּבוֹד מַלְכוּתוֹ לְעוֹלָם וָעֶד. אָמְרֵי רַבָּנָן הֵיכִי נַעֲבִיד? נֹאמְרֵהוּ, לֹא אֲמָרוֹ מֹשֶׁה רַבֵּנוּ. לֹא נֹאמְרֵהוּ, אֲמָרוֹ יַעֲקֹב. הִתְקִינוּ שֶׁיְּהוּ אוֹמְרִים אוֹתוֹ בַּחֲשַׁאי. אָמַר ר' יִצְחָק אָמְרֵי דְּבֵי רַבִּי אַמִּי. מָשָׁל לְבַת מֶלֶךְ שֶׁהֵרִיחָה צִיקֵי קְדֵרָה. אִם תֹּאמַר יֵשׁ לָהּ גְּנַאי. לֹא תֹּאמַר, יֵשׁ לָהּ צַעַר. הִתְחִילוּ עֲבָדֶיהָ לְהָבִיא בַּחֲשַׁאי.

*Ya'akov called his sons, and he said, "Gather together and I will inform you." Ya'akov wanted to reveal to his sons what would transpire at the end of days. However, the Divine Presence departed from him (thus removing his vision). Ya'akov said, "Perhaps, God forbid, there is a defect in one of my*

11. *Devarim* 6:4.

*offspring, just as with Avraham, who begot Yishmael, and Yitzchak, who begot Esav." His children reassured him, saying "Listen, Yisrael (another name for Ya'akov): The Eternal is our God, the Eternal is One." They thus conveyed the message that just as there was One in Ya'akov's heart, so in their hearts there was only One.*

*At that moment Ya'akov responded, "Blessed is the Name of His glorious kingdom forever and ever."*

*...Said Rabbi Yitzchak, "They used to bring a parable in the house of Rabbi Amai: There was once a princess who smelled a (distasteful) cooked raisin dish. To mention it would be beneath her dignity, but if she remained silent, she would suffer discomfort. Her servants therefore brought the dish in silently."*[12]

Our Rabbis debated on whether or not Ya'akov's response should be included in our prayers. On the one hand, how can we say it, since Moshe did not say it? Yet, how can we omit a praise uttered by no less than our Patriarch Ya'akov? In a balancing act, in which we attempt to satisfy both sides, it was decided that we must whisper this praise. It is for this reason that even today, in our prayers, we recite בָּרוּךְ שֵׁם in an undertone. However, there are two points that remain to be understood:

1. Why did Moshe not make this statement?
2. What is degrading about saying בָּרוּךְ שֵׁם in an audible voice?

If we compare the above scene at Ya'akov's deathbed with another account, we discern a few differences that shed light on our subject.

אָמַר ר׳ תַּנְחוּמָא: הֵאָסְפוּ וְאַגִּידָה לָכֶם. מִכָּאן שֶׁהָיוּ מְפוּזָּרִין וּכְנָסָן בְּרוּחַ הַקֹּדֶשׁ... בְּשָׁעָה שֶׁהָיָה יַעֲקֹב אָבִינוּ נִפְטָר מִן הָעוֹלָם קָרָא לי״ב בָּנָיו וְאָמַר לָהֶם: שִׁמְעוּ אֶל יִשְׂרָאֵל שֶׁבַּשָּׁמַיִם אֲבִיכֶם. שֶׁמָּא יֵשׁ בִּלְבַבְכֶם מַחֲלֹקֶת עַל הקב״ה? אָמְרוּ לוֹ שְׁמַע יִשְׂרָאֵל אָבִינוּ, כְּשֵׁם שֶׁאֵין בְּלִבְּךָ מַחֲלֹקֶת עַל הקב״ה כָּךְ אֵין בְּלִבֵּנוּ מַחֲלֹקֶת אֶלָּא ה׳ אֱלֹקֵינוּ

12. *Pesachim* 56a.

ה׳ אֶחָד. אַף הוּא פֵּרֵשׁ בִּשְׂפָתָיו וְאָמַר בָּרוּךְ שֵׁם כְּבוֹד מַלְכוּתוֹ לְעוֹלָם וָעֶד. ר׳ בְּרֶכְיָה חֶלְבּוֹ בְּשֵׁם ר׳ שְׁמוּאֵל הֲדָא הוּא שֶׁיִּשְׂרָאֵל מַשְׁכִּימִים וּמַעֲרִיבִים בְּכָל יוֹם וְאוֹמְרִים שְׁמַע יִשְׂרָאֵל אָבִינוּ מִמְּעָרַת הַמַּכְפֵּלָה. אוֹתוֹ דָּבָר שֶׁצִּוִּיתָנוּ עֲדַיִן הוּא נוֹהֵג בָּנוּ — ה׳ אֱלֹקֵינוּ ה׳ אֶחָד.

*Said Rabbi Tanchuma, "Gather and I will tell them." From here we learn that they were not unified, and he gathered them with Divine inspiration. When Ya'akov passed from the world, he called his twelve sons and said to them, "Listen to Yisrael [your father, who tells you] that your Father [God] is in Heaven. Maybe your hearts have some doubt in the Almighty?"*

*They responded, "Listen, Yisrael our father: just as in your heart there is no divergence from God, so there is none in our hearts. Rather, the Eternal is our God, the Eternal is One."*

*So he (Ya'akov) augmented their words, saying, "Blessed is the Name of His glorious kingdom forever and ever."*

*Rabbi Berechya Chelbo in the name of Rabbi Shemuel said, "This refers to the fact that the Jewish People arise and retire every day saying "Hear O Yisrael our father, from the Cave of Machpelah. We still fulfill that which you commanded us — the Eternal our God is One."*[13]

In this Midrash, it appears that Ya'akov introduced the subject, and uttered the words, "Listen to Yisrael your father." His children then responded by affirming their faith in God. However, in the earlier extract it is the children who begin, "Listen, Yisrael…" How can we reconcile the two accounts? Further, in both versions, Ya'akov first affirms the unity of his sons. What is the significance of their unanimity?

A different Midrash attributes the origin of the phrase בָּרוּךְ שֵׁם to yet another source:

*When Moshe ascended to the heavens, he heard the celestial angels lauding God, "Blessed is the Name of His glorious kingdom forever and ever." Moshe brought this praise down*

13. *Bereishith Rabbah* 98:3.

*to Yisrael, and introduced it into this world. Why do we not say it aloud? It can be compared to someone who stole a precious piece of jewelry from the palace. He gave it to his wife, with the following stipulation, "Do not adorn yourself with it publicly; wear it only inside the house." On Yom Kippur, The Jewish People are likened to angels, and are therefore given license to raise their voices aloft and declare, "Blessed is the Name of His glorious kingdom forever and ever."*[14]

The origin of this praise has still not been determined. The Oral Law brings us two different accounts, and attributes the source of this praise to two different individuals: Ya'akov and Moshe. It is interesting to note that this expression is visibly absent from the Written Law. This cannot be an arbitrary or accidental omission. Why is this the case?

To understand this omission, let us delve into the essential nature of both the Written Law and the Oral Law. The Written Law was transmitted to us through Moshe, the greatest prophet of all times. It was given to us through revelation; Godliness was present for all to experience. There could be no other explanation of what transpired, no other interpretation of events: God Himself spoke to the entire nation. The Written Law is thus a symbol of clarity, of incontrovertible truth, evident to all, impervious to denial.

In contrast to this mass exposure, the Oral Law has been the domain of each individual scholar for generations. It has been passed from teacher to student throughout the ages. While the Written Law represents unadulterated, undeniable truth, the Oral Law represents *emunah* — the faithful loyalty required by the chain of transmission. As the verse states in *Tehillim*: לְהַגִּיד בַּבֹּקֶר חַסְדֶּךָ וֶאֱמוּנָתְךָ בַּלֵּילוֹת — "To tell of Your kindness in the morning and Your *emunah,* faithfulness, in the nights."[15] The Midrash states that this verse refers to Moshe, who spent forty days and nights on Mount Sinai, learning the entire Torah. The Midrash asks a striking question: high up in Heaven, how

14. *Yalkut Shimoni, Va'ethchanan* 834.
15. *Tehillim* 92:3.

could Moshe distinguish between day and night? The answer:

בְּשָׁעָה שהקב"ה מְלַמְּדוֹ תּוֹרָה יוֹדֵעַ שֶׁהוּא יוֹם וּבְשָׁעָה שֶׁהוּא מְלַמְּדוֹ מִשְׁנָה יוֹדֵעַ שֶׁהוּא לַיְלָה.

*When God was teaching him the Written Law, he knew that it was day, and when God was teaching him the Mishnah (Oral Law), he knew that it was night.*[16]

The *emunah* that is referred to in the verse refers to the study of the Oral Law. This study has a particular connection to night ("and Your faithfulness in the nights"), when the cover of darkness obscures clear vision, and God's Hand is not clearly discernable. This is the study of Talmud: toil and labour to reconstruct the shards of light, re-form the fragments which will eventually lead us back to the clarity of the Written Law. It is *emunah*, for it details that which is outside the realm of human understanding, that which we must accept and believe, although we are unable to penetrate to its depths. *Emunah* — for the study of Talmud has accompanied us through the long night of exile in which light and goodness are obscured. Nevertheless, we remain loyal to that truth, to the declaration which is no longer overtly audible.

For example, we know about the future resurrection of the dead, which will occur after the coming of Mashiach, only through the Oral Law, having no explicit reference to it in the written tradition. It is a subject which by its very nature is obscure and distant from our lives and experiences, and we are unable to fully understand it while in this world. We nevertheless have full conviction in it due to our quality of faith, due to an unbroken tradition that it will be so. It is a subject that reflects the nature of the Oral Law, rather than the Written Law. Thus from the Written Law, it is absent.

It was only after the Sinai experience that the Jewish People were allowed to openly and audibly declare, "Listen, Yisrael! The Eternal is our God, the Eternal is One." In the rendezvous between man and God, the existence and Oneness of the Almighty was obvious to all.

---

16. *Midrash Shocher Tov* 19.

Thus, it was transcribed in the Torah, the Written Law, the work of lucid clarity. It is declared incumbent on every Jew to grasp and understand the existence of a Prime Force.

However, what lies in the expression בָּרוּךְ שֵׁם — "Blessed is the Name of His glorious kingdom forever and ever"? With this statement we are, in effect, negating the existence of anything apart from כְּבוֹד שָׁמַיִם, the glory of God. As the famous maxim states, הַכֹּל בָּרָא לִכְבוֹדוֹ — "Everything was created for God's glory." This precludes the existence of anything that does not lead to the glory of God. Although intellectually, we can accept this idea, it rings hollow in our depths. Every minute of every day, we encounter that which not only does not increase sanctity in the world, but actively opposes it. Although we utter, אֱמֶת מַלְכֵּנוּ אֶפֶס זוּלָתוֹ — "True is our King, there is none but Him," we constantly behold the existence of things "apart from" or "in addition to" the Almighty. As mentioned in previous essays, our own existence apparently contradicts this statement! Further, although we may know that true existence belongs exclusively to God, we continue to attribute reality to this entire physical world. All may be "vanity," but we live in an illusory world, in which honour, prestige, power, physical beauty, and other materialistic aims play a very important role.

Only in the realm of angels, a realm wherein spirituality is the only reality, can the statement, "Blessed is the Name of His glorious kingdom forever and ever," be heard unopposed. The world in which we live does not allow us to deliver this praise. Inhabitants of a dream world, we must enunciate the words in a whisper, waiting for the day on which we will be permitted to speak out each word clearly.

There is one day on which we raise ourselves up to the level of angels. On Yom Kippur, we disregard our bodily requirements, divorcing ourselves from physicality, extricating ourselves from the shackles of this world. On Yom Kippur, Satan is silent; the accuser, the evil inclination, is unable to speak. On Yom Kippur we raise our voices aloft and declare, "Blessed is the Name of His glorious kingdom forever and ever."

A thought-provoking maxim of our Sages reads, "Our Father Ya'akov did not die." Although his physical presence may have been removed, his spirit lives on. Indeed, we are told that Ya'akov's image is engraved on God's throne of glory. Ya'akov was able to say בָּרוּךְ שֵׁם in a manner that defies our understanding, and is far removed from any spiritual level to which we can relate. Moshe too, could make this declaration in a manner that accorded with his perception of the truth, with an understanding that is totally beyond us. Moshe was still not commanded to transcribe the praise in the Written Law, for the Written Law is the domain of explicit truth, truth that is accessible and comprehensible to the entire nation. For us, this concept is one of "*emunah*," not one of "truth," and it is therefore omitted from the Written Law; we do not have permission to enunciate the words audibly.

With this understanding we can return to our original question as to why it was necessary for Ya'akov to gather all the tribes together. To answer this, we will have to turn to a famous explanation of the Ramban concerning the blessing which Ya'akov bestowed on Yehudah.

**לֹא יָסוּר שֵׁבֶט מִיהוּדָה...**

*The (ruling) staff will not depart from Yehudah...*[17]

The Ramban relates this blessing to a period in history many hundreds of years later. After their victory over the Syrian-Greek army, the Hasmoneans re-established the Jewish monarchy by coronating members of their own clan. The Hasmoneans, however, were priests, descendants of the tribe of Levi. They thus contravened the command that Jewish monarchs should be exclusively members of the tribe of Yehudah. And we find that their entire dynasty either was killed or died untimely deaths.

*This was the punishment of the Chashmonaim. They were giants in their piety, and prevented Torah from being forgotten, lost from the Children of Yisrael. However, they were subject*

17. *Bereishith* 49:10.

*to a terrible punishment. We find that four Chashmonaim, who ruled consecutively with great success and might, fell to the sword of their enemy. Indeed, the entire dynasty was wiped out due to their sin: they ruled although they were not from the tribe of Yehudah, or from the progeny of the house of David... Their crime was augmented further because the Chashmonaim were from the tribe of Levi. Their mission was to be priests, serving God in the Temple, not leading the nation.*[18]

Quite apart from the fascinating historical insight with which the Ramban presents us, we learn from his words that every tribe has a particular purpose. By appointing themselves as monarchs, the Hasmoneans had effectively trespassed into Yehudah's territory. The consequence: destruction, which prevented them not only from fulfilling someone else's task, but even from their own allotted function of serving in the Temple.

On his deathbed, Ya'akov blessed each of his sons, informing each one of his individual life's work, the field of Divine service in which each must excel. The twelve tribes can aptly be compared to the branches of a tree, while Ya'akov, together with the other Patriarchs, corresponds to the tree's trunk. Each branch is given its own particular place, and each is important. However, all this is meaningless unless the branches are firmly attached to the trunk, to their lifesource. Although each tribe must work on his designated area of service, all must be bound up with the one purpose which unites them all — spreading the glory of God. Diversity can be encouraged as long as all the disparate parts ultimately lead back to one source.

The Maharal[19] elaborates upon this idea.

*The tribes declared, "Listen, Yisrael, the Eternal is our God, the Eternal is One." In making this statement, the tribes linked themselves to our forefather Ya'akov. They did this because Ya'akov was completely bound up with the Oneness of God;*

---

18. Ramban *ad loc.*
19. *Netzach Yisrael*, Ch. 44.

*his lofty spiritual stature was such that this was his essence, his hidden inner truth. Through associating themselves with Ya'akov, the tribes were indirectly associating themselves, and connecting, with God's Oneness. We find a hint to this in the word* אֶחָד*, one, where* א *corresponds to Ya'akov;* ח*, the numerical value of which is eight, corresponds to the eight tribes who descended from Rachel and Leah; and* ד*, four, corresponds to the four sons of the maidservants.*

The twelve tribes, connected to Ya'akov, were intimately linked to God's Oneness and singularity. It is noteworthy that the numerical value of the entire word אֶחָד is thirteen — corresponding to the twelve tribes with the addition of Ya'akov! It was through their sublime father that the tribes learned to declare God's Oneness in שְׁמַע יִשְׂרָאֵל ה' אֱלֹקֵינוּ ה' אֶחָד.

Ya'akov's words, שִׁמְעוּ אֶל יִשְׂרָאֵל שֶׁבַּשָּׁמַיִם אֲבִיכֶם — "Listen to Yisrael: your Father is in Heaven," are tantamount to the maxim, "The Holy One, blessed be He, the Torah, and Yisrael — they are one." Concurrently striving for excellence, each in their own field of Divine service, the twelve tribes were connected to their father, and thereby also to the Almighty. Together with Ya'akov, they formed אֶחָד: united on earth, connected to Heaven. Conversely, were there to have been contention or friction amongst the brothers, they would have broken the bond between them and would have been unable to connect with God.

In a similar vein, the Jewish People must converge as one, each fulfilling his particular mission, and by doing so, working for the good of the community at large. "Listen Yisrael, the Eternal is our God, the Eternal is One." Acceptance of the yoke of Heaven, of God as our ruler, must be preceded by national unity. Our Sages state, אֵין מֶלֶךְ בְּלֹא עַם — "There is no king without subjects." In order to coronate God as King over ourselves, we must declare our desire to be His subjects, to willingly allow Him to rule over us. As one people with one heart, we proudly utter, "Listen, Yisrael: the Eternal is our God, the Eternal is One."

# EKEV

AFTER THE FIRST set of tablets was smashed when Moshe saw the nation in an idolatrous frenzy around the Golden Calf, Moshe was asked to prepare another set of tablets. He reports:

**בָּעֵת הַהִוא אָמַר ה' אֵלַי פְּסָל לְךָ שְׁנֵי לוּחֹת אֲבָנִים כָּרִאשֹׁנִים וַעֲלֵה אֵלַי הָהָרָה וְעָשִׂיתָ לְּךָ אֲרוֹן עֵץ. וְאֶכְתֹּב עַל הַלֻּחֹת אֶת הַדְּבָרִים אֲשֶׁר הָיוּ עַל הַלֻּחֹת הָרִאשֹׁנִים אֲשֶׁר שִׁבַּרְתָּ וְשַׂמְתָּם בָּאָרוֹן. וָאַעַשׂ אֲרוֹן עֲצֵי שִׁטִּים וָאֶפְסֹל שְׁנֵי לֻחֹת אֲבָנִים כָּרִאשֹׁנִים.**

*At that time, the Eternal said to me, "Carve for yourself two tablets of stone like the first ones and come up to Me to the mountain; and you shall make for yourself a wooden ark. I shall then write on the tablets the [same] words that were on the first tablets which you smashed, and you shall place [the tablets] inside the ark." I made an ark of acacia wood and carved out two tablets of stone.*[20]

Close examination of these words reveals something strange. If the theme here is the tablets of stone, why is so much emphasis placed upon the wooden ark? Not only is the ark mentioned by God, Moshe also mentions that he carried out the command concerning the ark, seemingly a peripheral detail, not meriting mention in its own right.

To shed light on this question, let us digress to the following enigmatic description of an annual ceremony. On Yom Kippur, two identical goats were subjected to two very different fates:

**וְלָקַח אֶת שְׁנֵי הַשְּׂעִירִם וְהֶעֱמִיד אֹתָם לִפְנֵי ה'... וְנָתַן אַהֲרֹן עַל שְׁנֵי**

20. *Devarim* 10:1–3.

**הַשְּׂעִירִם גּוֹרָלוֹת גּוֹרָל אֶחָד לַה' וְגוֹרָל אֶחָד לַעֲזָאזֵל. וְהִקְרִיב אַהֲרֹן אֶת הַשָּׂעִיר אֲשֶׁר עָלָה עָלָיו הַגּוֹרָל לַה' וְעָשָׂהוּ חַטָּאת. וְהַשָּׂעִיר אֲשֶׁר עָלָה עָלָיו הַגּוֹרָל לַעֲזָאזֵל יָעֳמַד חַי לִפְנֵי ה' לְכַפֵּר עָלָיו לְשַׁלַּח אֹתוֹ לַעֲזָאזֵל הַמִּדְבָּרָה.**

*He shall then take the two goats and stand them before the Eternal... Aharon shall then put [two] lots on the two goats — one lot marked "for the Eternal" and the [other] lot [marked] "for Azazel." Aharon shall then bring near the goat on which fell the lot "for the Eternal" and designate it as a sin offering; while the goat on which fell the lot "for Azazel" shall be presented alive before the Eternal, to atone upon it and [then] send it away to Azazel, to the desert.*[21]

One goat was slaughtered and offered up in the *Mishkan* as a burnt offering. The other was taken to a precipitous cliff in the middle of the wilderness, and cast off to meet its death. It is interesting to note that in the Torah, goats are symbolic of the forces of evil and impurity. This is seen from the verse, "They shall no longer offer their sacrifices to goats."[22] Rashi explains that "goats" is a metaphor for the powers of evil. The goats slaughtered on Yom Kippur, then, signify the death and annulment of the influence of negativity. This being the case, it appears strange why one of these goats was sanctified and offered up to God. Why were not both goats, personifying the forces of darkness, cast off a cliff in the desert? On a universal level, can we infer from this that evil can be used as part of our Divine service? Further, if this is indeed so, the following incident becomes puzzling:

**עַתָּה לֵךְ וְהִכִּיתָה אֶת עֲמָלֵק וְהַחֲרַמְתֶּם אֶת כָּל אֲשֶׁר לוֹ וְלֹא תַחְמֹל עָלָיו וְהֵמַתָּה מֵאִישׁ עַד אִשָּׁה מֵעֹלֵל וְעַד יוֹנֵק מִשּׁוֹר וְעַד שֶׂה מִגָּמָל וְעַד חֲמוֹר.**

*Now go, and you shall smite Amalek, completely destroying all that is his. You shall not have pity on him; you should slay*

21. *Vayikra* 16:7–10.
22. *Vayikra* 17:7.

*man and woman, infant and suckling, ox and sheep, camel and donkey.*[23]

The prophet Shemuel commands King Sha'ul to utterly eradicate Amalek from the face of the earth. Sha'ul, however, did not completely obey this command, leaving alive the best sheep and oxen to sacrifice to God. Amalek, the symbol of evil, must be obliterated, but Sha'ul sought to utilise some negativity, "the best of the sheep and oxen," in his service of God. Sha'ul's desire was rejected, and he was subject to a harsh punishment for his deed. However, his action seems to mirror that of the High Priest on Yom Kippur, when one of the goats is indeed sacrificed to God. What was Sha'ul's terrible error?

Let us turn to the *Shema*, where examination of two injunctions will clarify the nature of evil itself:

**וְלֹא תָתוּרוּ אַחֲרֵי לְבַבְכֶם וְאַחֲרֵי עֵינֵיכֶם אֲשֶׁר אַתֶּם זֹנִים אַחֲרֵיהֶם.**

*And you must not be searching, following your heart and your eyes after which you [tend to] stray.*[24]

Our Sages elaborate that both "heart" and "eyes" in this injunction refer to two specific types of evil.

אַחֲרֵי לְבַבְכֶם — זוֹ מִינוּת, וְכֵן הַכָּתוּב אוֹמֵר "אָמַר נָבָל בְּלִבּוֹ אֵין אֱלֹקִים", וְאַחֲרֵי עֵינֵיכֶם — זֶה הִרְהוּר עֲבֵרָה, שֶׁנֶּאֱמַר "וַיֹּאמֶר שִׁמְשׁוֹן אוֹתָהּ קַח לִי כִּי הִיא יָשְׁרָה בְעֵינָי".

*After your hearts — this refers to heresy, as it says, "The fool has said in his heart, there is no God."*

*After your eyes — this refers to fantasies of sin (specifically immorality), as it says, "And Shimshon said, 'Take her for me, for she is good in my eyes.'"*[25]

(It is important to note here that Shimshon's main intention was to take the woman for spiritual reasons. However, because some

23. *I Shemuel* 15:3.
24. *Bemidbar* 15:39.
25. *Berachoth* 12b.

desire, albeit extremely subtle, was mingled with his admirable intentions, Shimshon was severely punished. Our Sages tell us that because of these words that he uttered, "she is good in my eyes," Shimshon's eyes were gouged out. However, the whole story is deserving of comprehensive analysis in its own right in order for us to understand exactly what befell this lofty figure.)

The Vilna Gaon delineates evil into two main categories: physical desire and pride (which also manifests as anger). He states:

> בָּרַע גּוּפֵהּ יֵשׁ טוֹב וָרַע. דְּהַיְנוּ תַּאֲוָה הוּא טוֹב שֶׁבָּרַע וְכַעַס הוּא רַע שֶׁבָּרַע. וְהַטּוֹב שֶׁבָּרַע, דְּהַיְנוּ תַּאֲוָה... כִּי הַתַּאֲוָה נִצְרָךְ קְצָת לְקִיּוּם הַגּוּף. וְצָרִיךְ לָזֶה רֹב הִתְחַכְּמוּת לִשְׁקֹל בְּמֹאזְנֵי שִׂכְלוֹ שֶׁלֹּא לִיקַּח רַק הַהֶכְרֵחִי. וְהוּא דּוֹמֶה לְמִי שֶׁרוֹצֶה לִלְכֹּד עִיר וּלְהַשְׁאִיר אוֹתָם בַּחַיִּים, שֶׁצָּרִיךְ לָזֶה תַּחְבּוּלוֹת גְּדוֹלוֹת.
>
> *In evil itself there are elements of good and bad. For example, physical desire can be classed as "the good that is in evil," and anger as "the bad that is in evil." Physical desire contains some good because it is necessary for sustaining the earthly body. Desire, therefore, requires much wisdom, so that one utilises it just enough to fulfill one's requirements, and no more. It can be compared to one who wishes to capture a city while leaving the inhabitants alive. To do so requires much strategy and planning.*[26]

The Vilna Gaon here states that physical desires must be used in conjunction with the recommendation of our Sages,[27] "The left hand pushes away, and the right hand draws near." While one's inclination should not be blindly followed, neither should it be completely rejected. For example, one must eat to sustain one's body, yet reveling in sumptuous foods only draws a person after physicality and sin.

The Gaon continues:

> אֲבָל כַּעַס דּוֹמֶה לְמִי שֶׁרוֹצֶה לַהֲרֹג אֶת שׂוֹנְאוֹ. שֶׁאֵין צָרִיךְ לָזֶה רַק גְּבוּרָה לְבַד.

---

26. *Even Sheleimah*, Ch. 3.
27. *Sotah* 47a.

*However, the inclination towards anger must be dealt with in a manner comparable to one who wishes to kill his enemy. For this, strength alone is needed.*

The commandment not to stray "after your hearts" refers to the pride that leads to heresy. As explained by the Vilna Gaon, this must be completely eradicated. Related to this, we can understand the following famous maxim:

כָּל אָדָם שֶׁיֵּשׁ בּוֹ גַּסּוּת הָרוּחַ כְּאִלּוּ עוֹבֵד עֲבוֹדָה זָרָה.

*Every person who possesses a haughty spirit can be considered as if he serves idolatry.*[28]

A seemingly drastic statement to make! However, our Sages understood the root of the human personality, and recognised that pride (and anger) stem from the same root as serving strange gods. For one who becomes filled with wrath is in effect denying the part God plays in events, that the Almighty engineered what transpired. He thus denies the Presence of God's hand behind all that befalls him. An angry person can be likened to one who, struck by a stone thrown by his enemy, proceeds to burn with wrath against the stone, while ignoring the enemy who directed the stone. The haughty person bows not to God, but to his own ego, pretentiously deluding himself that wisdom, strength, and wealth are his. He possesses the capability to do as he pleases. He thus denies his dependence upon God.

Returning to the two goats that are slaughtered on Yom Kippur, we can now specify that they do not only symbolize evil in a general way. Each goat corresponds specifically to one of the two main categories of evil. The goat that is sent to Azazel, which is cast off a rocky precipice, is an allegory for the sins of pride and anger, the source of heresy and idolatry. As stated by the Vilna Gaon, these sins, and their underlying character flaws, must be uprooted completely; sent to a desert and hurled to death.

Returning to the incident of Sha'ul and Amalek, let us determine the exact type of evil that Amalek personifies. Amalek is called

---

28. *Sotah* 4b.

רֵאשִׁית גּוֹיִם עֲמָלֵק — "The first of the nations." For the evil of Amalek is that it takes the concept of first, and subverts it for its own purpose. Amalek denies the true "first," the Source of everything that exists: God. Amalek prides itself on its independence, viewing itself as the source of its own strength. It thus instates itself as the "first," the source of everything. Amalek therefore represents "the bad that is in evil," the pride that is the source of heresy and idolatry, evil incarnate.

Against this force, we fight unceasingly; we banish feelings of pity and mercy to uproot evil from our midst. Thus we have the command, "Wipe out the remembrance of Amalek," an injunction to obliterate the nation completely. The Vilna Gaon writes of this, "The haughty person can never be cleansed from this sin, and his judgment will mirror his own reactions. Even if his pride lies only in his heart, he is still abominable and despised before God." Before the Almighty there is no place at all for pride. It follows that it was forbidden for Sha'ul to offer any of Amalek's livestock to God. The evil of pride cannot be utilised or uplifted; it can only be destroyed.

Let us turn now to the "good that is in evil." The goat that the High Priest offered on Yom Kippur was a symbol of this second type of negativity: physical desire. Interestingly, this goat, this inclination, was offered as a sacrifice to God. For physical desire does have a place in our Divine service; as earthly beings we all have bodily requirements, which must and should be fulfilled to enable us to devote ourselves to spiritual growth. In this manner, physicality itself becomes consecrated to the Almighty: food, drink, clothing — all become holy. It is notable that physical desire is shown to have a place in man's spiritual ascent specifically on Yom Kippur, the day where we abstain from any earthly pleasure. Eating, bathing, anointing oneself, and marital relations are all forbidden on this day. For it is only after we have severed the shackles binding us to materialism, when we have proven that we are no longer slaves to our desires, that we can safely utilise the physical world for our own benefit.

Concerning physicality, however, there is a spiritual level higher than the one we have discussed. Our Sages state:

וְהָאָרוֹן הָיָה שֶׁל עֲצֵי שִׁטִּים לְכַפֵּר עַל מַעֲשֵׂה שִׁטִּים.

*The ark was made from shittim (acacia) wood, to atone for the incident that took place in Shittim.*[29]

The incident that took place in Shittim is recorded in the book of *Bemidbar*:

וַיֵּשֶׁב יִשְׂרָאֵל בַּשִּׁטִּים וַיָּחֶל הָעָם לִזְנוֹת אֶל בְּנוֹת מוֹאָב.

*Yisrael were living in Shittim, when the people began to act immorally with the daughters of Mo'av.*[30]

Rabbeinu Bachya explains an important principle in connection to this. Already established is the fact that earthly desires can be uplifted, sublimated, and thereby utilised in a Jew's Divine service. However, Rabbeinu Bachya reveals that it is not only the tangible, visible item that can be used. The underlying desires, drives, and lusts are built into the human psyche, for they also have their place in the higher system. Man is given this capacity to be directed towards Torah, so that his service, and specifically his acquisition of Torah, should be done with burning passion, yearning, and desire. *Shittim* wood symbolizes the force of desire; in its negative form, it was the lust that embroiled the Children of Yisrael in impurity at Shittim. But it is precisely this wood that was used to construct the ark that contained the tablets of stone. For it is this force that supports Torah and serves as its receptacle. Righteous people plough their drives as a farmer ploughs his soil, using this power in their Divine service in order to reap Eternal seeds. In contrast, wicked people use this force to immerse themselves in the mire of this corporeal, transient world.

The Rambam uses this principle to give a palpable example of the level of love towards God that is expected of a Jew. He states that the profound love that is felt between people in this world is a parable for the deep bond that should exist between man and his

29. *Tanchuma*, *Vayakhel* 8.
30. *Bemidbar* 25:1.

Creator. He concludes: וְכָל שִׁיר הַשִּׁירִים מָשָׁל הוּא לְעִנְיָן זֶה — "All of the *Song of Songs* is an allegory for this matter." The famous *Song of Songs*, so often misunderstood, is termed as the "holy of holies." For by depicting the intense love between husband and wife, it provides some perception of the bond that should be felt between each Jew and God.

In the future world that will transcend this one, physical desires will dissipate, being irrelevant to a world that exists purely on a spiritual plane. However, the underlying power that exists in the soul will remain. And this power will be used for one reason: as a tool to increase a person's love of Torah.

The first level of physical involvement can be summed up by the words of the Vilna Gaon, "to take only that which is necessary." Strategy and guile are the tools with which to battle this inclination, for the fight is compared to "one who wishes to capture a city and leave the inhabitants alive." In his commentary on *Mishlei*, the Vilna Gaon expands upon this idea:

**זִבְחֵי שְׁלָמִים עָלָי הַיּוֹם שִׁלַּמְתִּי נְדָרָי.**

> *Peace sacrifices were incumbent upon me; today I fulfilled my vows.*[31]

He explains that the evil inclination does not spring upon a person and try to convince him to blatantly transgress a Torah law. The Satan knows that the key to success is to persuade a person to do mitzvoth, and thereby catch him in his snare. This is what the verse refers to with the words "peace sacrifices." Peace sacrifices were not offered because of sin, and it was a great mitzvah to eat the sacrifice in joy. Often, this would lead to sin, for a person is vulnerable to spiritual descent when he is eating and joyful.

"Today I fulfilled my vows." The Vilna Gaon explains that when bringing a free-will offering, a sacrifice given of one's own volition, one does not feel as much happiness as when bringing a sacrifice which one has vowed to bring. The verse states, "Today I fulfilled

---

31. *Mishlei* 7:14.

my vows," alluding to the obligation not to leave any remainder from the sacrifice.... And so it is with all matters, that the evil inclination seduces a person with a blend of good and evil, not with unalloyed negativity. There is no good thing that can be utilised to negatively influence a person more than eating and rejoicing for the purpose of a mitzvah. From this starting point, the evil inclination is able to seduce him.

The evil inclination is unable to overtly induce a person to sin, and so instead dons the garb of a pure conscience, and attempts to persuade one to perform a mitzvah. This mitzvah however, is merely sin in disguise, and the evil inclination has caught a person in its snare.

The joy in fulfilling one's vow is so great because it is accompanied by the relief that one is no longer bound by an obligation. As it is a mitzvah to finish eating the sacrifice within an appointed time, there is an opening for the evil inclination to influence a person to eat quickly, gluttonously, and for his own enjoyment. Yet he is fully convinced that all this is, of course, done only for the sake of Heaven! This danger applies not only to the sacrificial offerings. Every mitzvah that involves some physical pleasure is liable to be utilised by the forces of evil for their own ends, as they persuade a person to indulge in this world "for the sake of the mitzvah." The Vilna Gaon himself warns of this: "Let man not say that he has never pursued temptation and pleasure, but that everything in which he indulged was only for the sake of Heaven. For God possesses scales and measures to determine how much his intention was indeed for sanctity, and how much was for his own pleasure." Although we might try to convince ourselves of the rectitude of our actions, God knows our real motives.

The Torah's emphasis on the ark made of *shittim* wood teaches us the place of physical desire in our Divine service. Just as the ark was constructed only to be a receptacle for the tablets, physical desire must be used only as a tool in our climb to spirituality.

# RE'EH

**רְאֵה אָנֹכִי נֹתֵן לִפְנֵיכֶם הַיּוֹם בְּרָכָה וּקְלָלָה. אֶת הַבְּרָכָה אֲשֶׁר תִּשְׁמְעוּ אֶל מִצְוֹת ה'... וְהַקְּלָלָה אִם לֹא תִשְׁמְעוּ אֶל מִצְוֹת ה'...**

*Look! I am putting before you today blessings and curses. The blessings [will come so] that you shall heed the commandments of the Eternal, your God... the curses [will come] if you do not heed the commandments of the Eternal, your God.*[32]

The Seforno's famous comment reads as follows:

הַבִּיטָה וּרְאֵה שֶׁלֹּא יִהְיֶה עִנְיָנְךָ עַל אֹפֶן בֵּינוֹנִי כְּמוֹ שֶׁהוּא הַמִּנְהָג בָּרֹב. כִּי אָמְנָם אָנֹכִי נוֹתֵן לִפְנֵיכֶם הַיּוֹם בְּרָכָה וּקְלָלָה וְהֵם שְׁנֵי הַקְּצָווֹת. כִּי הַבְּרָכָה הִיא הַצְלָחָה יוֹתֵר מִן הַמַּסְפִּיק עַל צַד הַיּוֹתֵר טוֹב. וְהַקְּלָלָה הִיא מְאֵרָה מְחַסֶּרֶת שֶׁלֹּא יַשִּׂג הַמַּסְפִּיק. וּשְׁנֵיהֶם לִפְנֵיכֶם לְהַשִּׂיג כְּפִי מַה שֶּׁתִּבְחֲרוּ.

*Look and perceive that your affairs (as a people) will never be of an average nature, as is the case with other nations. For today I set before you either blessing or curse: two extremes. Blessing implies success even beyond that which is sufficient, and curse implies deficiency such that attainment even of requirements is out of reach. Both of these are before you to attain, according to what you choose.*[33]

Built into the nature of the Children of Yisrael is the drastic pendulum of their fortune. Either ceaseless blessing or unbearable curse is their lot. Yet, why should this be so? Why can the lot of the Jewish People not mirror that of the nations of the world, who live a more stable, average existence?

---

32. *Devarim* 11:26.
33. Seforno *ad loc.*

This question is not a new one; it was first asked by Esav when Ya'akov sought to buy the privileges of the firstborn from him:

**הִנֵּה אָנֹכִי הוֹלֵךְ לָמוּת וְלָמָּה זֶה לִי בְּכֹרָה?**

*I'm going to die [as a result of it], and so what is the birthright [worth] to me?*[34]

Rashi gives us a fuller version of the conversation between the brothers, bringing out the meaning behind Esav's question:

אָמַר עֵשָׂו מַה טִּיבָהּ שֶׁל עֲבוֹדָה זוֹ? אָמַר לוֹ כַּמָּה אַזְהָרוֹת וַעֲנָשִׁין וּמִיתוֹת תְּלוּיִין בָּהּ כְּאוֹתָהּ שֶׁשָּׁנִינוּ אֵלּוּ הֵן שֶׁבְּמִיתָה שְׁתוּיֵי יַיִן וּפְרוּעֵי רֹאשׁ. אָמַר אֲנִי הוֹלֵךְ לָמוּת עַל יָדָהּ. אִם כֵּן, מַה חֵפֶץ לִי בָּהּ?

*Esav said, "What is the nature of this service?"*
*Ya'akov replied, "Many warnings and punishments and death penalties result from it!"*
*Said Esav, "I would die through it! Therefore, why should I want it?"*[35]

Rabbi Yerucham Levovitz derives a fundamental principle from this exchange: "This issue really occurs on every level. Corresponding to the greatness of the spiritual level is the detriment of its loss."

The greater and more sublime the spiritual level, the more the lack in its absence. An example of this is a *Kohen*, who is obligated in a greater level of Divine service than ordinary folk. At the same time, however, he is subject to harsher punishment should he fail in his mission.

A crucial quandary thereby arises:

וְעַתָּה עוֹמֶדֶת בְּאֱמֶת הַשְּׁאֵלָה, מַה כְּדַאי לָאָדָם? מַה שָּׁוֶה יוֹתֵר, הַמַּעֲלָה וּשְׂכָרָהּ אוֹ שֶׁמְּפַחֵד הָעֳנָשִׁים וְהָאֲבַדּוֹן הַכְּרוּכִים בָּהּ יוֹתֵר שָׁוֶה לוֹ שֶׁלֹּא יִהְיוּ לֹא הֵן וְלֹא שְׂכָרָן?

*And now I will present you with a question: What is better for man — the heights of spirituality and the tremendous reward*

34. *Bereishith* 25:32.
35. Rashi *ad loc.*

*that it brings, or does the fear of punishment and personal degradation that are involved in this opportunity outweigh the benefits, so that he will prefer to give up the opportunity together with the reward?*[36]

Ostensibly, it appears that the Jewish People chose the second option when standing at Mount Sinai. "It is better that we should have neither the punishment nor the reward." It seems that they sought to renounce the sublime level that they merited. Forty years after the event, Moshe reports the words of the Jewish People at that time.

**וַתֹּאמְרוּ הֵן הֶרְאָנוּ ה' אֱלֹקֵינוּ אֶת כְּבֹדוֹ... וְאֶת קֹלוֹ שָׁמַעְנוּ מִתּוֹךְ הָאֵשׁ הַיּוֹם הַזֶּה רָאִינוּ כִּי יְדַבֵּר אֱלֹקִים אֶת הָאָדָם וָחָי. וְעַתָּה לָמָּה נָמוּת כִּי תֹאכְלֵנוּ הָאֵשׁ הַגְּדֹלָה הַזֹּאת... קְרַב אַתָּה... וְשָׁמַעְנוּ וְעָשִׂינוּ...**

**וַיִּשְׁמַע ה' אֶת קוֹל דִּבְרֵיכֶם בְּדַבֶּרְכֶם אֵלָי... שָׁמַעְתִּי אֶת קוֹל דִּבְרֵי הָעָם הַזֶּה... הֵיטִיבוּ כָּל אֲשֶׁר דִּבֵּרוּ. מִי יִתֵּן וְהָיָה לְבָבָם זֶה לָהֶם לְיִרְאָה אֹתִי וְלִשְׁמֹר אֶת כָּל מִצְוֹתַי כָּל הַיָּמִים...**

*You said, "The Eternal, our God, has indeed shown us His glory and His greatness, and we have heard His voice from within the fire. Today we have seen that God can speak with a person and he will [still] live. But now, why should we die, for this great fire will consume us?! If we continue to hear the voice of the Eternal, our God, anymore, we shall die! ...You (Moshe) should draw near and listen to whatever the Eternal, God, says, and [then] you tell us whatever the Eternal, our God, tells you, and we will listen and do [it]."*

*The Eternal heard the sound of your words when you were speaking to me, and the Eternal said to me, "I have heard the sound of the words of this people which they spoke to you. Everything that they have spoken, they have spoken well. If only they would [always] have this kind of heart, to fear Me and to keep all My commandments for all time, in order that it be well with them and their children forever."*[37]

36. *Da'ath Torah* 1, p. 169.
37. *Devarim* 5:21–26.

Rashi highlights the verse's use of the feminine form in reference to Moshe:

וְאַתְּ תְּדַבֵּר אֵלֵינוּ. הִתַּשְׁתֶּם אֶת כֹּחִי כִּנְקֵבָה, שֶׁנִּצְטַעַרְתִּי עֲלֵיכֶם וְרִפִּיתֶם אֶת יָדַי. כִּי רָאִיתִי שֶׁאֵינְכֶם חֲרֵדִים לְהִתְקָרֵב אֵלָיו מֵאַהֲבָה. וְכִי לֹא הָיָה יָפֶה לָכֶם לִלְמֹד מִפִּי הַגְּבוּרָה וְלֹא לִלְמֹד מִמֶּנִּי?

*You (feminine form) speak to us. You weakened my strength like a woman, for I grieved over you, and you loosened my hand, for I saw you were not anxious to draw near to Him from love. Would it not have been better for you to learn from the mouth of the Almighty than to learn from me?*[38]

Overawed by the fantastic revelation at the giving of the Torah, the Jewish People requested that Moshe convey the commandments to them, rather than hearing them directly from the Almighty. The greater the clarity of truth experienced, the greater the responsibility incumbent upon a person. Fearful that they could not live up to the awesome obligation of hearing truth from God Himself, the Jewish People requested a lower level: to learn from Moshe. Their rejection of this opportunity greatly aggrieved Moshe, yet God Himself reassured him: "They did well in what they spoke."

In this case, God did not object to the Jewish People's renunciation of a lofty level, with the accompanying potential punishment. Indeed, He praised them for "opting out." Is the behaviour of the nation here not similar to that of Esav, who exclaimed that the obligation of the mitzvoth would cause his death? Esav also gazed at potential blessing, but recognising the accompanying curse, discarded all that he saw.

Our Sages themselves engaged in this debate:

תָּנוּ רַבָּנָן שְׁתֵּי שָׁנִים וּמֶחֱצָה נֶחְלְקוּ בֵּית שַׁמַּאי וּבֵית הִלֵּל. הַלָּלוּ אוֹמְרִים נוֹחַ לוֹ לָאָדָם שֶׁלֹּא נִבְרָא יוֹתֵר מִשֶּׁנִּבְרָא. וְהַלָּלוּ אוֹמְרִים נוֹחַ לוֹ לָאָדָם שֶׁנִּבְרָא יוֹתֵר מִשֶּׁלֹּא נִבְרָא. נִמְנוּ וְגָמְרוּ נוֹחַ לוֹ לָאָדָם שֶׁלֹּא נִבְרָא יוֹתֵר מִשֶּׁנִּבְרָא. עַכְשָׁו מִשֶּׁנִּבְרָא יְפַשְׁפֵּשׁ בְּמַעֲשָׂיו.

---

38. Rashi *ad loc.*

*For two-and-a-half years, the schools of Shamai and Hillel were in dispute. These said, "It would have been better for man not to be created than to have been created." Those said, "Better that man was created." They calculated and concluded: "Better that man was not created; however, now that he has been created, let him scrutinise his deeds."*[39]

The Maharsha[40] elucidates the underlying meaning of this debate. He explains that God gave 613 commandments to the Children of Yisrael, of which there are 365 prohibitions and 248 positive injunctions. In this debate, Hillel and Shamai made the simple calculation that there are more prohibitions than positive commands. Thus, man is naturally more prone to sin, due to the many prohibitions. Concurrently, as the positive commands are fewer, it is harder for him to attain reward. Thus, they state, "Better that man was not created."

Obviously, our Sages differ fundamentally in their debate from Esav and his complaint. Yet, superficially, both seem to say, "Give me not its punishment, nor its reward." What is the essential difference between the two?

To answer this question, let us turn to a verse in *Parashath Toldoth*:

וְאֵלֶּה תּוֹלְדֹת יִצְחָק בֶּן אַבְרָהָם אַבְרָהָם הוֹלִיד אֶת יִצְחָק.

*These are the descendants of Yitzchak, the son of Avraham — Avraham had fathered Yitzchak.*[41]

The *Avnei Nezer* gives a metaphorical answer to the apparent redundancy in the verse. He prefaces his answer with an explanation of two types of fear. The first is fear of punishment. In this case, man fears the suffering that he will endure if he does not accept his responsibilities and fulfill his task in the world. The second type of fear stems from love. Man loves God to such a degree that he is afraid lest some distance come between them.

39. *Eruvin* 13b.
40. Maharsha on *Makkoth* 23b, "*Taryag Mitzvoth.*"
41. *Bereishith* 25:19.

Our three forefathers were the foundations upon which the entire world rested, each excelling in a different area of service. Avraham was the pillar of loving kindness, Yitzchak excelled in his awe of God, and Ya'akov developed the quality of truthfulness. Focussing upon Yitzchak, the *Avnei Nezer* explains that it is important to recognise that Yitzchak's fear was not merely anxiety about future punishment. It was on an altogether higher plane: reverence stemming from love. For this reason, the Torah stresses, "Avraham fathered Yitzchak." Yitzchak's fear of God was born from Avraham's devoted love of the Almighty. In contrast to Yitzchak's awe, Esav possessed a fear of future punishment, an emotion that degenerates into resentment and hatred. As it says, "Serve from love, for one who loves does not hate."[42] Fear is an uncomfortable feeling, growing more and more intolerable, causing the person to hate that which causes his consternation.

One whose service of God stems merely from fear of punishment is advised not to take on extra obligations and tasks. For, instead of feeling the privilege of his behaviour, he will constantly worry over the negative consequences that the obligations might bring: "How many warnings and punishments and death penalties result from it!"

Turning back to the Children of Yisrael's acceptance of the Torah, why did the nation request that Moshe, instead of God, convey the commandments to them? To conclude that they were scared of the responsibility that such revelation entails, would imply that the Jewish People were on a very low spiritual level. The Talmud relates:

בְּכָל דִּבּוּר... יָצְאָה נִשְׁמָתָן שֶׁל יִשְׂרָאֵל... הוֹרִיד הַשי"ת טַל שֶׁעָתִיד לְהַחְיוֹת בּוֹ הַמֵּתִים וְהֶחְיָה אוֹתָם.

*With every word, the souls of Yisrael left them. God brought down dew, which He will use in the future to revive the dead, and revived them.*[43]

This remarkable statement gives a glimpse of what transpired at

---

42. *Yerushalmi Berachoth* 89, halachah 5.
43. *Shabbath* 88b.

this great revelation. Rabbi Dessler explains[44] that the Jewish People were elevated to such a sublime level that they were divorced from even the slightest taint of, the most tenuous connection to, the world of physicality. With each word, their souls left their bodies and clung to God. With the conclusion of the speech, the Jewish People returned to a lower level, which could be termed as only a "taste" of the level just experienced. Even this lower level was far higher than we can fathom, far above the level upon which we live; it was a level on which they were intimately connected to God. In the words of Rabbi Dessler, "They ascended to a place that is beyond the capacity of any human being to attain through his own exertion."

Yet, with all this, the Jewish People still preferred that Moshe convey God's word to them indirectly. How could they fear death if they had already experienced a parting of the soul from the body? Their fear was not merely fear of punishment, of trepidation lest their corporeal bodies die. After having ascended to such sublime levels, the nation was worried lest they be unable to sustain the closeness that they had achieved. Theirs was a fear stemming from love, from total devotion and from ultimate closeness.

Fear stemming from love was also the motivation driving the dispute of the schools of Hillel and Shamai. The conclusion was reached through counting the number of prohibitions versus the number of positive commands. The prohibitions outweighing the positive commands, they both declared, "Better for man not to have been created." The schools of Hillel and Shamai calculated that man is more liable to sin than to draw close to the Creator. There are 365 different dangers from which man must guard himself, while there are only 248 opportunities to actively draw close to Him through fulfilling the positive commands. Thus one conclusion was reached by all; fearful that sin would isolate them from the desired closeness with God, that negativity would freeze the warmth that was yearned for so passionately, they declared that it would have been better for man not to have been created, for man never to have been given the

44. *Michtav MeEliyahu*, Part Two, p. 32.

possibility to sever the most important relationship that can exist.

Infinite blessing or torturous curse is the choice that the Children of Yisrael face at the start of this *parashah*. The Jewish People cannot live in the mediocre manner of the nations of the world; their fate belongs to one of two extremes. For the Jewish People stood at Mount Sinai, and accepted God's Torah. In doing so, they were elevated high above the rest of humanity, and subsequently were unable to live in a comparable manner. It is our very elevation, our lofty task, which, if remaining unfulfilled, can lead to our downfall.

Let us return to the question posed by Rabbi Yerucham Levovitz. Is it indeed desirable for man to strive to lofty heights, if he thereby risks plummeting to the depths? In answer, Rabbi Levovitz quotes Rabbi Moshe Chaim Luzzatto:[45]

> *There are some fools who seek only to lighten their burden. They say, "Why weary ourselves with so much saintliness? Is it not enough for us that we will not be numbered among those wicked who are judged in Hell?"*

These "fools" have not yet elevated themselves from the lowest level in which they fear potential punishment. They remain oblivious to the beauty and richness of a pulsating Torah life, poverty of experience causing them to content themselves with merely avoiding retribution. One who truly recognises the inestimable value of Torah will gladly commit himself to it, regardless of any difficulties and punishments that this might entail. In his ardour, he will be unable to restrain his devotion.

The real motivation of these "fools" who refuse to lead a life of growth is an underlying egocentricity. Like Esav, who repudiated the firstborn privileges, one who rejects a life of spirituality justifies his decision through his fear of the negative consequences that might ensue from taking on additional obligations. In truth, however, this rejection of spirituality stems from an attachment to the world of materialism.

---

45. *Mesillath Yesharim*, Ch. 4.

Rabbi Levovitz offers this advice to those who wish to attach themselves to a life of spiritual blessing, yet genuinely fear retribution:

הַאִם כְּשֶׁרוֹאֶה סוּס וְכָל בְּהֵמָה, גַּם כֵּן יְקַנֵּא בָּהֶם עַל חָפְשִׁיּוּתָם בֶּאֱמֶת? כִּי אֵין לָהֶם גַּם שׁוּם עֹל דֶּרֶךְ אֶרֶץ, פַּרְנָסָתָם מְצוּיָה לָהֶם בְּכָל מָקוֹם, וְאֵין לָהֶם שׁוּם דְּאָגוֹת כִּי אִם חַיֵּי תַּעֲנוּג וַהֲנָאָה גְּמוּרָה. וַדַּאי כִּי לֹא תִּמְצָא לֹא סָכָל וְלֹא טִפֵּשׁ שֶׁיֶּחְפַּץ לִהְיוֹת סוּס. כִּי אַחֲרֵי הַכֹּל, אַף עִם כָּל הַקְּשָׁיִים וְהָעֹל הַגָּדוֹל הַתְּלוּיִים בְּזֶה, הִנֵּה הַתַּעֲנוּג הָאֲמִתִּי וְהַהֲנָאָה הֲכִי גְדוֹלָה הִיא לִהְיוֹת אָדָם.

*When a person sees a horse, or any other animal, does man really envy the animal's freedom? Beasts do not shoulder the burden of a livelihood, their sustenance being available everywhere. Animals have no worries, living a life of constant gratification and recreation. However, no fool or simpleton would seriously desire to be a horse! For, ultimately, with all the difficulties and burdens it involves, man knows that the greatest satisfaction and pleasure is to be a man.*

# SHOFETIM

GATHERED AT THE border, about to go to war, the Jewish army would first hear a rousing speech from the כֹּהֵן מְשׁוּחַ מִלְחָמָה, the priest appointed to lead them in battle. His speech raised their morale, fortifying their belief and trust in God. The substance of the *Kohen*'s speech is recorded in the Torah:

> **וְהָיָה כְּקָרָבְכֶם אֶל הַמִּלְחָמָה וְנִגַּשׁ הַכֹּהֵן וְדִבֶּר אֶל הָעָם. וְאָמַר אֲלֵהֶם שְׁמַע יִשְׂרָאֵל אַתֶּם קְרֵבִים הַיּוֹם לַמִּלְחָמָה עַל אֹיְבֵיכֶם אַל יֵרַךְ לְבַבְכֶם אַל תִּירְאוּ וְאַל תַּחְפְּזוּ וְאַל תַּעַרְצוּ מִפְּנֵיהֶם.**
>
> *It shall be, as you approach the battle[front], that the [anointed] priest shall step forward and speak to the people. He shall say to them, "Listen, Yisrael! Today you are drawing near to battle against your enemies. Do not be fainthearted, do not be afraid, do not panic, and do not be demoralized because of them."*[46]

Rashi calls our attention to one of the implicit messages delivered by the priest:

> **שְׁמַע יִשְׂרָאֵל, אֲפִלּוּ אֵין בָּכֶם זְכוּת אֶלָּא קְרִיאַת שְׁמַע בִּלְבַד, כְּדַאי אַתֶּם שֶׁיּוֹשִׁיעַ אֶתְכֶם.**
>
> *Listen, Yisrael! Even if you have no merit in your favour but the recitation of the Shema, you are worthy that He should save you.*[47]

The Chafetz Chaim elucidates why the recitation of *Shema* has the power to save a person from his enemy. He explains that the *Shema*

46. *Devarim* 20:2, 3.
47. Rashi *ad loc.*

is essentially an acceptance of Divine authority and Kingship, of the yoke of Heaven. The merit of this acceptance has the power to save one from perishing in war. Further, even if it were decreed for a person that he die in combat, by saying these words, he would die on a high spiritual level.

Within this declaration of faith, the Maharal highlights the words ה׳ אֶחָד, "God is One," stating that this is the pivotal phrase of the entire declaration. For by uttering these words, man reiterates his conviction in the Oneness and exclusivity of God:

> זְכוּת קְרִיאַת שְׁמַע דַּי לָהֶם לְנַצֵּחַ, כִּי הָאַחְדוּת שֶׁהֵם מַאֲמִינִים בּוֹ — שֶׁהֵם מְנַצְּחִים אֶת כֹּחַ הָאֻמּוֹת, לְפִי שֶׁהֵם דְּבֵקִים בְּכֹחַ אֶחָד. שֶׁהָאֶחָד מוֹרֶה עַל שֶׁאֵין מִבַּלְעָדוֹ. וּמֵאַחַר שֶׁאֵין מִבַּלְעָדוֹ, נִמְצָא כִּי הוּא גּוֹבֵר עַל הַכֹּל, עַד שֶׁאֵין הַכֹּל נֶחְשַׁב אֶצְלוֹ, רַק כֹּחַ אֶחָד. וְיִשְׂרָאֵל דְּבֵקִים בְּאֶחָד, לְכָךְ הֵם גּוֹבְרִים עַל הָאֻמּוֹת.
>
> *The merit of the recitation of the Shema was sufficient to afford them victory, for the Oneness that they believed in would triumph over the strength of the nations, for they (the Jewish People) were bound up with the power of God's Oneness. Since there is nothing apart from God, therefore He triumphs over everything, there being no other power, only the One Power... Yisrael, being connected to this Oneness, could thus triumph over the nations.*[48]

The Maharal, then, sketches out a relationship between belief and victory. To the extent that the nation has internalised a belief in God's total dominion and strength, to that extent will they be saved from their enemies. Thus, the priest's speech to the people was intended to buttress their faith, bringing them to victory through the strength of their conviction. Does abstract faith, then, have the power to influence events of the battlefield, and indeed the entire world?

Let us outline a number of incidents in the Torah, in an attempt to answer this question. Our first episode concerns Ya'akov. Lavan would only allow the marriage of his daughter Rachel to Ya'akov

---

48. *Gur Aryeh* on *Devarim* 20:3.

after Ya'akov had completed seven years of labour for Lavan.

**וַיַּעֲבֹד יַעֲקֹב בְּרָחֵל שֶׁבַע שָׁנִים וַיִּהְיוּ בְעֵינָיו כְּיָמִים אֲחָדִים בְּאַהֲבָתוֹ אֹתָהּ.**

*Ya'akov worked for Rachel seven years, and in his love for her, they seemed to him like a few days.*[49]

Ya'akov did not seek to hasten the allotted time, in his eagerness to marry Rachel. Seven years passed in their normal cycle, yet in Ya'akov's eyes they appeared to be like a mere few days. Thus we see how a person's attitude towards events can change them in his eyes. Instead of viewing this employment as a necessary evil, he viewed it as a period of preparation for the awesome task that lay before him. His attitude determined the manner in which the time would pass, and indeed the verse states that it felt "like a few days."

A second incident develops this principle further. Not only does one's attitude determine the way one experiences the event — it is even within man's power to change the circumstances themselves. Fleeing from his brother Esav, Ya'akov traveled to Charan.

כִּי מָטָא לְחָרָן אָמַר אֶפְשָׁר שֶׁעָבַרְתִּי עַל מָקוֹם שֶׁהִתְפַּלְּלוּ אֲבוֹתַי וְלֹא הִתְפַּלַּלְתִּי בּוֹ? יְהַב דַּעְתֵּהּ לְמֶהֱדַר וְחָזַר עַד בֵּית אֵל, וְקָפְצָה לוֹ הָאָרֶץ.

*When Ya'akov arrived in Charan, he said, "Is it possible that I passed by a place where my fathers prayed, and I did not pray there?" He made up his mind to return to Beith El, and the journey was miraculously shortened for him.*[50]

At the age of seventy-seven, after fourteen years of intense study in the yeshivah of Shem and Ever (during which time we are told that Ya'akov did not lie down to sleep), Ya'akov made the arduous journey to Charan. Upon his arrival, he was filled with a deep regret that he had missed the opportunity to pray at a place that his father and grandfather had sanctified with prayer. Ya'akov resolved

---

49. *Bereishith* 29:20.
50. Rashi on *Bereishith* 28:17.

to retrace his steps, and tread the long path to Beith El once more. As soon as it was fixed in his mind to actualize his intention, the potency of his desire actually shortened the geographical distance that he would have to travel! His actual journey was considerably shortened. His very will was able to change reality. As it says, צַדִּיק גּוֹזֵר וְהקב"ה מְקַיֵּם[51] — because Ya'akov unified his heart, God manifested Ya'akov's will into physical reality.

Another example of this phenomenon is found concerning Bathyah, daughter of Par'oh.

> **וַתֵּרֶד בַּת פַּרְעֹה לִרְחֹץ עַל הַיְאֹר וְנַעֲרֹתֶיהָ הֹלְכֹת עַל יַד הַיְאֹר וַתֵּרֶא אֶת הַתֵּבָה בְּתוֹךְ הַסּוּף וַתִּשְׁלַח אֶת אֲמָתָהּ וַתִּקָּחֶהָ.**
>
> *Par'oh's daughter then came down to the River to bathe, while her maids were walking along the River's edge. She saw the box among the reeds, so she sent her maid [to bring it] and took it [from her].*[52]

> רש"י — וְהֵם דָּרְשׁוּ אֶת אַמָּתָהּ — אֶת יָדָהּ. וְנִשְׁתַּרְבְּבָה אַמָּתָהּ אַמּוֹת הַרְבֵּה.
>
> *Rashi: [Our Sages] interpret the word אַמָּתָהּ [translated on the simple level as "her maid,"] to mean "her arm." The length of her forearm was multiplied to that of many armspans.*

Bathyah, noticing the little cradle in which the young Moshe was lying, decided to rescue the infant. She stretched out her arm, yet the distance to the cradle was too great. A miracle occurred and her arm extended, enabling her to grasp the baby. But why did Bathyah trouble to stretch out her hand at all, since it must have been obvious that the cradle was beyond her reach? It seems that her inner urge to save the baby was so strong that it overcame the natural, logical response to the situation. And so, her heart's desire had the effect of transforming physical reality itself, causing her arm to miraculously extend. It was the potency of her will that led to this miracle, one

---

51. *Shabbath* 59b.
52. *Shemoth* 2:5.

which contains within it a faint echo of the shortening of the journey for Ya'akov.

A negative manifestation of this same principle is seen concerning Sarah's reaction to the news that she would bear a child:

**וַיֹּאמֶר שׁוֹב אָשׁוּב אֵלֶיךָ כָּעֵת חַיָּה וְהִנֵּה בֵן לְשָׂרָה אִשְׁתֶּךָ וְשָׂרָה שֹׁמַעַת פֶּתַח הָאֹהֶל וְהוּא אַחֲרָיו. וְאַבְרָהָם וְשָׂרָה זְקֵנִים בָּאִים בַּיָּמִים חָדַל לִהְיוֹת לְשָׂרָה אֹרַח כַּנָּשִׁים. וַתִּצְחַק שָׂרָה בְּקִרְבָּהּ לֵאמֹר אַחֲרֵי בְלֹתִי הָיְתָה לִּי עֶדְנָה וַאדֹנִי זָקֵן. וַיֹּאמֶר ה' אֶל אַבְרָהָם לָמָּה זֶּה צָחֲקָה שָׂרָה לֵאמֹר הַאַף אֻמְנָם אֵלֵד וַאֲנִי זָקַנְתִּי. הֲיִפָּלֵא מֵה' דָּבָר לַמּוֹעֵד אָשׁוּב אֵלֶיךָ כָּעֵת חַיָּה וּלְשָׂרָה בֵן.**

*[The man] then said, "I will surely return to you at about this time [next year, when you will be] alive and well, and Sarah, your wife, will then have a son..."*

*Sarah laughed about herself saying, "After I have become withered, will I [now] have smooth skin? And my master is [also] old."*

*The Eternal said to Avraham, "Why did Sarah laugh, saying 'Will I really give birth, for I am [already] old?' Is anything beyond the Eternal? I will return to you at the appointed time, at about this time [next year, when you will be] alive and well, and Sarah will have a son."*[53]

Rashi highlights the discrepancy between Sarah's actual words, and the manner in which God reported these words to Avraham.

וַאֲנִי זָקַנְתִּי. שִׁנָּה הַכָּתוּב מִפְּנֵי הַשָּׁלוֹם, שֶׁהֲרֵי הִיא אָמְרָה וַאדֹנִי זָקֵן.

*"I am already old." The actual words are changed for the sake of peace. For Sarah actually said, "and my master is old."*[54]

The Torah here teaches us the importance of peace, God changing Sarah's words to avoid any marital disharmony. However, why was this whole change necessary? Why did God not simply omit this detail of Sarah's speech? Further, why did God reiterate the promise

53. *Bereishith* 18:10.
54. Rashi *ad loc.*

that the angel had just delivered, that Sarah would indeed give birth to a son?

The Torah here presents us with another situation wherein a person's own thoughts and convictions have the potency to change reality. Through her lack of faith, Sarah depreciated the value and the potency of the blessing. Her laugh tarnished the influence of the prediction, rendering it ineffectual. Therefore, God blessed them anew, with a promise redolent with full force.

In order to reveal God's Oneness and exclusivity, man is obligated to constantly fortify his *emunah*, within the framework of his life and personal mission. This, until one attains the level upon which it is clear that אֵין עוֹד מִלְּבַדּוֹ, that nothing — no force or power — exists apart from God. One who lacks complete conviction in this axiom is liable to fall into the hands of his enemies, of nature, of those to whom he attributes power. Turning back to the scenario concerning a battle of the Jewish nation against their enemies, we read:

**כִּי תֵצֵא לַמִּלְחָמָה עַל אֹיְבֶיךָ וְרָאִיתָ סוּס וָרֶכֶב עַם רַב מִמְּךָ לֹא תִירָא מֵהֶם כִּי ה' אֱלֹקֶיךָ עִמָּךְ הַמַּעַלְךָ מֵאֶרֶץ מִצְרָיִם.**

*When you go out to war against your enemies and see horses and chariots (literally, a horse and a chariot), [and] a people more numerous than you, you must not be afraid of them, for the Eternal, your God, Who brought you up from the land of Mitzrayim, is with you.*[55]

The Hebrew verse actually refers to the "horses and chariots" in the singular. It seems incredible that the Torah describes a major battle in such casual terms, depicting the enemy as "a horse and a chariot." The verse seems to downplay the resources and might of the enemy. Rashi explains:

סוּס וָרֶכֶב. בְּעֵינַי כֻּלָּם כְּסוּס אֶחָד. וְכֵן הוּא אוֹמֵר וְהִכִּיתָ אֶת מִדְיָן כְּאִישׁ אֶחָד, וְכֵן הוּא אוֹמֵר כִּי בָא סוּס פַּרְעֹה.

עַם רַב מִמְּךָ. בְּעֵינֶיךָ הוּא רַב, אֲבָל בְּעֵינַי אֵינוֹ רַב.

55. *Devarim* 20:1.

*A horse and a chariot: In My eyes, they are all like one horse. And so it says, "You shall smite Midyan like one man." Similarly it says, "When the horse of Par'oh will come."*

*A people more numerous than you: In your eyes they are numerous, but in My eyes they are not numerous.*[56]

It is only when we truly believe in God's omnipotence, that He and only He can do anything, that we will merit the revelation of "He alone made, sustains, and will orchestrate all events." In light of this revelation, "other" powers are rendered futile, irrelevant. A mighty army becomes like merely one horse; earth-shattering missiles are like tin cans.

In this manner we can understand the warning issued to those entering the battlefield: "Listen, Yisrael… do not be fainthearted, do not be afraid, do not panic, and do not be demoralized because of them." The priest's rousing speech was designed to fortify the nation's conviction in God's Oneness and exclusivity — the only avenue to guarantee success in war.

This principle applies not only to a physical war of horses and chariots, or in modern terms, of tanks and missiles. It applies to the personal battle that each Jew wages with his spiritual foe, the evil inclination. It is incumbent upon us to recognise, concerning this combat, that we have been granted the ability to overcome all obstacles placed before us, and indeed conquer our gravest enemy — our own inclination towards evil. The principle also applies to our belief in the coming of the Mashiach. With the power of our conviction, we can actively usher in the Redemption.

Turning inwards, it is incumbent upon each person to cultivate a deep faith in his own talents and abilities, for only by believing in them can man transform his talents from potential to actuality. As the Mishnah states:

חָבִיב אָדָם שֶׁנִּבְרָא בְּצֶלֶם. חִבָּה יְתֵרָה נוֹדַעַת לוֹ שֶׁנִּבְרָא בְּצֶלֶם שֶׁנֶּאֱמַר בְּצֶלֶם אֱלֹקִים עָשָׂה אֶת הָאָדָם.

56. Rashi *ad loc.*

> *Beloved is man, for he was created in the image of God. It was a special love that was made known to him that he was created in the image of God, as it says, "In the image of God He made man."*[57]

Man's unlimited potential mirrors God's transcendence of limitation. However, God's tremendous love is manifest in the fact that man was informed of his latent strengths. The knowledge of man's unlimited potential must be constantly reiterated and reflected upon, thereby enabling that which at present is abstract, to infuse the world with light.

---

57. *Pirkei Avoth* 3:18.

# KI THEITZEI

THE HATRED OF AMALEK towards our nation is so extreme as to be suicidal. Let us investigate the reason for this venomous animosity.

> זָכוֹר אֵת אֲשֶׁר עָשָׂה לְךָ עֲמָלֵק בַּדֶּרֶךְ בְּצֵאתְכֶם מִמִּצְרָיִם. אֲשֶׁר קָרְךָ בַּדֶּרֶךְ וַיְזַנֵּב בְּךָ כָּל הַנֶּחֱשָׁלִים אַחֲרֶיךָ וְאַתָּה עָיֵף וְיָגֵעַ וְלֹא יָרֵא אֱלֹקִים. וְהָיָה בְּהָנִיחַ ה' אֱלֹקֶיךָ לְךָ מִכָּל אֹיְבֶיךָ מִסָּבִיב בָּאָרֶץ אֲשֶׁר ה' אֱלֹקֶיךָ נֹתֵן לְךָ נַחֲלָה לְרִשְׁתָּהּ תִּמְחֶה אֶת זֵכֶר עֲמָלֵק מִתַּחַת הַשָּׁמָיִם לֹא תִּשְׁכָּח.
>
> *Constantly remember what Amalek did to you on the way when you went out of Mitzrayim, that they encountered you on the way... and they did not fear God. It will be, when the Eternal, your God, gives you relief from all your enemies, all around, in the land that the Eternal, your God is giving to you as permanent property to take possession of, [then] you shall wipe out [any] evidence of Amalek from beneath the heavens; you must not forget.*[58]

The Ramban explains why Amalek exclusively is to be treated so harshly:

> וְטַעַם הָעֹנֶשׁ שֶׁנֶּעֱנַשׁ עֲמָלֵק יוֹתֵר מִכָּל הָעַמִּים בַּעֲבוּר כִּי כָּל הָעַמִּים שָׁמְעוּ וַיִּרְגָּזוּן וּפְלֶשֶׁת אֱדוֹם וּמוֹאָב וְיוֹשְׁבֵי כְּנַעַן נָמוֹגוּ מִפְּנֵי פַּחַד ה' וּמֵהֲדַר גְּאוֹנוֹ וַעֲמָלֵק בָּא מִמֶּרְחָק וּמִתְגַּבֵּר עַל הַשֵּׁם וּלְכָךְ אָמַר בּוֹ וְלֹא יָרֵא אֱלֹקִים, וְעוֹד כִּי הוּא נִין עֵשָׂו וְקָרוֹב לָנוּ, עֹבֵר מִתְעַבֵּר עַל רִיב לֹא לוֹ.[59]

To paraphrase the Ramban: When the news of the redemption of the Jewish People was publicised, the nations of the world were stricken with a profound fear of God. Only Amalek, in their audacity,

58. *Devarim* 25:17.
59. Ramban on *Shemoth* 16:17.

traveled from afar and brazenly defied God in their attack against His nation. To compound the situation, Amalek, the father of this nation, was a grandchild of Esav, our close relative. Yet his descendants came, unprovoked, to contend with the Jewish People. His hatred was indeed strong! What lies at the root of Amalek 's burning animosity towards us?

Rashi comments on the words which describe Amalek's assault:

אֲשֶׁר קָרְךָ בַּדֶּרֶךְ — ד"א לְשׁוֹן קֹר וְחֹם, צִנֶּנְךָ וְהִפְשִׁרְךָ מֵרְתִיחָתְךָ, שֶׁהָיוּ כָּל הָאֻמּוֹת יְרֵאִים לְהִלָּחֵם בָּכֶם וּבָא זֶה וְהִתְחִיל וְהֶרְאָה מָקוֹם לַאֲחֵרִים.[60]

To paraphrase Rashi: קָרְךָ is a derivation of the word קֹר, meaning cold. The miracles experienced by the Jewish People made a profound impact upon the rest of the world, imbuing them with an awesome reverence for God and His people. Then Amalek attacked. The effect was comparable to that of a man who enters a boiling bath; whilst scalding himself, he cools the bath for others who enter after him. Amalek's action left the world with a diminished veneration and awe towards God. Why did Amalek's hatred express itself in this action of "cooling off?"

An incident recounted in the Talmud will shed light on the issue:

תִּמְנַע בַּת מַלְאָכִים הֲוַאי, דִּכְתִיב אַלּוּף לוֹטָן אַלּוּף תִּמְנַע, וְכָל אַלּוּף מַלְכוּתָא בְּלֹא תָּגָא, הִיא בַּעְיָא לְאִיגְיוּרֵי, בָּאתָה אֵצֶל אַבְרָהָם יִצְחָק וְיַעֲקֹב וְלֹא קִבְּלוּהָ, הָלְכָה וְהָיְתָה פִּילֶגֶשׁ לֶאֱלִיפָז בֶּן עֵשָׂו, אָמְרָה מוּטָב תְּהֵא שִׁפְחָה לְאֻמָּה זוֹ וְלֹא תְּהֵא גְּבִירָא לְאֻמָּה אַחֶרֶת. נָפַק מִינָהּ עֲמָלֵק דְּצַעֲרִינְהוּ לְיִשְׂרָאֵל מ"ט דְּלָא אִבָּעֵי לְהוּ לְרַחֲקָהּ.

*Timna was a personality of royal descent. Seeking to convert to Judaism, she approached the Patriarchs, each of whom refused to accept her. In her thirst and enthusiasm to join our nation, she resigned herself to becoming the concubine of Elifaz, a son of Esav. Her rationale: better to be a maidservant to this nation then be a princess in any other nation. The result of this marriage was Amalek, our arch-enemy. It was the rejection of*

60. Rashi on *Devarim* 25:18.

*Timna by our Patriarchs that led to such devastating results.*[61]

The Maharal addresses the reason for Timna's rejection.

וְלֹא קִבְּלוּהָ — נִרְאֶה כִּי אַבְרָהָם יִצְחָק וְיַעֲקֹב לֹא קִבְּלוּ לְתִמְנָע שֶׁמִּפְּנֵי חֲשִׁיבוּת וּמַלְכוּת תִּמְנַע לֹא תִּהְיֶה נִכְנֶסֶת בְּגֵרוּת כַּאֲשֶׁר רָאוּי וְאֵין שֵׁם גֵּרוּת עַל אֶחָד רַק כַּאֲשֶׁר הוּא מִתְחַבֵּר לְגַמְרֵי עַל אוֹתוֹ שֶׁמִּתְגַּיֵּר. וְאַבְרָהָם יִצְחָק וְיַעֲקֹב הָיוּ מַשְׁפִּילִים עַצְמָם לִפְנֵי הַשִּׁי"ת וְתִמְנַע [שֶׁהָיְתָה חֲשׁוּבָה] מִכָּל מַלְכוּת לֹא תַּחְשִׁיב עַצְמָהּ גִּיּוֹרֶת לְכָךְ לֹא קִבְּלוּהָ.

*A prerequisite for conversion is total self-negation. It is this which enables a person to divest himself of his previous lifestyle and attitudes, and completely embrace his new identity as a member of the Jewish nation. Each of the Patriarchs had nullified himself before God. Timna, having royal blood flowing through her veins, would be unable to acclimate herself to this new lifestyle, which involved a subordination so antithetical to her previous existence. The forefathers therefore rejected her, feeling she could never truly become part of the Jewish nation.*[62]

Indeed, the devastating consequences of an insincere conversion are illustrated clearly in the following scenario depicted in the Torah:[63] Victorious in battle, a Jewish soldier converts one of the gentile captives in order to marry her. Our Sages comment[64] that the result of this marriage would be a wayward and rebellious son, for ulterior motives in conversion result in an evil which is continually magnified.

This concept is elucidated by Rabbeinu Bachya:

וְלָמַדְנוּ מִתּוֹךְ סְמִיכוּת פָּרָשִׁיּוֹת אֵלּוּ שֶׁעֲבֵרָה גּוֹרֶרֶת עֲבֵרָה שֶׁהֲרֵי נִשּׂוּאִין הַלָּלוּ אֵינָן רְאוּיִין ואע"פ שֶׁנִּתְגַּיְּרָה אֵין זֶה גֵּרוּת שְׁלֵמָה, שֶׁלֹּא עָשְׂתָה כֵּן אֶלָּא מִיִּרְאָה וּמִפַּחַד הַחֶרֶב, שֶׁאֲפִלּוּ מִי שֶׁבָּא לְהִתְגַּיֵּר מֵעַצְמוֹ אָמְרוּ חז"ל שֶׁבּוֹדְקִין אַחֲרָיו שֶׁמָּא בִּשְׁבִיל מָמוֹן הוּא מִתְגַּיֵּר,

61. *Sanhedrin* 99b.

62. *Chiddushei Aggadoth*, Part Three.

63. *Devarim* 21:10–14.

64. *Tanchuma, Ki Theitzei* 1.

אוֹ בִּשְׁבִיל שְׂרָרָה שֶׁיִּזְכֶּה בּוֹ, אוֹ בִּשְׁבִיל הַפַּחַד אוֹ בִּשְׁבִיל חֵשֶׁק וְאִם הוּא אִישׁ שֶׁמָּא נָתַן עֵינָיו בְּאִשָּׁה יְהוּדִית, וְאִם הִיא אִשָּׁה שֶׁמָּא עֵינֶיהָ נָתְנָה בְּבָחוּר מִבַּחוּרֵי יִשְׂרָאֵל. זֶה דֶּרֶךְ תּוֹרָתֵנוּ, לֹא כִּשְׁאָר הַתּוֹרוֹת שֶׁמַּחְזִירִין אַחַר הָאֻמּוֹת וְרוֹצִים לְהַרְחִיב אֱמוּנָתָם בָּהֶם.

*The Scriptural juxtaposition of the subject of a woman who converts after having been captured in battle, to the subject of a rebellious child, demonstrates how one sin incontrovertibly leads to another. This marriage is improper, for her conversion stems from fear of captivity. The motivation of any candidate for conversion is always fully investigated. Reasons for conversion could be tainted with monetary considerations, desire for formal office, fear, or passion. A candidate might be motivated by the desire to marry a certain Jew or Jewess. Unlike other nations, who exert every effort to procure new members to their religions, Judaism discourages converts.*[65]

When an improper conversion transpires, terrible consequence arise. An example of this is found in Scriptures. King David took a woman captured in battle as a wife. Resulting from this marriage was Avshalom, who attempted to usurp the Davidic dynasty. Fearing the potentially grave consequences of an insincere conversion, our forefathers rejected Timna, feeling she was not a sincere proselyte.

In this vein, the Maharal explains the reason for the venomous hatred possessed by Timna's progeny.

וְנִתְרַחֵק יוֹתֵר כִּי כָּל דָּבָר הַנִּדְחֶה נִדְחֶה לְגַמְרֵי, וְאִי אֶפְשָׁר שֶׁיִּהְיֶה יוֹצֵא עֲמָלֵק שֶׁכָּל כָּךְ הָיָה שׂוֹנֵא וְאוֹיֵב לְיִשְׂרָאֵל אֲשֶׁר כָּל הַנִּבְרָאִים טְפֵלִים אֲלֵיהֶם, וְאִי אֶפְשָׁר שֶׁיִּהְיֶה אֻמָּה אַחַת מִתְנַגֵּד לְיִשְׂרָאֵל כְּמוֹ שֶׁהָיָה עֲמָלֵק, לְכָךְ בֵּאֲרוּ כִּי הַדְּחִיָּה הַזֹּאת מֵאַבְרָהָם יִצְחָק וְיַעֲקֹב וְהִיא הָיְתָה בָּאָה לְהִתְגַּיֵּר וְלֹא קִבְּלוּהָ... וְאִלּוּ לֹא בָּאתָה לְהִתְגַּיֵּר אֵין זֶה הַרְחָקָה, אֲבָל מֵאַחַר שֶׁבָּאת לְהִתְגַּיֵּר וְנִדְחָה זֶה הִיא תַּכְלִית הַהַרְחָקָה שֶׁלֹּא הָיָה שִׁתּוּף כְּלָל וְיָצָא מִמֶּנּוּ עֲמָלֵק וְהָבֵן זֶה מְאֹד.

*Timna's extreme hatred towards the Jewish People resulted from an initial enthusiasm which was followed by complete*

65. Rabbeinu Bachya on the Torah *ad loc.*

*rejection... If she had never approached the forefathers, seeking to convert, animosity would not have welled up inside her. But her determination and persistence in her desire to become close to the forefathers led her to Avraham's close relative, Elifaz.*

The Midrash continues the story:

וְתִמְנָע הָיְתָה פִילֶגֶשׁ לֶאֱלִיפַז בֶּן עֵשָׂו....לְהוֹדִיעַ שִׁבְחָהּ שֶׁל בֵּיתוֹ שֶׁל אַבְרָהָם אָבִינוּ עַד הֵיכָן הָיוּ הַמַּלְכוּת וְשִׁלְטוֹנִים רוֹצִים לְהִדָּבֵק בּוֹ. וּמֶה הָיָה לוֹטָן הוּא הָיָה אֶחָד מִן הַשִּׁלְטוֹנִים שֶׁנֶּאֱמַר אַלּוּף לוֹטָן וּכְתִיב וַאֲחוֹת לוֹטָן תִּמְנָע וְתִמְנָע הָיְתָה פִּילֶגֶשׁ. אָמְרָה הוֹאִיל וְאֵינִי כְּדַאי לְהִנָּשֵׂא לוֹ לְאִשָּׁה אֶהֱא לוֹ לְשִׁפְחָה.[66]

Timna was willing to give up her royalty to enter the family of Avraham, and resigned herself to becoming a concubine of Elifaz. The sacrifice she made was mammoth; her subsequent disappointment when, nevertheless, she was rejected, was proportional. Disappointment causes a person to hate that for which he sacrificed. The focus of her own burning enthusiasm was transformed into the object of her hatred.

Relating this principle back to the monumental events of the exodus from Egypt, we can understand the implications of the words אֲשֶׁר קָרְךָ בַּדֶּרֶךְ. Hearing of the events that had occurred, the nations were filled with admiration and enthusiasm. But Amalek stepped forward and dampened their enthusiasm, just as their progenitor, Timna, had had her enthusiasm quashed. When one demonstrates great self-sacrifice, the bitterness of subsequent disappointment is equally great.

As a corollary of this, we can see how vital it is to welcome newcomers to a Torah institution, so that they will not feel this disappointment and the hatred which could potentially develop. Conversely, the gains to be had by welcoming someone warmly and thus improving his spiritual stature are enormous, as in the following analysis.

**כִּי תִקְצֹר קְצִירְךָ בְשָׂדֶךָ וְשָׁכַחְתָּ עֹמֶר בַּשָּׂדֶה לֹא תָשׁוּב לְקַחְתּוֹ לַגֵּר לַיָּתוֹם וְלָאַלְמָנָה יִהְיֶה לְמַעַן יְבָרֶכְךָ ה' אֱלֹקֶיךָ בְּכֹל מַעֲשֵׂה יָדֶיךָ.**

---

66. *Bereishith Rabbah* 82:15.

*When you reap your harvest in your field, and you forget a sheaf in the field, you must not go back to take it. It shall remain for the proselyte, the orphan and the widow, so that the Eternal, your God, may bless you in all your actions.*[67]

Rashi comments:

וְאַף עַל פִּי שֶׁבָּאת לְיָדוֹ שֶׁלֹּא בְּמִתְכַּוֵּן ק"ו לָעוֹשֶׂה בְּמִתְכַּוֵּן, אֱמֹר מֵעַתָּה נָפְלָה סֶלַע מִיָּדוֹ וּמְצָאָהּ עָנִי וְנִתְפַּרְנֵס בָּהּ, הֲרֵי הוּא מִתְבָּרֵךְ עָלֶיהָ.

*One who benefits others unintentionally, for example by dropping a coin which is picked up by a pauper and provides him with sustenance, receives reward. How much greater is the reward when the benefit is intended!*[68]

Rabbi Simcha Zissel Ziv elaborates on this point in his work *Chochmah U'Mussar*: A pauper, he says, receives mere transient benefit from this unintentional benefactor, yet nevertheless the benefactor is rewarded with bountiful blessings. How much more does the principle apply when spiritual rather than physical gains are to be had. One's behaviour should always follow the dictum: שֶׁיְּהֵא שֵׁם שָׁמַיִם מִתְאַהֵב עַל יָדְךָ, that love of the Almighty should be engendered by your actions, leading others in turn to appreciate the spiritual values your actions represent. Intentionally providing others with spiritual benefits, both through encouraging spiritual progress and through one's own personal example, results in unfathomable reward.

It is incumbent upon all who are part of an institution to realise the ramifications of their actions. Great caution should be taken by existing members of an institution to prevent any disillusionment of new members. For disappointment can lead to hatred, which in turn can result in dire consequences. Furthermore, every encouragement and aid should be extended to new members so that, living up to the role models presented, they too will proceed to take their rightful place as valued members of both the relevant institution and society as a whole.

---

67. *Devarim* 24:19.
68. Rashi *ad loc.*

# KI THAVO

REWARD OR RETRIBUTION; abundant goodness or severe affliction. The blessings and curses of this *parashah* demonstrate how life's conditions are dependent upon the deeds of the Jewish People. As it states:

> **וְהָיָה אִם לֹא תִשְׁמַע בְּקוֹל ה' אֱלֹקֶיךָ לִשְׁמֹר לַעֲשׂוֹת אֶת כָּל מִצְוֹתָיו... וּבָאוּ עָלֶיךָ כָּל הַקְּלָלוֹת הָאֵלֶּה וְהִשִּׂיגוּךָ... וְהָיָה כַּאֲשֶׁר שָׂשׂ ה' עֲלֵיכֶם לְהֵיטִיב אֶתְכֶם וּלְהַרְבּוֹת אֶתְכֶם כֵּן יָשִׂישׂ ה' עֲלֵיכֶם לְהַאֲבִיד אֶתְכֶם וּלְהַשְׁמִיד אֶתְכֶם וְנִסַּחְתֶּם מֵעַל הָאֲדָמָה אֲשֶׁר אַתָּה בָא שָׁמָּה לְרִשְׁתָּהּ.**
>
> *But it will happen, if you do not heed the voice of the Eternal, your God, to be careful to carry out all His commandments... then all these curses will come upon you and reach you... It will then be that just as the Eternal rejoiced over you, to do good to you and increase your numbers, so will the Eternal make [your enemies] rejoice over you, to make you perish and to destroy you, and you will be uprooted from the land which you are entering to take possession of.*[69]

Our Sages comment:

> רש"י: יָשִׂישׂ ה' אֶת אוֹיְבֵיכֶם עֲלֵיכֶם לְהַאֲבִיד. אָמַר ר' אֶלְעָזָר, הוּא אֵינוֹ שָׂשׂ אֲבָל אֲחֵרִים מֵשִׂישׂ. וְדַיְקָא נָמִי דִּכְתִיב יָשִׂישׂ וְלֹא כְּתִיב יָשׂוּשׂ.
>
> *Does God exult when evildoers fall? He is not happy, but He makes others happy. This can be seen in the verse, where the causative form* יָשִׂישׂ, *"He will make others happy," is written, as opposed to the active form of* יָשׂוּשׂ, *"He will rejoice." It is not that God rejoices in the downfall of the wicked, but He*

---

69. *Devarim* 28:15, 63.

*implants happiness over their descent into the hearts of other people.*[70]

One of the terrible things detailed in these verses is the jubilation of our enemies at the suffering and downfall of our nation. However, as expressed by our Sages, הוּא אֵינוֹ שָׂשׂ — "He does not rejoice." If God does not delight in the retribution, why does He cause our enemies to exult in the humiliation of our people?

This rejoicing over the downfall of an enemy is not exclusive to the gentiles, however. As Jews, we are told: וּבַאֲבֹד רְשָׁעִים רִנָּה — "At the fall of evildoers, there shall be song."[71] These words appear to state that when our enemies fall, we should burst forth in song. We have already established that God Himself does not delight in this situation. Why then should we, His people, experience happiness?

Rabbeinu Yonah explains another maxim from *Mishlei*, seemingly contradictory to the above, which has bearing on our theme:

בִּנְפֹל אוֹיִבְךָ אַל תִּשְׂמָח וּבִכָּשְׁלוֹ אַל יָגֵל לִבֶּךָ.

*Do not rejoice at the downfall of your enemy, and let not your heart exult in his stumbling.*[72]

The underlying reason for this injunction is that this feeling of joy cannot reach a true level of purity; one is unlikely to rejoice solely for the sake of Heaven. One's emotions will surely be affected by the fact that the individual is an enemy, the object of dislike. Thus, permissible though it may be to rejoice in the downfall of a wicked person, it is an undesirable sentiment when the individual is in the category of enemy. In this vein, an added nuance is seen in the following verse in the book of *Shofetim*: כֵּן יֹאבְדוּ כָל אוֹיְבֶיךָ ה' — "May all Your enemies be destroyed, O God."[73] The enemies referred to in this verse are specifically enemies of God, those who oppose the purpose of Creation. In the case of enemies of God, who

70. *Megillah* 10b.
71. *Mishlei* 11:10.
72. *Mishlei* 24:17.
73. *Shofetim* 5:31.

fight a purely ideological battle, one can wish for, and even rejoice, in their destruction. Only when the battlefront is distanced from any personal sentiment is rejoicing in order.

In this world of falsehood and confusion, we are faced with a constant desecration of God's Name, as we witness the success and prosperity of the evildoers. A similar profanation is caused through seeing the affliction of the righteous; the Heavenly system of reward and punishment, of justice and goodness, seems to be askew. An example of this desecration is seen in a famous work of art. The picture depicts a Jew, standing at the edge of a mass grave. With Nazi onlookers jeering, the man beseeches that he may die while wearing his tefillin. "There is no Judge and no justice!" is the cry of the picture, the ideology propagated by the artist. And so in every case in which those who seek to perform God's will are afflicted with suffering, we witness the desecration of God's holy Name.

However, when the perpetrators of these evil deeds are brought to retribution, then the balance is redressed, and the system of Heavenly justice is once again apparent. The punishment of evildoers retrospectively remedies any previous desecration, and thus serves to sanctify God's Name in the universe. With hindsight, it is clear that God's fairness and rectitude need never have been disputed. Thus we understand the rationale behind the injunction to rejoice upon the fall of the wicked. One's exultation stems from the light and goodness that have thereby been brought into the world, the glorification of God that has been caused.

When personal sentiments are involved, however, there is a danger that one's joy will result from the resolution of one's own resentments, and thus the feelings of happiness cannot be said to flow from higher ideals. One's primary concern is not the display of justice in the world, but one's own victorious emergence from a personal battle. Therefore, "Do not rejoice," we tell this man. The successful jousting of an enemy is no reason for happiness within the Torah's system of life.

God Himself makes others happy when enemies fall, though He Himself does not delight: הוּא אֵינוֹ שָׂשׂ. To understand this, we must utilise a principle elaborated upon in previous essays. While man lives within the parameters of a world governed by time, God transcends these constraints. Man sees events as they occur in sequence: one followed by another, followed by another. Man will feel searing pain at the picture of a pious Jew being led to his death by mocking, sadistic Nazis. The apparent absence of justice, of Divine retribution, will strike him. He will only later see the perpetrator's punishment, the evildoer's penalty, and only then rejoice in the evidence of Divine justice. However, God exists in a realm in which past and future melt into a unified oneness. God does not view events sequentially. Outside of time, only the present exists. Thus, at exactly the same time as evil is perpetrated, justice is being meted out, and the individual is being punished. No desecration has ever occurred; no denial of His justice ever transpired. From a perspective above time, the constant Godly light remains impervious to dark stains of evil.

Thus it is clear why God does not rejoice at the affliction of evildoers. Remaining to be understood, however, is why God makes our enemies happy while they are afflicting the Jewish People with the prescribed curses.

Rabbi Dessler explains[74] that God manifests His guidance in the world in a manner that is clearly recognizable to any intelligent person. It is evident that it is not the workings of nature, but the Hand of God that directs all events. This applies not only to the many miracles that God performed throughout our people's history, but also to the trials and suffering that we endure through the ages. The miraculous rise, the supernatural strength and power of our enemies, points clearly to Divine intervention on their behalf. This is referred to in Scriptures, in the statement, "God will make your enemies rejoice." In this case, God fortifies our enemies, giving them power which defies natural boundaries, so that they can be the staff with which Heaven strikes, so that they can visit the curses upon us, Heaven forbid.

---

74. *Michtav MeEliyahu*, Part One, p. 203.

A passage in *Yeshayah* dramatically illustrates this frightening prospect:

> **וְנָשָׂא נֵס לַגּוֹיִם מֵרָחוֹק וְשָׁרַק לוֹ מִקְצֵה הָאָרֶץ וְהִנֵּה מְהֵרָה קַל יָבוֹא. אֵין עָיֵף וְאֵין כּוֹשֵׁל בּוֹ לֹא יָנוּם וְלֹא יִישָׁן וְלֹא נִפְתַּח אֵזוֹר חֲלָצָיו וְלֹא נִתַּק שְׂרוֹךְ נְעָלָיו. אֲשֶׁר חִצָּיו שְׁנוּנִים וְכָל קַשְּׁתֹתָיו דְּרֻכוֹת פַּרְסוֹת סוּסָיו כַּצַּר נֶחְשָׁבוּ וְגַלְגִּלָּיו כַּסּוּפָה.**
>
> *When God's anger is kindled against His people, He will raise a banner for the nations of the world, who will whistle [send forth a signal] from the ends of the earth. They will come speedily from afar; none will tire, nor will any stumble. They will not slumber, nor will they sleep. They will neither have to [stop to] tighten their belts, nor to fasten their shoelaces. Their arrows will be sharpened, their bows bent. They will come like a whirlwind, roaring like a lion. When they grasp their prey, there will be none who can save the victim.*[75]

In this chilling narrative, Yeshayah depicts the help that God will bestow upon the enemies of the Jewish People, assistance transcending all natural boundaries. Human limitations are miraculously removed: the enemy needs no sleep and suffers no drowsiness. He is hastened on his way, with God's blessing.

Rabbi Dessler relates this form of Divine providence to the events of his generation:

> *In the normal course of events, it is the distinguished and intelligent, those knowledgeable in affairs of state, who become political leaders. Can it be a natural occurrence for a contingency of empty people, who hold meetings in beer cellars, to rise to political power? The Nazi party consisted of nonentities, who were thrust into a position in which they dominated international affairs. For tens of years, the members of the Nazi party were insignificant, involved in trivialities. Suddenly, they were catapulted into ruling positions, leading the country with utmost precision and efficiency — in fact, with*

---

75. *Yeshayah* 5:26–28.

*an evil excellence. This process is a demonstration of Divine providence, a miracle, to teach us and open our eyes.*

The יָשִׂישׂ, the rejoicing that God causes our enemies, was present not only in the conception and growth of the Nazi party, but it reverberated throughout the war years. Just one example is the manner in which Hitler overran Poland, thereby controlling a large country in just a few weeks. An echo of the יָשִׂישׂ can be heard. The aid and assistance God granted to our enemy enabled them to defy natural boundaries.

The words of *Eichah* ring true two millennia after the destruction of the Temple: הָיוּ צָרֶיהָ לְרֹאשׁ — "Her [Jerusalem's] enemies shall become leaders."[76] Our Sages elaborate:

מְלַמֵּד שֶׁכָּל מִי שֶׁבָּא לְהָצֵר לְיִשְׂרָאֵל נַעֲשֶׂה רֹאשׁ, אַתָּה מוֹצֵא שֶׁעַד שֶׁלֹּא חָרְבָה יְרוּשָׁלַיִם לֹא הָיְתָה מְדִינָה חֲשׁוּבָה כְּלוּם, וּמִשֶּׁחָרְבָה, נַעֲשֵׂית קֵסָרִין מֶטְרוֹפּוֹלִין.

*This teaches us that all those who seek to oppress the Jewish People become elevated, become leaders. Thus we find that until Jerusalem was destroyed, the conquering nation was insignificant. When Jerusalem was destroyed, Caesarea was transformed into a metropolis.*[77]

יָשִׂישׂ — God grants assistance and power to our enemies, whether that enemy be Babylonia, Persia, Media, Rome, or Germany.

In his work on *Tehillim*, R. Chaim Vital details the four exiles that the Children of Yisrael have endured.[78] "Through the oppression of Babylonia, Media, Persia, and Rome, have the Children of Yisrael journeyed, undergoing the cleansing process which each nation offered. However, in the future, the Children of Yisrael are destined to suffer a fifth exile: that of Yishmael. The other exiling nations had some dominion over other countries; not so Yishmael. The Arabs were always a nomadic nation, who had no dealings with other tribes. However, in the future they will prevail over the entire world and over Yisrael."

---

76. *Eichah* 1:5.
77. *Eichah Rabbah* 1:31.
78. *Eitz HaDa'ath Tov*, *Tehillim* 124.

These words, written hundreds of years ago, have, until recently, been shrouded in mystery. The Arab nations were always perceived as underdeveloped, dependent upon the aid and technological advancement of the Western world. But now, however, "יָשִׂישׂ," God has invested the Arab nations with tremendous international influence. The world petrol crisis is but one example of the power which the Arabs now wield, as the whole of England grinds to a standstill due to lack of fuel. School is cancelled, surgical operations postponed, factory production halted — for without petrol, goods cannot be transported and people are confined to their homes. The Arab countries possess a monopoly on oil, such that their refusal to supply the precious commodity cast the entire civilised world into turmoil. Every developed country depends on oil; the Arab nations thus possess the power to manipulate the world.

Indeed we see the realisation of the words of R. Chaim Vital, as the Arabs have the resources to prevail over "the entire world and Yisrael," Heaven forbid. It behooves us to take to heart the continuation of his words:

> וְאֵין לָנוּ תִּקְוָה אַחֶרֶת זוּלָתִי שֶׁנִּבְטַח בִּשְׁמוֹ הַגָּדוֹל יִת' שֶׁיּוֹשִׁיעֵנוּ מִיָּדָם... וְיִגְאָלֵנוּ גְּאֻלָּה שְׁלֵמָה הָעֲתִידָה בִּמְהֵרָה בְּיָמֵינוּ.
>
> *We have no hope other than placing our trust in God to save us from their hands, and bring the Ultimate Redemption speedily, in our days.*

Our present suffering under Arab dominion and our recent suffering in the Holocaust clearly point to the existence of God, if we only take note of the unnatural power of our enemies. Rabbi Dessler gives us the correct perspective on the suffering of the Holocaust. "Many people do not recognise the hand of Providence leading us through the birth pangs which herald the Mashiach. Instead, they resent the affliction, and are consumed with questions against God, challenging our faith. They attribute events to chance, to coincidence, and adhere to the ideology that, 'there is no Judge and no justice.' The influence of such an attitude is a danger even to those who do believe in God and His providence." In this manner the Maharal explains the statement of

R. Ulah, "Let Mashiach come, and let me not be present to see him."[79] R. Ulah feared that were he to experience the suffering and birth pangs of Mashiach, he would be brought to question God's ways.

The suffering that heralds the advent of the Mashiach has been visited upon us. Throughout the Holocaust, the tribulations experienced by our nation were surely a reflection of the ninety-eight curses detailed in this *parashah*. There are two responses to the brutal torture: "There is no Judge and no justice," a backsliding into heretical denial, Heaven forbid, or the search to find the Hand of God which lies within even the darkest hours of our history. If we only look carefully at the suffering of this century, we will clearly discern the echo of יָשִׂישׂ, realising how God plants exultation into our foes. Witnessing their supernatural success, beholding the aid that they receive from on High, we see clear evidence of the fulfillment of the Torah's words. We see the materialisation of the ninety-eight curses, and we glean inspiration from our conviction that the contrasting words of our *parashah* will also be effected:

> **וְהָיָה אִם שָׁמוֹעַ תִּשְׁמַע בְּקוֹל ה׳ אֱלֹקֶיךָ לִשְׁמֹר לַעֲשׂוֹת אֶת כָּל מִצְוֹתָיו אֲשֶׁר אָנֹכִי מְצַוְּךָ הַיּוֹם וּנְתָנְךָ ה׳ אֱלֹקֶיךָ עֶלְיוֹן עַל כָּל גּוֹיֵי הָאָרֶץ. וּבָאוּ עָלֶיךָ כָּל הַבְּרָכוֹת הָאֵלֶּה וְהִשִּׂיגֻךָ כִּי תִשְׁמַע בְּקוֹל ה׳ אֱלֹקֶיךָ.**
>
> *It will be, if you constantly heed the voice of the Eternal, your God, to be careful to carry out all His commandments that I am commanding you today, then the Eternal, your God, will make you supreme over all the nations of the earth. All these blessings will come upon you and reach you, because you heed the voice of the Eternal, your God.*[80]

If we will only fill our lives with Torah, if we will only adhere to God's command, then the Almighty Himself will rejoice in bestowing every good upon His children.

---

79. *Sanhedrin* 98b.
80. *Devarim* 28:1.

# NITZAVIM

COLLECTIVE RESPONSIBILITY IS incumbent upon every Jew. The pivotal nature of the community in Jewish life is evident through the following words:

> **הַנִּסְתָּרֹת לַה' אֱלֹקֵינוּ וְהַנִּגְלֹת לָנוּ וּלְבָנֵינוּ עַד עוֹלָם לַעֲשׂוֹת אֶת כָּל דִּבְרֵי הַתּוֹרָה הַזֹּאת.**
>
> *The hidden [sins] are [the responsibility of] the Eternal, our God, [to punish,] but the blatant [sins] are our and our children's [responsibility to punish], so as to carry out all the words of this Torah.*[81]

Rashi explains that these words refer to the covenant of collective responsibility, wherein each person is held responsible for the deeds of his fellow Jew. However, a logical objection immediately arises from this oath, which Rashi continues to detail.

> וְאִם תֹּאמְרוּ מַה בְּיָדֵינוּ לַעֲשׂוֹת, אַתָּה מַעֲנִישׁ אֶת הָרַבִּים עַל הִרְהוּרֵי הַיָּחִיד, שֶׁנֶּאֱמַר פֶּן יֵשׁ בָּכֶם אִישׁ וגו', וְאַחַר כָּךְ וְרָאוּ אֶת מַכּוֹת הָאָרֶץ הַהִיא, וְהַלֹּא אֵין אָדָם יוֹדֵעַ מַטְמוֹנוֹתָיו שֶׁל חֲבֵרוֹ, אֵין אֲנִי מַעֲנִישׁ אֶתְכֶם עַל הַנִּסְתָּרוֹת, שֶׁהֵן לה' אֱלֹקֵינוּ, וְהוּא יִפָּרַע מֵאוֹתוֹ יָחִיד, אֲבָל הַנִּגְלוֹת, לָנוּ וּלְבָנֵינוּ לְבַעֵר הָרַע מִקִּרְבֵּנוּ, וְאִם לֹא נַעֲשָׂה דִּין בָּהֶם יֵעָנְשׁוּ הָרַבִּים.
>
> *One could claim that the idea of collective responsibility is an unfair one. How can the community be held culpable for evil deeds that people have committed secretly, or for any fantasies of sin in which one individual might have indulged? On this point, the verse reassures us: the nation as a whole will not be blamed for hidden liabilities — these are in the hands*

81. *Devarim* 29:28

*of God. It is, however, the duty of the community to uproot any overt evil. Failure to bring the perpetrator to justice will bring punishment on the entire nation.*[82]

Let us focus upon Rashi's words to learn more about the nature of this responsibility that rests on all of our shoulders. Earlier in our *parashah*, the verses state as follows:

**וְלֹא אִתְּכֶם לְבַדְּכֶם אָנֹכִי כֹּרֵת אֶת הַבְּרִית הַזֹּאת וְאֶת הָאָלָה הַזֹּאת. כִּי אֶת אֲשֶׁר יֶשְׁנוֹ פֹּה עִמָּנוּ עֹמֵד הַיּוֹם לִפְנֵי ה׳ אֱלֹקֵינוּ וְאֵת אֲשֶׁר אֵינֶנּוּ פֹּה עִמָּנוּ הַיּוֹם... פֶּן יֵשׁ בָּכֶם אִישׁ אוֹ אִשָּׁה אוֹ מִשְׁפָּחָה אוֹ שֵׁבֶט אֲשֶׁר לְבָבוֹ פֹנֶה הַיּוֹם מֵעִם ה׳ אֱלֹקֵינוּ לָלֶכֶת לַעֲבֹד אֶת אֱלֹהֵי הַגּוֹיִם הָהֵם פֶּן יֵשׁ בָּכֶם שֹׁרֶשׁ פֹּרֶה רֹאשׁ וְלַעֲנָה. וְהָיָה בְּשָׁמְעוֹ אֶת דִּבְרֵי הָאָלָה הַזֹּאת וְהִתְבָּרֵךְ בִּלְבָבוֹ לֵאמֹר שָׁלוֹם יִהְיֶה לִּי כִּי בִּשְׁרִרוּת לִבִּי אֵלֵךְ לְמַעַן סְפוֹת הָרָוָה אֶת הַצְּמֵאָה. לֹא יֹאבֶה ה׳ סְלֹחַ לוֹ...**

*And not with you alone am I forming this covenant and [swearing] this oath, but with those who are standing here with us today, before the Eternal, our God, and with those who are not with us today... Perhaps there is among you a man or woman, a family or tribe, whose heart turns away today from following the Eternal, our God, by going to serve the gods of those nations? Perhaps there is among you a root sprouting gall and wormwood? And it will be, when he hears the words of this oath, and feels complacent, saying, "I will be all right, for I follow my heart's desires," so that [the Eternal will now] add [his] unintentional to [his] blatant sins; the Eternal will not wish to forgive him.*[83]

The Ibn Ezra explains the rationale behind this evildoer's complacency, the confidence he has despite his wrongdoing.

וְהַטַּעַם שָׁלוֹם יִהְיֶה לִי אַף עַל פִּי שֶׁאֵלֵךְ בִּשְׁרִירוּת לִבִּי, כִּי בְּצִדְקַת הַצַּדִּיקִים אֶחְיֶה, כִּי הֵם רַבִּים וַאֲנִי יָחִיד חוֹטֵא. עַל כֵּן כָּתוּב אַחֲרָיו לֹא יֹאבֶה ה׳ סְלֹחַ לוֹ.

82. Rashi *ad loc.*
83. *Devarim* 29:13–14, 17–18.

*[The sinner thinks,] "I will live through the goodness of the righteous. There are numerous righteous people, and I am but an individual sinner." For this attitude, God does not desire to forgive him.*[84]

Thus we can see that it is the very covenant of collective responsibility on which the evildoer relies. From one perspective, the righteous of his generation will be held culpable for his actions. However, the wicked person can simultaneously shelter in the blessings that the righteous will enjoy. God, however, views this "convenient" arrangement in the harshest terms. Indeed, God will withhold forgiveness from this wicked individual. Why should this particular attitude arouse such a powerful judgment against the sinner?

Let us digress to the cataclysmic event of the giving of the Torah:

**וּמֹשֶׁה עָלָה אֶל הָאֱלֹקִים וַיִּקְרָא אֵלָיו ה׳ מִן הָהָר לֵאמֹר כֹּה תֹאמַר לְבֵית יַעֲקֹב וְתַגֵּיד לִבְנֵי יִשְׂרָאֵל. אַתֶּם רְאִיתֶם אֲשֶׁר עָשִׂיתִי לְמִצְרָיִם וָאֶשָּׂא אֶתְכֶם עַל כַּנְפֵי נְשָׁרִים וָאָבִא אֶתְכֶם אֵלָי. וְעַתָּה אִם שָׁמוֹעַ תִּשְׁמְעוּ בְּקֹלִי וּשְׁמַרְתֶּם אֶת בְּרִיתִי וִהְיִיתֶם לִי סְגֻלָּה מִכָּל הָעַמִּים כִּי לִי כָּל הָאָרֶץ. וְאַתֶּם תִּהְיוּ לִי מַמְלֶכֶת כֹּהֲנִים וְגוֹי קָדוֹשׁ אֵלֶּה הַדְּבָרִים אֲשֶׁר תְּדַבֵּר אֶל בְּנֵי יִשְׂרָאֵל.**

*Moshe went up to God, and the Eternal called to him from the mountain, saying: "So shall you say to the house of Ya'akov, and tell the Children of Yisrael: 'You have seen what I did to the Mitzrim, and [that] I carried you on wings of eagles and brought you [near] to [serve] Me. So now, if you continually heed My [words] and keep My covenant, you [alone] will be a special treasure for Me, more than all the nations, [even though] all the earth is Mine. And you will be a kingdom of nobles and a holy nation for Me.' These are words that you shall say to the Children of Yisrael."*[85]

When we examine Rashi's comment on this passage, a striking difficulty is evident.

---

84. Ibn Ezra *ad loc.*

85. *Shemoth* 19:3–6.

לְבֵית יַעֲקֹב. אֵלּוּ הַנָּשִׁים , תֹּאמַר לָהֶן בְּלָשׁוֹן רַכָּה.

*The house of Ya'akov — this refers to the women, whom you should tell in a gentle manner.*

וְתַגֵּיד לִבְנֵי יִשְׂרָאֵל. עֳנָשִׁים וְדִקְדּוּקִין. פָּרֵשׁ לַזְּכָרִים דְּבָרִים הַקָּשִׁין כְּגִידִין.

*Tell the Children of Yisrael. The punishments and exactitude [required]. Explain to the men in harsh terms.*

Both men and women are addressed at this climactic moment. This is learned from Rashi, who highlights that the two expressions in the verse are not redundant, but that בֵּית יַעֲקֹב refers to the women, and בְּנֵי יִשְׂרָאֵל, to the men. This explanation arises from contrasting the use of the verb אֱמֹר, and the verb הַגֵּד. The verb אֱמֹר denotes gentle speech, and is used in conjunction with the women, while word הַגֵּד implies harsh speech, the approach to be used when instructing the men.

Turning to Rashi's other comments on this passage, a striking contradiction arises:

כֹּה תֹאמַר. בַּלָּשׁוֹן הַזֶּה וְכַסֵּדֶר הַזֶּה.

*So shall you say — In these words and in this order.*

אֵלֶּה הַדְּבָרִים. לֹא פָּחוֹת וְלֹא יוֹתֵר.

*These words — not more and not less.*

Moshe is instructed to transmit the Torah in a manner that will be appropriate and appealing to his audience — one way for men and another for women. Simultaneously, however, he is warned against deviating in any way from the text prescribed by God. He may not change the content or the language of his speech. How could these mutually exclusive obligations be simultaneously fulfilled? How could Moshe possibly tailor his words to each different group, while relaying God's message in its original form?

The *Sefath Emeth* resolves the contradiction:

אָמַר בַּלָּשׁוֹן הַזֶּה וּבַסֵּדֶר הַזֶּה שֶׁגָּלוּי לְפָנָיו ית' שֶׁבָּזֶה הַלָּשׁוֹן יִמְשֹׁךְ כָּל אֶחָד לְפִי דַּרְכּוֹ. הַנָּשִׁים בְּפִתּוּי וְהָאֲנָשִׁים בְּקַבָּלָה נוֹרָאָה.

> *[Moshe was commanded] to utter set words in a fixed order. For it was revealed before the Almighty that everyone would draw from these words as he or she required, relating to them according to their temperament and personality. Thus, women would feel they were being influenced through words of tenderness, and men would feel the awesomeness and gravity of Torah and mitzvoth.*[86]

The same words could prompt an entirely different reaction from each listener. For women, the story of God's tremendous kindness at the Exodus would elicit feelings of gratitude, leading to a greater devotion. The same story would cause the men to tremble in trepidation, lest they fail to complete their duties. Both parties received a spur to aid them in their Divine service from the set text, for men and women related to it each from their own perspective.

Another example of how two people can have different approaches towards the same thing can be seen in connection to our theme of collective responsibility. For the righteous, this is an onus that they feel lying heavily upon their shoulders; they are duty-bound to prevent any sin from being committed, and to punish any misdemeanor. The Chafetz Chaim was one such individual who saw himself as answerable for the sins of his generation. He once traveled to spend the Sabbath in a nearby town, hoping, in this manner, to strengthen the townspeople's Sabbath observance. When questioned concerning the reason for this trip, the Chafetz Chaim stated that, upon the day of reckoning, he could be accused of desecrating the holy day. He would protest, stating that he had never profaned the Sabbath, and that he had even authored a work detailing the numerous laws pertaining to it. This argument, however, would be quickly countered with, "Yes, but there were people in your vicinity who did not observe the Sabbath, and you did not take pains to reprimand them, and guide them back to the correct path."

This reasoning also prompted the Chafetz Chaim to make another journey to educate people concerning the laws of *kashruth* —

---

86. *Sefath Emeth on the Torah*, Part Two, p. 50.

he wished to avoid being held accountable for the sins that were perpetrated in this area. Such is the approach of the righteous to the covenant of nationwide responsibility. It is an obligation which is "קָשֶׁה כְּגִידִין," harsh, with frightening ramifications. The righteous relate to the idea of collective responsibility with the mindset of one under obligation — how much is incumbent upon them because of this covenant!

The evildoer relates to collective responsibility in quite the opposite manner. The covenant gives him license to continue in his perversity, for others will be held accountable for his sin. The righteous will bear his crime, and he will share their merits and thus their reward. To some, עַרְבוּת, responsibility, can be viewed in light of its alternative translation, "sweetness." The same words, the same concept, are either an awesome responsibility, or a sanction to further embroil oneself in evil.

However, we still have to understand the words of the Ibn Ezra, who informs us that God will not "desire to forgive" one who interprets the covenant in this manner of "sweetness." Why should this be so?

The underlying perversity of this attitude can be seen when we examine an entirely different law:

> **כִּי יִקָּרֵא קַן צִפּוֹר לְפָנֶיךָ בַּדֶּרֶךְ בְּכָל עֵץ אוֹ עַל הָאָרֶץ אֶפְרֹחִים אוֹ בֵיצִים וְהָאֵם רֹבֶצֶת עַל הָאֶפְרֹחִים אוֹ עַל הַבֵּיצִים לֹא תִקַּח הָאֵם עַל הַבָּנִים. שַׁלֵּחַ תְּשַׁלַּח אֶת הָאֵם וְאֶת הַבָּנִים תִּקַּח לָךְ לְמַעַן יִיטַב לָךְ וְהַאֲרַכְתָּ יָמִים.**
>
> *If you happen to come across a bird's nest on the road on any tree or on the ground, [with] chicks or eggs [inside it], and the mother bird is roosting on the chicks or on the eggs, you must not take the mother bird [while she is roosting] on [her] young. You must send away the mother bird and [then] you may take the young for yourself, so that it will be well with you and that you live a long time.*[87]

87. *Devarim* 22:6, 7.

The *Oznaim LaTorah* explains that this prohibition applies only if the mother is actually roosting on the birds. If the mother is flying around, the law does not come into force, and the mother may also be captured. In light of this law, the *Oznaim LaTorah* suggests a rationale for the prohibition.

Birds possess a natural survival instinct, and from fear of capture, will fly away as soon as they are approached by man. When the mother is roosting on her young, however, she will not abandon her nest and escape for her life. Instead, due to her love and compassion for her young, she will curb her natural instincts, leaving herself open to danger, and remain with her nest. In the face of peril, the mother is willing to sacrifice her own safety for the sake of her beloved offspring.

> וְגָזְרָה תּוֹרָה שֶׁלֹּא יִשְׁתַּמֵּשׁ הָאָדָם בְּמִדָּה טוֹבָה זוֹ שֶׁיֵּשׁ בָּאֵם כְּדֵי לְתוֹפְשָׂהּ... יֵשׁ לְךָ רְשׁוּת לָצוּד עוֹפוֹת בְּכָל מִינֵי אֶמְצָעִים... אֲבָל לֹא עַל יְדֵי מְסִירוּת נַפְשָׁהּ בְּעַד זַרְעָהּ.
>
> *The Torah decreed that man must not take advantage of this good quality, by using it to capture the mother with her young. Normally, one may capture birds through all kinds of means. However, one may not exploit the sacrifice, the stifling of the instinct of self-preservation, which the mother has made on behalf of her young.*[88]

The Torah prohibits capturing the bird only when, for the sake of its young, it would not fly away in the face of danger. Man may not take advantage of this element of "self-sacrifice" which the bird has demonstrated.

Returning to our subject of collective responsibility, we have established that this oath can be taken in a manner of "קָשֶׁה כְּגִידִין," as one tries to raise the standard of one's own behaviour and encourage one's fellow Jew along the correct path. Concurrently, the covenant works for the benefit of the sinner, as his fellows gently guide him to the path of rectitude. Castigation, rebuke, and encouragement will

88. *Oznaim LaTorah, ad loc.*

spur him to spiritual progress. On the other hand, the same prohibition against taking advantage of the mother bird's sacrifice can be applied here as well. A sinner who abuses the sacrifice of his righteous brothers to give himself permission to continue on his wicked path is castigated in the harshest possible terms.

Of direct relevance to our theme is our attitude towards God's trait of אֶרֶךְ אַפַּיִם, longsuffering. God waits, not meting out punishment immediately, but giving the sinner time to show his regret and repent from his evil ways. God considers everyone's potential, his shining inner core, and He waits, allowing one to harness one's latent strengths and devote oneself to His service. This great kindness can be abused, however, as the sinner, instead of returning to God, takes advantage of His benevolence and constantly delays repentance. The desecration caused by the sin itself is deepened, as it appears that the sinner has escaped unpunished. God's mercy parallels the care a mother bird shows for her young, overcoming her instincts and placing herself in danger for the sake of her dependents. He allows His Name to be profaned, for the sake of His beloved, wayward children. Yet, when the sinner refuses to repent, he abuses the Almighty's kindness, and thus God will not desire to forgive him.

It is only too easy for us to delay examining our deeds, to defer scrutinising our spiritual pathway. It is much more comfortable to avert our eyes from our shortcomings and misdemeanors. This inertia, however, effectively takes God's kindness and forbearance and uses it for one's own selfish ends. God delays punishment so that we can reach the goodness of sincere repentance, the joy of returning to God wholeheartedly. It is only too easy to take advantage and abuse the kindness, continuing in our sinful ways. In this case, however, we cut ourselves off from forgiveness.

Another application of this principle connects to Yom Kippur, the Day of Atonement. We find those who sin, relying on the forthcoming Yom Kippur to bring atonement. For these people, Yom Kippur will be ineffectual. Having sinned with the thought in mind that they could count on being forgiven on Yom Kippur, they have, as it were, made Yom Kippur party to their sin. Having thus abused the day's sanctity, having tried to take advantage of its opportunity, they can no longer reap its benefits.

The gifts of forbearance, repentance, and Yom Kippur are all tools to awaken us, calling us to dedicate our lives to the Almighty with fresh vigour and ardour. They must be viewed as awesome obligations, not as aids to our spiritual complacency and stagnation. Only then can we achieve true repentance, and God will indeed "desire to forgive us," His beloved children.

# VAYELECH

UPON CURSORY READING, the Torah describes in this *parashah* the transfer of leadership from Moshe to Yehoshua. Our Sages, from their deeper perspective, convey the essence of this event:

> **וַיֹּאמֶר ה' אֶל מֹשֶׁה הֵן קָרְבוּ יָמֶיךָ לָמוּת קְרָא אֶת יְהוֹשֻׁעַ וְהִתְיַצְּבוּ בְּאֹהֶל מוֹעֵד וַאֲצַוֶּנּוּ...**
>
> *The Eternal then said to Moshe, "Behold, your days are nearing [the time] to die. Call Yehoshua, and [both of you] shall stand inside the Tent of Meeting and I shall give him encouragement."*[89]

Our Sages comment upon the word הֵן, closely related to הִנֵּה, meaning "behold."

> הֵן קָרְבוּ יָמֶיךָ לָמוּת. לָמָּה נִגְזַר עָלָיו מִיתָה בְּזֶה לְשׁוֹן הֵן? לְמָה הַדָּבָר דּוֹמֶה לְאֶחָד שֶׁכִּבֵּד אֶת הַמֶּלֶךְ וְהֵבִיא לוֹ דּוֹרוֹן חֶרֶב חַדָּה. אָמַר הַמֶּלֶךְ הַתִּיזוּ אֶת רֹאשׁוֹ בָּהּ. אָמַר לוֹ אוֹתוֹ הָאִישׁ אֲדוֹנִי הַמֶּלֶךְ בְּמַה שֶׁכִּבַּדְתִּיךָ בָּהּ אַתָּה מַתִּיז אֶת רֹאשִׁי. כָּךְ אָמַר מֹשֶׁה רִבּוֹנוֹ שֶׁל עוֹלָם בְּ"הֵן" קִלַּסְתִּיךָ שֶׁכָּךְ כָּתוּב (דְּבָרִים י,י"ד) הֵן לה' אֱלֹקֶיךָ הַשָּׁמַיִם וּשְׁמֵי הַשָּׁמַיִם וּבְ"הֵן" אַתָּה גּוֹזֵר עָלַי מִיתָה. א"ל הקב"ה שָׁכֵן רַע רוֹאֶה אֶת הַנִּכְנָסוֹת וְאֵינוֹ רוֹאֶה אֶת הַיּוֹצְאוֹת. אָמַר לוֹ אִי אַתָּה זָכוּר בְּשָׁעָה שֶׁשְּׁלַחְתִּיךָ לִגְאֹל אוֹתָם מִמִּצְרַיִם וְאָמַרְתָּ לִי וְהֵן לֹא יַאֲמִינוּ לִי, הֱוֵי הֵן קָרְבוּ יָמֶיךָ.
>
> *Why was Moshe's death decree proclaimed with the word הֵן? The situation can be compared to one who sought to honour the king, and to this end presented him with a razor-sharp sword. With the gift, the king began proceedings to decapitate*

89. *Devarim* 31:14.

*the man. The man protested vehemently: "My master, O King! I presented you with a sword. Will you use this gift to cut off my head?"*

*Moshe's arguments were in this vein. "I praised you with the word* הֵן*. As it says,* הֵן *— 'Behold, the heavens and heavens of the heavens belong to God' (Devarim 10:14). Will you then decree my death with this word?" God replied, "A bad neighbour sees how another man earns his income, and all that he brings into his home, but does not see the expenditure. Do you not remember how, when I commanded you to take the Jews out of Egypt, you exclaimed* הֵן *— 'Behold, they will not believe me.' It is because of this that I use the same word* הֵן *when informing you of your death, and the transfer of leadership to Yehoshua, who will lead the people into the Land."*[90]

The key to our understanding of that which transpired lies in the small word "הֵן." This word was originally uttered by Moshe in Egypt, and after its usage at that time the word continually reverberated, eventually rebounding upon Moshe and precluding his entrance into the Land of Israel. When dispatched to tell the Jewish nation the news about the forthcoming redemption, Moshe protested: וְהֵן לֹא יַאֲמִינוּ לִי — "Behold, they will not believe me."[91]

Let us discover what lies in this word. Further investigation is also needed concerning why Moshe was judged and punished through the "gift that he brought the King." Additionally, why according to the parable in the Midrash, was Moshe termed a "bad neighbour," a שָׁכֵן רַע?

The word הֵן is always indicative of that which is crystal clear. Behold! Something is here, tangible, existing with a gleaming clarity. Thus we understand the usage of the word in the verse declaring God's clear and transparent existence and guidance: הֵן — Behold — the heavens and heavens of the heavens belong to God — a tangible and clear knowledge of God's omnipotence, that Moshe guided the

---

90. *Devarim Rabbah* 9:6.
91. *Shemoth* 4:1.

Jewish People in the wilderness. Wonders and miracles were experienced by all. The start of Yehoshua's leadership was punctuated by a descent from this transcendent level to the level of "nature" where the people were subject to the normal flow of cause and effect. This is emphasized in the Midrash:

אָמַר ר׳ סִמוֹן כָּל מָקוֹם שֶׁנֶּאֱמַר וַיְהִי אַחֲרֵי מוֹת חָזַר הָעוֹלָם לְאַחֲרָיו... וַיְהִי אַחֲרֵי מוֹת מֹשֶׁה מִיָּד פָּסַק הַבְּאֵר וְהַמָּן וְעַנְנֵי הַכָּבוֹד.[92]

The expression of וַיְהִי אַחֲרֵי מוֹת always implies a fundamental upheaval. Life with open miracles was a feature exclusive to the life and leadership of Moshe. The word הֵן was constantly on the people's lips as they experienced the miraculous Well of Miriam, the daily manna, and the protective Clouds of Glory. With Moshe's passing, life underwent a dramatic change as the people began life on a different plane.

This is clear from the instructions given to the people immediately prior to Moshe's passing:

**ה׳ אֱלֹקֵינוּ דִּבֶּר אֵלֵינוּ בְּחֹרֵב לֵאמֹר... רְאֵה נָתַתִּי לִפְנֵיכֶם אֶת הָאָרֶץ בֹּאוּ וּרְשׁוּ אֶת הָאָרֶץ...**

*The Eternal, our God, spoke to us at Chorev, saying, "...Look, I have put the Land before you! Enter and take possession of the Land..."*[93]

**רש"י — בֹּאוּ וּרְשׁוּ. אֵין מְעַרְעֵר בַּדָּבָר וְאֵינְכֶם צְרִיכִין לְמִלְחָמָה. אִלּוּ לֹא שָׁלְחוּ מְרַגְּלִים לֹא הָיוּ צְרִיכִין לִכְלֵי זַיִן.**

*Rashi — Enter and take possession. You will experience no hindrance in this matter, and warfare will be unnecessary. Had the Jewish People not dispatched the spies, they would not even have needed to carry weapons.*[94]

Had it not been for the sin of the spies, Moshe would have led

---

92. *Yalkut Shimoni, Yehoshua* 1.
93. *Devarim* 1:6, 8.
94. Rashi *ad loc.*

the people into the Land on the level of הֵן, openly miraculous guidance, as explained by the Malbim:

> תְּחִלַּת הַגְּזֵרָה שֶׁלֹּא יִכָּנֵס מֹשֶׁה לָאָרֶץ הָיָה בְּחֵטְא מְרַגְּלִים... שֶׁלֹּא הָיוּ יִשְׂרָאֵל רְאוּיִים עוֹד אֶל הַמַּדְרֵגָה הַזֹּאת שֶׁמֹּשֶׁה יַכְנִיס אוֹתָם לָאָרֶץ. שֶׁאִם הָיָה מֹשֶׁה מֵבִיא אֶת יִשְׂרָאֵל לָאָרֶץ הָיָה הַכִּבּוּשׁ שֶׁלֹּא עַל יְדֵי מִלְחָמָה, רַק עַל יְדֵי ה׳ שֶׁהָיָה מַפִּיל אוֹיְבֵיהֶם לִפְנֵיהֶם חֲלָלִים... וְעוֹד אָמְרוּ חז״ל, שֶׁאִם הָיָה מֹשֶׁה נִכְנָס לָאָרֶץ הָיָה בּוֹנֶה הַמִּקְדָּשׁ וְלֹא הָיָה נֶחֱרַב לְעוֹלָם... וְכָל זֶה הָיָה תָּלוּי עַל תְּנַאי שֶׁיִּהְיוּ יִשְׂרָאֵל שְׁלֵמִים בֶּאֱמוּנָתָם וְצִדְקָתָם... אֲבָל אַחַר שֶׁחָטְאוּ בִּמְרַגְּלִים שֶׁנִּתְבָּרֵר שֶׁאֵינָם שְׁלֵמִים בֶּאֱמוּנָתָם, לֹא הָיָה אֶפְשָׁר שֶׁמֹּשֶׁה יָבִיא אוֹתָם לְאֶרֶץ יִשְׂרָאֵל.
>
> *The Jewish People were not on a sufficiently high spiritual level to warrant Moshe's leading them into the Land of Israel. For, if Moshe had led them, they would have conquered the Land with open miracles, seeing their enemies fall before them with no effort on their part. Our Sages say further, that had Moshe entered, he would have built an indestructible Temple. However, this utopia was dependent upon the nation's spiritual perfection. After they sinned and revealed their spiritual weakness, it was no longer possible for Moshe to bring them into the Land.*[95]

Moshe died before entrance into the Land precisely because of his incredible stature, it being incompatible with the level of the nation as a whole. It was under Yehoshua's leadership, at the lesser level of natural law, that the people entered the Land of Israel. For, in this situation, when 850 years later the quota of God's "long suffering" had, as it were, been filled, it was possible for God to vent His anger upon the wood and stones of the Temple rather than destroying the people. When the possibility of destroying one of two items exists, it is always the weaker of the two which will be obliterated. If the people are strong, the weaker physical building will be the focus of the anger. If, however, a building had been constructed by Moshe on his transcendent level, this incredible structure could

---

95. Malbim *ad loc.*

never have been demolished, and the weaker nation would have had to be wiped out instead.

This leaves us with a striking question. Knowing the awful consequences his entrance to the Land would incur, how could Moshe have prayed so persistently to gain admittance? Did he want to see the destruction of the people rather than the destruction of the Temple?

The intention behind Moshe's prayers can be comprehended in light of a promise made by the prophet Yechezkel.

> וְזָרַקְתִּי עֲלֵיכֶם מַיִם טְהוֹרִים... וְנָתַתִּי לָכֶם לֵב חָדָשׁ... וְאֶת רוּחִי אֶתֵּן בְּקִרְבְּכֶם...
>
> *I will sprinkle you with purifying waters... and I will give you a new heart... and I will bestow My spirit among you.*[96]

Yechezkel teaches us the ability of a leader to reverse a situation and effect a radical change in the nation's essence.

Moshe was dispatched as an emissary between God and the Jewish People while they were still in the throes of the Egyptian exile. Feeling the bleak nature of the situation, Moshe declared, וְהֵן לֹא יַאֲמִינוּ לִי, that his message would fall on deaf ears, for the people would lack conviction in him. Moshe was reprimanded for these words. Instead of bemoaning the present state of the people, he should have attempted to transform them at root level. He should have prayed for them; implored God to give them a "new heart." His failure to do so withheld a degree of illumination from the world which could have brought the cosmos to a previously unexperienced level of iridescence. For the Jewish People could have been externally lifted to the level of Exodus.

Many years later, Moshe repeatedly pleaded before God to allow him to enter the Land. In essence, his prayer was for the people. He was imploring God to bequeath a new heart, a new spirit upon the nation, to lift them up, grant them spiritual elevation. In their elevated state, they would be able to enter into the Land of Israel in full glory, crowned with Moshe as their leader. Moshe desired the root

96. *Yechezkel* 36:25–27.

of the word "הֵן," the level of overt revelation of spirituality, for the entire nation, as a basis from which to lead them into the Land.

But it was too late. At the beginning of his leadership, Moshe, even on his incomprehensible spiritual level, had not fully believed in the power of this potential prayer; therefore the prayer at the end of his life would remain ineffective. If he had achieved perfection in his belief and absolute conviction that God hearkens to every prayer and performs the impossible in answer to man's plea, he would have beseeched on behalf of the people, until God would have transformed the people's heart and spirit, thus rendering them fit for immediate redemption. As he had blunted the sword at this stage, it could not be unsheathed at a later stage. Corresponding to the "הֵן" of Moshe's complaint concerning the people in Egypt, was the "הֵן" of God's refusal to lift up the people and allow Moshe entrance into the Land. Moshe was a "bad neighbour," for although he saw the income, he did not consider his neighbour's expenditure. With the word "הֵן," Moshe praised God, telling of His dominion over Heaven and earth, bringing God's glory into the world. The expenditure, the detriment to Heaven's glory effected by his "הֵן" in Egypt, however, was not considered. This slight deficiency rebounded upon Moshe when his death decree was later sealed with this word.

It is axiomatic that in order to benefit from something, one must have complete conviction in that thing. Having denied something, one cannot utilise its innate power. Moshe did not lift the people up to the perfection of the level of "הֵן," complete clarity, while in Egypt, and therefore his subsequent desire for "הֵן" was rejected.

The application of this idea is particularly pertinent during the days of Judgment, approaching Rosh Hashanah and Yom Kippur. These days hinge upon one's heartfelt prayers and internal toil to correct and achieve atonement and forgiveness at root level. However, a precondition for our exertion in this area is a total conviction in the achievements possible through this work. It can only come about with complete belief in the power of our repentance and prayer to effect a change. It is only when we cry with utter conviction, from the depths of our hearts, that God really will cleanse our essence, will rejuvenate our hearts and spirits. It is when we cry with utter conviction, from the depths of our hearts, that God will indeed grant us livelihood, and health with which to serve Him.

Preparing for these days fills us with shame, and sometimes even a sense of helplessness, as we consider the many areas in which we have stumbled. We have spoken unfittingly, been haughty, denigrated our parents and teachers in some way — the list goes on and on. However when we really believe in our repentance, really believe that we will forsake the sin in the future, and that we will expend effort in our future spiritual labour, we give a sense of reality to our repentance, thus facilitating its effectiveness. It is thus that we are given an entire work, the book of *Yonah*, for the sole purpose of demonstrating the power of repentance and prayer. For the more we strengthen our belief in these areas, the more we can benefit from them.

In these awesome days, as we are filled with trepidation at our forthcoming judgment, let us utilise our time to strengthen ourselves in our conviction in the power of sincere repentance and heartfelt prayer. For it is through utilising these tools that we will be inscribed into the Book of Life, and will merit a year filled with every blessing.

# HA'AZINU

THE SABBATH THAT falls between Rosh Hashanah and Yom Kippur is commonly known as *Shabbath Shuvah*, an appellation taken from the Haftarah which begins with the words, שׁוּבָה יִשְׂרָאֵל עַד ה' אֱלֹקֶיךָ — "Return O Yisrael, unto the Lord, your God."[97]

Our Sages distinguish between two genres of repentance: repentance motivated by fear of punishment, and repentance motivated by love of God. The particular passage that we read on the awesome Shabbath preceding Yom Kippur refers to repentance motivated by fear. On this subject, our Sages state:

> ארשב"ל גְּדוֹלָה תְּשׁוּבָה שֶׁזְּדוֹנוֹת נַעֲשׂוֹת לוֹ כִּשְׁגָגוֹת. שֶׁנֶּאֱמַר כִּי כָשַׁלְתָּ בַּעֲוֹנֶךָ. וְהָא עָוֹן מֵזִיד הוּא וּקָרִי לֵיהּ מִכְשׁוֹל. אֵינִי וְהָא אָמַר רשב"ל: גְּדוֹלָה תְּשׁוּבָה שֶׁזְּדוֹנוֹת נַעֲשׂוֹת לוֹ כִּזְכֻיּוֹת. שֶׁנֶּאֱמַר וּבְשׁוּב רָשָׁע מֵרִשְׁעָתוֹ וגו' עֲלֵיהֶם חַיֹה יִחְיֶה? לֹא קַשְׁיָא. כָּאן מֵאַהֲבָה כָּאן מִיִּרְאָה.
>
> *Said Rabbi Shimon ben Lakish, "Great is repentance, for willful sins are transformed into accidental transgressions. As it says, 'For you stumbled in your sins.'" The word* עָוֹן*, used here, refers to willful transgression, thus how can the verse apply the verb "to stumble," i.e. accidentally, to willful sins that have been committed?*
>
> *Said Rabbi Shimon ben Lakish, "Great is repentance, for willful sins are transformed into merits. As it says, 'When the wicked person repents of his evil.'"*
>
> *These two statements do not contradict each other. When repentance is stimulated by love of God, willful sins are transformed into merits. When it is motivated by fear of punishment,*

97. *Hoshea* 14:2.

*willful transgressions are considered as unwitting ones.*[98]

The rationale behind both of these statements is clear. The definition of true repentance is to reach the point at which, "The One Who knows all secrets will testify that he will never return to his error." The penitent raises himself to a spiritual state that precludes falling into his previous mistakes, a level higher than he was at previously. Proof of his elevation is that while on his previous level the person sinned, and after having engaged in the process of repentance, he will sin no longer. We can thus say that the very transgression became a stepping-stone for the sinner, a springboard causing him to spiritually exert himself. It is precisely because he sinned that he elevated himself, attaining a level on which he would no longer fall.

In contrast, one who repents due to fear implicitly demonstrates that had he known the gravity of his sin at the outset, he would not have fallen prey to his desires. The transgression stemmed from a clouding of clarity and priorities, from a lack of knowledge. After the repentance process therefore, his sins can be considered as unwitting transgressions, for essentially they can be traced to a lack of recognition of the awesome destruction he has wreaked through trespassing God's will.

In our Haftarah, the prophet assesses the willful sins of the nation as mistakes, thoughtless errors into which they "stumbled." Thus, the passage appears to deal with repentance motivated by fear of God, through which willful sins are reduced to unwitting sins.

The Haftarah continues:

**קְחוּ עִמָּכֶם דְּבָרִים וְשׁוּבוּ אֶל ה׳ אִמְרוּ אֵלָיו כָּל תִּשָּׂא עָוֹן וְקַח טוֹב וּנְשַׁלְּמָה פָרִים שְׂפָתֵינוּ.**[99]

Translated literally, this might read,

*Take with you words and return to the Eternal; say to Him, "Bear all sin and take good, and let us replace [sacrifices of] bulls [with the words of] our lips."*

98. *Yalkut Shimoni*, *Hoshea* 530.
99. *Hoshea* 14:3.

Let us turn to Rashi's explanation:

כָּל תִּשָּׂא עָוֹן. כָּל עֲוֹונוֹתֵינוּ סְלַח. וְקַח טוֹב. וְלַמְּדֵנוּ דֶּרֶךְ טוֹב. דָּבָר אַחֵר וְקַח טוֹב. וְקַבֵּל הוֹדָיָה שֶׁנֶּאֱמַר טוֹב לְהוֹדוֹת לה׳.

*Bear all sin — Forgive all our sins. And take good — And teach us a good way. An alternative explanation: Take good — accept our confession, as it says, "It is good to admit to God."*

Rashi's explanation remains unclear. What is the enigmatic "good way" to which Rashi refers? And why will it be taught to us if we return to God? Further, why is it that, in addition to beseeching God for forgiveness, we plead with Him to accept our confession?

Upon the phrase, "Take with you words," our Sages state:

בִּדְבָרִים פִּתִּיתֶם אוֹתוֹ בְּסִינַי שֶׁנֶּאֱמַר וַיְפַתּוּהוּ בְּפִיהֶם.

*At Sinai, you persuaded Him with words, as it says, "And they persuaded Him with their mouths."*[100]

The meaning of this startling statement is found by examining the explanation of our Sages on the cryptic statement,[101] "Like grapes in a desert, I found Yisrael." They state:

בְּשָׁעָה שֶׁעָמְדוּ עַל הַר סִינַי נִמְשְׁלוּ כַּעֲנָבִים. מָה הָעֲנָבִים מִבַּחוּץ נָאוֹת וּכְעוּרוֹת מִבִּפְנִים, כָּךְ הָיוּ יִשְׂרָאֵל בְּשָׁעָה שֶׁעָמְדוּ עַל הַר סִינַי וְאָמְרוּ: כָּל אֲשֶׁר דִּבֶּר ה׳ נַעֲשֶׂה וְנִשְׁמַע. הֲרֵי בְּפִיהֶם. אֲבָל לִבָּם לֹא הָיָה נָכוֹן שֶׁנֶּאֱמַר וַיְפַתּוּהוּ בְּפִיהֶם וּבִלְשׁוֹנָם יְכַזְּבוּ לוֹ וְלִבָּם לֹא נָכוֹן עִמּוֹ.

*At the time when they stood at Mount Sinai, the Jewish People were like grapes. Just as grapes are firm on the outside, and yet soft and pulpy within, so was Yisrael. When they stated, "We will do and we will listen," it was a declaration made with their lips. However, their hearts were somewhat deficient, as it states, "And they persuaded Him with their mouths, with their lips they deceived Him, and their hearts were not*

100. *Yalkut Shimoni, Hoshea* 533.
101. *Hoshea* 9:10.

*fully with Him" [Tehillim 78:36–37].*[102]

At Mount Sinai, in a manner subtler than we can comprehend, the heart of the Children of Yisrael was not fully consonant with their sublime promise. Our Sages connect the "words" from the phrase, "Take with you words," with the deceitful "words" of the Children of Yisrael as they stood at Mount Sinai. Is this what God desires, words of deceit, words that, in a subtle manner, are somewhat false? Is it this type of words that Hoshea desires to arouse from the people?

According to the following statement of our Sages, it appears that this falsehood is indeed desired by God!

מִי גָּדוֹל גּוֹנֵב אוֹ נִגְנַב? הֱוֵי אוֹמֵר נִגְנָב שֶׁיּוֹדֵעַ שֶׁנִּגְנַב וְשׁוֹתֵק. וְכֵן מָצִינוּ שֶׁהָיוּ יִשְׂרָאֵל עוֹמְדִין לְפָנָיו עַל הַר סִינַי בִּקְשׁוּ לִגְנֹב דַּעַת הָעֶלְיוֹנָה. שֶׁנֶּאֱמַר כָּל אֲשֶׁר דִּבֶּר ה׳ נַעֲשֶׂה וְנִשְׁמַע. כִּבְיָכוֹל נִגְנַב לָהֶם, שֶׁנֶּאֱמַר מִי יִתֵּן וְהָיָה לְבָבָם זֶה לָהֶם לְיִרְאָה אֹתִי.

*Who is greater, a thief or one who is stolen from? The one who is stolen from, for he knows that he is being robbed, and remains silent. So we find that Yisrael stood at Mount Sinai, and sought to deceive God, as it says, "All that God says we will do and we will listen." In this manner, God was, as it were, deceived by them. Yet it says, "If only their hearts were always like this to fear Me!"*[103]

We find that at their rendezvous with God at Mount Sinai, the Jewish People sought to "steal" (deceive in some way) God's knowledge when they accepted on themselves unconditionally to fulfill the entire Torah. Not only was the Almighty, being omniscient, fully aware that He was being deceived, He remained silent, and even praised their behaviour: "If only their hearts were always like this, to fear Me in this manner!" However, the heart of the Jewish People has already been criticised as not being "fully with Him." Let us investigate the meaning of these words.

---

102. *Yalkut Shimoni, Hoshea* 525.

103. *Devarim* 5:26; *Tosefta Baba Kama* 87:3.

As explained above, the type of repentance that we are dealing with is that of repentance stimulated by fear, not love. Nevertheless, Hoshea brings the message of God:

**אֶרְפָּא מְשׁוּבָתָם אֹהֲבֵם נְדָבָה כִּי שָׁב אַפִּי מִמֶּנּוּ.**

*I will heal their contrary ways [and] love them with a free love, for My anger is withdrawn from them.*[104]

Rashi elaborates on the meaning of this promise:

**אֶרְפָּא מְשׁוּבָתָם. אָמַר הַנָּבִיא כָּךְ אָמַר לִי רוּחַ הַקֹּדֶשׁ. מֵאַחַר שֶׁיֹּאמְרוּ לְפָנַי כֵּן, אֶרְפָּא מְשׁוּבָתָם וְאֹהֲבֵם בְּנִדְבַת רוּחִי. אַף עַל פִּי שֶׁאֵינָן רְאוּיִין לְאַהֲבָה (מִפְּנֵי שֶׁאֵינָם אוֹהֲבֵי ה' אֶלָּא יְרֵאִים מִפָּנָיו), אֶתְנַדֵּב לְאַהֲבָתָם כִּי שָׁב אַפִּי מִמֶּנּוּ.**

*I will heal their contrary ways. Said the prophet, "So I learned through Divine inspiration." After they say so before Me, I will heal their contrary ways and I will love them with My generous spirit. Although they do not deserve My love (for they do not love God, but fear Him), I will nevertheless love them, "for My anger has abated."*[105]

In the next verse, the Almighty promises, "I will be as dew for Yisrael." Dew is the metaphor used to describe God's love to Yisrael, an unconditional, boundless love that is the result of repentance motivated by fear. A parallel allegory of dew is also found at the opening of this week's *parashah*:

**יַעֲרֹף כַּמָּטָר לִקְחִי תִּזַּל כַּטַּל אִמְרָתִי כִּשְׂעִירִם עֲלֵי דֶשֶׁא וְכִרְבִיבִים עֲלֵי עֵשֶׂב.**

*Let my teaching drip like rain, my speech flow like dew; like stormwinds [blowing on] vegetation, and like raindrops on plants.*[106]

The Torah does not indulge in empty poetry; rather each phrase

104. *Hoshea* 14:5.
105. Rashi *ad loc.*
106. *Devarim* 32:2.

is employed to highlight a new angle of the message. לִקְחִי — "My teaching" (literally, my portion), refers specifically to the Written Law, which is called a לֶקַח טוֹב — "a good portion." The Vilna Gaon expands on this idea:

> לִקְחִי הוּא תּוֹרָה שֶׁבִּכְתָב, כְּמוֹ שֶׁנֶּאֱמַר מֹשֶׁה קִבֵּל תּוֹרָה מִסִּינַי, אִמְרָתִי הוּא תּוֹרָה שֶׁבְּעַל-פֶּה. קֵל אֶחָד אֲמָרָהּ מִפֶּה אֶל פֶּה.
>
> *"My teaching" refers to the Written Law, as it says, "Moshe received the Torah from Sinai." "My speech" refers to the Oral Law. One God said it from mouth to mouth.*

Let us investigate why the Written Law is compared to rain, and the Oral Law is compared to dew. On this theme, the Talmud states:

> כְּנֶסֶת יִשְׂרָאֵל שָׁאֲלָה שֶׁלֹּא כַּהֹגֶן והקב"ה הֵשִׁיבָה כַּהֹגֶן. שֶׁנֶּאֱמַר וְנֵדְעָה נִרְדְּפָה לָדַעַת אֶת ה' כְּשַׁחַר נָכוֹן מוֹצָאוֹ וְיָבוֹא כַגֶּשֶׁם לָנוּ. אָמַר לָהּ הקב"ה בִּתִּי אַתְּ שׁוֹאֶלֶת דָּבָר שֶׁפְּעָמִים מִתְבַּקֵּשׁ וּפְעָמִים אֵינוֹ מִתְבַּקֵּשׁ. אֲבָל אֲנִי אֶהְיֶה לָךְ דָּבָר הַמִּתְבַּקֵּשׁ לְעוֹלָם שֶׁנֶּאֱמַר אֶהְיֶה כַטַּל לְיִשְׂרָאֵל.
>
> *The congregation of Yisrael asked in a manner that was not fitting, and God answered them in a manner that was fitting. As it says, "We will know and we will pursue knowledge of God, like the fitting morning I found it, and it came to us like rain." The Almighty said to her [Yisrael], "My daughter, you requested a thing that is sometimes sought, and sometimes not sought. However, I will be to you something that is always sought, as it says, 'I will be as dew for Yisrael.'"*[107]

What is the deeper understanding of the difference between rain and dew, and how does this difference relate to the comparison between dew and God's kindness?

To answer this question, let us investigate the enigmatic, "deception of God," which is desired in Heaven. Rabbi Dessler's explanation may be paraphrased as follows:

---

107. *Ta'anith* 4a.

What motivates people to make promises and resolutions for the future? People desire to achieve that which is presently beyond their grasp. This yearning causes a person to take steps in an attempt to force himself into the desired course of behaviour. One of these incentives is a promise or oath. A promise transforms that which was an optional course of behaviour, into a requirement. It thereby forces a person to climb up further, to step forward to a level that is as yet unconquered. If a person were on a higher spiritual level, the course of behaviour would not be classed as "optional." The battle in this area would already be won, and promises to strengthen his resolution would be redundant. For example, it would be unnecessary for a great scholar to vow not to commit an act of murder. His spiritual level is high above such a coarse internal battle, and any promise would be unnecessary. A promise is only in place when there is a discrepancy between one's inner yearnings and one's true spiritual level.

At the moment of marriage between God and the Jewish People, the nation made the famous promise, "We will do and we will listen." Our Sages discern a subtle, almost imperceptible deficiency in the internality of the nation, such that they "deceived God." Our Sages label their position as כָּזָב, deceit, as opposed to שֶׁקֶר, falsehood. The distinction between deceit and falsehood can be understood from the phrase כְּנַחַל אַכְזָב. A "deceitful" river refers to a river that, while flowing in the winter, dries up in the summer heat. Although initially present, the river cannot withstand a change of circumstances. Similarly, deceit refers to a situation in which the correct sentiments are originally present. However, with a change of circumstances, the original intentions cannot be maintained. When the Jewish People sinned in the incident of the Golden Calf, they revealed that their promise at Mount Sinai was not completely matched by their inner conviction. They demonstrated that their original promise was כָּזָב — deceit.

Our Sages pose the question, "Who is greater, the one who steals, or the one who is stolen from?" The answer is not as straightforward as it seems. The "one who steals," here refers to one who makes a promise to improve an area of his Divine service. His vow demonstrates that his true level is not satisfactory; in his desire to grow closer to God, he spurns complacency. Thus, a promise indicates an inner life of vitality, a striving to transcend. What is greater — this, or the revelation of God's kindness, for "He knows that He is being deceived and is quiet." God ignores the contradiction between man's desires and his true level, and accepts the promises, in return bestowing abundant good. Indeed, God declares, "If only their hearts were always like this." Their resolve might be "deceitful" and incomplete; nevertheless, God desires that the underlying yearning should constantly burn in their hearts.

For, this is the upward path in spirituality. Man cannot elevate himself unless he possesses ideals exceeding his present state, exceeding his position as a mortal being. One who wishes to succeed in building his personality need not withhold himself from his aspirations, scared that he will be unable to actualize his dreams. Although the physical expression may not completely materialise, the inner desire is present and complete, and the desire itself is praised by God. An example of this is found concerning the Ten Days of Repentance. During this time, people are accustomed to accept stringencies and forms of behaviour upon themselves that they would be unable to sustain throughout the year. Although this behaviour might appear hypocritical, it is in fact desired by God. For it reveals an inner desire that pulsates with vitality; it indicates a soul yearning to grow, to attain closeness to the Almighty. God promises, "One who comes to purify himself will receive Heavenly assistance." God displays unconditional love towards those who seek Him.

Let us now turn to the distinction between rain and dew. Man recognises his dependence on rain; without it his work would be futile, his toil in vain. Drought would strike the land and extend its destructive claws over all its inhabitants. The farmer prays wholeheartedly that God keep the heavens open, and grant rain in the correct season. When the patter of raindrops is finally heard, it is seen and felt by all. Dew, in contrast, descends each day while most remain oblivious to it. The written Torah, which is revealed to all, is compared to rain, while the Oral Law, inextricably bound to the Written Law, is compared to dew. As with dew, the Oral Law requires meditation and consideration for it to be understood and appreciated.

Our Sages highlight a further difference between rain and dew. Rain is not sought in every season; it is not constantly the subject of our prayers. Dew, however, is always sought, and always present. It is constantly mentioned in our prayers.

This distinction parallels the difference between using the qualities of love and fear in the service of God. A famous dictum of our Sages states, "All is in the hands of Heaven except for fear of Heaven." Instilling oneself with true awe depends upon man's own toil and work. It can be compared to prayer for rain stemming from a fear of the damage that drought can inflict. It can also be compared to repentance motivated by fear of the punishment that sin will bring. The falling rain, then, is a symbol of a blessing that is evident to all, yet is given in response to the prayer and toil expended.

Dew is a blessing given irrespective of onlookers or prayer. Dew is thus the symbol of gifts from Heaven. Our Sages state, "All is from Heaven except for fear of Heaven." If we consider what "all" encompasses, it appears that even love of God falls into the category of that which can be bestowed from Heaven. Fear of Heaven must come from man's own work, but love can be bestowed from above, like dew, in a concealed manner.

The question that then arises is: how to merit this gift of love of God? How can one who has struggled to acquire fear of God reach the level of love of God? The Almighty Himself answers this question: אֹהֲבֵם נְדָבָה — "I will love them as an unconditional gift." Love is a gift implanted into man's heart. Indeed, the *Zohar* states, "One who serves God from fear will ultimately find himself serving from joyful love." Let us note that the wording of the *Zohar* indicates that man is passive in this transformation; he "finds himself" loving God, without effort on his part. Like dew, this change is not evident, nor immediately understood. Thus does the verse state, "I will be as dew for Yisrael." Love of God is bestowed upon man like the descent of dew: consistently each morning, waiting for man's heart to draw near to His Creator.

Now we return to Rashi's comment on the verse, "Take with you words." Rashi explains that these words refer to the confessions that are somewhat "deceitful," not stemming from a heart brimming with love of God. Even if the motive for repentance is fear, lest evil befall a person, God will accept the sentiments and indeed, forgive the person's sins. Rashi continues, informing us that "take good" means, "and teach us a good way." We ask God to teach us the path to true service: service out of love. It begins with the fear of God that is in man's own hands to acquire. It concludes however, with God implanting love in man's heart, unceasingly, unnoticed, as dew.

There is a fear that occupies our thoughts and feelings during Elul and the days in which we stand in judgment. However, the more discerning of us may wonder what occurs when this period of the year has passed. The question pricks us, "Has any real and lasting change occurred in the realm of my internality?" We might begin to feel that we too "deceived God with our mouths," that our behaviour does not match our uttered sentiments. However, God has made a promise: "I will heal their contrary ways [and] love them with a free love." God always loves His children; He always encourages us in the path of growth. With His boundless love, He will transform our hearts, filling them with love. God will be "as dew for Yisrael."

# VEZOTH HABERACHAH

WITH MOSHE'S IMMINENT passing, the time has come to appoint a successor:

**וַיְדַבֵּר מֹשֶׁה אֶל ה' לֵאמֹר. יִפְקֹד ה' אֱלֹקֵי הָרוּחֹת לְכָל בָּשָׂר אִישׁ עַל הָעֵדָה.**

*Moshe then spoke to the Eternal, [for the Eternal] to reply [to him], "May the Eternal, God of all people's characters, appoint a man over the community.*[108]

Rashi informs us that Moshe originally wanted his sons to assume his position after him.

יִפְקֹד ה' – כֵּיוָן שֶׁשָּׁמַע מֹשֶׁה שֶׁאָמַר לוֹ הַמָּקוֹם תֵּן נַחֲלַת צְלָפְחָד לִבְנוֹתָיו, אָמַר הִגִּיעָה שָׁעָה שֶׁאֶתְבַּע צְרָכַי שֶׁיִּירְשׁוּ בָּנַי אֶת גְּדֻלָּתִי. אָמַר לוֹ הקב"ה לֹא כָּךְ עָלְתָה בְמַחְשָׁבָה לְפָנַי. כְּדַאי הוּא יְהוֹשֻׁעַ לִטֹּל שְׂכַר שִׁמּוּשׁוֹ שֶׁלֹּא מָשׁ מִתּוֹךְ הָאֹהֶל. וְזֶהוּ שֶׁאָמַר שְׁלֹמֹה נֹצֵר תְּאֵנָה יֹאכַל פִּרְיָהּ.

*May the Eternal appoint. Moshe heard God's instruction that he should give an inheritance to the daughters of Tzelofchad [who had died without any male progeny to inherit his land], in order to carry on their father's name. Moshe then felt that the time was right to request that his own sons should inherit his position. The Almighty, however, said to him, "This is not what I have decided. Rather, it is fitting that Yehoshua collect the reward due to him for not moving from the tent [and continuously serving you faithfully]." This is what King Shlomo refers to when he says, "The one who guards the fig tree shall eat its fruit."*[109]

---

108. *Bemidbar* 27:15, 16.
109. Rashi *ad loc.*

God's instructions concerning Moshe's successor continue as follows:

**וַיֹּאמֶר ה' אֶל מֹשֶׁה קַח לְךָ אֶת יְהוֹשֻׁעַ בִּן נוּן אִישׁ אֲשֶׁר רוּחַ בּוֹ וְסָמַכְתָּ אֶת יָדְךָ עָלָיו.**

*The Eternal replied to Moshe, "Take for yourself Yehoshua the son of Nun, a man who has a [considerate] character, and put your hand upon him."*[110]

Rashi explains the manner in which Moshe was required to "take" Yehoshua.

קַח לְךָ. קָחֶנּוּ בִּדְבָרִים, אַשְׁרֶיךָ שֶׁזָּכִיתָ לְהַנְהִיג בָּנָיו שֶׁל מָקוֹם. וְסָמַכְתָּ אֶת יָדְךָ עָלָיו. תֵּן לוֹ מְתֻרְגְּמָן שֶׁיִּדְרֹשׁ בְּחַיֶּיךָ. שֶׁלֹּא יֹאמְרוּ עָלָיו לֹא הָיָה לוֹ לְהָרִים רֹאשׁ בִּימֵי מֹשֶׁה.

*Take for yourself. Persuade him with words: "Fortunate are you that you have merited to lead the children of God."*

*Put your hand upon him: Give him a disseminator [one who will convey his words to the masses when he gives a public lecture], so that he can teach in your lifetime. This is to prevent people from saying that Yehoshua would not have raised his head in Moshe's lifetime [thereby challenging Yehoshua's authority].*[111]

Rashi describes the necessity of Moshe actively persuading Yehoshua to accept the mantle of leadership. From his words, we learn something of the tremendous humility which was Yehoshua's hallmark. Turning to *Parashath Ha'azinu*, we can learn more about Yehoshua's personality.

**וַיָּבֹא מֹשֶׁה וַיְדַבֵּר אֶת כָּל דִּבְרֵי הַשִּׁירָה הַזֹּאת בְּאָזְנֵי הָעָם הוּא וְהוֹשֵׁעַ בִּן נוּן.**

*Moshe then came and spoke all the words of this song directly to the people — he, with Hoshea the son of Nun.*[112]

110. *Bemidbar* 27:18.
111. Rashi *ad loc.*
112. *Devarim* 32:44.

Rashi highlights:

הוּא וְהוֹשֵׁעַ בִּן נוּן. שַׁבָּת שֶׁל דְּיוֹזְגֵי הָיְתָה. נִטְלָה רְשׁוּת מִזֶּה וְנִתְּנָה לְזֶה. הֶעֱמִיד לוֹ מֹשֶׁה מְתֻרְגְּמָן לִיהוֹשֻׁעַ שֶׁיְּהֵא דוֹרֵשׁ בְּחַיָּיו, כְּדֵי שֶׁלֹּא יֹאמְרוּ יִשְׂרָאֵל בְּחַיֵּי רַבְּךָ לֹא הָיָה לְךָ לְהָרִים רֹאשׁ. וְלָמָּה קוֹרְאוֹ כָּאן הוֹשֵׁעַ? לוֹמַר שֶׁלֹּא זָחָה דַּעְתּוֹ עָלָיו שֶׁאַף עַל פִּי שֶׁנִּתְּנָה לוֹ גְּדֻלָּה הִשְׁפִּיל עַצְמוֹ כַּאֲשֶׁר מִתְּחִילָּתוֹ.

*He, with Hoshea the son of Nun. This was the Sabbath of two crowns [two leaders]. Authority was taken from this one, and transferred to that one. Moshe appointed a disseminator for Yehoshua, thus enabling him to deliver a lecture in Moshe's life, to prevent the people from saying, "In the lifetime of your teacher you would not have dared to raise your head." Why is Yehoshua here called Hoshea [the letter* י *being removed from his name]? To teach us that despite the prestige and position that Yehoshua received, he minimized himself, behaving as he had previously.*[113]

Thus we learn about Yehoshua's tremendous humility, his remaining unchanged by his promotion. However, the Talmud's account of a conversation between Moshe and Yehoshua casts aspersions upon this paragon of humility. The exchange took place on the day of Moshe's death.

אָמַר ר' יְהוּדָה אָמַר רַב: בְּשָׁעָה שֶׁנִּפְטַר מֹשֶׁה רַבֵּנוּ לְגַן עֵדֶן, אָמַר לוֹ לִיהוֹשֻׁעַ שְׁאַל מִמֶּנִּי כָּל סְפֵקוֹת שֶׁיֵּשׁ לְךָ. אָמַר לוֹ רַבִּי כְּלוּם הִנַּחְתִּיךָ שָׁעָה אַחַת וְהָלַכְתִּי לְמָקוֹם אַחֵר? לֹא כָּךְ כָּתַבְתָּ בִּי וּמְשָׁרְתוֹ יְהוֹשֻׁעַ בִּן נוּן לֹא יָמִישׁ מִתּוֹךְ הָאֹהֶל? מִיָּד תָּשַׁשׁ כֹּחוֹ שֶׁל יְהוֹשֻׁעַ, וְנִשְׁתַּכְּחוּ מִמֶּנּוּ שְׁלֹשׁ מֵאוֹת הֲלָכוֹת וְנוֹלְדוּ לוֹ שְׁבַע מֵאוֹת סְפֵקוֹת.

*Said Rabbi Yehudah in the name of Rav: When Moshe passed [from this world] to Gan Eden, he said to Yehoshua, "Ask me about any doubts that you might have."*

*He answered, "My teacher, have I left you and gone elsewhere for even an hour? Did you yourself not write concerning*

113. Rashi *ad loc.*

*me, 'His servant, Yehoshua son of Nun, did not move from inside the tent'?"*

*Immediately, Yehoshua's strength waned: he forgot three hundred laws and had seven hundred doubts [concerning what he had learned].*[114]

From this exchange, we seem to detect some flaw in Yehoshua's character for which he is punished. His claim to have learned everything possible from Moshe seems to indicate a degree of pride. Is this indeed the case? How can this be reconciled with our image of Yehoshua as one who personified humility?

In a Midrash that has bearing on our subject, our Sages state:

כְּשֶׁנָּתַן הקב"ה תּוֹרָה לְיִשְׂרָאֵל נָתַן בָּהּ מִצְווֹת עֲשֵׂה וּמִצְווֹת לֹא תַעֲשֶׂה, וְנָתַן לַמֶּלֶךְ מִקְצָת מִצְווֹת שֶׁנֶּאֱמַר לֹא יַרְבֶּה לוֹ סוּסִים וְכֶסֶף וְזָהָב... לֹא יַרְבֶּה לוֹ נָשִׁים וְלֹא יָסוּר לְבָבוֹ. עָמַד שְׁלֹמֹה הַמֶּלֶךְ וְהֶחְכִּים עַל גְּזֵרָתוֹ שֶׁל הקב"ה. וְאָמַר לָמָּה אָמַר הקב"ה לֹא יַרְבֶּה לוֹ נָשִׁים? לֹא בִּשְׁבִיל שֶׁלֹּא יָסוּר לְבָבוֹ? אֲנִי אַרְבֶּה וְלִבִּי לֹא יָסוּר. אָמְרוּ רַבּוֹתֵינוּ בְּאוֹתָהּ שָׁעָה עָלְתָה יו"ד שֶׁבְּ"יַרְבֶּה" וְנִשְׁתַּטְּחָה לִפְנֵי הקב"ה וְאָמְרָה: רִבּוֹנוֹ שֶׁל עוֹלָם, לֹא כָּךְ אָמַרְתָּ אֵין אוֹת בְּטֵלָה מִן הַתּוֹרָה לְעוֹלָם? הֲרֵי שְׁלֹמֹה עוֹמֵד וּמְבַטֵּל אוֹתִי. וְשֶׁמָּא הַיּוֹם יְבַטֵּל אַחַת וּלְמָחָר אַחֶרֶת, עַד שֶׁתִּתְבַּטֵּל כָּל הַתּוֹרָה כֻּלָּהּ. אָמַר לָהּ הקב"ה שְׁלֹמֹה וְאֶלֶף כַּיּוֹצֵא בּוֹ יִהְיוּ בְּטֵלִין, וְקוֹץ מִמֵּךְ אֵינִי מְבַטֵּל. וּמִנַּיִן שֶׁבִּטֵּל אוֹתָהּ מִן הַתּוֹרָה וְחָזְרָה לַתּוֹרָה? שֶׁנֶּאֱמַר שָׂרַי אִשְׁתְּךָ לֹא תִקְרָא אֶת שְׁמָהּ שָׂרַי כִּי שָׂרָה שְׁמָהּ. וְהֵיכָן חָזַר? וַיִּקְרָא מֹשֶׁה לְהוֹשֵׁעַ בִּן נוּן יְהוֹשֻׁעַ.

*When the Almighty gave Torah to the Jewish People, He gave them positive and negative commandments. God gave additional mitzvoth to a Jewish king, as it states, "He should not accumulate many horses, [or] silver and gold... he should not have many wives lest his heart turn aside." King Shlomo arose and considered himself wiser than God's decrees. He said, "Why did God give the command not to have numerous wives? It seems to be because of the continuation of the verse, 'lest his heart turn aside.' I will have many wives, and my heart shall not turn aside."*

114. *Temurah* 16a.

*Our Sages said: at that time, the letter* י *from the word* יַרְבֶּה *[many] ascended and prostrated itself before the Almighty. It said, "Master of the Universe, did You not say that no letter of the Torah would ever be nullified? Yet Shlomo has nullified me! Today he will abolish one letter, and tomorrow another, until the entire Torah will be abrogated."*

*The Almighty replied, "Let Shlomo and a thousand like him be nullified, yet not one crown (from on top of the* י*) will be abolished!"*

*From where do we see that it was removed from the Torah and yet subsequently returned? It states, "*שָׂרַי*, Sarai your wife will no longer be called Sarai, but Sarah,* שָׂרָה*." Where did it return? "Moshe called Hoshea, the son of Nun, Yehoshua,* יְהוֹשֻׁעַ*."*[115]

The eternity of Torah is absolute; even one letter can never be abolished. The letter י that was removed from Sarai returned, becoming part of Yehoshua's name. Considering this Midrash, Rabbi Shneur Kotler asked why Yehoshua specifically was chosen to demonstrate the Eternal, immutable nature of Torah, through having a י attached to his name. Yehoshua, he explained, never moved from the tent of Moshe, eagerly anticipating every word that Moshe would utter — לֹא יָמִישׁ מִתּוֹךְ הָאֹהֶל. He nullified himself completely before the Torah, which was his only priority. Not wanting to miss even one word of Torah, Yehoshua never departed from Moshe's tent. In his humility, Yehoshua had no other desire than to dedicate all his strength and time to learning the sublime words that Moshe uttered. Feeling the eternity and importance of Torah to such a degree, it was appropriate that Yehoshua was the means through which this lesson was taught to the world, and thus he had the י added to his name.

The instance where Yehoshua is called by his old name, Hoshea, has already been highlighted. Faced with his teacher's imminent passing, Yehoshua is given the opportunity to ask any question. He

115. *Shemoth Rabbah* 6:1.

refuses the opportunity, stating that he has absorbed everything that he could from Moshe. He is faulted for his refusal, for by doing so he limited Torah study to that which he already knew. He intimated that there is nothing more to know, that he has absorbed everything that Moshe could teach him. It is therefore appropriate that in this context he is called by his old name, Hoshea, not by the name with the added letter י, showing his quality of viewing Torah as Eternal, unfathomable, that for which one ever thirsts.

In contrast to this explanation, however, we have the words of Rashi, which state that Hoshea was called so in this instance to demonstrate his humility, the fact that he remained the same person after his appointment as before. How can this contradiction be reconciled?

Man's personality traits and characteristics are termed in Hebrew as *middoth*, a term which may be literally translated as "measures." Judaism does not seek to suppress the personality; rather, every characteristic a person possesses must be used in its correct time and place, in the appropriate measure. A classic example of this can be found in our forefather Avraham. Avraham earned the title אֵיתָן הָאֶזְרָחִי, a term denoting his fierce determination and strength. Indeed, Avraham had the courage to spread belief of monotheism in a world that was exclusively paganistic. As described by our Sages, Avraham was an iconoclast, possessing the spiritual fortitude to "stand on one side," while the entire world "stood on the other," entrenched in their own faith. Concurrently, we read Avraham's statement about himself, "I am dust and ashes," an attitude which seems to belie the image of Avraham as one who was supremely confident in his convictions. Avraham attained complete mastery over his entire personality, and he knew the correct measure of each character trait. When the hour required him to stand erect, and proudly proclaim his beliefs, he could do so. At the same time, he was able to declare, "I am dust and ashes," in his incredible humility before God. Avraham had the right measure of all traits, knowing the appropriate moment for each to be used.

In conjunction with the trait of humility, King Shlomo states,

**גַּם בְּלֹא דַעַת נֶפֶשׁ לֹא טוֹב...**

*Also, without knowledge of one's soul, it is not good.*[116]

Rabbeinu Yonah elaborates upon the meaning of this maxim:

לֹא טוֹב שֶׁלֹּא יֵדַע הָאָדָם עֶרֶךְ נַפְשׁוֹ וְהַשָּׂגָתוֹ בַּעֲבוֹדַת ה' ית'.

*It is not good for man to be ignorant of the value of his soul, and his potential attainments in Divine service.*[117]

While each person must, from one perspective, compare himself to dust and ashes, he must also have the ability to gird himself in strength, and stand against the rest of the world. Humility can sometimes be misplaced, for it is crucial to recognise one's boundless potential, and cherish the importance of one's soul.

Examining the circumstances surrounding the addition of the י to Yehoshua's name, it is notable that Moshe added the letter before Yehoshua was to embark on the mission of spying out the Land of Israel. Our Sages say that Moshe prayed, "May God save you from the advice of the spies." Moshe knew that, in his humility, Yehoshua would be particularly vulnerable to co-operating with the spies, for he would lack the courage and confidence to stand up against their plans. Moshe sought to protect Yehoshua from his character traits, to encourage him to use his quality in the correct "measure." Yehoshua was entering a situation in which humility and submission were incorrect; pride and confidence were required instead.

The Talmud informs us:

פְּנֵי מֹשֶׁה כִּפְנֵי חַמָּה וּפְנֵי יְהוֹשֻׁעַ כִּפְנֵי לְבָנָה.

*The face of Moshe was like that of the sun, and the face of Yehoshua was like that of the moon.*[118]

The relationship between Moshe and Yehoshua paralleled the relationship between the sun and the moon. While the sun is a ball

---

116. *Mishlei* 19:2.

117. Rabbeinu Yonah *ad loc.*

118. *Baba Bathra* 75a.

of fire that serves as a source of light to the universe, the moon only receives and reflects the light of the sun. The moon is not an independent source of light and energy; it relies completely on the sun. While Moshe emitted light — the light of Torah and Godliness, Yehoshua, like the moon, merely absorbed and reflected these teachings.

Immediately before his teacher's death, Yehoshua was thrust into a new position. Suddenly, he was told, "Ask me concerning any doubts that you have." Yehoshua's whole essence was to receive what Moshe wanted to teach him, to absorb his teacher's Torah. If Moshe were to have given him one last lecture, teach him one more subject, Yehoshua would have seized his last opportunity and thirstily absorbed his words, as he did throughout his life.

However, Moshe now asked him to behave as the sun, to become proactive and bring up a topic for study. In his humility, Yehoshua felt unable to initiate the topic that should be learned. In this instance, Yehoshua is referred to by his old name Hoshea, losing the י that Moshe added to his name. As Rashi explains, this case demonstrated Yehoshua's tremendous humility, which did not change even after he was conferred with leadership. Simultaneously, however, loss of the י symbolically indicates that Yehoshua lost his ability to recognise the limitless, Eternal nature of Torah. By refraining from questioning Moshe, Yehoshua subtly implied that Torah could be somehow restricted into a boundary, and limited to a finite span of knowledge.

Although Yehoshua's mistake stemmed from his humility, in this case humility was inappropriate. Rather, Yehoshua was now required to become active in the learning process, to become an instigator in his own right.

Indeed, Moshe assigned him a disseminator just for this purpose — so that Yehoshua himself could begin lecturing and teaching the masses. Yehoshua was now required to step into a position of leadership, something he was reluctant to do.

*Pirkei Avoth* counsels each person to recall both his origin and his destiny:

דַּע מֵאַיִן בָּאתָ וּלְאָן אַתָּה הוֹלֵךְ וְלִפְנֵי מִי אַתָּה עָתִיד לִתֵּן דִּין וְחֶשְׁבּוֹן.

*Know from where you come, and to where you are going... and before Whom you will one day have to give judgment and accounting.*[119]

This thought is meant to sober man, reduce his ego by reminding him that he comes from "a putrid drop," and his destiny is to become "maggots and worms." Further, on the day of death, man will have to stand and be judged before the Almighty, Who knows every action and thought. The Vilna Gaon makes a distinction between the two terms דִּין, judgment, and חֶשְׁבּוֹן, accounting. He explains that דִּין refers to the judgment of correct and incorrect actions. חֶשְׁבּוֹן, however, refers to the verdict concerning what man could have achieved. חֶשְׁבּוֹן is the measure of man's accomplishments against his tremendous potential.

While it is important to be cognizant of man's lowly station, it is crucial for each person to recognise and cherish "the value of his soul." While humility is laudable, it is a character trait which, like all others, must be used in the correct measure. To downplay the greatness that lies, latent, in each one of us, is humility misplaced. Instead, every person must realise that he possesses a Godly soul which is Eternal, and which has infinite potential. Further, through his actions, every person can have a tremendous influence on all those with whom he comes into contact. This should never be minimized, and the responsibility should be willingly shouldered. For each person is unique in his ability to change himself and to affect the entire world.

---

119. *Pirkei Avoth* 3:1.